TRANSITION ECONOMIES

POLITICAL ECONOMY IN RUSSIA, EASTERN EUROPE, AND CENTRAL ASIA

Martin Myant

Jan Drahokoupil

WILEY

JOHN WILEY & SONS, INC.

VICE PRESIDENT AND PUBLISHER:	George Hoffman
ACQUISITIONS EDITOR:	Lacey Vitetta
ASSISTANT MARKETING MANAGER:	Diane Mars
SENIOR EDITORIAL ASSISTANT:	Emily McGee
ART DIRECTOR:	Jeof Vita
MEDIA EDITOR:	Greg Chaput
PRODUCTION MANAGER:	Micheline Frederick
PRODUCTION EDITOR:	Amy Weintraub

Credit for the copyright page is: ©iStockphoto (top photo) Alexey Zaytsev/iStockphoto (bottom photo) Wiktor Bubniak/iStockphoto

This book was set in 10/12 Times Roman by Laserwords Private Limited and printed and bound by Courier Westford. The cover was printed by Courier Westford.

This book is printed on acid free paper. ∞

Evaluation copies are provided to qualified academics and professionals for review purposes only, for use in their courses during the next academic year. These copies are licensed and may not be sold or transferred to a third party. Upon completion of the review period, please return the evaluation copy to Wiley. Return instructions and a free of charge return shipping label are available at www.wiley.com/go/returnlabel. Outside of the United States, please contact your local representative.

Library of Congress Cataloging-in-Publication Data

ISBN-13   978-0-470-59619-7

Printed in the United States of America

10 9 8 7 6 5 4 3 2 1

C O N T E N T S

PREFACE

This book analyzes the economic transformation in former Communist countries of Eastern and Central Europe and countries of the former Soviet Union, from the end of central planning to the capitalist varieties of the present. It provides a comparative analysis of economic transformation and the political-economic diversity that has emerged from it. It covers differences between countries in terms of economic performance and integration into the world economy. It seeks to explain and deepen an understanding of these differences in terms of historical backgrounds, locations, and policies pursued, with attention to state forms and the role of the state in development, to political forms and interest representation, and to the development of new forms of business organization. This provides a basis for identifying and explaining differences between groupings of countries in Eastern Europe and the former Soviet Union and will thereby contribute to work on the varieties of forms of capitalism emerging in these countries and to an understanding of responses to the world financial crisis of 2008.

ACKNOWLEDGMENTS

This book took shape over a number of years. The collaboration between us was made possible by funding for a one-year fellowship for Jan Drahokoupil in 2007 from the Centre for Russian, Central and East European Studies, a consortium based at the University of Glasgow, with the University of the West of Scotland as a member, and funded by the United Kingdom's Economic and Social Research Council. In developing our ideas, we have benefited from the input of many friends and colleagues, and it would be impossible to name them all here. In many cases, we refer to their works in the text and in the references, although the contribution in terms of specific points, of comments on our ideas, and of general encouragement was often much greater. We would also like to make special mention of the comments at various stages from 20 anonymous publishers' referees, which helped us to improve the structure and clarity of the work, to avoid some possible sources of misunderstanding, and to eliminate many errors. We would also like to thank our students, who have provided very useful feedback on the manuscript. Finally, we would like to thank George Lobell and his colleagues at Wiley-Blackwell for their support, help, and advice. Without that, we would not have been able to write this book.

LIST OF FIGURES

LIST OF TABLES

LIST OF BOXES

ABBREVIATIONS

BEEPS	Business Environment and Enterprise Performance Survey
CARs	Central Asian republics
CEECs	Central-Eastern European countries
CIS	Commonwealth of Independent States
CMEA	Council for Mutual Economic Assistance
ČS	Česká spořitelna (Czech Savings Bank)
ČSOB	Československá obchodní banka (Czechoslovak Trade Bank)
EBRD	European Bank for Reconstruction and Development
EIB	European Investment Bank
EMU	Economic and Monetary Union
EU	European Union
FDI	foreign direct investment
FIG	financial industrial group
FSU	former Soviet Union
FYR	former Yugoslav Republic
GDP	gross domestic product
GDR	German Democratic Republic
GNI	gross national income
GNP	gross national product
IFAD	International Fund for Agricultural Development
IFIs	international financial institutions
ILO	International Labor Organization
IMF	International Monetary Fund
ING	Internationale Nederlanden Groep (International Netherlands Group)
IPB	Investiční a poštovní banka (Investment and Postal Bank)
IPF	investment privatization fund
KB	Komerční banka (Commercial Bank)
MEBO	manager-employee buyout
MNC	multinational corporation
MTZ	Minskii traktornyi zavod (Minsk Tractor Works)
NEM	New Economic Mechanism (Hungary)
NGO	nongovernmental organization
OECD	Organization for Economic Cooperation and Development
OPT	outward-processing trade
PAYG	pay-as-you-go
R&D	research and development
SEECs	South-Eastern European countries
SITC	Standard International Trade Classification
TNK	Tyumenskaya neftyanaya kompaniya (Tyumen Oil Company, Alpha Group)
TTR	total tax rate

UN	United Nations
UNCTAD	United Nations Conference on Trade and Development
USSR	Union of Soviet Socialist Republics
VAT	value added tax
VAZ	Volzhskii avtomobilnyi zavod (Volga Automobile Plant: Russian automobile manufacturer)
WB	World Bank
WC	Washington Consensus
WEF	World Economic Forum
WTO	World Trade Organization
ZAZ	Zaporizkyi avtomobilebudivelnyi zavod (Zaporizhzhia Automobile Plant: Ukrainian automobile manufacturer)

MAP OF THE REGION

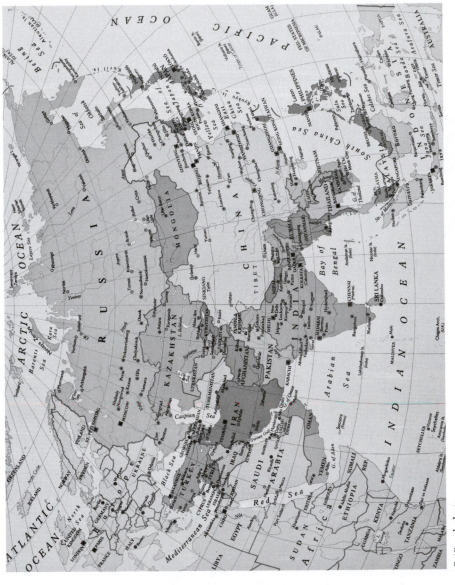

DETAILED MAP OF THE REGION

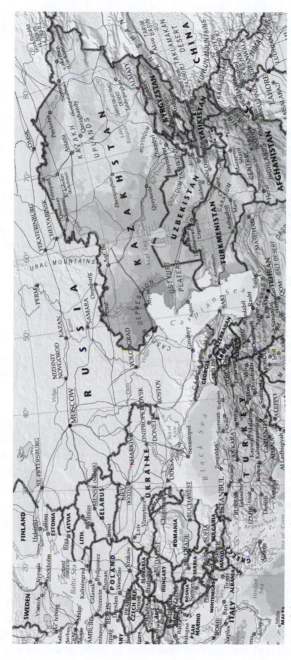

Detail from From H.J. deBlij and P.O. Muller, The World Today: Concepts and Regions in Geography, 5th edition. Originally rendered in color. H.J. deBlij and P.O. Muller. Reprinted with Permission of John Wiley & Sons, Inc.

This book follows the momentous transformations of the economies of the former Soviet Union and Eastern Europe in the 20 years after 1989. In that period, they abandoned their Socialist economic systems. They moved from economies based on state ownership and, with the partial exception of Yugoslavia, central planning—meaning that a central body allocated resources between producing units—to market economies with, in all but a very few cases, a predominance of private ownership. Alongside changes in their internal systems, they also opened their economies to a wide range of external contacts and influences. The impact of the world financial crisis, however, demonstrated the vulnerability of the growth models that developed in individual countries.

The so-called economics of transition is not a new subject. A great deal has been written on it from several different perspectives. On the basis of 20 years of development, it is possible to reassess past judgements and interpretations. It is possible to show how and why countries developed along a diversity of routes and why the end points, or at least the points reached after 20 years, deviated both from the systems of the past and from the market economies of advanced countries that served as an example for the development of transition strategies.

With so much diversity, it is an open question as to how the process should be characterized. The terms "transition" and "transition economy" gained currency from those who saw the process as simple and linear and leading to a clear and settled outcome. Reality proved more complex, with twists and turns that differed between countries and culminated in different outcomes. The term "transformation" was preferred by others who saw a more open-ended process, probably leading to a novel outcome that contained elements reflecting the heritages of the state Socialist past.

Neither term is ideal. The term "transition" emphasizes the common features in end results, and these were important. All the countries had moved toward market economies, generally with the dominance of private ownership, and all had become integrated in some way into the world economic system. The term "transformation" emphasizes the diversity and unpredictability of these outcomes and the powerful effects of starting points and past heritages. These, too, were important. Nevertheless, we stick with "transition," albeit partly as a convenient shorthand that has gained such wide currency as to be difficult to avoid. It also allows for convenient terms such as "transition economy."

Similarities and differences between countries, both in outcomes and in the course of changes, are recurrent themes in the following chapters. A striking common feature was a decline in gross domestic product (GDP) in the early years, widely referred to as the "transformation depression." Official data point to an exceptionally serious downturn. Only a few countries had passed their GDP levels of 1989 before 2000, and some still had not reached that level in 2008, albeit mostly ones affected at some point by internal wars. Any grouping of countries risks overgeneralizing, whether based on geography or economic structures, but the general picture was for shorter and shallower depressions in the countries of Central-Eastern Europe (referred to throughout the book as CEECs, as explained in the box below) and for longer and deeper depressions in countries emerging from the breakup of the Soviet Union. Thus, using approximate figures that are discussed in Chapter 4 (see also Tables 18.1 and 18.2), the low point of GDP in Poland was 18 percent below its 1989 level, and that was reached in 1991, with recovery coming before other countries and the 1989 level passed in 1996. This was among the most successful countries with the fastest recovery. Among the worst performers was Ukraine, which reached a low point at 60 percent below the 1989 level, and that occurred as late as 1999. Gross domestic product was still almost 30 percent below the 1989 level in 2008.

The countries covered

The countries covered in this book include all the successor states to the Soviet Union, the Soviet Union's former allies in Eastern Europe, and the countries of the former Yugoslavia. References are also made to Albania and Mongolia. However, no attempt is made to provide a comprehensive coverage of every country. That would be both tedious and unnecessary. Countries are given the greatest emphasis where they stand out or where their experiences illustrate general points for the overall discussion of transition.

At many points in this book, it is useful to classify countries into geographical groupings. This does not mean that all within one group followed the same course of development at all times. There were differences within, and frequent overlaps on specific issues between, these groups. At times, groupings that transcend geography prove more meaningful—for example, in relation to export structures when oil and gas exporters constitute a definable grouping. With that said, the following geographical groupings are frequently referred to:

- The Central-Eastern European countries are grouped together with Slovenia, a part of Yugoslavia until 1991, as CEECs. This group also includes Poland, Hungary, and Czechoslovakia, which split in January 1993 into the Czech Republic and Slovakia. Czechia is the grammatically correct geographic name for the Czech Republic, but we use the latter version throughout the book. These CEECs became European Union (EU) members in 2004 and shared many common features, including the highest per capita GDP levels and the best contacts to Western Europe.
- The Baltic republics—Estonia, Latvia, and Lithuania—broke from the Soviet Union in 1991 and became EU members in 2004. They were all small countries that had been forcibly incorporated into the Union of Soviet Socialist Republics (USSR) in 1940 and were quick to re-establish contacts with Western Europe.
- The South-Eastern European countries (SEECs) comprise Bulgaria and Romania and joined the EU in 2007. They were less developed than the CEECs, both economically and in terms of traditions of political democracy.
- The Commonwealth of Independent States (CIS) incorporates all former Soviet republics apart from the Baltic republics. It was formed in December

1991 with eleven members. Georgia joined in December 1993 and withdrew in August 2008. The CIS was a very loose organization with no significance for economic policies, but the countries had common features deriving from their pasts, from the experience of the collapse in state authority as the Soviet Union broke up, and from their limited heritage of contacts with the outside world. It is sometimes helpful to distinguish as a group the Central Asian republics (CARs) of Kazakhstan, Uzbekistan, Kyrgyzstan, and Turkmenistan. They shared common features in their pasts, but there were important differences in their paths of development.

- For some countries, geographical or historical groupings are of practically no relevance. Yugoslavia split up in 1991, and the successor states went through vastly different experiences. Slovenia belongs with the CEEC group. Croatia fits in some features with SEECs, as does Macedonia, referred to with its provisional name, the Former Yugoslav Republic (FYR) of Macedonia. Others were seriously hampered by instability, regional wars, and internal conflicts. This was most destructive in Bosnia-Herzegovina and had long-term consequences in Serbia. Montenegro declared independence from Serbia in June 2006. Other countries that do not fit easily are Albania and Mongolia, comparable to some poorer CIS countries in terms of income levels, but here, geography distinguished them, as Albania had much easier contacts with Western Europe.

Another common feature was a reasonably rapid growth in GDP levels up to 2008, albeit with some fluctuations. All countries were then hit by the effects of the world financial crisis, with some suffering much more than others. The causes of these similarities and differences are not simple. The faster-growing countries are rather diverse, including some with substantial oil exports and some without so strong a natural resource base; some that were criticized for limited reform steps and some that were credited as pioneers of radical reforms.

The approach adopted here to explain these outcomes can be characterized as "political economy." The transformation was always more than a change in economies. It involved the transformation of whole systems, characterized here as "state Socialist," for reasons explained in Chapter 1. The transformations involved changes in political systems and much deeper disruptions of social life, including, in some cases, violent internal conflict and wars with neighboring states. The aim is to explain economic phenomena, but economic theory alone does not provide an adequate basis. It is necessary to look also at history, geography, and political developments.

It is also necessary to adopt an eclectic approach to economic theories, using insights from neoclassical economics and accepting its conclusions on some points but noting its shortcomings on others. Similarly, insights are accepted from institutional and evolutionary economics where they prove the most useful. The structure of the book reflects this approach, starting with chapters on past history, which include a critique of the economic system before 1989.

Geography was also important, helping those countries that were closest to the economic heart of Europe. However, that cannot be separated from the political traditions that gave the CEECs the best prospects for democratic political consolidation. Inherited economic structures also helped countries starting from a higher economic level. This was most significant in CEECs, countries that had undergone a degree of industrialization decades earlier, and in countries with raw-material reserves, especially the oil-producing countries from the Commonwealth of Independent States (CIS), made up of most of the former Soviet Union. Many others, with weaker industrial bases inherited from their pasts, faced a more difficult road out of the transformation depression.

Political development and, above all, the nature of the states were important in the depression and in determining forms of recovery and subsequent development. This marked important dividing lines between countries. A market system cannot function without state activity, which, at the minimum, ensures a stable legal environment. The experience in much of the CIS included substantial weakening of the state's administrative apparatuses such that these preconditions could not be met in the early years of transition.

It can be added that even the minimum requirement of a functioning state apparatus is not enough on its own. Laws and rules have to be accepted and applied, and, as argued by institutionalist economists, this is not an automatic process but one that takes considerable time. That point can be illustrated from the slow evolution of institutions in the history of mature market economies. The exact processes that need time to develop are referred to at various points in the book, notably in relation to corporate governance and finance systems.

The effect of economic policies has been one of the most controversial issues in discussions of transition. Within countries, too, debates from the early 1990s led to entrenched positions, as individuals, including economic advisers, academic economists, and politicians, tied their colors to particular masts. The international aspect was particularly important. Transition was not a matter for the transition economies alone. It became a testing ground for the major international institutions—the International Monetary Fund (IMF) and World Bank—and their prestige was tied in with the success of particular transition strategies from the start. They developed their conception of the appropriate policy approach, and this set the agenda. They proved successful in influencing—often decisively and always to some degree—policy making in individual countries. This made transition an extraordinary experiment in the attempted application of a similar policy model across a range of very different countries. However, although they had considerable leverage with their prestige and with their ability to impose conditions, there were differences of opinion within those organizations, and their efforts met varying degrees of opposition within individual countries.

Debate focused on the broad strategy to be adopted, the speed with which measures should be implemented, and also the desired outcomes. Two opposing positions were caricatured as "shock therapy" and "gradualism." The former, focusing on speedy price and trade liberalization and macroeconomic restraint to limit inflation, was broadly the approach of the IMF and World Bank. The latter developed partly as a continuation of reform polices from before 1989 and partly as a reaction against shock therapy. In practice, policy mixes often appeared as a combination of the two.

The core of the policy package promoted by the IMF and World Bank was developed from the so-called Washington Consensus (referred to in what follows as WC), which had been the basis of advice to, and conditions for, Latin American countries previously seeking IMF assistance in the face of external and internal disequilibrium. Adaptation into a strategy for transition required a greater focus on privatization, and there were also references to the need to develop a framework of laws and other preconditions for a functioning market economy. It was not a rigid strategy and developed through adaptation in the light of experience, but in practice, the main focus at the start was on the liberalization and stabilization measures. In following years, the focus was on privatization alongside general liberalization and deregulation of business activities.

A discussion of the early years of transition, therefore, requires substantial discussion of the WC strategy. It was the basis for policies in many countries, starting with Poland in 1990, and it dominated much of the early analytical and academic writing on transition. Success was said to go with application of the WC strategy, while poor results were interpreted as penalties for deviating from that strategy. As already indicated, the conclusions of this book do not confirm so simple a relationship between one policy package and successful outcomes. Reality was more complex because other factors apart from policies were important, because other policies were also important, because application of the WC strategy varied between countries, and finally, because the effects of the WC strategy were not all positive. Its strengths and weaknesses, therefore, require a more careful assessment.

The WC strategy contained some clearly positive elements that would belong in any serious transition strategy. Some were embedded in part of the reform thinking in state Socialist countries before 1989, but their victory was not assured until the political changes of that and the following years. However, the application of the WC strategy revealed weaknesses that reflected a simplified and abstract view of a market system that was common to much of mainstream economics at the time. This was the era of "neoliberal" domination in economic thinking, meaning support for policies of deregulation, privatization, and free markets wherever possible.

Behind the WC strategy was an implicit assumption that a market needed very little more than liberalization and private ownership. The need for an active state and for a framework of laws and relationships within which a market system could function was sometimes given formal recognition but, in practice, was soon either given lesser prominence or ignored in total. That justified a mistaken emphasis on the need for speed above all else in reaching features recognized in mainstream economic theory.

Individual aspects of the WC strategy figure prominently in several chapters in this book, but a blanket assessment of the package as a whole is not possible. However, it is helpful to set out some key points at the start, outlining assessments that emerge from discussion in later chapters. Judgment on the strengths and weaknesses of the Washington Consensus strategy, and of the thinking that lay behind or came with it, can be set out under the following six points.

First, it was right to emphasize liberalization of prices and of international trade. The benefits of market-determined prices are beyond dispute. That is clear from the experience of central planning. Opening of trade to the external world was also clearly desirable in view of the experience of isolation under central planning.

Despite pressure for speed, these steps did not need to be adopted in total at once. In practice, price liberalization started in several countries before 1989, and all countries retained some central controls over some prices, typically energy and housing, over the following years. There was even more scope for a gradual approach toward trade liberalization. Countries that in the past have caught up with the most advanced in the world have always relied on forms of state help to protect new industries. Indeed, in practice, there was some protection in early years in all transition economies, although the pressure from the outside was to minimize this and to keep any period of significant protection as short as possible.

Second, it was right to emphasize the benefits of a stable macroeconomic environment, but it was wrong to set stabilization as an overarching priority. This was to be one of the most controversial parts of the WC strategy. The problem is that stabilization is never fully achieved—there are always some signs of macroeconomic imbalance—and driving down state spending and the money supply can be very harmful to other policy objectives.

Fiscal restraint by cuts in public spending threatened unnecessary destruction of productive capacity and further social costs from reductions in state spending. It could contribute to the destructive weakening of state apparatuses. Here, underlying theoretical positions influenced policy choices, as such concerns were not relevant to those who could not see a state ever playing a positive role.

Reducing and restricting the money supply was similarly problematic, as an overzealous approach undermined the development of a market economy. The heritage of central planning actually left enterprises poorly equipped to cope with restrictive monetary policies. However, that approach was pressed from the outside on the basis of a mistaken view that the principal problem was one of excess demand and an excess of money. In practice, many governments, by fudges and retreats, quietly relaxed restrictive policies as problems became apparent. In some cases, restrictive policies led to the strengthening of informal and barter relations between enterprises.

Third, it was right to remove restrictions on private enterprise as quickly as possible. This was underway in many countries before 1989 and hardly needed emphasis in international advice. It was a step justified by the evidence of inflexibility and failures to satisfy and respond to consumer demand under central planning. As long as the new enterprises could operate in a normal legal environment and as long as they were built genuinely from scratch and not by expropriation of state assets—neither of which was always the case—they were clearly beneficial to transition economies. The positive effects, therefore, depended on maintenance of a functioning state.

Fourth, it was wrong to emphasize the need for the maximum speed with privatization. This led, for a time, to active support for so-called mass privatization, based on distribution of vouchers that were then exchanged for shares in formerly state-owned enterprises. Support for this measure reflected two questionable theoretical views.

The first was the view that institutional and legal forms could wait until after privatization. That downplays the importance of the wider environment in which an economic system operates. An ingenious, but unconvincing, argument was developed to fill this gap. Privatization, it was suggested, should come first. That would create effective owners who would then demand new institutions to protect their property and regulate their relationships with each other. The state would then provide a framework demanded by private property, but there would never be much need for any larger role. This bears little relationship to the development of market economies in the past in which state authority always played an important role. The discussion in later chapters provides clear evidence of the negative effects of speedy privatization resulting in weak legal environments. These were particularly damaging when international financial flows were weakly regulated, making it easy for individuals and businesses to transfer wealth to other countries.

The second questionable view was that a successful market economy depends on incentive structures alone. A private firm, it was believed, would maximize efficiency so as to maximize profits. Managements would be forced to set this aim by private, profit-oriented owners. That ignores much of the complexity of modern businesses. They have complex internal lives in which different actors have varied incentives. Moreover, success does not depend on incentives alone. Managers need to know how to manage, how to develop new products, and how to access markets and networks. These are not simple tasks. Experience was to show that privatization alone often contributed nothing to solving these problems and in many cases left enterprises worse placed than under state ownership. Indeed, the incentive to seek quick profits was often highly damaging, leading to asset stripping and transfers of wealth abroad.

There were clear alternatives to mass privatization, and a varied array of countries avoided, or kept to a minimum, the reliance on that approach. One alternative was to target privatization so that it did help overcome the problems just mentioned, and the most promising way to do this was to seek out established multinational companies (MNCs) as buyers. This form of opening to the outside world did bring substantial benefits, although only when it was clearly associated with commitments to investment and development. That was not always the case. Simply selling off to foreign companies as quickly as possible and without attention to the terms was, therefore, not a wise policy. It can be added that finding desirable buyers was possible only for enterprises that were attractive to a potential buyer, and that was true only of some. Foreign ownership was, therefore, not a universal panacea.

Another alternative was commercialization under state ownership, allowing for later or gradual sale of shares as a means to raise finance and guarantee independence from political interference as the business environment developed and improved. That would have been in line with the significant levels of state ownership that persisted in many Western European countries in the years after 1945. There is some empirical evidence that private ownership has advantages over state ownership, although there are difficulties with comparing like with like under different ownership forms and strong evidence that other factors, such as a competitive environment, can be more important. There is no evidence that private ownership must be better in all circumstances, particularly not for the kinds of private ownership that emerged out of mass privatization in the 1990s.

Fifth, it was wrong to opt for speedy liberalization of banking. Hopes of creating a successful finance system in a short space of time were one of the most serious mistakes in transition strategies inspired by the WC, leading to substantial losses as new banking systems were engulfed by damaging crises. There was a theoretical basis for this policy in the view that banks are no different from any other business and would, therefore, similarly benefit from private ownership and minimal regulation.

In fact, their business activities can be very risky and the costs to the economy of their failure very large. The banking system is an area in which the institutionalist message—that the free market alone is not enough—has particular force.

The alternative here was clear. There could have been a much longer period of state ownership, ensuring that banks kept to the role of financing productive investment and to the gradual establishment of deposit bases as members of the public grew to trust this form of saving. This would have been consistent with practice in many market economies that developed with substantial state involvement in, and regulation of, banking. Comparisons between transition economies also show that there was greater stability where the growth of a private banking system was not rushed. New private banks came and went, often leaving the state to pick up the pieces.

Finally, it was wrong to argue against an active state role. The theoretical justification for this was the belief that a market system leads to an ideal allocation of resources such that any state intervention is an unnecessary distortion. It is seen as yielding to sectional lobbies or "rent seekers," meaning individuals and businesses seeking an income from state favors and subsidies without making any productive contribution. This ignores the many ways in which state intervention contributes to the functioning of a market economy, as justified by theories of market failure and as demonstrated by the history of active state roles in many countries' development and by state activity in mature market economies. Pressure for a greater state role was therefore likely in many cases to contribute to, rather than restrict, economic development.

There were businesses that survived thanks to state subsidies. In this sense, rent seeking was a real and important phenomenon. However, minimizing the role of the state and relying on private business often led to further problems. Apart from rent seeking as normally understood, it was often very easy to make rapid fortunes by exploiting the extreme freedom given to new private businesses and individuals.

In later years, policy debates shifted away from the early emphasis on shock therapy versus gradualism and on the WC strategy. That was partly because the WC strategy had itself developed, with parts from early versions universally accepted, parts implemented, and parts adapted or superseded. Problems caused by early policy choices had been handled and left in the past. New themes appeared more important, and policy debates were conducted on less-general themes—for example, shifting to tax and welfare policies and measures to attract foreign direct investment (FDI).

However, underlying theoretical differences continued to influence policy choices. There was continuing, lasting pressure from an approach that emphasized the benefits of the freest possible market with the smallest possible state role. Advocates of the neoliberal approach focused on new issues. These included low welfare spending and the "flat tax," which meant very limited progressiveness in tax systems. This was propagated and spread across transition economies, marking them out as still distinct in policy ideas from advanced market economies.

Another important theme was the liberalization of financial systems and opening to inflows of capital. These were to become more dangerous as economies developed, but the dangers were underestimated. There was an assumption that state debt could present a danger, but in fact, it was private debt that contributed most to the effects of the 2008 world financial crisis. These effects were quite devastating for some countries, although they appeared to have done well in the terms laid down by international agencies. They had followed the strategy of liberalization, privatization, low taxes, and limited state spending.

Thus, although the WC strategy as such became less relevant, neoliberal thinking continued to play a role, and policy choices continued to matter. They were still only one factor influencing outcomes, and that influence has to be set in the context of other factors—in particular, the geographical location of countries, their past development, and their political and state systems. These are brought together in the final two chapters, which set out to define the differences in the kinds of capitalism that emerged from 20 years of transition and to assess the effects of the world financial crisis. These can, in turn, serve as a basis for an assessment of the first 20 years of transition.

SECTION I

THE POLITICAL ECONOMY OF STATE SOCIALISM

CHAPTER ONE

The System of State Socialism

The purpose of this chapter is to introduce the economic system of the Communist period, showing how this was inseparably bound up with a particular political system. These rose and fell together, political changes often preceding economic ones. Nevertheless, the economic failures referred to in later chapters were also important in undermining the foundations of political power.

POLITICAL POWER

It was initially political change that brought the state Socialist system into existence, and it was political change that led to its downfall. The analysis, therefore, starts with the structure of political power that developed in the years after the Russian revolution of 1917 and was then imposed across the countries of Central and Eastern Europe that were incorporated into the Soviet bloc after 1945. Box 1.1 discusses concepts used to characterize the nature of the system.

The dominant common feature was the effective monopoly of power for one party. There are many descriptions of how the system worked, albeit with a bias toward following the Soviet Union rather than other countries, which, in some cases, had less monolithic power structures. Good descriptive accounts that also link political power to social and economic structures can be found in Lane (1978, 1985). The ruling party was usually, but not always, called a Communist party; that name will be used throughout this work. Its position was guaranteed with a constitutional provision for the "leading role" of the party.

This first appeared in the Soviet Union's constitution in 1936 and was later followed by the other members of the Soviet bloc. Its practical meaning was to rule out any opposition to the ruling party. This stood alongside constitutional guarantees of democratic rights, such as universal suffrage and the supremacy of elected bodies, but in reality, the party dominated, able to select candidates and determine the outcome of elections. At all levels, party bodies had supremacy over government and administrative bodies, able to arbitrate over important decisions and, above all, able to dictate important appointments. This was cemented in the so-called *nomenklatura* system, under which key appointments required approval from a relevant party body.[1]

The ruling parties grew rapidly in terms of membership (Berend 1996, 48–50), with a bias toward those in managerial and professional occupations. Membership tended to increase with economic and social development as the proportion of these occupations increased. In the last years of the USSR, membership was roughly equivalent to 7 percent of the total population, albeit with a much lower percentage among non-Slavonic nationalities and in less-developed republics of Central Asia. Thus, Uzbeks constituted 4.7 percent of the population but only 2.3 percent of party members in 1981 (Lane 1985, 228–29). Such differences could reflect both economic and social development and the extent of commitment to the system. For Czechoslovakia, a country at a higher economic level, the equivalent figure was 11 percent, while for Poland, it was 8 percent in 1980 prior to the political crisis at the start of that decade, after which it fell to about 6 percent.

Joining the party meant refraining from actively opposing the leadership or its aims. It did not need to mean much political conviction, although there was some committed support in all countries. It was a great help with, and even a precondition for, a range of careers. It implied little real political influence, as the party itself, despite formally democratic structures, was firmly controlled from above. Here, the merging of state and party were important, as state repression could be used to eliminate inner-party opposition. However, this was not all a one-way process. Party organizations could lobby for resources, as discussed later under the planning process, and there was scope for debate on themes allowed by the leadership, which sometimes included reforming the economic system.

The party was formally the bearer of an ideology, and members were expected to give verbal backing to this and to support efforts to encourage commitment and work effort from the rest of the population. They were expected to play the role of a support base for the leadership but often proved unreliable at times of crisis. In practice, official ideology was important for what it ruled out rather than for what it encouraged. It enabled the leadership to restrict the bounds of public debate, meaning, for example, that economic thinking was to be restricted within a Marxist framework, or it at least could not develop in open opposition to that framework. It ruled out much reliance on the private sector in the economy, although small-scale private activity was accepted pragmatically in many countries. It made contacts with capitalist countries much more difficult, leading to intellectual and economic isolation, and it stood as a barrier to relaxing central controls on the economy.

Members of society were encouraged to join organizations for social and sporting activities and for interest representation. However, these were firmly controlled from above and constituted a structure of "transmission belts," notionally carrying the

---

[1] The term *nomenklatura* originally referred only to the appointment system whereby key posts were filled by direct party appointment, or with the approval of the relevant party committee. In some, but not all cases, party membership was also a precondition for appointment. The term has also been used, less accurately, to refer to the social elite that benefited from the *nomenklatura* system. However, this differed from the elite in a capitalist society. The fact that elite status depended on appointment by a higher authority, rather than ownership of wealth or market power, meant that members of this elite had less freedom to pursue their own interests. They faced continual insecurity and had to accept subordination to those above them in the hierarchy.

leadership's thinking to the mass of the population. That did not rule out all autonomy, but it did rule out playing an independent, still less an oppositional, role. Indeed, these were societies with substantial voluntary involvement from activists at various levels. The largest mass organizations were trade unions, with near universal membership of employees and formally democratic structures. They played important roles in supporting individual members and in providing social and recreational facilities. They were expected to encourage work effort and commitment and did not undertake genuine collective bargaining with employers. That would have threatened the central control over the economy. The logic of this role within a planned economy, and how it marked out trade unions from those in market economies, is covered by Deutscher (1950), Ruble (1981), and Lane (1985, 25–37).

This characterization of political power leads to two questions relevant to post-Communist change. The first concerns how far political power and the ruling party were linked to material privilege, and the second concerns the nature of "civil society."

The nature and extent of privilege was different under state Socialism from developed capitalism. Information on the living standards of those at the top is fragmentary, but the highest earned incomes were not particularly high in relative terms, and there was no formal property income to widen the gap. The open atmosphere in Poland in 1981 led to publication of the salaries of the top party and government figures. They stood at five times the average pay, and only 0.1 percent of earners received over four times the average (Myant 1981, 62–63). Privilege depended more on goods and services acquired illegally thanks to positions of power or distributed informally or in special shops. It was not openly discussed in state Socialist societies but was studied by Mervyn Matthews (1978), using information from Soviet émigrés. Fragmentary evidence exists on CEECs (e.g., Mlynář 1980, 128–31), and some dramatic cases of personal corruption were exposed in Poland in 1980. All point to a very narrow group able to bypass shortages of high-quality goods and services.

There were benefits lower down the chain from political loyalty, such as priority in some recreational facilities, but this certainly did not turn all party members into a privileged elite. Nor did it give them a good start in the new system. Those with power, expertise, and contacts in some cases did have assets that could be converted into wealth under new conditions, but that describes only a minority of party members.

The nature of "civil society" under state Socialism was also different from its equivalent in societies with firm democratic institutions. The term has been used in different ways in the study of politics and societies. To the Italian Marxist Antonio Gramsci, it was a sphere distinct from the state in which a ruling class could nevertheless gain popular consent for the system's survival in periods of political crisis (1971). To much of political science, it represents a network of organizations ranging across the clearly nonpolitical to pressure groups and representatives of social interests. Society is thereby organized independently of the state, and this, so it is argued, provides a foundation for democratic politics.

In terms of the actual organizational forms implied, these two apparently very different conceptions had a great deal in common. However, the system of transmission belts and rigid control from above, over both party and nonparty bodies, meant that civil society was weak in either sense. Indeed, during periods of major crisis, the system seemed unable to survive without the use or threat of force from outside the country—most obviously, East Germany in 1953, Hungary in 1956, Czechoslovakia in 1968, and Poland in 1981.

Many members of society had experience within organizations, and this provided a basis for formal, organized activity in the post-Communist period. However, the system did not foster independent activities or initiatives, and there was no heritage of independent media that could help develop an informed, critical, and thinking public. Credit went to conformity with those in authority. Thus, in some views, civil society in any meaningful sense existed only in dissident circles made up largely of intellectuals who sacrificed careers, and hence access to information and the ability to publish, to develop their thinking independently. These individuals gained international prestige, but their numbers were very small. Overall, then, the dominant impact of the power structure and its ideology was to stunt independent thought and to isolate thinking in state Socialist countries from development elsewhere in the world. That was the background against which ideas on economic change were to develop after 1989.

Box 1.1 Totalitarian or state Socialist?

The system embodied one-party rule, an economy based overwhelmingly on state ownership and, at least in theory, central state direction. In the official ideology, it was a Socialist system, ensuring greater rationality than the capitalist alternative and providing a more equitable, stable, and prosperous future. Particularly from the 1970s, the terms "real" or "existing" Socialism were used as part of the effort by those in power to rule out discussion of alternative models of Socialism.

More critical perspectives have used a variety of terms that imply differing analyses of the system's strengths and weaknesses. "Communist" is an obvious term, taking the usual title for the ruling party and emphasizing the uniqueness of the system. It conveniently points to the subsequent period as "post-Communist." However, the term implies an exclusive emphasis on political power and on the system's uniqueness.

The term "totalitarian" is often used, albeit often rather loosely. Here, the focus is on the regime's use of repression—at times, very harsh—and on its efforts to control the population and its thinking through every aspect of social activity and to check on individuals' activities and opinions with the help of networks of informers. These were an important part of the system, which contributed to its longevity and stability over much of its existence. However, it has proved difficult to give it rigorous theoretical meaning.

The classic study claimed to produce only "a general descriptive theory of a novel form of government" (Friedrich and Brzezinski 1956, vii), showing common features of countries under Communist and Nazi power. This underplays the importance of the regimes' particular ideologies. Communist parties could gain some popular support, and even more acquiescence, thanks to their promises of development, security, and greater equality. This, too, was important to the system's longevity, and its demise followed, as, in its final years, those promises looked increasingly unconvincing. Theories of totalitarianism also exaggerate the extent of central control. Although the authorities were able to suppress opposition, their ability to impose their will on society was more limited. Society was, therefore, not as unchanging as early theories of totalitarianism had suggested.

Although differing in pace and precise form, the general direction of change has had common features across all countries, supporting an argument that totalitarian regimes tend to shift toward a "post-totalitarian" type. The regime still clings to features of the previous system but allows some relaxation toward social and economic pluralism (Linz and Stepan 1996, 38–51). That fits with developments in the Soviet Union and Eastern Europe, with maintenance of one-party rule alongside, for example, acceptance of widespread private agriculture in Poland or greater openness to nationalist ideologies in Russia and some other Soviet republics.

A possible match with totalitarianism for an economic system is the term "command economy," at one time popular and said to indicate a state taking over all initiative, while enterprises were left to carry out instructions (e.g., Wiles 1962, 18). This, too, exaggerates the nature of central authority and thereby misses many of the system's weaknesses.

Various writers from Marxist backgrounds (covered and discussed in Lane [1985, Chapter 3]), most notably Leon Trotsky, have used notions of a bureaucracy usurping control or even of a "new class" holding power under a form of "state capitalism." Trotsky saw the ruling "bureaucracy" as a cohesive privileged group that might seek to stabilize its privileges by reintroducing private property (Trotsky 1972, 254; Deutscher 1963, 460–66)—a prediction that was to find some support in developments in Russia in the early 1990s.

The first prominent exponent of a "new class" theory was the one-time Yugoslav leader Milovan Djilas (1957). It was also developed by authors with a Trotskyist heritage, especially Cliff (1964), into the theory of the Soviet Union as a "state capitalist" country. This exaggerates the similarity with countries with democratic politics and market economies; as is argued in the following text, different concepts are needed to understand the relationship between political and economic life and the sources of the system's ultimate weakness.

Others refer to "state Socialism," emphasizing that the system drew inspiration from Socialist thinking and remained true to that in some features but endured an overbearing state in all spheres of life. This is the best of the available characterizations, including a recognition of the system's ideological origins but also its distinctiveness from others within the Socialist tradition—most importantly, Western European social democracy. It also indicates that this is more than a system of political power. Political and economic structures were part of one coherent whole, and the links between them helped to shape its strengths and weaknesses.

FORCES FOR CHANGE

The authorities confronted three linked pressures for change. The first was the weakness of their social support base. The second was their inability to fulfill promises of economic performance. The third was pressure to make the system more effective—in other words, for its reform—from within the regime's own support base, meaning the specialists and intellectuals whom it believed it could rely on. In all of these, the system's official Socialist ideology was important, as there was a visible failure to live up to promises of superiority over the alternative capitalist system, a point that encouraged disillusionment and new thinking among committed supporters. The last of these three is taken up in more detail in Chapter 3, which deals with thinking on reforms to the economic system. The effects of the first two were felt increasingly acutely as the system experienced gradual economic stagnation.

The social support base was never fully secure in any country. In only a few cases was Communist power established with substantial popular backing. Generally, it was established with minority, or even minimal, public backing. A substantial account of Russian history (Hosking 2006) shows a continuing gap between thinking in the population and the regime's aims and ideologies. This was never a regime that could count on public trust, and the distance between regime and population appeared greater in other Soviet republics. Regimes in some Central European countries enjoyed some support at the start, possibly even a majority in Czechoslovakia at the time of the Communist takeover in 1948, but it was continually tested by economic disappointments and by repressive and discriminatory policies toward much of the population. These included imprisonment for public dissent and discrimination in employment or access to education on grounds such as class origin of parents, past political affiliations, or family contacts with countries outside the Soviet bloc.

There are no accurate means to monitor changing popular attitudes toward regimes, but there was a clear shift in the dominant rhetoric of the regimes' critics. The Socialist tradition, and accusations that the regime had not been true to its principles, were important in the early years and most obviously in the Czechoslovak reform movement of 1968. That kind of thinking had largely faded by the late 1980s.

The rigid monopoly of power and strict control of any sources of potential opposition could be seen as rational reactions to a likely lack of public support. This is also consistent with the speed with which commitment to a Communist cause disappeared after the regimes' downfalls. Communist parties survived in only a couple of countries and then with substantially different programs and aims. Indeed, the Russian Communist Party, founded in 1990 and commanding considerable electoral backing, dropped much of traditional Marxist thinking and adopted much of the symbolism of Russian nationalism (Hosking 2006, 396–97; March 2003, 122–25). The Czech Communists also retained their party's name and electoral support for more than 20 years after their fall from power from 10 to 13 percent of the population. Other former ruling parties shed much of their membership, changed their names, and claimed adherence to social democratic values; in Hungary and Poland, these parties, often referred to as "post-Communist," returned to government in the 1990s.

Political evolution in the Soviet Union was very clear from the terror of the Stalin period to less-arbitrary authoritarianism of later years. Indeed, the period under Brezhnev's pragmatic and rather colorless leadership, starting in 1964, is often characterized as establishing a welcome security for those in higher positions (Colton 1986, Chapter 1). The regime could allow itself a more relaxed approach, albeit only somewhat more relaxed, toward possible alternative ideologies, such as Russian nationalism (cf. Hosking 2006), that could make contact with more of the population. It has also been argued that this period saw a failure of, and hence a shift away from, extreme repression in other parts of the Soviet Union, meaning a greater dependence on forms of power relation derived from the pre-Communist period. In Central Asia, it meant implicitly allying with traditional clans that could rule under the Communist name and implement some of Communist economic and social thinking, linking this to more traditional forms of power and patronage (Collins 2006).

The regimes' weakness was most exposed when they could not satisfy employees' material expectations. Whenever possible, strikes and protest actions were not reported in the media, and leading participants were victimized. However, in some cases, they reached such a scale as to force concessions. They were in all cases a warning to the authorities that economic policy had to pay attention to consumers, and this held in check—and then ultimately ended—the high levels of investment and military spending of the industrialization drives of the 1930s and early 1950s.

Mass protests over living standards were most frequent in Poland, where they erupted in 1956, 1970, and 1980, and each one shifted the nature of the political regime and its economic policy. The first contributed to greater liberalization, attempts at decentralization, and employee involvement in planning and ended thoughts of collectivization of agriculture. The second led to a reorientation toward investment and consumption growth, financed in part by foreign borrowing. The third followed the failure of the previous strategy, which led to debts that could not be repaid and forced a massive cut in imports, hitting living standards and industrial production. Strikes led to the emergence of the independent union Solidarity, suppressed by military rule in December 1981. The Polish regime by then could seek legitimacy only by promising that it was aiming to reform the system. This, it signally failed to do. It appeared trapped between a recognition of the system's failure and a realization that the Soviet authorities would not tolerate abandoning the "leading role" of the party or allegiance to the Soviet bloc.

Mass protest in Poland was important to the weakening and breakdown of state Socialism as a whole. The country was the largest within Eastern Europe. It was incorporated into the Soviet bloc in the late 1940s but with a strong base for opposition and for alternative ideologies around Polish nationalism and the Catholic Church. This pluralism within society was met by a more liberal and tolerant attitude from the authorities toward public discussion than was usual in neighboring countries. Opposition also depended on workers' militancy in key periods. As indicated in the following text, the failure either to satisfy or to confront opposition led to economic paralysis in the 1980s, as covered by Myant (1982, 1989b) and Nuti (1981).

The decisive break for state Socialism as a whole came with the arrival of Mikhail Gorbachev as the Soviet party leader in 1985. His individual role was undoubtedly very important (cf. A. Brown 1996), but his arrival also reflected a view in the Soviet power structure that the system was failing to deliver and needed opening to new ideas and reform in order to achieve the desired modernization. Reform in the Soviet Union included loosening the grip on Eastern Europe, and this was followed by the regimes in Hungary and Poland—the two countries in which disillusionment with the system had penetrated the furthest into the power structure—initiating roundtable talks with opponents. They were soon relaxing power and allowing genuinely contested elections, opening the way for former oppositional groups to come to power. Communist power fell in some countries (East Germany and Czechoslovakia) when mass protests, inspired by events in their neighboring countries, were not suppressed. In Romania, a more determined attempt to use force failed in December 1989. A number of Soviet republics sought to break free from the USSR, and attempts at repression in Baltic republics—countries forced into the USSR after the Second World War—proved ineffective. Politics in the Soviet Union entered a chaotic phase, which, as indicated next, had important implications for the economic situation. The country definitively ceased to exist in December 1991 and was succeeded by 15 independent republics.

Thus, the transformations of political power took different forms. In all cases, the old regime ultimately yielded. In some (Poland and Hungary), it was effectively disintegrating with the lack of belief that the state Socialist system had anything more to offer. The old leaders lacked the ability or will to mobilize repression, and they could not offer much contest in free elections. In some, those in power were able to recycle themselves as new leaders, but commitment to democracy was often purely formal. In several former Soviet republics, the old leaders dropped any talk of socialism, but remained as autocratic rulers.

A spectrum emerged, as discussed in Chapter 8, with countries at one end adopting political democracy in forms familiar in Western Europe (Central Europe). In the midrange were regimes that some have considered close to an authoritarian model (Linz 2000; Way 2005), such as those of Russia and Ukraine, but others have preferred to classify these as "competitive authoritarianism" (Levitsky and Way 2002); they applied the basic rules of formal democracy, but those rules were routinely manipulated, and oppositional figures, seen as a significant challenge to the regime, were routinely bullied and harassed into cooperative behavior. At the furthest extreme were countries characterized by more clearly authoritarian regimes. Uzbekistan and Turkmenistan have also been characterized as "sultanist," meaning a rationalized form of traditional domination using the state apparatus (Linz and Stepan 1996, 51–54).

These differences in political regimes corresponded to countries' geographical locations, meaning their proximity to Western Europe, and to their pre-Communist political traditions. Multiparty systems had existed with varying degrees of embeddedness in Central Europe. Such a system had never taken root in Russia, and its basis was even weaker in Central Asia. The differences were to prove important for subsequent economic strategies but not in a simple equation between the extent of democracy and the extent of market-oriented reform.

CHAPTER TWO

The Successes and Failures of Central Planning

The economic system under state Socialism took shape after the establishment of a monopoly of power for a Communist party. It was successful at achieving economic growth and development and at securing, at least formally, full employment and a high degree of social protection. Material inequalities were less than in equivalent market economies. It was, then, a system that functioned.

However, despite promises of catching up and overtaking the world's most advanced economies, it failed to keep up in advanced technologies or modern consumer goods and failed even to provide adequate supplies of basic consumer goods to ensure market balance. There were clear signs of declining dynamism and, especially by the 1970s, of stagnation. The old, highly centralized economic system was failing to deliver, and countries that attempted to implement substantial reform, as was the case in the final years of the USSR, showed increasing signs of chaos and even collapse. It was political change rather than visible economic catastrophe that marked the end of the system, but economic failure was an essential stimulus to political change.

ECONOMIC SYSTEM AND ECONOMIC PERFORMANCE

Tables 2.1 to 2.3 show relative economic levels and growth performances in key periods for the Soviet Union, individual state Socialist countries, and, where possible, individual Soviet republics. Any figures of this sort are potentially controversial, and estimates of growth rates vary widely between sources. Economic levels cannot be compared with official exchange rates, for reasons explained later. Some measure of purchasing power parity is required, but that is also difficult to calculate in view of different price systems and the lack of detailed data.

Further difficulties with relying on official figures from the countries' statistical offices are discussed in an accessible way by Nove (e.g., 1992). These include difficulties in comparing outputs over time in countries undergoing substantial structural changes. There are also specific difficulties in state Socialist countries, which led statistical offices to overstate GDP levels and hence growth rates. These

11

TABLE 2.1   Per capita GDP of state Socialist countries compared with Western Europe and growth rates, 1950 to 1990

	1950	1973	1989	1990	Average annual growth rates		
					1950–1973	1973–1989	1973–1990
Albania	1,001	2,273	2,477	2,494	3.63	0.54	0.55
Bulgaria	1,651	5,284	6,216	5,597	5.19	1.02	0.34
Czechoslovakia	3,501	7,041	8,768	8,513	3.09	1.38	1.12
Hungary	2,480	5,596	6,903	6,459	3.60	1.32	0.85
Poland	2,447	5,340	5,684	5,113	3.45	0.39	−0.25
Romania	1,182	3,477	3,941	3,511	4.80	0.79	0.06
Yugoslavia	1,551	4,361	6,250	5,779	4.60	2.28	1.67
Total 7 Eastern European countries	**2,111**	**4,988**	**5,915**	**5,450**	**3.81**	**1.07**	**0.52**
USSR	**2,841**	**6,059**	**7,098**	**6,878**	**3.35**	**0.99**	**0.75**
Total 29 Western European countries[a]	**4,579**	**11,416**	**15,856**	**15,966**	**4.05**	**2.07**	**1.99**

Source: Calculated from Maddison (2006, 446–47, 479).

Note: Per capita GDP is measured in 1990 international Geary-Khamis dollars, a measure of purchasing power parity.

[a]The 29 Western European countries include: Andorra, Austria, Belgium, Channel Islands, Cyprus, Denmark, Faeroe Islands, Finland, France, Germany, Gibraltar, Greece, Greenland, Iceland, Ireland, Isle of Man, Italy, Liechtenstein, Luxembourg, Malta, Monaco, Netherlands, Norway, Portugal, San Marino, Spain, Sweden, Switzerland, United Kingdom.

follow from enterprises' desire to maximize reported, rather than actual, output. This could be done by false reporting, but more typically, it involved "pseudoinnovations," discussed later, which gave exaggerated impressions of product improvements. This again points to the need for estimates using purchasing power parity compared over time with relevant market economies.

The figures in Table 2.1 are taken from the Organization of Economic Cooperation and Development (OECD) comparative projects, which used detailed calculations to convert outputs of individual goods into international comparable prices, leading to estimates of GDP compared at purchasing power parity. These data may be preferred to the official figures from state Socialist countries, but they should still be treated only as rough estimates. Some of the results are very surprising and do not match data from either earlier or later periods. Above all, it is difficult to accept that the economic level of the Soviet Union was above that of several CEECs and barely behind the highest one. One likely explanation is that the comparisons could not make satisfactory allowance for differences in the quality of apparently similar products. Nevertheless, these are the best data available, and the broad picture of reasonably rapid growth followed by stagnation is consistent with other evidence.

The annual average growth rate of per capita GDP during the Soviet industrialization drive from 1928 to 1940, calculated in the same way as the figures in Table 2.1,

TABLE 2.2 **Per capita GDP levels in state Socialist countries relative to 29 Western European countries**

	Per capita GDP as a percentage of Western Europe				Arithmetic change in relative level	
	1950	1973	1989	1990	1973–1950	1990–1973
Albania	21.9	19.9	15.6	15.6	−2.0	−4.3
Bulgaria	36.1	46.3	39.2	35.1	10.2	−11.2
Czechoslovakia	76.5	61.7	55.3	53.3	−14.8	−8.4
Hungary	54.2	49.0	43.5	40.5	−5.2	−8.6
Poland	53.4	46.8	35.8	32.0	−6.7	−14.7
Romania	25.8	30.5	24.9	22.0	4.6	−8.5
Yugoslavia	33.9	38.2	39.4	36.2	4.3	−2.0
Total 7 Eastern European countries	**46.1**	**43.7**	**37.3**	**34.1**	**−2.4**	**−9.6**
USSR	**62.1**	**53.1**	**44.8**	**43.1**	**−9.0**	**−10.0**

Source: Calculated from Maddison (2006, 446–47, 479).

Note: Per capita GDP is measured in 1990 international Geary-Khamis dollars, a measure of purchasing power parity. The arithmetic change in relative levels shows the difference in GDP as a percent of the Western European level between the two years covered.

was 3.8 percent. The level of Soviet per capita GDP rose from 34.1 percent of the Western European average in 1928 to 47.1 percent in 1940. This, then, was a time of reasonably rapid growth, while Western European countries were stagnating.

However, after the immediate postwar reconstruction, few of the state Socialist countries kept pace with Western Europe's rapid growth, and declining growth rates took them into stagnation in the 1970s and, even more clearly, the 1980s. The figures show only Bulgaria, Romania, and Yugoslavia—three of the four with the lowest per capita GDPs—improving their relative position in the period from 1950 to 1973, and only Yugoslavia is shown to do so in the following period. Particularly, Poland, Bulgaria, and the Soviet Union suffered decline in this later period.

Figures in Table 2.3 for individual Soviet republics, available from 1973 and calculated from rather incomplete Soviet statistical sources, show substantial variations in the countries' economic levels. It is again surprising to see some Soviet republics ahead of CEECs in 1973 and 1990 and few very far below the average; this may reflect problems with the methodology used and difficulties of gaining truly comparable data. Other data give an impression of possibly larger differentiation at the bottom (cf. Myant and Drahokoupil 2008). The figures clearly show the slowdown after 1973 and the spreading stagnation, with poorer countries showing no sign of catching up. The available data use 1990 as the end year. This is not ideal for assessing long-term trends under state socialism as that system was by then at different stages of disintegration. That year alone saw particularly sharp drops in GDP in some countries, notably Tajikistan.

Populations of countries with particularly severe symptoms of stagnation might be expected to have been the most disillusioned with the state Socialist system and hence

TABLE 2.3   Per capita GDP of Soviet republics compared with Western Europe and growth rates, 1973 to 1990

	1973	1990	Average growth rate 1973–1990	As a percentage of Western Europe 1973	1990	Arithmetic change in relative level 1990–1973
Armenia	6,152	6,086	−0.06	53.9	38.1	−15.8
Azerbaijan	4,434	4,639	0.27	38.8	29.1	−9.8
Belarus	5,233	7,184	1.88	45.8	45.0	−0.8
Estonia	8,657	10,794	1.31	75.8	67.6	−8.2
Georgia	5,932	7,573	1.45	52.0	47.4	−4.5
Kazakhstan	7,625	7,319	−0.24	66.8	45.8	−20.9
Kyrgyzstan	3,727	3,596	−0.21	32.6	22.5	−10.1
Latvia	7,846	9,886	1.37	68.7	61.9	−6.8
Lithuania	7,593	8,646	0.77	66.5	54.2	−12.4
Moldova	5,365	6,165	0.82	47.0	38.6	−8.4
Russian Federation	6,582	7,773	0.98	57.7	48.7	−9.0
Tajikistan	4,095	2,979	−1.85	35.9	18.7	−17.2
Turkmenistan	4,826	3,626	−1.67	42.3	22.7	−19.6
Ukraine	4,924	6,023	1.19	43.1	37.7	−5.4
Uzbekistan	5,097	4,241	−1.08	44.6	26.6	−18.1
Total former USSR	**6,059**	**6,878**	**0.75**	**53.1**	**43.1**	**−10.0**
Total 29 Western European countries[a]	**11,416**	**15,966**	**1.99**			

Source: Calculated from Maddison (2006, 488–89).

Note: Per capita GDP is measured in 1990 international Geary-Khamis dollars, a measure of purchasing power parity. The arithmetic change in relative levels shows the difference in GDP as a percent of the Western European level between the two years covered.

[a]The 29 Western European countries include: Andorra, Austria, Belgium, Channel Islands, Cyprus, Denmark, Faeroe Islands, Finland, France, Germany, Gibraltar, Greece, Greenland, Iceland, Ireland, Isle of Man, Italy, Liechtenstein, Luxembourg, Malta, Monaco, Netherlands, Norway, Portugal, San Marino, Spain, Sweden, Switzerland, United Kingdom.

the keenest to support an alternative. To some extent, this is consistent with the data. Belarus was amongst the least enthusiastic reformers and also appeared to have done relatively well in the preceding years. Poland was a clear leader in transformation, and its economic performance in the 1980s was very poor. Its economy grew rapidly in the early 1970s, but that was bought at the expense of rapidly increasing foreign debt. The result was its dreadful performance, and deep public disillusionment, in the years up to 1989. However, some others, such as Uzbekistan, do not show the same relationship between stagnation and reform enthusiasm. The latter clearly did not depend on economic conditions alone.

The experience of stagnation after growth leads to the question of whether central planning may have been appropriate for rapid development from a low level but ultimately inappropriate for growth in a more advanced economy. The relationship cannot be simple, as relative decline was clear across countries despite widely differing economic levels. The following three points summarize the reasons for the system's different performances over time:

- In the first years, central planning was able to mobilize resources for rapid growth based on structural change and high levels of investment. The focus was on basic and heavy industries, intended to provide the foundations for growth across all sectors. This was often characterized as "extensive" growth, meaning that it depended on higher inputs rather than better use of those inputs—in other words, increased productivity. The distinction is somewhat misleading, as growth in the early years of Soviet planning depended on transferring labor from agriculture, and that was only possible if productivity increased there or, as was the case in the 1930s, if living standards in farming declined catastrophically over a number of years. In more advanced Eastern European countries in the 1950s, nationalization and rationalization of small-scale industry brought productivity gains, releasing labor for new projects. The early years, therefore, saw impressive growth rates in parts of the economies and increases in labor productivity in others.

- This extensive growth was based on one-off sources of labor for the favored sectors of the economy. Once they were exhausted, growth had to be based on technological advance in existing sectors and on further structural changes. The authorities partially recognized this, repeatedly emphasizing the need for "intensification," which means achieving more output from the same inputs of fixed assets, labor, and materials. The system failed to live up to leaders' hopes. Later sections discuss the key areas of innovation and international integration, demonstrating that central planning could not produce a high level of innovative activity, nor could it absorb imported innovations satisfactorily.

- There was also a general trend toward structural stagnation as interests became entrenched and as lower levels, meaning both enterprises and established sectors, learned how to manipulate, and hence dominate, the planning process. Planning thus shifted from a means to achieve change to a means to prevent change. This is described in the following sections. It was exacerbated by the political weakness of the regimes, which were able to suppress the minority of active and vocal opponents but remained scared to face the social consequences of structural change. Thus, a combination of political and economic factors contributed to creeping inertia, irrespective of the country's level of development.

THE NATURE OF THE ECONOMIC SYSTEM

The nature of the economic system varied over time and between countries, but the fundamental, initial thinking was the same, coming from Marxist theory. (Numerous studies exist on the organization of the system and on how it changed. Historical accounts are provided by Nove [1992], Berend [1996], and Kaser [1986]. The system is described and analyzed by Nove [1977] and, with an attempt to link to political and social issues, by Lane [1985]. A historical and analytical account of Czechoslovak development is provided by Myant [1989a].) A "plan," left without much definition in classical Marxist writing, was to replace the "anarchy" of the market, overcoming periodic crises and ensuring production to satisfy human need. This was interpreted as meaning state ownership, centralized control, and coordination by quantity indicators to replace markets and money. Classical Marxism gave very little further guidance on how a planned economy should be organized and proved to be of no practical value to later attempts to reform the system. Marxism provided interpretations for broad historical changes that could not be used for providing meaningful insights on management of an economic system.

The early days of Soviet power saw an attempt to introduce a fully centralized economy, without any role for money and all coordination by central allocation and decree, under the name of "War Communism." It remains a matter of debate as to how far this was a pure application of ideology and how far it was a response to economic collapse and necessity during civil war (cf. Nove [1992, Chapter 3]), but it was abandoned in 1921, and pragmatism led to the acceptance of the so-called New Economic Policy, which allowed substantial reliance on private enterprise and market relations. The system of central planning then evolved as industrialization accelerated in the late 1920s and 1930s. Private enterprise was once more suppressed, and the center, meaning the government and the structure of ministries and agencies that it established to direct and coordinate the economy, intervened to overcome perceived difficulties. The ideology of centralization was important, meaning that markets were not trusted and that the center was seen as carrying a responsibility for intervening whenever difficulties arose, but the emerging system of central planning was not based on any initial blueprint.

Production was undertaken in enterprises, the basic units in the economy, which were subordinated within a hierarchy to a supreme planning body. Enterprise incomes were related to fulfilling plan targets, formally sent down from above. Innovations and structural change were then the responsibility of the center, as was coordination of demand with production. There is an analogy here to the hierarchy within a firm in a market economy, but the organization of a whole economy on this basis had a number of implications that mark a clear difference from any market system.

The center's job included a complex balancing of supply and demand for individual products, a function elsewhere left to an impersonal market. Money and finance played a subordinate role, providing enterprise incomes when plans were fulfilled and providing resources for wages, which consumers could then spend as they wished on goods provided from enterprises.

Money was provided through a banking system based on a single "monobank" undertaking all central bank and commercial bank functions. There were often additional specialized banks, but they did not play independent roles and certainly could not compete with each other. Banks were subordinate agencies within the system, concerned with checking plan fulfillment but not with assessing business decisions or taking risks themselves. They checked enterprise spending on material inputs, wages, and other categories, all of which were subject to separate, centrally set limits. This meant that financial resources could not be transferred between uses—for example, between investment and wages. Money, therefore, did not play the role of a universal medium of exchange.

Prices were largely set by the center, with those of basic necessities often subsidized. This had proved a popular and egalitarian way to increase living standards. Indeed, on a number of occasions, major protests followed attempts to raise the prices of basic necessities. However, subsidization implied a distortion of consumer preferences and was associated with high consumption of, and relatively high demand within consumption patterns for, meat and other foods that the system then had trouble satisfying. Lower prices were, therefore, maintained at the expense of risking, or often continuing, market imbalance and shortages. Other prices were altered by variable rates of turnover tax, which raised state revenue but had the effect of separating prices received by producers from those charged to consumers. Adjusting supply to match demand, therefore, formally depended on central decisions, although in practice, enterprises to some extent had to make do with responding to quantity signals. An important consequence of this system was that the relative price structure differed substantially from that of market economies and from prices on world markets.

The system never functioned perfectly. Despite the nature of the power structure, the official media frequently distributed information on failings, initially with the assumption that they represented individual shortcomings rather than systemic problems. A great deal has been written, both in state Socialist countries and by outside experts using material published there, on the significance of these failings. A starting point for a general critique of central planning was the argument that it was impossible to plan a whole economy from one center.

This had an important practical implication in the toleration of apparently illegal activities. The plan was meant to be obeyed in every detail, but prominent roles were played by informal traders and lobbyists who could arrange for supplies of inputs that appeared unavailable or could bargain for changes to the plan. The *tolkach*, as these individuals were known in Russia, were highly valued by enterprise managements (Berliner 1957, 209–30; Welfens 1992; Harrison and Kim 2006). They were less well known in other countries, but the same practices occurred. The implication is that the system functioned by ignoring its own stated rules. That was likely to have implications for respect for laws and formal procedures in later years (see Chapter 7). It can be added that the legal framework left unclear, especially in the Soviet Union, exactly where authority lay (Sutela 2003, 28–29), and this encouraged an acceptance of informal methods if they were not actively prevented by those with effective power.

A number of features of enterprise behavior became well known across the countries. The impossibility of preparing a plan in perfect detail meant that plan targets were ambiguous and created perverse incentives (a target in weight leads to unnecessarily heavy products; a target in quantity leads to undesirably small products). Plans also had to be built from information that could come only from enterprises, and managements learned the benefits of concealing their potential in order to achieve lower and easier plan targets. In this, they exploited their superior knowledge of their own capabilities. Even if plans went badly, they could claim unforeseen circumstances, and the center would often concede alterations through the plan period. The "plan" thereby tended to become a framework for allocating enterprise incomes, reflecting the bargaining strengths of those enterprises, rather than a means for the center to impose its will on enterprises.

HAYEK AND PRICES

The theoretical argument that planning from one center is impossible was an old and a convincing one that played a central role in the so-called Socialist calculation debate of the 1920s and 1930s between supporters of Socialism and its opponents. The most prominent were members of the so-called Austrian school of libertarian, free market economists and particularly, Friedrich von Hayek. The starting point was the argument, taken up by Ludwig von Mises, another Austrian economist, in 1920 (Mises 1935, 87–130), that rational calculation would be impossible without prices derived from a competitive market. This was later expanded and clarified with the addition that only private ownership could provide the incentives to react appropriately to price signals to ensure economic rationality and efficiency.

Supporters of "market Socialism"—particularly the Polish economist Oskar Lange—proposed in response that a central body, given the same perfect knowledge assumed by neoclassical theory, could find market-equilibrating prices and could set appropriate rules for enterprises to overcome the problems Mises and Hayek had identified. Indeed, it seemed reasonable to assume that central planning would lead to a faster and more consistent reaction to price signals. (For important contributions to the debate, see Hayek [1935], Lange and Taylor [1938], and Lerner [1944]. A much later summary and analysis of the arguments is provided by Lavoie [1985].)

Hayek's important contribution was to return to the role of prices as a signal to which enterprises had to respond—for example, by adjusting output to match demand, saving on inputs that had become more expensive, or improving efficiency to cope with competitors that could cut prices. He thereby clearly differentiated himself from the mainstream of neoclassical thinking, which depended on an abstract model that assumed equilibrium had been attained. Hayek did not believe a stable equilibrium would ever be reached. For him, prices were a means of passing relevant information to actors so that the latter would know how to change their behavior. A central planner, he argued, could never process the volume of information required to give equivalent instructions to economic actors. The outcome would be a distorted and inefficient economy.

This argument was never officially accepted in state Socialist countries. However, the need for prices set in response to market pressures was an important element in thinking on reforms to the planning system in the 1960s. The need for private ownership was not accepted, but the need for some mechanism to protect enterprises' autonomy against arbitrary central interventions began to gain recognition with thoughts of enterprise councils or forms of self-management. However, as indicated later, reform attempts within state Socialism and the development of self-management in Yugoslavia did not lead to economic systems that could overcome all the weaknesses of central planning. After 1989, Hayek's view on the central role of prices proved central to thinking on economic strategies. It seemed that he had put his finger on a key problem and provided a good starting point for analyzing the weaknesses of a centrally planned economy.

There are, however, two important reservations. The first is the empirical point that Hayek and Mises, at the time they were writing, seemed to exaggerate the system's failures. Indeed, their critique was unpopular for a time, as planned economies experienced rapid growth, while Mises had referred to central planning as amounting to "no economy whatsoever" or "merely destruction and annihilation" (Mises 1935, 105, 125). The following sections demonstrate that the absence of market-determined prices and of possibilities inherent in a system with substantial private ownership did contribute to the failures of central planning, but they did not mean that the system could not function at all. Figures on performance rather imply that, for a time, it functioned quite well.

The second is that Hayek presented a model of an economy working effectively by price signals alone. This does not correspond to the reality of existing market economies. Prices are one signal and one coordination mechanism, but they are not adjusted immediately in response to supply and demand variations, and they do not provide all the information a firm needs for making rational decisions. Hayek's picture of an economy ignores the complexity of adjustments in a world of big corporations and in a world in which states can play different roles to correct for market imbalances and failures.

This has important implications for transition strategies. Following Hayek's thinking led to an exaggerated faith in prices and private ownership as panaceas and a dismissal of other issues. The strident and straightforward condemnation of central planning found a warm welcome in state Socialist countries, where economists were looking to find a comprehensible substitute for the Marxist approach they had been forced to adhere to before. It also found an easy resonance with outside advisers who knew very little, and saw no need to learn very much, about the actual workings of the planned economies that were disappearing. The oversimplified critique of state Socialism led to an oversimplified vision of future strategies.

KORNAI AND THE SOFT BUDGET CONSTRAINT

The basis for a more substantial line of critique of central planning was developed by the Hungarian economist János Kornai, who linked microeconomic behavior with macroeconomic imbalances. His inspirations were broad, including ideas developed by Marx and Keynes (Kornai 1992, 288) but also some adaptations of very standard economic theory. The strength of his analysis followed from a combination of empirical evidence and his eclectic approach to theoretical traditions. This enabled him to develop a systematic "empirical theory"—an analytical overview based on generalizations from empirical observation—of the actual workings of the planned economy. Key concepts within this are the "soft" budget constraint and "shortage." They are linked, with the former a possible cause of the latter, but both need to be interpreted carefully. The soft budget constraint will be discussed first. It was introduced in 1979 and formed a central part of the work *Economics of Shortage* (Kornai 1980).

The argument was that in an abstract model of a perfect market economy, all economic actors face a "hard" budget constraint, meaning that their financial resources are firmly limited. Under central planning, and under its reformed versions, consumers face a similarly hard budget constraint, but enterprises have considerable leeway that gives them, to varying degrees, a soft budget constraint. This means that they may not need to worry about overspending or making losses, as the center is likely to help them out. They can press for maximum demands for investment, inputs, wage payments, or other expenditures. The mechanism for ensuring a soft budget constraint is the enterprise's bargaining strength within the planning process plus the center's fear of adverse social effects from enterprise losses. Bankruptcy and subsequent employee redundancy were practically unthinkable.

The concept has proved extremely popular in analyses of planned economies and in inspiring transition strategies. It appears to make planned economies understandable with an original adaptation of mainstream economic theory. However, there are three important reservations.

The first is the assumption that the center will always yield to demands from enterprises. That was not always the case, and there were important differences between countries and between enterprises within the same country.

The interpretation of the soft budget restraint as a generalization to characterize the behavior of all enterprises faced considerable criticism in the 1980s. Kornai, as discussed in detail by Nigel Swain (N. Swain 1992, 124–26), was at times careful to emphasize that he was not claiming there to be no budget constraint. The budget constraint was rather an accounting relationship over which varying degrees of bargaining were possible. Some enterprises could make gains from such bargaining, but the ultimate locus of power remained the central authority. That could be unyielding but was most likely to make big concessions when facing mass protest, as at the times in Poland referred to previously.

The second reservation, following from the first, relates to the application of the concept of soft budget restraint to investment behavior. Kornai referred to an "almost insatiable" appetite for investment on the part of enterprises, but this was very often successfully resisted by the center.

The argument was that enterprises had various incentives to grow, and the soft budget constraint meant that they did not need to care about associated costs or risks. Such thinking had implications for the transition strategy and was used to justify sharply restrictive macroeconomic policies in the early 1990s. However, there are important arguments, discussed later, that enterprises had limited interest in innovation and modernization—they appeared to have suffered from under- rather than overinvestment—and this is difficult to reconcile with the notion of a generally soft budget constraint. Indeed, some other authors have argued that the incentive structure for enterprises meant that there was no incentive to change inherent within the old system; this point is taken up in the following text in relation to the weak incentive to innovate (referred to in Myant [1993, 27–28]). Thus, in contrast to Kornai's position, a common finding has been that a desire for modernization did not come from enterprises and instead had to be imposed, with limited success, from the center.

The third reservation is the timescale under consideration. Central planning imposed extremely rigid requirements on enterprises over a short time period. A plan covered one year, and there was formally no scope for financial overruns. Any deviation required special appeals and permission. The point in the concept of the soft budget constraint is that this was often possible, but it certainly was not automatic. Planning saw a hierarchy of priorities, with some sectors, such as military production, far more likely to get what they wanted. Moreover, the enterprise in a centrally planned economy should not be set against an ideal type from neoclassical analysis of a market economy.

The firm in a real market economy typically has considerable flexibility, too, thanks to scope for raising finance externally, for transferring money between uses, for delaying payment of bills, and for using bank overdrafts. Indeed, a key point made by Schumpeter (1954) in his account of great innovations is that firms can use external funding for projects that are not precisely calculated. They only face the hard budget constraint after a substantial time lag. Under central planning, there is a very tough short-term constraint, but the enterprise can turn a blind eye to long-term dangers. Experience teaches that it will not face bankruptcy, while the firm in a market economy is ultimately answerable for its market performance.

Kornai developed his concept of the soft budget constraint during the time of Hungary's New Economic Mechanism (NEM, discussed later), and it is more directly applicable to a partially reformed economy than to the traditional model of central planning. In the NEM, enterprises were free from detailed instructions, so plan targets were not the issue. However, they responded to difficulties by asking for financial help, and central authorities conceded when the alternative might be growing inequalities in enterprise incomes or even bankruptcy.

KORNAI AND SHORTAGE

Kornai's analysis of shortage provides a bridge between a commonly observed phenomenon and a critical analysis of the workings of a planned economy. The appearance of shortage was a permanent feature of the economic system, affecting enterprises, as they bargained with resources from the center, and consumers, as they searched for goods in shops.

In the first of these cases, shortage followed from rational behavior of enterprises. They feared plan changes that would suddenly cut inputs or lead to demands for higher outputs to cover for problems elsewhere in the economy. The soft budget constraint meant that they were not so constrained by the need to minimize costs. They therefore exaggerated demands during the planning process and hoarded any reserves they could. This included labor, meaning that employees were often taken on as protection against plan changes rather than because they were needed immediately. It also included other inputs that were accumulated in unnecessary stocks, covering against the danger of shortage but also creating shortage for other enterprises.

Shortage of consumer goods became a very visible phenomenon, affecting consumer attitudes and behavior and even social behavior. Consumer goods shortages were commented on in the Soviet Union in the 1920s after the authorities ignored the logic of the market and held down prices of goods in short supply (Nove 1992, 137–39). These shortages continued through the following decades. There were queues for both basic and sophisticated consumer goods, albeit the former kind severe in only some of the countries. This proves disequilibrium for individual goods, but not disequilibrium at the macrolevel, as specific shortages could, and did, coexist with surpluses of other goods. As Kornai (1982, 11–24; 1990b, 139), but not all who have interpreted and used his contribution, stressed, it is more complex than the disequilibrium of Keynesian analysis.

Although consumers faced shortages of some goods alongside excess supply of others, it was the shortages that governed behavior, leading to time wasted in queuing, forced substitution, or, it was widely hypothesized, forced saving. Shortages also altered personal relationships and gave greater importance to personal contacts in gaining access to products. One account describes a Hungarian experience of acquiring the necessary materials for building a house based on developing strings of contacts (Kenedi 1981). Another describes the rituals and contacts needed to cope with normal shopping in Russia (H. Smith 1976). Alena Ledeneva's (1998) analysis of the phenomenon in Russia shows deeply embedded personal-favor networks that complemented and subverted the formal economic system, providing alternative means for distribution and access to scarce goods through what was known as *blat*. Like the *tolkach* for the enterprise sphere, it could be officially frowned on, but few would choose not to be involved.

These practices and networks were probably only of indirect importance in later years. Ledeneva (1998, 2000, 2006) accepts that those practices linked to coping with shortage disappeared, and some people may even have regretted the passing of the social ties and camaraderie involved, but argues that other forms of informal and corrupt practices involving access to decisions by local and national politicians arose in their place. These appear more destructive. The link still remains unclear other than the dependence on a generally lax attitude toward formal rules, also reflecting to some extent their weak embeddedness at any time in Russia.

The extent of shortage is very difficult to measure, partly because shortage could lead to panic buying and to accumulating excess quantities when goods were available. It thereby altered buying behavior in ways that could exaggerate the extent and breadth of shortages. Rational consumers, for example, were said to be buying up all available skis in the summer and all swimming trunks in the winter.

The need to register in a queue for a product—for example, housing or a car—also gave an exaggerated appearance of the extent of shortage, as registration indicated the intent to pay at a future date, not the ability to pay immediately. It was, therefore, not the same as demand in the strict sense of economic theory. In practical terms, it means that an outward sign of shortage (a long waiting list) could disappear very quickly once supply matched demand (Myant 1989a, 181). The same is true of other forms of behavior provoked by shortage: they were good indicators that market imbalance existed but not good indicators of its extent.

However, various measures of intensity of shortage were used, based on opinion surveys, in Czechoslovakia in the 1980s (Myant 1989a, 214–15, 217–18), which helped the center plan to overcome shortages, particularly in sophisticated consumer goods. This was one of the most successful countries at maintaining market balance, but the evidence is clear that shortages were perceived at various times for many products.

More general and serious levels of shortage developed when the authorities' political weakness meant that they were losing control of the economy. The center could respond (1) by raising prices, an option that could be politically undesirable; (2) by raising domestic output of shortage goods if resources allowed; (3) by raising imports if the balance of payments allowed; or (4) by hoping the problem would be tolerated. Polish authorities used the first of these options in 1970, 1976, and 1980, but worker protests led to retreat. They used the third during the 1970s but then lacked the resources to repay debts at the end of the decade. They were left with the last option in the 1980s and backed it from 1981, with repression of popular protests.

The persistence of shortage of consumer goods led to debate over the possibility of an "inflationary overhang," caused by forced saving when there was simply nothing to spend money on. This is referred to later in the context of justifications for restrictive fiscal and monetary policies in the early 1990s and of the rise in prices, leading to very high rates of inflation in some countries. Kornai conceded that it was a possibility, while many others doubted it, and some insisted that it was the case and claimed to find econometric evidence, albeit only of a rather indirect form (Winiecki 1988, Chapter 2). Estimates exist for Poland and Czechoslovakia of the extent of forced saving, but they are highly speculative, with available data open to diverse interpretations (Myant 1989a, 215–17; 1989b, 8–9). More suggestive evidence for Russia is referred to in later text (p. 40).

The problem, as indicated, is that shortage was likely to lead to panic buying or precautionary buying of other goods not yet in short supply. It could also lead to spending on a black market, which grew in conditions of shortage. It can be added that actual levels of saving were generally low, and this was an argument used to justify privatization policies based on vouchers or free distribution of shares.

It seems right to conclude that shortages of many goods were persistent, caused popular anger or alienation from the regime, and led to behavioral responses that were not familiar in market economies, but it is not clear whether they left behind a backlog of forced saving or how far habits acquired for coping with shortage remained part of development in later years.

INTERNATIONAL INTEGRATION

For many reasons, international relations and contacts with other economies are considered essential for economic success. This was to prove a major weakness of centrally planned economies, as analyzed in great detail by Wiles (1968) and well summarized by Kornai (1992). The central planners' concern was to achieve balance within the system they controlled, and external relations were a complication to this. As the system evolved, it took on two particular peculiarities.

The first was that negotiation over foreign trade between state Socialist countries was conducted to a substantial extent in quantity terms, offering surplus products in exchange for goods that were needed for the domestic economy. Prices could then be negotiated to ensure bilateral balance.

The second was a system of foreign trade prices that bore no necessary relationship to domestic prices. There was no single exchange rate and certainly no currency convertibility. Hard (i.e., convertible) currency was strictly rationed and centrally allocated. The economic logic behind this was the implicit assumption that convertibility and free trade would lead to balance-of-payments deficits, while the central controls were also seen as protection against the influence of instabilities in the world economy.

However, the system of foreign trade pricing divorced export prices from domestic prices, making it impossible for enterprises to judge rationally between production for export or for the domestic market. That judgment could only be made by the central planners, who used the gap between the two prices as a guide to the "profitability" of exports. This made statistical data on foreign trade and domestic production incomparable, so the former cannot be used to derive reliable estimates of the economies' openness.

These peculiarities of the organization of foreign trade made international integration very difficult. The preference, therefore, was for autarky, even though official rhetoric continually recognized the benefits of integration and cooperation.

The Council for Mutual Economic Assistance (CMEA), the Soviet trading bloc also referred to in the West as Comecon, was established in January 1949. Its role evolved over the years, but it proved good only at coordination at a very global level—for example, over agreements for the long-term supply of basic raw materials.

To this end, pricing systems for raw materials and manufactured goods were formalized in the 1970s. The price of oil was set as a five-year moving average of world prices, eliminating sharp fluctuations and providing a substantial subsidy from the Soviet Union—the main oil exporter in the bloc—to Eastern Europe when world oil prices rose. Manufactured goods prices were also linked to world prices, again helping Eastern European exporters, as the penalty for low quality was removed (Marrese and Vanous 1983, 108–9). Recent calculations suggest that the subsidy may have been significant only for a short period in the early 1980s (Spechler and Spechler 2009), partly because the oil pricing system worked against the Soviet Union at times of falling world oil prices. Nevertheless, the winding up of the CMEA, meaning the end to a guaranteed export market and conversion to trade in world prices, in 1991 represented a massive shock to Eastern European countries that had imported oil from, and exported manufactured goods to, the Soviet Union.

Political leaders frequently spoke of the benefits of specialization in manufactured goods. This did develop but mostly in the form of one country producing and exporting a complete product, such as tractors from Czechoslovakia and combine harvesters from East Germany. This was out of line with the processes of integration among advanced market economies, which allowed competition between producers of end products and components and which involved complex integration of technology and production.

Even proposed forms of specialization were blocked by individual countries' attempts to maintain and develop manufacturing industries for prestige reasons. Thus, Poland developed its own tractor production. It invested in expansion and bought licenses from Massey Ferguson for the Ursus tractor manufacturer, which became one of the most notorious failures of the country's investment drive of the 1970s (Myant 1981, 108–9). Romania refused to accept a role as an exporter of agricultural goods and established its own heavy and engineering industries, with minimal scope to exploit economies of scale in the production of complex products. This was all possible because countries protected their domestic economies through the state monopoly of foreign trade, preventing enterprises from competing or cooperating across frontiers without state interference. Imports were always complementary to domestic production. They never provided competitors that could threaten domestic producers.

The problems with the system of international trade had three important consequences. The first was to limit access to modern technology and innovations. The second was to limit scope for specialization and economies of scale in manufacturing, and the third was to protect inefficient and uncompetitive enterprises.

State Socialist countries needed to export to earn hard currency—none could be self-sufficient, nor could the bloc as a whole produce all its needs—but for this, they had to rely on exports of raw materials or semimanufactures. Manufactured goods could be sold only at prices significantly below the levels of Western-made goods. Thus, Czechoslovakia, alongside East Germany—the country with the strongest industrial tradition—developed a dual export structure. Within the Soviet bloc, it exported apparently sophisticated machinery as part of its international obligations. Outside the bloc, it sold simpler products or manufactured goods at prices well below the levels of Western competitors.

The state control over foreign trade made this possible and ensured that an inefficient economy could earn the foreign currency needed for economic survival, but the state monopoly of foreign trade was also a major contributor to that economic inefficiency.

STRUCTURAL DISTORTION

As part of his critique of central planning, Hayek predicted that the lack of rational price signals would lead to a distorted sectoral structure. The outcome was slightly different from his expectation, but the broad principle was confirmed. The data demonstrate a strong bias toward manufacturing, particularly heavy industry, and raw material extraction when planned economies are compared with market economies at similar levels of development (Winiecki 1988, Chapter 3). This applied both during early industrialization drives, when it seemed sensible to accelerate growth by concentrating on the basic infrastructure, and in the 1970s and 1980s, when advanced market economies were shifting toward a greater emphasis on services. Stagnation in the sense of declining growth was matched by stagnation in sectoral structures.

This arguably was a feature of the planning system. Central planners noticed shortages in basic inputs that affected production across all sectors, and they felt forced to respond. They were less concerned over shortages in consumer goods and services, which were not inputs to other sectors. It might be added that some of those at the very top could be protected against such shortages by the special shops and services mentioned previously and would only have been reminded of difficulties when workers staged protests. These typically related to the most basic consumer goods—particularly food, which therefore remained a priority over more sophisticated consumer goods.

Suspicion of the private sector accentuated the bias toward large-scale production. Some activities, particularly in the service sector, are better and more efficiently provided on a small scale, and these were the activities that tended to be underrepresented. Attitudes toward the private sector varied with the ideological rigidity of the regime. Private enterprise was more significant in Poland, but private entrepreneurs there could not enjoy equal conditions with state-owned firms—for example, in access to scarce inputs or scope for investment. They often had to rely on informal contacts with the power structure in order to survive, let alone prosper. Such habits, it has been argued, contributed to the acceptance of business corruption in the post-Communist period (see the following text and Chapters 7 and 8). The link need not be that important, as forms of corruption also prospered in other countries that had minimal experience with legal private enterprise, such as Czechoslovakia.

Agriculture was a particularly important issue, and its failure in the Soviet Union was one of the reasons behind the system's difficulties. Unable to feed its own population, the Soviet Union became a major food importer in the 1970s and 1980s. The industrialization drive of the 1930s saw the forced collectivization of agriculture and a determined attempt to destroy the private sector. There were arguments that large-scale agriculture is more efficient, but Soviet experience at the time brought inadequate mechanization; the initial chaos and extreme repression rather led to the impoverishment of villages. The Soviet authorities made pragmatic concessions, allowing small private plots. These were always important in providing a range of foods, otherwise barely available, that were sold on free markets in towns and cities. Therefore, there was widespread experience of this very simple form of market activity throughout the period of state Socialism.

In CEECs, collectivization was also imposed, but it was more carefully prepared. In Poland, the government retreated after 1956, and small private farming predominated, also with low levels of productivity. In Czechoslovakia and Hungary, large cooperative farms were more successful (N. Swain 1985, 198–99; Myant 1989a), raising rural incomes to urban levels. Cooperatives, often with several thousand employees—or in formal terms, "members"—covering a range of skills and qualification levels, had greater freedom than state-owned enterprises once they fulfilled delivery obligations to the state, and their activities through the 1970s and 1980s provided services to society that would otherwise have been missing. Some even entered into contracts with foreign multinational companies, bringing in hard currency from exports of manufactured goods. They thereby started to fill gaps left by the rigidity of the planned economy and left a heritage of varied forms of entrepreneurial experience. They survived after 1989, although they were substantially slimmed down and restricted again to agriculture.

In all countries, the start of transition saw an explosive growth of new private enterprises. There clearly was considerable latent potential suppressed by the old system. The bias toward basic and manufacturing industries was associated with poor development of other sectors. The next section focuses on a primary source of weakness in technological development.

THE TECHNOLOGY GAP

Innovation and technological advance were themes continually stressed by the political leaders. That was consistent with their proclaimed allegiance to Marxism, which has traditionally seen science and technology as sources of human progress. Innovative activity was stimulated by exhortations from above and supported by a substantial backup in technical education and research institutes, albeit with questions over quality and over the effectiveness of coordination and links with production. However, the results were unimpressive, and the extent and causes of difficulties have been studied on the basis of published material, primarily for the Soviet Union and also to some extent for CEECs (Amann, Cooper, and Davies 1977; Amann and Cooper 1982; Berliner 1976; Myant 1989a, 226–29, 240–45).

Behind the disappointments lay three major weaknesses relative to market economies. The first was the lack of clear market signals for judging between projects and the associated lack of pressure from the market at all levels in the hierarchy.

The second was the absence of a means to raise finance independent of central approval, either at the enterprise level or for starting a new firm. As a result, ideas from science and research could be left unexploited. One of the best known was the development of the soft contact lens by the Czech chemist Otto Wichterle, who built prototypes in his own home in 1961. The license was sold to a U.S. company, as production was no part of any Czechoslovak enterprise's plan.

The third was the limited scope for international contact, reflecting the economic organization of foreign trade and the political constraints on travel, on contacts with any other country, and on allowing free rein to foreign companies. This restricted access to modern technology but also hampered implementation even of domestic innovations.

The disappointing outcome is confirmed from studies of total factor productivity, which show levels that were low compared with those of advanced market economies and also show a tendency for gradual decline. In other words, growth increasingly depended on greater inputs from labor and fixed assets, with a declining contribution for higher productivity of those factors. Far from switching from "extensive" to "intensive" growth, the trend was in the opposite direction, as structural stagnation prevented transferring resources from less- to more-favored sectors. This same trend was clear in the Soviet Union and in other centrally planned economies. Comparative data on patents also pointed to a low level of major technological advance (Hanson and Pavitt 1987), despite the high levels of research spending.

Case studies across sectors of Soviet industry showed delays at every stage, starting with the relative isolation of research institutes, which could not easily transfer ideas to decision makers. There were delays at high levels, where choices over the use of resources had to be made; although innovation was generally favoured, there was no particular pressure for urgency and no easy criteria for selecting between competing projects. There were delays in enterprises related to incentives. The management would gain little from improvements that were rewarded by higher plan targets and might even lose from disruption to current plans while they were being introduced. Against this were plan targets for innovation, although these could be satisfied by "pseudoinnovations" that amounted to trivial improvements with minimal risk of disruption.

There were also incentives to develop and use modern technology, which gave an enterprise prestige. Kornai saw this as driving pressure for new investment. However, implementing innovations also brought organizational problems, as new inputs might not be available. Limited access to foreign currency then blocked scope for importing complementary technology or for buying new materials and parts that might not be available domestically.

There were exceptions, and there was some technical progress in all sectors, but even Soviet military production and the space program, which might appear to have contradicted these criticisms, were held back by the weaknesses across the Soviet economy as a whole and devoured a substantial share of the economy's resources at the expense of development in other sectors. Overall, the net outcome was to leave industry—and particularly the most modern consumer-goods sectors—lagging some years behind the most advanced countries.

There was no easy solution in "importing" technology. This appeared to be the growth strategy in Poland in the 1970s following mass worker protests in December 1970, which ended thoughts of maintaining external balance with higher food exports. Instead, the country was allowed to run up a hard currency debt as it imported consumer goods and built new manufacturing capacity with the help of licenses from Western companies, albeit still with a share of production under license that was relatively low by international standards. The trouble was that the economy could not deliver investment projects on time or adapt to the production of new components and final products. Therefore, the 1970s ended with a debt that could not be repaid. (The failure of the attempt to import technology in Poland in the 1970s is analyzed in different ways by Winiecki [1988, Chapter 6], Myant [1981, Chapter 4], Nuti [1981], and Poznanski [1996, Chapter 2].) Indeed, this method of international integration was very much second best to fully free interchange, allowing enterprises to import technology for specific needs—and companies in advanced market economies, too, were very dependent on cooperation and licensing deals—or allowing foreign companies to undertake direct investment.

INEQUALITIES AND SOCIAL WELFARE

Despite all the negative features covered in the preceding text, the state Socialist countries did appear able to provide substantially lower levels of inequality and substantially greater levels of economic security than market economies. This appeared consistent with the regimes' claims to represent the working class and should have assured them of some solid support.

State Socialist states provided basic health care and education, subsidies for food and housing, pensions, and other types of social insurance. The welfare states were universalistic, but they also included a number of features that gave better access to social goods and services to privileged strata or restricted networks and allowed a great deal of administrative discretion in the awarding of benefits (Cook 2007). A distinct feature was a set of policies aimed at holding back decline in the birth rate while still maintaining women's employment. These included subsidized child care and extended maternity leave (Heitlinger 1979). Family benefits were nearly universal and provided substantial supplements to wages, particularly in Eastern Europe (Milanovic 1998, 21). As labor participation for both men and women was high, social insurance and pension coverage were also nearly universal. Retirement ages were low in comparison with capitalist welfare states, but so was life expectancy.

The state did not provide unemployment benefits, as full employment was formally guaranteed. Although this did not have the same meaning in all times and places (participation rates varied; particularly, that among women was slightly lower in the traditionally Muslim republics of the Soviet Union), important sectors did suffer persistent labor shortages, which, like other shortages, encouraged enterprises to hoard labor. Employees were, therefore, safe from the threat of redundancy and could feel closely tied to their enterprises.

Enterprises were major providers of social benefits, including recreational and sometimes housing facilities. Russian enterprises spent 3 to 5 percent of GDP on social provision, and enterprises in CEECs spent about half that amount. In some regions of the Soviet Union, large enterprises provided up to 40 percent of social expenditures, including public housing infrastructure (Wallich 1994a). States in CEECs appeared closer to Western European practice, relying much more than the USSR on social transfers in cash (Milanovic 1998, 13). This followed their prewar experience in developing occupational systems of social insurance, which were then integrated into state Socialist systems and expanded into universal coverage (Inglot 2008).

Data on inequality in individual earnings and in household incomes from both Central Europe and the USSR showed important similarities with and differences from market economies (Lane 1971, 1985; Krejčí 1972; Matejko 1974; Wesołowski 1979). There were similar trends toward higher skill levels and more white-collar workers. Qualifications and authority were generally materially rewarded. Men usually earned more than women, and sectors with high levels of female employment—services, caring, and much of light industry—received lower pay relative to qualification levels. Differences included the absence of income from property and generally smaller differentials for qualifications. Indeed, there was a substantial overlap between manual and nonmanual incomes, with relatively high pay for male-dominated manual work in mining and heavy industry.

The most comprehensive study showed considerable diversity across state Socialist countries. Czechoslovakia stood out for its exceptionally low level of inequality. The Soviet Union had historically higher levels of inequality, but the general trend was for these to decrease, albeit with some fluctuations. The country was clearly more egalitarian at the end of the Soviet period than at the beginning, which supports the argument that there was a "systemic" influence (Atkinson and Micklewright 1992).

In formal terms, income distribution in state Socialist countries was centrally decided, with wage scales, as well as wage bills, decreed from above. This included rules for minimum wages that were set high enough to help narrow the gap between the top and the bottom. However, in practice, much of the distribution pattern followed from the logic of central planning. Heavy and extractive industries were, as indicated, inevitably prioritized. Fulfilling immediate targets, therefore, depended on securing a labor force, and that meant providing attractive enough pay levels. The result was high relative pay for miners and for skilled labor in heavy industry. Lower-priority sectors could exercise less pressure for high pay, and consequently, these sectors suffered.

This pattern of security and inequality raises three questions. The first is a question of how far this pattern corresponded to the pattern of inequality in living standards. Some apparently poorly paid employees in retail could boost their declared incomes by taking tips or other favors in return for providing access to goods that were in short supply. Some manual workers could earn from a second or informal job, repairing consumer goods. State employees and some in public services, including health professionals, could benefit from gifts and bribes. Manual workers in mining and heavy industry probably had the least transferable skills and the least useful opportunities for pilfering from the workplace, putting their high relative pay in perspective. Indeed, such workers were often very prominent in the mass protests that did occur in state Socialist countries, notably in Poland in 1980. Thus, inequalities in consumption were not identical to the inequalities in formal pay, but the former were not clearly greater. Some aspects point to greater inequality and some to greater equality.

The second question relates to the argument that inequality is a functional necessity and that state Socialism suffered by not allowing enough of it. This view was prominent in Czechoslovakia in the 1960s around the slogan of "deleveling," but the case for relating poor economic performance to low levels of inequality was not convincing (Myant 1989a, 133–43). High pay for some kinds of manual work very clearly followed market pressures, while there was no shortage of candidates for higher qualifications.

The third question relates to the relations between managers and employees and to the ability, or desire, of managements to impose their will on the workforce. The manager in Soviet and CEEC enterprises had considerable personal power, but a substantial body of literature points to an inability to impose labor discipline—preventing petty pilfering or absenteeism—or to confront worker opposition to changes in the labor process.

This clearly varied over time. There were worker protests and opposition to the tightening of piece rates, meaning that more had to be produced for the same wage, in the early 1950s in CEECs (Myant 1989a). A detailed account of life in a Hungarian tractor factory in 1971 points to the continuation of conflictual relations (Haraszti 1977). However, protests over piece-rate changes and the demand for employees to speed up their work appear to have been rare in all countries in later years. Burawoy and Lukács (1992) followed another Hungarian machinery factory in 1984 and concluded that life was more relaxed. They hypothesized that this reflected the stable and guaranteed market for the enterprise's products and the lack of pressure for innovation (Burawoy and Lukács 1992, 9–10). Stagnation in the economy led, it seemed, toward easy industrial relations.

Others have presented slightly different arguments, but all lead toward compatible conclusions. Filtzer (1994), writing on the Soviet Union, set managerial powerlessness alongside politically atomized workers. The implication is that, even when not backed up by collective influence through independent trade unions, labor had some power both to influence the allocation of resources and to dissuade managements from innovations that might require substantial changes to the labor process. This, plus the welfare role of enterprises referred to previously, entrenched a "paternalist" style in managers, who saw their role as including defense of the interests of a community and a workforce. This had implications for the later transformation of enterprises, for the weak development of collective employee representation, and for the lack of managerial experience in negotiating with employees in order to achieve higher productivity.

CONCLUSION

The system of central planning suffered from comprehensive weaknesses that followed from the absence of market relations, including a price mechanism and freedom of enterprise, meaning that units could be created and destroyed without a decision from central planners. Ultimately, the system could not compete satisfactorily with market-based economies. It achieved rapid changes for a time but then headed into stagnation. Problems were clear from the start, but that was not enough to shake the system or to weaken the autocratic power structures. Problems were at first dismissed as difficulties with learning how to run a new system or as individual mistakes that would not be repeated.

In various periods, and very clearly in the 1980s, disillusion with the system was spreading to some of the political leaders. They reacted by becoming more open to ideas for systemic reform, and proposals became increasingly radical. This search for alternatives culminated in political breakdown in 1989, a process discussed in the next chapter.

CHAPTER THREE

From Reform to Breakdown

Awareness of persistent problems in the planning system led to continual ideas for improvement or reform. These started in the 1930s, albeit within a framework that viewed difficulties as problems within, rather than of, central planning (Sutela 1991). They continued through a series of systemic reform attempts, none of which overcame the weaknesses referred to in the previous chapter. Instead, reform attempts became increasingly intertwined with more sweeping political changes. The outcomes, therefore, depended to a great extent on the ability of elites to keep control over their economies and on their differing objectives. Nevertheless, as shown by the tables in this chapter, reforms in all cases left state Socialist countries far behind the capitalist rivals they had envisioned themselves competing with, and their economies were poorly prepared for the effects of a sudden opening to the outside world.

MARKET REFORMS

The obvious approach was to try to plug gaps by ever more instructions and centralization (cf. Kornai 1959, 216–17). As this repeatedly failed, economists in state Socialist countries began cautiously moving toward a critique of "overcentralization" (Kornai 1959). Voices were raised in the Soviet Union in the mid-1950s for abandoning the fulfillment of a directive plan as the success indicator for enterprises (Mau 1996, 19–21). From that came ideas for reintroducing some elements familiar from market economies, albeit within a phraseology of aiming to improve planning methods and with a conviction that the system would prove its superiority over capitalism. Broader theoretical works, such as that of the Polish economist Włodzimierz Brus, justified a limited introduction of market relations within the context of general state control and state ownership. His ideas were summarized in a book published in Poland in 1964 (Brus 1972).

This led to reforms in several countries in the early and mid-1960s involving greater emphasis on profit and meaningful prices but not a reintroduction of private property. Steps in this direction in the Soviet Union and Central Europe in the 1960s were mostly reversed after Leonid Brezhnev became Soviet party leader in 1964. A key development was the attempt to reform state socialism, combining political democratisation with economic changes, by the Communist regime in Czechoslovakia in 1968. This was suppressed after military invasion from the Soviet

Union. Brezhnev had always been cautious of allowing any political liberalization and ideas for market-oriented economic reform were condemned in the following years. Market reform then continued only with the so-called New Economic Mechanism, (NEM) introduced in Hungary in 1968.

Although the principal reason for reversal was political and ideological, economic experience also played a role. The center had retained the capacity to intervene in enterprises, setting prices and limiting spending on wages or investment. As soon as any imbalance appeared, such as inflationary pressure or shortages of materials as the level of investment was increased, the easiest and most effective instrument available to the center was its ability to reassert direct controls on enterprise pricing and wage payments and to issue instructions to limit the use of inputs in short supply. This contradicted and reversed steps toward enterprise independence and the use of market relations.

A number of authors have taken this further, arguing that the reforms to the system, as advocated in the 1960s, were internally inconsistent and would therefore always face powerful pressures for reversal. The point, argued persuasively by Brus and Laski (1989), was that reforms introduced market elements only into consumer goods markets while leaving investment broadly under central control. This followed from the continued faith that planning at this level would prove superior to the free market, particularly in avoiding the fluctuations and crises experienced in capitalist economies. However, the absence of a capital market—a logical consequence of central control over investment—created a range of further difficulties. The center was responsible for the formation of any new enterprise and also for the death of enterprises. These were potentially sensitive decisions and were difficult to make in the absence of meaningful estimates of future profitability, something that was ruled out as long as prices were subject to central control. The center also had to reallocate resources from profitable enterprises to ones favored for investment, as these need not be the same. Thus, the center was sucked into arbitrary redistributions of resources that restricted enterprise independence.

This fitted with experience. Market reform within a system of central power and full state ownership was always potentially under threat. It was quickly restricted in Czechoslovakia in the late 1960s, even with a government and party leadership that gave verbal backing to economic reform (Myant 1989a, Chapter 6), and there were frequent pressures for partial reversal in Hungary. That country's experience attracted considerable attention outside the state Socialist countries, as little else of interest seemed to be happening within that bloc during the 1970s. It was clearly viewed with suspicion in official circles in other members of the bloc. Works in English describing the system and its problems include Friss (1971); Hare, Radice, and N. Swain (1981); and Gadó (1972, 1976). Although the NEM did differ from the traditional system, especially in giving enterprises freedom from detailed instructions, the absence of a capital market left the same lasting weaknesses described in the preceding sections.

YUGOSLAVIA'S MODEL

Yugoslavia represented a somewhat different economic model within state Socialism. There were many distinctive features, but three appear particularly important. The first was that the absence of detailed central planning, and even less scope for central intervention than in Hungary's NEM, meant that there was no assurance of full employment and even less ways to achieve macroeconomic equilibrium. The second was that there was no equivalent central emphasis on research and innovation, and the third was that there was greater scope for international contact. Yugoslavs could work in Western Europe, their remittances helping the balance of payments and their absence helping to reduce unemployment, and some enterprises were becoming subcontractors for light industry in Western Europe. Yugoslavia could also cover its deficit by borrowing through the 1970s, thereby joining Poland with serious debt problems in the 1980s.

The origins of the different system were in the break from the Soviet bloc after 1948. Yugoslavia's Communist leaders then set about developing an alternative model of Socialism without the concentration of power and bureaucratic centralization that they claimed characterized the Soviet system. This played an ideological role in legitimizing a regime in a federal state, made up from six republics with very similar main languages but somewhat different histories and a wide span of economic levels. Therefore, there were always tensions between the constituent parts, and a claim to be developing a new and distinct model of Socialism could have given them a common purpose. In the end, the results were similar to those of other state Socialist countries, most notably with the declining growth rates shown in Table 2.1.

The Yugoslav system went through several stages. The idea of self-management played a prominent role from the early 1950s and was given greater potential importance with decentralizing economic reforms in 1961 and 1965, which, by placing greater emphasis on market relations, meant that enterprises had more scope for making their own decisions. Reforms in the mid-1970s moved in a new direction, creating a model of a whole economy that was meant to build from self-management. Economic units were split into so-called Basic Organizations of Associated Labor—as many as 80,000 in the early 1980s—which were then to negotiate agreements between each other as the basic links in the economic system.

Yugoslav claims to have created a novel economic system attracted considerable outside interest. One approach, developing from the neoclassical tradition, analyzed the behavior of self-managed enterprises on the assumption of a hard budget constraint, with the enterprise objective not of profit but of maximizing income per employee; that was assumed to be the logical common objective of the labor force. The result was a lower level of employment than in the traditional firm in a market economy. This, it has been argued with econometric support (Estrin 1983), was consistent with Yugoslav experience, as, unlike centrally planned economies, there was always significant unemployment.

However, there is substantial evidence suggesting that self-management, in the sense of bodies elected by employees with authority over management, was never very effective and was easily manipulated by management. (Research in Yugoslav enterprises is reproduced in Obradović and Dunn [1978] and Comisso [1979]. Work by Yugoslav researchers, which generally points in similar directions, is reported in Myant [1985]). The objectives at the enterprise level, judging from survey research, included high wages and employment from employees and growth, plus modern technology from employees and management. Indeed, there was an "unreasonable" obsession with growth from all levels (Granick 1975, 409–10).

There was little penalty for failure. A law on bankruptcy did exist, but it was very rarely applied. Instead, help almost always came to resuscitate enterprises in financial difficulty, often from banks that were swayed by the political strength of big enterprises. Here, then, the soft budget constraint applied in a very clear form. The incentive for all key actors was the wish for greater spending. Detailed central planning and precise limits on spending had been eliminated, but they had not been replaced by effective market mechanisms.

The self-management system from the mid-1970s probably made this even worse. Such a conception of massive decentralization appears quite unworkable, leading to a "maze of bureaucratic arbitrariness" (Brus and Laski 1989, 93). It appeared that the system functioned neither by a plan nor by a market mechanism or self-management. The result was a greater role for informal contacts. That gave even more power to the League of Communists (it had dropped "Party" from the title after the split with the Soviet Union, claiming to be aiming for a less-dominant role), which remained as an organization with unchallenged political power—it could even dissolve elected self-management bodies if it so wished (Comisso 1979, 205)—able to link between economic actors.

Taken over the whole period from 1948, the system showed remarkably steadily declining performance. High investment was associated with declining growth, declining total factor productivity, low levels of innovation, and rising balance of payments difficulties, as analyzed for the 1970s by Laura Tyson (1980, 1983). The systemic reasons are clear. There was no capital market to allow resources to flow to enterprises with prospects and no punishment for enterprise failure. Investment came from existing enterprises, irrespective of their prospects, and was encouraged by separate republics for prestige reasons.

Any thoughts of a central authority imposing a coherent economic strategy were ruled out by rivalry between the republics in the federation. The ruling party, rather than standing above such divisions, increasingly became a channel for each one to press its own demands. The paradoxical result was a degree of autarky in each republic rather than the creation of a unified market across Yugoslavia. A notorious example was the attempt of each republic to develop a motor vehicle industry, despite the fact that this could not be justified by the size of the market (OECD 1982, 39). Inefficiency and inflexibility meant that Yugoslavia, too, suffered from shortages of some goods alongside surpluses of others. Reform seemed only to have accelerated the trend toward breakdown.

However, self-management did leave a heritage for subsequent transition. This was clearest in Slovenia, the part of the old federation least affected by armed conflicts, which developed an economic system with a substantial voice for employees both within enterprises and at the national level.

CENTRAL EUROPE: FROM REFORM TO ROUNDTABLES

The last years of the 1980s saw rather different processes in different countries, depending on the extent of commitment to reform and of economic and political breakdown. Kornai (1992, 571) argued that attempts to press ahead with market reform led inevitably into instability. The old system ceased to function, but no coherent new system could emerge to replace it.

This partly matches experience; those countries that followed economic reform did seem to head into instability. However, the process of economic breakdown was closely tied in with political failure. The regimes could not command trust or support from their populations and were afraid to take tough measures that would risk public opposition. It was ultimately a failure both of an economic system that could not deliver on its promises and of a political system that shut out inputs from, and dialogue with, the population.

A distinction can be made between those countries that retained a broadly stable economic system, those in which radical reform ideas were associated with growing imbalances, and those in which confusion over policies coincided with signs of serious economic breakdown and more general institutional collapse. The latter applied mostly to parts of the Soviet Union and Yugoslavia, where an existing state did disappear and where, in several cases, political instability led to armed conflicts.

An example of stability was Czechoslovakia. There, the party leadership stuck to the centralized system reestablished after 1968 and shunned anything beyond cosmetic reform measures. Although much of the population was disillusioned with the system, the leadership insulated itself from those attitudes and continued to believe that it was running the best available system. Indeed, although growth had long since given way to stagnation, the economy appeared to be more stable than in neighboring countries. The center kept control over economic processes, avoiding budget deficits, generalized shortages, inflation, or a collapse in production.

Political change in Czechoslovakia came after the ending of Communist power in Hungary, Poland, and East Germany, and it was not associated with economic instability. The old regime allowed a peaceful transfer of power once confronted with massive popular demonstrations, and the new regime took over a functioning state machine, a functioning currency and central bank, and a stable economic situation. It then set about formulating and implementing new economic policies.

The cases that set the scene for development across the region were Hungary and Poland, countries in which radical reform was associated with deepening imbalances. In both cases, the regimes were verbally committed to serious reform throughout the 1980s, and in both cases, changes were made that moved the economies away from the model of central planning (described in the previous text).

An outline of Hungary's reforms before the Communist regime had been defeated in parliamentary elections in 1990 (N. Swain 1992) showed that the government had been able to liberalize most prices, covering 67 percent of consumer spending (N. Swain 1992, 10). Other changes included giving power in enterprises to elected councils or managements (1985), introducing a bankruptcy law (1986), splitting up the state monobank and replacing it with a two-tier banking system (1987), and allowing foreign direct investment (1988). By then, there was consensus that property reform was required, and a process of privatization began before the transfer of political power. In fact, rules introduced in 1988 allowed enterprise managers to pursue a very similar course to that foreseen by Trotsky (see p. 7) and to gain property for themselves. This was strongly criticized and even blocked by the opposition, who demanded a more open and slower approach to replace the so-called "spontaneous" privatization. Thus, gradual political liberalization—allowing informed debate over economic policy and allowing the public to protest policies that seemed unfair—set Hungary on the road to a slow and more cautious privatization policy in later years.

There were two weaknesses, however. The first was the failure to plug all loopholes that enabled some enterprises to soften budget constraints by state help or by price increases (N. Swain 1992, 150). Indeed, the concept of the soft budget constraint seemed most appropriate precisely in the context of systems experiencing decentralization with a weakening government that was scared of popular opposition. It was less useful for unreformed systems and for those in which political power was not challenged. The second weakness was the failure to improve export competitiveness. Reforms led to no visible gains in efficiency and left the country facing a severe external imbalance and high levels of foreign debt. However, the Hungarian economy in 1989 is better seen as one on the way to a major transformation rather than one in a state of collapse.

Poland faced more serious problems. A period of martial law in the early 1980s had been intended to eliminate the influence of the Solidarity trade union and to open the way for restoring market equilibrium through price increases. Instead, albeit with some fluctuations, inflation and shortages continued through the 1980s.

The Polish government made its most determined effort to overcome the opposition to price increases by staging a referendum for a general reform package in 1987, including a commitment to introduce "authentic prices" involving "substantial increases." Despite winning support from 66 percent of those voting, it failed to gain the desired majority of those eligible to vote (Myant 1989b, 22–24). The government continued with a reform strategy based on changes in enterprise independence and powers. That contributed nothing positive to economic performance and possibly even exacerbated signs of chaos by allowing enterprises greater freedom without the controls that a full market system would have provided.

Poland's ruling party recognized the pointlessness of trying to rule without reference to the opposition, which remained strong despite being illegal, and agreed to roundtable discussions in February to April 1989. There was agreement on political change, allowing elections in June 1989—which the Solidarity movement was to win—and on an agenda for economic changes. The discussions were difficult, and the conclusions left a lot open for the future, but there was considerable agreement on both sides of the table that the old economic system had failed and that moves toward freer prices, freer enterprise, and the market were the only way forward (Myant 1993, 74–78).

However, as finally agreed, the "dynamic" element was to come only from the abolition of monopolies, structural changes, and equality of conditions for self-managed state enterprises and the private sector. The government conceded to demands from Solidarity, backed by the state-sponsored union organization, to allow indexation so that wages would increase to cover 80 percent of price rises and to maintain employment levels and security for employees (Baka 2005, 51–52; Myant 1993, 76–77). There was therefore no dramatic progress toward achieving market equilibrium and a functioning price system. As in Hungary, the long-standing problems of internal and external imbalances remained to be resolved. These were left for the new government to try to clear up.

FROM REFORM TO DISINTEGRATION: THE SOVIET REPUBLICS

The Soviet Union followed a different course, with more elements of linked breakdown in political and economic life leading toward a collapse in the state. (For a succinct account, see Nove [1992].) The starting point was Gorbachev's policies of openness (*glasnost*) and restructuring (*perestroika*). Unlike the Czechoslovak case, the Soviet Union's leadership saw the need for major systemic change. However, the reform agenda was far less clear than in Hungary and Poland, and the economic policies of *perestroika* had much in common with an old-style, state-directed drive for acceleration of growth. Other old themes also persisted, such as attacks on profiteering and unearned incomes (Sutela 2003, 47; Mau 1996, 27). The focus by the late 1980s was on cementing enterprise independence, with a law clarifying the position and powers of state enterprises passed in 1987, but the question of ownership was left out of the debate. In 1988, a new law allowed cooperatives to operate as small private enterprises in services, manufacturing, and foreign trade. Some of these were to form the starting points for powerful capitalist businesses in later years. A new Soviet Joint Venture Law that went into effect in 1987 initially limited foreign investment: it was subsequently revised to allow majority foreign ownership and control. In other areas, reforms were slower than in Poland and Hungary. It was April 1991 before most prices were freed and before private enterprise was given equal legal status to state and cooperative enterprise.

This slower pace of reform, and the omission of price liberalization, in the Soviet Union reflected two factors. The first was an ideological attachment to past thinking. There had been far less contact here with the outside world than in Central Europe, and there was no consensus on the need for changes along the Hungarian or Polish lines. The second factor was the government's fear of imposing unpopular measures. Political liberalization was confronting those in power with the new and unfamiliar phenomenon of opposition and challenges from outside the power structure. Believing themselves to be popular, the new leaders could not bring themselves to take unpopular steps (Mau 1996, 43). They, therefore, shied away from price increases, price liberalization, and tax rises. The result was a very half-hearted reform.

Gorbachev turned in 1987 to economic advisers to come up with comprehensive proposals. The result was a flood, with estimates of the total number of reform programs in the following years ranging from 11 to 40 (Sutela 2003, 48). They became more radical after changes in Poland in 1990, including a "400-day" program in May of that year designed for rapid stablization, liberalization, and privatization and a "500-day" program later that year intended to achieve a full market economy in less than two years. In Poland and Hungary, there was more understanding of economic issues, and no such comprehensive, and unrealistic, programs were produced.

The formulation of reform programs had little relevance to the actual development of the Soviet economy in its closing years. It increasingly suffered from two problems.

The first was escalating macroeconomic disequilibrium. The state budget moved into massive deficit, possibly equivalent to 30 percent of GDP by 1991 (Sutela 2003, 55). This reflected rising subsidies, notably to hold back price increases, and falling revenues following a fall in oil revenues after 1986 and declining revenue from enterprises. Keeping control over prices was associated with a sharp rise in personal savings that has been interpreted as evidence of a "monetary overhang" or "inflationary overhang," meaning that citizens could not find the goods to spend their money on.

This interpretation was to have implications for future policies, as it implied a backlog of hidden inflationary pressure that justified strongly deflationary policies. As previously indicated, arguments that this was a general phenomenon in planned economies were unproven, at best. A massive study of the Soviet economy—jointly sponsored by the IMF, World Bank, the OECD, and the European Bank for Reconstruction and Development (EBRD)—accepted that there may have been no monetary overhang over long time periods but concluded that one almost certainly did develop in the late 1980s. The evidence for this was a rise in the personal savings rate from 7 percent of disposable incomes in 1985 to over 12 percent in 1989. There had been fluctuations before that, and the 1989 figure was not an excessive level by international standards, but the change appeared to the authors to be too large and rapid to be explained by a voluntary change in consumer behavior (IMF et al. 1991b, 396, 416).

The second problem was a more general breakdown in central control. This was much more serious than in Poland, let alone Hungary, and, it has been argued, must be seen as the main reason for the failure of a gradual reform strategy that had some similarities to the approach adopted with success in China. In the Soviet Union, GDP was clearly in decline in 1990 and then fell by 8 percent in the first quarter of 1991 (K.M. Murphy, Shleifer, and Vishny 1992, 900).

That was obviously not a normal feature of the central planning system, which had been characterized by a remarkable degree of stability. Economic breakdown came because Moscow was losing authority over economic policy across the country, as illustrated by the fact that even within individual cities local administrations were taking decisions on prices.

It lost more general authority as the Soviet Union began to fall apart as some individual republics pushed for independence, beginning in the Baltics and Georgia and including Ukraine. The motives for and implications of this differed. Some wanted to break from the Soviet system completely and were led toward radical thinking on market-oriented reform. In others, local elites were taking the opportunity to latch onto nationalist rhetoric to establish an independent power base. They did not necessarily have any commitment to economic reform and often had little knowledge of economics at all. Russia might have been expected to keep more of a central economic authority, as Moscow was the seat of central bodies. However, in 1991 Russia's leaders actively encouraged the breakup of the Soviet Union and that meant ending the power of the central bodies from the Soviet era. Thus, in Russia as in other republics, a vacuum was left, ending the means to coordinate much of the economic activity both within and between republics. Even the central bank could no longer control the increasingly chaotic financial system in Russia, while other republics were left to start out without a central bank at all.

Thus, the economic system of state Socialism ended with varying degrees of political and economic chaos. Both of these features were to influence individual countries' development in the next few years. However, the most important heritage from the old system was in the levels of economic development, the economic structures, and the experiences of international integration. These first three chapters on the period of state Socialism, therefore, conclude with summary details on those themes.

Results and Potentials

As shown in Tables 2.1 to 2.3, per capita GDP in state Socialist countries was considerably behind that of the world's most advanced countries. This section provides some additional data to show how the weaknesses covered in Chapter 2, and left uncorrected by reform attempts discussed in this chapter, led to economic structures with a bias toward industry and autarky. Thus, there were common structural features alongside some important differences in economic levels and in forms of international integration.

Table 3.1 shows the shares of industry value added in GDP at the start of transition. In all countries, industry was important, reflecting the significance attached to industrialization in economic development even in poorer countries alongside the slow development of modern service activities that have been replacing industry in more developed economies.

International integration is indicated in Table 3.2 by the share of exports in GDP and in Tables 3.3 and 3.4 by the share of exports outside the bloc. Here, the data from the World Bank source on republics within the Soviet Union is fragmentary and differs markedly from data derived from those countries' statistical publications. This was difficult to measure and dependent on the distorted and arbitrary prices under the Soviet system. Those figures have therefore not been included. Data from the countries that are included show the poorer countries as more autarkic. Small, industrialized state Socialist countries appeared to have lower export shares than countries of similar size in Western Europe, which rose to 71.67 percent of GDP for Belgium in 1989. Transition was later to lead to similar, or even higher, levels in some CEECs.

Table 3.3 provides more detail on the nature of principal export markets. Advanced market economies were already substantial markets for CEECs, albeit with Czechoslovakia rather more tied into the old Soviet bloc than Poland and Hungary. Exports of raw materials required relatively little contact between producer and customer and, therefore, little experience of international activity. Some CEECs exported semimanufactures (steel and heavy chemicals) and more sophisticated manufactured goods, albeit generally at very low prices relative to those of Western producers. This at least gave experience of international business contacts and provided a base for future exporting. However, Table 3.4 indicates the very low level of trade in machinery and transport equipment (Standard International Trade Classification [SITC] category 7; generally the most sophisticated manufactured goods) outside the bloc. This gives an indication of the limited nature of business contacts that could be built on in later years. Trade in manufactured goods within the bloc was to prove harder to maintain with the dramatic changes in the system of international trade after the breakdown of central planning. International integration of individual Soviet republics can be followed in some cases at the end of the 1980s, thanks to greater openness from statistical offices. However, these figures must be treated with caution. One major study reached different conclusions, with

TABLE 3.1 Percentage share of industry value added in GDP at the start of transition

	1989	1990
Albania	44.8	48.2
Belarus		47.1
Bulgaria	57.6	49.2
Croatia		35.7
Czech Republic		48.7
Estonia	40.6	49.7
Georgia	38.7	33.5
Hungary	43.7	39.6
Kazakhstan		44.6[a]
Kyrgyz Republic		35.8
Latvia	43.9	46.2
Moldova	39.2	36.7
Mongolia	38.8	40.6
Montenegro		
Poland		50.1
Romania		49.9
Russian Federation	50.2	48.4
Slovak Republic	58.5	59.1
Slovenia		42.4
Tajikistan	36.2	37.6
Turkmenistan	33.8	29.6
Ukraine	48.4	44.6
Uzbekistan	32.6	33.0
EEC plus EFTA	32.1	31.4
Germany	37.7	37.3

Source: World Bank (2008a).

Note: EEC = European Economic Community (members at the time were Belgium, Denmark, France, West Germany, Greece, Ireland, Italy, Luxembourg, Netherlands, Portugal, Spain, and United Kingdom); EFTA = European Free Trade Association (members at the time were Austria, Finland, Iceland, Norway, Sweden, and Switzerland).

[a]This percentage is from the year 1992.

somewhat higher levels of integration between republics (IMF et al. 1991b, 225). Using official statistics, the figure for Uzbekistan shows exports divided between those to the rest of the USSR, 27.9 percent of GDP in 1988, and those that left the union in total, which were equivalent to 5.3 percent of GDP. The structure of exports generally was strongly biased toward agriculture and raw materials. The Uzbek economy thus appeared to be serving its own needs—with garment output per capita around half the level of the USSR as a whole, reflecting generally lower living

TABLE 3.2   Exports of goods and services (percentage of GDP)

	1989	1990
Albania	17.9	14.9
Bulgaria	46.4	33.1
Czech Republic		45.2
Hungary	36.0	31.1
Mongolia	22.5	22.4
Poland		28.6
Romania		16.7
Slovak Republic	28.8	26.5
Western European 18	40.8	40.4
Germany	24.2	24.8

Source: World Bank (2008a).

Note: EEC = European Economic Community (members at the time were Belgium, Denmark, France, West Germany, Greece, Ireland, Italy, Luxembourg, Netherlands, Portugal, Spain, and United Kingdom); EFTA = European Free Trade Association (members at the time were Austria, Finland, Iceland, Norway, Sweden, and Switzerland).

TABLE 3.3   Percentage share of exports from state Socialist countries to key markets, 1989

	USSR	Other Eastern European countries	EEC plus EFTA
Bulgaria	65.2	17.1	5.2
Czechoslovakia	32.9	23.1	23.5
Hungary	25.1	15.9	35.6
Poland	20.8	14.0	43.6
Romania	21.9	10.7	33.7
USSR		46.2	17.2
Yugoslavia	21.7	12.9	44.2

Source: Calculated from United Nations ([UN]; 1993a).

Note: EEC = European Economic Community (members at the time were Belgium, Denmark, France, West Germany, Greece, Ireland, Italy, Luxembourg, Netherlands, Portugal, Spain, and United Kingdom); EFTA = European Free Trade Association (members at the time were Austria, Finland, Iceland, Norway, Sweden, and Switzerland).

standards—while also providing inputs to industry elsewhere in the USSR (Myant and Drahokoupil 2008, 606).

Evidence from other Soviet republics also points to high levels of autarky, albeit with more manufactured goods exports coming from the most advanced countries. Thus, total exports from Russia in 1989 were equivalent to 11.5 percent of GDP, of which exports to outside the Soviet Union were equivalent to 3.6 percent of

TABLE 3.4   **Percentage share of machinery and transport equipment exports from state Socialist countries**

	Share in total exports	Share outside the bloc in total exports
USSR	16.4	0.8
Other Eastern European countries	16.8	2.4

Source: Calculated from United Nations (1993a).

GDP. Machinery and metal products accounted for 33.7 percent of this latter figure. Ukraine's exports were a slightly higher share of GDP—25.9 percent in 1990—but those to outside the Soviet Union were only 2.5 percent of GDP. Belarus exported 25.9 percent of GDP in 1990, but only 2.4 percent of GDP went to outside the union. Machinery and metal products made up 50.6 percent of this latter figure.

TABLE 3.5   **External debt, total (percentage of gross national income)**

	1990	1992	1993
Albania		92.9	64.6
Belarus			5.9
Bulgaria	57.1	116.0	114.5
Croatia			15.0
Czech Republic	27.9[a]	28.3[a]	27.9
Estonia			
Georgia		2.2	21.1
Hungary	67.1	61.2	65.2
Kazakhstan		0.1	7.4
Kyrgyz Republic		0.2	14.4
Latvia		1.3	5.3
Moldova		1.7	11.7
Mongolia		34.7	77.0
Montenegro			
Poland	88.7	58.6	53.3
Romania	3.0	13.1	16.3
Russian Federation		17.2	26.0
Slovakia			25.0
Slovenia			
Tajikistan		0.5	23.6
Turkmenistan			8.6
Ukraine		0.7	6.0
Uzbekistan		0.5	7.9

Source: World Bank (2003), Federální statistický úřad (1992), and Czech Statistical Office (CZSO) (1994).

[a]Figures are percentages of GDP for Czechoslovakia.

These figures indicate just how unprepared Soviet republics were to become significant exporters to the outside world. They were bound to face great difficulties in finding new markets to compensate for loss of internal demand and for loss of trade between republics. Other indicators point to the likely costs of the breaking of links between republics and, above all, of the collapse of central, Soviet-level authorities. Iwasaki and Suzuki (2007, 401) used official Soviet statistics to follow the percentage of production under federal jurisdiction in individual republics. The average was 61 percent, with a high of 69 percent in Russia and a low of 28.5 percent in Estonia. Even for Uzbekistan, one of the lowest income countries, the figure was 35 percent, reflecting a considerable presence for industries of all-union significance.

These figures add a dimension that is not clear in data on trade between republics, but industries under federal control covered a range of types. Among these were ones with advanced technology, and they were likely to depend on inputs from other republics. However, this was not always true; much of basic industry was also under federal control. Still, the implication was that complex manufacturing processes were likely to face paralysis as supplies of parts and components failed to materialize.

A final, and rather different, problem inherited from past forms of international integration was international debt, which, in some cases, was a serious threat to economic stability. Poland, Hungary, and Yugoslavia had all borrowed extensively in the 1970s and were faced with burdens of external debt, which contributed to instability in the late 1980s and limited their choices in the 1990s. Czechoslovakia, with its less-liberal political regime, had borrowed less and even claimed to be a net creditor, although credits it had granted to many developing countries were unlikely ever to be repaid. The breakup of the Soviet Union left all of the former country's foreign assets and obligations with Russia. In the case of Yugoslavia, debts were shared between successor states, but there were disputes for some time over exact obligations. Table 3.5 shows the differing positions at the start of transition. For some countries, debt was a problem inherited from past policies. For a number of former Soviet republics, it grew rapidly from a base of zero in the following years as a result of policies discussed in the subsequent chapters.

SECTION II

MACROECONOMIC TRANSFORMATIONS: FROM SHOCK TO RECOVERY

CHAPTER FOUR

The Courses of Transition

All countries in Eastern Europe and the former Soviet Union that underwent transformation away from central planning endured some kind of sharp decline in output and some kind of subsequent recovery. Even if not applying the Washington Consensus strategy (discussed in Chapter 5), much less "shock therapy," they experienced a severe shock. This decline came to be known as the transformation, or transformational, depression. However, the depth, timing, and causes clearly varied between countries. In all cases, there was also a recovery, which again varied in form and strength between countries.

In what follows, it will be shown that these transformation depressions and subsequent recoveries are best understood as distinct processes. There is no useful analogy to theories of economic cycles, in which the decline phase creates the conditions for subsequent recovery. In these cases, recovery came from new economic structures and processes. It was in all cases the result of changes in state forms and enterprises and in the environments for business activity. These are themes for later chapters. This chapter sets out the visible changes in the key macroeconomic indicator of GDP. That, in turn, is related to forms of international integration. The ability to export, or to acquire foreign currency by other means, was a crucial element in transition and a precondition for recovery from depression. The story is outlined up to the period immediately before the world financial crisis of 2008, but more detail on how countries were prepared for that, or not, is left to Chapter 16, following discussion of other aspects of the transition.

THE TRANSFORMATION DEPRESSION

Figures 4.1 to 4.7 use data trusted by the EBRD to show changes in output, grouping together those countries that followed clearly similar trends (see also Tables A.1 and A.2 in the Appendix). These groupings frequently resemble geographical groupings, but that does not mean that geography was the determinant of performance (see Box 4.1). Groupings in this chapter are pragmatically chosen to show countries with similar performance profiles. The overall comparison between these groups and some key countries is shown in Figure 4.1.

The most successful countries—meaning those experiencing a relatively shallow depression and then steady recovery—were the CEECs, as shown in Figure 4.2. The

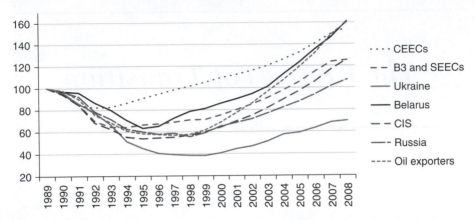

Figure 4.1 Gross domestic product as a percentage of the 1989 level. (*Source:* EBRD economic statistics and forecasts, available at http://www.ebrd.com/country/sector/ econo/stats/index.htm. *Note:* Figures for groups are arithmetic means. B3 refers to Baltic republics.)

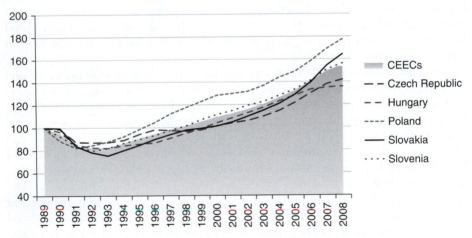

Figure 4.2 Gross domestic product as a percentage of the 1989 level: CEECs. (*Source:* EBRD economic statistics and forecasts, available at http://www.ebrd.com/country/ sector/econo/stats/index.htm.)

low point among these came latest in Slovakia, following the economic effects of the breakup of Czechoslovakia at the start of 1993, and earliest in Poland. Thus, despite differences in the details of policies, these countries performed very much as a single group. It will be argued that the causes of depressions were also broadly similar, deriving from identifiable economic factors. Processes of recovery and international integration also had striking similarities.

The next grouping, which included the Baltic republics, Romania, and Bulgaria (covered in Figure 4.3), suffered somewhat deeper GDP declines that lasted slightly longer. There were also downturns after the beginnings of recovery in Bulgaria and Romania. These countries appear as less successful than the CEECs, albeit with similar trajectories of decline and recovery. They followed the advice and policies

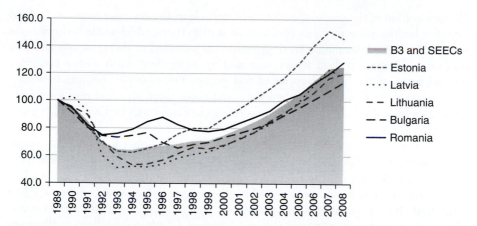

Figure 4.3 Gross domestic product as a percentage of the 1989 level: Baltic republics and SEECs. (*Source:* EBRD economic statistics and forecasts, available at http://www.ebrd.com/country/sector/econo/stats/index.htm. *Note:* B3 refers to Baltic republics.)

of international financial institutions (IFIs) at slightly different times—the Baltic republics were new and insecure states that took the advice more easily than did the SEECs—but depression broadly followed from identifiable economic factors. Recovery also had similarities to CEECs, albeit with less speed and certainty.

This contrasts with rather different trajectories followed by CIS countries. These experienced long and deep depressions, which are less easily attributable to familiar economic factors. More general breakdown in state machines and in the governments' ability to regulate economic processes played major roles, which cannot be directly quantified. These are divided in Figures 4.4, 4.5, and 4.6. The first to be separated out is the group of oil and gas exporters, shown in Figure 4.4. They experienced a long and deep depression, as did other CIS countries, but then very rapid growth.

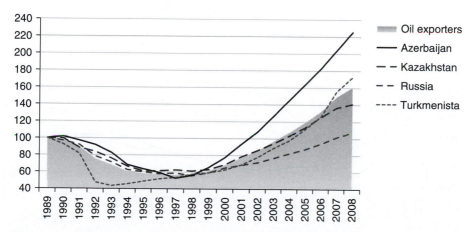

Figure 4.4 Gross domestic product as a percentage of the 1989 level: Oil exporters. (*Source:* EBRD economic statistics and forecasts, available at http://www.ebrd.com/country/sector/econo/stats/index.htm.)

The delineation of the grouping is not absolutely clear. Russia was a major oil and gas exporter, but there was much more economic activity there, which made hydrocarbons less dominant in determining GDP growth. It is included in this grouping and in a later one, reflecting both its importance and its ambivalent status. Other countries showed some of the characteristics of this group. For example, Belarus benefited from reexporting Russian petrochemicals, and there were also fuel reexports from Baltic republics. In those cases, however, other economic activities were much more important to GDP changes.

The fourth grouping, shown in Figure 4.5, brings together lower-income countries, mostly from the CIS, that suffered deep depressions. Recovery was most marked for countries outside the CIS—Albania and Mongolia—and least marked for countries that suffered from internal conflicts. Kyrgyzstan stood between the two subgroups. Its low point came very late and was followed by moderate recovery. The contrasts between countries shown in Figure 4.5, therefore, help to illustrate the particular difficulties of CIS countries, which can be related to the breakdown of their state machines. The different processes of recovery are also indicated by the course of international integration. Albania, unlike other low-income countries, showed some similarities to the early stages experienced in CEECs, reflecting both its degree of state consolidation and its geographical position.

Figure 4.6 shows four CIS republics that share the common feature of not fitting easily into any other category. This incidentally also illustrates the diversity among countries. Uzbekistan and Belarus were the most reluctant to pursue the WC strategy and to privatize their enterprises, yet they seem to have done better than many other CIS republics. Recovery came after 1995 and was strong enough to indicate that GDP in 2008 was further above the 1989 level than in any other transition economies apart from Poland, some oil and gas exporters, and a couple of low-income countries. This slightly flatters Uzbekistan, as the country benefited from an inflow of population

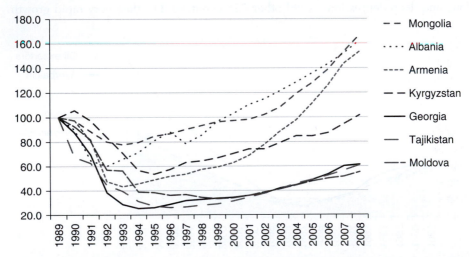

Figure 4.5 Gross domestic product as a percentage of the 1989 level: Low-income countries. (*Source:* EBRD economic statistics and forecasts, available at http://www.ebrd .com/country/sector/econo/stats/index.htm.)

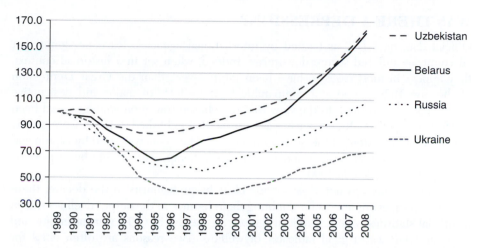

Figure 4.6 Gross domestic product as a percentage of the 1989 level: Belarus, Russia, Uzbekistan, and Ukraine. (*Source:* EBRD economic statistics and forecasts, available at http://www.ebrd.com/country/sector/econo/stats/index.htm.)

from neighboring republics in the early years; however, per capita figures, used in Table A.1 in the Appendix, show weaker growth. Nevertheless, there is a clear contrast with the deeper and longer depressions in Russia and, even more clearly, Ukraine.

The final grouping, as seen in Figure 4.7, shows some former Yugoslav republics, some of which suffered exceptionally severe depressions. These economies were affected by war that brought destruction and disruption and, especially in the case of Serbia, left a legacy of international suspicion, making it difficult to develop deep business contacts. Recovery was therefore also slow, and GDP levels here, as in Ukraine and the least successful of the low-income CIS countries, had not reached the pretransition level by 2008.

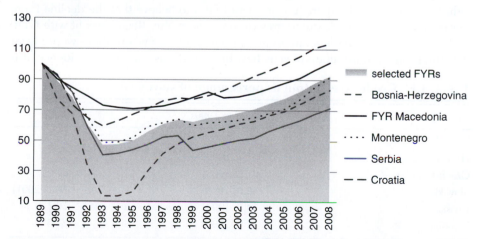

Figure 4.7 Gross domestic product as a percentage of the 1989 level: Selected FYRs. (*Source:* EBRD economic statistics and forecasts, available at http://www.ebrd.com/country/sector/econo/stats/index.htm.)

WAS THERE A DEPRESSION?

Official data on GDP, as trusted by international agencies, leave no doubt that all countries suffered severe downturns. Indeed, when set in a historical context, they appear in most cases to have been more severe than the Great Depression of the post-1929 period and comparable to the effects of major and destructive wars. That gave strength to the view that the chosen transition strategies had been woefully misguided. One response was to argue that published statistics were greatly exaggerating the extent of the declines in output. This claim was aired by Lipton and Sachs (1990a) as soon as the proponents of shock therapy were caught by surprise by Poland's GDP decline in 1990.

Although this was not always made clear by protagonists in the debate, there were two distinct arguments for doubting the relevance of the output declines shown in official statistics: whether official figures on the fall in GDP were accurate and whether GDP was a good indicator of welfare. Two reasons are often cited for doubting the accuracy of GDP figures.

- The first is a possible inflation of output figures under central planning, when enterprises wanted to claim plan fulfillment. In a market economy, underreporting would be more likely so as to minimize tax obligations.

- The second is a possible underestimation of the growth of a new private sector and of informal economic activities, which was very rapid once allowed by the authorities.

Although these complications do make it difficult to be certain of the full extent of the GDP fall, there is ample evidence of declines both in the most easily measurable forms of industrial output and in consumption from those industries. Table 4.1 shows the trends in steel output in a small sample of countries. This is easily measurable in physical terms, and the downturns fit reasonably well with movements in GDP taken from official statistics. Steel was one of the most successful parts of the manufacturing industry, and it would require a major act of faith to believe that the decline there was compensated by unmeasured growth somewhere else. Recoveries fit with GDP best for Ukraine but are less important in other countries where there were bigger structural shifts toward different activities. In view of this, and other, evidence, it is

TABLE 4.1 Crude steel output as percentage of start year

	Lowest in 1990s	2003
Poland	79.7 (1993)	73.1
Hungary	51.7 (1992)	62.7
Czech Republic	67.3 (1993)	67.9
Slovakia	82.0 (1993)	86.1 (2001)
Russia	54.5 (1994)	70.1
Ukraine	41.6 (1996)	71.6

Source: UN (1998, 2006).

Note: The start year was 1990 for all countries, apart from Poland and Hungary, for which it was 1989. The dates in parentheses show the years in which the lowest levels were reached.

reasonable to conclude that the reservations just listed cancel out only a small part of the recorded drop in GDP (Myant 1993, 92–95).

There are also several reasons for doubting the usefulness of the GDP indicator. One argument was that part of production may not have been saleable to domestic consumers, as it was produced only to fulfill plan obligations. This cannot explain much, as, despite its failings, central planning was not characterized by an unending escalation in stock levels. Nevertheless, a welfare loss could be assumed in so far as consumers felt obliged to accept a product mix they might not have considered ideal. They had to buy what was available.

Another reason given for doubting the GDP indicator is that the meaning of all index numbers becomes problematic in times of major change; thus, consumption of some goods was quite definitely declining, but consumption of others was increasing, and there is no fully reliable way of aggregating across different kinds of products when relative prices are also subject to substantial changes.

However, one immediate effect of the shock was to eliminate consumer goods shortages and, with that, the need to spend time and effort queuing. This was interpreted overwhelmingly positively. Another element of the shock was to eliminate the multiple exchange rate regimes, which had encouraged Poles to hold money as dollars, changing them on the black market into Polish currency when they wanted to spend. These inconveniences were no longer necessary (Myant 1993, 91–92). It is obviously impossible to put a monetary value on these changes, but it is reasonable to conclude that they went some way in compensating for the effects of declining GDP.

Anders Åslund, a Swedish economist who has advised Russian and other governments to adopt shock therapy and rapid privatization, has used these and other arguments to claim that the output fall in many countries did not happen or, in his words, that "the great post-Communist output collapse is a myth," the fall affecting only war-torn countries and those that failed to implement reforms. For this, he makes various arbitrary assumptions, excluding from earlier GDP figures production that he considers useless (Åslund 2002, 113, 125–26). It would be methodologically better to argue that GDP is not a perfect indicator, as his method is inevitably very subjective. He also argued that GDP was already declining before transition began, so the chosen strategy could not be blamed for all of the depression, and that the WC strategy was not adopted from the start in all countries. This, he argues, could justify considering a different start date for some countries—in other words, a date at which they were already in deep depression.

As indicated in the Introduction, the WC strategy was highly contentious, and Åslund has been one of those most determined to defend it. His argument is really about the contribution of that particular policy package to output decline. There is no serious doubt that a decline did take place, but the contribution of precise policies to the depth of depression remains difficult to determine. The WC strategy was never the only factor, but, as argued later in relation to CEECs, it did play a role—one that, at least in some countries, can be measured, albeit only approximately.

Having established that there really was a transformation depression, even if official figures may give an unnecessarily frightening impression of its depth, the next stage is to seek explanations. Comparisons across countries using econometric methods can provide some guidance but, as indicated in Box 4.1, these studies do not provide a full explanation for the diversity of experiences and can even lead to quite misleading conclusions. A frequent starting point has been a framework provided by Kornai (1995a, 1995b). He implicitly contrasted what happened with the instantaneous adjustment process assumed in neoclassical theory. The fall in output for which there is no demand is instantaneous, but recovery from new sectors or activities takes time, particularly when it depends on the emergence of new enterprises and, it can be added, if those new enterprises require a new infrastructure, including a finance system and state support, before they can grow.

This provides a general framework for comparing transformation depressions. Their depths and lengths depend on two quite separate processes of decline and recovery.

Box 4.1   Explaining recovery with econometrics

The relative success of the CEECs can give the impression of a natural process of recovery for countries that followed the WC strategy. Indeed, a number of authors have used econometric studies that show a correlation between rapid stabilization, liberalization, and structural reform and quick recoveries. Of these, early stabilization seemed to be the most important, even if other standard measures were delayed (summarized in Havrylyshyn [2006, 23, 62] and Mickiewicz [2005, 109]). The implication could be that CEECs did better because they got some specific policies right.

A major problem for econometrics is the choice of potentially relevant determinants of economic performance. Studies frequently start with a theory that is to be tested, such as links between performance and particular policy measures, and then look for the strength of a relationship. However, other variables may also yield good correlations, and it is often unclear what they really represent. Thus, as indicated in the following text, geographical position turns out to relate closely with economic performance, but that—and the choice of particular policies—need be no more than indicators that countries in Central Europe generally performed better than countries further east.

Unfortunately, standard statistical methods that lump together and compare all transition economies have proved to be only a very preliminary guide for assessing the reasons for differing outcomes between countries. There are too many possible variables, which frequently correlate with each other, and too much scope for arbitrariness in their use to know exactly what is being measured.

The attractiveness of finding an indicator for macroeconomic stabilization is clear, as that was a central part of the WC strategy. Unfortunately, it is very difficult to define and date stabilization in a way that can be used in econometric studies. In no country was there no macroeconomic instability at all. In a few, inflation was quickly reduced. It is frequently argued that Poland achieved stabilization with the Balcerowicz program of January 1990, but it was neither immediate nor total. Inflation rose to 586 percent in 1990 and fell below 10 percent for the first time only in 1999 (see Table A.3 in the Appendix). The Polish economy did experience a relatively rapid recovery from the transformation depression, but that could also have been due to corrections to the Balcerowicz program or to other factors such as the approach to privatization or the conditions for new private enterprises. Grzegorz Kolodko (2000), Poland's minister of finance from 1993 to 1997 of a government dominated by a Social Democratic party that emerged out of the old ruling Communist party, attributes growth to policies he was implementing beginning in 1994. These could have contributed, but his argument is not fully convincing, either. Recovery appeared to be underway before then.

It is even less clear how Russia should be judged. This is important, as its government appeared to attempt shock therapy, but the result was a decade of depression, inflation, and economic chaos. As shown in Chapter 5, an attempt at stabilization was made in 1992, but it did not prevent hyperinflation, which peaked in that year and coincided with declining GDP in every year from 1990 to 1996. The inflation rate (as shown in Table A.3 in the Appendix) fell under 10 percent for the first time in 2006. Successful stabilization has been dated by some as beginning in 2000 (Sutela 2003, 146–47)—a suggestion that would keep the appearance of the WC strategy's status as a key to economic success—although the economic environment and policy framework were by then very different. In some other countries, there was less sign of the attempt but the same phenomenon of hyperinflation.

One relationship that does stand up well in econometric tests is the relationship between GDP growth, or other indicators of successful performance, and geographical distance from Western Europe. That is broadly confirmed in the groupings of countries used in this chapter; at least once, allowance is made for the exceptional cases of oils and gas exporters.

It is less clear how this relationship should be interpreted. Geography does link directly to some sources of economic growth. Proximity was important for Western companies that outsourced activities or set up assembly plants, a point pursued in Chapter 15. However, it is also linked to past intellectual and political traditions, to attractions of a future within the European Union, and to inherited economic structures. It is therefore a proxy for a range of potentially important influences, some of which are difficult to separate from each other and most of which cannot be measured. A correlation between geographical position and economic performance, therefore, also remains only a starting point for further investigation rather than an indicator of clear causality.

However, the strength of the relationship between geography and performance does show problems with seeking to explain the latter in terms of policy choices. Thus, for example, Kyrgyzstan was a "radical" reformer in Central Asia, but its performance was far more like that of other CARs than CEECs. Similarly, Hungary avoided shock therapy, at least in its most extreme form, but did not obviously suffer, or benefit, as a result. If the relationship between a particular aspect of reform strategy and economic performance were decisive, then it ought to provide an explanation for differences between countries in the same geographical areas; it is not convincing in that. More factors, many of them not easily measurable, need to be taken into account.

THE CEEC DEPRESSION

Depression in CEECs can be related to two causes. We name the first cause the Washington Consensus depression, as it follows from the policies of stabilization and liberalization in line with advice from the IMF. This came in its purist form in Poland in 1990 and, as demonstrated in Box 4.2, can be understood using the most basic concept in macroeconomics: the circular flow of income. Enterprises paid less wages, when measured in real terms; consumers then spent less, and enterprises reduced their level of output.

Box 4.2 Poland under shock therapy

The process of output decline in Poland in 1990 can be explained in simplified form with the following steps, using data from Poland's statistical office at the time:

- In January 1990, imports were freed and the currency devalued. Domestic prices were largely freed and increased immediately to 179.6 percent over the level of the previous month (compare with Table A.3 in the Appendix).
- Restrictive policies meant that wages and consumption increased in monetary terms only to 101.8 percent and 104.3 percent, respectively, of the December 1989 level.
- This meant that, in real terms, wages fell to 56.7 percent and consumption fell to 58.1 percent of the previous month's levels.
- The fall in demand hit enterprises immediately, and industrial output fell to 68.5 percent of the December 1989 level.

The fall in output does not exactly match the fall in consumer demand because there were further elements of spending, on nonindustrial and imported goods, and because some of the industrial output went into exports, government demand, and stock building.

Over the whole year 1990, the effect was less dramatic. Real wages fell to 75.4 percent of the 1989 level, and real consumption fell to 81.6 percent of the previous year's level. Industrial output fell to 75.8 percent of the 1989 level. This improvement on the first month's figures can be attributed both to some relaxation of the restrictive policies later in the year and to growth in new enterprises that compensated for decline in other parts of the economy and created new spending power.

The process of rapid decline depended on a divergence in enterprise behavior from that predicted by Poland's policymakers, who were following the WC strategy of price liberalization alongside sharply restrictive policies to control spending power and hence inflation. They correctly foresaw that wages would be held in check, but they had expected lower demand to lead quickly to an end to price increases. Instead, enterprises continued with their past practice of cost-plus pricing and passed on higher input prices following the freeing of trade and currency devaluation. Later in the year, they did respond to the effects of falling demand by slowing the rate of price increases. The effect was a gradual reduction in inflation levels, but a degree of macroeconomic instability continued.

The second cause of the CEEC depression was the breaking of links within the CMEA. This was felt beginning in January 1991, as all payments had to be made in hard currency. Exports to the Soviet Union either ended or were unlikely to be paid for. Imports, principally of oil, immediately became more expensive. This affected all CEECs, delivering a sudden shock to all, irrespective of whether they were pursuing the letter of the WC strategy. The effect was greatest in Czechoslovakia, which had been the most dependent on the CMEA market. In that country, its impact was felt simultaneously with the impact of the WC depression following a liberalization and stabilization package introduced in January 1991.

The effects in Czechoslovakia were similar to those of the Polish package. A large devaluation led to import price rises, and enterprises passed on the costs in higher prices. However, there was no lasting inflation. The price level rose by 53.6 percent over the whole year, which was almost exactly the level that was predicted, albeit not acknowledged by the government, on the assumption that the higher input prices caused by devaluation would all be passed on by enterprises. Personal incomes then increased by 14.5 percent in monetary terms, held back by tight monetary policy and by wage controls, so that the real level of consumer demand fell substantially, leading to lower output from consumer goods sectors.

It is difficult to separate out the two negative influences on industrial output or to differentiate the effects of particular policies. It appears likely that the main internal source of falling output was declining domestic demand after monetary constraint prevented enterprises from increasing wages, even to the extent allowed by the wage-control policy. The key measures were high interest rates and, above all, direct control on the volume of credit that could be created. Thus, in Poland in 1990, EBRD data show a 160 percent increase in the money supply, while prices rose by 585.8 percent. A rough estimate made by the Czechoslovak Statistical Office of the relative importance of internal and external influences on demand suggested that the former explained 78 percent of the recorded fall in GDP—then estimated at about 16 percent for 1991—while falling exports to CMEA countries explained another 38 percent. Both were then partly compensated by the growth in exports to Western Europe as the process of recovery from depression began (Myant 2003, 32).

This account of transformation depression broadly applies to the other countries in the first group. Hungary did not adopt shock therapy but suffered from the shock of losing CMEA markets. It experienced a gradual price liberalization, successive devaluations, and monetary restraint to counter inflation, albeit with a growth in the money supply that was close to the inflation rate. The net effects were similar to those in countries that went for a more decisive blow and then later moderated its effects.

Slovenia had been part of Yugoslavia and was, therefore, not involved in the CMEA, but it suffered in an analogous way from the breaking of links with other Yugoslav republics as that country disintegrated and high inflation, partly inherited and partly associated with the end of Yugoslavia, was countered by restrictive policies.

The countries in Figure 4.3 followed this path with less consistency. Baltic republics were hit by the breaking of links with other former Soviet republics, but that was less important to the countries of southern Europe. The SEECs were not tempted by shock therapy but were persuaded to adopt elements of a similar approach later in the decade when Bulgaria opted for a very tight monetary policy.

THE CIS DEPRESSION

The much deeper depression in CIS countries cannot be explained by purely economic relationships. It followed from a much deeper "institutional collapse" that distinguishes these countries from other transition economies. The situation can be contrasted with Polanyi's framework, discussed in Chapter 6, in which a distinct economic sphere can function broadly independently once backed by a stable social and political order. Here, that precondition was absent.

There were some directly economic factors that may have put the CIS countries in a less favorable position than that of CEECs. Vladimir Popov (2007) referred to "pretransition distortions," meaning industrial and foreign trade structures that deviated substantially from those of market economies. Opening countries that suffered from "underopenness" could then lead to greater and more destructive shocks, particularly if liberalization was carried out quickly. It certainly was true that enterprises in CIS countries had less international experience and were, therefore, less equipped to cope in an open environment. This could, therefore, contribute to a deeper depression and to the difficulty of developing economic recovery.

Another attempt to relate the depression to economic processes led Blanchard and Kremer (1997) to use the notion of "disorganization" to explain decline in a sample of CIS countries. The evidence showed that output declines were greatest in products that required the widest range of inputs, as indicated by the sectors from which inputs came. The problem, therefore, appeared to be that established links had been broken and could not be reestablished. There was supporting evidence for this idea, as enterprises in CIS countries were likely to complain of difficulties in obtaining inputs as much as with selling their products. The authors found no evidence of greater difficulties with imported inputs, suggesting a very substantial breakdown in relationships within countries.

Blanchard and Kremer do not include CEECs in their study, and the disorganization hypothesis would be of less relevance where output declines were so clearly related to declining levels of demand for particular products. Nor do they explore the wider roots of disorganization in the CIS context, which should have led to consideration of the nature and effects of institutional breakdown. The activities they choose as ones requiring wide ranges of inputs roughly correspond to those planned from the all-union level rather than the republic level before the breakup of the Soviet Union (Iwasaki and Suzuki 2007, 392–402). As discussed later, there may have been bigger problems from trade between republics than Blanchard and Kremer suggest.

Notions of disorganization or systemic shocks as referred to by Blanchard and Kremer or by Iwasaki and Suzuki can be taken further with three points that go beyond purely economic factors.

The first is the breakdown of the state, legal, and enforcement apparatuses, covered in detail in Chapters 7 and 8. Without this infrastructure, a market system could not function satisfactorily. Recovery was, therefore, either very gradual or concentrated into a few sectors, such as oil and gas, which could function as enclaves within an otherwise chaotic economy.

In Tajikistan and Georgia, breakdown reached the scale of civil war. In other cases, the creation of new states brought to light ethnic tensions that led to sudden movements of population as members of national minorities headed for the country in which they could join a majority. Estimates vary as to the numbers moving, with possibly up to 9 million leaving one republic for another or leaving the area of the former Soviet Union in total during the 1990s (Sutela 2003, 218; Pilkington 1998, 5; Radnitz 2006, 653).

Many republics thereby lost part of their labor forces. These were not all the most skilled personnel—many moved for economic reasons as their workplaces closed—but there is evidence that the most qualified were among those likely to leave (Radnitz 2006, 671; Peyrouse 2007, 493). Therefore, this probably weakened more modern sectors of the economies, links with other republics, and the potential for developing new international contacts.

The second point is the breakdown of the financial and currency systems. All CIS countries (as shown in Table A.3 in the Appendix) experienced a bout of hyperinflation, a term that has been used to denote inflation above a level of 50 percent per month. On this measure, Poland suffered from hyperinflation in some months in 1989 and 1990, but this had largely identifiable economic roots, lasted only for a short period, and was relatively easily controlled. It took a different form in CIS republics, where it was associated with a more total loss of public confidence in the existing currencies. These countries were afflicted around the early to mid-1990s, at roughly the same time as their low points in GDP, and all had substantially reduced inflation rates by 1998. The record figures were 15,607 percent in Georgia in 1994 and 4,734 percent in Ukraine in 1993.

An explanation for hyperinflation, consistent with the WC framework, is that it is a result of high budget deficits creating excessive demand, and CIS countries were unable to raise enough in taxes to cover their spending. The deficits were generally not particularly high when compared with other countries, but the point was that they were not even covered by borrowing. Instead, the Russian central bank was soon covering government spending by printing money (Sutela 2003, 125). This, it can be assumed, contributed to rising inflation.

This cannot be a complete explanation. There has been remarkably little analysis of post-Soviet hyperinflation, but its fundamental cause probably lies in the general breakdown of confidence in the currency associated with the ending of Moscow's central authority. Existing banknotes were no longer trusted throughout the former Soviet Union, which is hardly surprising, as they were linked to a central authority that no longer existed. Restoration of public trust in money in CIS republics came gradually as individual republics established their own central banks and their own currencies. This process was delayed, as the IMF initially advised against it, doubting the ability of new countries to manage their own money, but was complete by 1994 (Åslund 2002, 205–6; Sutela 2003, 90).

Set in this context, focusing on the means of financing budget deficits and the quantity of money as the primary cause of inflation appears misplaced. These economies were very different from those of advanced countries. The quantity of money, measured as M2, was not high in CIS countries. In Georgia, when inflation peaked, it was equivalent to 5.6 percent of GDP. It was only 19.0 percent of GDP in Russia in 1993. By way of contrast, the equivalent figure for the Czech Republic, a country that experienced no serious problem of inflation, was 65.8 percent in 1993. The CIS economies were less monetized than CEECs and far less monetized than the most developed market economies. Attempting to cure inflation by ever tighter restrictions on the already limited money supply was, therefore, a policy that would cure inflation at the expense of restricting, if not stifling in total, the development of a money-based economy.

Indeed, hyperinflation had a number of consequences, encouraging flight from the money economy that was already limited by the heritage of central planning and by governments' attempts at restrictive monetary polices. Individuals, when possible, held savings in foreign currencies, and businesses took what money they could out of the country. Some money-based relationships were replaced by barter or by no relationship at all. This was, therefore, an additional factor contributing to disorganization.

The third element was the breaking of links between the Soviet republics. This was probably not the central issue in causing the downturn, as the declines in GDP were greater even than the shares of exports in GDP at the start of the transition, albeit with questions over the interpretation of the statistics of the time. Nevertheless, there were many reports of failures to deliver a particular component from another republic, thus paralysing a whole enterprise and thereby multiplying the effect of an apparently small drop in trade. Relations between republics were also very difficult to reestablish or develop, making any recovery more difficult. It would have appeared even more pointless to expect timely payment from another country than from one's own.

These points help to explain differences between CIS countries. Uzbekistan and Belarus underwent smaller political changes and kept more of their old state machines in tact. Authoritarian leaders soon established "order" states (Iwasaki 2004; see Chapter 9). Breakdown and disorganization were therefore more limited. Low-income countries outside the CIS, meaning Mongolia and Albania, also recovered more quickly from relatively shallow depressions. They did not suffer from the extent of state breakdown that came from membership in the former Soviet Union.

These factors were also important for the prospects for recovery, a process that can be divided into two elements: a consolidation of the domestic environment and an integration into the world economy. These two are closely linked, but discussion of the links is left to Chapter 16, following the discussion of specific elements of transition. The focus here is on international integration in measurable, quantitative terms.

INTEGRATION INTO THE WORLD ECONOMY

International integration was central to recovery from transformation depression in all countries. It can be followed in country groupings that are similar to those derived from GDP growth. Table 4.2 and subsequent figures keep the same groups as Figures 4.1 to 4.7, with the one change being that Croatia is placed with SEECs. The rationale for this change is partly one of convenience: meaningful comparison with other former Yugoslav republics is impossible due to the inadequacy of data in some cases. It is partly also a reflection of similarities in Croatia's performance to that of the SEECs.

International integration is introduced here with an outline of countries' positions in terms of four dimensions that relate to categories in balance-of-payments data, albeit not precisely. The first is trade in goods and services, which was usually freed early on, albeit with some tariffs retained, some restrictions on exports of particular commodities, and, in some CIS countries, the continuation of arbitrary administrative controls. The second is the movement of money and of capital. This had been liberalized slowly in market economies in earlier years but was implemented fairly quickly with CEECs removing all controls in the mid-1990s. The third was the movement of labor. Emigration became possible at once, but immigration was always subject to some constraints. Finally, the fourth is official financing from international agencies and through international aid. In each case, there was potential for gain and also potential dangers.

All countries needed to achieve overall external balance, and all needed to import. These imports could be covered by exporting goods and services, by an inflow of finance to cover a current account deficit, by remittances from citizens working abroad, or by foreign aid. Table 4.2 shows the positions of individual countries in 2006 alongside some further indicators of international integration. The end year is chosen to mark a point before the effects of the world financial crisis of 2008 were felt. Over the whole period from 1989, the current accounts of countries' balances of payments showed broadly three experiences of persistent deficits, periodic deficits, and rough balances or even surpluses. These in several cases correspond to the data on debt levels in the last column of Table 4.2, but the link is not precise, as countries inherited various debt histories, and some were able to write off past obligations.

These different experiences do not correspond precisely to geographical areas or transition strategies, although some links can be made. A number of poorer countries—notably Albania, Moldova, Georgia, and Kyrgyzstan—suffered from substantial and permanent deficits. Other countries that could not achieve balance were the Baltic republics, Romania, and Hungary, the last of these showing an important difference from other CEECs. Those faced by periodic or only relatively mild deficits included Poland, the Czech Republic, Belarus, Bulgaria, Slovakia, and Ukraine. Russia was generally in surplus, but Kazakhstan, despite oil exports, generally experienced small deficits. This means that most countries had some difficulties in covering the costs of their imports. Long-term failure to secure external balance points to persistent weakness in an economy, and obvious sources of this are the failure to develop competitive export activities and the failure to control consumption and spending levels to match the country's earning power.

TRADE AND EXPORTS

The second two columns in Table 4.2 follow this through the trade balance and the share of exports of goods and services in GDP (for which there are more complete data in Tables A.9 and A.10 in the Appendix). There are some problems, as comparable data are not available for all countries in all relevant years. There are also some large fluctuations for countries with narrow export structures that reflect no more than the changing prices of key exports, especially oil and gas. However, this indicator corresponds fairly closely to predictable groupings of countries. A few remained at low levels, and these were mostly poorer countries, exporting very little, even from low levels of GDP. Albania was among the lowest.

TABLE 4.2   **The international position of transition economies, 2006 (measured as percentage of GDP)**

	Current account	Trade balance	Exports of goods and services	Remittances Reported (WB)	Remittances Estimates (IFAD)	Official aid	FDI stock	Debt
Czech Republic	−2.7	3.5	76.6	0.8	1.2		54.8	40.9
Hungary	−5.8	−0.7	77.1	0.3	0.8		73.0	94.1
Poland	−2.8	−0.7	40.3	1.3	1.4		30.6	49.3
Slovakia	−5.7	−3.8	84.4	0.8	1.3		55.0	47.3
Slovenia	−2.8	−0.5	66.6	0.8			20.0	78.5
Bulgaria	−18.5	−18.8	64.5	5.4	3.8		65.8	78.2
Estonia	−16.8	−11.5	80.9	2.4	2.3		77.2	102.3
Latvia	−22.7	−21.5	44.9	2.4	2.3		37.5	117.9
Lithuania	−10.7	−10.2	59.1	3.3	1.6		36.7	63.4
Romania	−10.4	−10.4	33.7	5.5	3.9		33.6	34.3
Bosnia-Herzegovina	−7.9	−29.9	36.6	1.8	20.3	4.0	38.7	53.8
Croatia	−6.7	−7.0	43.4	2.9	3.3	0.5	29.2	85.3
Macedonia, FYR	−0.9	−18.6	48.1	4.2	8.4	3.1	38.3	38.7
Montenegro	−29.1	−28.3	49.4			3.6	47.8	38.3
Serbia	−12.9	−20.7	28.7	2.3	11.4[a]	5.0	31.8	68.2
Azerbaijan	15.6	27.7	66.5	4.1	9.3	1.0	66.9	9.6
Kazakhstan	−2.5	10.7	51.1	0.2	6.5	0.2	42.0	91.5
Russia	9.5	12.7	33.8	0.2	1.4	0.2	20.2	91.5
Turkmenistan	12.3	18.5	73.7		3.4	0.2	14.3	8.4
Belarus	−3.9	−4.2	60.1	0.9	6.3	0.2	7.4	16.6
Mongolia	5.6	5.7	65.3	5.7	7.5	6.4	27.5	42.9
Ukraine	−1.5	−2.8	46.6	0.8	8.0	0.5	21.1	46.9
Uzbekistan	18.6	10.1	37.5		17.0	0.9	8.4	22.7
Albania	−7.4	−24.1	25.1	14.9	21.7	3.5	14.1	20.0
Armenia	−1.8	−15.9	23.4	18.4	18.5	3.3	26.6	32.4
Georgia	−16.1	−24.2	32.9	6.3	20.2	4.7	43.0	25.4
Kyrgyzstan	−10.6	−37.3	41.7	17.1	31.4	11.0	21.0	84.5
Moldova	−11.3	−46.6	45.2	35.2	31.4	6.8	39.6	71.9
Tajikistan	−0.8	−34.2	23.3	36.3	36.7	8.5	23.0	41.1

Source: Calculated from the IMF International Financial Statistics, available at http://www.imfstatistics.org/imf/; WB (2008a); UNCTAD (2007); IFAD (2007); and EBRD economic statistics and forecasts, available at http://www.ebrd.com/country/sector/econo/stats/index.htm.

Note: For an explanation of individual measures, see the Appendix.

[a] Serbia and Montenegro

The CEECs saw rapid growth in the share of exports in GDP, with Slovakia being the most dramatic, rising from 56.3 percent in 1993 to 84.4 percent in 2006. Some of these countries were also recording a trade surplus in the last years up to 2008. The Baltic republics and SEECs had slightly lower export shares in GDP, with the exception of Estonia, which reached 80.9 percent in 2006. They also ran substantial and persistent deficits. Another group, including Russia and other CIS countries, retained more autarky, just as they had as republics within the Soviet Union. This applied even to Kazakhstan, despite its high level of oil exports.

FINANCIAL FLOWS

The financial account can balance deficits on the current account (complete data is found in Tables A.13 and A.14 in the Appendix). However, the components carry different implications. Short-term financial flows, much of which are associated with banks, are likely to be the most volatile. As they were freed in transition economies, this freedom brought benefits of access to international financial markets, but it also brought dangers. For countries trying to maintain a fixed exchange rate, money could be attracted by an interest rate differential and could be withdrawn quickly, frequently when devaluation is expected. For countries with an unstable exchange rate, money could be attracted by the expectation of appreciation, while the expectation of depreciation tended to lead to citizens taking money out of the country or holding it in foreign currency. These processes created the background for financial crises that amplified the problems of transition and the weakness of domestic economies (cf. Becker 2007).

There is no easy way to measure these problems that could be used in Table 4.2. A number of countries experienced crises linked to the free movement of finance, which served as signals for substantial changes in the orientation of economic policies, albeit in different directions that reflected the state of economic thinking in the countries at the time. Three examples can illustrate this point. In no case was the crisis purely one of external payments, but in each case, that was central to a subsequent change in policy direction and in the country's growth trajectory. The message should have been clear from these and other experiences that liberalized financial flows carry risks, especially, but not only, when they mask trade deficits. The lesson was not learned, as later years were to show.

The first case was the Bulgarian crisis of 1996 to 1997. Its roots were in a banking crisis caused by unsound lending to industrial enterprises. This was, therefore, tied in with a transition strategy that left state-owned enterprises struggling to survive, and which the government encouraged banks to help (Berlemann and Nenovsky 2004).

Fears of the collapse of banks led to a withdrawal of foreign currency deposits held by Bulgarian citizens, and this caused a sudden foreign currency crisis, even though trade and current account balances were positive in 1996. The crisis led to a spell of very high inflation, reaching 1,082 percent in 1997, and the government sought IMF help to stabilize its payments position. The agreement reached led to cuts in the budget, turning a deficit of 10.3 percent of GDP in 1996 into a surplus of 1.7 percent of GDP in 1998, and to an emphasis on rapid privatization that had not previously been a government priority. The crisis was reflected in the decline in GDP and the slower overall growth shown in Figure 6.2. It also brought Bulgaria into line with the transition strategies favored at the time by the IMF and World Bank. There was even a policy of fixing the exchange rate through a currency board, returning to the concept of an "anchor" for other macroeconomic policies, which had been abandoned in Poland shortly after its shock therapy.

The second was the experience of the Czech Republic in 1997, a country that was priding itself on maintaining a fixed exchange rate. In this case, the stimulus came from a current account deficit, as imports rose to support personal consumption, which reached the dangerous level of 8.3 percent of GDP in the first quarter of the year. Up until then, the deficit had been covered by inflows on the financial account, but external confidence in the currency collapsed following a negative IMF report on the economy in March 1997. Money was pulled out, causing an immediate financial crisis and forcing the central bank to abandon attempts to defend the exchange rate.

The government responded with a deflationary fiscal and monetary policy, leading to the decline in GDP in 1997 and 1998 shown in Figure 4.2. Recovery came later, when the balance of payments was secured by inward direct investment and by the exports generated from that. This also confirmed the ending of faith in past privatization strategies, as it was the firms privatized into Czech ownership that had failed to reach a level of international competitiveness that could ensure adequate exports to maintain external balance. Thus, the financial crisis brought a final end to faith in voucher privatization in the Czech Republic. Financial crisis in Bulgaria led to a very different outcome. The government accepted external advice from international organizations that still believed in the benefits of the voucher method.

The third was the Russian crisis of 1998. This followed from deeper weaknesses in Russia's transition. The state budget was always in deficit through the 1990s, and the gap could not be covered by taxation, for reasons explained in Chapters 7 and 8. Up until 1995, it was effectively covered by printing money. After that, it was covered by selling state debt at home and abroad, a policy supported by the IMF, which was encouraging a policy of maintaining a fixed exchange rate to give confidence to foreign investors (Sutela 2003, 140). This inflow was supplemented by lending to Russian banks and private companies. Remarkably, it was more than counterbalanced by an outflow of wealth, as Russian businesses and wealthy individuals took their money abroad by any means they could find. Evidently, foreign bankers and international agencies had more confidence in the Russian economy than the country's business leaders.

However, in 1998 in the context of a financial crisis affecting east Asian countries, foreign investors lost confidence in the Russian currency and ceased funding the government's debt (see Sutela [2003, 168–72] and Woodruff [2005]). The government was forced to announce that it could not repay outstanding debts, leading both to crisis for Russian banks and to massive pressure on the Russian currency, which had fallen by the end of the year to 29 percent of its value at the start of the year relative to the U.S. dollar.

An immediate consequence was the fall in GDP in 1998, shown in Figures 4.1 and 4.4. Devaluation also caused a renewed bout of inflation, reaching 86.1 percent 1999. Beyond that, consequences were overwhelmingly positive, and the following years saw big improvements in the Russian economy. The crisis allowed for a restructuring of debt such that debt servicing was no longer a problem. The fiscal position also improved thanks to the coincidence of rising oil and gas revenue. Domestic industrial producers also expanded their output following devaluation, which helped their competitive position relative to that of importers, at least for a time. Thus, the Russian financial crisis marked the start of a new period in the country's economic development.

FOREIGN DIRECT INVESTMENT

Direct investment is typically less volatile than the flows of money considered in the previous text, as it generally depends on long-term assessments of profitability. Figures for FDI show that, in some countries and periods, it could make a substantial difference in the overall balance, compensating for much of the current account deficit (see Tables A.11 and A.12 in the Appendix). Figures in Table 4.2 show the stock built up over preceding years, with higher levels in CEECs, some Baltic republics, and oil exporters. The lowest levels were in Uzbekistan and Belarus, with only 50 and 52 registered subsidiaries of foreign companies in 2006, respectively, while Russia and Ukraine also recorded low levels (1,176 and 367, respectively; United Nations Conference on Trade and Development [UNCTAD] 2007, 218).

Factors determining levels of FDI are discussed in Chapter 15. The issue here is its balance-of-payments impact. A positive side stems from the inflow of capital and the possible subsequent exports once an investment project is in operation. A negative side stems from the possibility of higher imports for components. Investment that targets the domestic market, as is the case for much of manufacturing and practically all of retailing and finance, may bring no exports to compensate for possible import requirements. There is also in all cases a negative impact from repatriated profits, which increase over time. This is an important source of differences between trade and current account balances in the years up to 2008, especially in Hungary and the Czech Republic, countries that had pioneered inward investment.

Foreign direct investment was significant first in Hungary, the country with the second-highest stock relative to GDP (as indicated in Table 4.2), and remained highest there for some time. Hungary's lead was quickly followed by other CEECs and the Baltic republics and then, with a significant lag, by Bulgaria and Romania. In all of these cases, a substantial proportion of inward investment was export oriented, and its most important impact is, therefore, discussed next in relation to export structures.

REMITTANCES AND AID

In later years, it became common in some countries for people to seek work abroad and to send back remittances. If recorded, these account for part of the difference between trade and current account balances. However, their importance is extremely difficult to measure, as a large proportion of remittances were not recorded by central banks. World Bank figures, therefore, underestimate the scale of this phenomenon. An alternative methodology, used by the UN International Fund for Agricultural Development (IFAD) agency, has relied on surveys of migrant workers, and the resulting estimates are set alongside World Bank figures in Table 4.2.

Together, these sources show a number of transition economies among the highest levels of dependence on remittances of any in the world. This was an especially important source for Tajikistan and Kyrgyzstan, both able to benefit from jobs created in the boom conditions in the years up to 2008 in Russia and Kazakhstan. The IFAD figures also show significant levels of remittances sent into Uzbekistan and Belarus, two countries for which central banks had reported very low levels. A number of countries received both migrant workers and incomes from their own workers abroad. Ukraine was an example, having workers in several EU countries while also receiving migrants from Moldova. Russia, and Kazakhstan also appeared in both categories.

This element appears in the balance-of-payments current account and is, therefore, incorporated into the calculation of deficits referred to previously. It is obviously not possible from these data to know what kinds of people are working outside their own countries, but other evidence suggests that they often were educated and skilled, taking considerably less-skilled jobs in the host country. The remittance-dependent economies were, therefore, failing to use the potential of their own labor forces. A very high dependence on remittances, therefore, suggests both a failure to develop a competitive economy and a limited scope for successful development in the future.

Some of the transition economies within the European Union—notably Bulgaria and Romania—were also heavily dependent on remittances, as was Albania from the very start of transition. Opportunities expanded in CEECs with EU accession. However, migrant labor was never as important there as in CIS countries. For the Czech Republic and Slovenia, incoming migration became important as a means to cover for labor shortages. Poland saw considerable emigration and temporary work abroad, but the money sent back made only a small contribution to its balance of payments. It was slightly more important in the Baltic republics, and, as indicated in the next section, those were countries that were less successful at building competitive export structures.

The final way to pay for the necessary imports is dependence on international aid. This was insignificant for all but a few countries. In Tajikistan, it provided 8.5 percent of GDP in 2007, and for Kyrgyzstan, 11.0 percent. The latter country's dependence on this source, and on credits from the IMF and World Bank, reflected both the weak state of its economy and its willingness to follow international advice on transition strategy. That at least brought aid, if not a means to successful economic development. That depended above all on integration by international trade.

INTEGRATION BY INTERNATIONAL TRADE

The ability to export goods was the most important factor in sustained and stable recoveries from the transformation depression. No other form of international integration provided such potential for rising GDP. Other forms of integration were important either in providing a basis for goods exports, as was the case for some FDI, or as a means for covering for a failure to export enough to balance import needs; this was not a basis for sustainable growth.

A considerable literature exists on forms of integration into the world economy through trade, and this leads to an approximate hierarchy of the forms that provide the highest incomes and greatest security. This has been set out by Porter (1990) in terms of stages of development, with the highest incomes going to the home bases of firms that are the sources of innovations, and by Gereffi (1995) in terms of integration into networks, with the highest incomes going to the originators of modern, branded goods.

Exports of raw materials generally provide unstable incomes, and, in most cases, these are low. Between that and the other extreme—the exporters of technologically advanced branded products—are a number of intermediate possibilities. Semimanufactures—steel and heavy chemicals—are produced with widely available technology and sold into competitive world markets. A country dependent on these products can therefore expect a middle-income level, threatened by price instability and the ease with which competition may arise from any other country with the ability to organize large-scale production and worldwide sales.

A range of simple manufactured goods can be produced as part of networks set up by MNCs. In Gereffi's terminology, these can take two forms: "buyer-driven" and "producer-driven" networks. Buyer-driven networks are characteristic of much of light industry—especially footwear and garments—that can be made to contract. Distributors in richer countries provide and control technology, distribution, and marketing. Skill requirements are not particularly high, and the scale of production can be small. These activities can, therefore, be undertaken in countries with little more to offer than geographical accessibility and a satisfactory environment for business activity. Moreover, for the simpler activities, strong competition can be expected from other countries. There is some scope for moving up to higher-quality products and high value added activity, but the most common trend is for participation in these networks to become less important as income levels rise (cf. Bair and Gereffi 2003).

Producer-driven networks are established by MNCs to undertake component-manufacturing or assembly tasks. Some can be simple, but in parts of the motor-vehicle and electronics industries, this can also bring more complex tasks as part of the integration of production processes. Subsidiaries are often involved in developing products for specific markets—for example, adapting a car model for a particular country—and even in research and development (R&D) for the company as a whole. This kind of activity can, therefore, bring rising income levels and considerable security.

Organizing the production of the final product provides the highest incomes. This is where several transition economies started. The enterprises they inherited were fully integrated operations that were producing their own branded products. However, these enterprises were hit by the shock of falling domestic demand and falling demand in traditional export markets. It can be added that they had been producing in protected markets without access to the most modern technology and were, at best, going to have difficulty competing in world markets.

CHANGING EXPORT STRUCTURES

Figures 4.8 to 4.22 show how different countries integrated into the structure of world trade. The chosen indicator is the share of product groups in total exports. A possible alternative would be the share of exports from those groups in total GDP, guarding against the effects of changing shares of total exports in GDP. In practice, that would make no difference to the general trends and conclusions. The product groups have been derived from the Standard International Trade Classification, with some alterations to the single-digit groupings in order to create groupings that correspond more closely to the likely technological level of products.

We combine SITC3 categories as follows: nonfuel primary products (0, 1, 2, 4); fuels (3); semimanufactures (5, 6, without 54); machinery and other complex (referred to as machinery-complex) activities (7, 54, 87, 88), which broadly corresponds to incorporation into production-driven networks; and light industry (8, without 87 and 88), which broadly corresponds to incorporation into buyer-driven networks. In the context of transition, it is useful to group SITC categories 5 and 6 together, as semimanufactures can compete by price without the need for substantial development of the product.

Any measures based on the commodity structure of exports can be misleading. A country may export sophisticated products, but that could reflect simple assembly tasks using complex imported components. Such is often the case in electronics. Similarly, a country could export apparently simple products, but made in sophisticated ways or to sophisticated designs that make them more competitive. Such can be the case even for basic consumer goods. This can partly be checked by using measures of relative export quality, such as unit values, and by checking export values against component import values. Such methods have been used in analyses of transition economies' exports, including those of CEECs and CARs (Landesmann and Burgstaller 1997; Myant 2003; Greskovits 2005; Myant and Drahokoupil 2008), and have been borne in mind in what follows.

The countries are grouped into CEECs, a second grouping of mostly SEECs and the Baltic republics, and a third grouping of CIS countries. This demonstrates the close links between GDP growth and international integration, maintaining the validity of the groupings developed in Figures 4.1 to 4.7.The CIS countries are put together in one set of figures, but there is a division into two groups, with one benefiting from rising revenues from fuel exports. However, the dividing line is not completely clear—Belarus takes an intermediate position, with partial dependence on fuel exports—and other raw materials also provided rising incomes in the years up to 2008.

Trends can now be followed across the three groups.

Central and Eastern European Countries

The most striking feature of trade restructuring in CEECs is the decline and then rise in the share of the machinery-complex category, as shown in Figure 4.8. The decline marked the loss of CMEA markets for heavy equipment. The later rise was not a restoration of previous exports but was related to two processes, described in Chapters 11 and 15, whereby existing enterprises shifted to exporting simpler products, and then enterprises under foreign ownership produced sophisticated goods, especially motor vehicles and electronics, for export. The rise in this category in the mid–and late 1990s was, thus, associated with integration through product-driven networks of MNCs seeking access to Western European markets. Motor-vehicle assembly was particularly desired, as the large-scale investment was likely to be secure and to attract an infrastructure of component suppliers, neither of which was so certain for electronics. There was a tendency toward producing cheaper cars and components in CEECs, but these were generally higher-quality products, as measured by unit values, than could be manufactured by domestically owned firms.

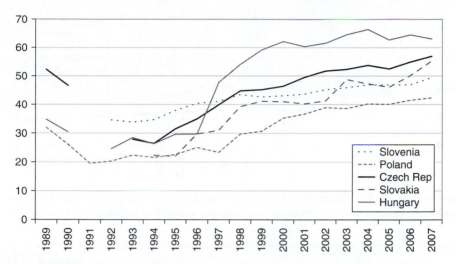

Figure 4.8 Machinery/complex (SITC 7, 54, 87, 88): Share in total exports in CEECs (%). (*Source:* Calculated from the UN Commodity Trade Statistics Database (Comtrade), available at http://comtrade.un.org/db.)

The initial fall in export share of the machinery-complex group was matched by increases in semimanufactures, light industry, and raw materials, shown in Figures 4.9, 4.10, and 4.11, respectively. The ordering of these increases roughly corresponds to the difficulty of adapting existing capacity and of finding new markets. Problems were smallest for raw materials that could be sold directly into international markets. Their share rose and fell first, declining in all countries after 1992 as they were pushed aside by the other categories. Semimanufactures fell beginning in 1994, and light industry, which needed to link up into the buyer-driven networks of Western companies but generally followed a course similar to that of semimanufactures, fell

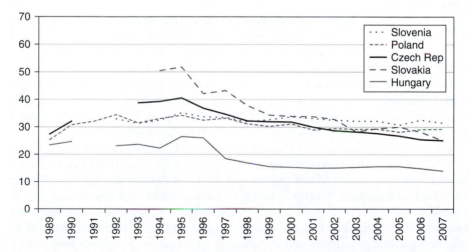

Figure 4.9 Semimanufacturing (SITC 5, 6, without 54): Share in total exports in CEECs (%). (*Source:* Calculated from the UN Comtrade database, available at http://comtrade.un.org/db.)

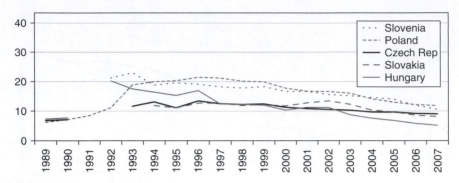

Figure 4.10 Light industry (SITC 8, without 87 and 88): Share in total exports in CEECs (%). (*Source:* Calculated from the UN Comtrade database, available at http://comtrade.un.org/db.)

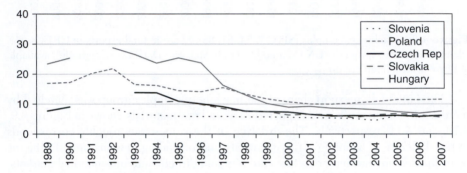

Figure 4.11 Nonfuel raw materials (SITC 0, 1, 2, 4): Share in total exports in CEECs (%). (*Source:* Calculated from the UN Comtrade database, available at http://comtrade.un.org/db.)

beginning in 1996. (Adjustment through fuels, as shown in Figure 4.12, was not an option in CEECs.)

In all cases, at the start, these were products that required little adaptation. In the case of light industry, they were usually made by existing equipment and labor according to precise instructions from foreign partners. The decline fits with Porter's notion of stages of competitiveness in which the simpler products are forced into decline by competition from lower-wage countries. However, the fall in the share in exports was associated with quite high absolute levels. This did generally depend on improving quality, as exports into the European Union were threatened by competition from companies from Asia and other European countries.

The differences among CEECs are relatively small. The revival of the machinery-complex category was fastest in Hungary, which was the first to welcome inward direct investment. Much of this growth was new and did not depend on adapting the inherited industrial structure. Hungary soon overtook the Czech and Slovak republics, which had been given a better start by the industries they inherited from state Socialism. Poland had coal to export and was slightly worse off in terms of its inherited machinery industry and in terms of attracting inward direct investment. The Czech Republic and Slovakia had stronger steel and petrochemical industries. Slovenia stood out, as it had not been integrated into the CMEA and had inherited

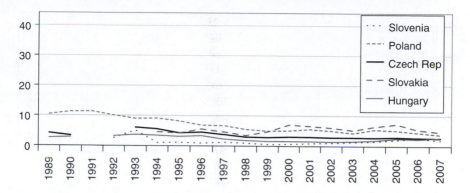

Figure 4.12   Fuels (SITC 3): Share in total exports in CEECs (%). (*Source:* Calculated from the UN Comtrade database, available at http://comtrade.un.org/db.)

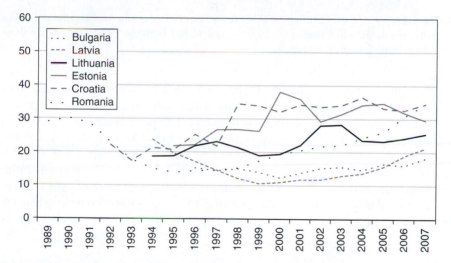

Figure 4.13   Machinery/complex (SITC 7, 54, 87, 88): Share in total exports in SEECs, the Baltic republics, and Croatia (%). (*Source:* Calculated from the UN Comtrade database, available at http://comtrade.un.org/db.)

a strong light-industry base. It was characterized by more stability while still broadly following the same trends as the other countries, albeit with much lower reliance on FDI.

South European Countries and the Baltic Republics

The second grouping is made up of countries that inherited export structures that were less oriented toward the machinery-complex category. Their development is also harder to follow due to the inadequacies of the available data. Nevertheless, as shown in Figure 4.13, the machinery-complex category was clearly growing by, or after, the late 1990s. Romania's pattern is the closest to the CEECs, with decline occurring as its uncompetitive products lost markets and then growth following FDI to a level above the initial starting point.

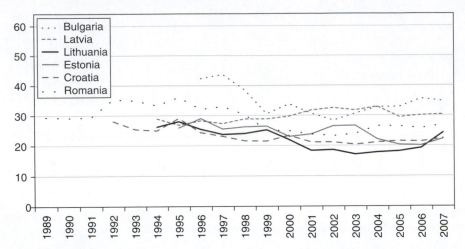

Figure 4.14 Semimanufacturing (SITC 5, 6, without 54): Share in total exports in SEECs, the Baltic republics, and Croatia (%). (*Source:* Calculated from the UN Comtrade database, available at http://comtrade.un.org/db.)

The other measures, shown in Figures 4.14 to 4.17, similarly show this group following the CEECs with a few years' delay. Light industry rose higher and peaked later; this was particularly important in Romania. The peak in absolute terms came as the European Union allowed competing imports from China (Pickles et al. 2006). Raw materials were consistently more important, and semimanufactures showed less signs of decline. It is remarkable that Albania clearly belongs within this group, rather than with lower-income CIS countries, due to its high export share of light industry. As with several other countries in the grouping, the exports were footwear, garments, and furniture, and this share was increasing up until 2000 as the same category was

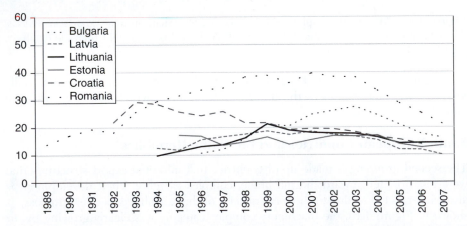

Figure 4.15 Light industry (SITC 8, without 87 and 88): Share in total exports in SEECs, the Baltic republics, and Croatia (%). (*Source:* Calculated from the UN Comtrade database, available at http://comtrade.un.org/db.)

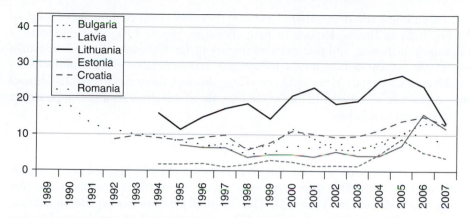

Figure 4.16 Fuels (SITC 3): Share in total exports in SEECs, the Baltic republics, and Croatia (%). (*Source:* Calculated from the UN Comtrade database, available at http://comtrade.un.org/db.)

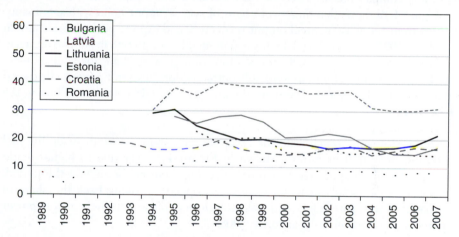

Figure 4.17 Nonfuel raw materials (SITC 0, 1, 2, 4): Share in total exports in SEECs, the Baltic republics, and Croatia (%). (*Source:* Calculated from the UN Comtrade database, available at http://comtrade.un.org/db.)

declining in CEECs. This would be consistent with Western firms choosing to switch to subcontract to countries that offered lower wages but were still geographically close.

The Baltic republics require more comment, as export structures alone give a deceptive impression of their international integration. As shown in Figure 4.13, Estonia saw rapid growth in exports from the machinery-complex group in the late 1990s, fueled by inward direct investment, but it then stagnated. Growth came from electronics—not motor vehicles, as in CEECs—and activity fluctuated with changes in thinking from the foreign companies. The significance of the manufacturing-complex category is further exaggerated, as exports also included a substantial share of used cars—rising to 4.0 percent of exports in 2007—imported from Western Europe and sold on to Russia. That item contributed 4.75 percent of Lithuania's exports in the same year.

Other items also demonstrated a strong dependence on continuing, or reestablishing, links to Russia. Exports of fuel, shown in Figure 4.16, were reexports of imports from Russia, and this was also important for Lithuania. A major Estonian export was car seat belts to Russia, following a division of labor in car manufacturing established across the old Soviet Union. Thus, although there was some international integration that was similar to that of CEECs, there was also a stronger emphasis on building from past links.

CIS Countries

The CIS countries can only be followed from when reliable data became available. Data from the mid-1990s show very low levels of exports in the machinery-complex category, as indicated in Figure 4.18. The inherited base was inadequate for a strong internationally competitive position, and there was minimal export-oriented inward investment in these sectors. Belarus was a partial exception, able to export heavy vehicles to other CIS countries without help from inward FDI, but its share of machinery-complex products declined as oil became more important.

Figure 4.19 shows that there were signs of success at one point with semimanufactures from Kazakhstan. Steel output recovered, and exports peaked as a share in the total in 1995 before falling. Ukraine experienced some growth in later years, again due largely to steel. Figure 4.20 shows a hint of a growing share for light industry from Kyrgyzstan, reflecting garments subcontracted for Western European firms and exported at very low prices. These are the only signs of CIS countries following the CEEC route.

Raw materials continued to be important to all countries. Figure 4.21 shows the nonfuel category, which, with the exception of Ukraine, fell only when the fuel category increased. This growth, shown in Figure 4.22, was due to higher world prices and higher output. Azerbaijan was a strong exporter throughout the period. Kazakhstan grew rapidly as new capacity was opened, pushing back the share of semimanufactures. Russia followed a slightly slower course, but fuels made up over 60 percent of exports in the years up to 2008.

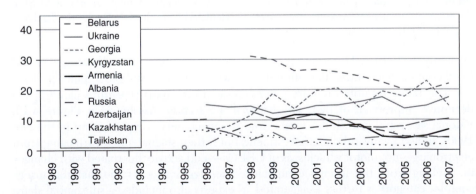

Figure 4.18 Machinery/complex (SITC 7, 54, 87, 88): Share in total exports in CIS countries (%). (*Source:* Calculated from the UN Comtrade database, available at http://comtrade.un.org/db.)

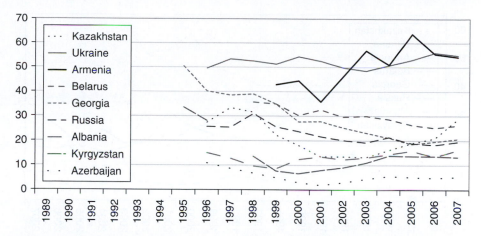

Figure 4.19 Semimanufacturing (SITC 5, 6, without 54): Share in total exports in CIS countries (%). (*Source:* Calculated from the UN Comtrade database, available at http://comtrade.un.org/db.)

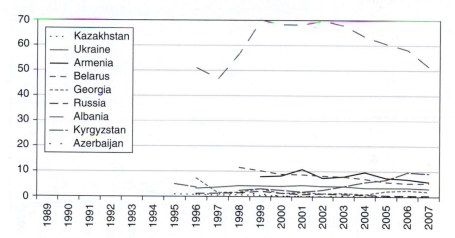

Figure 4.20 Light industry (SITC 8, without 87 and 88): Share in total exports in CIS countries (%). (*Source:* Calculated from the UN Comtrade database, available at http://comtrade.un.org/db.)

Oil and gas are quite specific among raw materials in view of the scale of the revenues they can generate and the relatively low levels of employment needed for their extraction. Some possible consequences of this are discussed in Chapter 7. A strictly economic effect is the so-called Dutch disease, whereby export revenues lead to exchange rate appreciation restricting the scope for export of other goods. It is possible to demonstrate that fuel exports do not lead to high price levels when taken across all transition economies (Kronenberg 2004). It still could have been important within groupings where it could have been one factor limiting the scope for following the early steps of the CEEC route in some CIS countries, but it was not the only one. Thus, in Central Asia, price and wage levels were higher in Kazakhstan and Turkmenistan, the biggest fuel exporters, than in Kyrgyzstan and Uzbekistan.

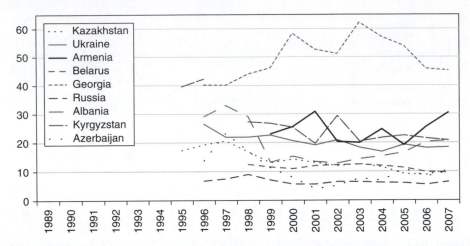

Figure 4.21 Nonfuel raw materials (SITC 0, 1, 2, 4): Share in total exports in CIS countries (%). (*Source:* Calculated from the UN Comtrade database, available at http://comtrade.un.org/db.)

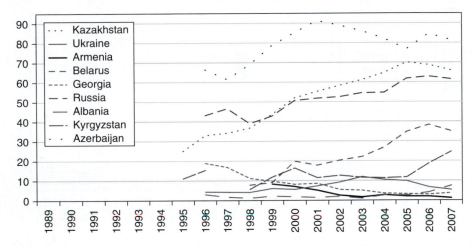

Figure 4.22 Fuels (SITC 3): Share in total exports in CIS countries (%). (*Source:* Calculated from the UN Comtrade database, available at http://comtrade.un.org/db.)

However, incorporation into international networks was limited in all these countries, suggesting that geography and unfavorable environments for international business activity were the most important constraints.

CONCLUSION

Forms of international integration show variation across countries that can be linked back to the growth in GDP. Integration by exports of more sophisticated products brought the most stable balance-of-payments positions—that meaning relative to other transition economies—and contributed to reasonably rapid growth for CEECs from the early 1990s. This generally required inward investment, which was attracted by stable states and sound business environments. It depended on a degree of macroeconomic stability but not on precise transition strategies other than opening to foreign investment.

The export of less-sophisticated manufactured goods into networks controlled by multinational companies was associated with slower growth and less external stability but required a business environment and access to outside businesses that was difficult in much of the CIS. Exports of semimanufactures and raw materials, the dominant feature in CIS countries, brought revenues and contributed to GDP recovery. However, in many CIS countries, the share of exports in GDP was relatively low. Therefore, GDP growth was to a greater extent driven by inward-oriented activities. Thus, the Russian acceleration after 1998 reflected successful oil and gas exports but also revealed firms that were producing for the domestic market. Ukraine followed a similar course, in this case based on the less-lucrative steel exports. It therefore remained some way behind Russia.

Thus, the courses of recovery from the transformation depression were linked to forms of international integration and depended on developments discussed in subsequent chapters, in both the state forms and in enterprises.

TRANSITION: POLICIES AND ALTERNATIVES

CHAPTER FIVE

A Strategy for Transition

The ending of state Socialism opened the door for more radical thinking on changes to the economic system. The aim was no longer reform of a Socialist economy but rather creation of a market system similar to the capitalist economies of the world's most advanced countries. This chapter is concerned with the early evolution of policies for transition, focusing on the dominant version, which was propagated by international agencies in the early 1990s. The starting point is the strategy itself, its international supporters—particularly the IMF and World Bank—and its theoretical underpinnings. The core of the chapter deals with early steps in Poland, Russia, and other countries, showing how and why strategies differed. This sets the scene for the discussion in Chapter 6 of criticisms of and adaptations to the strategy.

SHOCK THERAPY AND GRADUALISM

Debate at the time crystallized around two broad approaches, characterized as shock therapy, or "big bang," and gradualism. These terms are not ideal and were often used to stigmatize and condemn opponents. Behind the differences in strategy lay differences in understanding both of how a market economy can develop and of the essential nature of a market economy once it has developed.

Shock therapy was an approach that centered on achieving the most rapid possible changes in the direction of a market system. It was accepted that not everything could be done at once, but the general principle was to do anything that could be done as quickly as possible. Thus, no argument was accepted for delaying one step until another had been implemented. Macroeconomic stabilization, price and trade liberalization, and privatization of state-owned enterprises should come as quickly as was humanly possible.

Reasons given for favoring speed were both political—a fear that opposition would soon mobilize against reform, so measures had to be rushed—and economic, a belief that economic actors needed to be jolted into changing their behavior. Shock therapy also corresponded to a theoretical position, fitting with the view that a market system is essentially simple and can be created quickly. It matched an international situation in which the IMF and World Bank were advising and imposing conditions on transition countries. Clear and straightforward policy requirements suited them best, particularly as they were permanently suspicious that governments and populations were not really committed to the kinds of changes that they were advocating.

Gradualism did not necessarily mean opposition to the general agenda of liberalization and stabilization, but its advocates gave various reasons for taking steps more slowly. These included fears over the political and economic consequences of shock therapy. Gradualism was also often linked to a different understanding of the foundations and development of the market economy, placing more emphasis on the need for active state involvement and an institutional framework as had grown up alongside markets in the historical process of the development of capitalism elsewhere in the world. A rush to the maximum liberalization and privatization, it was argued, would prove counterproductive, harming economic prospects and generating political opposition to reform in general.

Neither the shock therapy nor the gradualist approach was set either as a clear or as an unchanging strategy. Reality was rather an evolution of thinking, differing between countries, in which pressures for speed jostled with arguments for more caution. However, the initiative in the early years was definitely with the view that rapid and decisive change was required. In view of the degree of flexibility and the important role in development of strategy played by international agencies, this is usually best referred to as the Washington Consensus (WC) strategy.

TRANSITION AND THE WASHINGTON CONSENSUS

The WC strategy was backed with a theoretical framework, supported by international agencies and propagated by teams of foreign advisers. Once the aim was the creation of a modern capitalist system, as existed in the world's most advanced countries, the attraction was obvious to seek advice from those well versed in modern economic theories from those countries.

Formulation of a strategy for transition came as neoliberal thinking was dominating policy making in some advanced market economies. Governments in the United States and the United Kingdom in the 1970s, and even more emphatically in the 1980s, based their policy agendas on the alleged benefits of deregulation, privatization, greater emphasis on use of the market, minimization of the role of the state, and reduction in the level of taxation. The firmest advocates of free market solutions latched onto this, presenting transition as part of a new worldwide trend that was sweeping away the past of an interventionist state in capitalist countries and of an even more dominant state in state Socialist countries. It made it sound like something that could be solved quickly, simply, and with the same theoretical apparatus.

However, transition from a state Socialist system was very different from a degree of deregulation in an advanced market economy. Creating a modern market system was as much about creating new rules and regulations as about demolishing ones that already existed.

The term "neoliberal" is imprecise and often poorly defined by its users. However, it is useful as a characterization of a merging of economic theories, discussed in Box 5.1, with a policy agenda that was given broad support by international agencies. It refers to a direction of policy—toward greater reliance on private enterprise and market forces, irrespective of the starting point—rather than to specific policies, still less a precise economic system. It is frequently lumped together with the so-called Washington Consensus, although that term is best reserved for the more precise policy agenda outlined next. The neoliberal label is of wider application and continued to be relevant after the first transition strategies had been implemented or forgotten.

Box 5.1   Theories for transition

Two slightly different branches of theory supported the neoliberal policy agenda—and within that, the Washington Consensus—giving them the appearance of enjoying a solid academic foundation. From the mainstream neoclassical tradition, starting from the basic assumption of isolated, self-seeking individuals, came the theory that exchange through a free market would lead to a stable equilibrium with an ideal allocation of resources and pressure for maximum efficiency in production. A different tradition, associated with Hayek and the so-called Austrian school, doubted the relevance of equilibrium but presented markets as the best available means for organizing a complex economic system. The implication of both was that any state involvement—by taxation, public spending, or regulation—would distort the workings of the market. Similarly, pressures from particular sectional interests—typically represented by trade unions or employers' organizations—were sources of distortion that reflected rent-seeking activity, meaning a search for financial benefits from state help or from state protection against competition rather than from improving efficiency.

Policy implications follow both from what is and what is not emphasized. Focusing on markets and equilibrium points to the primacy of liberalization and stabilization. Playing down market failures—the role of the state and institutions—points to the possibility of achieving a market system quickly with one decisive blow.

There are three important lines of criticism of this theoretical base of the neoliberal agenda, all pointing toward a similar conclusion.

The first relates to developments within the neoclassical tradition that provide strong warnings against simplistic and confident conclusions. Sophisticated theories point to many ways in which markets can fail to lead to equilibrium, in which equilibrium may not be stable, and in which an outcome may not be ideal. A number of prominent economists who had developed such theories came forward as critics of transition strategies that they felt gave inadequate recognition to the need for a state role in the economy. An open letter on strategy in Russia, signed by six Nobel Prize winners, is referred to in Chapter 6, p. 117. However, early influence went to those with the confidence to preach a clear message and to promise quick results rather than to those who warned of complexities and spoke of the need to accept the possibility that change could take a little time.

The second line of criticism relates to the implicit assumption within neoclassical economics of a stable institutional environment. The self-regulating market is presented as if it is the natural way to coordinate human activity, but serious historical studies of the development of markets, such as the classic works of Karl Polanyi (1957, 1977), demonstrate that it is only one possibility. Moreover, even the simplest markets require an external arbiter to impose rules and could, therefore, only develop in societies with a reasonably stable and secure political and institutional environment.

Free market enthusiasts generally show no recognition of the historical development of the market system. They do, however, typically follow Milton

Friedman (1962) in assuming the government will provide for "the maintenance of law and order, . . . the enforcement of contracts, the definition and meaning of property rights, [and] the interpretation and enforcement of these rights" (27). Friedman went somewhat further, also seeing a state role in providing "a monetary framework." As will be argued, there were some advising on transition policies—particularly related to privatization in Russia—who seemed to have forgotten these principles. Experience also showed that more is needed for a complex economic system to function, and one of the controversies, referred to later, was precisely over the importance of the creation of a legal and regulatory framework and whether this should be done before, simultaneously with, or after the liberalization of markets and development of private property.

The third line of criticism relates to the realities of advanced market economies. Despite rhetoric about small states and deregulation, governments actually played important and substantial roles. Reality corresponded not to abstract theories of a perfectly functioning free market but to a more nuanced approach to theory that recognized the complexities referred to previously. If the target was to follow what already existed, then transition could not be a simple demolition of the centralized elements of state Socialism. It also required the creation of new forms of regulation and the development of new forms of state activity. There were differences among capitalist countries, but the state always played a substantial role. In some European countries—Sweden was the example that attracted most attention—the state's direct role was very substantial, with shares of public spending in GDP passing 50 percent. There were some who advised on the benefits of following this Social Democratic model, which was also favored by some economists within CEECs. However, as in an example recounted by one active participant in debates in Poland (Kowalik 2008, 14), that sort of thinking was firmly rejected by those with political power. Preference was going to free market enthusiasts.

The WC strategy developed as a specific adaptation of the IMF view of necessary policies in Latin American countries suffering from major internal and external imbalances. The term "Washington Consensus" was first used by John Williamson to refer to the typical IMF conditions for financial help for these Latin American countries. This was not a policy recommendation but rather a synthesis based on an observation of what policies had been advocated. He concluded that they could be summarized in a 10-point package of "prudent macroeconomic policies, outward orientation and free-market capitalism" (J. Williamson 1990). The emphasis was clearly on macroeconomic stability and microeconomic liberalization, with measures relating to the institutional environment mentioned at the end.

The points can be summarized as follows:

- Fiscal policy discipline
- Redirection of public spending from subsidies to education, health care, and infrastructure
- Tax reform to broaden the tax base and reduce high marginal tax rates
- Interest rates determined by the market and positive in real terms

- Competitive exchange rates
- Trade liberalization, with any protection by low and relatively uniform tariffs
- Liberalization of inward foreign direct investment
- Privatization of state-owned enterprises
- Deregulation, but prudent oversight of financial institutions
- Legal security for property rights

The changes deemed necessary for a transition strategy were relatively minor. Stabilization, meaning minimizing budget deficits and controlling the money supply, still came first. There was more emphasis on price liberalization, reflecting the previously distorted price system. Privatization had figured in conditions for Latin American countries, although only with a very brief mention in Williamson's account. After some initial hesitation, this became far more central in transition strategies.

Several systematic versions of the WC strategy, with slightly different timescales, were developed, blending established IMF thinking with the first experiences in Poland (e.g., Gelb and Gray 1991; Fischer and Gelb 1991). Key figures in this were Stanley Fischer, chief economist at the World Bank until August 1990 and subsequently at the IMF, and Alan Gelb, who led the World Bank's research on transition policy. The packages they formulated were detailed in terms of policy measures and the recommended timetables. They differed from the Washington Consensus as outlined by Williamson in their greater attention to privatization, institutional changes, and measures dependent on an active state, but these generally came after, and were set lower in the hierarchy, than the classic Washington Consensus measures.

The recommended policy packages were not completely inflexible, and there was recognition that conditions would differ between countries, but the clear assumption was that international agencies knew better than the economists from the countries concerned. Consultation with economists from transition countries was selective, meaning that those broadly agreeing with Washington thinking were listened to.

Figure 5.1 shows one version of the recommended package. It is clear that everything was not to be done at once, but the reasons for different timescales were essentially pragmatic. Some measures could be taken quickly and, therefore, should be taken at once. Some would take time and, therefore, should be done as quickly as possible. Thus, institutional reform would take longer, but that did not mean delaying any other measures. However, in this version, there was a tight timetable for corporate governance, logically a precondition for successful privatization. The hope that a satisfactory system of corporate governance could take shape that quickly soon proved unrealistic, but when practical difficulties emerged, that did not mean delaying large-scale privatization. Instead, once rapid disposal of state property seemed like something that could be done quickly, advocates of speed quickly thought up reasons why changing the ordering would be beneficial (see the following text, pp. 117–18).

This and other adaptations demonstrated that the emphasis was always on the greatest possible speed with any measure that was considered generally desirable. The details of reform outlines, like the one set out previously, quickly proved less important than a more general insistence on speed. As the next two sections demonstrate, Washington had a powerful influence on policy making, but it was not the only source of thinking from outside the transition countries.

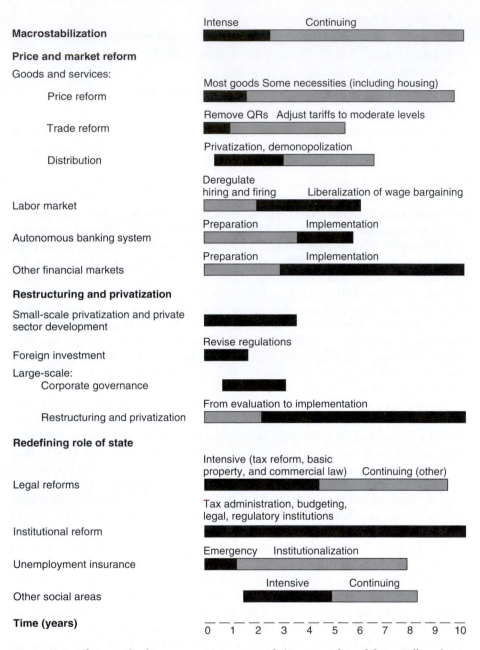

Figure 5.1 Phasing of reform over a 10-year period. (*Source:* Adapted from Gelb and Gray (1991, 13). *Note:* QR stands for quantitative restrictions.)

INFLUENCES FROM WASHINGTON

The most detailed and visible policy advice came from the Washington-based agencies. The IMF gave general advice on the development of financial institutions, and the World Bank took the lead on privatization and enterprise restructuring. The IMF was involved with Eastern Europe from the start but began helping most CIS countries only in 1995. They obviously had to first join, and they then had to comply with some very basic policy requirements. Net financial assistance to 12 CIS countries totalled $21.4 billion over the period from 1992 to 1999. The Baltic republics and all other Eastern European countries received $0.3 billion and $1.6 billion, respectively in the years from 1989 (IMF 2000b, 86). There were calls for much more, both from countries and from several prominent advisers. Some sought a repetition of the Marshall Plan, named after US Secretary of State George Marshall, implemented from 1948 to 1951. This had helped Western European reconstruction after the Second World War with aid equivalent to almost 5 percent of U.S. gross domestic product in 1948, the peak year, and generous repayment terms. No government in the 1990s was prepared to finance so grandiose a scheme. The IMF's contribution was the biggest source of finance, and the most important recipient was Russia.

Backing from the IMF was also a stamp of approval that enabled renegotiation of past debts. This was immediately important for the Polish government (Balcerowicz 1995, 360–63), which began negotiating for debt relief in September 1989 to the extent of using every available opportunity to lobby every available government and agency, even including the pope. In April 1991, the Paris Club, representing governments, awarded Poland forgiveness for 50 percent of its debts from the 1970s, although the Polish government had asked for 80 percent. Everything was conditional on IMF approval for the government's economic policy, and this was assured even though agreed targets for inflation and the state budget were at that time already unrealistic. The remainder of the debt was repaid from 2001.

As IMF support was conditional, this gave the agency formal power over much of policy making in a number of transition countries. It was most important for those with large inherited debts, and its impact was particularly clear in Poland and Russia. That did make a difference in Poland, but the country was able to renegotiate a number of points to make its own policies more flexible. For Russia, too, the IMF's power was not absolute. On the one hand, the fear of losing Western help, and the continuing hope that more might become available, ensured that outright opposition to the broad direction of IMF thinking never won a parliamentary majority (Sutela 2003, 127). Thus, U.S. backing was important to maintaining a broadly neoliberal policy agenda. On the other hand, governments frequently failed to keep precise conditions and commitments, a point used to argue that the IMF was not "dictating Russian economic policies" (131). The U.S. government, the main paymaster for the IMF, was determined to support Russian president Boris Yeltsin, and that meant continuing to provide financial support through the IMF even when there were deviations from IMF advice or conditions.

Alongside the IMF's partially effective "hard" power was the "soft" power of the neoliberal thinking that it, and the advisers financed from outside the transition countries, propagated. This included individual governments, often following the same agenda as the Washington agencies. The EBRD, a new international agency, was set up in London in 1991 to provide investment support to individual projects that were intended to support the transformation of former state Socialist economies into market economies. Its impact was small in relation to the extent of changes under way, but its message was broadly similar to that of the Washington agencies, and the strong consensus in advice from most of the external sources had a huge impact on internal policy making in transition countries.

The importance of this has been emphasized by advisers to the Russian government. Aid from the United States to Russia "was given to reformers to pursue reforms and hence gave them the advantage of both resources and know-how" (Boycko, Shleifer, and Vishny 1995, 144). It financed the team of foreign advisers who supported the Russian government's transition strategy and helped with its implementation. It should be added that they could depart from the details of IMF and World Bank advice at the time, as long as they kept within the free market agenda and propagated the most radical-sounding reform measures. Thus, they were able to move large-scale privatization higher up the agenda to give it priority over policies for macroeconomic stabilization (3).

Indeed, it was academics who became powerful advisers who pushed the simplest versions of a neoliberal agenda. Josef Stiglitz, chief economist at the World Bank from 1997 until he was pushed out in 2000, referred to "market fundamentalists" who preached "textbook economics" and ignored the need for laws and regulations that had been built up in advanced countries "over a century and a half, in response to problems encountered in unfettered capitalism" (Stiglitz 2002, 139).

David Ellerman, a colleague of Stiglitz at the World Bank, wrote disdainfully of "wunderkind professors in economics" who brought "the compounded arrogance of youth, academic credentials, and elite associations" (Ellerman 2005). They were then "unleashed" into "the real world of policy-making as 'experts.'" Advice was indeed given by groups of relatively young economists who brought an oversimplified version of mainstream economics, which led them to advocate a dangerously simple policy agenda. They cannot be blamed for the enthusiastic reception their ideas received, but their actions and prestige were important in undercutting any local reformers who advocated more gradualist approaches to transition. They found willing soul mates within Eastern Europe and Russia, who gained prestige from the same certainty.

INFLUENCES FROM BRUSSELS

The impact of the European Union was different in form and content from that of individual governments or international agencies. It was concerned with a much broader agenda of political, economic, and institutional changes. Its message was wider than, and therefore in some respects conflicted with, that of the Washington agencies. It has been characterized as the most prominent of a group of "transnational actors" that "turned out to be the dark matter that held the various aspects of post-Communist transition together in Central and Eastern Europe" (Orenstein, Bloom, and Lindstrom 2008, 6).

Formal links to the European Economic Community, as it was called until November 1993, started with so-called Association Agreements signed by CEECs in December 1991. These laid the basis for a range of forms of political and economic cooperation, including the gradual freeing of trade over a 10-year period. This was to lead to full EU membership at some point, which governments in CEECs generally expected to be within a very few years. Similar agreements were signed with Baltic republics and with Bulgaria and Romania in 1995. Agreements of far less significance were reached with CIS countries.

Association Agreements gave CEECs access to Western European markets, and this was the basis for much of their economic recovery from the depression of the early 1990s. There were limitations—steel exports were several times constrained by antidumping cases—but the EU connection became increasingly important to economic development, even before full membership. As argued in Chapter 15, it was the key to an inflow of direct investment in the mid- and later 1990s as multinational companies sought a base for exports into EU countries.

In 2004, CEECs and Baltic republics were accepted as EU members, followed in 2007 by Romania and Bulgaria. That brought benefits of aid from EU funds, equivalent to a net annual contribution of about 1 percent of GDP in the first years for CEECs. Free movement of people enabled citizens of new member states to work in Western Europe, although several major countries were able to delay this for some years.

Thus, links to the European Union brought economic benefits. From very early on, the prospect of those benefits influenced policy thinking. The links also brought strict requirements for the development of democratic politics and the institutional basis of a market economy. Direct EU influence was embodied in the *acquis communautaire*, the 31 detailed "chapters" to be satisfied before accession could be approved. These covered harmonization of many legal norms, adequate protection for business, and a satisfactorily functioning legal system. The implications for economic policies are set out in Box 5.2.

Box 5.2   What kind of capitalism did the European Union promote?

Countries could not join the European Union until they were judged to have functioning market economies and functioning democratic systems and to be following the rule of law, respecting human rights, and respecting minorities. The criteria were different from those of the Washington Consensus, with more concern for social policies and even such issues of political detail as functioning regional government structures as a basis for receiving assistance under various EU programs. This influenced policy making directly from the mid- and late 1990s and indirectly from 1990, when membership was set as a clear objective. This provided a different background to policy making for CEECs, and later SEECs, when compared with CIS countries.

However, the European Union did not promote a precise and definable "European" model of capitalism. Its message was partly contradictory, pointing toward a role for social policy and state intervention but also pressing policies that tended to limit that role. Despite the lack of detail, the pressure, especially on economic policy issues, during accession negotiations endorsed a neoliberal agenda, including privatization, a reduction of state involvement in the economy, and further liberalization. The socioeconomic system the European Union implicitly endorsed "had a more 'Anglo-Saxon' flavour than the 'Rhenish' social market economies of France or Germany or the 'Latin' economic systems in the southern EU" (Grabbe 2006, 24). Ambiguities in the European Union's message in relation to economic and social policies meant that the door was left open for other international players—in particular, the World Bank and the International Monetary Fund (e.g., Ferge and Juhasz 2004; Potůček 2008). This ambiguity was reflected in differences among Eastern European countries—for example, in relation to the "flat tax" as discussed in Chapter 9.

Western European countries have a higher degree of social protection than the United States, with greater spending on social welfare and public services and greater legal protection for labor. The European Union itself, particularly from the official launch of the so-called European Social Model in the mid-1980s, claimed to represent not just an economic and political but also a social union. Countries joining the European Union were, therefore, accepting general commitments to concern over social issues that went beyond the priorities of the Washington Consensus.

However, the degree of practical integration in the social field was always limited. It continued to be so in the *acquis communautaire* in which the social elements covered only some aspects of working conditions, gender equality, and nondiscrimination. There were also "soft" requirements of meaningful social dialogue.

The social dimension of accession and enlargement was, therefore, weak, with economic issues taking pride of place (for an overview, see Keune [2009] and Vaughan-Whitehead [2003]). There were also weaknesses in the implementation of social directives (Falkner et al. 2005), which often depended on the struggles between domestic actors, largely independent of the agency of the European Union (Falkner and Treib 2008; Meardi 2007). The same applies to issues of employment, social inclusion, and social dialogue. The policy influence was limited and shaped primarily by domestic power constellations (Keune 2009; Vaughan-Whitehead 2003). As an example, a directive on the need to inform and consult with employees, leading to the introduction of works councils, could undermine existing trade union powers (Meardi 2007, 507).

The economic *acqui*, meaning the body of European Union law regulating economic policy and organization, was enforced much more systematically, improving the quality of the regulatory environment, but it also contained features that weakened the impact of the social model. Economic integration encouraged competition to attract investors with low taxes and labor market deregulation (Bohle 2008; Vliegenthart and Overbeek 2008; Drahokoupil 2008a). The new member states were also required to enter the Economic and Monetary Union (EMU) and in doing so to accept the European common currency. Slovenia completed the process in 2007 and Slovakia followed in 2009, thereby giving up their autonomous monetary and exchange rate policies. The conditions for EMU accession included strict control of inflation, the state budget, and the level of public debt. This put pressure on public expenditure in general and on social expenditure in particular (Rhodes and Keune 2006).

However, formal rules and pressure on governments associated with EU accession understate the full influence of the "European" perspective on CEECs and hence the extent of their differences from CIS countries, which are clear from data on state capacities and the rule of law discussed in Chapter 7. Behind the EU conditions was a more general European influence. A guiding force in thinking in CEECs from the start was a belief that they belonged in the mainstream of European life, meaning that they belonged alongside Western Europe. They had a history of capitalist development from before the Second World War, and they wanted to return to that. This feeling was probably strongest in Czechoslovakia, which had been an industrialized country with political democracy in the interwar period. Others, too, looked to European pasts, and this provided an orientation for the newly independent Baltic republics, which had been incorporated into the Soviet Union only in 1940.

This identification with Western Europe ensured that formal democracy was taken for granted. It was also natural to look to Western European models for ideas on a wide range of issues spanning from the role of a central bank through the development of a system of support for the unemployed to methods of consulting social interests. This did not appear as imposition of an outside model but rather as a return to where they should have been anyway. In some cases, that was exactly how they started, reactivating laws on enterprise, bankruptcy, and the like from the prewar period. In other cases, they took newer ideas from Western Europe. This happened both at the central-government level and on a more decentralized basis—for example, with labor offices established with advice from similar bodies in Western Europe. Thus, again, the anchor that CIS countries lacked was as much one that pointed to modifying the free market model and establishing state organizations to ensure that it functioned as it was one that supported its unquestioned adoption.

POLAND'S SHOCK THERAPY

Poland was the trendsetter for transition strategy in the early years. It attracted international attention because it sought the help of international agencies from the very beginning. That was partly because its economic situation was so serious in terms of its level of international debt and the demands it was facing for repayment. The involvement of the Washington agencies meant that they in turn took the strategy they advised for Poland as a general basis for other countries.

There was less international interest in other options. Rather different roads were followed by East Germany and by Hungary. There policy making did not benefit (or suffer) from the same level of advice from international agencies and, therefore, attracted less attention from the economists who were to influence thinking in the next few years. Thus, it could be argued that it was the weakness of the Polish economy that enabled its transition strategy to attract so much international attention.

Leszek Balcerowicz, the minister of finance of Poland's Solidarity-led government formed in September 1989, had once presented himself as a believer in self-management, but by the time he took office, he was an enthusiast for free market economics. He favored the maximum possible speed for stabilization, liberalization, and privatization, even if other elements of transition would inevitably take longer. In all his writings (especially Balcerowicz [1995]), he asserted the benefits of the most radical possible strategy and the greater risks from delays.

He proved able, with minimal opposition, to sweep aside the commitments from the roundtable to a socially painless economic transformation. He could then take measures Communist governments had shied away from. He was helped in this by a surprising act from the last Communist government, which, shortly after the roundtable agreements, took the momentous step of freeing food prices. As had been agreed, a system of indexation allowed wages to rise to cover 80 percent of price rises, leading to a cycle of rapid price and wage increases. This was the cause of a 251 percent year-on-year inflation level in 1989, which gave the impression of still greater economic chaos when the new government came to power.

Balcerowicz was backed by the young Harvard professor Jeffrey Sachs, who addressed a parliamentary committee in August 1989. Sachs exuded absolute certainty in the correctness of his advice, claiming very wide international experience and arguing the need for "a sudden decisive jump" to which, he insisted, "there is no alternative" (Myant 1993, 82). On top of this, Sachs indicated that following his advice would mean following a tried-and-tested package that could expect international approval, opening the way to help with the burden of international debt. There was no explicit promise—Sachs was not in the position to make one—but many in Poland thought that one had been given. This could also have been read as a threat: failing to follow external advice would mean no help with handling the burden of debt that was threatening Poland's ability to continue importing.

A revealing further indication of how he gained credibility came in an interchange in parliament between two of Solidarity's members of parliament (MPs). One whispered that Sachs's optimistic confidence sounded like complete nonsense. Jacek Kuroń, a former left-wing dissident and prominent adviser to Solidarity from the time of its foundation, replied, "I don't know much about what he is arguing for, but listening to it, I know it has political value" (Myant 1993, 85).

Thus, the WC strategy had political appeal far beyond those who might understand its economic strengths and weaknesses. It was a godsend to the new government, which felt insecure—the Soviet Union was still in existence at the time—and uncertain. Here, from one of the best universities in the United States, came words of certainty. Balcerowicz could confidently counter those counseling a more cautious approach with a call to "shut our eyes and jump into the hole, without checking either the state of the water or the depth of the drop" (Myant 1993, 84). Strictly speaking, the attempt to restore market equilibrium by allowing prices to rise was not new, but it was presented as a complete change in economic policy, and this was made to appear credible because it came from a new government and because it was part of a package of measures (cf. Mickiewicz 2005, 19).

Thus, adoption of the program was compatible with political democracy, but formulation of the program was the affair of a narrow group of experts. Balcerowicz's team included friends and colleagues that he had known for many years, plus Sachs and David Lipton from the United States and several economists of Polish origin working in the West. There was also continual consultation with the IMF (Balcerowicz 1995, 296–304). The rest of the population was asked only to offer its trust.

Approval was achieved quickly, without much public discussion and without an explicit search for alternatives. That would not be the usual method for so momentous a step in a mature democracy, but state Socialism had left a heritage of a weak civil society, with neither the habits nor the organizational means for the public to become actively involved in the discussion of policies. Any opposition would also have needed to offer a solution to the problem of foreign debt.

Balcerowicz characterized this early period as one of "extraordinary politics." The government was enjoying a honeymoon period of popularity, disarming potential advocates of alternative strategies and making it possible to implement policies that would face serious resistance under normal conditions. He wanted to ignore any inclination to hesitate, or to protect living standards, and to press ahead with reforms as quickly as possible, before such forces—vilified as "populists" or "social demagogues"—could be mobilized. There was, therefore, neither the time nor the need for detailed discussion of policies. Normal politics would soon be resumed, with competition between parties and representation of interests. He saw those as negative features that would work against the successful implementation of systemic changes.

The Balcerowicz program, as it became known, was not presented as shock therapy. Balcerowicz himself preferred the characterization of "radical, but not dogmatic," as there were some continuing forms of state intervention "distorting" the working of the free market. The key points are set out in the following list, with some elaboration and commentary included.

- Price liberalization. Much of this had already been done, and some prices of basic goods and services were still set centrally. Uncontrolled prices increased from 58 percent to 83 percent of consumer spending.

- Trade liberalization, albeit initially with a 20 percent duty on imports, plus some further taxes. Import liberalization was partly justified by the argument that price liberalization would enable enterprises to exploit their monopoly positions. Freeing imports thereby circumvented arguments for delaying price liberalization until big, state-owned enterprises could be split up to eliminate monopolies, a step agreed on at the roundtable. Any danger that a flood of imports would lead to an unmanageable trade deficit was covered by an IMF standby loan.

- Devaluation and establishment of a single exchange rate with partial convertibility of the currency. The chosen exchange rate was roughly the black market rate from the previous year. This had always been well below the official rate used in formal trade. The effect was to reduce the currency's value relative to the dollar to less than 20 percent of its level in December 1988 and to well below the purchasing power parity level. This, in turn, created an effective barrier against imports. The exchange rate was to be held firm as an anchor for other macroeconomic policies.

- Fiscal restraint, including the reduction of subsidies for enterprises—with the aim of reaching a budget surplus in 1990 after a deficit equivalent to 7.4 percent of GDP in 1989—and monetary restraint through the use of high interest rates and direct controls to limit credits.

- A wage control system providing indexation for 30 percent of price rises in January, falling to 20 percent for the next three months. This, alongside monetary restraint, was expected to choke off inflationary pressures very quickly.

The government gave no information on any expected change in output prior to implementation of the program. A letter of intent to the IMF, the basis for the standby agreement reached on February 5, 1990, predicted an initial 75 percent rise in prices, followed by rapid stabilization, and a 5 percent fall in GDP, followed by recovery later in the year. It had by then already become clear that the shock would be painful, but these figures underestimated the pain. The immediate effects of the policies are shown in Box 4.1 in Chapter 4.

SHOCK THERAPY IN RUSSIA

The political context in Russia gave a slightly different background to shock therapy than that in Poland. Both countries were developing formal democracy, but the commitment to political democracy was weaker in Russia. In both, there was exasperation with the failure of reform attempts, but in Russia, there was even less agreement on what was needed. In Poland, there was no serious doubt among prominent economists about the need for market prices and market equilibrium; the debate was over whether it was politically feasible. In Russia, the centrality of a functioning price mechanism was not so widely accepted among economists, let alone political leaders. In Poland, advice from the United States gave a policy greater credibility, but that kind of outside stamp of approval had less appeal in Russia.

The decision to follow the WC model and its meaning in the Russian context depended on Boris Yeltsin, Russia's first president after the breakup of the Soviet Union. As described in Timothy Colton's biography of Yeltsin (Colton 2008), his early priorities were the political battle with Gorbachev and the need to consolidate his own position of power. He took very little direct interest in economic issues, apparently approving the radical "500-day" program for a free market economy in autumn 1990 without reading a page; he was impressed by the "zippy title and the taut timetable" (220). He followed that with opposition to price rises implemented by Gorbachev and appeared to promise an economic transformation requiring no hardships (209).

The key question was whom he chose to trust, and his choice was to sweep aside the reformers from the Gorbachev period and to seek new experts with no "mental and ideological blinkers" (Colton 2008, 226). He gave the key role to a group centered around Yegor Gaidar, a young economist from an orthodox Soviet background who had dropped his old blinkers but was putting on new ones, having become a disciple of Milton Friedman shortly beforehand (Kotz and Weir 2007, 123). Gaidar worked closely with the advisers from the United States and probably encouraged Yeltsin to promise in October 1991 that a new radical reform program, to start with price liberalization in January 1992, would lead to six months of hardship, after which prices would stabilize and living standards would begin to improve by the autumn of 1992 (Kotz and Weir 2007, 161).

It was a bold promise when set against the reality of difficulties already apparent in Poland, but Yeltsin was more interested in holding the political initiative and wanted to move quickly and dramatically (Colton 2008, 227). As in Poland, there was initially no serious opposition to shock therapy, and Yeltsin won parliamentary approval for rule by decree on economic reforms, meaning that he did not need parliamentary approval for individual measures, for a year beginning in November 1991. Doubts began to emerge only in April as enterprise directors raised the idea of a more gradualist approach, even quoting China as a possible example to follow (Kotz and Weir 2007, 194).

Continuation of the WC strategy at all times depended on support from Yeltsin, which was rather inconsistent. The president's exceptionally powerful position was confirmed in the 1993 constitution and in the growth of his presidential office to 7,000 staff members in 1995. This central bureaucracy had immense powers of discretion, with no political control or administrative oversight (Berglöf et al. 2003, 51–52). These conditions, conducive to pushing through policies without public debate or certainty of public support, also facilitated a high level of corruption, an issue pursued in Chapter 7. Enthusiasts for rapid reform welcomed these limitations on democracy. They felt the parliament had approved privatization policies only because it "did not take privatization seriously." Once a parliamentary bloc took shape opposing rapid privatization, "every subsequent major regulation of privatization was introduced by presidential degree" (Boycko, Shleifer, and Vishny 1995, 5).

To establish and maintain the power to make crucial decisions without outside scrutiny, the Russian president had to head off potential parliamentary opposition by bargaining to pacify various interests. One consequence of this was greater autonomy to regions, with the side effect of further weakening the central administration and its ability to implement polices effectively. Another was favoritism in privatization decisions. In Russia, then, a neoliberal economic policy was associated with—although not necessarily the main cause of—the strengthening of an autocratic presidential authority, an accompanying low level of state capacity, and a form of privatization that was, at best, highly controversial (see Chapter 13).

There is controversy over whether, in view of the need for such compromises, Russia did or did not follow the WC strategy. The point is important, as excluding Russia's experience and concentrating only on the CEECs where economic recovery was more rapid would make the WC strategy appear more successful. The reality is that prices were freed on 80 percent of wholesale and 90 percent of retail turnover in January 1992. The immediate impact on the price level was very substantial in view of the extent of previous distortions. Subsidies on food had been exceptionally high in the closing years of the Soviet Union (IMF et al. 1991a, 14). Transport and energy prices remained under government control, as they generally did in CEECs. Imports were freed, with tariffs commonly around the 10 percent level, somewhat lower than in Poland at the start of the Balcerowicz program. There was no wage control system, and that difference from Poland's package was clearly considered by Balcerowicz to be an important omission (Balcerowicz 1995, 366), but there was a very tough monetary policy. As indicated previously, pp. 58–59, the relative impact of these measures is difficult to estimate, but restricting the money available to enterprises was probably the main factor depressing demand in Poland and Czechoslovakia.

Implementation of the package in Russia was followed by very rapid inflation and a dramatic fall in output. In May 1992, the Russian government allowed an increase in the money supply, without which there would probably have been an even more dramatic fall in output and living standards.

Richard Layard, among others, concluded that "no attempt was made to stabilize the price level," so Russia's poor economic performance in the 1990s therefore could not be cited as an example of the strategy's failure (Blanchard et al. 1993, 18). A fairer assessment would be that Russia did not follow the letter of the WC package "in the pristine form in which it emerged from economic theorists' pens," but the government, at least for a time, "made a determined effort to pursue the basic outlines of that program" (Kotz and Weir 2007, 163). It accepted a retreat on monetary policy, albeit only a temporary one, because "no government could stabilize and survive"; the Gaidar team, it has been argued, would have been thrown out if it had pressed on with stabilization policy (Blanchard et al. 1993, 3, 16).

That would seem to indicate not that no attempt was made but that first results demonstrated that no sustained attempt could have been successful. There were further complicating factors, as the government in Russia had limited ability to control the actions of regional authorities and even the central bank. The issue was not simply one of government resolve and determination but of wider conditions and possibilities, including political pressures and the lack of state capacity (as discussed in Chapters 7 and 8), which should be considered before settling on a policy. The political context, despite Yeltsin's concentration of autocratic power, meant that a president and small group of advisers could not achieve full implementation of the WC strategy.

For completeness, this should be contrasted with experience in other CIS countries. They were generally slower to follow the WC strategy because their political and economic elites had little conception of economic policy making beyond continuity with the past. That is most true of the countries with limited, or very limited, formal democracy, where the old ruling group kept power, albeit dropping the Communist label. This kind of concentration of power was generally associated with continuity in economic thinking, in the sense that no new ideas were forthcoming. There was little heritage of thinking on economic reform—that had mostly taken place in the biggest Russian cities—and in some cases, there was not much interest in ideas from outside, either. Change was therefore slower.

That was not true in all cases. Listening to international agencies did also bring benefits in the form of economic assistance and outside recognition. In Kyrgyzstan, there was even enthusiasm for the WC strategy, but that seems to have been largely a matter of preference of a very few individuals at the top rather than a reflection of deeper social forces. The country stood out by joining the World Trade Organization (WTO) in October 1998, the first CIS member to do so (Åslund 2002, 177), and its pro-Western orientation brought support and aid from international agencies. Kazakhstan followed much of the WC strategy, albeit less consistently and, again, because those at the top were happy with it. There was not much depth of support, but neither was there much scope for opposition. The most important cases for the development of a transition strategy continued to be the CEECs and Russia.

SHOCK THERAPY IN CEECS

Political contexts led to different outcomes across other transition countries. Poland's package was followed a year later by Czechoslovakia, although it had slightly different political and economic conditions. In Czechoslovakia there was no major economic crisis, no major internal or external imbalance, and no need to seek help and support from the IMF. However, there was disillusionment among professional economists with past reform attempts. The need for a functioning price system and for the freeing of international economic relations had been discussed during the reforms of the 1960s, and were not seriously challenged once political life was freed.

There was the same process of a small group trying to dominate economic policy making, rejecting influences of social interests and rival economic policy ideas. The core was created around the new finance minister Václav Klaus, a committed and long-standing disciple of Milton Friedman who was to set his objective as "a market economy without adjectives," as distinct from a market economy that accepted social, environmental, or other concerns justifying some state intervention. Klaus was not completely successful in blocking rival policy proposals. Unlike Poland and Russia, outside advisers played relatively minor roles in Czechoslovakia. Those around Klaus were convinced that they could work out the best answers themselves and that the relatively stable political and economic situations meant that they did not need international approval to gain internal legitimacy, although praise from neoliberal thinkers abroad was definitely welcomed.

The key to the appeal of the WC strategy was not the need to overcome an economic crisis but was its appearance as the firmest available rejection of the Communist past. This was an important factor in Czechoslovakia, where the state Socialist period was widely portrayed as a deviation from a history within Central, or even Western, Europe.

The Czechoslovak package of liberalization and stabilization was implemented in January 1991. It differed from the Balcerowicz program of January 1990 only in points of detail. There was less protection against imports, and a greater proportion of prices were liberalized at one time. This reflected a different starting point, as almost all prices had been controlled before, but the end results were very similar. As in Poland, there was a sharp currency devaluation to protect against a possible inflow of imports, setting the exchange rate at about a quarter of the purchasing power parity level. Again as in Poland, the advocates of the policy did not foresee the extent of the output decline that took place. They chose not to notice the economic events unfolding in Poland, which should have given a clear warning of what was likely to happen.

In Hungary, there was a high level of international debt but also a strong community of economists with international standing and good contacts with economic thinking from outside the old Soviet bloc. They had the confidence to question policy ideas from outside. There were also pragmatic reasons for ignoring the WC strategy, as reform in Hungary had already taken the country a long way from traditional central planning. A single package, delivered as a shock, was therefore irrelevant both in economic terms and as a political demonstration of a change in direction. It was also seen as politically dangerous within the government to undertake a rapid transition that would, in the words of Finance Minister Mihaly Kupa in 1991, leave part of the population "abandoned along the way" (quoted in Pereira, Przeworski, and Maravall [1993, 150]). When asked why Hungary would want to proceed more slowly than Poland, he responded: "We cannot risk the social tensions that would put everything in question" (151).

The result was a more gradual approach. The currency devalued against the dollar by 46 percent between 1989 and 1993—against an 18-fold devaluation of the Polish currency—and this led to lower inflation, peaking at 35 percent in 1991 but remaining over 10 percent until 2000. The money supply, measured by M2, the definition that includes notes and coins and demand and time deposits, increased slightly more slowly than prices in the years of high inflation, suggesting a moderate tightening of monetary policy.

Thus, in Hungary, governments were persuaded to be cautious in the face of possible social unrest, while the same fears were used to justify abandoning caution in Poland. The Hungarian position reflected an assumption that transition would take some time anyway and the lack of an assumption that opposition would necessarily increase. Thus, it was primarily political rather than economic situations that led to different strategies in Poland and Hungary. The new Polish government saw the need to be presenting a dramatically new economic policy, but pressure in that direction was much weaker in Hungary.

Slovenia, despite its small size, occupies an important place in judging transition strategies because of its apparent success. There were the familiar debates over shock therapy versus gradualism, but there was no attempt to implement a comprehensive package along Polish lines. Instead, particularly in relation to privatization, Slovenia's transition was "more gradual than even the most enthusiastic 'gradualists' had suggested" (Mencinger 1995, 477). The new state proclaimed its independence from Yugoslavia in June 1991 and used monetary policy as the principle instrument for reducing a high rate of inflation inherited from the past. This appears to have been less vigorously applied than the policies in Poland and Hungary, as the money supply, measured by M1, the definition of money that includes notes and coins plus demand deposits only, fell in real terms to 60 percent of its September 1991 level in May 1992 and then rose back toward the previous level (478). However, the exchange rate was stable, and inflation fell more rapidly from a higher peak than in Poland, dropping below 10 percent in 1996.

THE SHOCK IN THE BALTICS

The case of the transformation depression and recovery in the Baltic republics is important, combining some features similar to CEECs and some similar to CIS countries. They were closer to the former in the speedy reorientation toward links with Western Europe, although that was by no means complete. They were closer to the latter in the weakness of state capacity, although the Western orientation helped there, too, in its consolidation and hence in the countries' ability to carry through policies. The depression, as indicated in Figures 4.1 and 4.3, was also deeper than in countries outside the CIS, but the recovery was relatively rapid.

The shock was primarily a result of the breakup of the Soviet Union, which led to massive falls in industrial output and GDP. Internal disorganization was less important than the loss of markets across the old Soviet Union and shortages of fuel inputs and other raw materials. Manufacturing industry declined particularly rapidly, with the hardest hit sectors being those that relied on contacts, for inputs and markets, with other former Soviet republics. There was no state help to keep enterprises afloat, and that was something of a contrast with the experience in CEECs (as indicated in Chapter 4). The decline in production, therefore, led to a sharp drop in living standards and domestic demand.

Stabilization was linked to the introduction of independent currencies in mid-1992, a step initially viewed unenthusiastically by the IMF. Inflation rates of around 1,000 percent in 1992 were reduced fairly rapidly following stabilization of the new states. That coincided with the acceptance of IMF advice for strict fiscal and monetary, but not wage control, policies. However, the key policy for macroeconomic stabilization was probably the linking of new currencies to major Western ones, a step that was again cautiously received by the IMF.

Estonia and Lithuania established currency boards, which not only pegged the exchange rates but also meant that the domestic central banks could not pursue expansionary monetary policies unless they were backed by the appropriate foreign currency. This prevented any further inflationary stimulus from currency devaluation. These restrictive policies further contributed to reducing real wages and hence the domestic demand level, but this was a lesser factor in causing depression and came after the main falls in output (cf. Knöbl and Haas 2003; Pädam 2007; Brīvers et al. 2007; Ramanauskas 2007).

In contrast to other countries, these measures proved to be reasonably politically acceptable. This followed partly from the weak development of economic thinking; there was no community of internationally experienced and respected economists, and the only alternative in the public eye seemed to be the Soviet past. It partly also followed from the situation of "extraordinary politics" associated with independence; pro-Western and market-oriented reform seemed to fit well with the countries' newfound orientations (see Bohle and Greskovits [2007]).

Unlike CEECs, there was little adaptation of existing manufacturing capacity to find new markets in Western Europe; that part of the heritage of the past was largely left to die. However, Baltic republics were helped in comparison with CIS countries by four factors. The first was the ability to shift exports of raw materials to new markets in Western Europe; friendly political relations and easy transport links helped here. The second was a rapid development of simpler manufacturing activities, subcontracted by Western European firms or based on inward investment. The third was a continuation of links with CIS countries; large-scale transit trade—selling on raw materials from Russia and exporting food to that country—and small-scale trading both grew rapidly. The fourth was an easy international debt position. The Baltic republics refused to accept responsibility for a share in Soviet debt on the grounds that incorporation into the Soviet Union had been illegal. Their position found international acceptance, and they could then build up international debts from scratch, with the bulk of credits in the 1990s from international agencies, led by the IMF. This enabled them to cover current account deficits that rose to over 10 percent of GDP in some years. The IMF tolerated this, being more concerned with inflation and budget deficits. The Baltic states thus became pioneers in the ultimately unsustainable "financialized" growth, covered in Chapter 16, that developed in more countries in the last years up to 2008.

THE EXTREME CASE OF EASTERN GERMANY

The German Democratic Republic (GDR) ceased to exist with German reunification in October 1990. The Washington Consensus, or indeed any other strategy developed outside Germany, was from then irrelevant. Reunification meant the effective takeover of the East German economy by the larger West German economy. Reunification meant adoption of the existing currency, of the economic and social system, and of the full legal system of the old Federal Republic. There were suggestions for a slower transition, allowing two currencies to coexist for a time, but they were rejected on political grounds, irrespective of their possible economic merits. Germany was to be reunited, and that meant economic reunification. Maintaining any kind of distinct economy would have been difficult once political reunification led to a completely free movement of people, making wide price and pay differences unsustainable.

The consequences of this extreme shock can be summarized by four points (following Myant et al. [1996, 8–15]):

- East German industry, although among the most productive in the state Socialist countries, could not compete once Western price and cost levels were introduced. Productivity in the manufacturing industry in 1990 was 18 percent of the level of West Germany, but wages were 28 percent of the West German level. Eastern wages rose rapidly with reunification, as did productivity, largely with the closure of much of the least effective manufacturing capacity. By 1994, productivity was 50 percent of the Western level, but employment had fallen by 44 percent. Employment in the economy as a whole had fallen by 37 percent by the end of 1995.

- Industry was also hit by the organizational incorporation of the East German economy. Privatization amounted to the takeover of firms by Western businesses and the downgrading of their activities. The core units of the GDR economy were eliminated, and the new owners of what was left frequently continued with established (i.e., Western) suppliers, undermining established markets for East German enterprises.

- The German state channeled resources into infrastructure development, doubling employment in construction and increasing employment in transport and public services.

- The key to the economy's survival was an extraordinary level of subsidization from the West. The total over the period from 1991 to 1995 was equivalent to over four times the area's GDP in 1995. This did not create a basis for sustainable growth and also constituted a massive burden on the state budget of the reunited Germany.

The implication is that a complete economic liberalization would not be sustainable in a country that could not rely on long-term subsidization from a rich benefactor. East Germany would have stood a better chance economically if it could have continued with its own currency and control over its own enterprises, but that option was not feasible politically.

WHO FOLLOWED THE WC STRATEGY?

We conclude this chapter with an assessment of how far the WC strategy was implemented. If the criterion is the implementation of a form of shock therapy, meaning one coordinated package of measures along the lines of Poland's Balcerowicz program, then there are few candidates. The strongest are Poland, Czechoslovakia, and the Baltic republics. Russia is another candidate but is questionable in view of its government's difficulties with implementing any coherent policy. The next chapter will show how far all of those countries deviated from, or adapted aspects of, the strategy.

Broad adherence to a liberal agenda can be followed by cataloging how and when countries implemented key policy measures, even if they were not part of a single coordinated package. Some elements can be measured in a reasonably uncontroversial way, and Table 5.1 shows the dates on which different countries

TABLE 5.1   Years in which transition economies reached EBRD score levels of 4 for liberalization of prices and of foreign exchange and trade

	Price liberalization	Foreign exchange and trade liberalization
Albania	2000	1992
Armenia	1996	1996
Azerbaijan	1997	2005
Belarus	1997[a]	
Bosnia and Herzegovina	1998	2008
Bulgaria	1991	1994
Croatia	1992	1994
Czech Republic	1991	1992
Estonia	1993	1994
Georgia	1996	1997
Hungary	1990	1991
Kazakhstan	1995	1996
Kyrgyz Republic	1994	1995
Latvia	1992	1994
Lithuania	1993	1994
Macedonia, FYR	1992	1994
Moldova	2005	1995
Mongolia	1997	1997
Montenegro	2001	2007
Poland	1992	1993
Romania	1994	1994
Russian Federation	2000	1996
Serbia	2001	2009
Slovak Republic	1991	1992
Slovenia	1999	1993
Tajikistan		
Turkmenistan		
Ukraine	1997	2008
Uzbekistan		

Source: EBRD transition indicators, available at http://www.ebrd.com/country/sector/econo/stats/timeth.htm.

Note: A score of 4 for price liberalization indicates that only a small number of administered prices remain. A score of 4 for foreign exchange and trade liberalization indicates the removal of all quantitative and administrative import and export restrictions (apart from agriculture) and all significant export tariffs, insignificant direct involvement in exports and imports by ministries and state-owned trading companies, no major nonuniformity of customs duties for nonagricultural goods and services, and full and current account convertibility.

[a] Belarus reached a score of 4 for price liberalization in 1997 but then dropped back to a lower level in subsequent years.

fulfilled set EBRD criteria for liberalization of prices and external relations. This, of course, does not necessarily mean adherence to Washington's advice, as the same measures were already underway in some countries by 1989 and were also advocated by many of its critics. These were not the most controversial parts of the strategy.

The two forms of liberalization hardly ever came in the same year but were often close. The results indicate broad distinctions between countries. Eastern Europe generally saw more rapid liberalization than CIS countries; Hungary could claim to be the absolute leader. Some countries in this group appeared to be going more slowly, but apparent delays were often unimportant. Thus, Slovenia appears somewhat slower with price liberalization but was only marginally below the score level of 4, meaning only a small number of administered prices, used in Table 5.1, from 1990.

Some CIS countries—those most amenable to outside advice—also liberalized reasonably rapidly. This group included Kyrgyzstan, Kazakhstan, Armenia, and, to a lesser extent, Georgia. Russia and Ukraine appear to be somewhat slower liberalizers, but again, prices were largely liberalized from early on. They differ markedly from the very slow reformers—Belarus and to a greater extent Uzbekistan, or the extreme case of Turkmenistan—in which foreign exchange and trade liberalization only began in 2008.

Measuring stabilization can never be so precise. There was never complete stability in any country. The differences were in degrees of disequilibrium, as indicated by continuing significant levels of inflation (shown in Table A.3 in the Appendix) and unemployment (shown in Table A.4). Government policies are also an inexact guide. Governments could implement, or try to implement, measures intended to achieve macroeconomic balance, but the results were never precisely as expected. Indeed, the initial effect of liberalization was often price rises much higher than were publicly predicted. When inflation was reduced, the restrictive policies used were associated with failings in other areas, meaning lower output, higher unemployment, worse prospects for enterprise restructuring, and substantial social costs. As argued in Chapter 4, the transformation depression had complex causes, but policies were a contributory factor.

It can be added that setting stabilization as a priority depended on a particular view of the state Socialist economies—that they were characterized by a fundamental macroeconomic disequilibrium that needed to be eliminated before other policies could succeed. That was not true in all cases.

In view of all these points, it is not surprising that implementation of the stabilization part of the WC strategy proved the most controversial and the most questionable. This is made clear in the next chapter, which deals with its criticisms and adaptations.

CHAPTER SIX

Alternatives and Adaptations

The Washington Consensus strategy was both criticized and defended from the start of transition, particularly as output fell dramatically—and much more than predicted—and as inflation either persisted or accelerated. Debates were the liveliest in CEECs, where critics and revisions followed fairly similar lines, and in Russia, where the economic difficulties were deeper and the strategy most clearly failed to produce the desired outcomes. There was less sign of public debate in other countries, regardless of whether they adopted the strategy.

In Poland, the negative voices grew louder after the first effects were felt, and some revisions were made to the policy package during 1990. In Czechoslovakia, Klaus had failed to gain government approval for his proposals before parliament had decided to put the policy out to open tender. Five groups of economists, largely from official research and academic institutions, expressed their positions, and all were, to varying degrees, critical of Klaus's original proposal. Nevertheless, parliament accepted a package that emphasized rapid liberalization and tight macroeconomic policies, albeit with concessions toward accepting a role for state intervention in promoting structural changes in the economy.

The alternatives that were proposed (covered in Myant [1993, 2003]) do not group easily into categories of gradualism versus shock therapy or in terms of allegiance to particular theoretical perspectives. Nor is it clear to what extent all shared the same objective in terms of the kind of market economy they wanted to see. The positions are, therefore, discussed for the CEECs—focusing on Czechoslovakia and Poland as the two that did pursue a form of shock therapy—under four headings that cover the main issues on which alternatives were proposed.

The first alternative was for stabilization but without such a dramatic shock. In other words, the policy was to be similar but more moderate. This merged in practice into a second alternative that was for stabilization supplemented with other policies to overcome its negative features. This alternative was often supported from fears of the social consequences of the shock leading to political opposition that could provoke a reversal of all changes. It also followed from rejection of the view that the free market alone is enough for a modern economy. The third alternative was for stronger state involvement, particularly in industrial restructuring. That could come before, or alongside, other reform steps and clearly implied greater scepticism in the power of markets and price signals as a basis for economic recovery. The fourth alternative was for accelerating privatization in the belief that this would solve problems revealed by shock therapy. Here, the theoretical starting point was precisely that a market, if given the maximum freedom, would solve all problems.

Developments in Russia followed a different course; both the political context and the results of shock therapy were different. Stabilization proved a much more elusive target. It is not possible to follow similar debates across other CIS countries. Even if they were developing formal democracy, which was often not the case, there was little serious debate on economic issues. The alternatives were largely undiluted acceptance of outside advice or continuity of past practices that suited an autocratic elite.

Two boxes are used to fill out the picture. Box 6.1 deals with the relationship between political and economic change, addressing the question of whether democracy helped or hindered the development of transition strategies. Box 6.2 deals with the contribution of institutional economics, which is found to be of value for criticisms of the WC strategy as it developed in practice, but it did not provide the foundations for a comprehensive alternative.

Box 6.1   Democracy and economic reform

Much of the early discussions of the political context of economic change addressed the questions of whether democratization helped or hindered economic change and, conversely, of whether economic reforms could undermine the development of democracy. This discussion took place within the context of debates over the WC strategy, the central theme in economic policy thinking in the early years and one presented by its supporters as synonymous with a serious commitment to market-oriented reform. In fact, as indicated in this chapter, there were viable alternatives and good economic arguments for modifying the strategy. The debate was, therefore, directed at only one possible version of economic reform policies.

A comfortable argument is that markets and democracy logically go together, both being associated with the removal of autocratic and centralized power. This is a familiar argument and is supported by a mass of quantitative studies consistently establishing a positive correlation between capitalist development and democracy (e.g., Lipset 1959; Cutright and Wiley 1969; Bollen 1979), but historical studies of the development of capitalism and democracy also point to complexity and varieties of experience. The relationship is neither automatic nor simple. There have been many dictatorships in capitalist countries. Moreover, it is often the pressure of social interests, something unwelcome to free market thinking, that has been important to the development of democracy (Rueschemeyer, Stephens, and Stephens 1992).

Indeed, one common theme in early debates of transition was the fear of an incompatibility between simultaneous economic and political transformations (Przeworski 1991, 190; Offe 1991; Elster 1993). Adam Przeworski argued that a protracted and painful reform, which he thought market-oriented reform would inevitably be, would lead to an erosion of support so that "the policy style typical of market-oriented reform tends to debilitate nascent democratic institutions" (Pereira, Przeworski, and Maravall 1993, 132).

Supporters and critics of the WC strategy alike expected economic hardship to threaten support for the new regime. Popular anger could be a breeding ground for authoritarian, nationalist, and demagogic political mobilization, provoking serious social conflict and even a breakdown of new democratic institutions (Ost 1992, 49; Åslund 1991, 19; Sachs and Lipton 1990, 48–49; Walton and Seddon 1994, 327). Moreover, the egalitarian logic of political participation was seen as conflicting with the exclusionary process of privatization, giving additional incentives to the elite to resort to nondemocratic means (Offe 1991; Elster 1993). For neoliberals, these contradictions and dilemmas represented a case for shock therapy; only rapid and radical implementation of the WC strategy could take advantage of the window of opportunity at the beginning of the reform and thus prevent the political backlash threatening economic reforms. They then predicted that an early recovery would provide an economic anchor to new democracies (Sachs and Lipton 1990; Balcerowicz 1995).

Assessing the first years of transition, Bela Greskovits concluded that what followed was neither a vicious circle leading to a systemic breakdown nor a virtuous circle of systemic consolidation triggered by a shock-therapy-induced "creative destruction." In fact, "democracy and market economy could be simultaneously introduced only because neither has been fully implemented" (Greskovits 1998, 18). Economic crisis and transformation meant that democracy could stabilize only at the cost of its substantive aspects in terms of political participation. Economic transformation, in turn, "remained feasible only at the cost of its speed and radicalism" (18). This is close to the experience of Poland, where governments softened the impact of restrictive policies, and of Hungary, where they were cautious of social opposition from the start.

The links between democracy and the WC strategy were not simple either in relation to the latter's adoption or in relation to its effects on political development. Its acceptance was often linked to the introduction of formal democracy; that broke the power of the old conservative elite to prevent economic liberalization. Adoption of a radical, neoliberal strategy was unlikely in an unchanged, autocratic political system, but even with the development of democracy, the neoliberal reformers still had to win control over the state (Drahokoupil 2008a, 88–95). In practice, the lead was taken by "lonely reformers"—allied with their foreign advisers—gaining considerable autonomy, taking advantage of the weakness of social forces, and often acting with limited democratic accountability (Greskovits 1998, 35). The WC strategy thus proved to be associated most frequently with formal democracy but also with an isolation of decision making from society. That was clearly the case in Poland. It should be added that similar policies could be adopted in countries with more autocratic regimes if the powerful rulers chose to follow outside advice. That was the case in some CIS countries.

In relation to the consequences for political development of economic changes, experience around the world does not show economic crises leading automatically to antidemocratic mobilization (Remmer 1991), although it can lead to a defeat through the democratic process for the government in power. In fact, in CEECs reformers often proved able to gain popular support for shock therapy policies. However, a more important issue was the modification of the strategy in the light of the development of democracy.

Formal democracy, in the sense of free and fair elections, was only part of the story. Discussions within, and influences from, society depended on the openness with which governments operated, on the extent and forms of interest and opinion representation, and on the degree to which the public was well informed by the media—not to mention the extent to which elections themselves were genuinely free and fair. Moreover, as indicated previously, the development of democracy to include active discussion of, and participation in, decision making—the development of an active civil society—led to criticism and modification of the WC strategy. Balcerowicz's window of opportunity was indeed short lived, lasting only until a voice from more of the population could be heard. However, the result was not, as he had feared, a reversal of the changes but was rather a strengthening of the advocates of a more considered and gradual approach. Shock therapy was moderated, but changes to the strategy did not reverse economic reforms. Instead, they led to adjustments that could improve the prospects of economic transformations. This marked a real difference between economic policy making in autocratic and more democratic political systems.

Thus, democracy was not a threat to market-oriented reform, but it was a threat to the rigid application of the WC strategy. Indeed, discussion of individual countries shows the peculiarities in the political situations of those that tried to adopt shock therapy. They did have formal democracy in the sense of accountability of political leaders through periodic elections, but their new governments were not responsive to pressures from society. They were unsure of their popular support and of popular support for changing the economic system. This led them to favor an apparently dramatic step in order to demonstrate that they were breaking from the state Socialist past and putting a final seal of defeat on the previous system. This was important in Poland and Russia, but it was less relevant in countries where political transformation was more gradual. The arguments used for economic policy were generally derived from economic theories, but the reasons for their adoption lie in political development rather than economic conditions.

Box 6.2   An institutionalist alternative?

The alternatives covered in this chapter are not based on a single theoretical perspective. They emerged partly as pragmatic reactions to the WC strategy, albeit with degrees of distrust toward unquestioning faith in a free market. A possible candidate to fill that gap is the contribution from institutionalist economics. The conclusion here is more modest; it provides helpful criticisms, and a counterbalance, to mainstream neoclassical economics but not a full alternative, particularly as far as the policy advice is concerned.

The issue is complicated by different uses of the term "institution." Some have used it to refer to laws and regulations and the authorities that can enforce them. For the "institutionalist" school of economics as represented by North (2005), institutions are habits, customs, and attitudes within society that are subject to only gradual change and, therefore, constrain the choices available to economic actors.

Using the first of these interpretations, the IMF accepted that it had failed to emphasize the need for an "institutional infrastructure" and cautiously accepted that "in practice such institution building was not always given adequate attention" (IMF 2000b, 84). The World Bank apologized at greater length (WB 2001) in its summary of the transition experience, recognizing the crucial role that should be played by rules, enforcement mechanisms, and organizations. The EBRD's "transition indicators," produced annually to show how well transition economies were progressing, were also amended in 2003 to incorporate institutions, albeit again only in the sense of laws and rules. They were also matched by the inclusion of some new indicators closer to the neoliberal agenda, such as private pensions and the commercialization of railways and water provision. Institutions were evidently recognized as important but were not given a clearly central place.

The policy implication of this revision to the WC strategy was that steps should have been taken to develop the necessary frameworks alongside, or before, other reform measures. That was particularly relevant as a criticism of rapid privatization. It was less important in relation to liberalization and stabilization, although there, too, the effectiveness of policies was limited by the weakness of laws for enforcing contracts and bankruptcy.

The more comprehensive institutionalist approach to economics points to a stronger case for gradualism, but it, too, fails to provide a complete alternative framework. The neoclassical assumption of a sphere of market exchange, separated off from social processes, is applicable for the most basic forms of activity, meaning small-scale trading and starting up small-scale business activities. In these areas, there is validity to the notion of the "institutionally separate economic system" referred to by Karl Polanyi, a pioneer of the institutional approach (Polanyi 1977, 53). It is, therefore, not surprising that in all transition economies, these basic forms of market activity emerged very quickly (as discussed in Chapter 11), without needing a new or complex institutional environment. A model based on little more than self-seeking individuals seemed adequate.

Some institutionalist writing has taken this further, emphasizing that the economic system cannot be treated in isolation from the society in which it is imbedded and from persisting influences from past habits and thinking (Hausner, Jessop, and Nielsen 1995). A new system, it is argued, could not be created by "rational design." Instead, it was marked by "path dependency" (Stark and Bruszt 1998). However, the fact remains that alongside a more path-dependent evolution in some areas, there were striking discontinuities in others. The problem, glossed over in this literature, is to identify where and why the former were important.

The search for path dependency has been particularly vigorous in Russia, where some economists have countered a "neoliberal turn" with "Russian institutionalism," seeking support in the very old theory that Western capitalism could never be appropriate to Russia (Zweynert 2007) on account of "deep civilisation differences" from Western Europe and North America (Shkaratan 2007, 156). Much of this is too vague and generalized to provide a useful basis for criticism of specific policies.

The institutionalist approach, therefore, does not provide a complete alternative to mainstream neoclassical economics. It does provide warnings against the WC strategy because it points to the importance of a legal framework, as later recognized by the IMF and World Bank, and because it points to the importance of social and institutional resources—including habits, customs, and networks—that develop only gradually.

The most important of these occur where economic activity depends on the development of confidence through long-term relationships rather than one-off transactions. This was analyzed by Artur Okun (1981), with a focus on labor markets. Other examples include the development of corporate governance, including control over management and protection of shareholder interests (as discussed in Chapter 8), and the establishment of a financial system. Relying purely on self-seeking individuals with short time horizons, uncontrolled by a regulatory system, would lead to disaster. Owners of banks would use deposits for their own enrichment; banks could even be set up for that purpose. Debtors would take credits they could not repay, and depositors would be defrauded of their wealth. Such phenomena became well known in transition economies.

The habit of saving and of trusting one's money to a bank, and even more to a newer form of financial institution, depends both on a legal and regulatory framework and on public trust that that framework is effective, something that develops with time and experience. Thus, depositors frequently preferred the state-owned savings banks, despite legal guarantees for private bank deposits, because they did not trust the latter; this was a rational response that followed the experience of new banks defrauding depositors. High savings rates were also discouraged in countries that experienced hyperinflation, wiping out savings in the early 1990s and, in Russia, again in 1998 (Berglöf et al. 2003, 36–37). A strong and effective banking system, therefore, depended on a combination of laws and regulations and engrained habits.

One policy implication of the institutionalist critique of the WC strategy is that governments needed to give a high priority to laws and regulations from the start. A further implication is that policies dependent on the existence of that framework should not be rushed. A third implication is that further policies should be sought to promote the development of institutions, habits, and thinking appropriate to a modern market economy. The shock, leading to a sudden and extreme increase in prices, was not conducive to nurturing confidence in saving and depositing wealth in banks. Overall, a case can be made for a more gradualist approach and for a broader approach, with a more active state supporting changes beyond just liberalization and stabilization.

STABILIZATION WITHOUT SHOCKS

The first alternative was essentially for putting a similar priority on stabilization and liberalization, but the implementation was to be less harsh. That could be seen as following the Hungarian example. An early criticism in Poland was that the restrictive macroeconomic policies had overshot, creating an unnecessarily deep depression without eliminating inflation. In fact, inflation accelerated as a result of the extreme devaluation in January 1990. A milder policy, so it was argued, could have achieved the same benefits at a lower cost.

Grzegorz Kołodko, Poland's minister of finance from 1994 to 1997, put forth this argument from early 1990. He did not advocate reversing the steps taken in the Balcerowicz period, but he did claim to have corrected them, replacing "shocks without therapy" by "therapy without shocks" (Kolodko 2000, 111). As a former participant in the roundtable negotiations on the Communist side, he stuck broadly with the party's position from that time, which meant achieving market equilibrium without unnecessary social pain.

Others, too—including Levcik (1995) and, more cautiously and with more reservations, Kornai (1995b)—argued that deflation had been too harsh and that reflation would help lift the CEEC economies out of depression. The evidence in Chapter 4 on the nature of the so-called transformation depression provides only partial support for this view. Depression was caused partly by government policies but also partly by structural problems, as export markets were lost and imports competed with domestic producers. A "Keynesian" solution, meaning higher public spending to raise demand, could therefore have lifted demand for producers oriented toward the domestic market, but it could not have replaced former export demand, much of which was for completely different kinds of products.

In fact, there was some macroeconomic easing in Poland while Balcerowicz was still in charge, following clear signs of discontent with the course of economic development. As early as June 1990, the government implemented an antirecession policy, despite some scepticism from the IMF, and relaxed the monetary, wage, and fiscal restraints. There was no reversal of price liberalization, although liberalization of coal prices was further delayed. This small move toward restoration of demand levels, and others that followed it, contributed to a lasting degree of macroeconomic instability, which stands as a reservation both to the view that Balcerowicz achieved stabilization and to the view that stabilization was an absolute precondition for economic growth. Inflation, shown in Table A.3 in the Appendix, quickly undermined much of the benefit of devaluation and continued at a significant level. Rising imports led to a continued balance-of-payments deficit and hence to gradual devaluation, which in turn raised costs and caused further inflation. The notion of a fixed exchange rate as an anchor for other policies was undermined by devaluation in May 1991, followed by a decision to allow the currency to float in November 1991.

There was also a return of the budget deficit that had disappeared in early 1990. This had been a paradoxical and unexpected consequence of the WC package as enterprises increased their profits—the main source of government revenue—following price increases and as they used up inputs bought at the previous, lower prices. However, falling demand and lower output soon led to falling profits, and the state budget deficit rose to 5.3 percent of GDP in 1992. Only very harsh spending cuts could have brought it back toward balance, and this was impossible, as social policy in Poland, as in other CEECs, was to maintain existing and newly established forms of welfare provision, as discussed in Chapter 10.

Reality in Poland, then, was more gradualist than initially intended. There were opponents of this softening of policies, including the deputy finance minister Marek Dąbrowski, who resigned his post and left to advise the Russian and other CIS governments on their strategies. His message was to avoid the kind of concessions the Polish government had been making, but he was soon also acknowledging that without policies to protect employees, there would be "a strong backlash against the reform process" (Blanchard et al. 1993, 112). Balcerowicz, writing some years later, preferred to leave it as an open question as to whether monetary and fiscal policies had been too tough (Balcerowicz 1995, 217–18).

In Czechoslovakia, the main alternative in macroeconomic policies was for a slower liberalization of international trade, maintaining a higher degree of protection; critics later referred to a "premature opening" of the economy (Myant 1993, 266–71). Their alternative would have been consistent with a smaller devaluation, and it was devaluation, through higher import prices, that fueled domestic price increases that in turn persuaded the government of the need for its highly restrictive macroeconomic policies. There were proposals in the following years from the political opposition for strengthening barriers to imports and partially reversing the extent of devaluation. Scope for this was limited by agreements with the European Union and commitments to other international agencies, but there was still some room for a more protectionist policy in the early and mid-1990s.

A slower pace of external liberalization would have improved the survival prospects of domestically oriented producers that were threatened by imports. Following the familiar "infant industry" argument used in many industrializing countries in previous decades, that would have given more time for them to adapt and improve their international competitiveness. It is impossible to predict the outcome of this alternative policy approach. Protection could lead enterprises to seek an easy life, or it could allow them to survive while functioning finance and corporate governance systems developed. Arguments that many could have done better with a little leeway and a little help are taken up in relation to the fourth alternative.

There was also support for this more gradual liberalization from the experiences of developing countries and China. The development economist Ronald McKinnon used this to argue for a 5- to 10-year adjustment period during which other internal changes, such as the development of capital markets, could take place and support enterprise development (McKinnon 1993, 9). There is a clear link here to the contribution of institutional economics, discussed in Box 6.2

STABILIZATION PLUS INDUSTRIAL POLICY

The second alternative, heard both in Poland and Czechoslovakia, amounted to acceptance of the primacy of liberalization and stabilization, albeit with preference for the more gradual implementation suggested by the first alternative but with a requirement for further complementary policies. It was claimed that the full WC package would lead both to unnecessary social costs and to the destruction of key parts of the economy. Depression, with the short-term drop in demand and tough financial constraints, would hit enterprises, irrespective of their long-term prospects. It would, above all, hit those with debts. Far from being the least efficient, indebted enterprises were often the most modern, repaying the costs of recent investment. It would hit exporting firms that had relied on government credits and other support, and these were often the big manufacturing enterprises with the best international contacts. It could also have random knock-on effects on other enterprises through nonpayment of bills by those facing difficulties. All of this was predicted before, and observed after, the shock in Czechoslovakia. The solution, according to critics of the government's policy, was industrial policy (Myant 1993, 183–86).

The development of rudimentary industrial policies required a continual battle. Industrial policy had been a major target of neoliberal thinking in Western Europe. The central argument was that governments could not "pick winners"—that was better left to the market—and that help to enterprises was generally a response to rent seeking from firms that were inefficient and should be left to fend for themselves. There was a clear trend from the 1970s away from selective help for firms, but governments were still actively involved in promoting innovation, new technologies, regional development, exports, and development of new and small firms.

The debate in CEECs built from Western European experience. One side insisted that the state should play no role, while the other side argued along two lines. One was that there were special problems in CEECs that justified more, rather than less, intervention. The second was that enterprises deserved at least the same support as in Western Europe, and this was being denied them by the neoliberal direction of policy making.

The first of these lines related particularly to debts that many enterprises inherited from central planning and that were exacerbated by the effects of the shock. These threatened them with early bankruptcy. The first concessions came from governments very soon after the introduction of the WC packages and are discussed in Chapter 5.

Easing conditions for enterprises amounted to a serious revision of the WC package. The initial conception had been that enterprises would face hard budget constraints and would be faced with a choice to adapt or die. How far they could and did adapt is discussed in Chapter 11. Death was a difficult option, partly because there were no satisfactory provisions for bankruptcy. Poland revived a 1934 bankruptcy law, but it led to long and complex processes that seemed best avoided (Blanchard et al. 1993, 146). An attempt to overcome this in Hungary in 1992 with a very tough law quickly proved unsuccessful (see later text, p. 220). Moreover, large-scale closures would threaten social catastrophe, and, despite all the tough talk of governments, this was not an acceptable option. The Hungarian government was aware of social discontent from the autumn of 1989, and there were protests in large enterprises facing financial difficulties in Poland and Czechoslovakia in early 1990 and 1991, respectively. Governments yielded in various ways, allowing enterprises to survive and to continue employing workers.

This modification to the WC strategy implied recognition from those in power of the need to respond to outside pressures and social interests. Balcerowicz's period of "exceptional politics" did not last for very long, although there was still some way to go to the development of a modern civil society in which a well-informed public could contribute to the development of policies.

At first, the softening of conditions on enterprises was badly received within the IMF and by Western experts prominent in giving advice. Governments were still advised to stand firm and to let state firms decline and close (Blanchard et al. 1993, 112). That message was soon mixed with the acknowledgement that past debts, often built up after implementation of the WC package, should be written off if they could not be repaid and written down if they could be partly repaid (146) and that firms needing capital restructuring should be given a chance (112). Gradually, and not very explicitly, the need for state involvement was recognized.

The public face presented to countries expected to follow the examples of Poland and Czechoslovakia was of a steadfast determination not to yield or soften policies. Years later, it was still claimed by an IMF official that CIS countries were failing because they were slower to seize on the need to close inefficient factories and put people out of work (Havrylyshyn 2006, 151–52). The truth is that this was not the approach in CEECs, either.

There were repeated rescue packages for Polish enterprises. They were politically important, lightening the social costs of transition. However, their long-term economic impact is harder to assess. Capacity and workforces were kept together, providing a basis for economic recovery in some enterprises. For some enterprises, ultimate failure appeared inevitable, but attempts to give them a chance persisted for many years. As late as 2002, the government presented a program for the conditional cancellation of debt for large enterprises facing difficulties, albeit without much evidence of subsequent success (Mickiewicz 2005, 153–56).

STRENGTHENING INDUSTRIAL POLICY

The third alternative here groups together proposals for a consistently more active state. This sometimes, but not always, meant delaying price and foreign trade liberalization to allow time for a range of preparatory measures (Gabrisch and Hölscher 2006, 23–25). Thus, it could be a complete alternative to the WC strategy, but it was usually an alternative only to the emphasis on stabilization, meaning restrictive macroeconomic policies, as the precondition for future economic recovery. The common feature was that the state was expected to play an active role at some stage.

Some questioned the value of market relations without a functioning financial system, an argument that gains strength from the previous discussion of the institutionalist contribution. The implication was a greater state role in developing a banking system, although the details were not spelled out. Another common argument was that monopolies should be broken up first, as agreed, for example, at Poland's roundtable. Advocates of the WC strategy hoped they had handled the issue with the freeing of imports. The question of monopoly occupies an important place in mainstream economic thinking and was, therefore, an obvious target of interest, but, in practical terms, it is not clear that it was an important issue. Enterprises did not compete under state Socialism, but, especially in consumer goods sectors, there were often several enterprises that easily could compete with each other once given the chance (Amsden, Kochanowicz, and Taylor 1994, 88–98).

The most important alternative under this heading was an argument for much more forceful state involvement in promoting development, rather than just warding off collapse, of enterprises inherited from the past. It came with deep scepticism about the value of macroeconomic restraint as the central element in economic policy, but it did not come with opposition to price liberalization. The argument that follows draws on the work of Amsden, Kochanowicz, and Taylor (1994).

Foreign consultancy firms, brought in by managements to offer advice, found many cases in which enterprises could have had prospects if they had had access to finance. This would have enabled the enterprises to go beyond overcoming immediate financial difficulties and to undertake investment and modernization. Without this, they had little chance of competing internationally. It should be added that modernization often also involved reductions in capacity, or complete closure, of some lines of activity that were judged to have no realistic chance. It was, therefore, not an option without possible social costs.

However, this option conflicted with the importance put on suppressing inflation, meaning imposing the most restrictive conditions possible on enterprises. The World Bank pressed the argument that *financial* restructuring was the priority, and that meant overcoming current financial difficulties by cutbacks. New development, it was argued, could come only from private enterprises, while state-owned firms could not be trusted, and their financial conditions should not be eased. The effects of the shock—including macroeconomic policies and the breaking of trade links, plus the effects of outside advice and conditions attached to help for IFIs—were, therefore, cutting enterprises off from possible recovery. In the view of Amsden, Kochanowicz, and Taylor, the solution was an active state policy, including subsidies targeted at enabling enterprises to finance some degree of modernization.

One criticism of this approach was that it amounted to picking winners. The market and price signals would be replaced by decisions from state officials, and they would yield to powerful lobbies, irrespective of business prospects of the enterprises. It is true that it would have been difficult for inexperienced officials and advisers to judge the prospects of enterprises, but, as indicated, many studies were undertaken and judgments made. It can be added that no effort was made to develop governmental capacity for such activities, while resources were available for, and devoted to, other activities, especially privatization.

Moreover, models did exist from the experiences of other countries—notably Japan, South Korea, and Taiwan. In those cases, governments gave general support to particular sectors—including advice, protection, and export promotion—and gave help to specific enterprises that showed results. There were economists in CEECs who favored looking at those examples to see how experience could be adapted to their conditions. Such views were at first firmly rejected, but persistent lobbying from large industrial enterprises and the failure of other policies to improve their position led governments to yield a little ground.

Thus, alongside emergency help to prevent financial paralysis, governments added in more elements of Western European interventionist polices, giving support to exporters in the form of credit guarantees, supporting credits to new enterprises, and developing systems of support to agricultural prices. Farmers' lobbies were particularly vocal, and they were able to stage effective and disruptive protest actions, setting aims and using tactics familiar from Western Europe. They also cited U.S. government policies as an example to follow. Balcerowicz was reluctant to waver, responding that U.S. agriculture "might be the most regulated [sector], but is it the healthiest?" (Myant 1993, 110). Ultimately, the Polish and other CEEC governments were compelled to recognize the case for helping the farming sector and manufacturing industry, conceding that a modern market economy required a new role for the state rather than no state role at all. The Polish government, particularly when Kołodko dominated economic policy, was slightly more enthusiastic than the Czech government—under Klaus as prime minister from 1992 to 1997—but international agencies continued to restrict options (see later text, pp. 266–267). Remarkably, the greatest help was given not to domestically owned firms but to inward investors that bought more successful established enterprises in Poland, Czechoslovakia, and Hungary. It seemed that they alone could succeed with arguments for protection, for better terms for importing equipment, and for investment in the necessary infrastructure.

ACCELERATING PRIVATIZATION

The fourth alternative, advocated in Poland both before and during the implementation of the Balcerowicz program, was for an even faster rush to a pure free market solution. That meant rejecting the central intervention to control wages—which Balcerowicz characterized as "not dogmatic," meaning that he recognized it was out of line with principles of a free market—and pressing immediately to privatization. The argument was that private owners would have the incentive to hold back wages in the interests of maximizing their profits. Privatization would, therefore, make wage controls an unnecessary distortion of the market mechanism.

This thinking followed a long tradition in part of the Solidarity movement, combining faith in free enterprises with the belief that living standards could be protected and that macroeconomic restraint was unnecessary. Armed with such thinking, Lech Wałęsa returned to the political stage to run in the presidential election against the prime minister in the first Solidarity-dominated government. His focus was on the "acceleration" of reform, and he won the election by a comfortable margin. This approach evidently had more mass appeal than the dry formulation of the Balcerowicz program. In practice, it brought two possibly contradictory elements to supplement the Balcerowicz program. The first was pressure for faster privatization, and the second was greater attention to social pressures in welfare provision and support for troubled enterprises, which led toward greater state involvement. However, there was no reversal of policies, and Balcerowicz remained as finance minister until August 1991.

Privatization also proved difficult and slow in Poland, as the period of extraordinary politics was replaced by a period of debate and disagreement. However, it was the measure that the IFIs came to see as the essential step, pressing it on all countries regardless of whether they had followed the WC strategy to that point. Discussion of this is left to Chapter 13.

RUSSIA'S TWO OPTIONS

The revisions to the WC strategy in Russia took a different course. As shock therapy seemed to be leading only to greater instability and still further decline in output, two broadly coherent alternatives emerged.

The first was for a considerably slower transformation, with greater protection against imports and less priority to macroeconomic stabilization. Many professional economists from outside the narrow circle that was setting policy—including advisers to previous governments and the emerging employers' organization the Russian Union of Industrialists and Entrepreneurs—argued that stabilization and balanced budgets were impossible in conditions of falling output, that preventing expansion of the money supply would lead to large-scale bankruptcies, and that liberalization of energy prices would fuel further inflation (Åslund 2002, 85).

To supporters of the WC program, this was a "proinflationary bloc" that had taken shape by the early summer of 1992 and that wanted a national protected economy rather than an open market economy. Gaidar, the acting prime minister at the time, compromised with them because he had no choice in view of the government's weak support base (Mau 1996, 73, 82).

The strength of the wish among leading economists for an alternative is indicated by a statement published in the Russian media in July 1996 and reproduced in amended form in English (Intriligator 1997) that includes the signatures of five leading Russian economists and eight leading U.S. economists, five of them Nobel Prize winners (Kenneth Arrow, Laurence Klein, Wassily Leontieff, Robert Solow, and James Tobin).

Their argument was that failures stemmed "directly or indirectly from the fact that the government has not assumed its proper role in a market economy," (226) leaving the way open for "criminals" (226) to fill the vacuum. Their central message was that the Russian government had to play a "much more important role in the economy, as in such modern mixed economies as the United States, Sweden, and Germany" (225). This was to include "a central coordinating role in establishing the public and private institutions required for a market economy to function" (225). There were points on the areas of government responsibility, including macroeconomic stability, social services, and technological advance. It was emphasized that "moving an economy in a different direction takes time" (227). This was to be a gradualist approach to correcting for the perceived mistakes of the early transition strategy; there were no precise details on policies to be pursued. This, then, was not a fully coherent alternative program, and the focus was different from that of alternatives in CEECs. Emphasis was on overcoming the breakdown and weakness of the Russian state rather than on specific macroeconomic policies.

This statement first appeared two days before presidential elections and was quickly condemned by opponents as an attempt to support Yeltsin's Communist adversaries. Such was the politicization of debates on economic policy at the time.

The second trend in Russia also amounted to accepting the impossibility of speedy stabilization. Instead, attention turned to very rapid privatization but with a different justification, or set of justifications, from that of Wałęsa's supporters in Poland. In Russia, it was a preliminary step in the development of an anti-Communist and anti-inflation coalition, which could then cement Yeltsin's position and ensure successful implementation of the WC package (Mau 2005, 71). The notorious loans-for-shares scheme (see later text, p. 250) was even justified in these terms as a vital step toward the consolidation of a proreform, or anti-inflation, bloc. In this version, then, privatization was intended to change the political, rather than the economic, system.

A similar, if more complex, argument came from the Russian government's advisers' version of free market ideology (Boycko, Shleifer, and Vishny 1995). Socialism was said to be "a system of extreme political control of economic activity" (21). It gave dominance to politicians who would pursue their own interests and yield to pressure from "interest groups" (27). The fundamental need was, therefore, for "depoliticization" (10–11). This justified the idea of the fastest possible privatization, handing property to anyone apart from the "official bureaucracy." Everything, including the creation of a framework of laws, was secondary to the aim of eliminating the state's influence. This was even presented as a positive innovation, with the view that emphasis on developing corporate governance had been "the fundamental conceptual error of the Polish approach to privatization" (83). It apparently led to unnecessary debate and delay. Such was the most extreme version of faith in a free market, albeit a kind of free market that was unlike any in advanced market economies, as it appears to give no role to the state at all, even in ensuring a legal framework.

Andrei Shleifer (1997) related the negative view of the state very powerfully in his condemnation of the joint statement referred to previously. The Russian state, he claimed, was "fundamentally predatory, disorganized, and hostile to growth," (228) coming to business with a "grabbing hand" (231). It should, therefore, not be allowed to grow or be given bigger roles, as that would simply give it more scope for predatory activities.

None of these responses to the joint statement by Russian and U.S. economists is convincing. "Depoliticization" was portrayed as countering the power of lobbies and interests, but it was to be achieved precisely by supporting and propagating a particular interest—that of enterprise managers rather than state officials. The boundary between the two in the Soviet system was rather blurred, anyway, and it was notable that some supporters of neoliberal positions saw the enterprise managers as the enemy of reform (Åslund 2002, 106). The perceived enemy shifted, but the remedy—very rapid privatization—remained the same.

The blanket condemnation of the state was used to justify giving property to individuals largely freed from the controls required to prevent them from becoming, to use Shleifer's term of condemnation of the Russian state, "fundamentally predatory." Indeed, part of Russian private business proved very good at grabbing what was available, both from the state and from any other source. A further irony, illustrating that a grabbing hand can be used by private firms and individuals as well as the state, is that Shleifer, a prominent Harvard economist who was advising the Russian government and allocating U.S. aid for reform policies beginning in 1992, was accused in 1997 of defrauding the U.S. government and of profiting from insider knowledge on Russian privatization. A legal case in the United States ended in 2005 after charges had been upheld (Kotz and Weir 2007, 228–30). However, rapid privatization without concern for controls against fraud and corruption did at the time win some international acclaim as a radical step, and that helped ensure continuing U.S. government, and hence IMF, backing for Yeltsin.

Thus, while CEECs were correcting aspects of their early reform strategies, the advice to Russia was to avoid those Central European mistakes and to head down a more chaotic and lawless road. This was broadly the road chosen, albeit wavering toward a looser monetary policy in 1992. The difference from CEECs reflected the weaker appeal of the Western European model and the low level of state capacity after the breakup of the Soviet Union. These factors applied also in other CIS countries. Some followed analogous paths but with even less—and in some cases effectively no—heritage of past debate and original economic thinking. Some made far smaller changes. A common feature was the weakness of coherent voices from society for developing strategies or seeking alternatives, and a common outcome was a formal transfer of property into private ownership without the accompanying development of an institutional framework, a theme pursued in the next few chapters.

CONCLUSION

This and the previous chapter have focused on describing and explaining what was done rather than speculating on what else might have been done or what would have happened under alternative policies. However, it is clear that there were alternatives to the WC strategy and to its application in the form of shock therapy. Debates and disagreements were not about support for versus opposition to fundamental change in the economic system, though some supporters of shock therapy portrayed them as such in their attempt to discredit and marginalize opponents. Unfortunately, international agencies helped, rather than hindered, this attempt to restrict policy debate.

There is no case for disputing the broadest aim of the WC strategy—the creation of modern market economies—but on almost every point of detail, there is a case for a more considered, and hence gradual, approach. The greatest possible speed was not justified by serious economic arguments; its attractions were largely political. The main one was the belief that social forces existed that would, once they had a chance, be able to reverse the changes and restore much or all of the economic system of state Socialism. Speed was also attractive for the international agencies, as they, too, were suspicious that local actors were not genuinely committed to the policies being recommended from outside. Therefore, setting clear and simple targets with tight timescales made sense to them.

The evidence here suggests that opponents of shock therapy were not necessarily opponents of systemic change. In CEECs, the evidence rather suggests that the development of democracy and of wide participation in well-informed debates on economic policy provided a better basis for sound economic policies than did rushing through dramatic changes worked out by a small group of isolated experts or based on advice or imposition from the outside. In CIS countries, outright opponents of change, or people in powerful positions who had no understanding of what a market system would mean, were more important. However, they were matched by supporters of market-oriented reform whose enthusiasm led to dangerous extremes. There, too, a higher level of public control and debate and a higher level of state capacity would appear to be a better basis for a successful transformation of the old economic system.

SECTION IV

THE STATE

CHAPTER SEVEN

State Capacity and the Rule of Law

Maintaining state capacity and the rule of law proved to be crucial to the prospects of individual countries. It quickly became apparent that transition was not about reducing the role of the state. States actually grew bigger in terms of administrative employees during the transition period (Brym and Gimpelson 2004). Rather than a "wasteful expansion of bureaucracy" (Åslund 2007, 232), the growth took the form of a convergence to a size consistent with countries' populations, reacting to new functions that governments had to assume in a market economy (Gehlbach 2008b). Transition required creating a new state with very different kinds of roles. The extent to which the countries succeeded in this challenge marks a major division between them.

It has been widely recognized since the times of Adam Smith that state institutions are fundamental to a market economy and, more broadly, capitalist social relations. Institutional provisions of the rule of law and property rights allow the exchange of goods and services as well as the accumulation of capital to proceed with a reasonable degree of security and predictability (cf. Weber 1968; North 1981). Historically, mobilization of state power was crucial in breaking down resistance to the emergence of a market economy both in the center of the capitalist revolution and in the peripheries (Marx 1990, 873–940; Polanyi 1957, 135–50; H. Schwartz 2000, 11–41).

State capacity can be defined as an ability to make and enforce collectively binding decisions across a territory (cf. Rueschemeyer and Evans 1985; Jessop 1990). Thus, as in the classical statement of Max Weber (1968), a successful claim for the monopoly on the use of violence within a territory is an essential aspect of the state. In this context, it is useful to distinguish between the "despotic power" of the state, enabling it to enforce a decision without consulting with civil society groups and possibly against their wishes, and the "infrastructural power" of the state to penetrate civil society and enforce its decisions within its territory (Mann 1993, 59). We, therefore, also refer to the "strategic capacity" to make and enforce strategic decisions, which depends on political processes, including the will, expertise, realism, and coordination of key political actors, and also on an effective administrative apparatus.

State capacity depends on a state apparatus organized along bureaucratic lines and also on the nature of its embeddedness in society (Weber 1968; Rueschemeyer and Evans 1985). The bureaucratic infrastructure guarantees a certain degree of coherence of the state as a corporate actor. The bureaucratic organization is necessary for the transfer of information and resources that make possible effective and coordinated action; it is also a means of control over state actors to ensure that state agents act as required for the goals pursued. One of the crucial aspects of the modern bureaucratic state organization is the maintenance of a private/public distinction so that the holders of power cannot use the state and its resources for private enrichment and patrimony. More generally, a certain degree of autonomy from dominant interests is needed to make a pursuit of any consistent policy possible. This often entails acting against the preferences and interests pressed by groups within society.

After comparing perspectives on the role of the state in the context of transition, this chapter analyzes the patterns of state capacity collapse and consolidation. Comparative measures of fiscal capacity, corruption, rule of law, and strategic capacities show a clear division between the CIS and Eastern Europe, although corruption remained a serious problem in both groups of countries. The available indicators are far from perfect, both as far as the methodology of their calculation and the thematic coverages are concerned. Nevertheless, they show major differences and trends. First, the CIS states often failed to undergo institutional reforms to adjust to the new environment and experienced a major crisis of state capacity, leading to a surge in crime, corruption, and general chaos. However, there were exceptions in this group; most importantly, Belarus and Uzbekistan retained state capacity and contained corruption. Second, Eastern European countries managed to adjust their states to the new environment. The states of the former Yugoslavia (with the exception of Slovenia and the FYR Macedonia) experienced problems with retaining state capacity due to wars. Third, despite their difficult starting position, the Baltic states progressively caught up with the rest of Eastern Europe. Finally, the end of the 1990s saw consolidation of the state also in the CIS, but experiences varied. Factors that explain the differences in outcomes are set out in the final section.

PERSPECTIVES ON THE STATE AND ECONOMIC PERFORMANCE

There is a wide consensus that state capacity is conducive to economic growth. First, it is a prerequisite for an institutional environment in which contracts are enforced and property rights can be established. Second, it provides abilities and capacities to pursue policies. Empirically, successful growth strategies differed as far as the specific policies pursued were concerned, but they were characterized by a state capable of enforcing its policies and by a professional and well-monitored bureaucracy (Rodrik 2006; see also WB [1997]). Inefficient and corrupt government, in turn, is likely to limit the growth potential of an economy, regardless of the policies pursued. Empirical studies indeed show corruption to have a negative impact on economic growth (e.g., Bardhan 1997; Kaufman 2004).

State capacity also proved to be a crucially important factor of success in the context of transition. The remarkable contrast between transition outcomes in Russia and China is commonly attributed to the different role of the government in the transition process (Burawoy 1996; Miller and Tenev 2007; Parker and Thornton 2007). It has also been argued that Gorbachev's *perestroika* of the late 1980s included gradual, dual-track reforms similar to policies pursued in China with considerable success (on *perestroika*, see Chapter 3). However, these reforms failed in the Soviet Union. This can be attributed to the decline of the power of central government and of the Communist Party in the Soviet Union (K.M. Murphy, Shleifer, and Vishny 1992, 900).

The depth of the transformation depression, it has been argued, was conditioned by the retention of capable institutions in some countries and the catastrophic incapability of government in others (see, for example, Kolodko [2000, 321–47]). Econometric evidence presented by Popov (2000, 28–42; see also Popov [2007]) has identified the strength of state institutions[1] together with the initial conditions to be the most important predictor of success in the post-Communist world (including also China, Vietnam, and Mongolia); the specific policies implemented seemed to explain relatively little. Using different indicators, Miller and Tenev (2007) found that state strength had the strongest impact on growth performance of all indicators they employed. A panel study by Hamm and King (2007) showed that the positive impact of foreign direct investment on economic development was dependent upon the presence of a strong, bureaucratic state.

However, there has been less agreement on how to transform the state and on the wider role state institutions should play. Neoliberals argued that the market functions best when state interference is minimized, as it is likely to cause market distortions and inefficiencies. State interference, it was argued, promotes rent seeking and thus a nonproductive use of resources. The WC perspective recognized the role of the state in providing a safety net targeted at new groups in need as well as the importance of securing property rights and other market-supporting institutions (Lipton and Sachs 1990a; Sachs 1990; Balcerowicz 1995), but the emphasis was clearly put on the need to reduce the role of the state. Government was not to have any discretionary power after the privatization phase.

The neoliberals did not argue for a weak state; they preferred a small and capable one. However, there was a strong distrust of the inherited state, which was associated with the old regime and thus considered as something that had to be destroyed and replaced by the self-regulating market (Boycko, Shleifer, and Vishny 1995; Shleifer and Vishny 1998). The old elites, it was believed, had a vested interest in the old order or a propensity to block reform in order to defend their rents. Thus, the task was to destroy the grabbing hand of the bureaucrats (Shleifer and Vishny 1993; Frye and Shleifer 1997), demolish the networks of old elites, and liberalize the countries by "taming the Leviathan" of the Soviet state (Åslund 2007, 117, 207).

The post-Socialist bureaucracy was perceived as inert, hardly reformable (Bunce 1999), and particularly dysfunctional and corrupt (e.g., Frye and Zhuravskaya 2000; Hellman, Jones, and Kaufmann 2000). Reducing the role of government, deregulation, liberalization, and privatization were seen as far more important for fighting corruption than was creating a bureaucracy that would function better, for instance, by improving the incentives and personnel selection (Shleifer and Vishny 1998, 12; cf. Rose-Ackerman 1999; Tanzi and Schuknecht 2000). New constituencies for the rule of law and property rights, it was argued, had to be created through privatization (Boycko, Shleifer, and Vishny 1995; Frye 1997; Gaidar 1999; Åslund 2007). The new owners were then expected to demand the new institutions that would create the institutional fabric of capitalism.

---

[1] The ability to raise taxes was used as the indicator.

In contrast, the statist perspective saw a major role for the state also in allocating investment resources, carrying out expansionary monetary policies, and in helping to create incentives for enterprise restructuring and upgrading through trade, competition, and technology policies. Rather than necessarily leading to a nonproductive use of resources, state intervention, it was claimed, can compensate for market failures in mobilizing resources and for the lack of know-how essential for catching up with technologically advanced countries. Such a perspective has been developed in the study of late industrializers—particularly the so-called developmental states in Southeast Asia (Amsden 2000; Kohli 2004; Mathews 2006). Amsden (2000) argued that the successful late-industrializing countries developed systems of conditional subsidies and careful performance monitoring. The statists also emphasized the importance of a state bureaucracy. Economic growth in less-developing countries was shown to be associated with capable bureaucratic state apparatuses that were sufficiently autonomous from social pressures (Evans and Rauch 1999; Rauch and Evans 2000). What is more, the statists argued, successful developmental states were characterized by "embedded autonomy," with bureaucrats constantly renegotiating state goals and policies in the exchange of information with the business groups (Evans 1995). State and business were not alternatives but actors that could benefit by working together.

In the context of transition, statists argued for an institutional reform empowering the government bureaucracy to take an active role in addressing the problems of transition economies by helping technological advances, structural change, and enterprise restructuring (Amsden, Kochanowicz, and Taylor 1994; Chang 1995). They were worried that the attack on the state and removal of experienced bureaucrats, who were condemned for their political association with the old regime, would in fact diminish the capacity of the states to deal with the new tasks and challenges. Within the statist perspective, concentration of ownership, as incidentally occurred in Russia, was seen as a threat to state autonomy, as it gave new owners resources to capture the state.

Statists accepted that the WC mantra of "getting prices right" and the introduction of a narrow set of institutions that supported the market and private ownership could succeed in inducing simple market exchange and small investment in services (e.g., retail and restaurants; cf. Kornai 1995a). However, the conditions for larger-scale capitalist ventures require institutional support to generate savings and to aid investment and technological advance. Such an environment had to be created through active state intervention. Chapter 9 will discuss the actual effects of such policies as pursued in the region.

The sections that follow look at the transition shocks and their impact on the state in different contexts and then compare the patterns of the consolidations that followed.

THE LEGACIES OF STATE SOCIALISM

The state under central planning gave the appearance of omnipotence, justifying the view that the principal need was to reduce its role. However, with government expenditures and revenues amounting to about 50 percent of GDP, the extent of public spending was roughly the same as among higher-spending countries in Western Europe. The administrative apparatus as such was comparatively small, even allowing for a substantial number of people working within the apparatus of Communist parties. Available comparative data for 1993 show that the mean size of public administration for Eastern Europe and the FSU was only 3.8 percent of the labor force in comparison to the OECD mean of 10 percent (Schiavo-Campo et al. 1997, 29–32; see also Brym and Gimpelson [2004] and Gehlbach [2008b]). In contrast to the OECD countries, the size of the administrative apparatus in the Soviet bloc was not positively correlated with the level of economic development. In fact, there was a weak tendency for larger public administration to be associated with poorer countries in Eastern Europe and the FSU. The size of public administration in Russia was particularly low (1.2 percent of the labor force in 1993).

In terms of ownership of the means of production and formal authority, the state Socialist state was powerful, but, as indicated in the discussion of central planning in Chapter 2, its real influence in economic management was more limited. More generally, it has been argued that the Soviet state had strong despotic capacity, but its infrastructural power to penetrate and coordinate civil society was more limited (Stoner-Weiss 2006, 6). Importantly, however, all countries developed some kind of relatively robust state bureaucratic infrastructure. Neoliberals have argued that the bureaucrats represented a "negative human capital," as they were promoted for political reasons (Åslund 2007, 231), but educational qualifications played an increasing role in career promotion in the post-Stalinist period (Linz and Stepan 1996; Eyal, Szelenyi, and Townsley 1998). The legacies thus gave some protection against descent into full-scale chaos and state collapse and provided some foundations for consolidation in the late 1990s (Way 2005).

Within this there was diversity. With past traditions of a market economy and reforms strengthening dependence on a legal infrastructure, CEECs could be expected to produce the most resilient state apparatuses. The Soviet project involved the creation of state infrastructural power in much of the Soviet Union. Similar to the experience of peripheries in the earlier empires, the Soviet domination in central Asia as well as in Belarus also led to the creation of new state boundaries and state-nation identities (on Belarus, see Marples [1996]). Relatively effective bureaucratic structures were thus created as new national identities were forged.

However, public confidence in a state was also most fragile where it was associated with an external power, as in some parts of the Soviet Union. In some, even the capacity of vertical control was limited, particularly in central Asia, where local clans colonized the newly created states and continued to enjoy considerable autonomy from the center (Collins 2006). However, states could survive intact where power was transferred without major internal conflict or where a new power structure emerged by former Communist rulers reinventing themselves under a nationalist label. Prospects were most bleak where political and national conflicts led to civil wars and hence the division or disintegration of the state's bodies of force and repression.

The ability of state apparatuses to survive and adapt to the new demands after the collapse of state socialism thus varied between countries. In no case was the rule of law established before 1989. Ruling parties were not prepared to limit themselves by accepting binding regulations, particularly in the political sphere, and the repressive forces were allowed a great degree of discretion (cf. Linz and Stepan 1996, 248–52). However, after the Stalin period in the Soviet Union, developing toward this was tempered by the strengthening of a legal infrastructure and by giving scope to a considerable degree of rule of law in the civil and economic spheres. Property rights and contracts between predominantly state-owned organizations were legally defined and enforced. This trend was considerably stronger in CEECs, countries with previous traditions of the rule of law.

However, to reemphasize, this was not full independence from political authority, as the judiciary could always be influenced by the ruling party as the effective supreme authority. Moreover, at least in the Soviet Union, the planned economy depended for its successful functioning on informal transactions and relationships that were formally illegal (see previous text, pp. 17, 20, 22, and also Welfens [1992], Goldman [2003, 117], and Harrison and Kim [2006]). These links between enterprises, bypassing the mechanism of central planning, helped to alleviate some of the difficulties in the planning systems and provided alternative means for distribution and access to scarce goods for the population. Functional to the old system to some extent, they can be assumed to have reinforced the lax attitudes toward formal rules and the reliance on informal and corrupt practices among the population (Ledeneva 2000, 2006). There was little direct continuity in the informal practices and ties, but new illegal practices and relationships emerged, with bribery becoming more widespread (Feige and Ott 1999; Whitten 2002).

The regime change involved continuity of the legal systems and infrastructures. While the most compromised security services were generally closed down, the state apparatuses and personnel were broadly retained. Only Estonia formally opted for a radical break, drawing up completely new government structures and laying off all civil servants, requiring them to reapply for the new government jobs.

THE TRANSITION SHOCK

The political and economic transition represented a major challenge for retaining state capacity. State revenues and expenditures as a proportion of GDP are the only comparative indicators of state capacity available as a time series covering the 1990s. These indicators illustrate state collapse accompanying the lengthy transformation depression of CIS countries. Each one contributed to the other, as depression led to fiscal crisis—rising costs and falling enterprise profits hit budget revenues—which in turn limited the scope to finance state machines that could raise tax revenue and counter temptations for officials to indulge in corrupt practices. The figures, however, underrepresent state failures in countries that suffered from the most profound GDP declines. These are precisely those countries where the state failure was most devastating—notably Ukraine, Russia, and most of the CARs.

Government expenditures shrank dramatically in most of the cases, dropping by 50 percent and more in real terms in Russia and other CIS countries in just a couple of years. However, CEECs retained and often even increased public spending, as indicated in Table 7.1, with expenditure reduction limited to subsidies and defense. Reducing government spending in Russia, in contrast, entailed not only lower spending on defense, investment, and subsidies but also reductions for "ordinary government," effectively undermining the infrastructural power of the state. The sudden drop in public spending recorded in most of the CIS thus cannot be

TABLE 7.1   General government expenditure as a percentage of GDP

	1989	1992	1996
Slovakia		58.0	60.7
Hungary	56.6[a]	60.2	52.6
Poland		50.5	51.0
Uzbekistan		29.8	49.8
Bosnia-Herzegovina			46.8
Slovenia		44.1	45.6
Russia		58.4	45.3
Moldova		49.0	43.8
Czech Republic	54.5[a]	49.6	42.6
Bulgaria	55.3	43.6	42.0
Belarus		47.8	40.7
Estonia			40.2
Ukraine		58.0	39.9
Croatia		38.9	38.5
Lithuania			37.4
Macedonia		49.1	37.1
Latvia			37.0
Romania		42.0	33.8
Kyrgyz Republic	24.5	35.1	28.6
Mongolia		24.5	28.4
Armenia		46.7	26.1
Albania	59.7[a]	46.7	24.3
Georgia			21.1
Tajikistan	40.3	57.8	19.0
Kazakhstan			18.6
Azerbaijan		48.4	16.7
Turkmenistan	42.7[a]	30.3	16.3

Source: EBRD economic statistics and forecasts, available at http://www.ebrd.com/country/sector/econo/stats/index.htm.
[a] 1990 figure

interpreted as reflecting a reassessment of priorities from a big government to a leaner one. On the contrary, almost all government programs and departments were retained, but the sudden drop in financing meant a general institutional collapse (Popov 2000, 29), leading also to the difficulties with welfare provision discussed in Chapter 10.

Tax revenues as a proportion of GDP decreased considerably in most of the countries (see Table 7.2). Only CEECs and Estonia managed to avoid the decline. Russia, Lithuania, Latvia, several southeastern European states, and CARs experienced the greatest reductions. Among the CIS states, only Belarus and Uzbekistan avoided such reductions, arguably retaining the strongest state institutions among all CIS states throughout the 1990s (cf. Iwasaki 2004; Popov 2007).

TABLE 7.2   The fiscal shock: Total revenues of consolidated government budgets (including budget funds) as a percentage of GDP

	1989	1992	1996[a]
Estonia	39.5	34.6	−38.9
Latvia	52.0	27.4	−38.8
Lithuania	50.0	32.1	23.3
Poland	41.4	44.1	−46.8
Czech Republic	61.7	49.5	44.5
Hungary	59.1	56.1	47.0
Slovakia			44.6
Slovenia	42.4	46.5	44.4
Romania	51.1	37.4	−29.8
Bulgaria	58.0	40.2	−34.2
Croatia		32.2	
FYR Macedonia		38.6	43.9
Albania	47.8	21.9	17.0
Belarus	38.2	43.6	
Russia	41.0	44.2	30.4
Moldova	35.3	20.2	23.0
Ukraine	26.4	33.0	37.2
Georgia	31.5	13.6	9.5
Armenia	52.2	4.2	10.1
Azerbaijan	25.8	49.1	16.4
Kazakhstan	35.4	24.5	16.0
Uzbekistan	35.0	31.4	32.3
Turkmenistan	32.4	55.4	−15.5
Kyrgyzstan	38.0	16.5	17.0
Tajikistan	40.3	26.6	12.3

Source: Popov (2000, 54, Table3A).
[a]These figures are estimates.

DEVELOPING FISCAL CAPACITY

Transition to a market economy required major changes to the tax system, much of which had to be created either from scratch or through a substantial reform of the inherited system. Taxation systems in command economies were relatively simple. Balance was maintained by taxes on consumer spending, typically combined with a complex system of subsidies, and by taxes on enterprises. Other sources of revenue included resource exports and profits from the foreign trade monopoly. Thus, the general public hardly needed to notice how state activities were financed.

Market economies typically required less-arbitrary tax systems. They could not rely on arbitrarily high levels of tax on certain commodities or enterprises. Raising

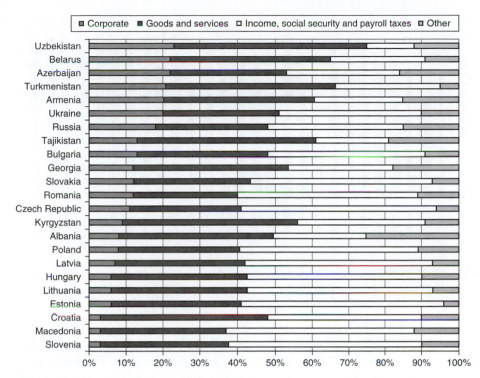

Figure 7.1   Mean tax structure, 1994 to 2000. (*Source:* Adapted from Gehlbach (2008, 52, Table 2.A.1).)

the same amount in revenue thus meant taxing more activities. Personal incomes, which could rise to very high levels for some earners, were a natural target in market economies. A reformed tax system would, therefore, be more varied and complex, requiring a considerable infrastructural power. It was also more likely to face the barrier of political opposition from people resenting tax demands.

As shown in Figure 7.1, CIS states continued to rely on the familiar sources of revenue: taxes on goods and services and on corporations, with the former gaining an increasingly important role in the late 1990s (Gehlbach 2008a). Eastern European countries, in contrast, were able to restructure their taxation systems early on, developing the capacity to collect revenue from taxation on personal income.

The continuing reliance on old sources of revenue indicates either a lack of will to reform or insufficient infrastructural power to monitor and tax general economic activity. One of the indicators of such power is the percentage of total annual sales that firms report for tax purposes (see Figure 7.2), which shows that Uzbekistan, Kazakhstan, Belarus, and Tajikistan were among the most efficient in monitoring companies. Uzbekistan, Belarus, and, to some extent, Tajikistan retained a high degree of control and oversight over large enterprises, which explains the effectiveness of monitoring for tax purposes. Other cases of efficient monitoring are the CEECs and Baltic republics, suggesting that their administrative apparatuses were able to cope with the new private sector and changed tax systems.

In fact, many of the CIS states were relatively effective in collecting corporation tax (Schaffer and Turley 2000). Importantly, however, the effectiveness of corporate

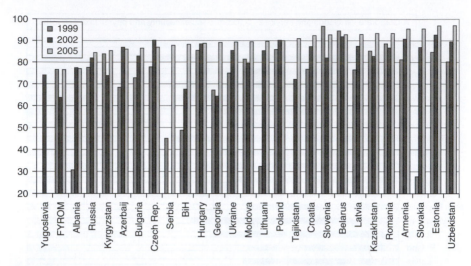

Figure 7.2 Revenue hiding: Percent of total annual sales estimated to be reported for tax purposes, 1999 to 2005. (*Source:* BEEPS dataset, available at http://www.ebrd.com/country/sector /econo/surveys/beeps.htm; based on self-reporting by management of respective enterprises.)

tax collection did not reflect good tax collection overall. Only Eastern European states showed consistent effectiveness in also collecting social security payments and payroll and income taxes (Gehlbach 2008a, 41). The point was rather that some of the states, also including Russia, developed some capacity to extract revenues through the corporation tax, but this was only achieved by concentrating their efforts on large Communist-era enterprises. They devoted less effort to taxing new economic activities (Ebrill and Havrylyshyn 1999; Mitra and Stern 2003). Firm characteristics such as size, monopoly position, and sector explained much of the variation in revenue hiding in the CIS, but explained less of that variation in Eastern Europe (Gehlbach 2008a, 46).

CORRUPTION: CORPORATE EXPLOITATION AND STATE CAPTURE

Bribe taking is a misuse of public power for private purposes, which indicates a malfunctioning of the state, undermining the private/public distinction. Comparisons of countries across the world show a strong association between levels of per capita GDP and corruption (Kaufman 2004) as well as between economic growth and lower levels of corruption (Kalyuzhnova, Kutan, and Yigit 2009). On the level of individuals, the studies have shown that corrupt behavior is likely to be triggered by a combination of opportunities on the one hand and by increased financial pressure, reduced individual prestige, stress, and psychological problems on the other hand (Fitzsimons 2009, 516). While transition reforms were likely to create opportunities for corruption, economic collapse led to pressures on state officials to take advantage of them. Thus, in the context of the fiscal crisis of the state and the emergence of the new private sector, corruption could be expected to thrive. As discussed previously, legacies of the informal activities under state Socialism may have played some role, but the forms taken by corruption were definitely new, and there was often a lack of regulation that would define them as illegal.

In this context, "corporate exploitation" and so-called "state capture" are distinguished as two distinct phenomena linked to the business environment. Corporate exploitation is defined as bribe taking by state officials who turn a blind eye to illegal conduct. It often also takes the form of extortion, with state officials taking advantage of the possibility to apply arbitrary regulations or to withdraw provision of a public service. State capture refers to the "actions of individuals, groups or firms to influence the formulation of laws, regulations, decrees and other government policies (that is, the basic rules of the economic 'game') to their own advantage through illicit or non-transparent means" (Fries, Lysenko, and Polenac 2003, 26; cf. discussion in Chapter 8).

It remains impossible to provide a perfect measure of these phenomena, as reporting of illegal activities is bound to be unreliable. Table 7.3 shows firm-level data from the Business Environment and Enterprise Performance Survey (BEEPS) on payments to state officials as a percentage of annual sales and on the frequency of bribery. The comparison with two other EU member states illustrates the generally high levels of corruption in transition economies. The level of bribery also proved to be strongly correlated to per capita GDP in the transition economies, albeit with Kyrgyzstan, Albania, Russia, Serbia and Montenegro, and Lithuania below the levels expected on the basis of GDPs. Predictably, countries most hit by fiscal crisis and economic downturn reported the highest frequencies of bribery and the bribe tax (i.e., bribes as a share of annual sales). Other studies found much wider differentiation between the CIS and Eastern Europe. According to an enterprise survey comparing Poland, Slovakia, Romania, Russia, and Ukraine in 1997 (S. Johnson, McMillan, and Woodruff 2002), 90 percent of the Russian and Ukrainian companies had made extra payments for public services or the acquisition of a license, while an average of 25 percent of firms had the same experience in the other three Eastern European countries. Moreover, 76 percent and 85 percent of enterprises surveyed in Russia and Ukraine, respectively, had previously been forced to make unofficial payments as a result of a tax inspection, compared with an average of 7 percent for the surveyed corporations in the other countries.

The surveys also showed that bribes and corporate exploitation to some extent worked as a substitute for taxation; the new private firms were most likely to pay bribes and to pay them more often, while larger or older firms, state-owned firms, and foreign firms—that is, those less able to dodge the tax system—paid less in bribes (Hellman, Jones, and Kaufmann 2000; Hellman and Schankerman 2000; J.H. Anderson and Gray 2006).

Similar patterns were observed also for state capture. The 2002 BEEPS showed 22.7 percent of enterprises surveyed in the FSU as being "captor firms"—that is, firms that declared an ability to influence state executives, legislative bodies, ministries, and regulatory agencies—compared against 16.6 percent in CEECs and SEECs (Iwasaki and Suzuki 2007, 396). The BEEPS-based studies also revealed that (1) enterprises with a high level of government participation were more likely to become influential firms; (2) the subsidiaries of Western multinationals were generally reluctant to become involved in state capture, but foreign-affiliated joint ventures captured the state more successfully than domestic corporations; and (3) captor firms showed better performance than noncaptor firms in terms of sales and investment rates, and the gap between the two was more substantial in countries with a higher

TABLE 7.3 Paying bribes

	Bribe tax			Frequency of bribery		
	1999	2002	2005	1999	2002	2005
Czech Republic	1.7	0.92	*0.63*	26	13.33	*9.93*
Hungary	0.9	0.97	1.06	32.3	22.56	*9.93*
Poland	0.7	1.22	*0.7*	33.2	18.57	*14.77*
Slovak Republic	1.3	1.45	*0.93*	33.6	36.02	*10.64*
Slovenia	1.4	0.8	*0.17*	7.7	7.15	*4.65*
Latvia	0.9	0.93	0.71	22	17.9	*7.49*
Lithuania	1.6	0.74	0.87	23.2	20.62	24.08
Estonia	0.9	0.34	0.29	12.9	12.14	*6.47*
Bulgaria	1.3	1.95	*1.58*	23	32.79	*15.7*
Croatia	0.6	0.64	0.76	17.7	12.86	11.27
Romania	1.7	2.57	*0.81*	50.9	36.74	*22.56*
Albania	1.7	3.31	*1.8*	46.7	36.37	46.11
Bosnia and Herzegovina	2.1	0.95	*0.39*	20.5	22.42	19.63
FYR Macedonia	1.4	0.79	0.62	33	22.7	25.28
Serbia and Montenegro		1.52	*0.67*		15.88	33.2
Russia	1.7	1.43	1.07	30.6	38.72	39.3
Ukraine	3.1	2.19	*1.52*	39.1	34.93	*27.53*
Belarus	1.6	1.49	*1.11*	14.8	23.97	*21.65*
Armenia	4.2	0.92	1.17	40.3	14.28	*10.1*
Azerbaijan	3.7	2.74	2.89	59.5	27.46	27.42
Moldova	3.2	2.07	*1.09*	34.4	34.32	*22.42*
Georgia	3.5	2.74	*0.46*	36.8	37.81	*7.38*
Kazakhstan	1.9	2.1	*1.42*	26.1	29.66	*23*
Kyrgyz Republic	2.4	3.7	2.46	28.2	43.7	52.85
Tajikistan		2.6	*1.07*		35.08	*21.33*
Uzbekistan	2.5	1.45	*0.99*	46.2	20.24	21.37
Germany			0.4			8.17
Greece			0.49			22.48

Source: BEEPS data set, available at http://www.ebrd.com/country/sector/econo/surveys/beeps.htm; based on self-reporting by management of respective enterprises.

Note: The *bribe tax* refers to typical unofficial payments/gifts to public officials as a percentage of annual sales. The *frequency of bribery* is the percentage of respondents who agreed they have to pay some irregular payments/gifts for activities related to customs, taxes, licenses, regulations, or services either frequently, usually, or always. Statistically significant changes in 2002 to 2005 are highlighted (with 90 percent confidence).

degree of state capture (Hellman, Jones, and Kaufmann 2000; Fries, Lysenko, and Polenac 2003; Hellman and Schankerman 2000).

Data from enterprise surveys were used to argue that the "rent-seeking bureaucrats" raised the cost of doing business, particularly in the CIS (EBRD 2005). The BEEPS data also showed that the level of state intervention in corporate management was associated with the level of corruption (Hellman and Schankerman 2000; Iwasaki and Suzuki 2007).

There is little doubt that corruption was rife, but the validity of such conclusions is questionable. Analyzing the World Bank's corruption perception indexes, Goel and Budak (2006) demonstrated that large governments in the transition countries were in fact associated with low corruption. What is more, J.D. Brown, Earle, and Gehlbach's (2009) analysis of enterprise registries and balance sheet data in a panel of Russian manufacturing enterprises has shown that privatization had more positive effects on productivity in those Russian regions that had relatively large bureaucracies. Introducing the bureaucracy-size variable into the BEEPS sample, their study found that "larger regional and local executive bureaucracies . . . contributed positively to the post-privatization business environment, reducing wait times and lowering costs for licenses and government contracts" (279).

Moreover, an inverted U-shaped relationship between concentration of power and corruption was noticed, with more authoritarian countries such as Belarus and Uzbekistan and some Eastern European countries reporting the lowest levels of corruption (J.H. Anderson and Gray 2006, 33). This casts doubt on the view that corruption is a "major cause as well as purpose of authoritarian rule" (Åslund 2007, 215). The lower corruption levels in these countries probably should be attributed to the better prevention of economic crisis and the structure of incentives for enterprise managers and state officials (Iwasaki and Suzuki 2007, 418) rather than to the degree of authoritarian rule.

Corruption seems to have declined in most of the countries by 2005 (presumably reflecting the economic recovery). Accession into the European Union was arguably the important factor in Eastern Europe (J.H. Anderson and Gray 2006), but notable improvements were also recorded in Ukraine (cf. Hellman, Jones, and Kaufmann 2000). Somewhat unexpectedly, the progress of economic reform appeared to diminish the frequency and degree of state capture in Eastern Europe only (Iwasaki and Suzuki 2007, 399). In the CIS, the states that reestablished direct control and oversight over major enterprises, referred to in later text as order states, proved to be able to prevent state capture (418; see Chapters 9 and 15).

RULE OF LAW

The advantage of using government revenue and spending as indicators of state capacity as presented in the preceding text is that it is clear what they measure, but these are only indirect proxies. They indicate the extent of institutional collapse, but its effects on the rule of law can only be assumed. Figure 7.3 shows a composite index of the rule of law, developed by the World Bank to measure the extent to which people and economic actors have confidence in and abide by the rules of society. The focus is on the quality of property rights, contract enforcement, the police, and the courts and on the likelihood of crime and violence.[2]

[2]The measure is constructed as a weighted average of the sources for each country as the best estimate of the rule of law for that country. The weights are proportional to the reliability of each source. The resulting estimates of governance have an expected value (across countries) of zero and a standard deviation (across countries) of 1. This implies that virtually all scores lie between—2.5 and 2.5, with higher scores corresponding to better outcomes (see Kaufmann, Kraay, and Mastruzzi 2009).

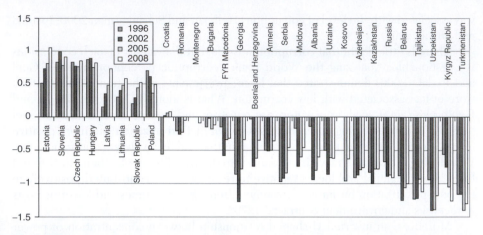

Figure 7.3 Rule of law, 1996 to 2008. (*Source:* Data in Kaufmann, Kraay, and Mastruzzi (2009).)

The measure is based on expert assessments, and its precise meaning is thus difficult to interpret (cf. Kaufmann, Kraay, and Mastruzzi 2009). Nevertheless, it indicates major differences and broader trends in the period from 1996 to 2008; comparative data for earlier periods are not available. In general, the rule of law has improved across the board in the 2000s. Official statistics in the CIS, however, show a doubling of the crime rate in Russia and Kyrgyzstan in the period from 1988 to 1992, in contrast to more gradual increases in Turkmenistan and Uzbekistan (Mikhailovskaya 1994).

The improvement was particularly rapid in the Baltic republics, which effectively caught up with the CEECs. Significant improvements have also been reported in the SEECs. Russia, along with Kyrgyzstan and Moldova, reported deterioration in the rule of law, but the Russian situation was more complex. As will be shown in Chapter 8, this period saw progress in the process of state consolidation that was made possible by the apparent abuse of state power. In this process, the legislative base and institutional infrastructure of the legal system improved considerably, giving rise to a "dual legal system . . . in which the courts can be relied on to handle mundane cases, but are likely to bow to the will of the powerful in touchier cases" (Hendley 2009, 340).

These indicators of the rule of law are well correlated with those of legal protection of property rights and institutional provisions for the private sector, which are used as indicators in a comparative study by the Bertelsmann Foundation. In this context, only Kazakhstan and Armenia exhibited relatively good protection of property rights and the private sector in the context of a poor rule of law (Bertelsmann Stiftung 2008). Again, these judgments are based on the subjective opinions of experts, but the available evidence tends to confirm the gap between Eastern Europe and CIS countries, with other transition countries frequently falling between the two groups.

STRATEGIC CAPACITY

Under state Socialism, strategic capacity of the state was increasingly limited by inertia among political leaders and by fear of popular opposition. Thus, alongside the weakness of a legal state and the absence of a state able to regulate a market system, there was little of an analogy to the developmental state of East Asian countries. If one were desired for the post-transition period, it would have to be created.

The creation of a market economy with a minimal role of the state as preferred by the neoliberal reformers also required an active state capable of designing and implementing market reforms, most notably privatization. Academic environments of Central European capitals, as well as that of Moscow, were a breeding ground for the young liberal intelligentsia that staffed reform teams. Soviet peripheries including CARs, the Caucasus, and the Baltic republics lacked such cadres.[3] Policy makers, except those who were most resistant to ideas from outside for a transition strategy, were thus much more open to advice coming from the IFIs as well as to more idiosyncratic influences. In the Baltic republics, for example, the lack of available expertise was an important concern justifying the choice for fixed exchange rate arrangements through currency boards and a currency peg in Latvia—meaning that they gave up the option to pursue an independent monetary policy. These arrangements were found suitable also because they were less demanding in terms of expert knowledge than the full-fledged central banks (cf. Alonso-Gamo et al. 2002; Knöbl, Sutt, and Zavoiceo 2002).

Figure 7.4 presents one of the expert-based indicators of strategic capacity for 2008, referred to by the Bertelsmann Foundation as "steering capability," as well as an indicator of infrastructural power, referred to as "basic administration." It shows that Eastern European laggards were able to catch up in strategic capacity. The steering capability indicator, however, is far from perfect, as it also reflects the normative beliefs of the experts about the policies implemented, thus arguably pushing down Belarus and Russia and pushing up Georgia and the Baltic republics. Nevertheless, the broad picture is of higher levels of strategic capacity in Eastern Europe and low levels in most CIS countries.

WHAT EXPLAINS THE DIFFERENCES?

Having established the differences in state capacities and the rule of law, this section sets out the background factors that led to those differences. They are very similar to the factors that led to differences in economic policies and performances, as outlined in preceding chapters, with economic performance during the transformation depression also proving to be important. The differences can be explained by five groups of factors: political systems and structures, economic effects of transformation, the level of economic development, the sectoral composition of the economy, and the pull of the European Union.

First, there were important differences in political systems and structures. In Russia and other CIS countries, controls on the old elite were weak, and it was

---

[3]At the border of Europe and Asia, the Caucasus refers to a region located between the Black and Caspian Seas. It includes Armenia, Azerbaijan, Georgia, and a number of Russian regions.

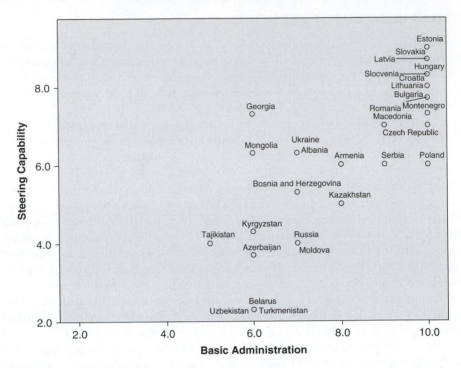

Figure 7.4 Steering capability and basic administration, 2008. (*Source:* Bertelsmann Stiftung (2008).)

possible for elements of that elite to profit from the weakness of those controls. Eastern Europe moved more quickly to a clear separation of economic from political power and to clearer forms of control over those with political power. Historically, divisions between the dominant groups and the pressure from other interests in society proved to be crucial sources of state autonomy (Rueschemeyer and Evans 1985, 63). In the context of transition, differences in elite strategies toward the state were also an important factor.

Russian elite groups, as has been often argued (e.g., Yakovlev 2006), were not confronted by a counter-elite that would protect the general interest and resist the tendency among the old elite to destroy public institutions. The old elite in Russia was much more successful in converting its positions in the old system into power or wealth in the new system than were political elites in Eastern Europe, which were largely replaced by individuals rising from outside the old power structures, the so-called technocratic intelligentsia (Szelenyi and Szelenyi 1995; Hanley, Yershova, and Anderson 1995; Frydman, Murphy, and Rapaczynski 1998; Eyal, Szelenyi, and Townsley 1998). There was, of course, even more continuity in the CARs, where the old elite groups retained their control of the state (Collins 2006) without promoting its disintegration.

The situation clearly differed from that in Russia in Belarus, Uzbekistan, Turkmenistan, and initially also in Tajikistan, where the elites opted to defend their control of the state and to recentralize state control over enterprises. This helped to prevent the collapse of the state and also limited corruption (Iwasaki and Suzuki 2007). Elite strategies apparently reflected differences in elite social structures between the few principal urban centers (most notably Moscow and St. Petersburg) and in the Soviet regions. While the former became the crucial constituency for the regime change, elites in the latter were much more conservative, with their mindsets shaped by their predominantly rural backgrounds (Vishnevsky 1999; Ioffe 2004, 107–8).[4] The views of Moscow liberals thus did not have much of a following in countries like Belarus.

The point in Russia was that within a demoralized and disorientated elite, the conviction grew that they would do better under capitalism and as individual capitalists (Dobbs 1997, 373–74). Thus, the elite abandoned its own system (Kotz and Weir 2007, 107–10). As part of that, they tried to rid themselves of centralized control mechanisms that were restraining their pursuit of control over the property earlier managed by the old Soviet bureaucratic establishment. There was thus no demand for the rule of law that would impose undesirable restrictions on the participants of the "big fight" (Pistor 1999). Similar pressures existed also in other transition countries (e.g., Staniszkis 1991; Hankiss 1990; Baylis 1994; Higley, Kullberg, and Pakulski 1996), but they were held in check in CEECs by mechanisms controlling those in power.

One of these was the rise of political movements—both Social Democratic and liberal—that took their cue from European experience. These confronted and also largely replaced old elites, particularly as far as the political positions were concerned. This ensured a greater separation of economic from political power. An early sign was opposition to spontaneous privatization in Poland and Hungary (see later text, p. 245), reflecting a more active media and a more active political life, including the role of Poland's Solidarity trade union, which functioned as an umbrella over the parties implementing economic transformation. This helped ensure that reform could not simply be a means to allow fortunate individuals to enrich themselves; a wider social dimension had to be recognized.

In other CEECs, independent interest representation was recognized in tripartite structures bringing together trade unions, employers, and governments. Their influence varied depending on governments and the power of trade unions, but these structures emerged more quickly and played bigger roles, especially in social and employment policy, than in CIS countries. The differences are discussed in a number of studies (e.g., Phelan 2007; Kubicek 2004; Crowley and Ost 2001). These confirm the extent of the span from countries in which trade unions could not raise an independent voice to, at the other extreme, Slovenia, in which governments saw the need for the maintenance of social dialogue and for discussion with representatives of social interests over important economic policies. Thus, a more pluralistic and open political life was linked to the development of a state that maintained, or developed, its capacity rather than abdicating in the face of rising new business interests.

These differences in political developments were reflected in differences in the impacts of antistatist ideologies that were popular in the CIS and in Eastern Europe (cf. Appel 2004; Drahokoupil 2008a; Miller and Tenev 2007, 556–57). In some CEECs (as discussed in Chapter 13), the mass privatization and the lack of will to exercise actual control over state assets hampered enterprise restructuring and undermined the quality of corporate governance, but it did not threaten the stability of states. In

---

[4]The main driving force in the Baltic republics was different; the opposition to the Soviet rule was an attempt at national liberation from the imperial rule.

the Russian context (as discussed in Chapter 8), the disintegration of the state helped those from the old elite wanting to take power and property for themselves.

The party-state elite, as Gel'man (2009) argued, found common ideological ground with neoliberal reformers, who advocated minimizing the state's role. Regionalization was also convenient in undermining the enemies of neoliberal policies (i.e., the Communist Party in the federal parliament) and in shifting responsibility for carrying out unpopular policies. State disintegration through decentralization was also backed by the proponents of a self-governing ideology (Yabloko and liberal parties), who interpreted the elimination of the Soviet legacy of centralism as democratization, even though it left autocratic power structures within regions.

The second groups of factors explaining differences in the development of state capacities cover the economic effects of transformation leading to different fiscal shocks for the state. As analyzed in previous chapters, there were important differences in the depths and lengths of transformation depressions. The problem was exacerbated as many firms coped by switching to hard-to-tax strategies such as barter (see Chapter 11). In addition, trade liberalization cut off important streams of revenue for the state from tariffs and from the profits of state-owned monopoly trading companies. As a result, tax revenues declined even more drastically than the GDP.

The level of development and the sectoral structure of the economy constitute the third group of factors influencing state capacity and opportunities for transition adjustment. Richer countries, meaning especially the CEECs that recovered more quickly from the transformation depression, could develop more effective state administrations that were better equipped to adjust to the introduction of the market economy, giving them the capacity to raise revenue through direct taxation of income as well as by monitoring and taxing emerging economic activities, including small businesses (e.g., O'Dwyer 2006). Thus, GDP was a major predictor of state capacity.

Fourth, economic structures also influenced opportunities for raising taxation, shaping the incentives for the state to develop capacities that enabled monitoring, regulating, and thus also taxing the respective leading sectors (cf., Shafer 1994). States could then be expected to respond primarily to the needs of those enterprises or sectors that they were able to tax effectively. More specifically, the prominence of large enterprises and heavy industries, including natural resource extraction in some CIS countries, led to a concentration on the taxation of large taxpayers, effectively allowing a continuation of the old practices for raising revenues (Gehlbach 2008a).

Eastern European states, in contrast, were less reliant on a few large enterprises in heavy industry, but this was compensated for by their ability to develop new tax systems (Easter 2002; Gehlbach 2008a). This seemed to have implications for how the state distributed collective goods and public services. The provision of collective goods to enterprises in the CIS—measured as satisfaction with public agencies or services such as police, justice, government, electricity, and water (Gehlbach 2008a, 89, 97)—was primarily determined by the degree to which they hid revenues (with the small enterprises in the new economy the least likely to report their turnover), by firm size, and by monopoly status. These were much less significant in Eastern Europe, where factors such as the degree of collective organization mattered (94–113). The poor provision of collective goods to the new sectors in the CIS could discourage migration of capital into these very activities, effectively further undermining incentives of politicians to provide them with institutional support (cf. Gehlbach 2008a, Chapter 5).

A high representation in an economy of profitable raw-material-exporting industries, especially oil and gas, had further implications for economic development, as it created new opportunities for those with political power. It is often argued that natural resource endowments are prone to give rise to "rentier states," effectively facilitating the perpetuation of resource-led development (Karl 1997). Such states focus on monitoring, regulating, and promoting the few critical firms, failing to provide institutional support to, and respond to the needs of, other sectors. Capital and, to a lesser extent, labor concentrate in the privileged sector, which thus tends to get even more support from the state. Long-term benefits from investment in human capital are likely to be ignored because of the immediate benefits offered by supporting the natural resource sector (Gylfason 2001). The availability of natural resources also provides opportunities for rent seeking in the government and the elite, having a negative effect on economic performance (Bardhan 1997).

Raw material export thus can support an autocratic elite and can enable its members to enrich themselves and to finance state spending without facing pressure for public representation and accountability, which would be likely if they had to tax the population (see Bräutigam [2008]). Other actors, lacking voice in the autocratic environment, are then left unsupported, struggling with corrupt state machines (cf. Gylfason 2001; Kalyuzhnova, Kutan, and Yigit 2009).

The so-called Dutch disease, whereby raw material exports raise the exchange rate and harm the prospect of other industries, is not easy to demonstrate for CIS countries (Kronenberg 2004; but see Merlevede, Schoors, and Aarle [2009] and our earlier discussion, p. 77), but the rentier-state effects led to similar outcomes. Natural resource endowments were thus associated with a neglect of education and with higher corruption, with negative implications for growth of other activities (Kronenberg 2004; cf. Franke, Gawrich, and Alakbarov 2009; Kim 2003).

The last but not least important factor explaining different levels of state capacity is the pull of the European Union, prompting the Eastern European countries to restructure, rather than simply cut back, their states, increasing their bureaucratic capacity and the rule of law (e.g., J.H. Anderson and Gray 2006). Requirements for accession into the European Union clearly played a major role in encouraging many countries to harmonize their tax systems with those of the European Union (Martinez-Vazquez and McNab 2000; Appel 2006). The direct influence of EU conditionalities on the rule of law and the quality of governance may have been more limited, with the political elites able to instrumentalize the vaguely framed requirements (O'Dwyer 2006; cf. Grabbe 2006). A 2005 WB survey thus reported little progress in judicial reform and strengthening, with few signs of the new member states catching up with the old members and idiosyncratic variations from country to country (J.H. Anderson, Bernstein, and Gray 2005).

However, the European Union did exercise some leverage over the laggard states, prompting them to implement institutional reforms after 2002 (Grzymala-Busse 2007). Bulgaria became a notorious example of the difficulties in enforcing such anticorruption measures. Because of repeated failures to curb high-level corruption and organized crime, the European Commission suspended €487 million of aid in July 2007. Several senior officials were then sacked, more than 150 investigations were launched, and a law to prevent conflict of interest was approved. The commission then unfroze part of the funds, but skepticism remained about the effectiveness of tackling the widespread corruption in the judicial system, in business, and in political life (Hope and Petrov 2009; Petrov and Hope 2009).

CONCLUSION

Geography and inherited political economic structures had major roles in conditioning the transformation of the states, as was the case with transition and its outcomes in general. Structural factors largely constrained possibilities, but specific policies mattered. First, the antistatist policies of neoliberal reformers had very different implications depending on the context, but in all cases, they led to weakening the capacity of the state to play new roles and address challenges of transition. Second, as discussed in Chapters 4 through 6, economic shocks that weakened the capacity of the state and its fiscal situation have been associated with WC strategies. As a consequence, the states that have avoided such policies, such as Belarus and Uzbekistan, were able to retain higher levels of state capacity. Finally, as will be discussed in Chapter 8, political strategies had an important role in the processes of state capacity consolidation.

The chapters that follow investigate the transformation of the state in more detail. Chapter 8 analyzes the process of state capacity breakdown and consolidation. Looking at the political and economic processes that are hidden behind the quantitative indicators, it also investigates the links between state capacity and political regime consolidations. Chapter 9 then analyzes the actual economic roles of the state, and Chapter 10 deals with its social role.

CHAPTER EIGHT

State Consolidation: Russia in a Comparative Perspective

The indicators in the previous chapter of the strength and effectiveness of states showed consistent differences between countries. In fact, states were subject to enormous changes over time. Put in their simplest form, there were three broad courses of transformation. One, typical of Eastern Europe, was for a small degree of disorganization followed by consolidation toward a Western European model, albeit generally with a somewhat smaller state role in the economy and in social provision. Another, common in the CIS, was for a partial disintegration of the state and then, often some time later, for its reconsolidation, albeit with a substantially smaller role than in Eastern Europe. Finally, in some CIS states, most notably Belarus and Uzbekistan, there was more continuity, with the state reestablishing control over the economy as well as the political sphere, effectively preventing state capacity disintegration.

State consolidation was intertwined with the consolidation of political regimes—that is, sets of formal and informal rules and institutions regulating access to state power. On a more general level, these can be analyzed on the continuum from the totalitarian regimes to democratic ones. The structure of power in society and the distribution of resources play major roles in shaping these regimes. An overview of different patterns of state and regime consolidation and their driving forces is provided in the next section. The remainder of the chapter investigates in detail the breakdown and consolidation of the state and political regime in Russia, a country where the crisis of the state as well as its reassertion was particularly spectacular. The detailed case study reveals the reality behind the composite indicators presented in the previous chapter and shows how the outcomes were shaped by the interaction of a number of ongoing processes. These are followed in the fields of law and enforcement, capacity to raise taxes, control over regions, and corporate governance. The forces driving changes in these spheres differed. In security and enforcement, reconsolidation depended both on government decisions and on developments within business. For taxation and control over regions, reconsolidation was much more clearly a matter of a reassertion of central power. Corporate governance is a more complex case, with some open questions remaining about the driving force for change.

STATES AND POLITICAL REGIMES

The political changes of the early 1990s gave exceptional power and autonomy to the groups of reformers within the state (cf. Greskovits 1998; Lane 2005, 2008). Policies implemented, thus, generally reflected ideological preferences and strategic concerns of the domestic leaders and influential international advisors rather than that of classes or autonomous interests in civil society (cf. Drahokoupil 2008a, 88–95). One of the main concerns of the reformers was to destroy the political and economic base of the old ruling elites and to create new constituencies for the market economy, particularly through privatization. The actual nature and consequences of these policies for the nature of the state and political regimes differed depending on the context, giving rise to the familiar distinction between Eastern Europe and the CIS. Figure 8.1 shows the variety of outcomes as far as the political regimes are concerned. Relying on expert assessments, it shows the extent to which the countries developed democratic institutions and stable patterns of representation for mediating between society and the state (for details on operationalization and measurement, see Bertelsmann Stiftung [2008]).

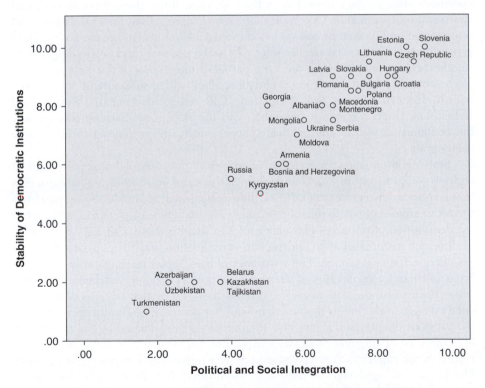

Figure 8.1 Varieties of political regimes.(*Source:* Bertelsmann Stiftung (2008).)
Notes: "Stability of democratic institutions" refers to the extent to which democratic institutions are capable of performing and are adequately accepted. "Political and social integration" refers to the extent to which stable patterns of representation exist for mediating between society and the state; this also includes a consolidated civic culture.

The factors explaining the underlying differences in state-capacity breakdown and consolidation were discussed in the previous chapter. Political regimes were shaped in closely interconnected processes, with state-capacity breakdown leading also to more political pluralism, but not necessarily to a representative democracy, as distinguished by "a participative policy process that integrates the diverse preferences of the population" (J.F. Anderson 2007, 827). Among the factors discussed previously, the pull of the European Union and the differences in political and economic structures then accounted for the different nature of consolidation in Eastern Europe and the CIS.

In Eastern Europe, it took a form of state-capacity building and democratic consolidation, intertwined with the process of class formation, in which control of productive assets became a source of social power. The outcome is close to a Western European model, albeit with some specific features. Labor remained a weak political actor (Kubicek 2004; Ost 2005; Phelan 2007). A new property class took shape, but its structural position and power was specific due to the heavy dependence on transnational capital (Drahokoupil 2008a, 2008b). Formal democracy found a stable anchor in the EU institutions but with periodic concerns about the fragility of democracy in the region. Even after some years, there were instances of the electoral rise of extremist and populist parties, political radicalization on both sides of the main political cleavage, unstable governments, increases in violent protests and attacks on minorities, and occasional violations of democratic rules and standards (see the special issue of the *Journal of Democracy* [2007]). Comparative historical evidence suggests that the relative weakness of labor as a political actor may be one factor explaining the weakness of democracy in the region (Ost 2005, 2009; cf. Rueschemeyer, Stephens, and Stephens 1992).

The CIS states followed a different pattern. Disintegration of the old regimes and the collapse of state apparatuses also opened political competition. Privatization, when implemented, gave rise to groups of "oligarchs" rather than a capitalist class. The distinction is made because owners of capital as a capitalist class owe their power to the ownership of economic assets (or control of the means of production); oligarchs, as discussed in Box 8.1, owe their power and wealth to clientelistic links with the state. The late 1990s saw processes of state-capacity reconsolidation intertwined with attempts by the political elites to consolidate their power and restrict political competition (Way 2005). In the context of oligarchic capitalism, consolidation of the state required building a strong presidential formal organization allowing for the subordination of oligarchs to state power.

Box 8.1   Russian oligarchs

The term "oligarch" is widely used to refer to Russia's richest businessmen. It reflects the privileged position of a few "clientelistic capitalists" (King and Szelenyi 2005), particularly in their heyday in the late 1990s. In the 1990s, the number of oligarchs was estimated to be only about 25 to 30 people, with most of them well known to the public (e.g., Kryshtanovskaya and White 2003). Oligarchs built their business empires by making use of their links to state officials, allowing them to obtain various sources of income—including government subsidies, preferential access to foreign exchange, allocation of export quotas, and provision of preferential import tariffs—and also state property. Thus, they typically made their first millions through commodity trading, importing scarce goods or financing brokering (Rutland 2010). The origins of some of the most prominent oligarchs, including Mikhail Khodorkovsky, could be traced to the so-called Komsomol economy organized by the officials of the Communist Union of Youth. They benefited from the privileges that allowed them to travel and to move money and goods in and out of the country. The banks run by the "kids of Komsomol" are also believed to have organized transfers of the billions of dollars held by the Communist Party to private foreign bank accounts (Hoffman 2002, 125).

Often unable to transfer ownership to themselves, those with political positions established patron-client relationships with businessmen, who then supported their patrons in their political careers and gave them access to consumption and wealth. Such patterns were reproduced on a smaller scale around the executive offices in regions and cities. The most influential oligarchs dominating the scene in the 1990s—the so-called seven bankers—were connected to the highest executive offices in Russia: the president (Yeltsin) and the mayor of Moscow (Luzhkov). The seven bankers included Boris Berezovsky (Sibneft; also controlled major media outlets), Vladimir Potanin (United Export-Import Bank, Interros metals), Mikhail Khodorkovsky (Yukos Oil, Menatep bank), Vladimir Gusinsky (Most bank; also controlled major television stations and other media), Alexander Smolensky (Bank Stolichny), Vladimir Vinogradov (Inkombank), and Mikhail Fridman/Peter Aven (Alpha Group). By the late 1990s, the "big seven" controlled 70 percent of Moscow's press and radio and 80 percent of national television (Goldman 2003, 2).

The loans-for-shares privatization program provided a major boost to the oligarchs (for details on the scheme, see Chapter 13). It was widely interpreted as a payback for the financial and media support the seven bankers provided to Yeltsin in the 1996 elections. The oligarchs emerged with their previous power as bankers transformed into control over key enterprises, most notably in the raw-material sector, acquired at prices well below any serious estimate of their values. Subsequent deals in later years, often secretive and just as blatantly manipulated to help favorites, further increased their power over key exporting enterprises. By the end of the 1990s, more than 50 percent of the economy's output was estimated to be concentrated in only ten "integrated business groups" controlled by an oligarch (Pappe 2000).

In order to succeed, Putin's state-building project had to tame the power of oligarchs. A deal was allegedly struck between the oligarchs and the administration in 2000, giving immunity from prosecution over privatization to the businesses that refrained from meddling in politics (cf. Hanson and Teague 2005; Tompson 2005). State power was used against those not willing to comply, starting with the oligarchs who were controlling major media outlets. In May 2001, Gusinski and his media empire were attacked; the state-controlled gas monopoly Gazprom led a hostile takeover of his group. Charged with embezzlement and money laundering, Gusinski fled to Spain. The authorities also closed down TV-6, which was controlled by Berezovsky, who was charged with embezzlement and money laundering and fled to the United Kingdom.

Khodorkovsky, chairman of Yukos, clashed with Putin over taxation, energy policy, and possibly also over selling a minority stake in his company to a U.S. oil firm (Yakovlev 2006, 1046; Sim 2008, 66–71). Khodorkovsky provided financial support to Putin's political opponents and gave the impression of being prepared to challenge Putin directly in the run for presidency. In his efforts to resist Putin, he also launched an international public-relations and lobbying campaign involving senior officials of the Bush Sr. administration (King and Treskow 2006, 88). Khodorkovsky was arrested in July 2003, found guilty of fraud, and sentenced in May 2005 to nine years imprisonment. Yukos was forced into bankruptcy and then sold to a state-controlled company. Charges against Khodorkovsky included fraudulent activities during privatization, contract killings, and tax evasion. Similarly to the charges raised against Gusinski and Berezovsky, there was evidence to support the accusations, but similar cases could have been constructed against many other prominent businessmen.

The Yukos affair seemed to represent a "comprehensive victory" of the state in the conflict with oligarchs (Yakovlev 2006, 1046). However, many oligarchs of the 1990s, such as Oleg Deripaska (Rusal aluminium), profited from the co-optation by those in power. In fact, the affair marked an end to the era of the oligarchic family around Yeltsin, but it did not lead to a shift from the clientelistic model. At the same time, oligarchs as a social group underwent important transformations. The financial crisis of 1998 was a significant blow to the Moscow bankers. The destruction of the media empires of Berezovsky and Gusinsky forced oligarchs out of the media. After the crisis, "the 'old' oligarchs of the Yeltsin period retired into shadows, yielding their place to a new generation of entrepreneurs" (Kryshtanovskaya and White 2005, 302), who learned to be more cautious and loyal to the leadership, preferring to relate to the state through intermediaries rather than directly.

The industrial enterprises emerged much more prominently in the period of recovery, increasing the representation of entrepreneurs from the regions among the economic elite. The political stability and economic growth of the Putin presidency allowed them to increase their wealth. The oligarchs benefited from the sustained boom in oil and metal prices and the soaring stock market, largely financed by foreign investors. The increasing involvement of the state in the economy also gave rise to "state oligarchs," whose power to extract resources under their management matched that of real owners (Rutland 2010). Business groups often also benefited from increased state-ownership stakes, as these brought them higher credit ratings (Malle 2009, 261–62).

The oligarchs thus became a larger and more diverse group of people, and they seemed to lack the means to challenge the state power directly. What did not change, however, was the merging of state and business in the clientelistic relationships of mutual dependence. According to the *Forbes* list, the number of individuals from Russia with personal assets above $1 billion rose from 33 in 2006 to 87 in spring 2008 (Rutland 2010, 171). This number dropped significantly only a couple of months later—not because of a political misfortune but due to the global financial crisis.

There was a considerable variation (see Figure 8.1). Some of the regimes could be characterized as "competitive authoritarianisms" (Levitsky and Way 2002). In such a regime, democratic rules were routinely manipulated, but, rather than openly violating the rules, the authorities opted for more subtle forms of persecution to harass critics into cooperative behavior. Opposition, thus, remained a significant challenge; this was the outcome in Russia. As discussed later, the capacity of the Russian state improved in the context of an effort to consolidate the political power of the president. Taking advantage of his networks with roots in Soviet military and enforcement ministries, Putin was successful in restricting the power of oligarchs and bringing regions under federal control.

Ukraine saw a similar pattern of state disintegration and the emergence of oligarchic groups. A form of competitive authoritarianism was consolidated at the time of Leonid Kuchma's presidency (1994 to 2005). However, his rule was not based on consolidating state power. The state was in fact very weak, and the regime was dependent on Kuchma's balancing of support from oligarchic groups (Kuzio 2007; Åslund 2008; Mykhnenko and Swain 2009). Following a shift of some of the oligarchic-group support to an opposition camp (Åslund 2006), Kuchma's departure in the Orange Revolution, referred to later, entailed an opening of the political system to political competition. In Belarus, in contrast, Alexander Lukashenko's victory in the 1994 elections meant an end to political and economic reforms that were associated with disintegration of the state in Russia and Ukraine. Control over the economy was reestablished and political plurality sharply curtailed.

Despite the severity of transition shocks hitting the state in CARs, the elites retained their control. Kyrgyzstan experimented with democratic reforms in the early 1990s, but personalistic authoritarian regimes controlled by "clan networks" consolidated throughout the region by the end of the 1990s (Collins 2006). These were states with low levels of capacity, which was further undermined by confrontations between rival clans, defined as "informal organization[s] comprising a network of individuals linked by kin and fictive kin identities" (cf. Collins 2006, 17; Lindholm 1986). An extreme form of patrimonalism developed in Turkmenistan, which could be characterized as a "sultanistic regime" with personalized domination and, thus, a minimal role for clans and special interest groups (Tsygankov 2007; on sultanism, see Linz and Stepan [1996, 51–54]).

Many of these authoritarian regimes met with popular pressures for democratization. This gave rise to movements that enjoyed political and financial support from external sources—particularly Western foundations supporting democratic institutions and processes (Bunce and Wolchik 2006). Most notably, in several of these countries, so-called colored revolutions took place: Serbia (2000), Georgia (2003), Ukraine (2004), and Kyrgyzstan (2005; see the special issue of the *Journal of Communist Studies and Transition Politics* [2009]). These revolutions gained popular backing from dissatisfaction with corruption, the quality of governance (Tucker 2007; White 2009), and falls in living standards (Mykhnenko 2009). The outcomes, however, were often rather disappointing; the revolutions brought personnel replacements, but change in the nature of the regime was usually limited (Lane 2009).

Why was the authoritarian consolidation accomplished in some cases and not in others? Way (2005) has argued that the failure of incumbents to consolidate authoritarian political control can be explained by the presence of an "anti-incumbent national cleavage" (as was the case in Ukraine) and by the weak capacity of the incumbent, which was dependent on four factors. First, authoritarian consolidation required a strong state capacity. Countries that were able to raise revenues could finance their apparatuses. As discussed in the previous chapter, creating a tax capacity was a major challenge in the CIS. However, the oil and natural resource price bonanza beginning in 1999 provided a revenue stream to natural-resource-rich countries, allowing them to finance the authoritarian consolidation.

Second, incumbents in the countries that reestablished control over the economy, such as Belarus and Uzbekistan, did not allow an emergence of oligarchic groups or a capitalist class that would challenge them.

Third, Russia, as a large country, was less susceptible to influences from outside, which played an important role in the colored revolutions covered on p. 148.

Finally, the incumbents had to develop know-how and organization of control to consolidate the state. While this took some time in most of the cases, Russia inherited such know-how and organizational capital from the highly centralized Soviet state. It was eventually mobilized for state building when Putin took power.

STATE COLLAPSE AND CONSOLIDATION IN RUSSIA

Two crucial periods shaped the process of state collapse and reconsolidation in Russia. The first was the disintegration with—and after—the rise of Boris Yeltsin at the time of the breakup of the Soviet Union. The second was the arrival of Vladimir Putin as president at the end of 1999 and an accompanying state consolidation, although this was already in process to some extent in Yeltsin's last years.

In the first, the slow erosion of the party state culminated in 1989 to 1991 in a concentrated effort to destroy the federal state apparatus, which was shaped in a struggle between the "procapitalist coalition" around Yeltsin and the Socialist reformers led by Gorbachev (see Kotz and Weir [2007, 126–49]). The procapitalist coalition drew its support from four overlapping groups: intellectuals, economists, private businesspeople from nonelite backgrounds, and, most decisively, the party-state elite (105–25). The struggle took place against the background of the efforts of much of the existing elite to take over property controlled by the centralized party state. Allowed at the time of Gorbachev's *perestroika*, political decentralization and the undermining of central authority were driven by the interests of regional party-state elites who took control over local bureaucracies, state enterprises, and raw materials (Stoner-Weiss 2006). The unsuccessful putsch of August 1991 by the hardline members of the Communist Party against Gorbachev sealed Yeltsin's victory over Gorbachev—Yeltsin crushed the coup—and broke the power of the once-dominant elite at the federal level (Yakovlev 2008a; for information on the August Coup, see White [2000, 28–33]).

The withering away of central control gave way to the conglomerates that organized the economy by sector and region, putting them into a position to extract subsidies from the center (Burawoy 1996). In the chaos of transition, power shifted to informal networks of influence among individuals who had political connections or economic resources at their disposal (Rutland 2010). On the federal level, oligarchic groups gained privileged access to the state through their clientelistic ties with senior officials and politicians, capturing numerous opportunities to secure easy sources of income from special privileges and benefits (e.g., Yakovlev 2006, 1034). A small group of oligarchs concentrated in the Moscow banking sector gained a particularly strong influence and control over resources (see Box 8.1).

As discussed in Chapter 7, a large part of the Soviet elite managed to retain positions of power in the new order. According to one study, 61 percent of the business elite came from the *nomenklatura* elite (see p. 4, n.1). Of that group, 13.1 percent came from the party nomenklatura, 37.7 percent from the Komsomol (Young Communist League) nomenklatura, 3.3 percent from the Soviet legislative nomenklatura, 37.7 percent from the economic nomenklatura, and 8.2 percent from other parts of the nomenklatura (Kryshtanovskaya and White 1996, 729). Other studies suggest similar continuity for the political elite but less for the economic elite (Szelenyi and Szelenyi 1995; Hanley, Yershova, and Anderson 1995; Lane and Ross 1999, Chapter 9). There was certainly scope for recruitment from outside, particularly from the Soviet shadow economy. According to Goldman (2003, 117), most of those involved in such activities were members of non-Russian ethnic groups, such as Jews, Armenians, Georgians, and Muslims, who were excluded from the positions of authority.

The fiscal crisis was a symptom as well as a cause contributing to the collapse of the state in the 1990s. With budget deficits averaging 9.7 percent between 1992 and 1998 (EBRD 2001), the receipts of the consolidated budget declined from 41 percent of GDP in 1990 to only 26.8 percent in 1997, while GDP contracted by about half in the same period (Vorobyov and Zhukov 2006; EBRD 2007).[1] An investigation of large corporate taxpayers commissioned by Yeltsin in 1996 found that these enterprises paid less than 8 percent of their tax bill with money; 63 percent was paid in the form of offsets and bartered goods, and 29 percent was not paid at all (Karpov [1997], in Gaddy and Gale [2005, 984]). Even some of the transfers and remittances between different bodies of the state apparatus were settled with noncash offsets and barter, effectively denying the federal budget cash revenues to pay public-sector employees and pensioners and to meet other fiscal responsibilities (Woodruff 1999, 130–37).

The second period that shaped the process of state collapse and reconsolidation in Russia, the reconsolidation phase, depended on new political priorities. It also reflected changes in society. In the business sphere, there was pressure from owners to secure their positions with a firmer legal framework. The devaluation following the 1998 crisis raised the profile of the productive enterprises relative to those involved in finance and financial dealings. The crisis also brought forward middle-range bureaucrats with long-term career interests, unbound by previous networks and, therefore, looking for more regularized forms of state activity (Yakovlev 2008a). The collapse of welfare programs (discussed in Chapter 10) and the economic hardship and suffering inflicted upon most of the population throughout the 1990s also created a popular demand for a strong state and the rule of law, supplanting the discourse of individualism and freedom that was popular in the early 1990s.

Putin's success capitalized on these sentiments, but it was by no means pre-determined. On the contrary, handpicked by the family of oligarchs around Yeltsin

---

[1] In August 1998, the government was not able to sustain borrowing any more, defaulted on its rouble debt, and implemented a four-fold devaluation, triggering the major financial crisis.

(Kryshtanovskaya and White 2003), Putin was seen as a part of Yeltsin's corrupt inner circle and, thus, fared very poorly in the polls. An attack by Chechen fighters on Dagestan and deadly September 1999 bombings in two Moscow apartment buildings allowed Putin to rally around war and nationalism and to mobilize massive popular support.[2] After his election in March 2000, the Russian superpresidential system allowed him to pursue virtually any policy (Fish 2005). He relied on support from very influential networks with backgrounds in the military and power ministries (the so-called *siloviki*). This, along with the massively growing popular support, gave him a greater degree of independence from business than that enjoyed by the Yeltsin regime. This was a precondition for the shift to applying general rules across business rather than yielding to lobbying from individual businesses. At the same time, it was not a complete change from the clientelistic regime organizing the relationships between the state and business.

The political strategy for reconstruction included the legal prosecution of those who resisted the state-building project and/or supported political opposition, including the so-called inner-circle oligarchs—Boris Berezovsky, Vladimir Gusinsky, and Mikhail Khodorkovsky. Putin also neutralized potential resistance in the regions by co-opting local strongmen through direct appointments, with regional and local authorities making pacts with financial-industrial groups, despite their criminal origins. Where he failed, the uncooperative groups were removed through criminal investigations, effectively mobilizing the coercive power of central authorities (Volkov 2002). In 2003 and 2004, a federal program of administrative reforms was implemented, limiting administrative discretion of executive bodies and individual officials. The reforms also introduced the idea of "conflict of interest" into the Russian law on civil service (Konov [2004], in Miller and Tenev [2007, 550]). The state was, thus, strengthened in a contradictory process in which a selective application of legal regulations challenged the property rights of new owners, but this in turn was instrumental in strengthening state institutions and, hence, it could be argued—and despite the implication of the data in Table 7.3—the rule of law.

The state consolidation under Putin was often discussed in terms of a shift from "state capture" to "business capture" (cf. Hellman, Jones, and Kaufmann 2000; Fries, Lysenko, and Polenac 2003; Yakovlev 2006), but neither term characterizes the relationships between the state and society adequately. Yeltsin did rely on certain business supporters (most notably in his 1996 reelection), but they did not dictate policy and were themselves dependent on the regime. In fact, they needed support from state officials in obtaining various licenses and subsidies and in accumulating assets through privatization. The state-business relationships, as the following sections demonstrate, were more complex and took different forms, depending on the type of enterprise. Rather than capturing the state, enterprises struggled with an environment in which the state was often not functioning. Many, thus, opted for the strategy of "keeping a distance from the state" and relied on private solutions to the state's failure to deliver basic collective goods (Yakovlev 2006).

Nor is "business capture" a helpful characterization. The authorities under Putin did assert greater, and sometimes arbitrary, power over oligarchs and business in general, but there were limits to the actual capacity of the state or the officials

---

[2]There was much speculation that these were directed by Russian security forces possibly to enable Putin to enhance his popularity.

to bring private business under their control. First, major Russian enterprises had undergone the process of internationalization, in which a large part of their assets and activities were brought outside of the Russian national jurisdiction. At the same time, many businesses had entered into strategic alliances with foreign partners, some of them also launching public offerings on foreign equity markets. Internationalization, thus, provided better exit opportunities and actual protection of property rights. Second, the state bureaucracy remained divided in the competition over resources and power, both horizontally between different government agencies and vertically between middle and top levels (Yakovlev 2006). Vertical control over regions was established, but the economic recovery after 1998 also saw a consolidation of regional conglomerates of local oligarchies in all Russian regions. Finally, business corporations were able to exert considerable direct influence on politics through their representatives in the State Duma, the lower house of parliament, and in local administrations (Kryshtanovskaya and White 2005, 303–5; Rutland 2010).

The Putin presidency, thus, marked a shift within the clientelistic regime organizing the links between politics and business. State power and central control was reestablished, with the contested nature of property rights making business vulnerable to state pressure. The state used its power against those representing a direct challenge to the leadership and began to exclude oligarchs from the media. The property rights of those remaining loyal to the leadership were not challenged. The lack of popular legitimacy of the ownership claims by the oligarchs, however, proved an important factor in limiting the possibility of them dominating over politics. As discussed in Box 8.1, the oligarchic groups themselves underwent a transformation, with membership expanding and power shifting to the industrial and financial groups in the regions. The state and business related through less-conspicuous, but firmer, clientelistic links of mutual dependence, with the merging of business and politics continuing both on the federal levels and in the regions.

LAW AND ENFORCEMENT

A major symptom of the decay of the state in the early 1990s was a surge of violence on the everyday level, with the state unable to claim a monopoly for the use of force and hence unable to arbitrate between economic actors. Violence became an essential accompaniment for much of Russia's emerging business activity and the origin of many new business leaders. This peaked in the mid-1990s; in 1995, 14,050 criminal groups were officially identified, with a total of 57,545 members (Volkov 2002, 74). Survey evidence from 1997 and 1998 showed that fully 40 percent of entrepreneurs had been subjected to threats of violence, and 11 percent admitted to using violence when they felt cheated (Radaev 2002).

The fiscal crisis was a major blow to all institutions, but the law-enforcement function suffered also from a concerted effort by the Yeltsin administration to destroy the state security services (or force-wielding ministries, *silovye ministerstva* — shortened to *siloviky*) embodying the coercive power of the Soviet state. The determination of some of these forces to defend the old regime was confirmed by their participation in the August 1991 putsch to remove Mikhail Gorbachev (see White [2000, 28–33]). The disintegration that ensued generated an outflow of personnel from security agencies, estimated at 50,000 people, who could join army veterans, former professional sportsmen, and criminals to become "violent entrepreneurs," working for various violence-managing agencies whose activities included racketeering, protection, and contract enforcement functions (Volkov 2002).

In the absence of state capacity to protect property and enforce contracts, private networks were used as a primary mechanism of conflict settlement. One survey in 1994 showed 20 percent of enterprises preferring to appeal to the state justice system, while 15 percent used "bandits" and private protection companies, and 11 percent relied on themselves to resolve disputes (Volkov 2002, 45). These were judged by the users to be faster, cheaper, and more reliable methods than using the formal authorities. In particular, new small businesses needed private protection, but even large and established enterprises became dependent on the services of criminal organizations.

The survey results suggest differences among the companies in relating to the state. Former Soviet business managers could take advantage of extensive networks with other businesspeople, as well as state officials. Large former-Soviet enterprises, thus, tended to appeal to state militia and authorities for protection, mobilizing their old networks (Radaev 2000). They were also likely to get preferential treatment, as they represented the main source of tax revenue. Paying little in taxes, new private-business operators tended to avoid the state also in dispute settlement and security provision, using private providers instead. For most of these businesses, there was little choice, as a company without an appropriate "roof"—meaning an organization paid to provide protection—was likely to be targeted by another criminal group offering its protection services under the threat of violence (Volkov 2002).

Crime rates in Russia stabilized and gradually fell from 1996. This was partly a natural process occurring as crime groups consolidated their positions, established links to the state, and moved toward legitimate activities. It was partly also a reflection of the gradual competitive success of formally recognized private security companies, often employing former employees of the police and security forces. In 1992, the government legalized private enforcement. The immediate motivation was the need to provide employment for the former staff of power ministries. The measure had important unintended consequences, leading by stages toward a partial reconstruction of the state. Private security agencies proved able to outcompete criminal syndicates, providing higher-quality services at a lower price. These groups were often created from informal private providers that took advantage of links with state agencies, giving access to the state's enforcement power. Purely criminal organizations, therefore, lacked long-term sustainability, putting pressure on them to become legal.

This allowed the state to regulate and codify the private enforcement sector, which it indeed did from 1995, thereby gaining the instruments for conflict resolution and protection of property rights. In the process of developing market consolidation by the end of the 1990s, territories controlled by syndicates were gradually connected into unified spaces and "state roofs" organized around regional power holders, typically linked to an oligarchic business group (Volkov 2002).

The efforts to rebuild this aspect of the state after the 1998 crisis thus could focus on targeting a limited number of unified roofs. Consolidation of the private protection market gradually brought private operators within the scope of new regulations, reinforcing the rule of law as well as cooptation by the state. This, then, was not simply a matter of a more effective and assertive state. Consolidation also reflected developments within the businesses as they worked to rules that limited and regulated violence. They not only realized the need to protect what were often their past victims, but they also reacted to the need for protecting assets they accumulated and often invested in "standard businesses." However, the reassertion of the state in these areas of property-rights protection and conflict management left many protection functions privatized. The reassertion of state authority was, therefore, still constrained by the effects of its previous disintegration.

FISCAL CAPACITY

Economic shocks of the 1990s were only one of the factors contributing to the fiscal crisis of the state. Crucially, the state lacked administrative resources to monitor economic activities and collect taxes, even though the State Tax Service had been established in 1991 and the Federal Tax Authority in 1992. With unrecorded cash turnover constituting the most common means of tax evasion, the state was virtually unable to tax the rapidly growing base of small businesses. Criminal agencies and security providers were quick to step in to tax the unreported turnover in a very effective way (Volkov 2002). A coherent framework of tax laws was only enacted in the 1998 to 2002 period. Before that, central and regional governments could set and change tax rules arbitrarily and negotiate their application. As a consequence, the official combined tax rate on business rose enormously, exceeding 100 percent according to some estimates (Dolgopiatova [1998], in Volkov [2002, 175]). As compliance was a practical impossibility, consistent application of tax regulation could, thus, function as a form of punishment or as an instrument of coercion, giving the authorities considerable blackmail power. Personal connections could completely alter tax obligations (Easter 2006; Turley 2006). It is estimated that tax exemptions and concessions reached 7 percent of GDP in Russia by 1996 (Grafe and Richter 2001).

The actual tax levy was in effect negotiated between the firms, regional governments, the federal administration, and the criminal agencies, each competing for their share from tax collection (Busse 2000; Volkov 2002, 173–78). In the medium- and small-enterprise sector, the regional and local tax authorities competed with private violence-managing agencies, with the hidden part of turnover taxed by the latter. The large-enterprise sector was targeted by federal authorities that competed with regional and local governments; the latter often endorsed barter, which was difficult for federal authorities to monitor and, thus, tax (as discussed in Woodruff [2000]). The lack of a clear single authority and the resulting competition among several actors reduced the effective tax rate to 10 to 30 percent, comparable to what was charged in the informal sector (Paneyakh [2000], in Volkov [2002, 177]).

In 1996—and, therefore, with Yeltsin still in power—the federal authorities established an Emergency Tax Commission to coerce tax collection in cash. As a result, 1997 saw a 61 percent increase in tax debt collection, reestablishing the priority of Moscow over regional tax authorities. However, this could not prevent the practice of personal negotiations over taxation (as suggested by Woodruff [2000]).

The 1998 financial crisis prompted the Yeltsin government to implement an enterprise tax reform and stabilize the fiscal flows between the federal and regional governments. With a recovery of energy prices, the government began to enforce tax payments from Gazprom and the large petroleum exporters. Tax exemptions were cut, tax revenues increased, and the federal government started to reduce its own payment arrears (IMF 2000a, 59–74). The reform of the fiscal system gathered momentum under Putin with a complete overhaul and simplification of the tax system: A flat tax replaced the progressive income tax system (see discussion in Chapter 9), a unified regressive social tax replaced separate social taxes, the corporate tax rate was lowered and many loopholes were closed, turnover taxes were eliminated, and a mineral-extraction tax was introduced. The budgetary reforms improved the capacity of the Ministry of Finance to control and implement budget policy across individual ministries and state-owned companies (Parker and Thornton 2007, 530–31).

New regulations, however, would have made little difference had they not been accompanied by reforms increasing state administrative capacity and strengthening the state overall. These included the training of tax officials and the introduction of personal tax identification numbers. What is more, this also involved the strengthening of the coercive institutions, including the tax police, which contributed to greater compliance with tax laws (Appel 2008).

Importantly, Putin was in a position to confront oligarchs who controlled the oil and gas sector, the most important source of revenue. Oligarchs, however, were not enthusiastic about complying with the tax legislation, effectively insisting on continuing the old practice of tax avoidance by taking advantage of legal loopholes and various preferential treatments. The oligarch-controlled oil companies—most notably Yukos, Sibneft, and the TNK (Alpha Group)—paid much less taxes than the companies controlled by the state or privatized by management from the oil sector (King and Treskow 2006, 80). Yukos's chairman Mikhail Khodorkovsky continued to pressure the government against the attempts to tax the energy sector, and he was successful in stopping a 2002 law to raise oil excise tax in the Duma (Easter 2006, 45). The nationalization of Yukos not only stopped Khodorkovsky (see Box 8.1) but also sent a strong and well-understood signal to other large businesses, encouraging them to pay taxes and to avoid taking advantage of existing loopholes (Hanson and Teague 2005, 664; Easter 2006). This did not solve all problems in monitoring oil companies (Rossiaud and Locatelli 2009), but it allowed the state to benefit from the surge in hydrocarbon prices in the early 2000s (Appel 2008).

CONTROLLING REGIONALISM

The regional dimension played a crucial role in the collapse and consolidation of the Russian state. Fiscal decentralization and recentralization were closely linked to the disintegration and subsequent improvement of state fiscal capacity (Parker and Thornton 2007, 528–31). Gorbachev's reforms in the 1980s loosened oversight over regions, which had enjoyed different administrative status but had been tightly subordinated to the center through the vertically integrated Soviet power structures. The weakening of central control gave regional elites the opportunity to grab state assets for themselves and to consolidate control over local bureaucracies, state enterprises, and raw materials (Solnick 1998). The interest of the former regional power structures in keeping control over key assets has been seen as the major driving force for regionalism, leading to a complete breakdown of the Soviet institutional order in a number of regions (Stoner-Weiss 2006).

Gorbachev tried to maintain central control with the use of force but succeeded only in encouraging anti-Soviet movements, often mobilizing over issues of nationality and ethnicity. Yeltsin then struck bilateral deals with individual regional leaders, exchanging regional autonomy for political support at the federal level (Treisman 1999). As a result, the ability of the center in Moscow to enforce its decisions and rules and to extract resources from regions became very limited. In 1993, 20 regions out of 89 did not meet their tax remittance obligations (Wallich 1994b). Some regions even prohibited the Federal Treasury from opening local branches (Rutland, Gitelman, and Sakwa 2005). The turning point came in the 1999 elections when the major regional leaders, such as Moscow's Yury Luzhkov and Tatarstan's Mintimer Shaimaiev, and allied interest groups took part in an electoral bloc, which suffered electoral defeat by a Kremlin-backed bloc. Some of the regional leaders then began to desert the bloc of regional leaders to join the camp of the victor. The regional leaders, thus, lost the ability to formulate and assert a collective interest and could do little to hinder the recentralization that ensued (Gel'man 2009).

The regional reform aimed to reassert state capacity through the subordination of regions. It was intended to lead to an improvement of delivery at the central level—through loyal regional elites—and to increase administrative capacity through the acquisition of the resource bases of regional elites. In the first phase, federal districts were created as a tool to monitor regional compliance.

Putin also changed the composition of the Federal Council of Russia, the upper house of the parliament of the Russian Federation. This meant a sharp decline in the influence of regional elites on central policy making (Gel'man 2009, 10). Further, the president was given power to remove elected officials in certain circumstances. In 2002, budgetary reforms integrated extrabudgetary funds—such as the pension, social welfare, employment, medical insurance, and roads funds—into a consolidated treasury system, eliminating regional control over these funds (Parker and Thornton 2007, 230). Budget reforms also transferred most revenue-raising authority to the federal level, making regions more dependent on transfers from the center.

The Putin administration used the familiar mechanisms of enforcement through the selective application of norms and sanctions as well as by striking individual deals and co-optations. Multiple, overlapping, and competing centers of power and regional patrimonies were brought under central control; the capacity of vertical steering to link central and regional administration was reestablished, and the ability to extract taxes from the provinces improved significantly (Hyde 2001; Zudin 2002; Shlapentokh 2004; Easter 2006). What is more, regionalism was virtually eliminated from political life. All regional political processes were vertically integrated, with regional parties effectively prevented from operating. Formally approved by regional elites, regional officials became de facto appointees of the center (Gel'man 2009; see also the special issue of the *Journal of Communist Studies and Transition Politics* [2010]).

The reestablishment of vertical control over the state apparatus, however, was accompanied by the consolidation of autonomous oligarchic groups in the regions, which forced out Moscow oligarchs weakened by the 1998 crisis, often expanding economically in the neighboring regions (Kryshtanovskaya and White 2005, 303–5).

CORPORATE GOVERNANCE AND PROPERTY RIGHTS

Changes in the sphere of corporate governance and private-property protection took the familiar course of a somewhat chaotic period followed by a degree of consolidation. A key initiator of the chaotic period was the mass privatization program implemented from 1992 (see Chapter 13). This was intended to create, after some concentration of ownership, a coherent system of private ownership. The architects of Russian privatization believed that the state would have no interest in providing institutions to secure property rights and corporate legality until property owners were created through privatization. As discussed in Chapter 7, the new owners were expected to form a constituency for the rule of law, exerting pressure on the state to develop the legal framework required to sustain property rights (Boycko, Shleifer, and Vishny 1995; Frye 1997; Åslund 2007; Gaidar 1999).

An opposing—and pessimistic—expectation, as put in later years, was that those who benefited from the weak rule of law had "become so powerful as to block further reform such as tax reform, government reform, stronger law enforcement, and stronger security of property rights" (Roland 2000, 337). Both of these expectations made sense from the perspective of abstract equilibrium models used by economists (Woodruff 2004), but the first found few parallels in the history of modern state formation (cf. Tilly 1990; H. Schwartz 2000). The optimistic expectation proved unrealistic in the early years, albeit with some signs of hope in later years. Roland's pessimistic expectation proved accurate on the point about taxation but ultimately less clear on the point about security of property rights.

Mass distribution of shares meant that enterprises were up for grabs at very attractive prices by expanding business groups. An inevitable result, Woodruff (2004) argued, was conflict, and conflicts ultimately had to be settled through legal processes. However, laws that might in another context function as part of a stable system of corporate governance were manipulated, with any possible loopholes found, so that they could be used by business groups to aid in the accumulation and concentration of wealth. Court decisions could also be influenced by those with money and power and were hampered by the sudden flood of cases thrust before them. Bankruptcy laws, in particular, were used to resolve conflicts over ownership (Woodruff 2004, 96); they could be used by the oligarchic business groups acting in accord with government officials to target virtually any enterprise. Government officials could freeze the bank account of an enterprise following a trumped-up charge of tax evasion or criminal activity. This allowed an allied business group to initiate bankruptcy proceedings by demanding payment of some outstanding debt, eventually enforcing a "hostile takeover" (see Goldman [2003, 32–33])

In Woodruff's view, the key point was not the inadequacy of laws; they could be derived from foreign examples and implemented after the best available advice. However, in no country are they free from all ambiguities. Moreover, an enormous volume and intensity of conflict developed out of the outcome of Russian privatization. By way of contrast, there were far fewer conflicts in countries with more straightforward methods of privatization, such as Hungary's emphasis on direct sales to foreigners, or in which interests were better represented in deciding over privatization, as in Poland, where management or the council of employees had a veto right. The implication for Russia is that rising business groups had no interest in plugging the loopholes in corporate governance laws that they were using to concentrate wealth in their own hands. However, once they were successful, so it is argued, their views could change, as they were not eager to see others repeating their accomplishments. Many oligarchs, thus, became active promoters of the rule of law and private-property protection, supporting 2002 changes in corporate governance regulations, which closed many of the loopholes (Medvedeva, Timofeev, and Iukhnin [2003], in Woodruff [2004, 46]).

In the same period, however, the Yukos affair (see Box 8.1) demonstrated the ability of the Putin administration to challenge ownership gains by selectively applying charges only against businesses targeted for other reasons (as indicated in Hanson and Teague [2005]). The authorities could, thereby, use their ability to influence court decisions to reassert their power over any oligarch that acted against the interest or desires of those in power. This probably explains the poor performance of Russia on composite rule-of-law indicators discussed in the previous chapter, although there were other benefits from this method of reconsolidation of the state that the quantitative indicators do not capture.

In sum, the state consolidation in the corporate governance sphere depended partly on a reassertion of central state authority and partly on developments within the business sphere, where interests in maintaining loopholes declined in favor of interests in protecting property that had already been acquired. This was predominantly a Russian process. Generally, CEECs avoided such a chaotic period. The Czech Republic had some similarities, at least in the method of privatization, but the consolidation process was more clearly directed from the state, as businesses created out of voucher privatization generally failed and left the scene (Myant 2003; Drahokoupil 2008a, 82–86, 109–12). Other CIS countries also generally avoided the extent and complexity of Russia's privatization program.

CONCLUSION

Although Russia is the most studied case of the process of state collapse and reconsolidation, it is worth emphasizing its specific features. State breakdown was common across CIS countries. The old country collapsed, and new states had to be created. Internal wars led to greater breakdown, while in other cases, maintenance of power by the existing elite under a new title—as, for example, in Kazakhstan—prevented chaos in central bodies.

Russia's course was only one of those possible. The reconsolidation process was clearly driven by internal forces, reflecting internal interests. It was also complicated by the extent of regional power bases, an issue that was less important in most other countries. Putin could rely on the *siloviki* groups with roots in the centralized Soviet apparatus and subordinate oligarchs with links to state power. This constitutes a major difference, for example, from developments in Ukraine, where the executive could not take advantage of an analogous enforcement infrastructure. In several other countries, there was also a stronger tendency to accept ideas from outside—for example, on tax or corporate governance systems. These were sometimes effective but often amounted to no more than formal changes. Laws were passed but then ignored or proved difficult to operate. Thus, the balance of internal and external influences, the roles of key actors, and the degrees of authoritarian regimes varied. Nevertheless, in all cases, some kind of reconsolidation of states took place.

CHAPTER NINE

Economic Role of the State

The state plays an enormously important role in any modern economy, as indicated partly by the share in GDP raised in taxes or spent directly by government, partly by the extent of regulation and coordination of private-sector activity, and partly also by direct involvement in providing infrastructure and other elements essential to economic activity in general.

The previous two chapters focused on state capacity as linked to political regimes and the social embeddedness of the state. This chapter analyzes the specific economic roles of the state. The central theme is the policies pursued, but this is conditioned by the revenues raised. As indicated in Chapter 7, the general ability to raise taxes and the structure of taxation is an important aspect of state capacity. This chapter investigates further the structure and levels of taxation. It also analyzes the barriers to raising taxes in the post-state Socialist environment, including the so-called flat tax, which sets limits on the active role of the state.

The state and market have frequently been counterposed and the transition portrayed as primarily representing a reduction in the state's role. That obscures the extent to which a functioning market—and even more, a modern market economy—is dependent on state activity, albeit of a different kind from that of a centrally planned system. The state is, in all cases, a complex and diverse entity playing different roles in different spheres of economic and social activity. It has also played substantially different roles in economic development in different countries. A state may appear prominent in promoting economic development but play a relatively small role in the welfare sphere, as has typically been the case in east Asian countries. Referring to large, active, or interventionist states can, therefore, appear as dangerous overgeneralizations. The need is to look at the state in a disaggregated way. This chapter focuses on those activities that could be seen as directly promoting economic development, meaning education, research and development, the economic infrastructure, and the promotion of industrial development. Approaches to the state and its role in economic development are discussed in Box 9.1.

The first part of this chapter analyzes the levels of public spending and how this spending is balanced with revenues; further, it compares the roles of the state in the promotion of knowledge and the provision of infrastructure and explores state involvement in industrial development policy. The second part then looks at the revenue side in more detail; it compares tax systems and the levels of taxation.

159

Particular attention is given to the nature, the role, and the implications of the flat tax. Adopted in the 2000s by many countries in the region, the flat tax became a distinctive post-Communist phenomenon.

Box 9.1 Perspectives on economic intervention: Beyond state and market failures

The standard economic thinking on the role of the state has centered on two rather simple frameworks, each with a fairly direct policy message. The theory of market failure is based on an acceptance that the market provides an optimal static allocation of resources, albeit with a number of exceptional cases in which state intervention is, therefore, justified (see Ledyard [2008]). Beyond that, the state should restrict itself to providing a legal framework such that business can function and, with varying degrees of conviction, to redistributing income to counter the extent of inequality that may be generated by a free market.

With less recognition of forms of market failure, neoliberal approaches put emphasis on a counterbalancing concern that there may also be government failure. This leads to greater confidence in dismissing state intervention as a response to sectoral lobbies, or rent seekers, and in rejecting redistributive policies as distortions of the market that will reduce incentives and harm economic growth.

Both of these frameworks can be related to practical aspects of state activity. There are clear cases of market failure and of state spending responding to sectional lobbies. Indeed, state spending could almost always be interpreted as a response to particular interests, but that does not mean that it is an unwelcome distortion of an allegedly perfect market mechanism. The state and market failure frameworks appear rather simplistic and incomplete in the light of the extent and variety of state activity and of its importance in many successful economies.

The theoretical case for the neoliberal perspective was already weakened by developments in mainstream economics at the time that it achieved a political victory as the dominant frame of reference for policy advice on transition. In the 1980s, new growth economics demonstrated a need for more public investment in education than the market might determine (Romer 1986; Barro 1997). At the same time, new trade theories (e.g., Krugman 1991) have shown that free trade is not always optimal for technological laggards, given the market structures, product development modes, and location preferences of producers in mature capitalist economies.

In 1990, the publication of the *World Development Report on Poverty* (WB 1990) provided an opening for welfare-state research to be heard in international economic policy-making circles. This body of research showed the importance of public policy for social development, promoting equality of opportunity and social integration (for an overview, see Gough [2008]). The reception to these ideas in actual developmental practice, however, was rather lukewarm (Dani and Haan 2008). The social role of the state was still seen, in line with the neoliberal thinking, as a cost and social spending seen as "unproductive" (e.g., WB 2007, 88).

The social role of the state will be discussed in Chapter 10, but two observations are important in this context: (1) part of social spending, if that includes education, should contribute directly to competitiveness, and (2) the highest-spending EU countries have tended to be among the more successful. Regarding the first observation, there is a large body of literature that argues that state spending on education and R&D can increase the growth rate (Klenow and Rodríguez-Clare 1997). The point that state expenditures on education, and also health care and infrastructure, can enhance the efficiency of production factors and thus promote economic growth was accepted also among international policy-making circles (e.g., WB 2007, 76). The empirical evidence indeed shows that while the impact of fiscal policies on growth is generally rather slim, education expenditure has a positive impact (Nijkamp and Poot 2004). The second observation does not illustrate a generally positive relationship between public spending and growth. At the same time, the empirical evidence shows that public spending does not generally impede growth, either (Agell, Lindh, and Ohlsson 1997, 1999). It can be added that studies of the relationship between the size of government and economic growth in transition economies were inconclusive (Chu and Schwartz 1994; Campos and Coricelli 2002; Beck and Laeven 2005; Åslund and Jenish 2005).

The World Economic Forum (WEF; Lopez-Claros et al. 2006) recognized the different roles state intervention can play in economic development, taking up Porter's (1990) notion of "stages of growth," each with a specific role for the state to play. The first is factor-led growth (competing on price by exploiting raw materials or cheap labor without direct access to customers), followed by investment-led growth (competing by using efficiency in modern industries developed with imported technology) and innovation-led growth (competing by developing new products and processes). Roles for the state are not set out for each stage explicitly, but paramount needs are identified as infrastructure (electricity, communications, and transport) in the first stage; investment incentives, improving skills, and access to capital for investment in the second stage; and boosting the importance of education and spending on it, plus efficient use of, R&D in the third stage. Here, the government plays a role, but it is not obviously one of strategic leadership, so it appears "less and less able to build a competitive economy" (Lopez-Claros et al. 2006, 56).

The WEF's stages of growth model should not be taken too precisely. The state's role in providing infrastructure remains important in all economies. It is deeply involved in energy policy, even when providers may be under private ownership, because of the long-term nature of decisions and their importance for the whole economy due to the impact on the environment and security. Successful "developmental states" (see p. 126) often pursued competitiveness strategies that combined factor, efficiency, and innovation advantages. They implemented diverse measures to ease supply and demand constraints. On the supply side, the policies to facilitate the availability of capital, labor, technology, and entrepreneurship included repressing labor to provide cheap, flexible, and disciplined workers and promoting technology by bargaining with foreign firms to enable technology transfer and/or by investing in education and R&D. The demand side measures often included expansionary monetary and fiscal policies and a combination of import substitution and export promotion in selected target industries, often through tariffs and exchange rate policies, subsidies, and administrative support (C. Johnson 1982; Wade 1990; Evans 1995; Woo-Cumings 1999; Kohli 2004).

Industrial policy of the developmental states often relied on the strategy of "linking, leverage, and learning" (see Mathews [2006]). Learning occurred through a repeated process of tapping links with more advanced firms to acquire knowledge, technology, and market access. In order to obtain the most from these links, entry into an industry was forged through a strategic leverage of knowledge, technology, and revenue extraction. There is, it can be concluded, a continuing potential for a developmental role of the state also in the innovation-led economies, but growth in those cases also clearly depends on initiatives from other actors.

PUBLIC SPENDING AND GOVERNMENT BALANCE

Throughout the world, the level of public spending and revenues is closely related to per capita GDP (WB 2007, 47). This, as shown in Figure 9.1, was also the case in the post-state Socialist countries, although the relationship was not very close and there was also considerable variation among similar countries. The levels of social spending, analyzed in Chapter 10, accounted for most of the differences (4). Table 9.1 provides figures on general government expenditure, accumulated debt, and the balance of the budget for 2007, just before the financial crisis led to important fiscal adjustments in many cases (see Chapter 17). Table A.16 in the Appendix provides complete data for general government balances. Hungary and Belarus, perhaps surprisingly in view of other differences between them, stood out with the highest levels of public spending relative to GDP, but only middle-income Belarus managed to balance its budget and recorded only moderate debt levels. In contrast, the high-income Hungary accumulated very high public debt, and its deficit reached 9.3 percent of GDP in 2006; it was brought below 5 percent only a year later in the context of a (local) financial crisis. As discussed in Chapter 3, Hungarian public (foreign) debt dates back to the state Socialist era, and debt repayment constituted a significant strain on the state budget, leading also to several financial crises.

Ukraine was another overperformer among the middle-income countries, with government spending exceeding levels in some of the high-income countries. The high levels reflect an introduction of expansionary fiscal policy that accompanied the Orange Revolution in 2004, which included also a significant rise in social expenditures (see Chapter 10). This was matched by revenues coming not only from (re)privatization but also from a sharp increase in tax revenues following an elimination of sectoral tax privileges and subsidies for special economic zones (Economist Intelligence Unit [EIU] 2008b; Mykhnenko and Swain 2009).

Among the high-income countries, the Baltic republics Bulgaria, Romania, and Slovakia recorded relatively modest levels of state expenditure. This reflected not only low commitment to social protection but also, as will be shown later, low levels of taxation, particularly on capital. In the middle-income countries, the level of spending in Kazakhstan was very low relative to its level of development. Finally, general government expenditure in low-income Moldova reached the level of high-income countries. Economic recovery of the 2000s allowed the financing of public spending from domestic resources in this remittance-driven economy, as reflected by the moderate level of public debt reached by 2006. In contrast, low-spending

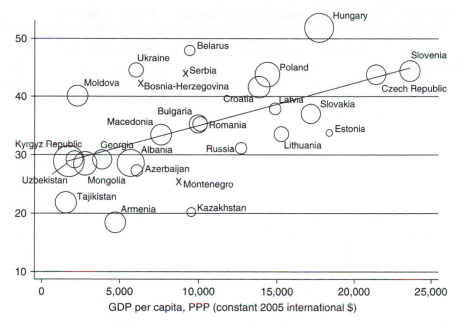

Figure 9.1 General government as a percentage of GDP, 2006 *Sources:* GDP per capita data are from WB (2008a); general government data are from EBRD economic statistics and forecasts, available at http://www.ebrd.com/country/sector/econo/stats/index.htm.
Note: Area of symbol proportional to government debt (% of GDP).

Kyrgyzstan continued to suffer from high indebtedness and debt-servicing costs. A 2004 debt-restructuring deal helped to contain the income debits.

These outcomes are the result of important transformations in public finances, reflecting the processes of state consolidation and different forms of recovery from the transformation depression. As discussed in Chapter 7, transition brought fiscal shocks, with dramatic drops in real levels of spending in the CIS and more stable patterns of public spending in Eastern European countries (see also Tables 7.1 and 7.2). The CIS countries, thus, found it much more difficult to balance their budgets. In the early 1990s, fiscal deficits in low-income countries in the CIS, comprising Armenia, Azerbaijan, Georgia, the Kyrgyz Republic, Moldova, Tajikistan, and Uzbekistan, averaged 9.4 percent; middle-income CIS countries, including Belarus, Kazakhstan, the Russian Federation, and Ukraine, reported a 6.9 percent deficit on average, but the average deficit reached almost 10 percent in Russia, and the average in southeast Europe was 6.1 percent. The situation was much better in CEECs and the Baltic republics where the average deficit was only about 2.4 percent (WB 2007).

Ten years later, the situation changed dramatically. In general, tax revenues picked up, fiscal deficits narrowed, and public debt ratios fell. What is more, the CIS countries brought their public deficits below CEEC and Baltic levels. In 2002 to 2005, low-income CIS states reported average deficits of just 1.1 percent; the middle-income CIS countries even achieved an average surplus of 1 percent. The low-income CIS countries consolidated their budgets by large revenue increases in the context of economic recovery and the increasing ability to tax economic activities. They

TABLE 9.1   General government as a percentage of GDP, 2007

	Expenditure	Balance	Debt
Hungary	49.8	−4.9	65.8
Belarus	49.6	0.4	11.6
Ukraine	44.3	−2.0	13.4
Bosnia-Herzegovina	44.1	1.3	
Serbia	43.7	−2.4	
Czech Republic	42.5	−0.6	28.9
Slovenia	42.4	0.5	30.0
Croatia	42.3	−2.0	33.1
Poland	42.0	−1.9	44.9
Moldova	41.8	−0.3	28.3
Mongolia	38.1	2.8	36.3
Bulgaria	37.2	3.5	19.8
Romania	36.9	−2.5	20.0
Estonia	35.5	2.7	3.5
Latvia	35.5	0.1	9.0
Lithuania	34.9	−1.0	17.0
Slovakia	34.6	−1.9	29.4
Georgia	33.5	−4.2	22.9
Russia	33.0	5.1	9.5
Uzbekistan	32.7	5.7	15.8
Macedonia	32.6	0.6	24.7
Kyrgyz Republic	31.0	−0.7	56.8
Albania	29.1	−3.8	52.7
Tajikistan	27.8	−6.2	35.2
Azerbaijan	27.4	2.4	9.4
Montenegro	24.8	6.3	
Kazakhstan	24.2	4.7	5.8
Armenia	19.2	−2.2	20.0
Turkmenistan	13.4	4.0	

Source: EBRD economic statistics and forecasts, available at http://www.ebrd.com/country/sector/econo/stats/index.htm. Data for the Czech Republic is from the Eurostat database, available at http://epp.eurostat.ec.europa.eu/portal/page/portal/statistics/search_database.

stabilized primary expenditures at 25 percent of GDP. In the middle-income CIS, expenditure reduction played an important role in budget consolidation, bringing it to 35 percent of GDP. There was more continuity in CEECs, SEECs, and the Baltic republics where expenditure increases in the early 2000s raised the average deficit to 3.1 percent in 2002 to 2005 (WB 2007). The average reflects the conflicting pressures in central European countries for retaining public expenditures at levels comparable to what is known from Western Europe and for undercutting the levels of taxation in European tax havens such as Ireland. The low-spending Baltic republics and SEECs did not have problems with balancing public spending before the 2008 financial crisis.

THE STATE AND EDUCATION

The level of public spending does not provide a full picture of the impact of the state on economic development because it contains such varied activities with varied effects. Spending on education and R&D are areas of state activity that are commonly understood to improve developmental prospects of a country. As indicated by the World Economic Forum (WEF) framework in Box 9.1, these are major fields of state activity in developed countries and were particularly relevant for more advanced countries in Eastern Europe. These countries could benefit from upgrading their relatively complex industrial structures and from human capital levels to attract higher-value FDI (see Chapter 15). At the same time, the experience of some developing countries, such as India, showed that state education spending can be used as a core component of the developmental strategy also in the lower-income countries (Kohli 2004).

Education was not typically set as a priority to lead a transformation toward a more advanced economy, and, in some cases, it was clearly constrained by the limited ability of governments to raise taxes. Large fiscal imbalances were often associated with lower education spending, even in the countries with high overall expenditure (WB 2007, 88). However, spending figures indicate continuity in the importance attached to education in general. In some cases, serious cuts in spending were also held in check partly by protests over pay from teachers, which have been a frequent feature in CEECs in particular. Thus, a provider group could help ensure that education spending was protected but not that it was given a substantially higher priority. In countries with weaker interest representation, particularly in the CIS, state education went into decline.

Table 9.2 shows state spending on education across the region, comparing 1990 with 2000—which was the low point in many cases—and 2006. The comparison shows some differences in trends. Eastern Europe is characterized by more continuity. Private payments played increasing roles in covering costs of tertiary education, particularly in the Baltic republics and SEECs. Data on private contributions in the CIS are missing, but these countries were characterized by high levels of informal payment, particularly in tertiary education. Hungary, Estonia, and Kyrgyzstan inherited a high level of public spending, but only Hungary was able to sustain it. Slovenia is the only case that appears to have moved from significantly behind to higher Western European levels (Denmark was the highest, at 8.3 percent in 2005). Russia remained very low by international standards, despite improvements in the 2000s. As tax revenues increased in the 2000s, some of the CIS countries—that is, Moldova, Ukraine, Kyrgyzstan, and Russia—increased their spending on education, albeit to different extents. The spending increase in Ukraine reflected wage increases across the public sector, as explained in Chapter 10.

Perhaps surprisingly, Moldova appears as a leader in public education spending in the region. Education is also one of the leading recipients of state expenditure in Moldova, accounting for 19 percent of the total in 2007. At the beginning of the 1990s, the Moldavan government was reported to be spending about 15 percent of GDP on education (EIU 2008a, 12). The level shrunk to 4.4 percent, the lowest point, in 2000. Despite the improvements, education was still said to be underfunded, the quality of service and infrastructure were poor—especially in rural areas—and teachers' salaries were extremely low. A low pupil-staff ratio indicated failure to adapt to a shrinking student population rather than a high quality of service (Munteanu et al. 2008).

TABLE 9.2   Public expenditure on education

	As a percentage of GNI			As a percentage of total spending on education, 2005/2006	
	1990	2000	2006	All levels	Tertiary
Moldova		4.4	6.7	93.3[m]	
Ukraine	5.2	4.3	6.3		
Belarus	5.0	6.0[a]	6.1		
Slovenia	4.8[b]		5.9	87.0[l]	76.9[l]
Hungary	6.1	5.1	5.8	91.3[k]	78.5[k]
Mongolia		5.8	5.2[c]		
Kyrgyzstan	7.4[d]	3.7	5.6		
Poland	5.5[e]	5.1	5.6[f]	90.7[k]	74.0[k]
Latvia	3.8	5.4	5.2	88.0[l]	60.8[l]
Estonia	6.2[e]	5.6	5.1[f]	92.4[k]	69.9[k]
Lithuania	4.8		5.0	90.8[l]	65.9[l]
Czech Republic	4.6[g]	4.1	4.8	87.6[k]	81.2[k]
Croatia		4.6[h]			
Macedonia		4.2[i]			
Bulgaria	5.6		4.3	84.8[l]	56.3[l]
Russia	3.5	3.0	4.0		
Slovakia	4.6[g]	4.0	3.9	83.9[k]	77.3[k]
Romania	2.8	2.9	3.6[f]	87.7[k]	64.4[k]
Kazakhstan	6.5	3.5	3.0	78.3[m]	
Georgia		2.1	2.9		
Armenia		2.7	2.6		
Azerbaijan		4.1	2.3		
Albania		2.8[j]			

Source: UN (1995, Table 11) for 1990; UNESCO Global Education Digest database for 2000 and 2005–2007, available at http://www.unesco.org/unesdi/index.php/eng/repertoire/education.html.

Note: GNI = gross national income.

[a] Statistics are from UNESCO Institute for Statistics (2009, Table 25) estimate, share of public spending.

[b] Statistics are for 1991.

[c] Statistics are for 2007.

[d] Statistics are from Pomfret (2006); relates to GDP.

[e] Statistics are for 1992.

[f] Statistics are for 2005.

[g] Statistics are for Czechoslovakia as a whole.

[h] Statistics are for 2001.

[i] Statistics are for 1999.

[j] Statistics are for 2002.

[k] Statistics are for 2005.

[l] Statistics are for 2006.

[m] Statistics are for 2007.

TABLE 9.3   Number of students enrolled in tertiary education as a percentage of the 1990 level

	1993	2000	2004	Percentage of population, 2004
Hungary	130.8	299.9	412.3	4.1
Poland	137.2	289.9	375.2	5.3
Romania	129.7	234.7	355.6	3.1
Slovenia	119.9	249.7	311.0	5.2
Latvia	82.5	198.5	277.8	5.4
Czech Republic	129.3	214.6	269.8	3.1
Estonia	95.6	207.0	253.5	4.8
Slovakia	110.2	205.9	249.5	3.0
Lithuania	79.5	137.5	206.0	5.2
Russia	89.9		169.1	6.0
Belarus	89.4	122.8	151.3	5.0
Ukraine	92.8	105.2	149.2	5.0
Kazakhstan	91.9	68.9	123.6	4.5
Bulgaria	109.4	138.6	121.2	2.9

Source: Calculated from UN (1995, Table 10; 2006, Table 9).

Trends in student enrollment, shown in Table 9.3, point to a determined and consistent trend toward improvement in Eastern Europe, which began as early as 1990. Participation in tertiary education, as indicated in Table 9.4, reached the levels common in Western Europe and North America. The Czech Republic and Slovakia were lagging in this respect, albeit with questions over the comparability of figures that might explain some of the gap. Expansion of tertiary education often found backing from regional interests, seeking a prestigious form of development. As this was started from a low base, it still left the share of the labor force with higher education relatively low in a number of countries. In 2007, it amounted to 13.1 percent in the Czech Republic, 14.0 percent in Slovakia, and 11.1 percent in Romania, as compared to an average of 22.9 percent for the whole EU at the time (Eurostat 2009).

Some of the additional students were in private universities—for example, making up about a third of the number in Poland. Data on private enrollment can be found in Table 9.4. The extremely high figures in Latvia and Estonia reflect the organizational autonomy of universities rather than a full privatization of tertiary education. There are substantial payments from the students, but public budgets cover about 60 percent of spending in the Baltic republics and SEECs (see Table 9.2). Thus, with some variation, the general picture is still of a state commitment to fostering a well-qualified labor force, or at least a highly qualified group within the labor force.

Increases in student numbers can be seen as a clear case of states putting priority on promoting knowledge. However, the explosion of student enrollment was not matched by the increase in funding for higher education. The infrastructure and

TABLE 9.4   Tertiary education: Enrollment rates and student-teacher ratios, 2007

	Gross enrollment ratio			Private enrollment (%)	Student-teacher ratio
	Total	Male	Female		
Slovenia	86	70	102	10	20.7
Lithuania	76	59	93	9	12.5
Ukraine	76	68	85		14.3
Russian Federation	75	64	86		14.3
Latvia[a]	74	53	95	96	21.1
Belarus	69	57	80	13	13.3
Hungary	69	56	82	15	18.8
Poland	67	56	78	32	21.7
Estonia	65	50	81	84	10.8
Romania	58	50	67	31	29.9
Czech Republic	55	49	61	12	15.8
Slovakia	51	41	61	7	15.6
Bulgaria	50	45	55	20	12.3
Mongolia	48	37	58	34	16.1
Kazakhstan[b]	47	39	56		17.6
Croatia	46	41	51	5	10.8
Kyrgyzstan	43	37	48	9	18.4
Moldova	41	35	48	15	17.2
Bosnia and Herzegovina	37				
Georgia	37	35	39	21	8.8
Macedonia	36	31	40	17	20.7
Armenia	34	31	37	23	8.2
Tajikistan	20	29	11		18.8
Azerbaijan	15	16	14	16	8.4
Uzbekistan	10	11	8	0	12.6
North America and Western Europe	70	60	80		13.0

Source: Calculated from UNESCO (2009, Table 8).

Note: The *gross enrollment ratio* refers to the number of pupils or students enrolled as a percentage of the population in the theoretical age group for the same level of education. For the tertiary level, the population used is the 5-year age group following on from the secondary school-leaving age. A *teacher* refers to a person who is employed full-time or part-time in an official capacity to guide and direct the learning experience of students, irrespective of their qualifications or the delivery mechanism (i.e., face-to-face and/or at a distance). This definition excludes educational personnel who have no active teaching duties (e.g., headmasters, headmistresses, or principals who do not teach) and persons who work occasionally or in a voluntary capacity in educational institutions. *Private enrollment* refers to the percentage of students enrolled in private educational institutions that are controlled and managed by a nongovernmental organization (church, trade union, or business enterprise), regardless of whether they receive financial support from public authorities. In countries where private institutions are substantially subsidized or aided by the government, the distinction between private and public educational institutions may be less meaningful.

[a] Data are for 2006.

[b] Data are for 2008.

teaching staff in many universities remained more or less the same, or increased only very moderately, while the number of students doubled or tripled (e.g., Hrubos 2000; Bučar and Stare 2006). As a consequence, there are claims of a declining standard of education, particularly higher education, in several fields (United Nations Educational, Scientific, and Cultural Organization [UNESCO, 2006, 121], in Berend [2009, 230]). This observation is supported by high student-teacher ratios in many East European countries, far exceeding the average for Western Europe and North America.

The structure of education changed, as courses in economics, social sciences, and business were expanded both in the private and public institutes of higher education. At the same time, the strongly specialized and vocational character of secondary education was retained. In the early 2000s, the majority of the students enrolled in upper-secondary education in the Czech Republic, Slovakia, Croatia, Slovenia, and Romania were in vocational education. By 2005, only Estonia, Lithuania, and Hungary reduced their share of specialized vocational training below 30 percent, the level common in the West (UNESCO 2006, 96, 104). However, the number of science and engineering graduates in Eastern Europe in 2006 remained below the EU average (PRO INNO Europe 2009).

All the CIS countries experienced a fall in student numbers after 1990 and less dramatic expansion in the following years, suggesting a more limited commitment to expanding higher education than in Eastern Europe (Table 9.3). However, according to figures in Table 9.4, tertiary education enrollment rates in Ukraine, Russia, and Belarus had reached the levels of leading East European countries. In the most extreme cases of Tajikistan and Moldova, the proportion of 15- to 18-year-olds in education halved to about 20 percent (Pomfret 2006, 69). Turkmenistan experienced a fall in higher education enrollment from 40,000 in 1991 to less than 10,000 in 2004, with those more affluent students studying outside the country, in Moscow in particular (99).

RESEARCH AND DEVELOPMENT

While the state retained a major role in education, its role in the promotion of knowledge through R&D is less obvious. What is more, as will be evident from the comparison with advanced, technology-intensive economies in the West, the heavy reliance on the state in R&D spending may indicate the weakness rather than strength of high-tech sectors in the economy. At the same time, state activities play an important role in promoting innovations in the advanced economies. State involvement in R&D may thus be important for creating a potential for technology-intensive growth.

Figures for people employed in R&D showed substantial falls in the years immediately after 1989 (UN 1992, 1993b, 1995, 1997, 2006). It appears from this that the potential of a substantial research base was lost, but the original figures indicate little about quality, and there are availability problems as well as questions about the comparability of figures. The data also indicate major differences between countries, which reflected policy choices and activities of multinational companies. Continuity in state support could prevent R&D employment declines, but increases were associated with the recovery in the private sector (covered in Chapter 15).

The number of scientists and engineers employed in R&D in Russia fell in 2004 to 46 percent of the 1991 level, and a comparison with more recent data indicates some stabilization, but not a reversal in the decline. The decline in Ukraine seemed to be even steeper, with 2004 employment reaching only 25 percent of the 1989 level. R&D employment in 2004 dropped to 25 percent of the 1987 level in Bulgaria and to 20 percent of the 1989 level in Romania. Subsequent data indicated a stabilization of R&D employment in both of these countries (UN 2008).

The CEECs saw less dramatic declines in R&D employment, which were followed in the 2000s by increases in the Czech Republic and Hungary and stabilization elsewhere. Employment in R&D in Slovakia in 2006 was 38 percent of the 1989 level (FSU 1992). Data on Poland are more equivocal, but national sources indicate only a moderate decrease in R&D employment, falling in 2004 to 80 percent of the 1989 level (Central Statistical Office of Poland [GUS] 1990, 451; 2008, 284). In Hungary, R&D employment shrunk to 52 percent of the 1989 level in 1993, but this was followed by recovery, bringing it to 66 percent of the 1989 level in 2004. In the Czech Republic, R&D employment had recovered from 38 percent in 1997 to 50 percent of the 1989 level in 2006 (CZSO 1993, 2008).

In many Eastern European countries, there was a shift toward a more active role of the state in promoting innovation. In some countries, such as Estonia, EU accession brought the innovation policy onto the agenda. In others, including Slovenia and Hungary, the changes in policy focus occurred even earlier. Attempting to imitate the advanced industrial countries, the innovation policies focused on R&D-related activities, such as the commercialization of public research and the development of technology parks for start-ups. However, such policies were often accompanied by relatively little increase in actual funding and left the bulk of local industrial base out of consideration, leaving only a limited impact on target regions (Piech and Radosevic 2006; Tiits et al. 2008).

Table 9.5 compares expenditures on R&D and the role of the government in financing it in 2005. This allows comparison of levels across countries. The highest-spending levels, recorded in Slovenia and the Czech Republic, still lagged behind the advanced economies in Western Europe. The high levels in Slovenia reflected a more gradual buildup of R&D spending throughout the 1990s and 2000s. The Czech Republic was somewhat exceptional, with growth from 0.95 percent in 1995 to 1.41 percent of GDP in 2005 (CZSO 2008). The increase followed a Czech government policy of encouraging research activity, but, as the figures in Table 9.5 indicate, research spending by private companies was more important, mostly in the motor-vehicle sector controlled by the multinationals (Pavlínek, Domański, and Guzik 2009). Indeed, as in Finland or Germany, the private sector accounts for most R&D spending in the leading East European countries.

Russia is among the countries with the highest R&D spending and also the highest R&D employment per capita (WB 2008a). However, in this case, this is largely accounted for by the state, a pattern common among many countries with low overall R&D expenditure and low levels of foreign ownership of manufacturing industry. In contrast, Ukraine has a similar level of R&D expenditure, with the private sector playing a major role.

TABLE 9.5 **Expenditure on R&D, 2005**

	As a percentage of GDP	Percentage spent by government	Percentage spent by higher education
Slovenia	1.49	37.2	0.7
Czech Republic	1.41	40.9	1.1
Russia	1.07	61.9	0.4
Ukraine	1.03	40.1	0.1
Croatia	1.00	58.1	4.9
Hungary	0.94	49.4	
Estonia	0.94	43.5	0.8
Lithuania	0.76	62.7	5.7
Belarus	0.68	71.9	0.7
Poland	0.57	57.7	2.9
Latvia	0.56	46.0	1.2
Slovakia	0.51	57.0	0.3
Bulgaria	0.49	63.9	0.4
Romania	0.41	53.5	4.0
Kazakhstan	0.28	51.2	
Macedonia	0.25		
Azerbaijan	0.22	77.5	
Armenia	0.21	53.8	
Kyrgyzstan	0.20	63.6	
Georgia	0.18		
Tajikistan	0.10	91.9	0.3
Finland	3.48	25.7	0.2
Germany	2.49	28.4	

Source: UNESCO Global Education Digest database, available at http://www.unesco.org/unesdi/index .php/eng/repertoire/education.html.

INFRASTRUCTURE

The quality and availability of economic infrastructure—power, water, railways, roads, and communication—contributes positively to economic output, growth, and productivity (e.g., Briceño-Garmendia, Estache, and Shafik 2004). The positive effect of infrastructure seems stronger in low- and middle-income countries (Canning and Bennathan 2000). Although it was never doubted that the state would play a key role in infrastructure development also in the transition countries, this was not seen as a priority. The transition countries inherited more infrastructure stocks than typical in countries at similar levels of per capita income, but the quality and reliability was poor, close to the average of developing countries (WB 2007, 112; see also EBRD [2004]).

The output contraction in the transformation depression led to overcapacity problems, making it difficult to maintain the systems. The share of railways in surface transport declined in almost all countries (WB 2007, 131); the effect was to leave much of the transport infrastructure in a dismal state due to the inability to fund normal operations and to the neglect of maintenance throughout the 1990s. Most of the countries in the region transferred responsibility for managing certain types of infrastructure to municipal governments, but these often lacked the capacity to supervise the operation effectively and to provide appropriate fiscal support. Some mainline modernization was undertaken in CEECs, following from the aims of European integration and largely financed by the European Union. Only in Eastern Germany did infrastructure investment appear as a major part of a revival strategy. In the low-income countries of the CIS and SEECs, shortage of electricity became a major concern, with blackouts and reduced periods of service even in capital cities (WB 2006).

With the economic recovery of the late 1990s, many of the countries began to outgrow their asset bases, especially in power production and distribution. The poor conditions of infrastructure then became a significant hindrance to growth, particularly in the low-income CIS countries (WB 2007; EIU 2008a). The extent of infrastructure privatization varied (for an overview, see EBRD [2004, 77, Table 4.2]). It went furthest in telecommunications, urban transport, and utility transmission and distribution, with CIS countries more reluctant to allow private operators to operate, but there is little systematic evidence on the effect of privatization (see EBRD [2004, 84–86]). Performance improvements after privatization were most frequently claimed in the telecommunication sector.

International financial institutions such as the EBRD and the European Investment Bank (EIB), a body controlled by EU governments with the mission of making long-term investment loans, increased lending to infrastructural projects in the CIS from the mid-2000s. Central projects included transport and road rehabilitation. The EBRD focused on transport links that fostered regional integration, such as the Trans-European Network Corridor IX, which connects Moscow, Kiev, and Bucharest. The biggest promise of a major further modernization in any post-Communist country was, appropriately enough, in Russia, with plans in 2007 for a huge expansion in electricity production, funding for high-tech sectors, and the development of roads, ports, and waterways. In view of constraints on the Russian state budget, despite revenues from oil and gas, and of the passivity of the state in economic development in previous years, so ambitious a project may prove impossible to implement (EIU 2007, 19).

INDUSTRIAL DEVELOPMENT POLICY

The notion of a developmental state was firmly rooted in thinking and practice in state Socialist countries. Alexander Gerschenkron's (1962) study of earlier Russian economic history led to the notion that in a "late developer," the state had to substitute for free market and private-enterprise processes; it had to lead industrialization by providing financing and by substituting for private entrepreneurship (see H. Schwartz [2000, 47–49, 85–90]). Clearly very different from the developmental state known from east Asian countries, the Soviet model can be considered as the most globally influential exemplar of the developmental state, a project aimed at transforming Russia's feudal social structure into a "proletarian" one (Derluguian 2005).

The brutal tyranny imposed during the Lenin and Stalin eras notwithstanding, the post-Stalin Soviet Union achieved a high degree of social stability and progress for the majority of the Soviet population. In less than one lifetime, it seemed to many of the country's inhabitants, the Soviet Union was rocketed from the periphery of the world system into a position to be able to compete, at least in some fields, with the United States. The generation born in the Stalin era saw their life chances improve rapidly with expanding educational opportunities and material advance (Derluguian 2005).

The Soviet project exported modernization also to peripheries of the union. In Eastern Europe, the Czech lands and some parts of Hungary and Poland had undergone modernization and industrialization under the auspices of the Austro-Hungarian empire in the nineteenth century (see Berend [2003]), but it was only the Soviet project that brought industrialization to much of the region. The temporary success of Soviet modernization led to a catch-up process, societal security, and, consequently, transient legitimization for the regimes (Berend 1996; compare with discussion in Chapter 2).

The notion of the developmental state, therefore, left two possible heritages: It could be associated with past modernization, or alternatively, it could be associated with the negative features of the repressive states under state Socialism. In practice, the collapse of state Socialism quickly led away from any thoughts of an active, strategically based industrial policy that could set objectives for structural and technological modernization. The reason for this was partly ideological—the belief that the state should play no such role, while privatization and new private owners would solve the basic strategic economic problems. There was also a practical issue with the collapse of the state (discussed in Chapters 7 and 8). Even where state collapse was not an issue, the erosion and subsequent collapse of state-led modernization in the state Socialist era left the elites with little strategic capacity to conduct industrial policy in a market economy.

Industrial policy, albeit not a full state commitment to promoting industrial development, gained a higher profile in CEECs when employment was threatened. That led to ideas for preserving existing enterprises and, in some cases, to a large number of programs encouraging new enterprise development and innovation in existing enterprises. These were never given serious financial backing and came to very little, as, in one country after another, the main hope shifted toward salvation first from privatization and then from inward investment (see Chapters 11, 13, and 15).

As the developmental prospects in CEECs became dependent on investment decisions made by foreign investors, providing the infrastructure and support for inward investment became the most important state role in development of the manufacturing industry. That required no input to business plans; all of that was left to the companies. The state's job was simply to attract them. The economic role of what can be called the "competition state" thus became limited to attempts to manage the position in transnational investment flows (see Drahokoupil [2008a]).

In the four central European countries, the Czech Republic, Hungary, Poland, and Slovakia, these competition states pursued some low-profile developmental strategies, attempting to attract higher-quality FDI through targeted subsidies and then to embed it in local economies. In the Baltic region, the states relied on providing a low-cost and flexible environment in attracting foreign investment. Only Slovenia initially pursued some protective policies, attempting to develop its domestic industrial base, but restrictions on FDI had to be removed during its accession into the European Union (see Bandelj [2004]).

The Russian state seemed to gain capacity to play a developmental role. The Yukos affair (see Chapter 8) was an important step, confirming that private entrepreneurs could amass vast fortunes only as long as the state allowed them to. It also marked an end to the private oil oligopoly, with two state-owned, vertically integrated companies—Rosneft and Gazprom—gaining control of more than 30 percent of oil production by 2008. The state also exerted control over oil production by applying tougher conditions for access to hydrocarbon resources. The new law—signed by Putin's successor, Medvedev, in July 2008—restricted access to continental oil and gas deposits only to the state-owned companies (Rossiaud and Locatelli 2009, 434).

The state also proved to be able to exert influence over the private sector by other means. Putin increased representation of central government not only in regional governments but also in nonfinancial corporations, with some evidence suggesting that this led to some improvements in the quality of corporate governance (Yakovlev 2009). The federal government not only slowed down privatization but also increased state ownership by buying assets, particularly in the oil industry. Ideologically, there was an increased emphasis on nationalism. This generated a debate on the nature of a state-led capitalism in Russia (e.g., Lane 2008; Sakwa 2008; Appel 2008; Hanson and Teague 2007; Woodruff 2007; Gel'man 2009; Yakovlev 2006), which could also be associated with the Russian institutionalism referred to in Chapter 6.

The increasing involvement of the state in the oil sector might have helped to overcome some of the key coordination problems linked to the uncertainty over property rights to major oil companies, the partial nature of the rights of access to hydrocarbon deposits, and the suboptimal structure of taxation that reflected the inability of the state to monitor oil companies effectively (Rossiaud and Locatelli 2009). Longer-term strategies of oil exploitation thus could possibly replace the short termism underinvestment, and risk aversion that characterized the sector when it was a private oligopoly (see Wolosky [2000] and King and Treskow [2006]). However, the Yukos affair did not mark a switch to an active state role in economic development. State intervention indeed also gained in prominence outside the oil sector, but it tended to take the form of a "rescue state" (Iwasaki 2004, 231–33; Iwasaki and Suzuki 2007, 403); if in trouble, enterprises deemed important would be rescued through state intervention, including by the injection of public capital and by temporarily depriving the companies of decision-making authority. The primary issue, so it seemed, was political power and the consolidation of a state in general.

A careful study of the changed role of the state in this period shows some continuing privatization alongside a switch toward some conscious efforts from the state to strengthen and consolidate military-related industries (Durand 2008). In the motor-vehicle sector, a slightly active state also sought cooperation with MNCs by offering minority shareholdings, but they targeted domestic rather than export markets. In many cases, run-down factories were finding a chance by assembling cars from kits, as was also happening in Ukraine.

Putin spoke frequently of a stronger state role in economic development and in 2007 put forward ambitious plans for using oil and gas revenues to finance a program for creating a transport and energy infrastructure and for promoting high-tech industries. This was not underway in 2008, when the management of the economic crisis became a priority. The state then provided liquidity to failing banks and bailed out a number of large enterprises by buying controlling stake in the conglomerates or by refinancing their foreign debt. Nevertheless, there was little interest in the state taking a more active role in the governance of the companies it effectively controlled;

there was more of a concern with shielding key Russian assets from foreign control, particularly in finance, defense, and energy and mineral extraction (Malle 2009, 260).

The state played a more active role in Belarus, Uzbekistan, Turkmenistan, and, at the beginning of the 1990s, in Tajikistan. These "order states" (Iwasaki 2004, 230–33) recentralized economic control, with the government or its appointees having the final decision over the strategic management issues in major enterprises, which were, in contrast to the situation in rescue states, constantly and actively monitored. Iwasaki (2004, 245) observed that such government-led management of the transformation depression, based on systemic monitoring and control over enterprises, underpinned an annual average GDP and industrial production growth of 2.7 percent and 7.0 percent, respectively, from 1992 to 2001, a performance superior to the rest of the CIS (compare with Chapter 4).

Belarus developed what has also been described as a command economy without central planning (Nuti 2007; cf. Korosteleva 2007; Iwasaki and Suzuki 2007, 401–2). There was some move toward market, some degree of enterprise decision-making decentralization, and prices were near market clearing and not too distant from relative international prices (Nuti 2007). The economy was stimulated by an expansionary monetary policy of credit expansion through negative real interest rates. Further policy tools included the continuation of price control over energy and other major products, the maintenance of a state order system and a centralized trade regime for major exports, the reintroduction of a multiple exchange rate system, and a mechanism of mandatory sales of foreign currency export earnings. Repeatedly criticized by IFIs, this strategy shielded the economy from the transition shocks experienced elsewhere (Iwasaki and Suzuki 2007). By the end of the 1990s, there were some signs of success also in enterprise restructuring, with some state-run enterprises, such as the Minsk tractor producer MTZ, experiencing an export-led recovery, allowing the MTZ output in 2008 to recover to 65 percent of the 1988 level, with production runs diversifying from two to 60 models (see Chapter 15).

Uzbekistan also reestablished greater central control, ameliorating the transition shocks (Spechler 2008; Iwasaki and Suzuki 2007). The Uzbek state implemented also what could be called a developmentalist project, linking up with a foreign partner in car manufacturing, but with only mixed success (Myant and Drahokoupil 2008). In Turkmenistan, there were state-organized attempts to develop textile manufacturing, but that did not seem to take off at all. In the early 2000s, there were attempts to stimulate industrial modernization in Kazakhstan; an Industrial and Innovation Development Strategy for 2003 to 2015 was introduced (Franke, Gawrich, and Alakbarov 2009, 128), but its actual meaning remained to be seen. However, some measurable success was recorded in the context of the 2003 to 2005 Agriculture and Food Program, effectively contributing to the reversal in decline and to greater diversification in agriculture (Pomfret 2009).

TAXATION

The state consolidation and revenue increases in the late 1990s brought some convergence in the overall size of tax revenues relative to GDP. The low-income CIS states caught up with rates common among other low-income countries. Government revenues in Belarus, Russia, and Ukraine were well above the average of comparable upper-middle-income countries. Eastern European countries, if compared with the rest of the European Union, generally belong in the low tax-and-spend category. There was also a considerable variation within country groups. The level of government revenues in southeastern Europe varied from 47 percent of GDP in Bosnia and Herzegovina to 26 percent in Albania; varied in the middle-income CIS from 22 percent of GDP in Kazakhstan to 51 percent in Belarus; and varied in the low-income CIS from 22 percent of GDP in Armenia to 42 percent in Moldova (IMF 2009c).

In the low-income CIS countries, the revenue increase came through an expansion of indirect taxes on goods and services and international trade, reflecting in part the introduction of a value added tax (VAT), the primary source of indirect tax revenues. Social security contributions were a particularly important source of revenue in the Eastern European countries and middle-income CIS, where they were equivalent to, or even exceeded, the share of direct income taxes (WB 2007, 46; see Figure 9.2).

After the fiscal consolidation of the late 1990s, there was a trend of cutting taxation on companies and individuals—high-income groups in particular. This was driven partly by the liberal ideology, according to which taxation decreases incentives for individuals to engage in productive activities, and partly by the weak acceptance of personal income tax, which was a new phenomenon in former state Socialist countries. Attempts to cut taxes thus also reflected the rise of high-income groups and their representation in the political system. Finally, corporate taxation was often slashed in order to attract foreign investment, triggering a race among Eastern European states (Bohle 2008; Vliegenthart and Overbeek 2008; Drahokoupil 2008a; cf. Cassette and Paty 2008).

Trends over time confirm a differentiation of the post-Communist countries. Table 9.6 shows effective taxation on business, including a "total tax rate" on

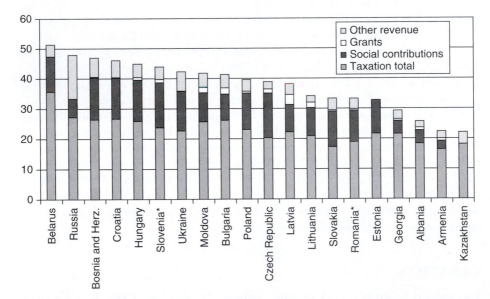

Figure 9.2 Variation in revenue (general government) as a percentage of GDP, 2007 *Source:* IMF (2009c, 18–19, Table W4) Data for Albania are from 2006.
Note: Data for Albania are from 2006.

TABLE 9.6   Effective taxation on business, 2008

	Profit	Labor	Total (TTR)
Belarus	22.0	39.6	117.5
Uzbekistan	1.9	27.1	90.6
Tajikistan	17.7	28.2	85.5
Kyrgyzstan	3.0	23.7	61.4
Ukraine	11.5	43.3	58.4
Hungary	9.1	39.4	57.5
Albania	16.7	28.6	50.5
Russia	10.7	31.8	48.7
Estonia	8.8	38.3	48.6
Czech Republic	6.0	39.5	48.6
Romania	10.4	35.5	48.0
Slovakia	6.8	39.5	47.4
Lithuania	8.3	35.2	46.4
Bosnia-Herzegovina	21.5	17.2	44.1
Moldova	10.4	31.4	42.1
Azerbaijan	13.8	24.8	41.1
Poland	13.0	23.5	40.2
Georgia	14.1	22.6	38.6
Slovenia	13.0	21.1	36.7
Armenia	12.1	23.4	36.6
Kazakhstan	15.6	17.9	36.4
Bulgaria	4.2	26.8	34.9
Serbia	11.6	20.2	34.0
Latvia	2.2	27.2	33.0
Croatia	11.4	19.4	32.5
Montenegro	9.6	20.0	31.8
Macedonia	14.0	0.8	18.4
CEECs	*8.2*	*32.6*	*44.1*
CARs	*9.6*	*24.2*	*68.5*
Baltic republics	*6.4*	*33.6*	*42.7*
Czech Republic, Hungary, Poland, and Slovakia	*8.7*	*35.5*	*48.4*

Source: WB and PwC (2008).

Note: The total tax rate indicator (TTR) of the WB and PricewaterhouseCoopers measures the amount of all taxes and mandatory contributions borne by a business in the second year of operation, expressed as a percentage of commercial profits. This is a comprehensive measure that looks at the cost of all such contributions borne by business rather than focusing only on corporate income or profit taxes (WB and PwC 2008).

TABLE 9.7   **Direct taxes as a percentage of GDP in Eastern Europe**

	Personal income tax			Corporate tax		
	1995	2005	Top rate, 2006	1995	2005	Adjusted top rate, 2007
Czech Republic	4.8	4.6	32.0	4.6	4.5	24.0
Hungary	6.7	6.6	36.0	1.9	2.1	18.6
Poland	8.4	3.9	40.0	2.7	2.5	19.0
Slovakia	3.7	2.8	19.0	6.8	2.8	19.0
Slovenia	6.0	6.0	50.0	0.5	2.9	23.0
Bulgaria		3.0	24.0		2.9	10.0
Romania		2.4	16.0		2.7	16.0
Estonia	8.3	5.6	23.0	2.4	1.4	22.0
Latvia	5.3	5.8	25.0	1.8	2.0	15.0
Lithuania	6.5	7.0	27.0	2.1	2.1	18.0
Ireland	10.3	7.3	42.0	2.7	3.4	12.5
Sweden	16.5	15.6	56.6	2.6	3.8	28.0
EU-25, arithmetic average	8.7	8.3	40.0	2.8	3.2	25.5

Source: Eurostat (2007, 32, 250, 252).

profits (TTR).[1] As indicated by the TTR, Belarus and CARs (with the exception of Kazakhstan) levy much higher taxes on business than the rest of the post-Communist states. Effective taxation of profits varies significantly also within country groups.

Tables 9.7 and 9.8 show the trends in taxation levels in Eastern European EU members. Corporate tax levels were, on average, slightly above the average EU level in 1995 (both close to 2.8 percent of GDP), reflecting the role they had played as a major source of tax revenue in the period of central planning. They had fallen to 2.5 percent of GDP in 2005, while the EU average had risen to 3.2 percent. This reflected approximate constancy in the Czech Republic, Latvia, Lithuania, Hungary, and Poland, an increase in Slovenia, and dramatic falls in Slovakia and Estonia. The Baltic republics kept the lowest corporate taxation levels in Europe, with Estonia introducing a 0 percent tax on reinvested profits in 2000.

As far as the taxation on personal income is concerned, the average was 6.2 percent of GDP in 1995 (against 8.7 percent for the EU-25) and was 5.3 percent of GDP in 2005 (against 8.3 percent for the EU-25). This again reflected variations between countries. There was approximate constancy in Slovenia, Hungary, and Lithuania, a small decline in the Czech Republic, and much more marked declines in Estonia (falling from 8.3 percent to 5.6 percent of GDP from 1999 to 2000), Slovakia (falling over the whole period from 3.7 percent of GDP to 2.8 percent, albeit with a

---

[1] The total tax rate indicator of the WB and PricewaterhouseCoopers (PwC) measures the amount of all taxes and mandatory contributions borne by a business in its second year of operation, expressed as a percentage of commercial profits. This is a comprehensive measure that looks at the cost of all such contributions borne by business rather than focusing only on corporate income or profit taxes (WB and PwC 2008).

TABLE 9.8   Implicit tax rates in Eastern Europe

	Capital		Labor		Consumption		Corporate income, adjusted top rate	
	1995	2006	1995	2006	1995	2006	2007	Change 1995-2007, %
Estonia	25.6	8.4	39.2	33.9	20.8	23.6	22.0	−4.0
Latvia		9.6[a]	39.2	33.5	19.3	20.0	15.0	−10.0
Lithuania	15.1	14.1	34.5	34.1	17.7	16.7	18.0	−11.0
Poland	20.9	22.2[a]	36.8	34.4	21.3	20.2	19.0	−21.0
Czech Republic	26.4	24.9	40.5	41.0	22.1	21.2	24.0	−17.0
Hungary			42.6	39.0	30.8	25.8	29.6	−11.3
Slovakia	35.3	18.1	38.5	30.3	26.0	20.2	19.0	−21.0
Slovenia			38.9	37.6	25.2	24.2	23.0	−2.0
Romania				29.1[a]		17.7	16.0	−22.0
Bulgaria				30.9		25.9	10.0	−30.0
EU-25	*25.8*	*33.3*	*36.9*	*36.7*	*20.0*	*19.9*		

Source: Eurostat online database, available at
http://epp.eurostat.ec.europa.eu/portal/page/portal/statistics/search_database.
Note: The implicit tax rate is calculated by dividing the revenues from taxes on a special activity or good by an appropriate corresponding aggregate tax base from national accounts statistics.
[a]Data are from 2005.

rise to 5.0 percent in 1997), Poland (falling from 8.4 percent of GDP to 3.9 percent, with big drops in 1999 and 2004), and Latvia. The comparison of taxation levels shows that while CEECs and Slovakia brought personal income tax to extremely low levels, the low-corporation-tax Baltic republics levied relatively high levels of tax on personal incomes.[2]

THE FLAT TAX FAD

The idea for a flat tax is attributed to Robert E. Hall and Alvin Rabushka, beginning with an article they wrote in 1981 (see R.E. Hall and Rabushka [2007]). The proposal was originally for the United States. The authors advocated one tax covering all forms of income, thereby replacing existing personal income, corporation, inheritance, and capital gains taxes. There would be one 19 percent tax rate and a significant allowance on personal incomes. They justified this in terms of administrative simplicity by rejecting the view that progressive taxation could be linked to fairness or justice and by claiming that "high tax rates reduce economic output" (44). The idea attracted some interest but also very widespread condemnation, not the least of which became

[2]The 2008 flat tax reform in the Czech Republic is not reflected in the figures. It included an apparent 15 percent basic rate, but that came with an innovative expansion of the income tax base to include "supergross income," including also all health and social insurance contributions. In effect, the actual tax rate amounted to 23.1 percent. The reform meant significant tax reduction for top-income groups only (Večerník 2009, 108–116). The Czech story also points to the importance of the symbolic dimension of tax cuts.

apparent when the authors acknowledged that they favored a reduced tax base and a substantial retreat of the state in traditional welfare activities. That appeared to be an inevitable corollary of their proposals for a narrowing of the tax base.

However, they claimed success in the introduction of flat taxes in an increasing number of former state Socialist countries, none of which previously had particularly high top rates of income tax. The popularity of the flat tax in the post-Communist area does not reflect serious evidence of any negative effects of income tax on personal incentives; nor are low corporation taxes particularly relevant to inward investors, for whom total costs, especially wages, are more important. Furthermore, it is not a response to economic difficulties. On the contrary, it may partly be a response to growing prosperity and high growth rates that make possible either tax cuts or new forms of spending.

As indicated in Table 9.9, there were two identifiable waves with rather different features. The first covered the Baltic republics, beginning with Estonia and Lithuania in 1994, followed by Latvia in 1997. They set relatively high standard tax rates, and in two cases, the following year saw an increase in revenue from personal income tax. The second wave came in the context of state-capacity consolidation and increasing tax competition in Eastern Europe. It was started by Russia in 2001, which was later followed by a number of further countries. In this context, the Baltic republics slashed

TABLE 9.9 **Countries introducing a flat tax**

		Previous	Flat tax rate	
	Year introduced	highest tax rate	Year of reform	2008
Estonia	1994	33	26	22p,c[a]
Lithuania	1994	33	33	27p/15c
Latvia	1997–2009	25	25	25p/15c
Russia	2001	30	13p	13p/24c[b]
Serbia	2003		14c	10c
Ukraine	2004	40	13	15p/25c
Slovakia	2004	38	19	
Georgia	2005	20	12p/20c	
Romania	2005	40	16	
Kyrgyzstan	2006	20	10	
Macedonia	2007	24	12	
Albania	2007/2008	30p/20c	10	
Mongolia	2007	30	10	
Czech Republic	2008	32p/24c	23.1p/21c	
Bulgaria	2008	24p/15c	10	

Source: R.E. Hall and Rabushka (2007, viii–x) and Eurostat (2007), as well as the authors' own elaboration.

Note: The letter "p" appearing after a figure indicates that it is the personal tax rate; the letter "c" indicates that it is the corporate tax rate.

[a]Here, there was a 0 percent tax on reinvested profits (since 2000) and a social tax of 33 percent.

[b]Corporate rate was lowered to 20 percent in 2009.

their tax rates, particularly those on corporate profits. Among CEECs, Slovakia took the role of reform leader in 2004 by introducing a 19 percent flat tax. It was followed by Romania, with a flat tax at an even lower level.

In Russia, personal income tax revenues substantially increased after the reform. This was attributed to higher compliance among higher-income taxpayers (Ivanova, Keen, and Klemm 2005). The tax reform came in the context of the attempt to consolidate state capacity in general, analyzed in the previous chapter. It was tied to the so-called Gref Program—named after the minister for economic development from 2000 who formulated it—the first aim of which was budget and macroeconomic balance. This depended on short-term cuts in real wages and government activities, which confirmed the commitment to a "small" state (Mau 2005, 93–94, 223). However, this was also closely linked to improvements in state capacity, and it is difficult to differentiate possible positive effects of the flat tax on tax collection from other factors, such as the improvement of the capacity of the tax-administering bureaucracy (cf. Appel 2008).

Russian experience, however specific, contributed to the emulation of the reform in Eastern Europe. In other countries, including Slovakia and Ukraine, personal tax revenues declined with the lower tax rates. (WB 2007, 16). As far as corporate income tax is concerned, revenues collected two years after the reform shrank to one quarter in Lithuania and by one quarter in Russia. There was a slight revenue increase in Slovakia and Ukraine, but it can be attributed to other factors, such as rapid GDP growth in that period (WB 2007). Thus, any rhetoric about gaining from improved compliance, or from newly released entrepreneurial incentives leading to higher overall tax revenue, proved illusory, at least within that timescale.[3]

REALITIES OF THE FLAT TAX

The flat tax has a specific meaning and form in the context of transition countries. First, the tax reforms in the region do not fully match Hall and Rabushka's proposal. They generally do not have equal rates of tax on different forms of income, and in Russia and Ukraine, a further progressive element was added by a tax allowance that varied with income levels (Keen, Kim, and Varsano 2006). Only the Slovak reform came close to the original proposal, with the same rate of personal income tax, corporate taxation, and VAT.

Second, although the idea first became visible in the United States, countries in Eastern Europe that adopted it were actually following the example of countries from the former Soviet Union rather than any advanced market economy. Moreover, they were competing with each other and fighting to keep up with the tax-cutting agenda of their peers, even when different priorities seemed to apply in Western Europe. This won support from a substantial political constituency in the transition countries, but it had far less appeal in countries of Western Europe.

Third, the flat tax was associated with rather different shifts in the distributional impact of personal income tax. In all the later versions, it led to gains for those with

[3]Yet, while the personal income revenue fell considerably the year after flat tax reform in Slovakia, there was a 14.6 percent increase in the number of personal income tax returns. A similar effect was not observed in Ukraine (WB 2007, Chapter 8).

the highest incomes. In some, such as Slovakia, it led to gains also for the lowest incomes, thanks to an increase in the basic allowance. It was therefore not a matter of simply reducing progressiveness. This accentuates the impression that the flat tax was largely about a slogan or about sending a message to the outside world. However, it produced two groups of losers. The first group was frequently made up of those with middle incomes—a realization that contributed to the defeat of the Slovak government in elections in 2006 and to the loss of electoral support for the Right in the Czech Republic in 2008. The second group was those who depended on other aspects of state spending that were cut, most notably in Slovakia, as part of a reform package that included the flat tax.

Fourth, it was an issue of intense controversy in Eastern Europe, where, much more than in the CIS, it was confronted by the alternative of a European social state. The idea of a flat tax summarized the view of the state's role in the economy as minimal and nonredistributive and appeared in numerous election programs. It was not a policy slipped in through the back door but was a core of the reform program, analyzed in Chapter 10 as "neoliberal restructuring." Advocating parties in some cases were defeated in elections, and even when they appeared to have won, they were forced to backtrack on occasion—as in Poland after 1998, when divisions within a right-wing coalition led to inaction—or to make substantial compromises. In Slovakia, trade unions staged a symbolic general strike in protest and raised enough signatures in a petition to force a referendum in April 2004 in which 31 percent of the registered electorate supported speedy parliamentary elections. It was not enough to make the result binding, but it was more than had supported the then-government parties and was followed in 2006 by the election of a left-dominated government. In Slovenia, the proposal from a new right-wing government for a 20 percent flat tax was abandoned after mass protests from trade unions and others in November 2005. Evidently, the flat tax aroused both strong support and strong opposition.

However, although easy to arouse opposition, it proved extremely difficult for governments to reverse direct-tax-cutting policies. Instead, the pressure was for further reductions in flat tax rates, as advocated in 2007 by governments in all the Baltic republics, albeit held in check by the need for a balanced budget and for continued public spending. The new Slovak government in 2006 made only small changes, largely to restore a progressive element with differentiated rates of VAT. There was talk, both from the opposition and from within the coalition, of a possible further reduction in the flat tax rate. The flat tax, however, proved to be unsustainable in Latvia, where it was scrapped in 2009 in the context of drastic spending cuts adjusting to the shocks of the financial crisis (analyzed in Chapter 17). The trend, nevertheless, had clearly been for a reduction in direct taxes, and that set limits on government spending and hence on any active roles that the state could play.

CONCLUSION

The comparison of different trajectories of state transformation in the last three chapters has also shown the variety of factors limiting the active role of the state as known from many West European countries. Eastern European states developed state apparatuses with strong bureaucratic capacity, including the separation of the economic and political spheres. However, internal political factors as well as the competition for mobile investors put considerable limits on the levels of taxation and thus also on the role of the state in promoting competiveness and, as will be analyzed in the next chapter, on its social role.

State capacity proved to be the major limiting factor in the CIS. Some of the states, most notably Russia, managed to consolidate their capacity to some extent, and state intervention started to play an important role. While Russian statism might be considered "better than anything else tried so far" (Lane 2008, 182), the weak separation of the politics from business and the related rescue state policy approach militated against effective state economic intervention. The natural resources bonanza of the early 2000s apparently freed Russia and some other states from fiscal constraints, but the collapse of natural resource prices accompanying the global financial crisis revealed the vulnerability of dependence on natural resources.

Finally, reestablishing control over economic and political spheres, the order states prevented the state-capacity collapse and the extent of clientelistic links between business and political power that accompanied transition elsewhere in the CIS. They also proved to be capable of effective transition-crisis management, hindering the level of corruption. It remains to be seen if they would be able to continue the gradual, or very gradual, state-led transformation into a market economy, particularly when their relative isolation from advanced markets limited their potential for economic development.

CHAPTER TEN

Welfare States and Regimes

This chapter focuses on changing "welfare regimes" during economic transformations. This means analyzing how state activities are interlocked with market and family roles in social provision (cf. Esping-Andersen 1990). Welfare regimes, or welfare systems, thus, include both the formal welfare state institutions and the security regimes where community, family, patronage, and other informal institutions are sources of welfare support (Alcock and Craig 2009, 2, 17–19). Welfare regimes thus refer to institutions, both formal and informal, that protect against life-cycle and labor market risks, regulate employment and labor market participation, and organize the distribution of resources. In a broader sense, they also include economic policies that shape the nature and levels of employment (cf. Adserà and Boix 2002).

The introduction of the market mechanism at the beginning of transition entailed a reorganization of welfare regimes. Organized around employment as the basic social right (and obligation), Communist welfare regimes included universalistic social services, with provision linked to the workplace (see discussion in Chapter 2). Major proponents of shock therapy understood that reforms would incur significant social costs and argued for "reinforcing the social safety net" targeted at new groups in need as a part of the policy package (Lipton and Sachs 1990a, 1990b; Sachs 1990, 1993; Balcerowicz 1992, 1995; see also Åslund [2007, 33]). They also understood that a political backlash from the reform losers could threaten the successful completion of the reforms (e.g., Balcerowicz 1995). Public welfare provision provided some social cushion to economic costs incurred by transition, but the level and nature of adjustment varied. The transition meant a considerable deterioration of life standards for significant parts of certain populations and led to large-scale human suffering, particularly in many of the CIS countries.

Welfare regimes and the role of formal welfare state institutions were shaped by three principal processes. First, where formal welfare state institutions failed to adjust to the new environment, welfare regime adjustments—that is, efforts to organize social protection—went through a continuing reliance on old institutions and informal provisions. This was the development common in the CIS, with variation linked to the patterns of state collapse and consolidation. With states retaining institutional capacity in the context of transition shocks, countries in Eastern Europe adjusted their welfare states, providing a social cushion for transition through formal institutions.

Second, attempts at neoliberal restructuring were made to reduce commitments to formal redistributive arrangements created in welfare regime adjustments. Neoliberal restructuring thus aimed to dismantle the redistributive elements of existing welfare regimes and appeared on the agenda in Eastern Europe in the late 1990s.

Third, the IFIs—the World Bank, in particular—had a major role in helping to organize a policy campaign, which included input from semi-independent think tanks and led to a "silent revolution" in pension systems. This was the crucial social policy field in the post-Communist world.

After outlining the patterns of employment, inequality, and poverty, this chapter discusses the three processes and factors that conditioned them. Then, the transformation of welfare regimes in Eastern Europe and the CIS and the variation within the country groups is analyzed in more detail. The final section sets out the variety of welfare regimes that took shape in these transformations.

THE WELFARE CHALLENGE: EMPLOYMENT, POVERTY, AND INEQUALITY

Economic transition meant the end of full employment, a core element of state Socialist welfare regimes. Figure 10.1 shows the falling levels of labor force participation, which were generally more rapid in Eastern Europe than in Russia and other CIS countries. Transition also brought about a drastic increase in poverty. By WB standards—equivalent to $2.15 per head per day at 1996 purchasing power—on average, 2 percent of the population in the state Socialist countries of Europe and central Asia lived in absolute poverty in 1988. Ten years later, in 1998, the WB estimated the number of people living below that standard to be 21 percent of

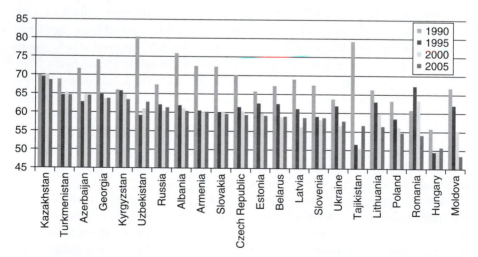

Figure 10.1 Labor force participation rates (ages 15+). (*Source:* ILO Economically Active Population Estimates and Projections (EAPEP) database, 5th edition (2008 revision), available at http://laborsta.ilo.org/applv8/data/EAPEP/eapep_E.html.)

Notes: The workforce is calculated as a percentage of the population in each age category.

the population (WB 2000, 31). These are rough approximations, with country-level data suffering serious deficiencies, but they provide strong evidence of an increasing problem of social deprivation.

In the CIS countries, transition was accompanied also by large (male) mortality increases. Estimates of the number of premature deaths that accompanied the systemic change vary between 3 and 10 million (Stuckler, King, and McKee 2009).[1] Table 10.1 provides estimates of poverty levels in 1995 to 1999. These were the highest levels in most of the countries, and poverty then appeared to decline. As indicated in Figure 10.2 (and also in Table A.17 in the Appendix), inequality, as measured by Gini coefficients—and with some questions over the reliability of data—increased in all countries and most markedly in Georgia, central Asia, Russia, the Baltic republics and Poland. These differences reflected the severity of depression and were linked to per capita income, but they were also related to the differences in welfare regimes.

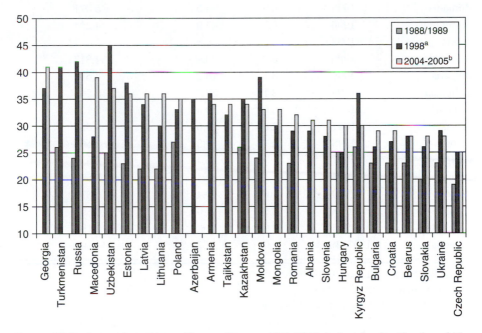

Figure 10.2 Inequality: Ginicoefficients.(*Source:* WB (2008a); data for the Czech and Slovak republics for 2006 are from the Eurostat database, available at http://epp.eurostat.ec .europa.eu/portal/page/portal/statistics/search_database.)
Notes: [a]The year is 1995 for Azerbaijan; 1996 for the Czech and Slovak republics and Kazakhstan;1997 for Albania and Bulgaria; and 1999 for Armenia, Tajikistan and Ukraine.
[b]The year is 2003 for Armenia, Bulgaria, the Kyrgyz Republic, Macedonia, Moldova, Kazakhstan, and Uzbekistan; 2002 for Mongolia and Russia; and 2006 for the Czech and Slovak republics.

[1]The pace of economic transition was found to be a key driver in increasing mortality rates (M. Murphy et al. 2006; Leinsalu, Vågerö, and Kunst 2003). There is even econometric evidence showing a correlation between rapid and mass privatization and mortality increases (Stuckler, King, and McKee 2009). However, caveats on the limits of econometrics also apply in this context (see Box 4.1).

TABLE 10.1 Absolute poverty rates of transition economies in Europe and Central Asia, 1995 to 1999

	Survey year	$2.15/day	$4.30/day	1998 GNP in dollars per capita
Tajikistan	1999	68.3	95.8	1,040
Moldova	1999	55.4	84.6	1,995
Kyrgyz Republic	1998	49.1	84.1	2,247
Armenia	1999	43.5	86.2	2,074
Azerbaijan	1999	23.5	64.2	2,168
Georgia	1999	18.9	54.2	3,429
Russia	1998	18.8	50.3	6,186
Albania[a]	1996	11.5	58.6	2,864
Turkmenistan	1998	7.0	34.4	2,875
Romania	1998	6.8	44.5	5,571
Macedonia	1996	6.7	43.9	4,224
Latvia	1998	6.6	34.8	5,777
Kazakhstan	1996	5.7	30.9	4,317
Bulgaria	1995	3.1	18.2	4,683
Lithuania	1999	3.1	22.5	6,283
Ukraine	1999	3.0	29.4	3,130
Slovakia	1997	2.6	8.6	9,624
Estonia	1998	2.1	19.3	7,563
Hungary	1997	1.3	15.4	9,832
Poland	1998	1.2	18.4	7,543
Belarus	1999	1.0	10.4	6,318
Croatia	1998	0.2	4.0	6,698
Czech Republic	1996	0.0	0.8	12,197
Slovenia	1997–1998	0.0	0.7	14,399

Source: WB (2000, 35, Table 1.1).

Note: GNP = gross national product.

[a]The survey did not cover the capital city, Tirana.

Transition presented new challenges for the welfare sphere, but they were met in different ways.

There was no direct relationship between employment, income distribution, and poverty, on the one hand, and the recorded changes in economic output, on the other hand. As far as employment is concerned, two patterns can be distinguished. Russia and other CIS states adjusted to the economic downturn primarily through large real-wage reductions and substantial wage arrears (EBRD 2000, 98; Clarke 1999; Gimpelson 2001). Thus, they experienced only modest employment decreases relative to GDP contractions. Russia and Ukraine, in particular, recorded only very low unemployment levels. In the low-income CIS states, migration abroad became an important coping strategy for significant parts of the workforce (see pp. 190-91). Probably at its lowest point in August 1998, the average real wage in Russia was less than a third of its December 1991 level (Clarke 1999, 120). Fearing failures of large enterprises and the political implications of mass unemployment, the Russian government introduced neither punitive fees for delayed payments nor an effective bankruptcy framework. The enterprises, thus, operated in an environment of a soft budget constraint that was monetized through debt (see Chapter 11) and protected as enterprises opted out of the money economy in the early 1990s and again in the period up to 1998, exchanging by barter and often paying wages in kind (Woodruff 1999). The state did not provide reliable or adequate unemployment benefits, so there was little incentive to register as unemployed, leading to the low recorded levels. Employees continued to gain access to social provisions, which often included housing that was provided by the enterprises. Thus, new social needs were to some extent handled by an informal continuation of the old Soviet-style system of welfare provision through enterprises.

In contrast, employment in Eastern Europe fell sharply as the region adjusted to transition shocks through employment shedding rather than wage cuts. Welfare institutions, modeled on Western European experience, played a major role in compensating for real income falls. Unemployment, as shown in Figure 10.3 (and also in Table A.4 in the Appendix), peaked in the early 1990s in most of these countries and then stabilized or fell. The Czech Republic was something of an exception, as detailed in Box 10.1.

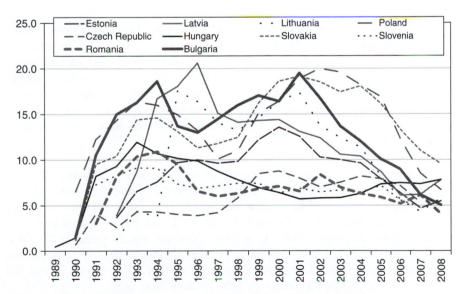

Figure 10.3 Unemployment in Eastern Europe (%). (*Source:* EBRD economic statistics and forecasts, available at http://www.ebrd.com/country/sector/econo/stats/index.htm.)

Box 10.1   Czech employment miracle?

With unemployment levels lower than in many advanced capitalist countries, the Czech Republic kept an exceptional unemployment record throughout the 1990s. It is often argued that rising unemployment was held in check by maintaining soft budget constraints in established industries through the absence of a strong bankruptcy framework and by extending credit through state-owned banks. However, this well-known and popular argument is partly myth.

There were delays in implementing a bankruptcy law passed in 1991, and this followed from fears of the impact that a similar law had in Hungary. Similarly, banks did provide support to some inefficient firms. Nevertheless, other financial constraints on enterprises were severe and led to as rapid employment declines here as in other countries. More specifically, from 1989 to 1993, the workforce in industry fell by 31 percent in Poland and by 35 percent in the Czech Republic (Myant et al. 1996). Czech coal mining employment fell over the same period by 51 percent, compared to 28 percent in Poland. Apart from the wage-employment trade-off, the distinctive Czech features were the lighter unemployment effects of employment declines. Part of the labor force had been made up of pensioners who simply lost their jobs and from Slovaks and even Poles who returned home, putting the cost on another country. More importantly, there was a very rapid expansion in a new service sector. These activities had been particularly weakly developed in the 1980s.

Emigration had important consequences for labor markets and general welfare in the sending countries. Data on remittances shown in Table 4.2 indicate the importance of part of the labor force working abroad to a number of CIS states. In general, migrants working abroad tended to be people with higher-than-average education who were from urban backgrounds. Consequently, remittances tended to be beneficial to the wealthier members of society, not to the worse-off households. This has been confirmed by case studies also in the transition countries (e.g., Uzagalieva and Menezes 2009).

According to an International Labor Organization (ILO) estimate, more than 9 million former Soviet citizens moved to live in another country between 1990 and 1996. Among them were many ethnic Russians who found themselves unwelcome in what had become new republics and/or who sought better opportunities in Russia; some 2.7 million returned to Russia between 1993 and 1996 (Stalker 2000, 95; cf. Radnitz 2006; Peyrouse 2007). In another estimate, Russia received 7 million immigrants by December 2002 (Sutela 2003, 218; Pilkington 1998, 5). Outside the CIS, Germany was a major destination, receiving 2 million ethnic Germans from the former Soviet Union from 1988 through 1994 (Stalker 2000, 96).

Remittance data are worse indicators for Eastern European countries, where the character of migration differed, generating also less remittances. The number of citizens of CEECs and Baltic republics working abroad increased sharply after the EU accession in May 2004. Some EU countries, such as Germany, kept transitional arrangements restricting employment of workers from the new member states. That increased the share of countries that freed their labor markets, most notably the United Kingdom and Ireland, among the recipients of migrant workers, but there was no simple link between the transition arrangements and migration flows. For instance, the main destination countries for emigrants from Lithuania in 2002 were Germany, Estonia, Russia, Ireland and the U.S.; in 2004, the bulk of emigration moved to the United Kingdom and Germany. In general, Germany, the United Kingdom, and Ireland were the main destination countries for migrant workers from CEECs and the Baltic republics. A similar pattern was evident in the SEECs even before they entered the European Union in 2007, with migrants often finding unregistered employment in Italy, Spain, and other countries (see Kahanec and Zimmermann [2009]). Precise figures are difficult to estimate due to the temporal character of the substantial part of the migration and to difficulties in registering the migrants. According to one estimate, the largest shares of emigrants in proportion to the home population in 2007 were in Romania (7.2%), Bulgaria (4.1%), Lithuania (3.8%), and Poland (3.4%; Brücker and Damelang [2009], in Kahanec, Zaiceva, and Zimmermann [2009, 17]).

Labor immigration within the European Union, however, was not limited to the new member states. Many workers in other countries neighboring the European Union were able to find jobs in the European Union. The same estimate of immigration to old member states, thus, shows the share of migrants in the home population as 7.1 percent in Croatia and an extraordinary 25.5 percent in Albania. In absolute numbers, emigration from Poland was most substantial, with the number of Polish residents who stayed abroad for at least two months tripling from early 2004 to early 2007, increasing from around 180,000 to 540,000 (Kaczmarczyk and Okólski 2008). Emigration coincided with changes in the labor market structures in home countries, leading to shortages of highly skilled professionals, wage increases, and increasing employment of migrants from non-EU countries—Ukraine, in particular. However, these changes were linked also to other, arguably more important, causes such as economic recovery (Kaczmarczyk and Okólski 2008).

WELFARE ADJUSTMENTS

Welfare adjustments, meaning steps to adapt inherited forms of social protection in response to new needs, were the natural response at the beginning of transition. Even in this, countries' responses varied enormously. It took CIS countries nearly a decade to adjust their welfare state institutions.

Based on the full-employment principle, inherited welfare systems could not address new risks created by transition, most notably to provide assistance to the unemployed. What is more, a large part of social services were provided by enterprises for their employees only. The high inflation of the early 1990s also made cash benefits without the appropriate adjustment irrelevant, and the benefit levels in the Soviet system were low, giving little scope for reductions without serious damage to welfare (Milanovic 1998; Cook 2007). Even in the more stable environment of the late 1990s and after, a lack of sustained efforts at maintaining real levels of social provision meant a retrenchment "by decay" (Saxonberg and Sirovátka 2009).

Welfare state adjustments, meaning changes specifically to that part of welfare regimes constituted by the state provision of benefits, were conditioned by state capacity to implement social policies and to maintain administrative control over the welfare infrastructure, both dependent on the ability to raise revenue. This, as discussed in Chapter 7, was a major problem in many of the CIS countries. There, the initial welfare adjustments, thus, involved reliance on the remnants of old institutions and on informal solutions. Welfare state adjustments came only in the context of state-capacity consolidation.

The efforts at welfare state adjustment were not directly related to the severity of shocks, be they hyperinflation, slumps in output, or falls in employment. Formal welfare state institutions were adjusted where the executive was effectively accountable to electoral constraints, as was the case in much of Eastern Europe, and/or where social interests were represented in the political system, as was the case particularly in Slovenia. State Socialist welfare arrangements gave rise to a popular expectation of an active state role in providing social protection and services, and, in Eastern Europe, also in reducing inequality (Cook 2007, 42–44; Murthi and Tiongson 2009). Effective representation thus led to efforts at welfare state adjustments, reflecting the strength of the welfare state constituency. The adjustment of the welfare state was then likely to produce a "ratchet effect" (Huber and Stephens 2001, 28), with social policies recreating its political constituencies and reproducing popular expectations that the state would provide social protection.

In authoritarian regimes, such as Turkmenistan, Uzbekistan, Kazakhstan, and Belarus, the outcomes in welfare state adjustments were variable. In some of these countries—most notably in Belarus—welfare provision appeared to be a key element of regime legitimation. Another factor, as argued by Cook (2007), may be the strength of bureaucratic-statist welfare interests in relation to the presidential power.

Adjustments of formal welfare state institutions tended to be path dependent, making old systems compatible with the new environment. New institutions were introduced to counter the effects of unemployment and to regulate the labor market. In some cases, existing institutions were used to address new social problems. The main actors shaping institutional change during the welfare adjustment were welfare bureaucrats who were drawing on policy legacies of incremental welfare adjustments (Inglot 2008, 214). Sustaining welfare efforts in the context of deep structural transformation and economic crisis was a fiscal challenge also for the CEECs. In the accession countries, the requirement to meet the Maastricht criteria was providing an additional fiscal constraint by the end of the 1990s (Rhodes and Keune 2006).[2]

Economic crises increased the influence of liberal technocrats and the IFIs (Haggard and Kaufman 2008, 11), but these considered welfare reforms of secondary importance in the early 1990s. Dominant ideas, such as the "targeted safety net"

---

[2]The Treaty of the European Union was formally signed in Maastricht in the Netherlands in February 1992 by members of the European Community to create the European Union. It included conditions for membership of the European Monetary Union and adoption of its common currency, the euro which required members to keep state budget deficits below 3 percent of GDP and the level of state debt below 60 percent of GDP. The national currencies of 12 EU member states were fully replaced by the euro in 2002. All new EU members were required to enter the European Monetary Union at some point, even though no specific entry date was set. The first two transition economies to join were Slovenia, in 2007, and Slovakia, in 2009. Estonia was scheduled to join in 2011.

principle, were mainly influential in designing new policies. The idea of a safety net became prominent later when the WB began to focus on social policy, arguing for targeted welfare policies.[3] The WB, as discussed in the next section, played a major role in the reform of the pension system that was implemented across the region.

NEOLIBERAL RESTRUCTURING

In the late 1990s, in the context of neoliberal restructuring, social policies moved to the center of policy attention, but not because of fiscal problems with existing welfare schemes or because of their failure to deliver socially acceptable benefits for constituencies. Attempts to restructure welfare regimes came as a part of a broader political agenda to transform existing regulatory and institutional frameworks and their underlying political arrangements. Aiming to dismantle existing redistributive regimes, cuts in taxation, including the flat tax, and loosening of labor regulation constituted the core of these reforms. Cuts in budget revenues were to be financed through a reduction of state commitment to the welfare system. Driven by political rather than economic considerations, neoliberal reform attempts typically came only after existing programs had been consolidated and possible crisis averted.

The political pressures for neoliberal restructuring could be observed all around Eastern Europe, but the restructuring took a more radical form only where the executive had a particularly strong position and where the party opposition as well as the representation of broader social interests were weak (for the importance of party systems, see O'Dwyer and Kovalčík [2007]). The election of a right-wing party representing these groups was one of the preconditions for neoliberal restructuring to take place. These conditions were fulfilled in Slovakia after 2002, which became an emblematic case of neoliberal restructuring.

The reforms can, therefore, be interpreted as political projects that reflected the rise of new social groups that were enjoying high incomes and of these groups' ability to establish themselves politically. However, their social support and appeal was broader; the post-Communist conditions shaped and provided advantages to neoliberal restructuring.

Thus, personal income tax, as a new phenomenon lacking the acceptance brought by the passage of time in mature market economies, was particularly resented. This helped to give the flat tax and the minimal role of the state much bigger popular appeal in the post-Communist context, particularly among the intellectuals and middle classes that were more exposed to policy debates in the media.

The political Right was able to reproduce an association of redistributive policies and the state's role in social provision with the past. The Right seemed to feel the need to keep reasserting its will to reform, even when it was "reforming"

---

[3]The experience of advanced capitalist states, however, showed that such targeting ultimately undermines political support for the welfare state, as it narrows the group of beneficiaries. Moreover, with benefits being withdrawn as incomes rise, means testing can create a "poverty trap." Welfare for the poor is, thus, prone to become a poor welfare, ultimately making the needy worse off (Atkinson 1995; Cornia and Stewart 1995; Moene and Wallerstein 2001).

from a weak version of EU practice rather than from the state Socialist past. Examples of radical reform then turned these "purification rituals" (see Eyal, Szelenyi, and Townsley [1998, 104–6]) into a symbolic race among post-Communist right-wing parties.

The IFIs had an important role in promoting ideas that informed these reforms, in facilitating policy learning and transfer, and in conferring legitimacy to the proposals of domestic reformers. The initiative, however, was with the domestic actors, who could even be found to be "too radical" by the IFIs.[4]

THE SILENT REVOLUTION: PENSIONS

By 2009, 15 post-Communist countries had implemented a partial privatization of pension systems that was influenced by the WB thinking (see Orenstein [2008]). The reforms toward the WB three-pillar pension system, discussed in Box 10.2, aimed to address the long-term fiscal challenges of the aging crisis. The actual reforms differed, and the individual pillars played varying roles (see Table 10.2). Pension reform was often put on the agenda by the IFIs—and from quite an early date, particularly in the context of financial crisis, which lent the latter hard power in the form of loan conditionalities. Poland, for instance, had already pledged to undertake a pension reform in a 1994 standby agreement with the IMF. However, the ability to implement these reforms was dependent on the ability of the executive to forge compromises with the welfare bureaucracy and on its political support (similar arguments also in Cook [2007] and Inglot [2008]).

Box 10.2   Putting the three-pillar pension system in its place

Pension privatization was first adopted in Chile in the context of its neoliberal revolution of the 1980s. The Chilean Pinochet government abandoned a pay-as-you-go (PAYG) defined-benefit system in 1981 and introduced private individual pension accounts (more specifically, a mandatory, privately managed, fully funded, defined contribution personal pension scheme). The reform became a template for many reforms elsewhere in Latin America (Madrid 2003), but the example had little influence in Eastern Europe and the former Soviet Union.

A turning point in the development of the pension reform in the post-Communist world came in 1994, when the World Bank published *Averting the Old Age Crisis: Policies to Protect the Old and Promote Growth*. The report argued that existing PAYG schemes were unable to cope with demographic aging (i.e., when the number of pensioners increases while the number of workers declines, a phenomenon that became widespread in Eastern Europe and the CIS around the turn of the millennium). Moreover, it claimed that publicly administered systems are vulnerable to moral hazard on the part of politicians, who tend to promise more

---

[4]This was the experience of the Slovak minister of finance, whose ideas were found to be too radical by the WB (Mikloš, quoted in O'Dwyer and Kovalčík [2007, 11]).

pensions than the systems can deliver. State administrators, it was also argued, administer funds in a less efficient way than the private providers.

As a solution, the report proposed a three-pillar model, which the World Bank subsequently campaigned for across the region (Orenstein 2008). The model included (1) a first pillar of state-provided benefits of a redistributive nature (such as a flat, minimum pension, or reduced social security system); (2) a second pillar of mandatory pension savings in private individual accounts (funded, defined contribution); and (3) a third pillar of voluntary, funded-individual, or occupational pensions. Such a solution, it was argued, would also bring an additional benefit of creating a large pool of domestic pension capital and would, thus, finance private-sector development and growth (WB 1994)

However, the economic superiority of the three-pillar model and its ability to overcome problems identified in *Averting the Old Age Crisis* is questionable (for a detailed discussion, see Holzmann and Stiglitz [2001] and Barr and Diamond [2008]).

First, transition from PAYG to a funded system is extremely costly. Such a shift turns the buried implicit pension debt of the PAYG system (i.e., pensions of today's contributors and of pensioners whose contributions had been used for paying pensions to others at the time they were paid in) into an explicit real claim on current government resources. These claims do not represent a problem and can remain buried unless a transition from PAYG to another system is contemplated. In such a transition, individual accounts are effectively financed from the revenues that would be used to pay off the hidden intergenerational debt. Substantial resources, thus, have to be raised to cover today's pensions. This makes the transition to a funded scheme ill-equipped to address the problem of declining returns in the PAYG framework caused by population aging.

Moreover, the experience of Chile and the United Kingdom showed that decentralized, privately managed accounts also involve substantial administrative costs, a drag on investment returns that consumes about 20 percent of the value of the account accumulated over the career (Diamond 1998; Murthi, Orszag, and Orszag 2001).

Second, inefficient and corrupt governments represent a major problem also for private systems, which need complex regulation and public oversight. As far as fund administration is concerned, comparative literature on public pension funds shows that those with sound corporate governance protection may avoid some of the pitfalls associated with public investing (Munnell and Sundén 2001; Iglesias and Palacios 2001).

Third, while privatization shifts risks to individuals, it does not make pension systems immune from public bailouts in case of a major failure (Heclo 1998). Pensions represent a key welfare policy. In a political system with some public accountability, a failure of a private pension system is likely to lead to some sort of government solution to prevent social costs and/or in response to demands for a pension from those who contributed to the failing pension scheme.

Finally, prefunding can indeed increase domestic capital formation, but similar, if not superior, effects can be achieved with publicly managed prefunding (Stiglitz 1988).

The three-pillar model is problematic also from the welfare perspective. First, privatization leaves individuals dependent on stock market performance. Even diversified stock portfolios are not immune from periodic declines and systemic crisis. This became apparent in the context of the 2008 financial meltdown, when the portfolios of mandatory private individual accounts that had been introduced through the WB-inspired reforms in Eastern Europe recorded substantial year-on-year losses: 30.5 percent in Estonia, 35 percent in Hungary, 48.4 percent in Lithuania, and 12.4 percent in Slovakia (all percentages are from October 15, 2008; WB 2008b).

Second, a shift to a defined contribution scheme eliminates redistribution to low-income earners and those with shorter employment histories (typically women with caring responsibilities). This is not just a problem of the second, prefunded pillar. Some countries have restructured their first, PAYG-scheme pillar into a notional defined-contribution model in which benefits are still paid from current contributions, but their levels are directly linked to individual contributions (see J.B. Williamson and Williams 2003).

In sum, a funded system may (or may not) be considered superior to the PAYG system if compared as an alternative for a society without any pension system. This, however, is not the relevant issue in the real world, and the costs of transition from existing PAYG systems need to be taken into account. This tilts the equation in favor of alternative solutions to the challenges of the old-age crisis (see Barr and Diamond [2008, 2010]). In accessing these alternatives, it is important to distinguish, and not to conflate, the effects of privatization (the extent to which private operators manage the system), prefunding (the extent to which assets are accumulated against future pensions), diversification (the extent to which assets are invested in a variety of resources), and the degree to which benefits are linked to the performance of the system (see Orszag and Stiglitz [2001]). Privatization can shift some responsibility from state administrators, but it does not solve fiscal problems caused by population aging. This can be addressed only through prefunding (regardless of whether it is organized by private or public operators), contribution increases, or cuts in pension benefits.

The immediate fiscal stabilization was usually achieved by (temporal) welfare retrenchment through "parametric" measures, meaning changes in the levels of benefits rather than in the principles underlying the system. After the loans were provided, the pledges countries had made were not easily enforceable. It was then the IFIs' soft power through policy campaigns spreading reform ideas that shaped the reforms and made compromises among policy-makers more likely.

This was enough to ensure that the three-pillar system came to be seen as a solution in countries with very different demographic situations, economic problems, administrative capacities, and political constellations and despite good grounds for arguing that other welfare reforms might have been more pressing. Once put on the agenda, privatization of pensions, and also health care, mobilized (would-be) private providers, who would then consistently push for marketization. These originally included mainly transnational financial groups such as Citibank and ING

TABLE 10.2 Outcomes of pension system reforms

Country	First pillar	Percentage of wage to funded scheme	Proportion of total contributions to funded scheme (%)	Year funded scheme began	Participation in funded scheme (by age)	Year funded participants retire
Bulgaria	PAYG	5	21.7	2002	Mandatory <42	Full cohorts by 2023
Croatia	PAYG	5	25.0	2002	Mandatory <40; voluntary 40–50	Partial cohorts of women by 2008 and of men by 2013; full cohorts of women by 2022 and of men by 2027
Estonia	PAYG	6	20.0	2002	Voluntary	Partial cohorts by 2012
Hungary	PAYG	8	23.9	1998	Mandatory for new entrants; voluntary for all others	Partial cohorts by 2008; full cohorts by 2035
Kazakhstan	Minimum	10	100.0	1998	Mandatory for all	Full cohorts by 1999, but acquired rights in old system in addition
Kosovo	Minimum	10	100.0	2002	Mandatory <55	Full cohorts by 2012
Latvia	NDC	8	24.0	2001	Mandatory <30; voluntary 30–50	Partial cohorts by 2013; full cohorts by 2033
Lithuania	PAYG	5.5	22.0	2004	Voluntary	Partial cohorts by 2014
Macedonia	PAYG	7.42	35.0	2006	Mandatory for new entrants	Partial cohorts by 2016; full cohorts of women by 2043 and of men by 2045

(continued overleaf)

TABLE 10.2 Outcomes of pension system reforms (*continued*)

Country	First pillar	Percentage of wage to funded scheme	Proportion of total contributions to funded scheme (%)	Year funded scheme began	Participation in funded scheme (by age)	Year funded participants retire
Poland	NDC	7.30	26.1	1999	Mandatory <30; voluntary 30–50	Partial cohorts of women by **2009** and of men by **2014**; full cohorts of women by **2029** and of men by **2034**
Romania	PAYG	2, increasing to 6	6.7	2008	Mandatory <35; voluntary 36–45	Partial cohorts of women by **2023** and of men by **2028**; full cohorts of women by **2033** and of men by **2038**
Russia	basic PAYG + NDC	6	30.0	2002	Mandatory <35	Full cohorts of women by **2022** and of men by **2027**
Slovakia	PAYG	9	31.3	2005	Voluntary for all (originally mandatory)	Partial cohorts by **2015**
Uzbekistan	PAYG	1		2004	Mandatory	
Ukraine (in preparation)	PAYG	2, increasing to 7			Mandatory	
Czech Republic	Voluntary third pillar, subsidized from state budget (1999)					
Slovenia	Voluntary occupational pension schemes (2000)					
Belarus	One-pillar PAYG system					

Source: WB regional staff (personal communication, April 30, 2009), updated and elaborated by the authors.

Note: NDC = notional defined contribution system.

(Orenstein 2008, 79), but similar agents established themselves also in individual countries by the end of the 1990s (e.g., Cook 2007, 77).

The reforms redefined social rights to different extents, particularly for future clients, but they did not lead to an immediate and radical change in the nature of social provision. The reforms represented a shift toward a reliance on the market in the long term, but they were often accompanied by an immediate increase in the level of public provision, coming as a concession in the reform compromises. Often presented as a response to fiscal problems, pension privatization did not necessarily reverse trends in overall spending on pensions and welfare in general. On the contrary, the considerable costs of the shift toward a prefunded pension system created immediate difficulties for state budgets (e.g., Fultz 2004).

REFORMING EAST EUROPEAN WELFARE STATES

The differences in welfare state efforts in the early 1990s are shown in Table 10.3. The levels of social spending varied across the region, with the Baltic and southeastern European states providing social protection on very low levels and only Slovenia coming close to the levels typical in Western Europe. Two reasonably good indicators are total expenditure on social protection, shown for EU members in Figure 10.4, and the ratio of average pensions to average pay, shown in Table 10.4. The former shows three groups of countries. At the lower end are the Baltic republics and Romania; they also had low pension levels. Welfare state adjustment in these cases typically meant the introduction of new benefits, such as for unemployment, at very low levels. The middle group of CEECs had high levels of provision. Slovakia saw a rapid decline in later years, which was linked to neoliberal restructuring. Slovenia was again at the top, with a welfare state along Western European lines that was protected by powerful interest representation.

Electoral concerns were an important factor explaining the nature of welfare state adjustments in Eastern Europe throughout the 1990s and 2000s, occasionally leading to pre-election surges in social spending in some countries. In Slovenia, legacies of self-management led to the high organizational strength of labor (see Stanojevic [2003]), which strengthened the political support for consistently high welfare spending. In contrast, the strategic use of nationalism and anti-Soviet sentiments against the Left in the context of state- and nation-building projects in the Baltic republics led to very low welfare state efforts there (Steen 1997; Smith-Sivertsen 2004; Sommers 2009, 135–36). Ideological and political factors responsible for labor and the Left's weakness in CEECs (Meardi 2007; Ost 2009; cf. Bohle and Greskovits 2006) can arguably explain the lower level of social provision there than in Western Europe.

Another important factor distinguishing development in these countries is the extent to which fiscal constraints and financial crises allowed IFIs to exert pressure for welfare reforms—most notably that of the pension system. Immediate fiscal pressures were particularly strong in Poland and Hungary, which used pensions as a transition cushion and, thus, created large budget obligations.

In Poland, social spending in 1991 increased to 32 percent of GDP from 25 percent in 1990. Hungary was spending about 27 percent of GDP on social

TABLE 10.3   Social spending as a percentage of GDP in the 1990s

| | Social assistance | | | | Social transfers | | | | | |
| | Health expenditures | | Education expenditures | | Pensions | | Family and maternal allowances | | Social assistance and unemployment | |
	1990–1991	1994–1995	1990–1991	1994–1995	1990–1991	1994–1995	1990–1991	1994–1995	1990–1991	1994–1995
Estonia		5.5		6.7				1.9	0.0	1.5
Latvia	2.5	4.2	4.5	6.7	6.8	10.3	0.6	1.8	0.0	0.5
Lithuania	3.0	4.5	4.8	6.1	5.8	7.0	1.3	1.1	0.7	1.2
Poland	5.0	4.7	5.2	5.2	10.3	13.6[a]	1.9		1.2	
Czech Republic	5.9	7.6	4.2	4.5	8.0	8.3	3.5	3.6	2.3	0.9
Hungary	6.7	7.0	5.6	5.9	10.1	11.4	4.1	3.3	0.8	2.7
Slovakia	5.4	7.1	6.0	4.8	8.2	8.5	3.5	2.6	0.8	1.8
Slovenia	5.8	7.0	4.7	4.8	11.0	13.7	1.4	1.5		2.0
Romania	2.9	2.5	3.1	3.0	7.1	7.0	2.1	0.8	0.3	1.1
Bulgaria	5.1	3.5	4.5	3.9	9.1	8.8	3.0	1.5	0.6	2.8
Albania	4.0	2.8	6.7	4.0	8.8	8.5	0.8			
Ukraine	3.3	4.7		6.0	5.9	6.8	0.2	0.7	0.0	0.1
Belarus	3.5	7.0	4.9	7.0	6.2	6.4	2.5	2.2	0.0	0.1
Russia	2.6	4.8	3.6	3.4	5.9	6.3	1.2	0.8	0.0	0.1
Moldova	5.3	5.1	7.0	6.5	5.5	6.5	2.5	0.7		
Georgia	3.2	0.3	7.2	0.4	6.4	3.0	1.2	0.2	0.4	0.5
Armenia	2.7	1.7	7.0	2.7						
Azerbaijan	2.6	1.3	7.7	3.5	7.4	3.4	3.2	1.3	0.1	0.2
Kazakhstan	4.4	2.5	4.0[b]	2.1	8.2[c]	4.0[c]				
Uzbekistan	5.9	4.5		9.7						
Turkmenistan	5.0	2.2		3.3						
Kyrgyzstan	5.0	5.8	8.4	6.6						
Tajikistan	6.0	1.5	9.1	2.4						

Source: Unicef TransMONEE database, reported in United Nations Development Program (UNDP; 1998).

[a]Data are for 1994 from the Polish Social Insurance Fund, cited in Inglot (2008, 256).

[b]Data are from the IMF (2004).

[c]Data are for 1992 and 1996, respectively, from the WB (1998).

expenditures in 1993 (Inglot 2008; compare with Table 10.3). The countries fought transition unemployment by expanding coverage of their pension schemes, with Poland relying largely on early retirement and Hungary on disability pensions. Between 1989 and 1996, the number of old-age pensioners increased by 20 percent in Hungary and by 46 percent in Poland, in contrast to a 5 percent increase in the Czech Republic (Vanhuysse 2006). Such targeted welfare expansion arguably disarmed potential social protest (Vanhuysse 2006; cf. Greskovits 1998).

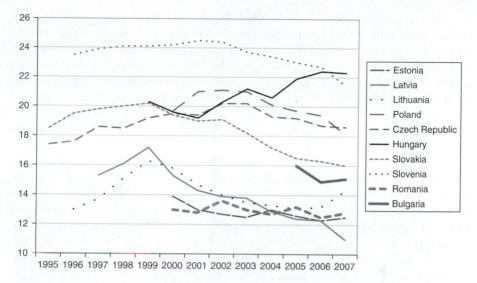

Figure 10.4 Total expenditure on social protection in Eastern Europe as a percentage of GDP. (*Source:* Eurostat-ESSPROS database, available at epp.eurostat.ec.europa.eu.)

TABLE 10.4 Average pension-wage ratio

	1976/1978	1989	1990	1991	1992	1993
Georgia		43.5	48.1	60.2	75.6	109.7
Slovenia		75.2	89.2	73.6	77.8	73.9
Poland	52.5	44.6	65.0	76.1	72.0	72.0
Hungary	60.6	63.1	62.6	64.3	60.9	59.6
Armenia		43.6	43.6	42.5	68.3	83.6
Azerbaijan		43.6	43.6	42.5	68.3	83.6
Albania		76.9	74.2	74.6	45.5	44.0
Moldova		39.5	40.5	36.4	60.3	60.3
Czech Republic	44.0[a]	52.2	54.3	55.6	49.2	48.6
Romania	59.2	54.9	46.5	44.6	43.1	50.3
Bulgaria	49.4	57.3	48.2	53.5	43.5	44.1
Lithuania		40.7	43.9	44.3	52.5	49.4
Slovakia		44.9	44.6	47.2	44.4	43.3
Russia	32.3[a]	33.5	33.7	33.8	25.8	33.6
Ukraine		34.5	34.5	43.9	61.1	42.3
Belarus			25.7	38.3	21.8	37.2
Latvia		37.6	29.8	26.0	34.6	30.7
Estonia		37.2	28.7		30.3	28.5

Source: Unicef TransMONEE database, reported in UNDP (1998); data for 1976/1978 is from Porket (1982, 255–60).

[a]Data is for Czechoslovakia and the USSR, respectively.

This could have been an unintended outcome of welfare policy legacies (Inglot 2008) rather than a conscious "divide and pacify" strategy of the reformers (as in Vanhuysse [2006]), but one outcome was to create a strong lobby for maintaining the newly created pension provision (discussed previously as the ratchet effect). The reform package approved in December 1989 also included unemployment benefits with broad coverage, but the expansion of pension spending associated with early retirement was the most striking feature of Poland's welfare adjustment. Pension spending reached 13.6 percent of GDP in 1994, accounting for most of the welfare expenditure increases.

Fiscal problems in combination with a dependence on IFIs in managing debt and balance-of-payment problems created pressures for cutting social spending and reforming social policies—most notably pensions and also health care. In Poland, the government made some adjustments to cut costs of welfare as early as 1995—particularly by family-benefits reductions. The IFI hand, then, is clear in the focus on the WB-favored method of pension reform (Orenstein 2008; Inglot 2008).

External persuasion and internal debate culminated in a pension reform compromise in 1997, with a fully funded second pillar to provide for almost half of the benefits for workers entering the labor force (Haggard and Kaufman 2008, 313). The 1997 health care reform replaced financing through general taxation with a payroll tax, and regional insurance funds were to negotiate contracts with both public and private providers. These funds, however, remained within the public sector, and universal coverage was secured by a constitutional law. Following these reforms, political and social resistance to further substantial change ensured that the Polish welfare state went through only parametric adjustments (Inglot 2008)

Hungary was similarly open to IFI influence when faced with financial crisis in 1995. However, to the disappointment of the IMF and WB, many cuts in the austerity package of the time were restored in the following years (Inglot 2008, 282–87). Nevertheless, fiscal stabilization provided an opening for a compromise on partial pension privatization as well as on shifting health financing to compulsory insurance (Haggard, Kaufman, and Shugart 2001). This was the limit of what could be achieved in terms of reducing state provision. Indeed, governments sought popularity in the following years by expanding welfare provisions, and Hungary, as indicated in Figure 10.4, became an outlier in spending trends.

Prompted by fiscal deficits at 10 percent of GDP, as well as problems in the current account, Hungary faced another financial crisis beginning in 2006 and then also in 2008 in the context of the global credit crunch, eventually forcing the country to seek a standby loan from the IMF. The government introduced a number of austerity measures, including tax increases and the reduction of public employment and wages, but these did not amount to a neoliberal restructuring. Hungary's welfare provision was still essentially the result of welfare adjustment and reforms that were compromises among domestic actors in response to IFI advice and pressure. In 2008, the packages also included nominal fees in health care and an increase in the retirement age. An attempt to introduce fees in tertiary education failed due to massive protests against further welfare retrenchment.

Pressure for neoliberal restructuring was felt across all countries in the early 2000s, backed by a rising group of high-income earners represented by right-wing parties. Electoral constraints and, in the case of Slovenia, the power of social interests played against major pathbreaking changes. In the Czech Republic, an attempt at neoliberal restructuring with tax cuts for the wealthy led to electoral setbacks for the conservative government elected in 2006 and eventually to a no-confidence vote, putting the political viability of reforms in question.

A major breakthrough was achieved in Slovakia after the 2002 elections that secured a majority for the Right, which had been leading the coalition government after the 1998 political turn. In 2000, the government agreed to a WB loan conditioned by the EU accession targets as well as to labor market deregulation, health care reform, and an overhaul of the pension system. However, the neoliberal restructuring took place only after the imbalances of the old systems had been reduced and stabilized in 1998 to 2002 (see Fisher, Gould, and Haughton [2007]).

The Slovak reform package of 2002 included the flat tax (discussed in Chapter 9); copayments and the introduction of private insurance in health care (Hlavacka, Wágner, and Riesberg 2004); pension privatization, with half of the contributions diverted toward a privately managed pillar; and a comprehensive overhaul of the labor code (EIROonline 2003). Unemployment benefits and basic welfare payments were halved, with means-tested family benefits replaced by a flat-rate contribution, tax deductions, and social grants. Some of the benefits were increased after a series of violent protests by Roma,[5] a group that was hit hardest (Kvapilová 2007), but, as indicated in Figure 10.4, expenditures on social protection decreased rapidly (Eurostat 2008). The electoral defeat of the Right in 2006 led to some adjustments, but not to a policy U-turn. Slovakia remained similar to low-spending Baltic republics.

THE CIS PATTERN: FROM STATE COLLAPSE TO BELATED ADJUSTMENTS

Economic shocks and state-capacity breakdown in Russia and other countries of the CIS led to welfare adjustments through informal practices rather than welfare state institutions. Families remained reliant on old institutions—most notably in-kind transfers and pensions (for pension levels, see Table 10.4). Reforms pursued by the executive often failed to make a difference, as the state lacked the infrastructural capacity to deliver, and the center was not able to impose changes on lower levels, particularly in the regions. The executive pursuing a liberalization agenda in Russia was virtually unconstrained by societal or statist welfare interests, particularly from 1991 to 1993 (Cook 2007). The autonomy of the executive was even higher in

---

[5]Roma are a sub-group of the Romani people (also known as Gypsies), an ethnic group living mostly in Europe, who trace their origins to medieval India. Dispersed across much of Eastern Europe, Roma constitute the largest minority that commonly suffers from social exclusion and discrimination. The largest Roma minorities as a percentage of population were estimated in Macedonia (10.7 to percent 12.7 percent; 220,000 to 260,000 people), Romania (8.3 percent-11.5 percent; 1,800,000 to 2,000,000 people), Bulgaria (9 percent-10.4 percent; 700,000 to 800,000 people), Slovakia (6 percent-7 percent; 350,000 to 380,000 people), Serbia (6 percent-6.7 percent; 450,000 to 500,000 people), and Hungary (5.3 percent-5.8 percent; 550,000 to 600,000 people) (UNDP, 2006, 2007; REF, 2007). Surveys show the majority of Roma households to live in absolute poverty ($4.30 per day PPP) in Kosovo (79 percent), Albania (72 percent), Romania (67 percent), Serbia (58 percent), and Macedonia (52 percent) (UNDP, 2010). Roma unemployment rates in individual countries have been estimated at 45 to 71 percent (UNDP, 2006).

authoritarian Kazakhstan, where pension privatization is attributed to a conversion of one key Kazakh official at a 1996 WB-sponsored conference featuring a Chilean reformer (Orenstein 2008, 130–31). Kazakhstan took an active approach also to other welfare reforms, cutting benefits across all categories in the early transition years (Cook 2007). Unemployment benefits were established, but their coverage was limited, and levels were well below the subsistence level (WB 1998). Spending on health care shrunk by half, and significant parts of the health care infrastructure were dismantled.

Russia, similar to other CIS states, began to improve the delivery of its welfare system around 1998 in the context of state-capacity consolidation and economic recovery. In the 2000s, electoral concerns became important in many CIS countries, leading to belated welfare state adjustments. Most notably, Ukraine implemented massive spending increases in the run up to the 2004 Orange Revolution, doubling pensions and raising public-sector wages (Åslund 2005; cf. Mykhnenko 2009).

As discussed in Chapter 7, very few CIS countries—particularly Belarus and Uzbekistan—were able to avoid state breakdown. In these countries existing welfare provision could be retained, but the institutional adjustment was lacking. In Belarus, welfare efforts were generally maintained or, if compared to GDP, substantially increased. However, there was only a small reaction to new social problems. No effective assistance was provided to the unemployed throughout the 1990s. There was very little institutional reform; a large part of social services continued to be provided by enterprises, and utility subsidies played an important role. Uzbekistan also managed to maintain high spending on education, public health, and utility subsidies (Pomfret and Anderson 1997), and the government also introduced some targeted social assistance (Coudouel and Marnie 1999). While limiting political competition, these authoritarian regimes were subject to electoral or plebiscitary pressures, encouraging their leaders to maintain social stability and old social contracts (March 2003; Rudra and Haggard 2005).

The weakening of Russia's central state capacity in the 1990s was supported by IFI advisers, who saw decentralization as a means to reduce the fiscal deficit. Reformers shifted responsibilities for, and financing of, welfare services, education, health care, and social assistance to the regions (Wallich 1994a, 6; Martinez-Vazquez 1994, 105). That meant that coordination mechanisms at the federal level disintegrated, while regional governments were left without adequate resources. Levels of provision deteriorated, and an informalized system of welfare provision—a mix of weak state and shadow markets—emerged (Cook 2007).

As welfare efforts relative to GDP remained relatively stable, neoliberal analysts concluded that the welfare state in Russia was relatively protected, with social support deemed to have expanded beyond a sustainable level (Åslund 2007, 197–201; Dmitriev 1997). Estimates of real spending, however, point to a dramatic decline, with spending on education, health, and pensions falling by 40, 30, and 50 percent, respectively, between 1990 and 1995 (Dmitriev 1997, 22, 47–48; Milanovic 1998, 199). The unreformed system was not able to address new needs and left many behind: unemployment benefits were marginal, the two lowest-income deciles received the least in state subsidies, and one-fifth of poor households received no public transfers at all (Cook 2007, 129–43; OECD 2001). It was estimated that the wealthiest 30 percent of households received 70 percent of social transfers (Dmitriev [1999] and

Misikhina [1999], quoted in Åslund [2007, 198]). Pensions were the only redistributive social program; pulling 20 percent of households above the poverty line, they constituted a major source of income for households, amounting to an average of 61 percent of household income for those households that were fortunate enough to have a pensioner (Clarke 1999, 139–46).

These improvised solutions were associated with changes in households and families. Women were particularly prominent in small-scale trade (see Chapter 12), a phenomenon that was far less important in Eastern Europe, where formal business activity took shape quickly. Formal employment continued to bring benefits, but pensioners enjoyed an enhanced status from their access to money.

Decentralization was most profound in social assistance, leading to a wide dispersion of coverage and levels of social assistance in the country. In 1998 to 2003, social expenditure in regions was *negatively* correlated with the number of needy and with the unemployment rate (Parker and Thornton 2007, 536). With Moscow receiving significantly higher social expenditures than other regions, some regions were left without any social assistance at all (Milanovic 1999). Health care reform transferred much of the financing from public budgets into insurance funds, and the implementation led to variable outcomes. Private providers were only allowed to operate in some regions. The outcome was an uneven, disorganized, fragmented, and poorly regulated public-private mix, with multiple institutions and little competition or control (Yudaeva and Gorban 1999).

Families had to rely on improvised solutions presented by the new economic situation, including the scope for small trading and other informal activities, and on inherited institutions, most notably on the pension system and in-kind provision, often linked to the workplace. A large part of services depended on the ability of struggling enterprises to continue the provision of social services (Clarke 1999, 95). Enterprise subsidies allowed for the continuation of in-kind provision, such as housing and utilities. Amounting to a subsidy of about 4 percent of GDP, price regulations on housing and utilities were maintained throughout the 1990s. In total, enterprise subsidies were estimated at 8 to 10 percent of GDP (EBRD 1997, 38; Pinto, Drebentsov, and Morozov 2000, 12).

There was a renewed drive for welfare state reform in Russia in 1997 in response to the continuing fiscal deficits as well as the falls in real expenditures. The WB stepped in to help the government in its reform efforts with an $800 million Social Protection Adjustment Loan linked to welfare state reforms and complemented by social-sector conditionality in an even larger IMF Extended Fund Facility (Sanford 2003). The reformers proposed a broad package of entitlement reductions, user fees in health and education, privatization of social security, liberalization of the labor code, and replacement of the existing system of social transfers with means-tested antipoverty measures. Yet, the executive was not able to forge a reform compromise. The reform found resistance within the government, and it was eventually stopped by the Duma; the government was only able to enforce spending reductions. The 1998 crisis put an end to the WB's strategy and, it turned out, to this reform attempt.

Economic recovery and Putin's efforts to consolidate the state, to recentralize political control and administration, and to reorder fiscal relations within the federation increased state capacity also in the social sphere and improved the delivery

TABLE 10.5   Pension replacement rates

Country	Year	Replacement rate (pension/wage, %)
Ukraine	2007	48.32
Poland	2007	47.05
Slovakia	2005	44.70
Slovenia	2005	44.30
Bulgaria	2004	42.90
Belarus	2002	41.60
Romania	2005	41.45
Czech Republic	2005	40.70
Uzbekistan	2005	40.00
Hungary	2005	39.80
Estonia	2007	35.42
Latvia	2005	33.10
Lithuania	2005	30.90
Russia	2003	29.20
Kyrgyz Republic	2003	27.50
Tajikistan	2003	25.70
Kazakhstan	2003	24.90
Moldova	2003	20.90
Armenia	2007	20.27
Georgia	2003	13.00

Source: WB regional staff (personal communication, April 30, 2009)

of basic welfare guarantees as well as remunerations in the public sector. Control over social assistance and the financing of selected-benefit programs were recentralized. Social spending increased moderately, but not enough to compensate for the retrenchment of the previous years. Most importantly, child benefits—the only federal program of poverty relief—became standardized and means tested; yet, they remained very low, only at about 5 percent of the subsistence level. Pension arrears were paid back in 2000, and the average pension began to increase in 1999, reaching the subsistence level in 2002. It could still be judged as very low, as indicated in Table 10.5, especially if that pension had to support a large household, but coverage of pensioners was almost universal, keeping most of them out of poverty, as defined by the WB (2005, 20, 88, 93).[6]

The general picture was of gradual improvements in the levels and reliability of spending, but not by enough to alter the essence of the system. In education and health care, low public spending, high private expenditure, and official tolerance of informality had become, and remained, institutionalized, and the government was not committed to sustaining public expenditure increases (Shishkin et al. 2003;

[6] Poverty was defined with reference to a normatively defined consumption basket, and information was collected through surveys (see WB [2005, 7–15]).)

Cook 2007). There was some consolidation of the state's capacity in the context of the Gref Program, launched in the spring of 2000 (see p. 181). This appeared to be inspired by a neoliberal agenda, with emphasis on the flat tax, and reducing taxes and state spending in general, and on increasing charges on the population. However, these reforms differed from the neoliberal restructuring in CEECs because the starting point was not a functioning system created by reforming a previous one. The issue in Russia and other CIS countries was of creating a functioning system after a period of low state capacity in which the inadequacies of the old system had been patched up improvization by enterprises and families.

In Russia, these reforms also coincided with economic growth so that potential resistance could be reduced by higher spending on some areas, increasing the salaries of those who benefited from existing provisions and investing into new institutions (Cook 2007). However, the general direction of reform was clear. The 2000 labor code reform allowed the broad use of temporary contracts, expanded employers' rights to dismiss workers, and reduced the powers of trade unions in dismissals. Financing responsibilities in housing, health care, and pensions were transferred to individuals, markets, and insurance mechanisms. Cofinancing was required for educational services above a state minimum, effectively legalizing some of the informal practices.

In 2004, the government began to dismantle the system of in-kind benefits inherited from the Soviet period, including access to public transport, housing, utilities, and other goods and services, which had been partly expanded in 1994 to 1999. Approximately one-quarter of the population—mainly labor and war veterans, pensioners, the disabled, single parents, and other vulnerable groups—benefited from this system (Ovcharova [2005], in Cook [2007, 179]). The attempt to remove housing subsidies, which benefited over 40 percent of the population, was most difficult to implement. In 2003, a Housing Reform Law was approved, envisioning major rent increases in 2004 to 2005 and a gradual elimination of subsidies by 2010.

Restructuring of the system through monetization and retrenchment was met with massive popular resistance, unprecedented in the Putin presidency. Political parties, trade unions, and nongovernmental organizations (NGOs) joined in support of large street demonstrations and transport blockades across more than 70 cities in early 2005. To compensate for cuts, pensions and payments were substantially increased. In the end, most benefits were monetized or transferred to the regions, and the provision of housing for some groups of employees was largely eliminated under a separate piece of legislation. While making many entitlements subject to devaluation, the reform failed to achieve what was presented as its main goal: a better targeting of social assistance (Alexandrova and Struyk 2007). However, in 2006 to 2007, the government seemed determined to increase spending on education, health care, and housing (Davidova and Manning 2009, 198).

VARIETIES OF WELFARE REGIMES

The outcomes of these different courses of change can be followed most clearly by their effects on the levels of welfare provision. Key indicators are presented in Figures 10.5, 10.6, and 10.7 and in Tables 10.2 and 10.6. Social- and health-related

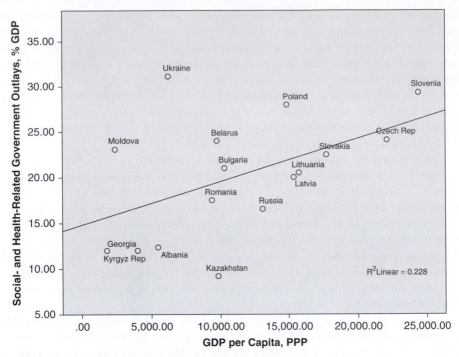

Figure 10.5 Social- and health-related government outlays as a percentage of GDP, 2006. (*Source:* Calculated from IMF (2007) and WB (2008a).)
Notes: PPP = purchasing power parity.

state spending (Figure 10.5) is only a very imperfect proxy for welfare efforts, but it is the best comparable indicator available across a large number of the countries. Figure 10.7 compares private and public health expenditure in the post-Communist countries, showing the trend toward a greater state role in CEECs and the very small presence in a number of CIS countries. As could be expected, welfare efforts were largely conditioned by the level of development (measured here as per capita GDP in purchasing parities). Yet, even when controlling for GDP levels, there is a large variation reflecting policy choices.

Relatively high levels of spending in Ukraine and Hungary, for which comparable data were not available and can, thus, be found in Figure 10.6 only, are linked to the electoral importance of welfare constituencies that shaped the nature of welfare state adjustments (cf. Mykhnenko 2009; Tóth 2009). This is reflected in the high levels of pensions relative to average pay. The capacity of these countries to sustain social spending in the context of post-2009 structural adjustments remains to be seen. It can be expected that there will be strong political pressures in these countries to sustain (or go back to) higher levels of provision in the future; such was the Hungarian experience in the aftermath of an earlier crisis. The feasibility of such adjustments, however, will be dependent on early economic recovery.

Other countries above the trend line followed slightly different courses of development. Belarus sustained relatively high spending levels, but it went through little adjustment in its formal institutions. Poland experienced high pension payments

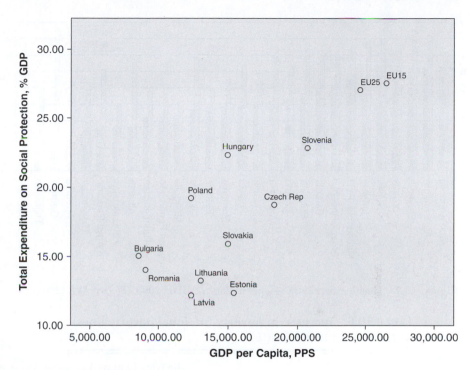

Figure 10.6 Total expenditure on social protection in Eastern Europe as a percentage of GDP. (*Source:* Eurostat database, available at eurostat.ec.europa.eu.)

Notes: PPS = The purchasing power standard (PPS) is the name given by Eurostat, the EU statistical agency, to the artificial currency unit used for comparing between EU member countries. It is intended to represent an equal purchasing power in terms of physical goods and services in each country.EU15 = European Member states before the 2004 enlargement: Austria, Belgium, Denmark, Finland, France, Germany, Greece, Ireland, Italy, Luxembourg, the Netherlands, Portugal, Spain, Sweden, and the United Kingdom. EU25 = European Member states before the 2007 enlargement: EU15 + Cyprus, Czech Republic, Estonia, Hungary, Latvia, Lithuania, Malta, Poland, Slovakia, and Slovenia.

from the early 1990s, possibly to satisfy and later defended by a powerful labor lobby. Slovenia moved closer to the European social model with its higher levels of spending and provision.

Countries below the trend line include Kazakhstan, a case of an authoritarian regime that minimized the scope for interest representation and in which decisions could be made without much external scrutiny. The power of welfare constituencies to influence the government in Russia was also weak, but sustaining the existing levels of social provision became an important political issue in the 2000s, and governments seemed to be determined not to allow decreases in social spending. The weakness of state capacity in these and other CIS countries meant that formal commitments to levels of provision needed not be reflected in reality.

It is, therefore, possible to characterize welfare regimes in former state Socialist countries around three ideal types, each of which is in a process of evolution and in each of which there are conflicting pressures for change.

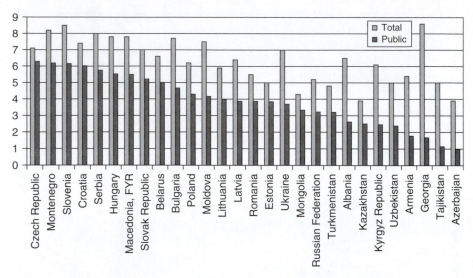

Figure 10.7 Health expenditure as a percentage of GDP, 2005. (*Source:* WB (2008a).)

TABLE 10.6 Increase in poverty (national poverty lines) without social transfers (%)

Country	Year	Increase in poverty without social transfers (%)
Bulgaria	2001	156
Belarus	2002	143
Poland	2001	141
Kazakhstan	2002	100
Bosnia and Herzegovina	2001	68
Russia	2002	68
Romania	2002	49
Serbia	2003	41
Montenegro	2002	34
Armenia	2001	12
Kyrgyz Republic	2001	10

Source: Alam et al. (2005, 131, Table 3.3); simulations of hypothetical "no transfers" situations are based on the WB's poverty assessment surveys.

Note: Simulations use national poverty lines. Some behavioral response is assumed in Romania (50 percent of transfer income is replaced) and Serbia (72 percent of transfer income is replaced in rural areas, 87 percent in urban areas).

The first is the "informalized" model, in which the welfare state institutions went through limited adjustments only. The state, thus, does not provide social protection that the population implicitly demands. It may have legal obligations to do so, but it fails to honor them. Improvised solutions are then found by enterprises and individuals, who make informal payments for what may formally be publicly provided services. Russia has roughly fit with this ideal type, and its evolution has been toward a system of low formal provision alongside formalization of the need to pay for much of welfare provision (cf. Davidova and Manning 2009). Some of that has been resisted, but resistance points to delay as much as to any alternative general direction of development. In fact, enterprises remained major providers of social services, including health care and housing. This was particularly true in the towns in which employment was heavily dependent on a single industrial plant of which there were still 460 in 2008, with a total population of 25 million (Malle 2009, 259).

Some of the countries approximating the informalized model recorded relatively high social spending (e.g., Ukraine and Moldova), but this went to pensions and public-sector wages, squeezing spending on services. Out-of-pocket payments, both formal and informal, thus constitute a major source of financing for health care. While they contributed around 50 percent of expenditure in Russia and Kyrgyzstan, out-of-pocket payments were estimated to constitute 70 to 80 percent of total health expenditure in Georgia and Azerbaijan (Shishkin et al. 2003; Lewis 2000; cf. Figure 10.7). In the context of mounting inequalities, health care ceased to be a public service with universal access, with more serious illness or injury representing a disproportionate or unaffordable financial burden for the unfortunate households (Lewis 2000). At the same time, as indicated in Table 10.6, existing social transfers (primarily pensions) had some poverty-reducing effects, even in some of the low spenders such as Russia and Kazakhstan. Ukraine, in particular, saw a significant reduction in poverty along with the 2004 social-spending increases. Yet, public welfare institutions failed to make a significant difference in Kyrgyzstan and Armenia (Alam et al. 2005). In these cases, improvised solutions remained more important, such as the dependence on remittances, which, as shown in Chapter 4, constituted an important source of income in these low-income CIS countries.

The second is the "minimal welfare state" model, in which there is greater formal dependence on private provision and payment for services than is usual in Western Europe. The state and its welfare institutions went through adjustments. Therefore, unlike in the informalized model, the state fulfills its formal obligations and ensures that a private sector can supplement its activities to provide what is considered an adequate level of provision. This roughly corresponds to the Baltic republics and SEECs, countries that underwent gradual welfare state adjustments, with low levels of overall provision. Social transfers, thus, made only a small difference to income distribution in the low-spending Baltic republics, which also record high poverty and inequality levels; in Bulgaria, they seem to make a difference mainly for the poorest (Sutherland, Figari, and Paulus 2007).

The Baltic countries appeared to have developed formal institutions that provided a high degree of protection to the labor market, exceeding levels in CEECs (Gebel 2008, 55), but the evidence from social surveys and case studies reveals a significant degree of informalization, with actual employment relations characterized by precariousness and undeclared work (Eamets and Masso 2005; Woolfson, Calite, and Kallaste 2008).

The minimal welfare state corresponds also to Slovakia, which underwent neoliberal restructuring. Opposition to restructuring was relatively strong there, as this is a country with significant interest representation, and other CEECs have not yet followed the same route. Further development either could be toward the European social model or could continue in the neoliberal direction.

In the aftermath of the financial crisis, the Baltic republics saw their financialized economic models brought to what appeared to be a possibly terminal crisis (see Chapter 17). This has meant a major challenge for the political arrangements underpinning their welfare regimes, and, in the longer term, the search for an alternative economic model may also involve additional welfare adjustments. The rescue package in Latvia included not only massive spending cuts in the defense of the existing economic model but also the scrapping of the flat tax, the symbol of the Baltic model.

The third is the "European" social model, as advocated especially by the Social Democrat–oriented political forces in CEECs. This model has been seen as a definite aim and alternative to the neoliberal restructuring advocated from the political Right. The nearest example is Slovenia, with considerable applicability to other CEECs. However, it is clearly under threat, with pressures for reductions in tax levels and welfare provision.

SECTION V

MICROECONOMIC EVOLUTION: NEW FORMS OF BUSINESS

CHAPTER ELEVEN

Enterprises: Shock and Survival

Enterprises are the basic units for business activity in a market economy. This chapter explores the diverse ways in which enterprises emerged and developed after the end of state Socialism. In an abstract neoclassical world, the transformation is largely about creating the right incentive structure. Private ownership will lead to a profit motive for owners, who will in turn ensure that managers seek to maximize efficiency. From such logic followed the enthusiasm through the 1990s for the speediest possible privatization, no matter who the new owners might be. If the theory was correct, the outcome should have been modern and efficient economies in all former state Socialist countries. The reasons why this did not happen, and why measures adopted could in many cases make enterprise survival and recovery more difficult, can be summarized under three points.

1. The enterprise under central planning does different things than the enterprise in a modern market economy. In the latter case, the enterprise's existence is not guaranteed. It can be formed, and it can go out of business. It has financial autonomy. It can raise capital, incur debts, and extend credits to other enterprises. It has independent access to technology. It has to find its own markets and suppliers, and this means linking into networks of other firms. The important point is that these are not simple issues that any manager can solve once they are imbued with a profit motive. They depend on expertise built up over time.

2. The enterprise in a market economy operates within a business environment that has also developed over a period of time. To raise finance, it needs access to banks and a capital market. To develop technology, it needs access to research and researchers. To develop many areas of expertise, it needs contact with private and public bodies that can give help and advice. This business environment develops over time as enterprises develop.

3. Private ownership requires a complex legal framework. This is acknowledged within neoclassical theory with references to the need for a state to maintain law and order. However, that understates the problem. There is no simple analogy between the hierarchy of central planning, in which every enterprise is clearly subordinated to a higher authority and every manager subject to discipline within the enterprise, and the modern market economy with complex forms of ownership and webs of credit.

These three points indicate the complexity of the transformation of the enterprise sphere. The problem is often presented as the difficulty of "creating capitalism without capitalists." There were, at the start, no significant accumulations of wealth and, therefore, no one available to buy up enterprises that might be privatized. However, even when property was handed to private owners, it solved very little. It could not ensure the emergence of an institutional and legal framework, nor could it ensure the evolution of other elements in the desirable business environment—such as access to credit—or that those with power over enterprises had the expertise or desire to develop them as businesses.

This chapter follows the first phase of transformation of the enterprise sphere, with a focus on the impact of the shock of the early 1990s. Many existing enterprises had to struggle for survival, but contacts to Western Europe for CEEC enterprises, either inherited or rapidly developed, meant that many could survive. In CIS countries, the shock was more severe, including the breakdown of the state, and there was no survival strategy based on integration into a Western European economy. Solutions emerged that were unfamiliar to the dominant trends in economic theory—particularly the growth in barter and the continuation of high levels of employment despite a failure to pay wages.

THE SHOCK IN CEECS

Enterprises in CEECs were hit beginning in 1990 by rapidly falling demand. There were, as indicated in Chapter 5, some advocates of rapid reform who assumed that that alone could force a change in enterprise behavior. There was also the strongly held neoliberal view that only private ownership could lead to a change in the behavior of state-owned enterprises. The first of these views was closer to the truth in terms of immediate adaptation to the effects of the shock. There were already some very substantial changes under state ownership, but they did not provide a basis for lasting recovery.

A pioneering study of 75 Polish state-owned enterprises in 1991 and 1992 showed them to be quickly seeking new markets and shedding labor in response to the pressures created by trade liberalization; privatization did not seem to the authors of this study to be an essential early step (Pinto, Belka, and Krajewski 1993). There was a brief period of serious payment difficulties in which inter-enterprise debts grew rapidly, but firms could soon rely on the banking system for working capital. Carlin, Reenen, and Wolfe (1994) summarized the early literature. A reasonable conclusion is that enterprises moved rapidly to find new markets and to build new contacts, but they did less in terms of large-scale modernization. This further stage was more difficult, requiring finance, international contacts, and expertise of kinds that were lacking. As studies from Hungary indicated, many enterprises drifted, allowing the erosion of assets as they made ad hoc attempts to establish useful contacts (Ernst, Alexeev, and Marer 1995, 200).

This early research relied heavily on case studies and on responses from enterprise directors. Not surprisingly, these individuals often appeared in a positive light, as leaders of restructuring efforts and constraints on their powers—as imposed by the self-management system in Poland, which frequently held managerial pay in check—were presented as negative phenomena (Pinto, Belka, and Krajewski 1993;

see also the studies on Poland in Estrin et al. [1995]). It is only possible to assess managements' strategies by following enterprises over a longer time period. Such studies (Myant 1997, 1999a, 2003) do not confirm the early expectation of those with a neoclassical background that "the absence of a profit motive" would lead to "few reactions from state-owned firms" (Estrin et al. 1995, xix). Nor, as indicated in Chapter 13, do they confirm that privatization was necessarily the key to success.

State-owned enterprises actively sought to adapt to the new environment, but they did this without an overarching aim of maximum profit. The closest thing to a single unifying aim, shared by management and employees alike, appeared to be survival of the enterprise, and that depended on overcoming the cash flow difficulties created by the shock. The same goal of survival has been used as a central objective for Russian enterprises, even under private ownership, with survival meaning the continued functioning of the enterprise as a collective (Clarke 1996, 2007).

However, there are two reservations to setting survival as the universal aim. The first is that managers were also capable of seeing to their own private interests. In the liberalizing economic systems, this could mean transferring the enterprise's money and other assets into companies they had set up for themselves, leaving the parent company to its fate. Such practices were made exceptionally easy for a short early period in Poland and Hungary and became known as "nomenklatura privatization." They were blocked by post-Communist governments in view of their unpopularity. Czechoslovak enterprises were also prevented from transferring property to new owners during the privatization process. Thus, survival was not the only objective of management, but it was an objective that could be shared across the enterprise and the best option for all if there were effective barriers to other possible managerial objectives.

The second is that survival also did not mean maintaining employment levels. Many workplaces disappeared, and there were some employee protests against closures, especially in Poland. However, managements did generally try to keep their enterprises together and may even have encouraged strikes to strengthen their bargaining position with governments. This partly reflected a feeling of social responsibility, a heritage of paternalistic management, and the wider social role played by the enterprise under central planning. It also partly reflected pride in the enterprise and a desire not to let traditions die.

As will be indicated, there were substantial differences between CEECs and the CIS, but survival, with recognition of these two caveats, is a reasonable first approximation to the enterprises' core objective in the first period after the shock.

However, even accepting survival as the principal aim need not point to only one strategy. It could be associated with a refusal to change very much, with a determined call for state help, or with vigorous changes in production profiles. Generally speaking, these alternatives were chosen when they were the most plausible option, but there were variations in how managements interpreted their objective situations. The following three forms summarize the most important options that were found in the studies referred to previously. First, the production of established products could continue with good results. This was straightforward for staple utilities, such as electricity, and generally possible for raw materials and semimanufactures that could be exported to new markets in Western Europe without significant changes in the product (cf. Pinto, Belka, and Krajewski 1993, 241). Therefore, these enterprises required minimal internal restructuring and did relatively well in the new environment.

Second, the production of established products could continue, but with poor results as demand collapsed. This strategy of continuity failed for manufacturers of more complex products, such as motor trucks, tractors, railway locomotives, and heavy machinery, which had previously been sold within the Soviet bloc. These were cases for which access to established international networks and the technological level of end products really mattered. There was little chance of penetrating new markets with existing products or of developing new and sophisticated products that would be internationally competitive. One option for these enterprises was to seek links with a foreign company, which often meant abandoning the technology, brand names, and reputation that they had developed and also could mean substantial job losses. This, then, was not a popular choice, and survival was often interpreted as maintaining proud traditions in the hope that good times would return. Another option was to seek state help to ease survival by covering past debts and then to support efforts to find new markets by guaranteeing export credits. The CEEC governments went some way to satisfying these demands.

However, persisting with established products in these cases brought only very limited results. Many of these enterprises endured very lengthy periods of crisis and contributed to the escalation of "payment arrears" throughout the economy. Some left the scene altogether. No substantial enterprise from the state Socialist period in the engineering, transport equipment, or electronics sectors could remain in domestic ownership and emerge as a significant player on the European stage.

Third, firms with no alternative switched, when possible, to producing simpler products for Western partners. This included outward-processing trade (OPT, whereby materials and designs are imported from a Western partner and finished products are returned to that same partner) in garments and footwear, sectors that suffered very rapid decline in Poland and then significant recovery, without seeking, or receiving, state help (Ernst, Alexeev, and Marer 1995, 95–96). Major engineering firms could adjust to produce simpler components, even as they hoped for a possible revival based on the more sophisticated finished products they had previously exported within the Soviet bloc. It meant rapid adaptation and effective diversification away from sophisticated end products and/or own-branded goods. This was largely a trial-and-error process, described in one study as "probing" (McDermott 2002, 111), as enterprises experimented with different products for different Western European firms that might provide a useful cash flow.

This was not a strategy with long-term prospects. It provided little basis for independent innovation and was successful only because of low relative labor costs that could come under threat from countries further east. Enterprises, therefore, combined probing with attempts to maintain or reestablish past products and brands. Garment manufacturers tried to set up their own outlets, and engineering firms tried to develop new, albeit fairly simple, products and to establish new outlets in China, then still a rather novel idea, and elsewhere to replace the lost CMEA market.

STATE HELP IN CEECS

When the shock hit CEECs, the original thinking was that the state was withdrawing from the economy, forcing enterprises to fend for themselves. In fact, governments soon felt forced to step in again. They were confronted by potential protest and potential social catastrophe, as major enterprises appeared to be on the brink of collapse. In Poland, these included the shipyards on the Baltic coast and the Ursus tractor plant in Warsaw, which had special significance as the scenes of worker protests in the past and were scenes of continuing militancy in the early 1990s (Myant 1993, 257–60). In Czechoslovakia, crisis hit major engineering enterprises that were important for employment and also seen as symbolizing the nation's past economic successes. Governments could not realistically hope to retain political credibility if they stood by as these enterprises disappeared.

However, they at first had no conception of how the state should intervene. Some were convinced that they should oppose any intervention, as was well expressed by Tadeusz Syryczyk, Poland's minister of industry in 1989, who believed that the only good industrial policy was no policy at all, even if that meant allowing output to fall to zero (Myant 1993, 84). This was ultimately not a tenable position, but the thinking behind it ensured that solutions evolved in an ad hoc manner. Steps were taken to prevent the closure of key enterprises, and then, gradually, systematic steps were taken to resolve problems of enterprise debt.

This was a problem inherited from the state Socialist period, when finance had played a lesser role. Many enterprises carried forward debts from investment projects, financed nominally by loans but formally decided on by the center. Others had outstanding credits linked to export deals with little chance of repayment; again, the central planners had made the decisions in the past and could, therefore, be judged responsible for the debts. Even some current spending was covered by bank credits, and that suddenly became a problem as monetary policy tightened and interest rates rose.

Problems from the past were exacerbated by the effects of the shock. Some enterprises continued producing the same products, anyway, hoping for the fulfillment of contracts that were entered into in the past. Debts that could not be covered were then translated into inter-enterprise arrears as the level of payment obligations escalated, with no sign of how they would be honored.

Delays in payment are not unusual in a market economy, but they rarely cause a problem because access to various forms of credit ensures adequate means of payment, and the small proportion of enterprises that cannot honor obligations over a long time period are subjected to bankruptcy proceedings. State Socialism left no adequate system to smooth over short-run payment difficulties, and tight monetary policy further worsened the situation. Delays in payment to one enterprise, therefore, led to immediate cash flow difficulties. There was also no adequate bankruptcy process inherited from the past, although that would have offered no solution, anyway, when large numbers of enterprises, rather than a small minority, were simultaneously failing to pay their bills.

Cash flow difficulties pressured enterprises to seek out new sources of revenue, leading to the dependence on low-level exports to Western Europe, referred to previously, which typically brought immediate payment. However, the extent of payment arrears also quickly became a concern to governments, as it threatened paralysis and ultimately the collapse of major enterprises, irrespective of whether they were the original source of the chains of debt and whether they might have prospects of a successful future.

One option was to write off all past debts, and this was advocated from outside the region. That would have required a purely internal accounting procedure within all-encompassing state sectors. It made sense if linked to the simultaneous imposition of hard financial conditions so that enterprises could not expect to be helped out repeatedly (Begg and Portes 1992). Others, including those presenting alternatives to Klaus's strategy in Czechoslovakia (Myant 1993, 218–20), advocated a more selective writing off of debts so as to favor enterprises with prospects and credible plans for the future. However, neither of these views won approval from free market purists. The former seemed to contradict the hope of benefits from a hardening of budget constraints, and the latter implied that a state body could judge which enterprises should be helped—an anathema to those who believed the market was the only means to provide a verdict. In this view, the solution was to force payment or bankruptcy, thereby cleaning out enterprises with financial problems and leaving the market to determine what might emerge.

Such an approach was roughly the one followed in Hungary. An exceptionally tough bankruptcy law was introduced in 1992, but the effect was to swamp inexperienced courts with more than 10,000 cases. The law was softened in 1993 (Ernst, Alexeev, and Marer 1995, 192–93) and a process of consolidating old debts undertaken in the following years. The absence of an effective form of bankruptcy had been identified as a source of the soft budget constraint under central planning, but its application on a grand scale when so many enterprises could not pay their bills proved to be an ineffective means to impose discipline and a measure that could have massive and random effects on enterprise survival. A similar Czechoslovak law was delayed following Hungary's experience and was introduced only gradually in much weaker forms in later years.

The urgency of the debt problem became clear in Czechoslovakia in early 1991, immediately after the tightening of monetary policy. A sharp squeeze led some big enterprises to declare that they could no longer pay employees' wages. Although this was to become a normal practice in CIS countries, it was unacceptable in Czechoslovakia, and workers' protests were enough to press the government to ensure the survival of key enterprises alongside a functioning monetary system. The key was an emergency measure that enabled enterprises to transfer part of their debts into a newly created state-owned institution, the Consolidation Bank (Myant 1993, 217–18). This body took on a wider role through the 1990s, quietly helping out key enterprises that faced otherwise insoluble financial problems.

A more permanent solution was still opposed by Klaus and his allies, but it was decided at the end of 1991, following pressure from the central bank and part of the government, to provide funds for eliminating past enterprise debts and for recapitalizing banks, albeit by considerably less than the idea's advocates had originally proposed. Help was to be administered through the banking system in the hope that it would be targeted at enterprises with prospects. In fact, it was allocated unconditionally and evenly across all, showing that judgement between enterprises' business plans was, at least in that situation, indeed impractical (Myant 2003 147). This still left many issues from the past unresolved—for example, the state railways had ordered but no longer wanted to pay for locomotives—but significantly cleared the financial atmosphere.

Inherited debt was a less serious problem in Poland thanks to higher inflation rates, but governments there, too, were forced by employee protests to recognize that they could not leave the fate of enterprises to the market and could not rely on privatization to solve the problems. The solution that emerged was similar to the Czechoslovak one, but it was adopted later and was more decentralized. The IMF was by then willing to allow part of its stabilization fund to be used for this, although it would have preferred the more centralized Czech method (Epstein 2008, 107).

Under the Polish plan, enterprises were to receive financial help if they were judged to have presented credible business plans that were formulated in agreement with employees and in coordination with banks. In practice, plans included substantial job reductions. However, flexibility in the means of implementation, and scepticism from within governments and enterprises, meant that the process was rather gradual, spread throughout the 1990s as employment reduced in key sectors. It was also supplemented by more direct state help, on a case-by-case basis, for some enterprises that did not receive help from banks, while others faced eventual bankruptcy and elimination. There was rhetoric about more systematic industrial policies, and studies were conducted of sectors, albeit with little sign that they led to any action (Myant 1993, 258–59; Ernst, Alexeev, and Marer 1995, 114; King and Sznajder 2006).

Thus, across CEECs, the state had some involvement in supporting enterprise survival. Even when there was rhetoric about linking help to long-term prospects, there were no cases of genuine state-led growth or of state support for full recovery, and there was little involvement in full-scale enterprise restructuring. Governments rather gave ad hoc help when they felt forced to do so. The enterprises inherited from the past had to try to find their own solutions, and this kept them concentrating on means for survival, with limited prospects of a future of independence and prosperity.

THE SHOCK IN THE CIS

Compared with CEECs, enterprises in the CIS countries faced greater disruption from the breaking of established links, which was exacerbated and compounded by the breakdown of state apparatuses. This ruled out systematic government support, meaning that any such help was unreliable and unsystematic. It was linked with a failure to develop an effective financial and payments system, leading enterprises into improvised solutions unfamiliar to developed market economies. It also meant that the legal system was far less effective, and this was another factor pushing enterprises toward dependence on nonmarket relationships.

The breakup of the Soviet Union caused greater disruption to economic links than anything experienced in CEECs. What follows is based largely on evidence from Russia, on which much more information is available. There were some very similar developments in Ukraine, but in some smaller republics, the survival of enterprises from the Soviet period was more of a short-lived phenomenon, and survival of the economies depended to a greater extent on the new business activity, discussed in Chapter 12.

Survival strategies for enterprises in the CIS, in comparison with those in CEECs, can be summarized in three points that indicate why CEEC solutions were not available and in three points that indicate CIS solutions specifically.

1. Those enterprises that could export to world markets did so, but this was limited by the lack of established contacts. Political chaos and economic

breakdown led to declines in output, even for raw materials that were in demand elsewhere in the world. Oil from Russia could continue to sell, and cotton from Uzbekistan did well, but many other basic products could not find new markets. Uzbek cotton exports depended on new trade links, but transport was even possible by air, avoiding the difficulties of negotiating with neighboring states. Semimanufactures suffered in all cases from the lack of experience on world markets, from problems with gaining essential inputs, and from the general chaos and social and economic breakdown. Thus, one of the means of survival for many CEEC enterprises was harder to exploit from the CIS.

2. Some enterprises tried to link up with foreign partners, but the probing method was effectively impossible. Contacts were weaker, the technological level was lower than in CEECs, geographical distance was greater—an important consideration for OPT and for many components in mass production industries—and, perhaps most crucially, the legal framework was uncertain. Indeed, even Czech companies were cautious in the Ukraine right through the mid-1990s following bad experiences due to the lack of clarity of ownership of enterprises (Myant 1997, 558).

3. Many enterprises persisted with established products, albeit after a time producing only for stocks (Ernst, Alexeev, and Marer 1995, 247). Russian enterprise managers appeared more likely than those in CEECs to see the future as a return to the past, although this may partly have reflected the lack of any attractive alternatives. However, continuing with the same products led to a rapid escalation of inter-enterprise arrears. This grew in early 1992, when money was especially tight, and then eased when the central bank allowed an expansion of credits. Debts then rose again in 1994.

Thus, unable to follow the same strategies as CEEC enterprises, three distinct elements appeared in enterprise survival behaviour, which grew out of a situation with poor business prospects, weak state control over the economy, and a weak role of the state in welfare provision. These were (1) the development of networks and new business forms, (2) the growth in barter relations between enterprises, and (3) an employment relationship in which wages were often paid late, or not at all.

The first was the stronger role for internal networks that pushed producing enterprises into an especially weak position and that later led to the creation of the financial industrial groups (FIGs), as discussed in Chapter 14. The quest for means of survival meant finding the necessary contacts within the country so that existing capital and labor could be used to continue production. Studies of Russian enterprises in the mid-1990s show the importance of networks and political contacts (Clarke 1996, 2007). One frequent solution was linking to a domestic trading company—with likely origins discussed in Chapter 12—that could provide inputs and markets for outputs.

There was some analogy to the dependence of CEEC enterprises on Western partners. In both cases, enterprises had to be ready for rapid adaptation to new orders, and that required diversification and downgrading toward less sophisticated products. However, the Russian enterprise was in an even weaker position, with even less scope for reestablishing its independence. It was moving further away from the form of a firm in an advanced market economy, which would ideally combine production with other activities in sales, marketing, R&D, and strategic planning. In comparison with CEECs, it implies even weaker prospects for independent enterprise development and even less chance of controlling its own outlets and brands.

The second distinctive element in enterprise survival behavior was the growth in systems of inter-enterprise barter. There were some cases of CEEC firms surviving with no cash resources so that they paid in kind with their outputs, but that never reached the scale found in Russia. There, barter became pronounced in 1992, described in detail by David Woodruff (1999), as tight monetary policy and weaknesses in the availability of bank credit restricted the money supply at a time of rapid price rises. Enterprises stuck to the practice of cost-plus pricing precisely because they were being allowed by other enterprises to delay payments. In this, they were continuing an element of practice from the Soviet period, when inter-enterprise debts had been periodically canceled out and written off by a central authority. This, alongside a general relaxation of monetary policy, was precisely what the enterprise managements expected and lobbied for.

The first half of this was conceded in mid-1992, but, as Woodruff emphasized, the center simultaneously scrapped the Soviet-period system of recording transactions, thereby eliminating hopes of a future cancellation of debts. There was, then, an analogy to solutions to the debt problems in CEECs, but the Russian version was less systematic and definitely not linked to any attempt to identify enterprises with prospects. Barter, which had been developing in the preceding months, did decline for a time.

Barter grew again in late 1993 after a tightening of monetary policy and as enterprises found that they could not sell their output and had no money with which to pay bills. They began paying in kind first for electricity. The alternative would have been not to pay essential bills and presumably face closure. Barter escalated as enterprises withdrew from the money economy. Even local authorities and then the central government were prepared to accept forms of payment in kind to meet tax obligations.

Barter was then supplemented with new means of payment as credit notes were issued by enterprises, banks, and even government bodies, obviously with only limited exchangeability. In all, it has been estimated that barter grew to reach 50 percent of enterprise sales by early 1998 (Woodruff 1999, 148), with another 25 percent of transactions conducted by "veksels," the informal credit notes, all operating outside the control of the formal monetary system.

Apart from Woodruff's studies, enough detail exists on the growth of barter to reveal its root causes (Commander, Dolinskaya, and Mumssen 2002; Olsson 2008). One factor, as argued by Gaddy and Ickes (2002), may have been development from an "informal" economy emerging in the closing years of state Socialism as central planning ceased to function. Past practices may have laid a basis, but there were also clear links to some specific features of transition in Russia and also in other CIS countries. This growth in barter can, therefore, be explained primarily by four factors.

The first was the government's tight monetary policy, which restricted means of payment. Anatoly Chubais, one of the key converts to free-market economics who was supported by Yeltsin and dominated economic reform and privatization policies from November 1991 to 1996, adamantly denied that government policy could be to blame, asserting instead that barter was criminal behavior and should be stamped out (Woodruff 1999, 187). His tough talk proved ineffective. Others sympathetic to his views also could not accept that a restrictive policy aimed at reducing inflation could not be the right course. They had difficulty understanding barter and often wrote about the Russian economy as if it were not a significant phenomenon. They were right that tight monetary policy alone was not the full explanation, but they were wrong to imply that it played no role. The fact that barter increased as overdue debts rose and then declined very rapidly after 1998 as access to money improved—down to 10 percent of sales by 2004 (Olsson 2008, 723)—demonstrates its central importance. The real issue for Chubais and his allies was probably their conviction, derived from mainstream economic theory, that restricting the money supply was the key to reducing inflation. Barter simply did not fit into their theoretical framework.

The second factor was the nature of the banking system, as discussed in Chapter 13. It failed to extend credit to enterprises or to create a functioning payments system. In the later 1990s, banks became even less interested in lending to enterprises as they found lucrative opportunities to lend to the government. Therefore, enterprises had to get by without money.

The third factor was the nature of state-business relations. One aspect of this was the potential for arbitrary and punitive interventions from the state, imposing impossible tax demands. Barter and opting out of the money economy could, therefore, be a means to evade the reach of the tax authorities. This is often cited as a key reason for the growth of barter, but its importance is unclear. The prices that were formally registered for barter transactions were often higher than prices for cash transactions, so tax obligations could have been increased rather than decreased.

A different aspect of state-business relations undoubtedly was important. By allowing the payment of taxes and utility bills in kind, government bodies supported the survival of the enterprises that were the core of local economies. The cutting off of electricity or the imposition of widespread bankruptcies, as was threatened in Hungary, would have led to a massive level of closures, with no gain to the utilities or the tax authorities. The spread of barter, therefore, followed from the willingness of government bodies to give informal support to business. This was even less systematic than support offered in CEECs, but it held back mass unemployment and substituted for the social safety net that the state was proving incapable of creating.

The fourth factor was the absence of other means for enterprises to find revenue, as was possible from exports for many enterprises in CEECs. It is notable that enterprises earning revenues from selling internationally traded goods, such as oil and nonferrous metals, had the lowest involvement in nonmonetary transaction.

The effect of the growth in barter was to make exchange more difficult and more cumbersome, operating through multiple networks with no necessary consistency in effective prices. It was symptomatic of a situation in which enterprises could not resolve problems of access to finance or to markets for their goods. They were finding the means to survive, but they were locked into existing networks, with little scope to develop new contacts and certainly no ability to invest and modernize their activities.

Finally, the third distinctive element in enterprise survival behavior was the employment policy followed by Russian enterprises. Reductions in employment were much smaller than reductions in output, but this was not a matter of simple inertia. Enterprises continued recruiting, and there was significant labor turnover. However, many were unable to pay employees' wages in full and ran into substantial arrears, to an extent and with a persistence that was unknown in CEECs. This appears irrational from both sides in the neoclassical framework; employers should reduce employment, and employees should leave voluntarily.

There was logic from both sides. Employers often hoped to return to their past production levels and did not want to lose their workforces. More immediately, they had to respond quickly to orders from trading companies. Moreover, wages in less successful enterprises were very low, insofar as they were always paid, and maintaining employment levels was, therefore, manageable.

For employees, there was little alternative in view of the weakness of social protection for those not in formal employment. Enterprises retained roles in catering, in providing housing, and in providing goods through their shops, which also ensured an outlet for some of the results of barter. These forms of welfare provision were always more substantial in the Soviet Union than in CEECs and declined more rapidly in the latter as welfare states were created. In the CIS, they could substitute for the failure of the states to develop and finance such services, and regional governments were in turn happy for enterprises to relieve them of that potential responsibility. Thus, it was employment that gave access to benefits in money and in kind—tax rules created incentives to conceal these—and opportunities for pilfering, either for consumption or to help small-scale business activity.

Thus, deep difficulties for enterprises, a weak financial infrastructure, and a weak state welfare role all contributed to an apparent divergence from standard economic behavior of firms in a market environment. The implication was that enterprises across the CIS, or at least those inherited from state Socialism, paid even less attention to long-term strategy than those in CEECs. There were frequently hopes of returning to past product ranges, but the narrowing to a purely production role made any thinking on a more comprehensive strategy highly problematic. Nor was there scope for thinking of innovation and competitiveness when enterprises were struggling to arrange for inputs and to dispose of outputs.

CHAPTER TWELVE

The Growth of New Business

The emergence of completely new enterprises was in all countries an important part of the development of a market economy. Some work has, at least implicitly, counterposed new enterprise formation to the privatization of existing enterprises as a means to create a new private sector. Kornai (1990a), sceptical of the possibility and benefits of rapid privatization, saw new enterprise formation as the most important source of private-sector growth. The emphasis shifted during the early and mid-1990s toward privatization, but some subsequent assessments have put new firm formation back as the more important engine of growth, at least in Poland and Hungary, where attempts at rapid, massive privatization were avoided (Gehlbach 2008a, 141; Jackson, Klich, and Poznańska 2005, 10–17). The evidence in this chapter points to a more nuanced conclusion. Creating new enterprises from scratch led only to very small-scale business activity, and growth into larger businesses was severely constrained by the underdeveloped nature of the business environment. Cases of rapid growth typically required gaining control of enterprises through privatization, meaning that it is difficult to separate growth driven by privatized enterprises from growth driven by newly created firms.

This chapter follows the overlapping processes of the creation of new companies, the emergence of very basic—but also very widespread—forms of small-scale business activity, and the differences in environments for smaller-scale business activity in different countries. Past history played a role, as did the course of early transition and the ability of the state to establish and maintain a monopoly on enforcement.

The approach here takes account of two perspectives in the literature. A substantial body of work has followed entrepreneurship in former state Socialist countries with an assumption that the heritage of the past system created barriers to new enterprise. This, it has been hypothesized, led to conformist and unenterprising attitudes, a habitual dependence on seeking help from the state, a willingness to seek solutions outside formal rules, and a likely hostility toward capitalism from part of the population (Rapacki 1996). This might be expected to lead to a low desire to set up new firms. However, empirical evidence does not confirm a consistently low interest in new business activity and points instead to new entrepreneurs tending to avoid contact with state authorities rather than continually looking to them for help.

Other authors have concentrated on how new businesses behave in apparently unfavorable business climates, identifying common features across former state Socialist countries. These include a preference for activities with low capital requirements, dependence on networks of family and friends for capital and business contacts, evasive attitudes toward state officials and larger organizations, and strategies of diversification to take advantage of limited entrepreneurial possibilities (cf. Estrin, Meyer, and Bytchkova 2006; Smallbone and Welter 2008). None of this is unique to transition; small businesses in other economies show all these forms of behavior. Nevertheless, empirical evidence does support the view that the bias toward such practices has been strong in transition economies.

However, it is also necessary to explain the substantial differences among countries in transition. Although they related in part to factors familiar from studies in market economies, such as the demand for products and services and the skills of potential entrepreneurs, they also related to specific conditions of the kinds of states that emerged in the early 1990s.

INFORMAL AND STREET TRADERS

The creation of significant new businesses took some time in all countries, but new business *activity* developed very rapidly. Much of this was very small-scale trading undertaken by individuals, often on the street, with minimal requirements for fixed capital. These activities filled gaps that had been underdeveloped under state Socialism and that required the smallest financial, and in many cases also human, capital inputs. The pattern was also similar across countries in terms of overall growth, although data do not exist to make possible exact comparisons.

So-called shuttle trade developed in Poland in the 1980s. International travel made possible purchases and sales in different countries, and profit could be made from exploiting the price and scarcity differences both between state Socialist countries and with neighboring market economies. Once fully freed from central control, street trading expanded rapidly from 1989. Exactly who was involved, or what happened to them, remains unclear; the phenomenon was too short-lived for much detailed research. Some were desperately selling personal possessions to earn a little money and presumably soon exhausted their supplies. Other small traders set up shops—converted wooden garden sheds appeared across parts of Polish cities—but many disappeared into unemployment or other kinds of employment. Such opportunities disappeared in later years with the freeing of international trade and the formalization of goods import.

Retailing in CEECs followed a pattern of repeated transitions, first including some informal trade, then to more stable formalized domestic firms, and finally to large-scale foreign-owned supermarkets, which easily triumphed over domestically owned rivals. There were further waves of small-scale traders, often foreign nationals. Thus, in the Czech Republic, further small traders came from Vietnam and gradually developed more permanent networks and supply chains, supporting family businesses. The continual generation of new businesses demonstrates that there was plenty of enthusiasm for independent business activity, but small businesses were constrained by features of their business environments and had difficulty competing when foreign investors arrived.

Greater and longer-lasting opportunities for informal trade opened up beginning in 1989 in the Soviet Union, as freer movement of people was allowed, while international trade was still centrally controlled and restricted. As many as 3 million people may have been involved at that time. In the mid-1990s, there were estimated to be 10 million people dependent on shuttle trade, bringing in one-third of the country's imports from outside the CIS (Eder, Yakovlev, and Çarkoglu 2003; Yakovlev 2008b), including much of the modern consumer goods that reached domestic hands. The typical shuttle trader was educated and frequently female (this was also true of other countries; for Lithuania, see Aidis [2006]). They worked on a cash-only, no-tax, and no-credit basis, but that meant paying bribes to state and customs officials, and they frequently also had to make payments to criminal organizations. The overall cost savings gave them an advantage over formal importers, but it was just as important that Russia's internal trade system was very poorly developed.

The crisis of 1998 led to an approximate halving of the volume of shuttle trade, measured in U.S. dollars, as consumption increased for domestically produced goods. However, rising consumer demand meant that there was still room for informal importers, often bringing expensive consumer goods, such as cars from the Baltic republics (see above p.75), to satisfy the wishes of a particular customer. They were very gradually edging toward more formal practices, which depended on long-term business arrangements made possible by the establishment of a degree of trust. Successful shuttle traders began to use transport companies to import goods, thereby incurring customs duties, albeit kept down by understating the value of the goods. They were gradually squeezed out by formal importing companies, but up until 2008, they still had clear advantages outside of the biggest cities.

Shuttle trade played similar roles in other countries, providing employment to an educated and enterprising part of the population and providing a wider range of goods to consumers. Its development toward more complex forms of business activity was extremely slow. The important difference between countries was whether more sophisticated businesses could take over its role, sweeping small traders off the economic stage. In CEECs, that happened much sooner than in Russia.

In Kyrgyzstan, a country with an unfavorable infrastructure for business growth and with little by way of useful assets from the past, small-scale trade was a basis for much of the continuing economic activity. Stable employment was difficult for much of the population in view of the severe downturn in industrial and agricultural employment. Traders established cross-border links, systematizing shuttle trade between China, Russia, and other CARs. They could expand their businesses, bringing in family members to increase trade contacts and to produce at home some products for sale (Özcan 2006). It was a very basic form of market activity. Set against the history of modern market economies, it corresponds to forms that were most important centuries ago, before the Industrial Revolution and large-scale manufacturing, which required the means to concentrate finance through banks and other institutions.

CREATING FORMAL SMALL BUSINESSES

More substantial private businesses could develop legally before 1990 in Poland and Hungary. The road was slightly more complicated in the Soviet Union, where individual labor activity was allowed in November 1986, and new cooperatives could be formed beginning in May 1988. Overwhelmingly, these were created to be closely tied to state-owned enterprises, and many were effectively capitalist firms with an owner and employees. An estimated 2.9 million people were working in 133,000 cooperatives by July 1989 (Kotz and Weir 2007, 89; Buyske 2007, 61). The end of state Socialism led in all countries to clearer legal rules that formally, and usually also in reality, guaranteed equal status for different forms of ownership. A new private sector could then grow rapidly.

This was further encouraged by policies of "small" privatization, whereby smaller public enterprises, mostly in retailing and small-scale services, were transferred to private hands. This was generally done early on and quickly, but the impact was rather small, largely because there were few small units in economies dominated by large organizations—for example, about 100,000 to privatize in Russia and 25,000 in the Czech Republic.

The aims and methods differed between countries (Earle et al. 1994). In Czechoslovakia, and subsequently the Czech Republic, the aim was explicitly to create a class of small-scale entrepreneurs as quickly as possible. It followed restitution of some property to former owners. Small privatization proceeded by open public auctions in which former employees had no advantage and from which foreign companies and individuals were formally excluded. In practice, only 22,345 units were sold and often only with a right to lease premises. There were some cases of intimidation during and prior to auctions, and sources of money were unclear, probably often coming from silent foreign partners, but the most striking point was the relatively small impact on the economy. Retailing was transformed rather by the emergence of completely new enterprises and then, from the later 1990s, by the penetration of foreign retail chains, which overwhelmed most emerging domestic capitalists (Earle et al. 1994; Myant 1993, 2007).

Hungary and Poland followed different courses, with the former giving greater weight to maintaining the integrity of established retail enterprises and allowing sale to private companies. It already had a private sector, and space in large shops was often leased out. In Poland, more weight was given to transferring ownership to "insiders," meaning employees of the enterprises.

Moreover, in all of these cases, a formal small privatization policy was less important to new business development than were laws that removed direct restrictions, plus scope for the commercialization of economic activities so that new businesses could buy, or more likely rent, basic premises from existing enterprises and state organizations. The typical new enterprise then grew from scratch on the basis of assets brought by a founder.

ORIGINS OF NEW ENTREPRENEURS

There are variations between countries in which one could emerge as a successful entrepreneur, depending on the assets—in terms of skills, competence, contacts, and access to resources, such as finance—that could give the greatest advantages. In all cases, technical, commercial, or scientific abilities from state-owned enterprises proved useful (Smallbone and Welter 2008; Estrin, Meyer, and Bytchkova 2006), although they often had little relevance to the precise activities the firms undertook; entrepreneurs had to adapt to any opportunities available.

Enterprise was not typically an activity for the poorest sections of society, who were suffering the most from the economic downturn, although the struggle for individual survival led into activities that could verge on business activity, albeit with little chance of accumulation and development of bigger businesses. Thus, some Russian collective farm workers could continue in nominal employment, albeit with minimal pay, as a basis for pilfering food for a few of their own animals. Other authors, looking at Bulgaria, Romania, and Russia, traced a retreat from the cash economy into growing one's own food and relying on exchange within very limited networks of contacts (contributions in Neef and Stănculescu [2002]). The implication is that having some private property meant for some not the start of business activity but the opportunity to survive in a "household" economy, covering for the absence of formal employment or a social safety net by producing for oneself (cf. Wallace and Latcheva 2006, 90).

Economic realities restricted the scope for wealth accumulation to certain sections of the population, but for some of them, prospects were very good. Accounts from Russia point to starting points for more substantial businesses in wealth from the black market or illegal activities and in experiences in the Komsomol, the Communist youth organization (Yurchak 2002). This brought scope for international contacts and trading in the last years of the Soviet Union. As trading became more systematic, it still depended on political connections to gain export licenses. Direct and indirect links to the former power structure were, therefore, important for many emerging Russian entrepreneurs (Kotz and Weir 2007, 111–21). That source was less important in CEECs, where international contacts were less restricted.

In Poland, some entrepreneurs did build up from illegal trading activities before 1989, but the typical route was for a well-qualified individual in a state enterprise to branch out on their own when the opportunity arose. According to statistical evidence, a background in the ruling party before 1989 was a serious disadvantage for entrepreneurial activity. Success was more often associated with involvement with the political opposition in the 1980s. In Hungary, party membership was neither a help nor a hindrance (Osborn and Słomczyński 2005, 85–86). Czechoslovakia also differed from these experiences. Travel was more restricted than in Poland and Hungary, and there was less opportunity for any significant business activity up to 1989. The transformation was more sudden than in those countries or the Soviet Union so that new enterprises began life in an environment of freer movement of goods and people, giving no obvious advantage to those with political contacts.

It can be added that in CEECs, the more stable state structures meant that links to political power in the new system were also less important to building a business than they were in CIS countries. Entrepreneurs there who did build significant businesses refer to a "wild" early period in which rules were unclear or unimportant. There were some acts of violence and the use of private means to settle business disputes, but there was a qualitative difference from the Russian case. There was never a point where private enforcement became a standard practice that was widely preferred to formal means.

DATA ON NEW ENTREPRENEURS

There are no comprehensive and reliable data on the numbers and growth of new enterprises across all transition economies. Nevertheless, what is available, plus the results of other kinds of research, point to differences between countries that are outlined here. Explanations for those differences are suggested in the next section.

The most precise measure for the first years was the number of legally registered businesses, but this depended on laws specific to individual countries. In some cases, one individual could own several businesses, and not all need be undertaking business activity. In other cases, business activity need not be formally registered.

More meaningful and comparable data became available with standardized labor force surveys in the early 1990s, but even these are incomplete. Table 12.1 shows the self-employed plus employers as a percentage of the total working population where data are available. The immediate impression is that there was no general barrier to independent business activity, although it is unfortunate that data are not available for Belarus and Uzbekistan, where authoritarian regimes might have imposed more effective constraints.

For some countries, the ILO provided data using a methodology intended to exclude those who were formally self-employed while still effectively in an

TABLE 12.1   Self-employed plus employers as a percentage of the active workforce in transition economies, 2007

Country	Self-employed plus employers in active workforce (%)
Czech Republic	15.6
Hungary	11.8
Poland	19.2
Slovakia	12.8
Slovenia	11.5
Azerbaijan	58.2
Kazakhstan	33.4
Russia	7.1
Bulgaria	11.2
Estonia	8.7
Latvia	9.1
Lithuania	11.9
Romania	21.1
Armenia	36.2
Georgia	34.9
Kyrgyzstan	35.2
Moldova	31.0
Mongolia	32.5
Ukraine	18.9
Bosnia-Herzegovina	22.6
Croatia	19.3
Macedonia, FYR	17.6
Montenegro	17.3
Serbia	20.1

Source: ILO LABORSTA database, available at http://laborsta.ilo.org.

Note: Figures for Poland and Bulgaria include members of cooperatives. The figure for Mongolia is from the census in 2000, and the figure for Montenegro is for 2005. Comparable data were not available for other transition economies.

employment relationship. This could be important, as employers often prefer to convert an effective employment relationship into a contract with a formally self-employed individual, thereby avoiding various financial and legal obligations. Formal self-employment can, therefore, be a less secure and lower-status position than traditional employment. In practice, the data suggest that this was not an important enough phenomenon to justify doubts about the data used in Table 12.1.

The data point to very high levels of self-employment in some former Soviet republics, where agriculture was transferred to individual farmers and where there were substantial service sectors—notably Azerbaijan, Kazakhstan, and Kyrgyzstan. There were much lower figures for Russia and somewhat lower figures for most CEECs, where the heritage of collectivized agriculture was partially continued in large-scale agricultural units. Poland, with largely individual farming, recorded a maximum figure of 20 percent in 2002, and, as shown in Table 12.1, the share of self-employed plus employers in the workforce was only slightly below that level in 2007.

Insofar as trends can be followed over time, they typically show rapid growth at some point in the 1990s, followed by stagnation or, quite often, clear decline. This suggests a one-off growth, with new businesses emerging in services and private ownership in agriculture and then hitting constraints following the penetration of retail and service activities by bigger domestic or foreign-owned companies. There was also some conversion of the individual self-employed into employers. Hungary was the clearest case, with employers reaching the unusually high figure of 6 percent of the labor force in 2005, alongside 7 percent for the self-employed without employees.

Other sources make it possible to separate out nonagricultural self-employment, but only for some countries. The OECD (2008) provides such data for member countries. The ratio of nonagricultural employers and the self-employed to the total workforce grew especially rapidly in the Czech Republic, from a minimal level in 1989 to reach 8.6 percent of the labor force in 1993 and a peak of 15.7 percent in 2003 before dropping back to 15.0 percent in 2007. The figure also grew rapidly in Hungary, already reaching 15.1 percent in 1994 and then declining gradually to 10.6 percent in 2007. The process was slower in Slovakia, reaching 5.8 percent in 1994 and 7.2 percent in 1999. However, it continued to grow and reached 12.1 percent in 2007. Growth in Poland was less dramatic, beginning from a significant base of 4.9 percent of the labor force in 1989. It peaked at 10.0 percent in 1999 and then declined back to 9.6 percent in 2007. Thus, these figures, too, confirm different starting points, rapid growth in some, and delayed growth in Slovakia. Estimates for Russia point to a lower figure of 4.3 percent of the labor force in self-employment outside agriculture in 1998 (Clarke 1999, 28). Conditions appeared to be less favorable there than in CEECs. In all cases, there were much higher densities in bigger cities and substantial regional variations. Thus, the Czech level was roughly twice the Slovak level in the mid-1990s, despite the countries' common pasts and legal frameworks.

It would be useful to be able to compare employment creation in new enterprises with the performance of those inherited from the past. However, this is very difficult to estimate. The first problem is to define a new enterprise, when many arose from the previous, state-owned enterprises. This was explicit in the Polish method of privatization through liquidation, which amounted to the sale of existing enterprises, frequently to employees. It was less explicit for many smaller firms that arose out of parts of existing enterprises. Figures on employment in small firms are, therefore, only a rough indication of the contribution of new firms. Using this estimate, 15 percent of employment in Poland in 1997 was in firms with fewer than six employees, including the self-employed in this figure. Another estimate suggests that 31 percent of the labor force may have been working in firms that had been founded after 1989 (Jackson, Klich, and Poznańska 2005, 30–31). An estimate for Russia was about 15 percent of total employment in the new private sector in the late 1990s (Clarke 1999, 28) or 20 percent in another estimate for the years after 2000 (Ahrend 2006, 8–9). The share of GDP from small businesses, meaning those with fewer than 100 workers, was reported to be only 17 percent in 2007, an extraordinarily low figure by international standards (Rutland 2010, 176) and one that is consistent with a very low share of employment in these businesses.

LEVELS AND FORMS OF ENTREPRENEURSHIP

The differences in numbers of the self-employed and the ability of new businesses to grow and increase employment can be explained in general terms around the following five themes, which also give indications of the forms business activity could take in different countries:

1. The scope for new enterprises depended on demand, and hence income levels, and on competition from established or incoming firms. This explains the growth trajectories in CEECs and the decline in the numbers of small businesses in many countries as larger businesses asserted themselves.

2. New businesses, and particularly new businesses that could grow, were typically started by qualified people, and this meant a bias toward more developed and urban areas, which were also likely to be areas with higher demand. Transferable skills depended also on sectoral structures, with traditional industries, especially coal mining and steel, providing a particularly poor starting point. The best environment was, therefore, likely to be a large administrative center in a country with higher levels of education.

3. Past traditions may have been important. New entrepreneurs in CEECs often referred back to family traditions from before state Socialism; there was obviously less of such potential in CIS countries, which lacked traditions of a market economy, and what traditions they did have were from a more distant past. Survey evidence from Poland shows a much greater likelihood for entrepreneurs to have had an ancestor involved in business than among the population as a whole (Osborn and Słomczyński 2005, 66). Entrepreneurs also often talked of encouragement from friends and family. Tradition could explain the much higher level of self-employment in the Czech Republic relative to Slovakia, despite the countries' common recent pasts and legal frameworks, as there was a stronger history of nonagricultural small businesses in the former case. However, it is not easy to find further evidence to support the hypothesis, and other explanations, in terms of economic structures and education levels, are easier to identify (Myant et al. 1996, 139).

4. Access to finance was a constraint in all countries, and evidence in Chapter 14 suggests that it was likely to have been particularly severe in Russia and other CIS countries. It was likely to have been least severe in the Czech Republic,

owing to the high availability of credit in the early years. However, the general effect of constraints on credit was not to prevent all business activity. Instead, it biased entrepreneurship toward smaller-scale activities and toward particular forms and methods. Initial growth depended on financial help from individual savings, from family and personal contacts, or from access to financial institutions that, to varying degrees, depended also on personal contacts. Combined with other sources of instability, this left many new enterprises struggling to develop, explaining the need for flexibility, diversity, and a willingness to seize any new opportunities that might arise rather than concentrating on a single strategy for expansion. Smallbone and Welter (2008) emphasize this with particular reference to Belarus, but it is true of other countries, too. Finance clearly was accessible in all countries to some enterprises, although this often depended on bribes or more extreme illegal activities.

5. The legal framework was important. This can both protect and constrain business activity. A weak state in Russia created the scope for violent entrepreneurs, as covered in Chapter 8. That in itself was a form of business and a basis for creating part of the new business elite. It was an elite with a background, attitudes, and expertise that arguably were not conducive to creating a business environment in which firms could compete freely and fairly. More immediately, the extent of intertwining business with violence and crime made life difficult for growing businesses, as they were constrained in their freedom to establish wide networks and to enter into business relations beyond the reach of their roofs. A weak state was, therefore, not a barrier to all business but a factor that created a bias toward particular kinds of entrepreneurial activity.

The impact of administrative regulations also requires careful interpretation. International agencies have been particularly concerned with the theme of avoiding unnecessary restrictions, an issue that has aroused interest in advanced market economies. This is followed by the Business Environment and Enterprise Performance Survey (BEEPS), established by the EBRD and World Bank and covered in detail on their web sites.[1] Results are unimpressive for a number of former state Socialist countries, notably including Poland, but the implications are unclear. A favored measure is the time required for, and the administrative complexity of, setting up a new business. However, to judge from the number of businesses established, this is not a consistent barrier. Indeed, it is frequently possible to buy a preregistered business with a minimal time lag, meaning that the cost is only financial. Thus, as a market economy becomes more sophisticated and complex, private businesses can find ways to minimize the effects of restrictions.

A large number of formal rules can be a serious problem for business in a corrupt environment. Regulations imply a need for contact with officials, who may exploit their positions of power to speed up processes or to impose unnecessary delays, demanding bribes for fulfilling their jobs. Thus, as the state reestablished itself in Russia, the need to pay bribes increased (Smallbone and Welter 2008, 77). It is a state that is unable, or unwilling, to ensure control over its own employees. The demoralization caused by the need to confront a huge number of different offices in Russia has been cited as a barrier to business development (76). There is also some survey evidence

---

[1] Available at http://www.ebrd.com/country/sector/econo/surveys/beeps.htm.

citing corruption as a major barrier to business expansion (Aidis and Mickiewicz 2006, 874). Even tougher administrative controls in Belarus, often applied arbitrarily, may also explain an apparent reversal in the growth of small businesses there after 1996, leading to a level of registered entrepreneurs in 2004 equivalent to 2.35 percent of the population—an exceptionally low level (Smallbone and Welter 2008, 104–8).

Regulations, then, can mean a small additional financial cost, or they can be a more serious source of arbitrariness in obstacles to undertaking enterprise. Such a situation raises questions about the purpose of rules that are effective only in enabling state officials to gain additional income. Indeed, it has been suggested, in a study of the Georgian case, that some political elites may deliberately create inconsistent and contradictory rules as a means to generate insecurity that they can then exploit (cf. Christophe 2007, 184). Irrespective of precise political motivations, it seems obvious that officials at all levels would have no interest in recommending any reduction in the administrative complexity from which they can profit.

CONCLUSION

Summarizing across these experiences, three points can be made. The first is that new businesses emerged quickly in all transition economies and provided employment and services to the population. Without them, depression would have been deeper and recovery even less impressive. The second is that their role varied between countries, depending on the institutional and economic environments. They required support from a business infrastructure, and even then, they proved weak when faced with competition from bigger enterprises. The third is that much of the information in this chapter relates most easily to an early stage in the development of capitalism. Small businesses emerged from scratch by means ranging from very hard work to violent crime; they did not look like part of a modern market economy. There was still a substantial gulf, even in the most successful transition economies, to the environment for small business development in the most advanced market economies. There was very weak development of such features as policies to support innovation, the availability of venture capital, or a network of business angels who could help promising entrepreneurs. International comparisons of detailed indicators of international competitiveness (e.g., Research Center for Competitiveness of Czech Economy [RCCCE] and National Observatory of Employment and Training [NOET] 2008) consistently showed CEECs well behind the EU average, in some cases with absolutely minimal access to venture capital that could support innovative new businesses.

That weakness partly reflected policy choices. As indicated in Chapter 6, state involvement in anything that could be interpreted as systematic industrial policy was generally not favored. The weakness also partly reflected the difficulty of developing these elements of a modern business environment from scratch over a short time period. Thus, for example, business angels—rich individuals willing to invest to help promising new businesses—could only exist and be effective after wealth had been accumulated from previous successful business activities. However, the effect of the weakness of the emerging new enterprises was to make transition economies even more dependent on inward investment by multinational companies if they were to improve their levels of international competitiveness. That theme is taken up in Chapter 15.

CHAPTER THIRTEEN

Privatization

This chapter follows so-called big privatization, the transfer into private ownership of large, state-owned enterprises. The means used varied between countries, but much of the debate about method focused on the experiences of the Czech Republic and Russia as the pioneers of the use of vouchers. This was then enthusiastically propagated by the World Bank, and teams of international advisers persuaded other countries to follow similar methods. A number of countries resisted that pressure and pursued alternatives. Evidence on the consequences of voucher privatization suggests that their scepticism was justified. This is backed up with brief assessments of the impact of privatization on the performance of enterprises and on the creation of other features of a developed market economy.

This, then, is a more questioning approach than the once-dominant insistence that any transfer to private ownership should be judged positively. That view was epitomized by the EBRD and others by using the percentage of GDP from the private sector and the progress in "small" and "big" privatization as key indicators of the seriousness of reform intentions and of the success in achieving reform. The evidence here points to less positive conclusions about privatization. The big exception, which generally had positive effects, was privatization into foreign ownership, which is followed in Chapter 15.

METHODS OF PRIVATIZATION

The EBRD and others classified and assessed the different possible methods for transferring enterprises into private hands. The three main possibilities were defined as manager-employee buyout (MEBO), mass privatization by vouchers, and direct sale. None of these is a very precise definition.

The MEBO category spans methods that give substantial shareholdings to all employees and those that give shares effectively just to managers. Neither method gained favor from neoliberal purists, who sought the benefits of outsider ownership and control, fearing that insiders, especially rank-and-file employees, would oppose restructuring that involved job losses. In fact, substantial shares to employees were the norm in the early 1990s across most countries (Uvalic and Vaughan-Whitehead 1997). This followed partly from political judgments—that employee support was needed—and partly from the perceived dangers and difficulties with other methods. Even some of those with doubts at the time came later to appreciate the benefits of some power for employees who had an interest in their enterprises' survival and could therefore create a barrier against asset stripping by managements (Nellis 2002, 17).

The voucher method involved distributing vouchers, either for free or at a nominal price, to the adult population. These could then be exchanged for shares. Advocates presented this as the quickest way to eliminate state ownership, even leading directly to a capital market as found in mature market economies. It was at least considered in all countries and implemented in some form in almost all, although the extent of property transferred varied considerably. Thus, in some cases, vouchers were limited to minority stakes, and in some, there were favorable terms for employees. The exact method also varied, depending on the degree of central control over the transfer of property, the scope for trading vouchers before their exchange for shares, and the role of investment funds, which, in some cases, were created as compulsory intermediaries between firms and shareholders. These differences influenced the complexity of the process, the scope for its manipulation, and the scope for participation by foreign companies.

Direct sale, unless simply to an existing management, appeared to bring in outsiders, but scope for this method was limited by available domestic financial resources. It frequently meant sale to a foreign company. In some cases, it created the conditions for enrichment for the new domestic business elites.

The EBRD has classified countries by their primary and secondary methods of privatization, albeit with considerable scope for arbitrary judgements. Thus, the Czech Republic was classified as primarily using the voucher method, although less than half of property set for privatization in the early 1990s was exchanged for vouchers. There, as elsewhere, a variety of methods was used. It can be added that the method used was not always decisive in determining the longer-term outcome. Property changed hands quickly, and concentrated ownership emerged fairly soon in all countries. Substantial variations in subsequent ownership structures then depended less on the method of privatization than on the economic viability of the enterprises emerging from it and on the scope within the institutional and legal framework for a rapid concentration of wealth.

A substantial literature grew up on the theory of privatization. Much of this was a discussion of how to transfer ownership (e.g., Frydman and Rapaczynski 1994) and of plans and first steps in different countries, often with multiple contributions from policymakers and advisers (Frydman, Rapaczynski, and Earle 1993b, 1993a; OECD 1995). Work on the subsequent performance of enterprises, which came after important decisions had been made, is taken up in the following text. A frequent conclusion of the early works was that the voucher method was best, as it was the quickest means to get rid of state property. It was first tried in Czechoslovakia, continuing in the Czech Republic after the old country split.

CZECH PRIVATIZATION

Czechoslovak, and then Czech, privatization became the starting point for a model taken up by international agencies for implementation in other countries. This was where the voucher method was applied first and, so it seemed, in its purest form.

The idea was taken from the writings of Polish economists Janusz Lewandowski and Jan Szomburg in 1988 and gained strength when Czech economist Jan Švejnar returned from emigration in the United States with a plan for transformation that involved handing shares to the public (A. Schwartz 2006, 102). Initially cautious, Czech economists around Klaus then quickly set about developing their conception. It differed from Švejnar's in providing an intermediate stage at which the public could trade voucher points for company shares. Klaus's initial hope was that a transfer of practically all corporate wealth into private hands could proceed very quickly.

The advantage of the method was its speed, allowing transfer to a population that lacked significant savings with which to buy shares. It also bypassed the need for valuing assets; that could be done through the free market by purchasers bidding with voucher points. Moreover, it appeared egalitarian—enabling all citizens to acquire property—and could, at least initially, prevent assets from ending up in the hands of foreigners, a point that was important to Klaus and his circle. It was therefore likely to be politically popular. If implemented properly, it should avoid favoritism for those bringing power, and possibly some wealth, from the past. It was presented as a step to creating a share-owning society in which citizens would have a financial stake in their own country.

As soon as the idea was mooted, it met doubts and opposition. The most common argument was that the outcome would be highly dispersed ownership, providing minimal control over management. It was also argued that many new owners would probably sell their shares, which would both increase consumer spending with inflationary consequences and depress share prices so that new issues would be difficult. They could also sell to foreigners, so the hope of creating a national capitalism would be frustrated.

There were two more fundamental criticisms. The first, voiced by the critics of the Czech transition strategy referred to in Chapter 6, was that voucher privatization was irrelevant to enterprise restructuring, as it brought in no new finance, no new market contacts, and no new expertise. Its advocates were unmoved, believing that creating a new incentive structure based on profit-seeking owners would quickly create the basis for solutions to all other problems.

The second was that the voucher method was based on a misunderstanding of how modern market economies work. The complexities of the separation of ownership from control in modern corporations, which typically left the mass of shareholders powerless, were ignored. The contribution of Berle and Means (1968), discussed in Box 13.1, was either forgotten or denigrated by the advocates of abstract models of a market system, as was the thinking behind Stiglitz's warning that the stock market should be seen for transition economies as no more than a "sideshow" (Stiglitz 1994, 228).

There was ambiguity in what the advocates of the voucher method were expecting it to lead to. Sometimes, they foresaw a system with owners managing their own enterprises, modeled on an early version of capitalism built around individual entrepreneurs. Voucher privatization, then, would be just a first step, followed by a rapid period of concentration as an entrepreneurial elite emerged and took control. At other times, they foresaw shareholders turning up in huge numbers at general meetings to impose discipline on managers. Among the key policymakers, it was the former view that predominated. That meant allowing an uncontrolled stock market to facilitate a very rapid concentration of wealth. They therefore consciously linked voucher privatization to weak regulation and saw the development of a solid legal framework as something that could be left until ownership had been consolidated into a few hands.

Box 13.1 Corporate governance and the separation of ownership from control

Interpretations of the roles and nature of shareholders, stock markets, and joint-stock companies were an important part of the debates over the form of privatization in transition economies. A body of literature on corporate governance has followed the means whereby shareholders can impose discipline on managers, thereby enforcing efficiency- and profit-seeking activity from managers who are formally company employees. A relevant survey article (Shleifer and Vishny 1997) concluded that this is possible for dispersed owners, if backed by a satisfactory legal framework. Concentrated ownership can be effective with less rigorous legal controls.

Other studies show that no system of corporate governance is free from dangers of theft by managers of shareholders' property (Allen and Gale 2000). Thus, forms of concentrated ownership give little protection against the majority owners using the wealth of minority shareholders as they choose. However, in established companies in many European countries, they use their power to build successful organizations and not purely for personal enrichment (Faccio and Lang 2000). Managers—with, at most, minority shareholdings—often had ambitions to build and run a successful enterprise, which overrode a thirst for the maximum short-term financial gain. That is consistent with the famous view of Joseph Schumpeter (1952, 132) that the entrepreneur was the key agent driving innovations, motivated by the long-term desire to found an empire or build a position of wealth.

Systems of corporate governance therefore functioned even when a simple reading of incentive structures would suggest that they should not. Nevertheless, although maximizing immediate personal financial gain is not the only important motivation in established companies, it often can play a destructive role, and legal frameworks have evolved to keep it in check.

This is confirmed by the historical evolution of joint-stock companies, which shows how institutions—in the sense of formal rules, plus less formal habits and forms of behavior—evolved alongside each other to create a key foundation of modern business. Established companies, controlled by their owners, were initially cautious of offering shares for sale. It was a means to raise finance, but it risked diluting their power. Members of the public were also cautious of buying shares, with no guarantee that their money would not be taken by managements or majority owners, leaving them with nothing (for the UK experience, see Hannah [1983, 21]). The modern corporation with dispersed ownership gradually evolved alongside a legal framework and an acceptance of that framework. Evolution took different forms in different countries, with more concentrated ownership in some, complex forms of cross-ownership in others, and structures that obscured exactly who held power in still other cases. There evidently is no single ideal type, reflecting again the extent to which systems of corporate control are the results of trial and error and pragmatic decision making.

The concept of the separation of ownership from control was popularized after the work of Berle and Means (1968), first published in 1932. Their study of U.S. companies showed both the process underway—toward more dispersed ownership—and some of the reasons for it. They showed that a very specific legal framework that defined and limited shareholder and managerial powers was a necessity. Thus, for example, a system of direct control by a majority of shareholders could not function satisfactorily, as it would allow the expropriation of minority shareholders. Management had to be legally obliged to respect the interests of *all* shareholders.

Some economists could not reconcile themselves to the implication that management was not under full control of owners. Mises (1949, 304, 709) continued to insist that there had to be an entrepreneur carrying the risks and making the big decisions. Harald Demsetz (1988, 230), a major writer on theories of the firm, also saw no alternative to "the having of *private* wealth" as the driving force for improving productivity. He consistently doubted the extent and importance of the separation of ownership from control. However, studies of business history point in the opposite direction. Some of the most substantial of these suggest that there are proven benefits of keeping owners in the background and leaving management duties to professional managers (Chandler 1977, 1990).

Private ownership in transition economies could bring benefits if it was able to bring methods of professional management that could help solve the long-term problems set out at the start of Chapter 11. A weakness of much of the thinking behind arguments for rapid privatization was that all the emphasis was placed on creating an incentive structure linked to financial returns for owners. That was not enough for long-term business success.

The form taken by Czechoslovak voucher privatization followed compromises between its firmest advocates and others who favored alternatives of commercialization and restructuring under state ownership, direct sales (possibly backed with credits), or partial or full sales to foreign companies. All of these were included as possibilities in a broad legal framework, but implementation was largely in the hands of Klaus's allies, with no direct control from parliament over individual privatization decisions. Therefore, they could try to maximize the weight of the voucher method. This depended on attracting the maximum interest from the public and on ensuring that enough shares could be offered to match the likely level of demand.

Thus, one side to the process was the issuing of voucher books at a nominal price to the public in late 1991. There was at first limited interest, and voucher privatization might have been relegated to a minor role alongside other methods. However, things picked up when former Czech émigré Viktor Kožený returned to establish his group of investment funds under the Harvard name. He offered to handle individuals' voucher points and to buy the shares, once distributed, at an attractive price. Suddenly, voucher privatization looked like a free cash gift, and Kožený's example was followed by other similar entrepreneurs and by established

Czech banks and enterprises. In the end, 77 percent of the adult population took part, with 294 investment privatization funds (IPFs) controlling over 70 percent of voucher points. This had not been foreseen when the voucher method was first proposed, although the possibility of such intermediaries had been discussed in Poland. In Czechoslovakia, the government rushed through a rough legal framework, which was to prove ineffective when some prominent fund managers ignored obligations to ordinary shareholders and took the wealth for themselves.

The IPFs saved Klaus by giving Czech voucher privatization mass appeal. They also gave greater international credibility to the voucher method, as this looked like a possible response to the criticisms of dispersed ownership. Suddenly, there were hopes that funds would impose discipline on managements, forcing restructuring, and enthusiastic observers even thought they could see that happening. Unfortunately, this is not how the new owners behaved.

The other side to the process was the formulation of enterprise privatization plans. This had seemed irrelevant at first, when the conception was to put all enterprises into the process unchanged, leaving any changes to future owners. However, it mattered once it was accepted that enterprises could be privatized in a variety of ways. This, and the possibility of combining different privatization methods, was satisfied by allowing any individual or organization to submit a proposal for any enterprise. A rushed and somewhat farcical process followed, in which proposals were assessed by inexperienced officials, often with little more than minutes for each one. They were under pressure to work quickly because Klaus wanted the whole thing underway before parliamentary elections in June 1992. They were under pressure to ensure that a significant proportion of shares were to be exchanged for vouchers so that voucher holders would be able to bid for attractive enterprises. They did bend rules, altering proposals even when the law did not allow this. They also frequently bowed to outside lobbying and pressures. Overwhelmingly, they accepted proposals from enterprise managements (A. Schwartz 2006; Myant 2003, Chapter 7).

The first wave, with voucher holders bidding for shares, was centrally organized, with prices determined in five rounds of auction bidding. There is no evidence of manipulation of this process. After the breakup of Czechoslovakia, the Czech government proceeded with a second wave, which proved roughly as popular, with 74 percent of citizens buying voucher books and bidding for shares. The process was completed at the end of 1994.

This helped raise the prestige of the Czech Republic, making it the apparent leader in economic reform. The World Bank was impressed by their seeming success. However, this needs to be set against six important reservations.

The first reservation relates to the extent of privatization. Vouchers accounted for 35 percent of the property set for privatization by 1996. The Czech government then claimed that privatization had essentially been completed in time for the next round of parliamentary elections. Not all privatization during the two waves had proceeded by the voucher method, and not all property set for privatization could be disposed of. Privatization continued in later years, largely through direct sales. There was no thought of another voucher wave in the Czech Republic.

Second, the government was modifying its plans even in the course of the first wave, moving toward its later strategy of selling on favorable terms to individuals judged to be potentially dynamic entrepreneurs. The direct impetus was the impending financial collapse of the giant Škoda-Plzeň engineering combine—an enterprise with 40,000 employees before 1989, unconnected to the Škoda car manufacturer—in September 1992. Klaus personally intervened to push through a change in the privatization plan, to remove the incumbent management—even as shares were being offered for vouchers—and to enable a new and apparently dynamic manager to gain a substantial minority shareholding (Myant 2003, Chapter 11). This so-called entrepreneurial privatization became the model for key enterprises in later years, implicitly demonstrating the government's own lack of faith in voucher privatization as the key to better enterprise management.

Third, voucher privatization led to a concentration of wealth, but with much going to share dealers and speculators and not to the enterprises that needed investment and modernization. The months after shares had been distributed saw rapid share trading in what became known as the third wave. The aim of key traders was to buy from individual shareholders, to acquire majority control over enterprises, and then to sell for a substantial profit. There was a random element in who was accumulating wealth and who was acquiring control, but the latter often went to managements who bought, with the help of bank loans or by ignoring company law in order to use the enterprise's own resources. This whole process was made easier by a deliberately lax legal environment, allowing the secrecy of transactions and offering no protection to minority shareholders. As controlling share blocks were accumulated, the third wave drew to a close. Share prices fell well below their nominal values, and any citizens who had not sold when they could were likely to be left with worthless assets.

Fourth, investment funds played no significant role in pressing for, or enabling, enterprise restructuring. Some studies have found a degree of involvement in management (e.g., Schütte 2000), but these were rare. Nor could funds play much of a role in corporate governance to ensure that firms were well run. One positive element was that they could keep an eye on managements at least to ensure that they did not tunnel assets into their own hands. This was particularly true of the funds established by big banks. However, the lax environment meant that there was minimal control over the behavior of the funds themselves. Indeed, the easiest and most attractive way for a fund management to maximize its wealth was by share dealing or by exploiting the lax legal environment to use the fund's wealth as their own (cf. Ellerman 2001). Kožený achieved this in spectacular style, moving the wealth of the funds he controlled out of the country. He broke laws along the way, but the Czech state proved incapable either of bringing him back for trial or of regaining the wealth he had taken.

Fifth, voucher privatization and the scope for dealing in shares created a more complex structure of business, with greater scope for the unproductive use of assets and a greater variety of possible aims and strategies. Privatization removed control exercised by the ministry, and that was not replaced by control by shareholders—they were weak, dispersed, and inexperienced—or by a legal system. There were formal laws preventing managers from taking their enterprise's resources for private purposes, but they were rarely enforced by inexperienced and poorly informed courts, and there was often little will to intervene from a police force unfamiliar with new forms of business activity. Managers, therefore, had more freedom to "tunnel" from the enterprises they controlled, a term gaining currency in the Czech media as the phenomenon became widespread. Managers were still often motivated by a desire to maintain the traditions of their enterprises, but the objective of enterprise survival was complemented by greater scope for personal enrichment at the expense of the enterprise rather than by innovations and productive investment.

New kinds of firms also appeared, trading in shares and aiming purely for financial profit. They drove forward the third wave, and one small firm, Motoinvest, moved close to creating a dominant financial empire after quietly gaining control of several banks and investment funds. This was made possible by the scope for secrecy in transactions and by the great willingness of owners of shares acquired from vouchers to sell for the best price they could get, even if well below the shares' nominal values.

Limits were set by the central bank using existing laws to hold back Motoinvest. In this case, the new legal framework—setting limits on banks' activities—was used to effect once the main commercial banks complained that they were under threat from a new upstart company. Further limits were set by the introduction in 1996 of rules on share dealing that included some protection for minority shareholders, and these were further strengthened in later years. Thus, unlike the experience of CIS countries, the Czech state and central authorities were absent only for a short period.

Finally, as indicated in following chapters, voucher privatization did little to improve enterprise performance. It did not address either the long-term issues set out at the start of Chapter 11 or the specific problems that were afflicting enterprises as they struggled to survive after the shock.

THE LURE OF VOUCHER PRIVATIZATION

World Bank official John Nellis wrote an assessment of the organization's thinking on privatization, showing how its experts became "infatuated" with the Czech privatization method. At first, they were sceptical, but they were soon caught up in the logic of the possibility of, and need for, speed. They were selective in who they spoke to and listened to and behaved as if they believed the warnings from those around Klaus that doubters of the voucher method were actually trying to reverse the whole reform process (Nellis 2002, 21).

Thus, the World Bank's role was definitely not to encourage, or participate in, debates taking place within countries. It was in contact with one side only and became convinced that the results were "tremendously encouraging" (Nellis 2002, 22), meaning that the voucher method seemed to have proceeded without major political problems and to have led, at least in formal terms, to private ownership. They and the IMF then pushed the method vigorously as an example for others to follow, using available leverage with countries seeking financial help (Appel 2004, 23–30) and deploying Czech "experts" to advise in other countries; Bulgaria then quite explicitly followed the Czech example in autumn 1996, albeit using investment funds from the start (Appel 2004, 32; Helmenstein 1999, 47–48). Much of expert and academic opinion willingly followed the new fashion.

The effect was to make the voucher method the obvious choice wherever countries lacked the intellectual armoury to resist. In practice, it was often applied in hesitant and disorganized ways, with some backtracking and reversals. Moreover, other countries did not follow the details of the Czech method. They often avoided the danger of excessive fragmentation of ownership by including IPFs from the start. They frequently allowed vouchers to be traded before they were exchanged for shares, again serving to hasten the ownership concentration. The rounds of share auctions were also not followed. A more usual method was for the public to be able to spend their voucher points as enterprises came forward with offers. This avoided the need for the rushed preparation of the Czech and Slovak cases, where large numbers of enterprises were offered simultaneously. However, enthusiasts were concerned that the absence of a set timetable created scope for delay—for example, in Ukraine (Frydman, Rapaczynski, and Earle 1993b, 122–23). It also gave incumbent managers a more obvious initiative, but they had generally come out on top under the Czech method, anyway.

Disillusionment with the voucher method in international agencies set in during the later 1990s. The Czech economy ran into difficulties, and the crisis in 1998 in Russia shifted the opinion of the World Bank toward Stiglitz's view, which had always been one of extreme scepticism. However, even after that, there is evidence that the World Bank backed a voucher scheme up until 1999 for Azerbaijan that would have opened the way for substantial corruption. Koženy was involved, seeking to gain still more profits from a lax privatization scheme and lobbying—for a time, successfully—for the World Bank's backing of the plan he supported (Government Accountability Project [GAP] 2008).

VOUCHER SCEPTICS

The voucher sceptics are worth noting here. Among these were countries with the strongest traditions of serious economic debate and wider involvement in policy making. There were also countries that were inclined to reject imported reform models, anyway.

Hungary was the clearest, taking a cue from Kornai's very strong opposition (Kornai 1990a) but also reflecting a more general scepticism within the community of professional economists and political leaders. Privatization in that country had started before 1989, and hostility toward incumbent managers using privatization for their personal enrichment led to the reestablishment of central controls (N. Swain 1992, 11, 29; Lajtai 1997, 138). This came amid considerable public debate over the means and aims of privatization, including a greater willingness than in other CEECs to sell to foreign owners (Stark and Bruszt 1998, 54–77). The prime minister in June 1988, Károly Grósz, even famously stated in California that he would be happy to see some Hungarian enterprises sold to U.S. companies. Much of the motivation was the need for help in repaying Hungary's foreign currency debt, although not much was achieved in that direction from the first companies sold. There were then delays and changes over the next few years, during which most large-scale privatization did involve sales to foreign companies (Ernst, Alexeev, and Marer 1995, 52). A plan for voucher privatization was worked out, with British help, in 1994 (Lajtai 1997, 143), but it was dropped the next year, with the emphasis back on sales to foreigners as a means to raise state revenue.

Poland was another major voucher sceptic. The same pressures there led to the government reestablishing control to prevent spontaneous privatization. It then won parliamentary approval in July 1990 for a policy that allowed for a variety of methods of privatization. There were strong advocates of the voucher method, but there were also plenty of doubters and disagreements within the pro camp over how to proceed. Lewandowski, an original author of the voucher method and Poland's minister for privatization for a period in 1991, concluded that it was either irrelevant or positively harmful to recovery in large enterprises, and he was scathingly critical of Czechoslovakia's approach (Myant 1993, 144). However, continual debate without much action strengthened the view outside that the Czechoslovak method was better. That was the message taken to Russia and other countries by international agencies and foreign advisers, including several with experience in Poland.

A further element in Poland was that employees retained some power in enterprises. The heritage of self-management—previously propagated by the Solidarity union, partially introduced during the state Socialist period and enjoying high prestige as an alternative after 1989—meant that employees could veto privatization proposals for their enterprise. This was not welcomed by outside advisers. World Bank staff, Sachs, and Lipton feared that it would lead to paralysis (Nellis 2002, 10). In practice, however, all of the forms of privatization in Poland in the early 1990s contained an employee presence (Nuti 1997, 169). The most important was known as privatization by liquidation, which involved the liquidation and sale of a state-owned enterprise, frequently to the incumbent management and employees.

Following twists and turns from 1990 onward, a form of voucher privatization was approved by parliament in May 1993 and was implemented in diminished form in 1995. This involved putting 530 state-owned enterprises, accounting for about 10 percent of production of the state sector, under the control of investment funds—vouchers for which were finally distributed in November 1995 (Kokoszczynski 1999, 156). The impact was low, not least because the funds could provide no financial help to firms, and their presence effectively blocked off the more attractive option of foreign ownership, albeit only until the funds could sell the shares they held. As a result, Poland appeared as a continual laggard in the privatization of large enterprises, a status that harmed its standing in EBRD tables of performance in transformation, but that did not harm its economic performance.

Another sceptic was Slovakia, which abandoned the second voucher wave after breaking with the Czech Republic. This reflected both serious criticisms of the voucher method and a desire to break with what was perceived as a Czech policy. Instead, privatization proceeded by direct sales, often to favored entrepreneurs. This was, in fact, essentially a more vigorous version of the entrepreneurial privatization that gained favor in the Czech Republic in the mid-1990s. Both led to privatization into domestic ownership and left enterprises ill equipped to finance modernization and to face international competition.

Slovenia followed a more individual course. The heritage of self-management in Yugoslavia left a powerful employee voice in the new company structure created in 1990. The form of privatization was then decided from conflict between two versions. One foresaw gradual privatization by sale to employees and managers, leaving large shares to the state for the foreseeable future. The alternative—propagated by Sachs and Lipton, who came to Slovenia in late 1990 hoping that the government would accept their quest for a model of rapid privatization—foresaw privatization partly to small private owners and partly through vouchers and investment funds. These outside advisers met very strong opposition from the country's leading economists.

The outcome was a compromise that was slow, lasting throughout the decade, which transferred most of the property of large enterprises to employees, with varying discounts on the prices they paid, to pension funds and to private investment funds. There was scope for selling some shares to foreign strategic partners, but Slovenia's method made it difficult for foreign firms to gain control. Therefore, the results differed significantly from those of other methods in Eastern Europe. Distribution of shares in exchange for vouchers or direct sales to outsiders or employees in other countries eventually gave way to widespread foreign ownership, as the domestically owned firms lacked the financial strength to invest and compete.

RUSSIA: FROM VOUCHERS TO OLIGARCHS

Russian privatization began from the changes in the Gorbachev period, reforming enterprise powers in 1987 and allowing the new cooperatives in 1988. While he was in power, and while the Soviet Union continued to exist, there was no firm choice for any particular form of ownership change. The "500-day" program, formulated in September 1990 as the basis for accelerated economic reform, outlined possible paths for ownership change, but the preference seemed to be for leasing or selling rather than vouchers or free handouts (Appel 2004, 73–74). Leasing was actually started in 1990 and applied to 9,500 enterprises by early 1992, accounting for 8 percent of total employment and 13 percent of production (Black, Kraakman, and Tarassova 2000, 1785).

This was changed when Yeltsin sought a decisive break from the Soviet Union and from the economists who had worked on reform projects with Gorbachev. He turned in November 1991 to the untried group of young neoliberal economists who believed that eliminating state control over the economy was the key to future success. World Bank officials quickly buried any doubts and, along with other international advisers, gave backing to the team's proposals.

The outcome of these plans, following compromises with representatives of management interests and those supporting a bigger role for employees, was a law passed in June 1992 allowing three methods of voucher privatization (Blasi, Kroumova, and Kruse 1997, 39–49), with enterprise general assemblies able to choose which one they would adopt. The first option gave 25 percent of shares to employees, with the possibility for employees to acquire 40 percent of the shares in total. The second option allowed employees to buy up to 51 percent of the shares at the full nominal price and a possible further 5 percent at a discount. A third option gave employees the possibility for ownership conditional on enterprise performance. In all cases, remaining shares were to be sold in exchange for vouchers distributed to the public. Advocates of the pure voucher method clearly preferred the first option, but that was chosen by only 25 percent of enterprises, while about 75 percent opted for the second. There was minimal interest in the third.

If the aim was to transfer out of formal state ownership, then the Russian method of voucher privatization was a resounding success. Strategic enterprises were held out of the scheme, but more than 50 percent of industrial production was put into private hands in just over two years, covering 16,500 enterprises. More than 41 million citizens became shareholders.

There were similarities to the Czech voucher privatization, but there were also important differences. These are indicated in the following six points.

First, although Yeltsin established, and relied on, a narrow group of enthusiasts, voucher privatization faced far more scepticism in the Russian parliament. Advocates accepted the need to buy off potential enemies, meaning managers and workers, by allowing scope for them to acquire substantial shares (Appel 2004, 84–87). Thus, while nominally inclined to follow the Czech model, the strengths of entrenched interests led to differences in the method adopted. This was accepted within the neoliberal camp. Although insider control was unappealing, the priority was seen as private rather than state ownership, irrespective of who the private owners might be.

The perceived need for these compromises has been explained by the differing political atmospheres in the two countries (Appel 2004; A. Schwartz 2006). The Czech Republic was more clearly gripped by an anti-Communist sentiment, a desire to end the old system as quickly as possible, and suspicion easily aroused toward anyone who counseled caution. In Poland, as indicated, the voice of employees was respected. In Russia, too, employees had been given more power in the late 1980s. Their direct voice was weak, but there were visible threats of social discontent, and there was a substantial group in parliament that could only be brought on board if employees' interests were recognized. Managers also came with more authority and had backing in parliament when they pressed their demands.

Second, the Russian implementation process was far more decentralized, with auctions for individual enterprises organized at different times and places. This was an inevitable result of the state's fragmentation. It could appear to mean a more open process, with more scope and time for voucher holders to assess the enterprises. However, the fragmentation and decentralization of auctions also created scope for the manipulation of outcomes. Any authority that might have intervened seemed very relaxed about allowing incumbent managers to find ways to influence auctions to their own advantage (Black, Kraakman, and Tarassova 2000, 1739–41).

Third, the outcomes in terms of who held power in the enterprises had much in common. Enterprise managers did well. In Russia, they could gradually buy up impoverished employees' shares. They could even ignore the employees' voices and run enterprises as if they were the sole owners. Outsider shareholders generally had even less chance of influence. One survey showed that 74 percent of Russian workers believed that the top managers were the real owners of their enterprises (Lissovolik 1997, 220). However, in neither case did this lead directly to the emergence and consolidation of a new economic elite.

Fourth, like Czech privatization, Russian privatization was followed by battles for enterprise control, but they took different forms (covered for Russia in Clarke [1996 2007], Morrison [2008], and Woodruff [2004]). There was not the rush toward concentration of share ownership as seen in the Czech third wave; nor was share dealing such an important source of wealth accumulation. Russia's employee shareholdings were a stabilizing factor, for a time. The main early victors were the incumbent managements, albeit often by somewhat obscure means. From the late 1990s, ownership often moved to holding companies and financial groups, emerging out of trading and other companies. They provided producing enterprises with the lifeline of inputs and markets and were therefore the firms that were able to set their own prices and to accumulate wealth. However, their first concern was typically not with modernization and investment but rather with making profits from trading. Ownership thereby cemented the subordination of the productive enterprises noted in the discussion of enterprise survival.

Fifth, privatization increased the scope for conflicts of interest, conflicting enterprise objectives, and battles for control. The separation of ownership from control created greater scope for a separation between the interests of the enterprise, meaning its long-term survival and business success as a collective, and of the managers and owners. Those with control over an enterprise could benefit from tunneling out resources for themselves. There were examples of this in many countries, but destroying the company in total and selling off its assets with the proceeds going to the owners was difficult to do where employees had any strength, be that through trade unions, through share ownership, or through access to the media.

In Russia, there is evidence of more systematic and extensive asset stripping than in the Czech Republic. It cannot be blamed only on voucher privatization, as there were cases of this as soon as managers were able to form their own private companies to which they could transfer assets by a wide range of means. However, privatization removed any administrative controls that had existed before, and there was no replacement in the form of a satisfactory legal and enforcement system. Laws did exist, as in other countries, but there was neither the will nor ability from courts and politicians to enforce them to control managements.

This points to increasing reservations about setting a general enterprise objective of survival. According to Black, Kraakman, and Tarassova (2000, 1766–67), managers' primary interest was in taking from the enterprises they controlled. Based on experience as observers and as advisers during the Russian privatization program, they were sceptical as to whether there were any "honest" Russian enterprises (1776). Survival remained relevant for enterprises inherited from the past that were struggling to survive in the new environment, and it was necessary for managers who wanted a personal cut. However, it was less relevant for those with improving financial results, which provided greater scope for managers to benefit at the expense of the enterprise. It was of no relevance to the new kinds of rising businesses that were built from trading, speculating, and operations of doubtful legality and that were given new opportunities by privatization. For them, short-term profit was the clearly dominant objective.

The most vigorous asset stripping probably afflicted smaller CIS countries. It was effectively advocated for Georgia by the country's one-time minister of the economy (Papava 2005) on the grounds that everything inherited from central planning should be considered a burden that restricted the scope for new growth. Such destruction of the economy's base indeed appears to have been particularly important in the Georgian transformation (Christophe 2007). It was also important in Kyrgyzstan, one of the more enthusiastic followers of the voucher fad. Again, this cannot be blamed entirely on voucher privatization. It is an open question as to the extent to which enterprises in these smaller republics had serious prospects once contacts with their former partners had been broken.

Finally, Russian voucher privatization did not end the transfer of state property. At first, the most important enterprises—oil, gas, and other raw material producing and processing enterprises—were held back, in view of their strategic importance.

Their ultimate disposal helped create the new group of business leaders that, in terms of wealth and power, had no analogy in other former state Socialist countries.

The best-known episode in the development of the new business elite was the so-called loans-for-shares deal. In March 1995, a group of prominent bankers came to the government and offered to finance the troublesome budget deficit, with shares in key enterprises, meaning especially fuel and metal producers, as collateral. After some discussion, Yeltsin accepted, although the extent of the scheme was less than the bankers had originally wanted. The right to manage these shares would be allocated by auctions, and, should the government fail to repay, creditors would then be able to sell the shares at further auctions. In practice, the government did fail to repay the loans, and auctions at all stages were manipulated in favor of buyers who were close to leading politicians. Neither political nor legal authorities prevented their business allies from using any available means to eliminate possible rival bidders (Black, Kraakman, and Tarassova 2000, 146–47).

The episode has been interpreted in various ways by different authors (for two reasonable but opposing views, see Allan [2002] and Sim [2008]). It may have been motivated by budget problems, but there were alternative solutions; this is not convincing as a full explanation. It also may have reflected a desperate effort by the government to reinvigorate its privatization program. The bankers were offering a solution that would enable transfer into private hands at a time when no other solution was on the horizon. This, too, may provide a partial explanation, but it remains unclear why privatization of these enterprises should have been such a pressing matter at that particular time.

Many authors have interpreted the episode as part of Yeltsin's reelection plan (e.g., Sim 2008). He faced a serious threat of defeat at the hands of Communists, and the oligarchs emerged in 1996 to give support with finance and through the media they controlled. Evidence of the political maneuvrings do not prove that this was the primary motivation from the start, but it is undeniable that loans-for-shares helped Yeltsin strengthen his political position and made the oligarchs even more dependent on the government. They would only receive the property after the outcome of the elections and could not be confident of the outcome after any future change in government.

Privatization by sales on generous terms to friends of those with political power gained the most outside publicity for the case of Russia, but it was common in other CIS countries. Kazakhstan set out on a scheme to exchange vouchers for shares in IPFs in 1993, but, in contrast most obviously to the Czech Republic, there was no serious control over the implementation of the process, and it amounted to the "spontaneous alienation of state assets by anybody in a position to steal them" (Pomfret 2006, 45). Preference went by 1995 to sales of enterprises at very low prices, largely to foreign companies. In Kyrgyzstan, a voucher method appeared to give quick and easy results, as there was not much property involved. It soon gave way to sales to "outright crooks" (Åslund 2002, 272). Ukraine, too, appeared to follow the Russian road from 1996, but much of the property found its way into the hands of political leaders and their friends.

Uzbekistan was a country more determinedly reluctant to listen to outside advice, and its government rejected pressures for a full voucher method. Nevertheless, a gesture was made with the acceptance of World Bank help in 1996 for a very gradual scheme based on investment funds, but neither this nor a case-by-case approach led to the rapid privatization of larger enterprises (Pomfret 2006, 31; Spechler 2008).

Thus, privatization was important in the creation of great concentrations of wealth, where that took place, a point taken up in the concluding section of this chapter. The sections preceding that also take up the consequences of privatization in different countries around themes of the extent of transfer to private ownership, the economic success of enterprises privatized by different means, and the creation of part of the infrastructure of a market economy.

SIZE OF THE PRIVATE SECTOR

An accessible indicator of an outcome of privatization is the share of the private sector in GDP or employment. Both are provided in EBRD data, but the latter is fragmentary, and the former is, at best, extremely approximate. It is also rather generous, counting as private enterprises those still with substantial state, as well as private, shares. Moreover, as already indicated, privatization was not the only means for growth of the private relative to the state sector. It cannot be separated completely from the autonomous growth of new enterprises, which also bought assets of state-owned enterprises and joined in privatization processes.

Table 13.1 shows a selection of transition economies that indicate the different trends. The available data make it possible to group countries at three points. At the start, Hungary and Czechoslovakia were estimated to have 5 percent of GDP from the private sector. Soviet republics were the same or slightly higher. Poland stood out above all others at 30 percent, reflecting the extent of private trade and private farming. This ordering changed by 1996, after some countries had pushed ahead rapidly with privatization. Most CEECs and the Baltic republics then appeared in front. Poland, Russia, Bulgaria, and some others lagged, reflecting their slower paces of privatization, and some countries lagged much further behind, reflecting a more general reluctance to privatize large-scale enterprises; Belarus already stands out, along with Turkmenistan, Tajikistan, and Azerbaijan. The other CARs were also slow to privatize.

Taking 2008 as the end point shows almost all with 70 to 80 percent of GDP from the private sector; laggards in 1996 had largely made up the lost ground. Two groups were still left with lower levels. The lowest are in the "nonprivatizers" group: Belarus, Turkmenistan, and, to a lesser extent, Uzbekistan. The second-lowest group is made up of Russia and Ukraine, slightly below the main group. There is some association here with other aspects of countries' development and performance. Privatization was accepted as a key aim across almost all countries, albeit with clear resistance in a few and the continuation of state control over key enterprises, especially in Russia. Other fuel exporters—Azerbaijan and Kazakhstan—were more willing to allow foreign ownership.

ENTERPRISE PERFORMANCE

An enormous number of studies were undertaken in the 1990s with the aim of assessing the performance of privatized enterprises. They came after the World Bank had already broadly committed itself to support for voucher privatization.

TABLE 13.1   **Approximate share of the private sector in GDP in selected transition economies (%)**

	1989	1996	2008
Azerbaijan	10	25	75
Belarus	5	15	30
Bulgaria	10	55	75
Czech Republic	5	75	80
Estonia	10	70	80
Hungary	5	70	80
Kazakhstan	5	40	70
Poland	30	60	75
Russia	5	60	65
Slovakia	5	70	80
Tajikistan	10	30	55
Turkmenistan	10	20	25
Ukraine	10	50	65
Uzbekistan	10	40	45

Source: EBRD structural change indicators, available at http://www.ebrd.com/country/sector/econo/stats/index.htm.

That judgment was based on application of theory rather than consideration of evidence, but support was soon claimed from empirical studies in which there was a significant, but not universal, bias toward demonstrating that privatization was leading to better performance. The evidence from subsequent development suggests that this was plausible for sales to foreign multinational companies, but privatization into domestic ownership ended in disappointment across CEECs. This raises questions about individual studies and also about the appropriateness of the methods used for evaluating privatization.

World Bank officials were understandably enthusiastic when econometric work seemed to back their policies. The studies generally used samples of companies and set an indicator of performance against ownership or the form of privatization. One used data from 6,300 enterprises in seven countries over the period from 1992 to 1995 and showed higher productivity growth in privatized firms as opposed to state-owned firms in all cases (Pohl, Claessens, and Djankov 1997, 11). There seemed to be no effect from the form of privatization, and this could therefore justify the fastest possible method, which meant using vouchers. Another study that pleased World Bank officials analyzed results from 190 enterprises, each with 100 to 1,500 employees, in the Czech Republic, Hungary, and Poland (Frydman et al. 1997). The time period ended in 1993, and that meant that privatization for those enterprises included in the study had to be complete by the end of 1992, which allowed into the study the first wave of Czech voucher privatization. The conclusion was that privatization led to a very rapid change in performance. Sales grew in privatized firms, with those controlled by investment funds doing particularly well.

These and similar studies faced, and often failed to eliminate, three pitfalls:

- The first is the time period. Studies inevitably followed changes over short periods, and those that ended in the early 1990s could easily be misleading. Firms with long-term strategies, which were typical of those under foreign ownership, need not show a rapid change in indicators of performance, nor need immediate results be a reliable guide to long-term prospects.

- The second is a likely bias toward finding privatization to correspond to better performance precisely because firms with better prospects could be easier to privatize. This was not always true; Czech voucher privatization was deliberately designed to include both good and bad enterprises. Nevertheless, the danger of selection bias was often ignored, as by Pohl, Claessens, and Djankov (1997), or was considered only for a small sample of cases, as by Frydman and colleagues (1997).

- The third is that performance, as measured by standard indicators, depends on factors other than ownership. The branch of industry was particularly important, but this was very rarely recognized in econometric studies that were based on the implicit assumption that adaptation and restructuring processes could follow essentially the same course in all sectors. This was not the case. As indicated in Chapter 11, enterprises selling raw materials or semimanufactures could do well, with minimal adaptation, by exporting into new markets, and they often remained under state ownership. Enterprises making complex engineering products often faced enormous difficulties as traditional markets disappeared, regardless of whether they were privatized or left in state ownership.

Djankov and Murrell (2000a, 2000b) summarized the results of 125 econometric studies on enterprise performance that they judged to have used sound methodology. In fact, many were from short, early periods and did not recognize the importance of differences between branches of industry, and only 24 were judged to have minimized the dangers of selection bias. Results varied widely, but the authors combined studies to produce aggregate conclusions. For CIS countries, they found no significant evidence that privatization had brought benefits. For other countries, however, they found clear benefits. That would be a reasonable finding, as there is plenty of evidence that privatization into foreign ownership did usually bring benefits, and that was a more important form in countries outside the CIS. Oddly, their summary suggested that firms owned by funds almost matched the performance of those under foreign ownership, a claim that is at odds with subsequent evidence and development.

Experience in the Czech Republic by the late 1990s so clearly conflicted with the implications of studies that had impressed the World Bank that the Ministry of Industry and Trade undertook as exhaustive a study as it could as an input to a government report on the results of the transformation strategy of the 1990s (covered in Myant [2003, 226–29]). An immediate stimulus was the dire financial condition of the big enterprises that had been privatized into Czech ownership. The aim was to follow how *all* the enterprises previously owned by the ministry had fared, depending on the chosen form of privatization. Table 13.2 shows performance indicators for manufacturing enterprises against the method of privatization. There are reservations to defining a single privatization method where different ones were used for shares in

TABLE 13.2   **Indicators of the performance of Czech manufacturing enterprises privatized by different means, 1997**

	Turnover, percentage of total	Profit, percentage of share capital	Productivity, percentage of average	Overdue debt, percentage of turnover
Public sector	19.3	4.33	109	6.4
Voucher privatization	25.3	−0.16	84	5.8
Standard methods	8.2	9.12	92	9.1
Foreign owner	14.6	18.58	205	3.9
Others	32.6	5.08	95	8.9
All	100.0	4.84	100	6.9

Source: Calculated from Czech government data (Myant 2003, 227).

the same enterprise, but the main overlap is between standard methods—meaning direct sale to domestic owners—and vouchers, and this makes little difference to the key conclusion. There is also an uncomfortably large "other" category, which is made up largely of enterprises for which the Ministry of Industry lacked clear information on the original method of privatization.

The key conclusion is that foreign ownership was clearly superior across important indicators. State ownership was better than domestic private ownership for labor productivity. Voucher privatization was the worst for profitability, and standard methods, which included entrepreneurial privatization, were the worst in terms of indebtedness. It can be added that statistical yearbooks also gave a breakdown of performance by ownership type and differed only by giving even better results for state-owned firms.

These results need to be used alongside other information on enterprise transformation. State-owned firms were largely big chemical firms and other producers of semimanufactures. They were capital intensive, and labor productivity was therefore high. They had been able to export broadly the same products that they had been making in the 1980s. The good performance of foreign-owned firms is explained in Chapter 15; the poor performance of firms privatized into domestic ownership reflected their inability to compete on international markets and their dependence on bank credits, which, by the late 1990s, they were proving incapable of repaying. This could be related to the method of privatization, which provided little new finance and often led managers to use their enterprises' financial resources to buy shares, even though this was illegal.

The government's conclusion was to abandon Czech capitalism, meaning the attempt to build a modern economy based on domestic private ownership, and to give maximum support to inward direct investment. However, there was not such a queue of willing buyers as there had been for the best enterprises that were offered at the start of the decade. The most important failing domestically owned firms were taken back into state control, slimmed down, and sold to foreign companies, but they survived only as shadows of their former selves and were never again to play major roles in economic development. That is the clearest indicator of the failure of privatization into domestic ownership.

A MARKET INFRASTRUCTURE

The failure to create successful domestically owned enterprises could have been counterbalanced if privatization had led to other benefits associated with a market economy. Thus, apart from the performance of enterprises directly privatized, it could create scope for organizational flexibility and, once share dealing and a stock market were fully established, for raising finance provided by new share issues. This was a frequent hope for voucher privatization.

Data is available on stock market capitalization and on the volume of share trading for most transition economies. Table 13.3 summarizes changes in representative countries for which figures are significant. Countries in which the stock market was never significant are omitted in total. This group includes Uzbekistan, Turkmenistan, Tajikistan, Albania, and Belarus. Among these, Albania was a rapid privatizer, but in the others, private-sector growth depended predominantly on new firm formation.

Other countries followed some slightly different trends. In Hungary and Poland, stock markets appeared very early on, and there was significant trading in some years. In the Czech Republic, voucher privatization was important, leading to a sharp rise in capitalization and trading in the mid-1990s. This was followed by a decline after the completion of the phase of ownership concentration and as share trading was better regulated. The outcome was similar to those in Poland and Hungary, with a very small number of companies quoted and a low level of share trading, which was heavily concentrated in firms with a large public-sector share. This was in line with Stiglitz's prediction that the stock market would be no more than a sideshow, with little relevance to economic development as a whole.

The trend in Russia had something in common with Czech development. There was a peak and then decline as ownership concentrated. However, growth resumed quickly, and Russia then led the way in increasing stock market capitalization in the

TABLE 13.3 Stock market capitalization as a percentage of GDP

	1996	2001	2007
Bulgaria	0.2	3.7	51.3
Czech Republic	29.2	14.1	37.4
Estonia	23.1[a]	24.1	26.9
Hungary	12.4	18.7	32.4
Kazakhstan	6.1[a]	5.6	39.2
Poland	5.7	13.2	44.1
Romania	0.2	5.8	27.3
Russia	10.4	26.0	111.8
Slovakia	10.8	7.4	8.6
Slovenia	7.7	16.8	57.2
Ukraine	7.4[a]	3.6	79.2

Source: EBRD structural change indicators, available at http://www.ebrd.com/country/sector/econo/stats/index.htm.
[a]Data are for 1997.

years up to 2007, reflecting the rise of large conglomerates controlled by oligarchs. This trend was also strong in countries that were enjoying an inflow of foreign money; Ukraine, Bulgaria, and Slovenia stand out. Growth was less dramatic in others, and Slovakia was the most obvious case of a country bucking the trend. In some cases, then, the stock market may have been more than a sideshow: It was part of a dangerous financial boom that left some countries exposed to international financial crisis.

THE CREATION OF CAPITALISTS

A concluding theme on privatization is its role in creating a new business elite. That was one of the explicit aims in the Czech Republic for some of its leading exponents. Privatization would generate the capitalists essential to a capitalist economy and society. State property would be transferred into the hands of individuals, who would then become very wealthy.

An irony is that, although the development of capitalism in transition economies did involve the creation of private fortunes, this concentration was often in the hands of people who were not interested in using it in the most productive way. In the Czech Republic, voucher privatization separated share ownership from entrepreneurship, and the wealthiest individuals were share owners. Some took their wealth abroad, while others constructed diversified financial empires. Many of the heads of industrial companies proved incapable of creating internationally competitive companies and disappeared from the scene at the end of the 1990s. Their place was taken by foreign companies. In this case, then, the predominant forms of privatization led to a short-lived period of Czech capitalism, with big firms inherited from the past under domestic ownership, but it proved economically unviable.

Alongside this, there were homegrown capitalists who built up businesses from trade, banking, construction, real estate, and other activities. There was a similar pattern across CEECs. These were rich individuals, albeit, to judge from evidence in the *Forbes* rich lists, not in worldwide terms. A few in the Czech Republic could trace their wealth back to IPFs. Others across CEECs benefited from the results of privatization, insofar as they bought and sold private companies. However, they were hardly ever major players in modern technology sectors or in driving forward international competitiveness. That role was almost exclusively the affair of foreign multinational companies

Russia followed a more complicated course. Great concentrations of wealth were built from the economic potential inherited from the Soviet Union. However, the abilities required to become wealthy were very different from those required to develop a modern, internationally competitive company. Oligarchs were individuals with the skills to master a lawless environment and to stay in favor with the holders of political power (see Box 8.1). The numerous studies of their rise show with embarrassing consistency catalogs of unexplained murders (Kotz and Weir 2007, 178, 222–23; see also Satter [2003]). These entrepreneurs also knew how to transfer wealth from their enterprises to their own pockets, again without encountering problems from courts and while stifling much of the potential media criticism, either by violence or by their own control over media outlets. The blatancy with which they enriched themselves is chronicled in many sources (Black, Kraakman, and Tarassova 2000,

1769–76). Enormous amounts of wealth were taken out of the country so that they contributed nothing to Russia's development.

The behavior of these businesses partly reflected the kinds of business leaders that could build up wealth in the Russian business environment of the 1990s. The persistence of a short-term orientation, aiming for maximum profit with little investment and taking earnings out of the country, also reflected lasting features of the Russian system. Taking wealth abroad made sense, as the property of oligarchs was not ensured by a reliable legal system. As confirmed by Putin's measures to control oligarchs (see Chapter 8), it depended on the goodwill of political leaders. The only security was therefore a good personal relationship with political leaders, and that could not be guaranteed.

However, favored businesses could accumulate wealth very rapidly. The result was a high level of business concentration, albeit one that, according to an estimate from 2003, may not be unprecedented in the history of capitalism (Guriev and Rachinsky 2005). Oligarchs brought together trade, production, construction, real estate, banking, and the control of media, promising political as well as economic power. Productive investment was limited, but, unlike the businesses that emerged out of privatization into domestic ownership in CEECs, this Russian wealth was not threatened by international competition, as it was linked to the export of raw materials. As long as raw material prices were rising, the oligarchs faced only political, and not business, threats. In other CIS countries, too, equivalents of the Russian oligarchs based their wealth on commodity exports or on production for the domestic market. They did not compete internationally in modern manufacturing sectors, and the main threats they faced were political rather than economic.

CHAPTER FOURTEEN

A New Banking System

A developed banking and financial system is essential for a functioning market economy. In transition economies, banks were the most important element in financial and capital markets; other features such as stock markets were substantially less important, as indicated in Chapter 13. Moreover, although banks are in one sense similar to other businesses seeking to make a profit, their position in an economy makes them absolutely central to its performance.

This chapter follows the development of banking during transition, beginning with a brief discussion of the problems of banking in general, followed by broad indicators of development in transition economies. Similarities in trends are clear, but familiar differences emerge between countries—most markedly between CIS countries, CEECs, and the Baltic republics. The Czech Republic and Russia are given special attention as cases in which banks had particularly important implications for the development of economies as a whole. The Baltic republics followed the course of extreme deregulation and reliance on free market relations. Overall, banking was not a success story in transition economies. The best cases ended with relatively solid foreign ownership, but even that was not enough to ensure stability unless the domestic population was saving enough to cover for the internal demand for credit.

BANKING IN MARKET AND TRANSITION ECONOMIES

Banks are a key enabler of economic development, channeling individual savings into credits to businesses and hence productive investment. However, as the holders of deposits for all kinds of businesses and households, they also stand at the center of the interlocking web of transactions, payments, and debts, often requiring trust that obligations will be met, without which a market economy would function only at a very low level. The granting of credits with no absolute certainly of repayment carries high levels of risk, leading to periodic failures and banking crises. The position of banking in the payment system means that such crises can quickly spread into crises for the whole economy. Banking, as argued on the basis of historical evidence, is "the critical destabilising phenomenon" in a market economy (Minsky 1982, 86).

Financial intermediaries have no place in a model of a perfectly functioning market economy. Where there is perfect knowledge, individuals should be able to judge for themselves where to invest their savings. Banks in this framework, therefore, arise from a lack of information on the part of individual savers. With their superior knowledge, they can better judge where to invest. However, that assumes the ability to predict future results for business activities with uncertain outcomes. Judgments are made without precise knowledge; they are based to a great extent on past experience and practices built up over time. Moreover, banks are always on the lookout for any profitable investment and transaction and may indulge in various forms of speculation and dealing in assets that carry further risks, which can threaten the stability of the financial system.

The riskiness of the business, and the severe consequences of failure for the economy as a whole, mean that the history of banking has been punctuated by periodic crises countered, in some cases, by periods of state ownership and, in all advanced market economies, by forms of regulation. The complexities of banks' roles and of their regulation raise special questions for transition economies. Past experience—the basis for so much of banking practice and for public confidence that banks, too, will fulfill their obligations—could not be a guide for sound practice in the new market environment. However, perhaps in line with their place in basic neoclassical theory, there was little regarding banks in the major reform packages or in advice from international agencies.

The message was largely to follow free market principles, meaning privatization, competition, and free entry, supplemented by advice from recent practice in advanced market economies—particularly central bank independence. A continual fear among those offering analysis and advice was that, if not freed from state control, banks would follow the desires of politicians. Other greater dangers were largely ignored. Thus, Bonin and colleagues (1998, 13) warned that regulation was not a substitute for market discipline and that only new owners—any new owners, as long as they were not the state—could prevent the consolidation of the domestic banking system into "a cartel beholden to its political parent" (54). The best solution was, therefore, the fastest possible privatization, meaning the use of the voucher method. This was similar to Sachs's (1992, 47) advice for Russia that commercialization and privatization of large banks needed "special and urgent attention." This was, according to Sachs, proven by Eastern European experience, although there had at that time been no experience to prove the benefits of rapid bank privatization.

The approach here follows the course of these policies and of the differing banking practices in groups of countries. Policy development was punctuated by periodic crisis, which in almost all cases reflected an underlying problem of nonperforming loans. Crises of varying degrees of severity were experienced in all countries, but their consequences differed. These included allowing banks to fail, bailing banks out in emergencies, taking over failing banks, systematically developing regulatory frameworks, and arranging sales to established foreign banks. These reflected differences in policy thinking between times and countries.

These developments can be followed to some extent by two sets of indicators of banking development. The first follows the number and ownership of banks, which was closely related to differences between countries in how the banking system was regulated. Explosive growth in the number of banks was invariably associated with weak regulation of their activities. Owners also ranged from the state through domestic shareholders to foreign banks. The first of these was associated with a degree of stability, albeit in some cases, as predicted by critics of state ownership, with favored treatment to particular enterprises or sectors. Domestic private ownership was associated with some of the most damaging forms of bank behavior. Foreign ownership brought banking practices from established market economies, and in some cases, that meant stability and caution. However, it also created easier means for inflows of finance from outside the countries, and this was to prove a source of dangerous instability, especially in the Baltic republics and SEECs.

The second set of indicators followed is the relationship of credits and deposits to GDP. A high level of credits is frequently taken as an indicator of the level of development of a market economy. Results from transition economies are consistent with that, with the most advanced countries typically showing higher levels of credit relative to GDP, albeit levels well below those of the most mature market economies. However, the volume of credit also indicates the potential severity of crises that can develop within the financial sector as the economy develops and grows. The extent to which credits are balanced by deposits also varied between countries, and this was important for vulnerability to the effects of the world financial crisis of 2008.

Credits and deposits are both related to habits and customs developed over long time periods. However, they are determined by different actors responding to different incentives. Deposits might be expected to set an upper limit to credits, but it was relatively easy in the years up until 2008 to finance credits from external sources. In a few cases, deposits exceeded credits, creating pressures in banks to find ways to lend more.

TRENDS IN BANKING

Banking in all state Socialist countries was undergoing changes at the end of the 1980s. The trend was to split the monobank into a single central bank and a number of commercial banks, sometimes differentiated by function or sector. Personal deposits were largely in a savings bank, continuing its old traditional function and controlling a large network of branches. Other newly independent banks were expected to concentrate on credits to enterprises.

Changes in the following years are outlined in Table 14.1. The structure of banking followed three trends. The first was a rapid increase in the number of banks, reflecting liberalization of the environment. The table is organized in descending order by the number of banks in 1994, which was frequently the peak level. The second trend was a stabilization or decrease in the number of banks, as many newly established banks proved unviable, and central banks reasserted some regulations. This was inevitably later in CIS countries, as central banks took time to be established and to assert themselves. The third trend was a growth in foreign ownership, both as foreign banks set up branches in the countries and as state-owned banks were privatized by sale to established foreign banks.

An explosion of new banks was most marked in Russia, even allowing for its large population, and was followed by other CIS countries. It was less marked in the Baltic republics and CEECs and in some of the lowest-income CIS countries. The subsequent reduction in numbers was common to all countries, albeit leaving Russia and some other CIS countries still at high levels. This followed the closure or

TABLE 14.1 Structure of banking in transition economies, indicated by the number of banks registered and the share of assets in foreign ownership

	1989	1994	1998	2007	Year of 50% foreign ownership	Foreign-owned assets in 2007 (%)
Russia	130	2,456	1,476 (30)	1,136 (86)		17.2
Ukraine	133 (92)[a]	228 (1)	175 (12)	175 (40)		39.4
Georgia		226 (1)	44 (10)	19 (14)	2004	90.6
Kazakhstan	30 (90)[b]	184 (8)	71 (20)	35 (18)	2003	38.5
Azerbaijan	13	164 (1)	79 (4)	44 (6)		7.5
Poland		82 (11)	83 (31)	64 (54)	2000	75.5
Latvia		56 (16)	28 (14)	25 (14)	1996	63.8
Czech Republic		55 (23)	45 (25)	26 (15)	2000	84.8
Belarus		48	37 (2)	27 (16)		19.7
Hungary	26 (7)	43 (18)	44 (28)	40 (27)	1997	64.2
Bulgaria	65	40 (1)	34 (26)	29 (21)	2000	82.3
Slovakia		29 (14)	27 (10)	26 (15)	2001	99.0
Uzbekistan	21[b]	29 (1)	33 (4)	29 (5)		4.4[c]
Estonia		22 (2)	6 (3)	15 (13)	1998	98.7
Lithuania		22	12 (5)	14 (6)	1998	91.7
Romania		20 (5)	36 (16)	31 (26)	2001	87.3
Slovenia		20 (5)	36 (16)	31 (26)	2001	87.3
Kyrgyzstan	6[b]	18 (3)	23 (6)	22 (10)	2002	58.7

Source: EBRD structural change indicators, available at http://www.ebrd.com/country/sector/econo/stats/index.htm.

Note: The figures in parentheses show the number of banks in foreign ownership.

[a] Data are for 1992.

[b] Data are for 1990.

[c] Data are for 2004.

takeover of many of the newly established banks, a trend that is partly masked in the figures in Table 14.1 in CEECs by the growth in foreign-owned banks.

The extent of foreign ownership grew rapidly in the late 1990s in those countries that were stable enough to attract foreign buyers for their state-owned banks and that were willing to allow foreign penetration. Countries that were to join the European Union generally led the way, sometimes in response to external pressure. The first to have a majority of bank assets in foreign hands was Latvia, followed by other Baltic republics, Central Europe, Bulgaria, and Romania, and then some CIS countries. Some followed the trend more slowly—Russia with considerable reluctance—leaving domestically owned banks very clearly dominant in terms of numbers alone. Azerbaijan and Uzbekistan are examples in which the trend was altogether very weak. Hungary and Poland started on the trend early but retained a significant minority of banking assets in domestic ownership in 2007. Slovenia stands out for rough stability in bank numbers and a low final share in foreign ownership.

TABLE 14.2   Bank deposits and credits as a percentage of GDP for transition economies with higher deposit bases

		1990	1996	2002	2007
Croatia	Deposits	20.6[c]	29.8	58.7	73.0
	Credits	103.5[c]	44.9	62.1	82.9
	Net government	37.3[c]	13.6	8.3	5.6
Czech Republic	Deposits	62.9[b]	58.3	61.5	63.7
	Credits	74.3[b]	67.2	42.3	52.9
	Net government	1.0[b]	−1.6	10.6	4.1
Bulgaria	Deposits	64.3[b]	67.4	29.6	62.2
	Credits	118.2[b]	108.7	23.6	59.2
	Net government	35.7[b]	45.7	3.8	−8.0
Slovenia	Deposits	27.8[b]	35.3	54.9	54.3
	Credits	33.6[b]	33.1	45.3	84.3
	Net government	11.4[b]	6.2	5.2	3.1
Slovakia	Deposits	61.8[b]	56.6	55.5	50.7
	Credits	79.7[b]	53.9	51.2	51.5
	Net government	16.1[b]	10.6	11.9	8.1
Hungary	Deposits	33.3	40.7	39.2	46.0
	Credits	82.6	72.5	52.9	74.3
	Net government	35.6	49.9	17.4	10.7
Poland	Deposits	25.8	27.4	36.8	41.6
	Credits	19.5	31.5	37.2	46.8
	Net government	−1.6	12.1	8.3	5.3
Romania	Deposits	49.4	22.9	20.8	31.3
	Credits	79.7	28.8	13.9	35.7
	Net government	0.0	4.2	2.0	−1.8

Source: Calculated from the IMF International Financial Statistics database, available at http://www.imfstatistics.org/imf/.

[a] = 1991, [b] = 1993, [c] = 1994.

Tables 14.2 and 14.3 show the importance of banking systems in different countries in terms of their deposits and credits in relation to GDP. Countries are ordered in the tables by the level of deposits in 2007, which roughly corresponds to ordering at the start of the period. This indicator reflects the willingness of citizens to trust their money to banks, which in turn provides banks with an internal source for financing credits. The net government position in relation to banks is an indicator of the volume of bank credit that is issued to governments, helping to cover budget deficits, rather than to businesses and households. A negative figure suggests a higher level of government deposits into the banking system than of credits from banks to the government.

Table 14.2 groups countries characterized by higher deposit bases. This covers the CEECs, some former Yugoslav republics, and SEECs. A figure is also included for the first year of available data from the IMF, and this confirms that relatively

TABLE 14.3 Bank deposits and credits as a percentage of GDP for transition economies with lower deposit bases

		1991	1996	2002	2007
Estonia	Deposits	62.6	18.7	31.6	45.8
	Credits	60.6	18.8	43.9	93.4
	Net government	−4.9	−3.6	−2.5	−2.1
Mongolia	Deposits	43.3	11.9	26.3	43.8
	Credits	68.5	14.0	16.0	29.0
	Net government	0.5	2.9	−2.4	−15.1
Latvia	Deposits	21.2[b]	12.4	23.4	39.3
	Credits	18.3[b]	11.4	35.7	94.8
	Net government	−0.2[b]	3.9	2.4	0.4
Ukraine	Deposits	20.3[a]	6.3	16.7	39.2
	Credits	41.9[a]	14.8	28.1	61.7
	Net government	15.0[a]	7.3	8.5	−0.5
Moldova	Deposits	63.0	9.0	18.8	38.7
	Credits	62.6	23.4	29.1	40.2
	Net government	30.3	4.6	10.0	0.9
Lithuania	Deposits	16.2[b]	10.7	21.3	37.4
	Credits	15.5[b]	11.4	17.8	61.1
	Net government	−1.9[b]	0.05	1.1	−1.0
Russia	Deposits	17.2[b]	12.6	19.1	31.8
	Credits	25.8[b]	27.8	24.8	24.9
	Net government	4.9[b]	15.5	5.7	−14.4
Kazakhstan	Deposits	19.8[b]	5.3	15.9	30.2
	Credits	51.7[b]	8.3	14.0	41.5
	Net government	0.3[b]	1.7	−7.0	−20.9
Belarus	Deposits	34.4[c]	10.9	12.1	20.9
	Credits	39.8[c]	15.1	18.0	27.2
	Net government	6.0[c]	3.6	2.4	−6.4
Georgia	Deposits		2.3	6.4	16.8
	Credits		8.1	20.5	31.6
	Net government		4.8	10.5	2.4
Azerbaijan	Deposits		4.9	7.3	12.3
	Credits		13.0	8.7	19.3
	Net government		−0.8	1.6	0.5
Kyrgyzstan	Deposits		3.3	5.5	11.8
	Credits		25.1	11.6	14.2
	Net government		16.5	7.4	−1.1
Armenia	Deposits	0.02[b]	2.9	9.0	11.6
	Credits	0.02[b]	9.1	7.4	12.1
	Net government	0.01[b]	3.4	0.0	−1.8

Source: Calculated from the IMF, International Financial Statistics database, available at http://www.imfstatistics.org/imf/.

[a] = 1992, [b] = 1993, [c] = 1994. No entry in the column for 1991 indicates that 1996 was the first year for which reliable data is available.

high levels of deposits are often inherited from the state Socialist past, reflecting a willingness to save that had already developed in that period. This frequently increased, but not by much. Fluctuations were often due to inflation reducing the value of savings.

In all of these countries, there were significant levels of credits, again often inherited from the past. Only in Poland, Croatia, and Slovenia is there much sign of a clear trend toward growth. In other countries, growth was interrupted by the effects of financial crises, causing temporary reductions in the level of credits relative to GDP. These downturns were very clear in the Czech Republic, Slovakia, Bulgaria, and Romania. In these countries, even when banking systems played the role of channeling savings into credits, they often did so badly, leading to credits that could not be repaid.

A final feature is a trend toward renewed growth in credits, running ahead of deposit bases in a number of countries, in the years up to 2008. Foreign-owned banks led the way in this in several, but not all, transition economies. In the Baltic republics and SEECs, most of the credits were denominated in foreign currency, and this informal "euroization" implied an enormous vulnerability of the financial system in those countries. The lending was predominantly to businesses and households, as the net government position typically improved. A rapid rise in credits did not affect all countries and was one factor differentiating their susceptibility to the effects of the financial crisis in 2008, although even some with high levels of credit were to prove relatively safe.

Table 14.3 covers countries that started with, or were soon characterized by, relatively low deposit bases. Data are so incomplete for several countries that they are excluded from the tables. The Baltic republics fit at the top of this group. The deposit base fell from the year when data are first available, reflecting the high levels of inflation in those countries. Estonia appeared to experience a bigger fall, but that may reflect no more than an earlier start date in the figures. In all of these cases, there was a respectable recovery in deposits and growth in credits, the latter escalating ahead of deposits in the years up to 2008. In the other countries, the deposit bases were lower, reflecting less willingness from citizens to put their small amounts of wealth into banks, and credit levels almost always ran ahead of deposits in the years up to 2008. In a few cases, the gap was small, and in a few, deposits remained ahead of credits.

Three countries shown in Table 14.3 warrant special attention. Russia's development shows the effects of the 1998 crisis, holding back the growth in credits while the deposit base could increase thanks to renewed confidence from the public that they could trust their money to banks. The government also became a net creditor to the banking system, at the time when it was building reserves from the proceeds of oil and gas exports. Kazakhstan, another hydrocarbon exporter, also saw an increase in deposits, and its government became a creditor to the banking system, but total credits grew more rapidly than deposits. The country was more dependent on financial inflows and was also running current account deficits. Ukraine showed the same trend toward higher levels of deposits, but credits rose even further ahead. They were predominantly to businesses and households, with, unlike earlier years, little to the government.

Of the other countries, Belarus appears like Ukraine, albeit on a smaller scale. Despite its slow pace of reform and state control over the banking system, there was growing reliance on financial inflows to fund credits, compensating for the low domestic deposit base. Data on other countries generally show lower levels of development of financial intermediation, and credits often exceeded deposits in all periods. The cases of Uzbekistan and Turkmenistan could not be covered at all from IMF data, but other sources point to a small role for banking in their economies.

The following sections present the details of bank development in countries, starting with the CEECs and followed by Russia, and then comment on some individual cases. Differences in banking development are set in the context of the changes of the late 1980s and early 1990s, of how far and which outside advice was followed, of the strength and nature of regulation, and of other policies during transition that affected the environment for banking.

BANKS IN THE CEECS

In the CEECs, new governments generally trusted the emerging central banks, rather than economic theoreticians, to work out a new framework. They quickly followed practices from Western Europe, especially Germany. This gave central banks a role in regulating banks but also left them with considerable independence from governments within their defined areas of competence, such as setting interest rates and the exchange rate. Rules quickly allowed the establishment of new banks, albeit under requirements set down by a central bank. Table 14.1 shows the growth in numbers.

The explosion of new banks ended as it became clear that they were a threat to the stability of the financial system. In CEECs, that mattered. They never provided competition for established banks, as they never had substantial deposit bases. Some fell victim to frauds, while others were established to perpetrate fraud or to channel finances to their owners. However, the important point from the comparative point of view is that this boom was relatively small and short lived thanks to a willingness and ability of central banks to exercise control, taking over some failing banks and imposing tougher rules to limit new registrations. Thus, by the mid-1990s, new bank registrations were largely branches of foreign banks, which initially served primarily foreign multinational companies. They, too, typically did not compete with domestic banks. The core issue in these countries was, therefore, the fate of the established state-owned banks.

As in other spheres, Polish and Hungarian policies were at first careful and eclectic but based on the assumption that banks should be run on strictly commercial principles; there was no thought of a more active role in economic development. Policies combined bank reorganization with gradual privatization—including a search for foreign partners to bring in capital strength and new expertise—and the elimination of past debts. Poland chose to split banks into regional units that could then seek means to privatization. Sales were slow at first, but they accelerated in the later 1990s as larger foreign banks became convinced that the economies were stable. A key turning point was in 1995, when the minister of finance Grzegorz Kołodko formulated a plan to delay privatization and to create a strong Polish-owned bank that could have played a role in developing Polish businesses. The IMF and EBRD were strongly opposed, and direct pressure was applied from the U.S. government by Lawrence

Summers, then deputy secretary of the Treasury. The Polish government agreed to an aim of full bank privatization in 1996, and that realistically meant selling to foreign banks (Epstein 2008, 110–11). By 2000, the majority of assets of the banking sector were in private hands (Górski 2001, 167–71).

Hungary decided on a privatization strategy in April 1992 that aimed to reduce the state's share to less than 25 percent by the end of the decade, following a cleanup of banks' portfolios (Bonin et al. 1998, 33–34). There was no initial assumption of foreign domination, but, as interest from abroad grew, the share of foreign ownership in Hungarian bank assets passed 50 percent well before the end of the decade. Czech banks were partially privatized by vouchers, but three of the four inherited from post-Communist reforms were still majority state-owned through the 1990s.

In all of these countries, banks were able to finance enterprises' current transactions, but they did not provide much finance for investment. Table 14.2 shows their role in domestic credit creation, which grew through the 1990s but remained below the level of advanced countries with the most developed financial sectors. Further data, providing more detail than just the volume of credits, show that there were differences in how far credits went to the private sector. In Hungary, credits to the government were five times the level of credits to the corporate sector in 1993, meaning that the banking system was channeling household savings into covering budget deficits (Bonin et al. 1998, 169).

Czech banks played the clearest role of financing transformation, with personal deposits backing loans to the corporate sector. By the end of the 1990s, the banks were in serious trouble. The share of nonperforming loans, according to the EBRD, rose to 37.8 percent of the total in 1999. This was very unusual among transition economies and particularly serious due to the high level of Czech credit relative to GDP. Bad debt had generally declined in CEECs after the resolution of enterprises' problems at the start of the decade. Comparable figures for 1999 are 7.9 percent for Hungary and 14.7 percent for Poland. Slovakia, a country that also followed a strategy of privatization into domestic ownership, was similar to the Czech Republic, with a figure of 32.9 percent. In both of these cases, the crisis was overcome by selling the banks off to Western European banks on the best terms available. Czech and Slovak banking, thus, rejoined the trend toward foreign ownership. The result was a decline in nonperforming loans, as the ratio of credits to GDP also fell back toward the levels of its neighbors and did not grow again in the years up to 2008. The Czech case is covered in more detail in the next section.

Foreign ownership also followed continual difficulties with bad credits and banking crises in Romania and Bulgaria, both following pressure for a change of policy in that direction from international agencies. Foreign ownership was established even more rapidly in the Baltic republics. After resolving crises in their banking sectors, these countries were seen by international agencies as relative success stories, and dangers from their forms of international integration were not considered serious.

THE FATE OF CZECH BANKING

The Czech Republic was exceptional in the central position of banking in its transformation strategy in the 1990s (Myant 2003, Chapter 8). It started with the most promising base for a solid banking system thanks to the strong deposit base, the recapitalization in 1991, and a continuing high domestic savings rate. This good start was squandered throughout the 1990s, leading in the next decade to a solid enough banking system that was overwhelmingly in foreign ownership, only a few large Czech-owned enterprises that were seeking finance from domestic banks, and a burden of bad debts, variously estimated at up to 25 percent of GDP, which would trouble the state budget for some years.

The story of Czech banking in the 1990s led within that country to misleading interpretations of "bank Socialism" or "bank capitalism," the term "Socialism" obviously carrying a pejorative tone in that period. The argument was that banks, predominantly under state ownership, had set up and controlled investment funds, which gained control of other enterprises through voucher privatization. Privatization had, therefore, led back to state ownership, and the state-owned banks could be assumed to be supporting inefficiency by delaying painful restructuring in industrial enterprises so as to minimize social discontent. It is an argument that had immediate appeal for those who expected privatization to lead directly to greater efficiency. The Czech problem, it could be argued, was that privatization had not taken place at all.

Despite its simplicity and appeal, the argument does not match reality and misses both the diversity of banks' behavior and the ways in which that behavior did cost the country so much. Bank development in the Czech Republic in the 1990s, like banking development in certain periods in other countries, was a story of governments and regulatory authorities learning as they faced a series of crises.

The first crisis hit the so-called small banks, which were those established from scratch from 1990. The number was never large by international standards—22 at its peak in 1993—even though initial rules for their foundation were very lax. Unlike the Russian case, there was no powerful urge for established enterprises to set up their own banks. Nevertheless, the central bank quickly became aware of difficulties in this sector, and rules on founding new banks were tightened in late 1993; no new bank was formed after that.

In September 1993, the central bank used its powers to take over the first of the new banks in serious trouble. In July 1994, a deposit insurance scheme was established to reassure depositors that their money would be safe, even if a bank collapsed. During 1996, two schemes were devised to resolve banks' problems, generally by merging them into larger banks. Only two of the small banks survived the decade, as independent entities and the losses of the others were taken over by the state.

The problems that were arising almost invariably aroused suspicion of law breaking. Some banks had been used to grant credits to owners that would not be returned, and others had found illegal means to seek credits from abroad. Criminal cases were filed in relation to most bank failures, but none brought a speedy conviction. Thus, the creation of new small banks had left both a significant price for learning the benefits of an active and watchful central bank and stricter rules to control banking behavior.

The four big banks were at the center of voucher privatization, setting up IPFs and, in three cases, undergoing partial privatization by the voucher method. However, no simple model covers their behavior, as each one was a unique case. One—the foreign-trade bank (Československá obchodní banka [ČSOB])—behaved as a rather orthodox bank and remained in state ownership throughout the 1990s.

The best placed in terms of deposits was Česká spořitelna (ČS), the old savings bank, and it was left in majority state ownership after partial privatization through vouchers. It had no past experience of lending to enterprises but was under pressure from the government to lend. This was not part of any conscious strategy to prop up failing industrial enterprises but rather was guided by the government's view that new growth depended on credits. In some cases, under pressure from the government, it financed the privatization of industrial enterprises by lending to the new buyers.

The ČS lent to enterprises, to local government, and also to other banks, including the small banks. When that still left a large deposit base, it engaged in riskier investment, financing deals in Russia that marked the downfall for early Latvian banks some years before. As loans were not repaid, the ČS was unable to comply with the banking rules, and it was ignominiously taken back under full state control in March 1999 and sold in February 2000 to the Austrian bank Erste Bank Sparkassen. The bad debts were transferred to the government and were greater in value than the price received from the Austrian partner. Its downfall, therefore, followed from granting unsound credits, reflecting partly its lack of banking experience in an uncertain environment and partly the prevailing strategy of emphasizing speedy privatization and credit-based growth of new private businesses.

The commercial bank (Komerční banka [KB]) was also partially privatized by vouchers. Its deposit base covered its credits, and it was persuaded by the government to help finance big enterprises that were sold to apparently promising entrepreneurs. However, it was not concerned with keeping them in business once it became clear that hopes of their rapid success under private ownership were illusory. Credits to big enterprises fell from mid-decade and had effectively stopped by late 1997; this precipitated crisis in those enterprises. The failure of enterprises to repay their debts also contributed to paralysis in the KB, but not before it had sought alternative means to make profits from its deposit base. In one disastrous deal, suggesting serious incompetence within the bank, it lent to an Austrian business that had even failed to repay a previous substantial loan to the KB. The company defaulted again in November 1999, and the KB was soon faced with massive losses. The government reasserted full control over the bank and sold it to the French bank Société Générale in October 2001. The government took responsibility for bad debts, the value of which was greater than the sale price of the bank.

The nature of those bad debts revealed the sources of the bank's failure. Credits had been given to all kinds of enterprises, big and small, old and new, without checking their creditworthiness. In many cases, there were signs of bribery to bank officials, who could operate with considerable independence. The primary aim was not to protect employment; it was rather to grant credits whenever possible.

The investment and postal bank (Investiční a poštovní banka [IPB]) was again a different case. At first, it had a small deposit base and depended on loans from other banks. It was partially privatized by vouchers, and the state then lost its majority control after a new share issue. Who in the government was responsible for this was never established. The effect, however, was to leave the IPB politically closer to those around Klaus, and it was very active in giving credits to finance the privatization of enterprises that were proving difficult to sell.

The management's control over the bank was built by gaining direct control over shares and by building a symbiotic relationship with friendly businesses. The management gained control of some shares through the bank's investment funds, which bought the bank's shares; although laws were intended to prevent this, the management was able to find a loophole, which the government saw no need to close. The other banks did not follow this practice. The IPB also gave credits to businesses that appeared to be the bank's own shareholders so that those businesses could be expected to support the existing management. With their position secured, the management set about creating their vision of an investment bank, using its IPFs to acquire shares and adding to this with debt-equity swaps as enterprises ran into difficulties. The other banks kept more distance between their commercial activities and the investment strategies of funds they had set up.

The central bank judged the IPB to be following a dangerous course, not least because the prices paid for shares appeared high. It can be added that, as indicated in Chapter 13, share prices fell in the Czech Republic as the rapid trading of the third wave subsided. A solution was offered when the government sold its remaining minority shareholding to the Japanese investment bank Nomura in 1997. The promise of bringing modern banking practices was upheld in the worst way possible. The IPB set up companies in the Cayman Islands, to which it tried to remove bad loans from its balance sheet. Nomura also found the means to transfer into its own ownership and then sell one of the IPB's most valuable enterprises, the Plzeň brewery. The bank's difficulties became so severe and visible that depositors moved to withdraw their money in June 2000. The central bank used its legal powers to take control of the bank, and it was quickly sold to the Belgian bank KBC (Kedietbank Company), which by then also owned the ČSOB, following an orthodox privatization of that bank by direct sale. There followed years of acrimonious legal proceedings, as Nomura sued the Czech state for compensation and as the Czech state sued Nomura for bleeding the IPB.

Thus, Czech banking, following a stormy decade in the 1990s, settled down under foreign ownership. There was less scope for lending to large enterprises, as they were largely under foreign ownership, too, and could raise finance from their home countries. With fewer shares to trade, there was little chance of fulfilling any dream of establishing an investment bank. It was still possible to give bad loans to smaller businesses and households, but the foreign owners were more cautious, under no pressure from a government to lend. They could also benefit from the lengthening period of experience of lending to Czech enterprises, which helped in assessing creditworthiness. The banking crisis of the late 1990s, thus, brought a paradoxical benefit: It kept the growth of credits in check while not seriously harming the deposit base—the state budget bore the costs of banking losses—and there was, therefore, no pressure on the foreign banks to finance credits with money from outside the country.

RUSSIAN BANKS

The banking system in the Soviet Union was reformed at the start of 1988, creating a central bank and five specialist banks in place of the old monobank. Although that start appeared similar to that of CEECs, Russian banks played a completely different role than banks either in those countries or in a modern market economy.

Their early activities were shaped by their emergence before the whole system had changed. Completely new banks were created under the law on cooperatives, but they were never going to provide competition for established banks. They were set up by enterprises, with practically no deposits from individuals, and based their initial activities on enterprise financial surpluses. Thus, it was enterprises that created banks rather than banks—using individual savings—that created enterprises, as in the industrialization processes in some European countries (Lane 2002, 18). They developed to meet enterprise needs and to take advantage of new opportunities that were created as the system of central planning disintegrated, and they continued to profit from a lax environment with minimal state or central bank control following the loosening of all such ties at the time of the breakup of the Soviet Union.

Banks could, therefore, use their funds for highly lucrative trading and currency speculation, supporting rapid enrichment for ambitious young individuals. This has been described as a "parasitic" banking system that diverted resources that could have contributed to economic modernization (J. Johnson 2000, x). It was also dependent on, and linked to, political patronage, which was useful for getting highly lucrative government contracts and for avoiding sanctions when ignoring tax and other regulations. Benefits of state help could be enormous. The Menatep bank of the future oligarch Khodorkovsky handled funds for military and reconstruction operations in Chechnya, part of which somehow disappeared before being spent (Black, Kraakman, and Tarassova 2000, 1743). Banks, like the oligarchs that emerged out of some of them, were dependent on those with political power who effectively appointed their owners as millionaires and in turn benefited from banks' financial support.

The number of banks escalated, as indicated in Table 14.1. Licenses were easily granted, and new banks were set up predominantly by existing enterprises. More came with the subdivision of state-owned banks, which thereby suffered spontaneous privatization. A crucial factor, as in the development of business in general, was the weakening of central authority at the time of the breakup of the Soviet Union. The Russian central bank created a deliberately relaxed regulatory environment so as to encourage banks to break links with the Soviet central bank and to recognize the new Russian authority. This ensured the death of the Soviet central bank (Buyske 2007, 102–3; Lane 2002).

The new Russian central bank in turn emerged with strong independence from the government (J. Johnson 2000, 68). Lack of clarity over its forms of accountability and over its responsibilities—it was run by insiders who were giving little information on how decisions were made, reminiscent of Soviet times—meant that it could make major decisions alone; for example, by taking the initiative in releasing credit to solve the inter-enterprise debt problem in 1992 (86–87). It was itself involved in major international currency transactions and had little idea on how to regulate other banks. Indeed, other banks frequently ignored central bank rules and resented any background checks that it conducted; one banker reportedly complained that the questioning was arbitrary and ultimately so intrusive as to include questions about his criminal record (72), an issue that was not normally considered important.

The decline in bank numbers after 1994 shows the central bank reasserting some authority. It began, albeit cautiously and somewhat inconsistently, to withdraw bank licenses in 1993, with significant numbers by 1995 (J. Johnson 2000, 134).

However, the continuing high number of banks—and published figures were not always complete—testifies to the continuing laxness relative to other countries. Moreover, reduction in numbers did not alter the nature of Russian banking.

For the general development of the economy, banks were remarkable primarily for what they did not do. They did not provide much credit to enterprises, especially smaller ones. Enterprise credits fell from 33.6 percent of GDP in 1992 to 12 percent in 1995 (J. Johnson 2000, 100), as banks became more selective in deciding to whom they would lend. They did not become involved in voucher privatization, nor did they attract new individual deposits. Private banks accounted for 0.4 percent of bank liabilities in 1998 (Lane 2002, 13). Deposits remained concentrated in the established state-owned savings bank, which also handled individuals' transactions.

However, banks were important as the source of money for enterprises, and this made them enormously powerful in an economy where money was scarce. Informal exchange could never cover all of an enterprise's needs. Larger enterprises, therefore, needed close links to a bank, and for a time, the government did encourage the remerging of banks with enterprises into the so-called financial industrial groups (FIGs).

These arose from two broad purposes. Some were set up by enterprises struggling to survive in the face of cash flow difficulties; recreating something like the conglomerates of the past made barter easier to organize (J. Johnson 2000, 163). Others were set up by banks as they expanded their power by taking shares in enterprises, primarily in sectors with strong export potential. There was a conscious analogy from some supporters of FIGs—and the government was giving some active encouragement from 1993—to the industrial groupings in Japan and South Korea, but the content was very different. In those countries, banks raised funds from outside the enterprises with which they were associated and could give long-term loans. In Russia, banks had different interests and activities, did not provide capital for investment, and had no ideas on enterprise restructuring (158–60, 163–64, 196).

Two events changed the role of banks in Russia. The first was the loans-for-shares deal and subsequent privatization measures, which converted bankers into oligarchs. The second was the financial crisis of August 1998. Many of the Russian private banks, following currency devaluation, were effectively bankrupt. This ended many of the FIGs and the unique power of banks and the regime of minimal regulation.

However, Russian banking still did not follow the CEEC road. There had always been suspicion toward foreign ownership, irrespective of whether foreign banks would have wanted to step in to save Russian banking, and the level remained persistently low right up to 2007. More generally, the Putin government did not put much emphasis on banking reform, and there was no determined strategy to change past practices. However, the financial crisis marked a change in two respects. The first was that, with private banks severely weakened, financial-sector recovery depended on the state (Mizobata 2002, 45). The dominant banking institution again became the old savings bank, which controlled 85 percent of deposits at the end of 1998 (Lane and Lavrentieva 2002, 85), compared with 60 percent in January 1995. The second was that banks found that the old means of making money had disappeared, and they began to lend to enterprises, which were benefiting from the effects of devaluation. This is consistent with EBRD figures, which show lending to the private sector rising from 13.3 percent of GDP in 2000 to 38.5 percent in 2007.

OTHER EXPERIENCES

Banks in the Baltic republics had a similar starting point to those in Russia. Their development was tempered by a greater degree of central bank control and more willingness to respond to international advice, but it was still a rather rocky road. Latvia was important in setting the trends, with policy initially aiming to create a "Switzerland of the Baltics." However, that could never have been a realistic objective; Switzerland's reputation was based on centuries of banking. Nevertheless, that target led Latvia to adopt a very liberal disclosure and regulatory framework in which anyone could set up a bank, and this served to attract deposits from the local population and also from CIS countries. Much of the banking structure inherited from the Soviet period was sold off quickly, and those parts that remained under the formal control of the newly established Bank of Latvia were allowed a free rein from central control.

Banks were free to lend as they wished, but opportunities for investment inside the country were much more limited than was the case in CEECs. Latvian industry suffered rapid decline after the breakup of the Soviet Union, and markets were yet to develop for the activities familiar in mature market economies for long-term credits, such as housing and real estate. Credits were therefore used to finance trade deals, often involving exports from Russia, and to finance the business activities of shareholders—legal loopholes made this relatively easy—who, again, were often closely linked to Russian businesses. It soon became apparent that many credits would never be repaid. The central bank took some steps to establish control, requiring that banks cover for bad loans in December 1993, but by late 1994, a number of banks were clearly failing.

The Latvian banking crisis (followed in Fleming and Talley [1996a, 1996b] and Bank of Latvia [1995]) reached its peak in the spring of 1995 with the failure of Bank Baltija, which had rapidly grown to become the largest commercial bank in terms of assets and deposits, the former equivalent to more than 10 percent of the country's GDP. Its failure was obscured for some time by the bank's unwillingness to reveal its balance sheet, a point that soon aroused suspicion. The central bank intervened rather belatedly, enabling the owners to ensure that large sums of money disappeared, and it was April 1996 before Bank Baltija was firmly declared bankrupt and put into the hands of the receiver. The banking crisis of the time affected a number of further banks, and about 40 percent of deposits and assets were compromised.

The Latvian authorities took steps to establish more powers of regulation, and the number of banks in the country declined, as shown in Table 14.1. World Bank officials drew further conclusions, noting that privatization had left banks exposed to the danger of the sudden withdrawal of deposits, as the public had no confidence in their permanence. They, too, argued for a more active central bank role. The trend in later years was rather toward trusting in foreign ownership and hoping that credits for housing, construction, and real estate would prove safe. The Latvian authorities still focused on keeping the regulation of those banking activities to a minimum. Latvian, and other Baltic, banking thereby moved away from its post-Soviet heritage to come closer to CEEC experience, albeit still with a narrower base for its domestic credit activities and with a low level of domestic deposits relative to credits.

Other CIS countries also failed to develop banking systems that could mobilize substantial resources for credits and investment. However, they differed from the

Russian example in a number of respects. The scope for a parasitic role and for a clearly negative impact on the balance of payments—by helping transfer money out of the country—was smaller in countries with less wealth from natural resources. Russia was also not typical in the extent of opposition it experienced to foreign ownership. Higher levels of foreign ownership of Ukrainian banks led that country toward the CEEC model, with a rapid expansion of domestic credit. Banking thereby became a driving force in the economic boom in the years up to 2008.

Experience in Belarus followed a distinct course after privatization policies were reversed in 1996 and presidential authority was established over the central bank in 1998 (Korosteleva 2007). The state's priorities were exercised through six "system-forming" banks, designated in 1996. Each had an effective monopoly in particular sectors. The level of domestic credit remained relatively low but was growing rapidly up until 2008. Despite the low level of foreign ownership, credits were backed by financial inflows from abroad. Banking thereby retained some features of the pretransformation period alongside exposure to the effects of the world financial crisis.

In Uzbekistan, movement away from the monobank system was slow, and, even after the formal establishment of a two-tier structure in 1992, the central bank continued to give credits as it had in the past (Akimov and Dollery 2009). The state continued to control three big banks, and 67.7 percent of the assets of the banking sector remained in state hands in 2004. This reflected Uzbekistan's reluctance to accept outside influence. It was also justified by the government's stated aim of playing a direct role in determining the direction of economic development so that it could channel finance to favored sectors or projects. However, the practical extent of this was very limited. Public confidence in banking was low, and the deposit level, and hence also the ratio of credits to GDP, remained relatively low. The striking feature here, even more than in Belarus, was the low level of development of the banking sector. Private commercial banks were allowed; there were consistently about 30 throughout the period from 1992 to 2006. Although, or because, their banks contributed little to economic development, this left Uzbekistan better placed than other countries to ignore the financial aspect of the economic crisis beginning in 2008.

CONCLUSION

The best outcome would appear to be a banking system that benefits from a domestic deposit base, lends to domestic businesses but is relatively cautious, and avoids involvement in speculative and short-term profit-making activities. The closest examples of this are in CEECs, but in no case were banks a major force in the successful development of modern domestically owned businesses. The picture across CEECs followed, to varying degrees, from an experience of setbacks and crises, leading to the development of an ownership structure, of a regulatory framework, and of habits and attitudes that could support reasonably sound banking practices. Caution meant that this provided a level of domestic credit relative to GDP that was low by the standards of advanced market economies. In countries where there was light, or nonexistent, regulation and freedom for private enterprise, banks turned toward practices that helped to destabilize the economy or toward parasitic activities that supported the rapid concentration of wealth without ensuring that it was used for productive investment.

The slow pace of development toward a modern banking system, and the even slower development of other elements of a capital market, stands as a major reservation to hopes for speedy transition, as embodied in the WC strategy. These are arenas where the institutionalist approach has the most credibility. Change takes time and depends on changes in habits, ways of thinking, and legal frameworks and on developing respect for those frameworks. In terms of overall transformation strategy, there was no chance for a mature and effective banking system to emerge quickly. The strategies of speedy liberalization and privatization led, in some countries, to a demonstrable and quantifiable cost. A slower pace of privatization and tighter restrictions on the activities of banks could have avoided those costs.

CHAPTER FIFTEEN

Enterprises in the Period of Economic Recovery

The years up to 2008 saw recovery and growth in all transition economies. This chapter covers the different ways in which that related to changes in the enterprise sphere. The picture presented at the start of transition—that enterprises would undergo privatization, followed by restructuring and recovery—proved to be too simplistic. Recovery followed rather different courses, often based on new enterprises that can be related only vaguely to the preceding privatization. In all cases, it was linked in some way to forms of integration into the world economy.

In some cases, export-oriented inward investment was a driving force for wider economic growth. In others, domestically owned firms brought in revenue from exports that could in turn raise domestic demand and support growth from domestic-oriented enterprises, including ones under foreign ownership. In all types of countries, including those with more limited export potential, other forms of financial inflows could support economic recovery and thereby stimulate some changes in the domestic enterprise sphere.

In CEECs, the dominant trend was a growing dependence on foreign ownership. With the death of faith in mass privatization into domestic ownership, the new panacea became foreign MNCs. Enterprises inherited from the past were either improved under foreign ownership, or their place in the economy was taken by new investment. In Russia, state consolidation coincided with other influences, leading to some stabilization in the enterprise sphere around the domestically owned private companies with financial and political power. There was growth, even if not full recovery, for all kinds of enterprises. Much of the same applies in those other CIS countries that could also benefit from rising prices for raw material or semimanufacture exports. In a very few, the state played a larger role, but characterizing this as state-led growth would be an exaggeration. These three experiences are followed in turn, with FDI given the greatest attention. It was particularly important in the period of economic recovery but began in some countries with the very beginning of transition.

INWARD DIRECT INVESTMENT

Direct investment is understood to mean taking a share in ownership with the intent to control a company. Statistics use a 10 percent share in a company as the cutoff for classifying investment as direct rather than portfolio, but this is rarely important. Direct investment generally took the form of much larger shares, often of 100 percent. It came on a large scale first with privatization and then, especially from the later 1990s, with greenfield projects, meaning building completely new plants on previously vacant sites. Table 15.1, which lists selected countries in order of their per capita stock of FDI in 2007, shows the broad trends and makes possible a comparison across countries.

The measure of FDI relative to population is a good indicator of the relative attractiveness of countries to inward investors. This shows a group of CEECs and Estonia leading the way and ending with the highest figures. There is some change in ordering between these countries over time—notably, Slovakia moves up and Slovenia moves down. A second group includes Poland and other Eastern European countries, overlapping with CIS countries. These are led by Kazakhstan and Russia, countries with higher income levels than others in the CIS and with valuable raw materials. As indicated later, only part of the recorded FDI in CIS countries was investment by genuinely foreign companies. At the bottom are countries that are the least attractive or that have been most resistant to inward investment.

The measure of FDI relative to GDP is a good indicator of the importance of foreign-owned firms within domestic economies, but it is harder to use for comparisons over longer time periods on account of exchange rate changes and fluctuations. This is shown for one year in Table 15.1 and leads to small changes in the ordering of countries; more complete data is shown in Table A.11 in the Appendix. Slovenia drops down, emphasizing the low weight to foreign ownership relative to domestically owned firms. Minor changes in the ordering of CIS countries confirm the importance of FDI for the oil and gas exporters and for Georgia, which was involved in the same industry through the construction of a pipeline. The positions of Belarus and Uzbekistan are also confirmed as countries with a low weight for foreign-owned firms.

Differences between countries depended both on the thinking of MNCs and on policies and situations in individual countries. The first companies to come chose countries with which they already had established contacts and bought firms that they had already been working with. That meant that the first acquisitions were established manufacturing exporters in CEECs, followed later by public utilities, starting with telecommunications. By the later 1990s, the success of pioneers encouraged others to come, spreading into sectors with widely varying characteristics. Entry by acquisition also increasingly gave way to greenfield investment, which had some different implications for the domestic economy.

The differences among CEECs indicated in Table 15.1 also reflected different privatization policies (Drahokoupil 2008a; Bandelj 2007). Economic pressures played some role, but there were differing levels of political and social resistance to what opponents described as "selling out to foreigners." Hungary was the first country to welcome in foreign companies. This may have reflected less fear there than in other countries of foreign domination of the economy. It definitely reflected the

TABLE 15.1 Stock of FDI in U.S. dollars per capita and relative to GDP for selected transition economies

	1993	1998	2004	2007	FDI/GDP, 2007 (%)
Estonia	170	1,315	7,460	12,347	78
Czech Republic	331	1,396	5,610	9,825	60
Hungary	542	2,050	4,783	9,671	70
Slovakia	121	542	3,884	7,735	56
Slovenia	970	1,400	3,801	5,152	23
Bulgaria	295	193	1,299	4,742	92
Latvia	85	646	1,958	4,586	39
Lithuania	37	458	1,859	4,325	38
Poland	60	587	2,269	3,727	34
Kazakhstan	77	432	1,490	2,834	42
Romania	9	201	945	2,823	37
Russia	1	87	850	2,274	25
Georgia	3	114	426	1,196	52
Ukraine	9	56	203	814	27
Turkmenistan	18	143	395	786	30
Belarus	2	70	209	462	10
Kyrgyzstan	2	80	101	158	23
Uzbekistan	3	21	43	64	7

Source: Calculated from the UNCTAD Foreign Direct Investment database, available at http://stats
.unctad.org/fdi.

closeness of economic contacts with foreign companies and the need to find a means to pay off its foreign debt. Estonia and Latvia also legitimized FDI from early on (Bandelj 2007, 73), reflecting enthusiasm in those countries for linking with Western Europe. Czech voucher privatization was linked with the political aim of keeping firms under domestic ownership and caused a temporary slowdown in inward investment in 1993 and 1994. Poland's lengthy debate over methods and then its choice of a limited version of voucher privatization also delayed sales to foreign companies. Slovenia's gradualist approach to privatization, keeping management and employees as major shareholders, limited the scope for private ownership (48–49).

The figure rose in all the CEECs and Baltic republics at the end of the decade, partly because foreign investors were becoming more willing to invest across a range of sectors, partly because any opposition to inward investment faded with the approach of EU accession, and partly because governments were following Western European models of financial and other incentives. Active encouragement of greenfield investment began with the establishment of inward-investment agencies in Poland and Czechoslovakia in 1992, with the creation of industrial zones in Poland beginning in 1995—an example later followed by other countries—and with the use of benefits and subsidies as allowed under EU rules in all CEECs as they prepared for EU accession (for further information, see Drahokoupil [2008a]).

Multinational companies thereby became absolutely dominant in modern export-oriented sectors, particularly motor vehicles and electronics, in the CEECs and Baltic republics. In passenger-car production, European transition economies as a whole moved from an output of 2.1 million units in 1990 to 1.6 million in 1994, the low point of the transformation depression, and then back to 4.4 million in 2007. The most dynamic were the CEECs, following inward investment first by privatization and then overwhelmingly by greenfield projects (Pavlínek, Domański, and Guzik 2009, 45). Foreign companies also dominated banking and financial services in those countries, largely following the privatization of established enterprises, and were strongly placed in a number of inward-oriented sectors of manufacturing. They moved to dominate large-scale retailing, beginning in the bigger cities in CEECs and then reaching into big cities in Russia and to smaller settlements in CEECs.

This spread of foreign-owned companies in CEECs appeared as a culmination of a process of transformation of the enterprise sphere. In some sectors, notably retailing, it was associated with the progressive elimination of enterprises that emerged from scratch or from the privatization of former state-owned enterprises. The CIS countries followed a different and more gradual pattern, with foreign penetration more focused on raw material and semimanufacture exports and on sectors targeting domestic markets. The foreign-owned, export-oriented manufacturing sector was largely absent.

The quality of data that could give detail to these points varies enormously between countries, partly reflecting the different levels of interest in the theme and partly reflecting the need to maintain confidentiality, as it is often possible to identify individual companies. The most complete has been produced in CEECs, and this makes it possible to follow the spread of foreign ownership across those countries' economies, albeit not with fully comparable data. The trends showed similarities, though not without differences over the extent of investment in export-oriented industry and in real estate and business services.

The Czech Republic was more oriented toward the first of these. Precise figures for 2006 show financial intermediation accounting for 16.8 percent of the stock of inward investment, followed by real estate and services to businesses at 14.3 percent. Trade and repair accounted for a further 10.2 percent, followed by motor vehicles at 9.4 percent; electricity, gas, and water at 9.0 percent; and transport and communications at 7.6 percent (Czech National Bank [CNB] 2008). In Hungary, real estate and further unspecified business services—mostly the latter—accounted for 59 percent of the FDI stock, albeit reflecting specific financial conditions in that year and later falling to 26 percent in 2007 (HNB 2009b). Other sectors, despite substantial volumes, took correspondingly smaller shares, with all manufacturing at only 17.5 percent and transport equipment at 5 percent. In Lithuania, the breakdown was closer to the Czech pattern, with a substantial share in manufacturing (34.5%), but no major investor in motor vehicles (Lithuanian Development Agency [LDA] 2006). In Poland, manufacturing was similarly important but more widely spread across activities than in the Czech Republic, and transport equipment took only 5.6 percent of the total (NBP 2006).

Table 15.2 shows the importance of foreign-owned firms to the Czech economy. The main contributions to employment and value came from the manufacturing industry. The extent of foreign domination was greater in some other sectors, especially

TABLE 15.2   The place of foreign-owned firms in the Czech economy, 2006

	Employment	Value added	Exports	Imports
Raw materials	0.7	0.7	0.6	0.1
Manufacturing	12.1	10.1	29.4	18.8
Trade and repair	3.0	2.2	3.1	8.0
Transport and telecommunications	0.9	2.2	0.7	0.7
Financial intermediation	1.6	2.2	0.2	0.2
Real estate and business services	1.3	1.4	0.8	0.5
Other	2.0	2.1	0.7	2.6
Total	21.6	20.9	35.5	30.9

Source: Calculated from CNB (2008, Table 6.2.1).

Note: Employment is calculated as a percentage of total employment. The remaining columns show percentages of GDP.

financial intermediation, which contributed less to employment and total value added. The figures on exports and imports show an overall surplus in trade and a very substantial share in the trade balance. The significance of this is taken up in later text.

The situation in CIS countries differed from that of CEECs and the Baltic republics due in the first place to the lower stocks of FDI relative to GDP, as shown in Table 15.1. Figures for Russia for 2008 covering all inward investment show that 73 percent was made up of credits and only 26 percent was from direct investment; there clearly were substantial inflows that were not connected to ownership. Within that broader total, manufacturing took 32.7 percent and motor vehicles took 2.5 percent. That is in line with the weaker development of foreign ownership and foreign financial inflows, in general, and in that sector, in particular. There were also high representations for trade and repair (23.0%), real estate and business services (14.8%), and raw material extraction (12.0%). Financial intermediation accounted for only 4.8 percent (Russian State Statistics Service [GKS] 2009, Table 24.9).

Less comprehensive data specifically for inward direct investment, with a breakdown by sector, show the low place for the machinery and equipment sector, accounting for only 4 percent of the stock in 2002. Mining and petroleum was then the fastest-growing sector, accounting for 73 percent of the total inflow in the period from 2001 to 2006. A substantial proportion of that was returning capital that had been taken out in preceding years by Russian businesses. This is even clearer for 2008, when oil accounted for 50 percent of the total inflow at a time of no major acquisitions or investment by foreign companies. As much as 72 percent of all FDI in that year came from tax havens and countries with conveniently lax rules for business regulation; Cyprus was the most important. Another important source was Holland, the country from which the Russian gas company Gazprom was channeling money back from its financial services affiliate (UNCTAD 2009, 74). The reason for these financial transfers was probably partly because of the preferences of privately owned Russian businesses for keeping their wealth safe from the unpredictability of Russian politicians. The choice of tax havens may also have enabled Russian businesses to continue to avoid paying taxes in Russia.

Among other CIS countries that could attract inward investment, Kazakhstan was more open from the start to MNCs. Ukraine created a welcoming environment in later years, but there were also cases of Ukrainian businesses bringing wealth back from safe havens abroad. Therefore, as in Russia, figures for FDI in this case are not a precise guide to the extent of genuine foreign ownership. Development in these countries was predominantly a matter for domestically owned firms, with foreign ownership playing a less central role than in CEECs and other Eastern European countries. This is taken up later in the chapter, while the next section concentrates on the effects of foreign ownership in countries where it was most important.

THE PROS AND CONS OF FOREIGN OWNERSHIP

There was strong international pressure for countries to open up to inward investment. International agencies and their advisers favored this, as, not surprisingly, did the MNCs that could hope to profit from their investments. However, there was also suspicion toward foreign ownership across all transition countries in the 1990s (Drahokoupil 2008a, Chapter 4), only some of which was based on well-established arguments. The strength of opposing arguments varied depending on the exact kind of FDI they were addressing. A simple blanket assessment that all could be judged positively or that all could be judged negatively appears unsustainable.

Table 15.3 summarizes the hopes and fears typically associated with FDI, following a heritage of studies across other countries. These themes, divided into three broad groupings, are then assessed against the experience in CEECs.

Balance-of-Payments Effects

The effect on the balance of payments should be immediately positive due to the inflow shown on the financial account. The long-term effect depends on the activities undertaken by the foreign company and has sometimes been associated with a worsening, rather than an improvement, in current account performance, as argued by Mencinger (2007). Overall, data show MNCs in CEECs to be substantial importers. The data on exports and imports in Table 15.2, covering the Czech Republic, show the varied balance-of-payments effects of FDI in different sectors. Foreign-owned companies appear as substantial importers. This was more than balanced by exports in the case of export-oriented sectors, but not in the cases of retailing, construction, parts of manufacturing, or finance. The initial capital inflow was also gradually balanced by an outflow of repatriated profits, meaning that, over time, the effect on the balance of payments could be increasingly negative unless balanced by a continuing inflow of new capital or by a strong trade surplus from export-oriented manufacturing.

For the Czech Republic—and even more clearly for Slovakia, which experienced its FDI inflow somewhat later—the net effect of FDI on the balance of payments, taking account of all financial flows on both the current and financial accounts and of exports and imports for those firms, was still positive. For Hungary, it was almost certainly negative. The net outflow associated with repatriated profits increased from 0.4 percent of GDP in 1995 to 4.1 percent in 2000 and 5.7 percent in 2007. In the last of those years, the current account deficit was equivalent to 6.4 percent of GDP, and the inflow of FDI shown on the financial account was equivalent to only 3.4 percent

TABLE 15.3 Potential positive and negative effects of FDI in host countries

Potential positive effects of FDI	Potential negative effects of FDI
Balance-of-payments level	
Financial inflow as investment comes	Repatriated profits as investment matures
Higher exports from MNCs	Higher imports from domestic-market-oriented investors
Enterprise level	
Enterprise survival and continued production	Closure of enterprises to eliminate competitors
	Sale at low prices, while firms could have been successful under domestic ownership
Access to investment capital, technology, and management know-how, leading to increased labor productivity and expansion of output	Labor shedding and reduced scale of production
Increased R&D brought by firms in high-tech activities	Transfer of R&D, marketing, and strategic decision-making activities abroad to companies' main centers
Access to worldwide sales and distribution networks	External control leading to dependence on decisions made abroad
High-tech activities leading to higher skill levels, increased labor productivity, and higher wages	Concentration on activities requiring lower skill levels and labor-intensive production
Whole-economy level	
Spillovers to local firms of higher productivity and wages and better management methods	Attraction of skilled and semiskilled workers away from local companies
	Suppression or destruction of local firms unable to compete with MNCs that have additional support from government incentives
Development of permanent new economic activities and sectors that can improve overall economic competitiveness	Subordination of economic development to the strategies of foreign multinational companies that may favor their home bases in times of difficulty

Source: Substantially adapted from Pavlínek (2004a, 48, Table 1).

of GDP (HNB 2009a). This does not provide the full picture, as foreign-owned manufacturing companies were substantial exporters, and companies involved in real estate and business services were also involved in other international transactions.

Enterprise-Level Effects

The first negative point on changes within enterprises—claims that foreign companies would want to eliminate a potentially troublesome rival—was not confirmed by clear examples. It reflected an exaggerated belief in the strength of the inherited technological bases. However, there were more persuasive arguments that sale prices, particularly for some raw material producers, were very low and that domestic producers could have done just as well by continuing to produce products that were relatively easy to sell.

This was less of an issue for major export-oriented manufacturing enterprises, which had no other future without a foreign partner. The best deals were achieved by bargaining between prospective buyers, as in the case of Škoda, the car manufacturer in the Czech Republic in which a number of companies were interested. Bargaining was primarily over the investors' business strategies and investment aims, rather than over the price they would pay, and was also over any help that they might be offered by the government. Volkswagen was successful in its bid after promising to maintain the existing brand name and to investment in expansion; in return, the government promised to undertake infrastructure investment and to provide some forms of temporary protection against imports.

The positive effects on enterprises are easier to document. The first cases of inward investment in manufacturing by acquisition showed benefits that can be set against the problems of enterprise transformation, set out in Chapter 11, and the experience of firms struggling with survival. Foreign ownership brought clear strategic objectives and, where major multinational companies were involved, prevented asset stripping. It brought financial strength and the resources to overcome difficulties from inherited debt. These firms could invest in new technology and modernization. It also brought access to outside markets through international networks and brand names; the probing or dependence on the OPT of domestically owned firms was, therefore, unnecessary. Foreign-owned firms could be more focused on a long-term strategy. Therefore, they were characterized by narrow product ranges sold into secure markets, high levels of investment, and the use of more modern technology (Myant 1997, 553).

These general points were illustrated by some of the first big sales to foreign companies. The Hungarian lightbulb manufacturer Tungsram was offered to the U.S. company General Electric in 1989, and a controlling share was sold the next year. This was already a company capable of exporting to Western Europe, but GE brought financial stability, with investment moving up from 1 to 2 percent of sales to 10 percent and with R&D rising to 5 to 6 percent of revenues. It also increased production in later years by transferring capacity from other European countries.

The Czech car manufacturer Škoda was sold to Volkswagen in stages beginning in 1991, and this was followed by financial stability and capital investment through the 1990s, while firms privatized into domestic ownership were able to undertake very little modernization. The number of cars produced fell at first but then almost doubled from 1989 to 1997, and it reached 3.7 times the 1989 level in 2008.

These successful cases demonstrated the benefits of linking up with a foreign multinational company, but they did depend on the requirement that the CEEC enterprise appeared attractive to an MNC. The two mentioned previously, albeit not world leaders, were established exporters into Western Europe with clear development potential. Many other enterprises were less attractive—the case of tractors is covered in Box 15.1—but the first pioneers did encourage followers. They showed to other MNCs that investing in CEECs was safe and profitable and provided an ideal base for exporting into the European Union, with good transport links and a reasonably skilled labor force at wage levels at half or less of those in Western Europe.

Box 15.1   Contrasting fates of tractor manufacturers

Tractor production was well developed across state Socialist countries, but all the manufacturing enterprises faced enormous difficulties through the 1990s as demand fell from agricultural enterprises that were themselves in crisis. All were dependent on state help for their survival. The Minsk tractor producer MTZ, as described in the text, was well placed because the state in Belarus was committed to the survival of inherited industries. Others followed complicated paths, which reflected the difficulties for governments in supporting enterprises alongside the difficulties in accepting their demise. Three examples—from Kazakhstan, the Czech Republic, and Poland—illustrate different ways of handling this dilemma.

Kazakhstan's tractor producer in Pavlodar, capable of producing 55,000 vehicles annually, had been heavily dependent on parts supplied from other republics in the Soviet period. This became problematic after the breakup of the Soviet Union both because of payment problems and possibly also because other manufacturers were happy to see a competitor in trouble. The enterprise's narrower product range was also less attractive to farmers in the 1990s. The World Bank tried to help find a foreign partner that could bring revival, but Pavlodar was too remote, and the factory was judged to need too much investment if it were to become viable. The U.S. firm John Deere had some interest but was prepared only to set up a service center for the equipment it exported to Kazakhstan. The enterprise was then declared bankrupt in 1998, and $40 million in state backing was offered to revive some of the remnants. The only potential partner that seemed consistently interested was MTZ, and there were several promises up to 2008 that small-scale production of its tractors would be revived.

Another example was the Czech tractor producer Zetor, which had had a strong presence in some Western European markets before 1989. Output quickly fell from 27,000 units to less than 20 percent of that year's level as domestic and export demand, the latter taking up to 90 percent of output, disappeared. The government helped three times: It helped with inherited debts in 1991, took Zetor back into state ownership in 1994 after voucher privatization had made no positive impact, sold the company again in 1997, and then took it back under state control in 1999. Each time, financial difficulties were caused by the failure to restore sales to anything approaching their pre-1990 level. Despite attempts, especially from the enterprise's management, no foreign buyer could be found in the 1990s. Although John Deere had seemed genuinely interested for a time, the deal fell through. Zetor was finally sold off to a Slovak holding company in 2002. Some new markets were found and output increased but remained too low to ensure viability (Pavlínek 2008, 221–22). This, then, was an extreme case of state-supported survival. The clearest differences from MTZ were in the smaller inherited product range and the lack of a foothold across the potentially vast CIS market. Privatization into domestic ownership contributed nothing to solving the enterprise's fundamental problems, and the state ultimately contributed nothing beyond fending off complete collapse of the enterprise. Unable to develop new products and unable to access completely new markets, its chances were always more limited.

Poland's Ursus followed an even more extreme course. This was the country's only tractor producer before 1990, and it was hit by falling domestic demand in the 1990s as farmers stopped buying new equipment in the face of the shock. Nevertheless, Polish governments were swayed by employee demands for support and would not let Ursus close or be sold to a foreign buyer, should a willing one appear. Plans were formulated for gradual restructuring, but, in view of financial constraints, this had to be achieved without developing new models. Restructuring, then, amounted to privatization in 2002 by incorporation into a Polish arms trading company, in the hope that it could find new outlets, and then the sale in 2007 to the Turkish tractor producer Uzel. Output fell to 1,578 units in 2006, compared with 60,000 in 1980.

This had always been a less promising enterprise than Zetor, with more limited sales outside Poland, minimal presence in Western Europe at any given time, a history of problems through the 1970s and 1980s, and a product range that appeared unattractive to farmers. It was definitely worse off than MTZ. Both were also helped by their respective states. In Belarus, this did not achieve a full modernization of MTZ and other enterprises so that they could compete in all markets, but it did enable them to take advantage of opportunities that arose and to undergo some kind of recovery in the years up to 2008.

Aggregate measures confirm the higher productivity of MNCs relative to domestically owned firms. This is illustrated with the figures in Table 15.4 for Czech industry, which include extractive as well as manufacturing industries. The share of foreign-owned companies increased rapidly after 1998, corresponding to the failure of the big firms privatized into domestic ownership. Comparing their shares in gross output and value added to their lower shares in employment indicates a considerably higher level of productivity.

Measures of the impact of inward investment on international competitiveness are less clear cut. A detailed study of the effects of foreign ownership in sectors of Polish industry showed marked improvements for most sectors (Weresa 2008). Competitiveness was calculated using the revealed comparative advantage method, which measures the ratio of exports to imports for a particular product in relation

TABLE 15.4   Percentage shares of foreign-owned companies in output, value added, and employment in Czech industry, 1998 and 2006

	1998	2006
Gross output	17.6	51.8
Value added	15.5	46.6
Employment	11.0	35.0

Source: CZSO (2002, Table 16-9; 2008, Table 16-9).

to the country's total exports and imports. However, there were cases, notably for parts of the food industry, in which foreign ownership led to the worsening of competitiveness. This could be expected, as multinational companies in these sectors were the most likely to be attracted to Poland because of its domestic market, meaning that they imported materials that were not balanced by exports.

Among the possible negative effects shown in Table 15.3 are possible social costs. Foreign owners, entering through privatization, often did reduce the labor force as they restructured their enterprises. In the case of a number of major engineering and truck-producing enterprises in the Czech Republic, the prospect of this was used as an argument in the early 1990s for rejecting offers from established MNCs and for trying to seek domestic owners who could promise business success without such changes. In Poland, there were cases of even stronger opposition to seeking foreign owners. However, firms in these sectors left under domestic ownership had generally failed catastrophically by the end of the decade. There were failures from foreign owners, but domestic ownership was a more frequent recipe for a slow death among firms that faced international competition.

The remaining items under the "enterprise level" heading in Table 15.3 relate to the extent to which foreign ownership leads to an increase or decrease in the activities that require higher skill levels, which contribute most to value added, and the extent to which it brings, or destroys, the higher-level activities that are typically concentrated in companies' home bases.

There were initial fears that acquisition would be followed by a general de-skilling as enterprises were "hollowed out," leaving only the lowest-level activities. However, evidence from the motor-vehicle sector points rather to an increase in R&D activity, albeit much of it relatively routine and transferred to CEECs because of the lower wages for the skilled labor required there. Much was also concentrated into a few larger establishments.

This is highly variable between countries, with far more in the Czech Republic, concentrated on Škoda, the car manufacturer that was bought by Volkswagen as a manufacturer of established models and that continued as a base for new model development. Car plants in other countries were more dependent on strategies, research, and product development coming from company head offices. The share of R&D in value added was 6.6 percent for MNCs and 3.3 percent for domestically owned firms in the Czech Republic in 2006, but it was much lower in other countries (Pavlínek, Domański, and Guzik 2009, 51–54; Pavlínek and Ženka 2010).

These differences reflected inherited bases. Greenfield investment was less likely to be associated with significant R&D, and that was particularly true of smaller-scale production activities, especially with small plants set up in industrial zones in the later years, which required only basic skill levels. These were also more footloose and could easily be moved to a country with even lower labor costs once that appeared favorable. This provided employment and exports, but not a general upgrading of technological levels. It could appear as downgrading relative to the production of independently designed finished products in the state Socialist period, but, as already indicated, a somewhat similar downgrading took place in many domestically owned enterprises.

Whole-Economy Effects

The final set of issues in Table 15.3 covers effects beyond the individual foreign-owned company. Both poaching skilled labor and squeezing domestic firms out of the market were referred to by Czech-owned firms in the motor-vehicle sector. The former was a frequent complaint as the economy grew in the years up to 2008, but its impact has not been quantified.

Another possibility is that inward investment need have little impact on the wider economy, creating only what have been described as "cathedrals in the desert" (Grabher 1992; cf. Hardy 1998). Studies have looked in many countries for spillovers to domestically owned firms in terms of better technology and management practices (e.g., Knell 2000; Pavlínek 2004b; 2008, Chapter 6). However, attempts to show this in CEECs have come up with very little.

Following spillovers alone misses the extent to which FDI brought revival and development across whole sectors. Evidence from the Czech Republic shows that component manufacturers in the motor-vehicle sector privatized by vouchers or by direct sales lacked finance and contacts, and, when investment funds were the dominant owners, there was no prospect of input of new expertise or capital. They, therefore, could not benefit from the stimulus from inward investment in other enterprises. Recovery and growth became possible only after they linked up with foreign companies, in some cases encouraged by Volkswagen (Pavlínek 2008, Chapter 7; Myant 1999b). The spillover effect was, therefore, not so much a stimulus to domestically owned firms as it was a stimulus to further inward investment by MNCs that led to a more general transformation of the whole sector.

The extent of foreign ownership in CEECs brought dangers if the investors had only limited commitment to the economies; the extent of investment in passenger-car production could be dangerous, should that sector face a general decline in demand. It would then be for the MNCs to decide where to cut capacity, and more peripheral operations would be likely to suffer first. However, commitment to a country is likely to be greatest for large-scale investments. This was particularly true of capital-intensive projects, for which lower labor costs in other countries would be less of an attraction. The big car assembly plants were the most welcome, both for these reasons and because they attracted an infrastructure of component suppliers that helped to embed the main investor in the domestic economy. Needless to say, that also meant that their failure would be more catastrophic for the economy than would that of a smaller, and less firmly embedded, project.

These points generally confirm the positive assessment of much of FDI. It has been the most successful means of creating enterprises with the potential for growth and hence the key distinguishing feature of CEECs as opposed to other transition economies. However, even in those countries, this is only one part of the total inward investment. It is not as simple to demonstrate such clear benefits for the sale into foreign ownership of telecommunications, utilities, and many activities targeting domestic markets. Alongside very likely improvements in productivity and service to customers, there could be costs in worsening the external balance. Especially in the case of retail, foreign MNCs were associated with the occurrence of more imported goods in shops replacing sales from domestic producers, although that trend was already clear without foreign ownership. Banking is also a different case, as discussed in Chapter 14. It had very little immediate direct impact on the balance of payments beyond the initial capital inflow. Foreign ownership made further financial inflows easier, bringing immediate benefits and also longer-term risks.

The SEECs followed behind CEECs and the Baltic republics, but without the base for creating the substantial electronics and motor-vehicle sectors, that could raise their exports in the machinery-complex group (shown in Figure 4.13) to the levels reached in CEECs. Serbia did have potential from its inherited base in car manufacturing, but that lay dormant through years of international isolation during the wars associated with the breakup of Yugoslavia; multinational companies understandably held back. Estonia did well for a time with electronics, but that did not have the permanence of motor-vehicle production.

FOREIGN AND DOMESTIC OWNERSHIP IN THE CIS

In CIS countries, there was little sign of the same trend toward export-oriented inward investment in manufacturing industries. There were differences in privatization policies, but the primary reason was that the countries were less attractive to those kinds of MNCs. There was less of a history of enterprise-level contacts, the countries were geographically further from established industrial centers, and their institutional and legal environments gave less confidence. This was particularly discouraging for activities that needed a wide range of contacts with an economy, something that would apply to motor-vehicle production and its need for reliable links to a large number of component suppliers.

Inward investment was therefore much slower to develop here. The first MNCs came for raw material extraction and to produce for domestic markets. Established firms in the food and drink industries were prominent in this. Motor-vehicle production was well established in the Soviet past, but its revival was almost exclusively to serve local markets, with only cautious involvement from MNCs.

Ukrainian car production was an example of this (Pavlínek 2008, 16–17). Total output was down to 2,000 units in 1997 and then grew to an annual figure of 380,000 units in 2007. The biggest producer was the ZAZ enterprise in Zaporizhia (Zaporizkyi avtomobilebudivelnyi zavod, Zaporizhzhia Automobile Plant), which was privatized to a local businessman in 2002. There had been involvement by the South Korean firm Daewoo in a joint venture, but it ended in 2002 when the Korean firm suffered bankruptcy. All production in the following years was essentially the assembly from kits of models from MNCs and from the Russian company VAZ (Volzhskii avtomobilnyi zavod, Volga Automobile Plant), which manufactured Lada-brand cars, and the market was restricted to Ukraine. Foreign MNCs had little interest in taking control of such operations.

Uzbekistan presents a slightly different case, with a motor-vehicle industry built up by the state and the South Korean company Daewoo, which soon withdrew its interest. The operation continued with cooperation from General Motors, and cars accounted for 9.5 percent of Uzbek exports in 2006, with Russia by far the largest market. However, the Uzbek operation was also assembly only, and the value of imported components, mostly from Korea, was almost equal to the value of finished car exports (Myant and Drahokoupil 2008, 614). This was not an activity firmly embedded in the Uzbek economy. It depended on imports over expensive and unreliable routes, and it was likely to be threatened by penetration of MNCs into the Russian market.

Russia's car output remained depressed through the 1990s, with major companies struggling to survive. By 2007, output had reached 106 percent of the 1990 level, and rising domestic demand was encouraging inward investment from major MNCs. However, inward investment was more important in other sectors and also in other branches of industry, such as food production. The arrival of MNCs in passenger-car production could eventually be expected to threaten the position of domestic manufacturers, of the Uzbek manufacturer, and also of the small traders bringing cars from Western Europe, often via the Baltic republics.

Export-oriented inward direct investment in Russia and other CIS countries was most visible in raw materials or semimanufactures, but energy often stayed in domestic ownership in those countries. Kazakhstan was something of an exception, happy to leave foreign companies with 85 percent of its oil output. This followed the unexplained generosity toward foreigners of its privatization policies in the 1990s.

Steel remained under domestic ownership, often state ownership, throughout the 1990s in Poland, Slovakia, and the Czech Republic, but in Kazakhstan, foreign ownership was welcomed in 1995 with the sale of the mining and steel complex Termitau to the expanding Mittal Steel Company, led by Indian businessman Lakshmi Mittal. There were strong criticisms of the price and of conditions that freed Mittal from tax payments or fines under new environmental laws. However, foreign ownership may have been important for gaining the access to world markets, a problem that CEEC firms had been able to solve for themselves on the basis of past experience. Privatization was more definitely important for opening the way for an EBRD credit in 1997, which, in line with EBRD policy, was intended specifically to support the growth of a private sector. This was also clearly beneficial to the expansion of Mittal's company, helping it to take on an even bigger role in transition economies in later years, as indicated later.

REORGANIZATION BY DOMESTIC COMPANIES

Unlike the CEECs, growth in the years up to 2008 in Russia was based predominantly on domestically owned enterprises. There was a clearer division here between domestically oriented and export-oriented enterprises, the latter producing raw materials and semimanufactures. Recovery from these firms was the most consistent. Two background factors were important for the changed environment of business in Russia, and these applied, albeit less clearly, in other CIS countries.

The first was the changed economic environment. Russia's financial crisis of 1998 led at first to devaluation. More enterprises could compete with imports, and banks lost the old means to make money, so they became more willing to lend to domestic firms. In later years, higher oil and gas prices encouraged expansion of output and brought profits to that part of industry, but Russia's growth still took a rather limited form (cf. Ahrend 2006). It was driven to a great extent by oil exporters but largely by making the most of capacity built up in the 1980s, as levels of investment by private companies in that sector were low. A common explanation is that oligarchs were discouraged from investing inside Russia by their uncertain property rights, especially after the Yukos affair. There were also some further institutional factors that worked against expansion from private companies (Rossiaud and Locatelli 2009; also see above pp. 256–57). At the same time, the revaluation that followed from rising export revenues limited the earlier positive impact on domestically oriented enterprises, and rising consumer demand was largely satisfied by imports in the years after 2002.

The years up to 2008 also saw high world prices for steel—benefiting especially Ukraine and Kazakhstan—and for other raw materials and semimanufactures. These benefits spread to other countries that depended on remittances from abroad, and several could benefit from financial inflows in the lax financial world of the years up to 2008. Thus, the limited improvement in the environment for business was not purely a Russian phenomenon; there were positive influences in this respect also in other CIS countries.

The second was the restoration of a greater degree of state authority, as covered for Russia in Chapter 8. There was an apparent increase in the state's direct role in the economy, reflected in the renationalization of part of the oil industry as Putin demonstrated his power over the oligarchs. The state's share, having fallen from over 80 percent in 1995 to 13 percent in 2004 following the loans-for-shares deal and subsequent privatizations that favored individuals friendly to those in power, was back in 2005 to one-third of production. Putin spoke in April 2007 of increased spending on electricity and transport and of support to high-tech sectors, alongside promises of higher social spending. There was the appearance of the beginnings of state-led growth, as discussed in Chapter 9, using oil revenues to stimulate other parts of the economy, but the first results up to 2008 were less impressive.

Despite these two positive aspects of development, domestically oriented enterprises had great difficulty in moving beyond a survival stage. There were substantial shifts in ownership and control, but none that could overcome in full the difficulties left behind from the transformation depression.

Following Russia's rather specific form of privatization, there was a gradual shift toward outsider control. An estimate relying on 97 investigations conducted over the period from 1992 to 2003 (Iwasaki 2007)—and with important reservations, as enterprises need not have reported ownership accurately—is reproduced in Table 15.5. It shows that workers' shares fell as they sold out to managers and outsiders. The state share also reduced with further privatizations; it was down to 15.4 percent in surveys conducted in 1994, with outsiders and managers the main beneficiaries.

The studies do indicate that private firms probably did better than state-owned firms after 2000, and worker ownership appeared inferior (Iwasaki 2007, 873). Of course, that could be because outside investors were more interested in buying into successful companies, and the others were left either with the state or with the employees who held large shareholdings at the start. An important question is whether outside owners could bring financial strength and access to networks, providing some analogy to the foreign companies in CEECs, albeit with more of an orientation toward domestic markets. That role could be played by the financial industrial groups, also known as industrial business groups, as covered in Chapter 14. These were formally encouraged by the Russian government, and 90 were registered in 2000, alongside many more that operated informally. Thanks to their diversification, they could, at

TABLE 15.5   The evolution of the ownership structure of Russian industrial enterprises

	Percentage share immediately after mass privatization	Percentage share in 2003
Workers	43.0	22.0
Managers	10.4	28.0
Outsiders	9.4	45.0
Foreign investors	0.0	2.0
State	35.8	4.0

Source: Iwasaki (2007, 856–57).

least in theory, play a role in transferring profits from raw material exports into other sectors (Berglöf et al. 2003, 31–33).

In the Russian case, larger firms were more likely than small ones to be owned by FIGs, and some evidence suggested that those firms were performing better. However, a massive survey of 5 percent of all Russian manufacturing enterprises conducted over the period from September 2005 to February 2006, which showed one-third of enterprises integrated into a group, did not find consistent differences. It seemed that any possible benefits from FIGs had by then been exhausted, although there were some firms within FIGs that appeared to be investing and following longer-term plans (Golikova et al. 2008, 47).

In general, it rather appeared that Russian firms had benefited from the changed environment after 1998, but those oriented toward the domestic market had soon afterward stagnated or even declined, again proving increasingly unable to cope with foreign competition, even within their own country. Russian enterprises were still poor in terms of investment, were suffering from outdated production facilities, had little access to outside finance, frequently lacked any long-term strategy, were not undertaking important innovations, and were poor exporters. There were some so-called leaders that were able to sell products abroad, but even then, much went to CIS countries. Many of the remaining firms were left to live out a "life-after-death existence" (Golikova et al. 2008, 56).

Evidence on other CIS countries is sparse, but enterprises in smaller countries had even greater difficulty exporting outside the CIS, and when they could export to other CIS countries, they depended on the ability to maintain or establish key political business relationships for market access (Gorton and White 2009). For Ukraine, there is some information on the role of FIGs in the steel and coal industries. Control was concentrated after capital had been accumulated by small companies that were able to trade. They acquired power over industrial enterprises and initially used this to enrich themselves. However, there are clear signs that at some time after 1998, the largest investors in the Donbas, the main steel and coal mining area, were the powerful businesses that had previously taken wealth out of the country. They were bringing it back to invest in producing steel for export, as that promised rapid returns (Lyakh 2007, 91; A. Swain and Mykhnenko 2007). Despite that, the Ukrainian industry remained remarkably backward, with 40 percent of output in 2005 from the long obsolete open-hearth method; the equivalent figure for Russia was 22 percent but the method was quite insignificant in all other major producers (International Iron and Steel Institute [IISI] 2007, 29).

Ukraine's political development then brought a new direction to the steel industry. The leading steel maker, Krivorozhstal, was privatized in June 2004 to a consortium including the son-in-law of the then president Leonid Kuchma. This decision was annulled after the change in government following the Orange Revolution of November 2004 to January 2005. An open auction was then won by the Mittal Steel Company, which in 2006 received an EBRD loan to support technological modernization. The EBRD was enthusiastic about the possible encouragement this would give to further inward investment and about the possible progress in more transparent management methods. Ukraine, it could be hoped, might eventually follow the path set out by CEECs. More immediately, it marked a new stage in the restructuring of the steel industry across the transition economies.

By 2008, the company ArcelorMittal, the successor to Mittal Steel, had 10 percent of the total world steel output and production facilities in 20 countries. It was by then presenting itself as a progressive company concerned with improving health and environmental standards. It was dominant in the industry in Kazakhstan, Ukraine, and Poland and had activities in other transition economies, too. That meant that those producers had access to its worldwide sales network and could benefit from its financial strength and political links. There was further backing from the EBRD. The Polish state also provided support as part of a 2004 privatization deal. However, incorporation into this MNC also meant that the fate of countries' steel industries depended on the world strategy of a company that they could not control. It could decide which production facilities to favor and which, in times of economic difficulty, might be sacrificed.

STATE-LED RECOVERY

As indicated in Chapter 6, the state played an important role in ensuring enterprise survival in many countries. In CEECs, this declined in the era of dependence on inward direct investment. It continued in CIS countries, with surveys of Russian enterprises pointing to some form of subsidies given to a significant minority of firms alongside help from state contracts given to another significant minority. Together, these firms accounted for about half of industrial employment (Golikova et al. 2008, 48). This help generally went to more successful firms that were likely to be investing. It was, therefore, not just about survival.

However, the notion of state-led recovery implies a more active, if not dominant, role in creating an internationally competitive enterprise structure. The closest to that in terms of government thinking can be found in Belarus, but even then, the penetration of completely new markets was limited, and new technology was an incremental development of what already existed, supplemented by some use of imported sophisticated components. The state's role was primarily in ensuring some unusually promising examples of enterprise survival in the face of difficulties. The term "order state," as used by Iwasaki and Suzuki (2007) and covered in Chapter 9, is therefore appropriate, indicating the state's role primarily in restoring some stability to economic relations.

Belarus inherited a strong base in heavy motor vehicles—trucks and tractors—and the key enterprises survived under state ownership through the 1990s. These were activities that did very badly in CEECs and other CIS countries, as indicated for tractors in Box 15.1. Demand fell sharply across these economies, and the enterprises were unattractive to foreign MNCs. This was a much worse base than a passenger-car industry.

The flagship of Belarus manufacturing was MTZ, the Minsk tractor producer, which suffered a substantial drop in output, down to around 25 percent of the level of the 1980s in 1995. This was not a bad performance in relative terms among former state Socialist countries, but even this level depended on barter schemes for Russian oil and gas. Belarus's economy was tied in closely with the country's international political orientation and its ability to gain favor in Moscow in exchange for avoiding a clearly pro-Western stance.

Growth was also dependent on the state's commitment to the enterprise's survival, and it provided various forms of financial help, as it did for other parts of the country's inherited industrial base (Nuti 2007). Alexander Lukashenko, president from 1994, was actively involved in MTZ's management, removing those who at one time opposed him politically and who had advocated privatizing the plant. The enterprise director was given a 10-year prison sentence in 2002. Such interventions characterized the arbitrary use of power by the Belarusian president. However, they also confirmed state backing for the enterprise's survival, enabling it to develop its product range to fit with market demand, producing more models than in the Soviet period. Sustained recovery came only from 2004, and sales then increased back to 63,000 tractors in 2007 (G. Smith 2008).

This success was possible because the enterprise held together through a difficult period, avoiding tunneling and asset stripping that could have followed privatization. It was also helped by a strong product range and, above all, by reoccupation of markets across the CIS, which were easier to penetrate as demand rose as other tractor producers faced even greater problems. By 2008, it had a presence in Central and even Western Europe, Asia, and the Middle East. It was not an isolated success, as the Minsk truck manufacturer was also competing well in the CIS heavy goods vehicle market following a cooperation agreement with the German company MAN (originally Maschinenfabrik Augsburg Nürnberg AG). These companies were certainly not world leaders, but they had used good starting points and state help to ensure survival and then output recovery, while privatized firms in other countries had struggled. They could then exploit rapidly expanding CIS markets, which had yet to be penetrated by major Western companies. This is contrasted with the fates of other tractor manufacturers in Box 15.1—truck manufacturers would point toward similar conclusions—which helps to confirm that the state's role was not the whole, but a significant part, of the difference.

CONCLUSION

The varying performance and behavior of enterprises during recovery from the transformation depression points to a more complex picture than does the simple model of privatization leading to restructuring and then to growth. For many, it proved impossible to move beyond a survival phase. Privatization often contributed nothing positive. Some enterprises—raw material exporters and producers of semimanufactures—could do reasonably well under state or domestic private ownership, while some others, notably those exporting modern manufactured goods, were internationally competitive only under foreign ownership.

This diversity of experience demonstrates the inadequacy of setting privatization in general as the key to enterprise transformation. It sometimes required less and sometimes more than that. Successful integration into the international economy was relatively easy for enterprises producing homogeneous products that were in continual demand. Even outdated technology and limited knowledge of world markets were not absolute barriers. For enterprises producing modern manufactured goods, integration into the international economy required links to international networks that were dominated by established producers with their own brands and access to the most modern technology, which in turn meant access to finance for investment. In practical terms, that was rarely possible without foreign ownership.

As a final conclusion, it should be emphasized that the process of enterprise transformation never reached a definitive end. International integration brought continual changes, with new prospects for investment and modernization and also new sources of instability. The most successful forms of transformation—those involving FDI—left uncertainties over the future strategies of the multinational companies, which had a wide range of choices for the location of future investment. Other types of transformation, often with opaque forms of domestic ownership, left questions about the future of enterprises that were not keeping pace with modern technology, should they face more international competition. Indeed, the continuing strong weight to small-scale trading activities and locally oriented manufacturing in CIS countries was largely ruled out in CEECs, where it was destroyed by the penetration of more sophisticated forms of business. Further transformations, therefore, await the enterprise spheres in transition economies as they become fully exposed to international development.

SECTION VI

CONCLUSIONS

CHAPTER SIXTEEN

Emerging Varieties of Capitalism

The countries of the former Soviet Union and Eastern Europe underwent enormous changes in their economies after the collapse of Communist power. The process can be characterized as "transition" or "transformation," depending on whether it is seen as a movement toward a defined end result, similar to the advanced market economies of the world, or a process of change without a clear end result. Neither term is ideal. There has been an end result in the development of forms of capitalism and in substantial integration into global economic relationships. However, the end results are diverse and rather different from the advanced market economies that were set up as the examples to aspire to. There was no single post-Communist variety of capitalism.

This chapter brings together the preceding discussions of individual aspects of transition to suggest how the transition economies, after 20 years of systemic change, could be classified in relation to other capitalist economies. It first discusses the extent to which the countries are different from those in the advanced capitalist world and the implication of these differences for characterizing the capitalist diversity in the region. The central topic of such characterization—the different forms of international integration and their internal preconditions—is analyzed in the second section. Finally, we produce a tentative classification made up of five varieties of capitalism that emerged in transition economies, linking the forms of international integration to other key features of these economies, including the nature of property rights (as constituted through the rule of law), the role of the state, and the nature of relations between the state and main economic actors. The five varieties then link into an analysis of the effects of the world financial crisis of 2008 in the final chapter.

VARIETIES OF CAPITALISM AND TRANSITION ECONOMIES

Differences in the kinds of capitalism emerging out of transition should not be surprising. A great deal has been written about differences among the world's most developed market economies, including the important contribution from Hall and Soskice (2001), which focuses on two important types that are broadly based on the United States and Germany. However, the "varieties of capitalism" paradigm that is used to analyze those differences is little help for analyzing the diversity among transition economies.

The explicit aim in much of this existing literature on varieties of capitalism is to find the causes of comparative economic performance. International competitiveness, in effect the dependent variable, is linked to "comparative institutional advantage," the independent variable, which leads to success for different kinds of economic activity. These institutional forms are then classified into a small number of important types. Hall and Soskice (2001) identify the liberal market economies (LME) and coordinated market economies (CME), which are broadly based on the United States and Germany, respectively. They focus on the stability of employment relations, the scope for cooperation between firms, the forms of corporate governance, and, linked to that, the means of raising finance. They thereby aim to explain Germany's success in establishing world leadership in certain kinds of modern products and the success of the United States in a different group of modern products, both characterized by different kinds of innovation processes. Institutional forms thereby help to resolve, in different ways, the basic coordination problems on the level of the firm and thus provide specific comparative advantages underpinning patterns of innovation in respective economies.

Other authors have concentrated on somewhat different themes as key distinguishing features among advanced market economies, including the role of the state in leading economic development and the extent and forms of welfare provision (e.g., Schmidt 2002; Amable 2003; Boyer 2005). It is possible to follow many of these indicators in transition economies, and comparisons have been made on this basis (e.g., Feldmann 2006; Knell and Srholec 2007; Mykhnenko 2007; Buchen 2007). However, these are not the key factors in distinguishing the kinds of capitalism in transition economies. There are four important factors that make a direct application of the established approaches inappropriate.

The first difficulty is in the choice of the dependent variable. For Hall and Soskice, that variable is the ability of a country to reach a leading position in the world in a particular branch of economic activity on the basis of innovation. No transition economy has reached such a position. Instead, they earn the foreign currency with which to pay for imports by exporting less sophisticated products, typically relying on imported technology, and from a variety of other means. The appropriate dependent variable is, therefore, the more general form of international integration, as covered in Chapter 4. Indeed, the attempts to apply the varieties of capitalism framework to the post-Communist context demonstrate that it does not provide a basis for following the key differences in the forms of integration into international economic relations (for an overview, see Drahokoupil [2009]).[1] As shown in Chapter 4, all of the transition economies experienced problems with achieving external balance, and the varied forms of recovery relate to different solutions to the problem of financing the persistent current account deficits, ranging from exports of manufactured goods to exports of natural resources to remittances and foreign aid.

---

[1] A similar critique of the varieties of capitalism framework can be made also for its utility in the context of advanced capitalist countries (e.g., Pontusson 2005; Panitch and Gindin 2005)—a point that became particularly relevant in the context of the global financial crisis.

The second difficulty relates to the independent variable. As previous chapters in this book have demonstrated, themes that dominated in analyzing transition economies differ from those for advanced market economies. More basic issues, ones that appeared to have been resolved and were, therefore, taken for granted in today's most advanced countries, remained important. These include state capacity, the rule of law, a functioning system of corporate governance, a stable financial system, clarity in the ownership of enterprises, and a separation between the spheres of business and politics, leading into the implications of political systems for the behavior of actors in the economic sphere. These issues are broadly assumed to be resolved in mainstream economic theory, and they are also either taken for granted or given little attention in varieties of capitalism literature.

However, they were more problematic in transition economies. Formal rules sometimes appeared to play little role. Where and when they did make a difference, it is important to ask how far they were applied, how far they were distorted by corruption or uncontrolled and unseen links between business and politics, and how far rules and laws were enough to ensure the functioning of a complex economic system. Following these issues requires treading on ground unfamiliar in much of mainstream economics, where it is assumed that rules are followed, that debts are paid, that credits are returned, that depositors can trust a banking system, and that government policies, once decided, will be implemented. Institutionalist writing frequently includes the recognition that informal rules may be as important as formal rules, but that issue is so much more important in transition economies that it points to the need to focus on a different set of themes.

The third difficulty is that institutional preconditions are not the only determinant of forms of international integration. Other determinants include inherited economic structures and the potential they provided. Nor is one form of international integration uniquely associated with one internal institutional framework. Many internal features that do appear in characterizations of the variety of capitalism may play no role as preconditions for the international competitiveness of transition economies. Among these are the scope for new business development, as followed in Chapter 12, and the nature of welfare regimes, followed in Chapter 10. The first of these is important in the Hall and Soskice framework, as it ties in with the forms of innovation in liberal market economies. The second of these is considered in Amable's (2003) analysis. The discussion that follows shows that they often are not directly linked to the forms of integration found in transition economies.

The final difficulty in applying the varieties of capitalism framework to transition economies is that it is built on an assumption of long-term continuity and the permanence of relationships (cf. Crouch 2005). Transition economies were characterized by continual, substantial changes. It is, therefore, difficult to distinguish which features were permanent, or would have lasting consequences, and which were transient.

One important difference between transition economies and the capitalist economies that developed by a process of growth, accumulation, and innovation was that the former were countries in which wealth and productive capacity had already been created within a former economic system. Transition, therefore, created scope for novel forms of wealth accumulation based on gaining control over resources that already existed. From that emerged the Russian oligarchs. Somewhat similar possibilities existed, and still exist, in more mature market economies, but they did not overwhelm the processes of development requiring productive investment, innovation, and the development of normal business practices. The question is whether, in the Russian case, oligarchic capitalism, linked to international integration through commodity exports, became a lasting feature or whether it was just one phase in development that would rapidly be superseded by another, possibly leading Russia toward something more similar to the capitalisms of the most advanced market economies.

This ties in with the assessment of the permanence of political systems. The rise of oligarchic capitalism was closely linked to a political structure based on a president with strong executive autonomy. Different degrees of authoritarian politics in other CIS countries were similarly associated with different forms of linkage between political and economic life, typically—insofar as privatization took place at all—in which selected business leaders could be favored. Changes in the political sphere can, thus, bring substantial changes to economic life, as could be argued for Ukraine after the Orange Revolution, when foreign ownership became more acceptable.

It is much more plausible to assume permanence in political forms and in the direction of development of the relationship between business and politics that have evolved in those countries that joined the European Union. They were committed to following the model of a law-based state, democratic politics, a secure welfare state, and a stable business environment. There were still differences from Western Europe, but there had been considerable convergence toward that general model. Transient elements in the capitalist variety in these countries were, therefore, more likely in the economic sphere alone rather than in the need to disentangle it from political structures.

FORMS OF INTERNATIONAL INTEGRATION AND THEIR PRECONDITIONS

The first step in adapting the varieties of capitalism framework is to distinguish six different forms of international integration, drawing on the analysis of the differences in the current account of the balance of payments and in export structures, presented in Chapter 4 (see Table 4.1 and Figures 4.8 through 4.22, respectively). These are then set against the internal features of individual countries that, it is argued, were their preconditions. These do not provide a basis for pure varieties of capitalism, as every country combined more than one form of international integration. Differences were in the weights of the different forms. There are also differences in the permanence of forms of international integration, some being important for only relatively brief periods. Moreover, while these internal preconditions represent key characteristics of the respective economies, they do not exhaust the important features of individual economies that are analyzed in detail in the preceding chapters. We discuss how they relate together in the five varieties of capitalism in the concluding section.

The important internal preconditions include the inherited economic structure and its level. These constitute a "structural comparative advantage" that played an important role particularly in the countries with similar "generic institutional advantages," as was the case in Eastern Europe (cf. Greskovits 2005). Preconditions also include state capacities, which in turn are related to political forms, and the institutional infrastructure for private business, which goes beyond formal privatization to include social norms and the acceptance of a legal framework. These can be understood as a comparative institutional advantage but of a much more generic nature than the specific institutional advantages analyzed within the varieties of capitalism framework.

Geographical location and a sense of European traditions are linked to all of these points. Specific policies did matter at some points, but it is not a matter of the application of the WC strategy opening the road to success. Choices made in the early 1990s, over the pace of liberalization and stabilization measures and over the speed of privatization, appeared to make less difference by the late 2000s, as long as there had been an opening to international economic contacts. By then, other important policy issues loomed larger, such as the steps taken to attract FDI and policies toward the financial sector that could increase exposure to the financial crisis of 2008.

Export-Oriented FDI in Complex Sectors

The most secure form of international integration, offering the highest incomes, was the export of high-value products into Western Europe, manufactured in branches of large multinational companies.

The internal preconditions for this form of international integration were demanding. Multinational companies required a complex web of links to other organizations; they required an economic environment in which they could guarantee their own operations and in which they could be sure of links to many other firms and to local and central government bodies. Foreign direct investment by MNCs that were aiming to export complex manufactured goods, therefore, required a high level of state capacity and a developed environment for business. All of those were broadly achieved in CEECs, the Baltic republics, and, to a growing extent, southeast Europe. However, none of these countries had the full environment for business in an advanced market economy, including access to large-scale finance for their own firms and to a research base appropriate for systematic innovation activity.

The MNCs were attracted to countries with which they had been in contact in the past, which had heritages of reasonably modern industry, good physical infrastructures, and links to Western Europe. Political stability was important to companies undertaking long-term investment, and the likelihood of EU accession served as a useful stamp of approval. The MNCs needed a secure legal and business environment, giving confidence that contracts would be honored. Policies could also influence the structural comparative advantages to the extent that maintaining industrial bases attracted investors seeking to acquire companies operating in similar activities to their own (cf. Greskovits 2005, 117–19; Kurth 1979, 3–4).

Other policies specifically aimed at attracting FDI also mattered; MNCs were sought out by governments that offered to provide help with infrastructural development, subsidies, and other concessions. Therefore, there had to be a stable state and also one with an agenda for supporting this form of economic development. The MNCs were attracted first to CEECs, and that gave those countries further structural advantages, which became increasingly permanent. Indeed, the dominance of MNCs in determining economic success justified Nölke and Vliegenthart (2009) in proposing the introduction of a third model to the varieties of capitalism framework:

the "dependent market economies," with intrafirm hierarchies within transnational enterprises constituting a distinctive coordination mechanism (cf. King 2007). That is broadly accepted in the following text, although we prefer a different term to characterize these economies to highlight this model's superiority over other forms and the associated potential for economic development.

This type of international integration does not fit into the Hall and Soskice framework. The prominence of foreign ownership means that themes of enterprise finance or corporate governance, or the specific institutional advantages, are of much less relevance and need not be well developed in the transition economy; those issues are resolved by the MNCs in their home bases. Issues of labor stability and training were also less problematic. There was an influence from practices and laws in EU countries, but it was also important that MNCs could offer higher pay and better conditions than was available from domestically owned firms. They could solve their labor problems without the complex institutional forms that had developed in Germany and other EU member countries. It made little difference to them whether they bargained with unions or set pay unilaterally, and practices of incoming MNCs varied in line with their preferences.

This meant that there was more scope for variation between countries and between firms within countries. A supportive framework for new domestic businesses was largely irrelevant to incoming MNCs. Social, and even employment, policies were often not major concerns. Countries could be closer to following a European social model, with significant labor protection, bargaining over wages, and substantial welfare states. Others could favor a minimal welfare state model, as in Slovakia after 2002. It made little difference to the operations of MNCs when they invested in major projects that required a permanent labor force, although it could affect their choice of location for more flexible and potentially short-term investment activities. This contrasts with the Hall and Soskice framework, in which some of these issues appear as primary preconditions for forms of international competitiveness.

Export-Oriented Complex Sectors without FDI

There were very few exceptions to setting integration through MNCs as absolute requirements for integration through exports of machinery-complex products. Indeed, the small number of successful domestically owned and privately owned exporters of these products serves to highlight the difficulties they faced. There was an adequate inherited productive base, but enterprises lacked the means to generate their own innovations and to compete on that basis. They lacked access to established international networks, to established brand names, and to financial resources for investment. A small number of Czech firms, and a significantly larger number of Slovenian firms, survived with their own products in modern sectors, but the trend was either toward outright failure and bankruptcy or toward seeking dependence on established foreign companies that could overcome the weaknesses mentioned previously. State ownership usually led to the same outcome, but there were some exceptions. Russian armament manufacturers were able to retain a position in international markets and to undertake some product development.

A more striking exception was found in Belarus, where exports of vehicles continued on the basis of what is characterized in this text as an order state (Iwasaki 2004), with state ownership of key enterprises and state direction of banks' lending policies. These provided some financial resources and a greater level of managerial stability than in countries where similar enterprises were privatized. They benefited from some international cooperation to gain access to modern technology, but there was also substantial autonomous product development. However, these products were able to compete only in less demanding markets that were not dominated by established MNCs, and it remains to be seen whether that model will prove to be more than transient. Attempts to promote the development of complex sectors in other contexts, as was the case in Uzbekistan, achieved much less impressive results.

Simple Manufacturing Subcontracting to MNCs

The export of garments, footwear, and simpler components depended on subcontracting from MNCs, typically with very precise specifications as to what was required and, in some cases, direct investment. There also had to be an adequate transport and communications infrastructure, but required skill levels were low—all product development took place in a richer country—so that low labor costs were a key attraction. The inherited industrial structure was also important, as it typically provided the productive capacity and labor force that could quickly be adapted to satisfy new orders. Issues of corporate governance or privatization policies were of little significance to the foreign company, but the MNC did need a secure enough legal framework to give it confidence that contracts would be honored.

This form of integration was important in CEECs in the early 1990s and in SEECs and the Baltic republics in later years. It also spread to lower-income countries, including CARs, but on a very small scale. Very low wage levels were not enough to attract MNCs when other internal preconditions were missing and when long distances added to transport costs. Kyrgyzstan appeared to do slightly better than other CARs, exporting some simpler garments to Western Europe. It is significant that Uzbekistan, despite its low wages, cotton production, and some inherited industrial capacity, made very little headway. In that case, the order state could prevent collapse and ensure continued production of raw materials, but it appeared less appropriate where contacts with, and confidence of, foreign MNCs were required.

In CEECs, this form of integration appeared to be a temporary phase. Countries typically moved through it fairly quickly and on to exporting more sophisticated products. This is not surprising, as the institutional preconditions are not that different from those required for the first form of international integration just covered. Once foreign companies had confidence in those countries, they took advantage of low wage levels by undertaking large-scale investment. However, that lead established by CEECs may limit the scope for similar investment in SEECs and other transition economies, meaning that they remain for longer as exporters of simpler manufactured goods.

Commodity Exports

Commodity exports were important in CEECs in the early years but became less important as inward investment provided a new export potential. They played some role across many more countries but were most important for the oil-exporting countries and for Ukraine, a steel and chemicals exporter. These products provide less stable incomes than high-quality manufactured goods and generally also lower incomes, albeit with oil and natural gas something of an exception. Export activity was built from industries inherited from the past, and the old enterprises often needed little by way of transformation. Simple, homogeneous products could be exported, even when produced from outdated technology.

Exporting raw materials and semimanufactures, therefore, required a less sophisticated business environment. This was compatible with lower levels of state capacity and with institutional environments that did not provide a basis for secure links between enterprises, much less for the development of newer innovative firms. The themes of employment relations, links between firms, or the development of a finance sector were, therefore, not important to international integration. Exporting firms could prosper in the absence of a stable legal and business environment, as long as they were favored by those with political power.

There are differences between oil and gas exporters and other commodity exporters, owing to the exceptionally high revenues and low employment needs of the former. That makes oil and gas exporting even more compatible with a weak environment for the rest of the economy. Exporters can create their own physical infrastructure, raise capital from abroad, and rely on very limited contacts to local businesses. Preconditions for this, therefore, have no direct implications for labor relations, welfare provision, and the environment for business overall. Oil and gas exporting is, therefore, compatible with an authoritarian regime that need not listen to voices from society or promote other forms of economic development. This potential limitation to other forms of growth means that domination of commodity exports need not be a transient feature of international integration.

Dependence on Remittances and Aid

The fifth form of international integration is dependence on remittances, aid, and borrowing from IFIs to compensate for often substantial trade deficits. These were common methods for the lowest-income countries. The enterprise sphere failed to provide competitive exports and also to compete with imports. Integration into the world economy was, therefore, by citizens working in other countries—often Russia and, in some cases, Central or Western Europe—and sending earnings home.

A remittance-based economy is compatible with a very low level of internal institutional development. It depends on employment conditions in another country, which implies no internal institutional prerequisites. Nothing is needed beyond transportation links to get to a country offering employment and to a bank to convert earnings into a local currency. If that brings back enough earnings to significantly increase domestic demand, then it can be a stimulus to wider economic growth, but the forms of business activity that develop can be very basic. It was a long road from this to a modern, mature market economy. Dependence on remittances creates no basis for other forms of international integration. When remittances fail due to lower demand for labor in other countries, the only remaining options are international aid or poverty.

Dependence on Financialized Growth

International integration by foreign borrowing and financial inflows to support private-sector activity, including consumption and imports, covered the deficits on many countries' current accounts, though this was never the only form of integration. Nevertheless, it became an important driver for economic development in the years up to 2008.

The most basic indicator for financialized growth is the surplus on the financial account, excluding the contribution of FDI. This distinction is important partly because FDI was less likely to be withdrawn and also because FDI promoted economic development. A large part of this was in export-oriented manufacturing in Eastern Europe and in raw materials in CIS countries and thereby contributed to export growth. Other financial inflows were usually promoting development that brought no future benefits for the balance of payments.

Table 16.1 shows the breakdown by countries, grouping them in the order used in Chapter 4. In a very few cases, these financial inflows were of little relevance. This includes the Czech Republic, Slovakia, and, to a lesser extent, Poland, countries in which, as shown in Table 14.2, bank deposits were largely adequate to cover the demand for credits. For another group of middle- and higher-income countries—spanning geographical areas and export structures to include Hungary, Belarus, Ukraine, and Kazakhstan—they were more important. A number of low-income countries also depended significantly on financial inflows, including Armenia, Georgia, Tajikistan, and Kyrgyzstan, but much of this came in the form of official aid, with rather different implications for economic development. Russia was unique among countries, with a significant financial inflow alongside substantial current account surpluses. This was an unusual feature of its form of oligarchic capitalism. Private businesses were keen to borrow from abroad to finance growth by acquisitions while the state was accumulating reserves from export revenues.

A first prerequisite for financialized growth was the interest of lenders, and that increased with the abundance of liquidity in the world. This often entered the transition economies through branches of foreign-owned banks, seeking what they believed were reliable and lucrative credit opportunities. That implied an attractive enough institutional environment in the transition economy, often including light regulation and low taxes. Fixed exchange rates guaranteeing macroeconomic restriction and real exchange rate appreciation, capital account liberalization, light-to-no-touch regulation of lending, and low-to-zero taxation on capital gains (including housing market speculation) were particularly favorable to financialized development. Bankers also judged countries on their political reputations, and inflows clearly escalated in the Baltic republics and SEECs around the time of EU accession, and they also increased to Ukraine and Belarus, as those countries' standing improved in the West.

A second prerequisite—or rather a precondition, as it was hardly a positive feature—was an inadequate domestic deposit base. This could be seen as an institutional failure rather than a positive institutional precondition, as it followed from the low level of willingness from domestic households to save money in financial

TABLE 16.1 **Surpluses on the financial account, including and excluding the contribution from FDI, as a percentage of GDP**

	Financial account, total			Financial account without FDI		
	2002	2006	2007	2002	2006	2007
Czech Republic	14.1	3.0	2.8	3.1	0.1	−1.7
Hungary	3.9	10.7	7.3	−0.2	9.7	3.9
Poland	3.6	3.8	9.4	1.7	0.7	5.1
Slovakia	15.1	1.7	8.4	3.3	−3.8	4.8
Slovenia	9.1	−0.3	5.7	2.2	0.3	5.9
Bulgaria	22.5	28.1	47.1	16.9	4.2	18.2
Estonia	10.3	18.1	16.7	8.2	14.0	11.4
Latvia	7.4	30.8	24.6	4.7	23.3	17.9
Lithuania	7.4	15.5	16.1	2.5	10.3	12.5
Romania	8.9	15.4	17.7	6.4	6.5	11.8
Bosnia and Herzegovina	8.9	10.1	14.4	4.6	4.3	0.6
Croatia	10.3	13.1	11.2	8.2	6.6	3.2
Macedonia	6.6	6.8	6.0	3.8	0.2	1.9
Serbia			18.8			21.1
Russia	0.6	0.3	7.4	0.8	−0.4	6.7
Kazakhstan	5.5	20.0	8.0	−3.3	11.7	0.4
Belarus	5.2	4.6	11.6	2.1	3.6	7.7
Ukraine	−2.5	3.6	10.7	−4.2	−1.7	4.2
Albania	4.8	5.8	6.8	1.8	2.3	2.6
Armenia	6.2	6.8	10.7	1.5	−0.2	3.3
Georgia	0.4	17.3	21.6	−4.2	3.5	5.3
Kyrgyzstan	6.9	11.9	9.3	6.6	5.5	3.8
Moldova	1.2	10.5	22.2	−3.8	3.2	11.2
Tajikistan	6.0	9.8	21.9	3.0	−2.2	12.2

Source: Calculated from the IMF International Financial Statistics database, available at http://www .imfstatistics.org/imf/.

institutions. Only in some CEECs, following the long-term development of banking systems, were domestic deposits at a high enough level to cover the demand for credits. These countries were, therefore, not affected by financialized development. As shown in Table 16.2, the gap was greatest in the Baltic republics and was also high in Ukraine and Belarus. The order state in Belarus could not ensure a balance between domestic savings and the demand for credits, as it was in fact associated with an extremely low level of deposits.

A third prerequisite was a demand for credits from the domestic economy. Inflows generally went to private businesses and to households and are associated with small-state liberal policies as much as with welfare spending. The governments did not seem to see a danger in the process and often actively encouraged inflows and the expansion of credit. In Hungary, part of the inflow financed state budget deficits,

TABLE 16.2 Domestic credit

	Domestic credit (percentage of GDP)			Loan-deposit ratio	Domestic credit to households (percentage of GDP)		Mortgages (percentage of domestic credit to households)	
	2000	2007	2008 (Q1)	2009	2002	2007	2002	2007
Czech Republic	49.4	52.9	51.1	0.8	7.3	20.1	41.1	62.2
Hungary	53.5	74.4	72.9	1.4	7.4	21.6	55.4	75.9
Poland	34.4	46.6	46.0	1.1	9.4	20.0	25.5	49.5
Slovakia	56.6	51.6	48.2		5.5	16.3	18.2	27.6
Slovenia	8.9	79.0			10.5	19.2	19.2	32.3
Bulgaria	17.8	59.2	53.4	1.3	3.7	23.0		45.2
Estonia	34.9	95.1	90.4	2.1	10.6	43.3	51.9	87.1
Latvia	23.3	94.8	86.0	2.8	7.3	42.7	56.2	78.9
Lithuania	15.2	60.2	55.7	2.0	2.4	24.4	79.2	70.5
Romania	14.0	35.7	31.9	1.3		17.7		7.9
Bosnia and Herzegovina	5.6	50.6			11.0	26.2		
Croatia	47.2	82.9	76.6	1.1	23.8	41.1	28.6	39.9
Macedonia, FYR	10.5	36.8			2.4	13.5		19.3
Serbia	7.6	35.3				12.6		30.2
Azerbaijan	9.6	18.2	10.7		1.4	5.8		12.1
Kazakhstan	12.3	41.0	30.1	1.7	1.6	17.4	12.5	28.2
Russia	24.7	25.2	19.5	1.3	1.0	9.0		21.1
Belarus	19.2	27.2	21.6	1.5[a]	1.8	8.2	88.9	54.9
Ukraine	37.9	48.7	44.4	2.0	1.6	22.5	88.9	28.9
Albania	3.0	28.9				10.6		
Armenia	11.5	12.1	11.2		1.5	7.1		23.9
Georgia	21.6	31.6	29.6		3.0	8.8	16.7	29.5
Kyrgyzstan	12.2	14.2			0.3	3.3		72.7
Moldova	25.2	40.2	36.3		0.5	5.5	180.0	72.7
Mongolia		32.4				18.1		17.7
Tajikistan	11.3	29.7				3.6		

Source: IMF (2008b), Moody's (2008), EBRD (2009), and author's own calculations.

Note: Domestic credit to households is the ratio of outstanding bank credit to households, at end-of-year, to GDP; mortgage lending is the ratio of mortgage lending to households, at end-of-year, to GDP; asset share of foreign-owned banks is the share of total bank sector assets in banks with foreign ownership exceeding 50 percent, end-of-year. Q1 = first quarter.

[a] Data are for 2007 from Raiffeisen Research staff (personal communication, October 20, 2009).

which reflected high social spending as parties competed through welfare spending. A similar political phenomenon in Ukraine followed the so-called Orange Revolution of 2004 and led to higher consumer spending and hence current account deficits that were covered by financial inflows. The start to serious competition between parties in Serbia's political system after 2000 led to similar consequences.

Demand for credits came in Hungary as domestically owned businesses grew and were considered creditworthy and as households felt secure enough to take out loans for house purchases. The latter trend was even more important in the Baltic republics and SEECs, and in these countries, it led to pressure on real estate prices, in turn increasing the demand for credits. Financialized growth thereby escalated in the years up to 2008 in those countries that had the preconditions just listed and that lacked sound export structures and domestic deposit bases. This, then, was a transient phase that ended with the world financial crisis, leaving a number of countries with uncertain futures.

FIVE VARIETIES OF CAPITALISM IN TRANSITION ECONOMIES

These six forms of international integration provide a partial basis for defining the types of capitalism in transition economies. It is partial, as a number of key features characterizing a political economy are not important as preconditions for forms of international integration. It is also necessary to reiterate the caveat that each country had a mix of different forms of integration, in some cases including a contribution from every one of them. Nevertheless, by combining forms of integration and key internal features such as the nature of property rights, the role of the state, and the nature of the relation between the state and main economic actors, an approximate classification into five types can be made. In some cases, there is overlap between them, and none is fixed. All are, to varying extents, in a process of change. The suggested varieties are listed next.

The first are *FDI-based (second-rank) market economies*. This characterizes the CEECs, distinguished by democratic political systems, integration into the European Union, and export structures increasingly built around manufactured goods produced by foreign-owned MNCs. These economies developed complex export structures, but they had only a second-rank position in international production networks. Nevertheless, there was a considerable potential for upgrading and development, making this variety more promising than other outcomes of transition. There was also flexibility of other features, with a range from quite substantial labor protection and welfare provision to a more neoliberal approach. Although these countries lacked the business infrastructure for high-level innovations, they did have sound environments for other domestic business development. Hungary's involvement in financialized growth did not reflect weakness of export structures but rather peculiarities of its political system.

The second type of capitalism is found in *peripheral market economies*. This applies to SEECs and the Baltic republics, although they may be joined by others, and some of them may develop toward the first category. Estonia, for instance, ranked among the first group in terms of its per capita GDP, but its export structure and reliance on financialized development puts it, on balance, into the peripheral group. Peripheral market economies had democratic political systems and basic legal and institutional conditions for business, but they relied on less stable manufactured-goods exports. Weakly developed domestic economies were also often associated with financialized growth and significant dependence on remittances. They were thus less equipped to withstand external shocks. The forms of economic development fit best with highly liberalized market conditions, which are likely to lead to a good reputation in international financial circles. That is also often associated with low levels of welfare provision. It should mean there were light restrictions on setting up new businesses, but the numbers were actually low relative to CEECs.

The third type is *oligarchic or clientelistic capitalism.* These terms apply to much of the CIS. Neither is ideal, and one seems more appropriate for some countries and the other for other countries. This group was characterized by relatively authoritarian political systems and a closer merging of business and politics than in the previous two groups. Social and employment protection and an environment for dynamic new businesses were generally very weakly developed, not because they would harm the forms of international integration that dominate but because they were irrelevant to those forms.

There clearly was evolution in all CIS countries. The Russian case is the best documented, as summarized in Chapter 8. Lawlessness and domination by a few flamboyant oligarchs gave way to a more ordered structure that included many new business leaders, often with closer links to regional- than federal-level politicians. However, some key features remained unchanged. Under Putin, the wealth of the oligarchs was confirmed, but only by negotiation between business and political leaders. It continued to lack the solid backing of an independent legal system, and, as Putin was able to demonstrate, the state could eliminate individual business leaders when it so wished. Wealth was formally in private hands, but it was there for only as long as the business leaders were favored by political leaders.

Despite the apparent strengthening of the Russian state, the label of "state capitalism" is not appropriate. As explained in Chapter 8, political leaders were also limited in how far they could exercise more detailed power over business and were tied by the weak development of other sources of political support to particular powerful business leaders. In turn, business leaders sought political backing, partly to cement their property rights, partly to protect monopoly positions, and partly also for direct benefits through subsidies or state contracts.

Even the major state-owned firms often behaved like Russia's private businesses, creating foreign-trading subsidiaries and using them to earn the profits from exports that could then be transferred into the hands of private individuals. Such transfers were simpler in Kazakhstan and some other CIS countries with more authoritarian regimes, where the state very clearly served as a source of private income for select individuals.

Oligarchic capitalism was characterized by low investment levels, particularly long-term investment levels—businesses preferred to take their wealth abroad—and by a poor environment for other new businesses. Inward investment was at times also opposed by established businesses that feared competition. Therefore, there were forces locking in the dependence on raw material exports and restricting the development toward other forms of international integration.

Upgrading export profiles depended on improving the environment for development of a wide range of businesses, a clear weakness in Russia and other CIS countries (as outlined in Chapter 12). That, in turn, depended on consolidating state-business relationships through regularized rules and laws to replace informal understandings between a few political and business leaders. Evolution in that direction depended on political development. Without strong and varied interest representation and an active political life and civil society, the established concentrations of wealth could be expected to retain enormous power and influence, even within formally democratic systems and even when formal laws exist to control them.

The fourth type of capitalism is found in *order states*. This term applies to the CIS countries that underwent the most limited reforms. Classifying them as capitalist at all can be questioned, but they clearly underwent substantial transformations since 1989, as indicated by the degrees of integration into the global economy, the use of a price mechanism and prices at least close to the world level, and the scope for private enterprise, even though substantial state ownership remained. They were characterized by authoritarian political systems that also dominated in the main economic decisions. International integration depended on state support for export either of manufactured goods or of commodities. The environment for business from outside the state sector was poor. The authoritarian and arbitrary states and the low levels of development of finance made the growth of new businesses difficult. Welfare provision reflected continuity with the past, leading to relatively high levels of public spending. This distinguished them from many other CIS countries, in which welfare provision was drastically reduced in the turmoil of the early 1990s. High spending in order states helped secure the necessary popular backing for political survival of the authoritarian regimes.

Finally, the fifth are *remittance- and aid-based economies*. This applied to a number of low-income countries in the CIS and Eastern Europe. It was a weak base for future development. Moving into another group, the most likely being the peripheral market economy, depended on an adequate environment for business and probably also a geographical location and level of infrastructure that was attractive for subcontracting from MNCs. Much of this was missing, and much of domestic business activity remained at the level of small-scale trading.

The permanence and viability of these capitalist varieties that emerged in transition economies was severely tested by the financial crisis of 2008. That is analyzed in the next chapter, which concludes by using the effects of the crisis to point to a final verdict on transition, or at least on its outcomes up to early 2010.

CHAPTER SEVENTEEN

The Financial Crisis and a Verdict on Transition

The world financial crisis that began in 2008 affected countries in different ways, depending on their forms of international integration (on its origins, see IMF [2009b, 2009f], Wade [2008, 2009], J. Friedman [2009], and Stiglitz [2009]). The impact of the crisis highlights vulnerabilities and strengths of the different forms of growth and international integration that evolved in the region.

The first IMF predictions for the world economy pointed to a relatively limited period of economic decline, but they were accompanied by warnings that the area of uncertainty was large and that there could be more prolonged and severe depression with more serious consequences for individual countries. A major reason for pessimism was the observation that previous financial and banking crises in individual countries tended to be long lasting, with recovery dependent on strong demand from the outside—in other words, from the rest of the world (IMF 2009f; see also Reinhart and Rogoff [2008]). Levels of credit have tended to recover very slowly. Experience of crises precipitated by unsound lending in transition economies was fully consistent with that (as discussed in Chapter 13), as credits relative to GDP always grew slowly, at least when based on domestic deposit bases, and recovered only gradually from periodic crises. The implication in the context of a world downturn is that, as demand fell in almost all parts of the world, recovery based on financial and credit systems would be very gradual. Indeed, the complexity of the effects of the initial financial difficulties points to a strengthening of forces leading toward deeper depression rather than to an awakening of forces for recovery.

FOUR STAGES OF CRISIS

The approach here uses an interpretation of the effects of crisis divided into four stages, which are then dealt with separately to discuss their implications in the transition economies. In some countries, they are easily separable and follow in sequence; in others, the separation is less clear.

The first stage was the "credit crunch," the crisis in banks caused by unsound lending to households. This began in the finance sector in the United States and spread around the world, first through the interlinking of financial systems and then, thanks to opaque interlinkages, through new forms of financial instruments. The credit crunch in the United States began to unfold in July 2007, but the decisive break came in mid-September 2008 when, following the collapse of the U.S. banks Washington Mutual and Lehman Brothers, institutions became very reluctant to trust, and hence lend to, each other. The effects of this stage were then spread rapidly around the world to countries dependent on capital inflows.

The second stage, the "demand slump," was an extension of the financial crisis into reduced demand for products that were dependent on credit—especially housing, construction, motor vehicles, and other consumer durables. Some other sectors could stand up reasonably well, such as food and small-scale services. State provision also continued largely unaffected, even with higher spending, in some cases, as public services bore the costs of recession or as governments deliberately sought to generate fiscal stimuli. For raw materials and semimanufactures, the effect of lower demand was often a very substantial fall in price from July 2008, provoked by a much smaller drop in demand in physical terms. Revenues to firms and countries dependent on these sectors were, therefore, hit very hard. For more sophisticated manufactured goods, the effect was a fall in quantities that could be sold, albeit without so great a drop in prices.

The third stage was driven by pressure for further depression, following from the effects of the previous two stages. Standard Keynesian theories lead to an expectation of a downward multiplier, as lower demand for products leads to lower employment and incomes and hence a further decline in demand. In the post-2008 context, the pressures for further depression were more complicated and varied than this simple framework would suggest. Apart from the simple multiplier effect, lower sales could also limit the ability of businesses and households to repay loans, providing a further threat to the stability of the financial system. Government policies in many countries were intended to counter this threat, supporting the banking system, encouraging the continuation of new credits, and stimulating output through expansionary stimuli. The third stage also included some diverse international effects. Countries previously dependent on financial inflows were threatened by pressures for devaluation, which, in some cases, had very serious implications. Countries heavily dependent on FDI faced a threat, should that source of financial inflow cease. Countries dependent on remittances could lose that source of foreign currency if employment opportunities in other countries dried up.

The fourth stage, the "fiscal" and/or "solvency crisis," is in some cases effectively a continuation of stage 1, but even those not affected at the start were at least potentially at risk here. Governments can be expected to have to accept budget deficits through a period of depression, reflecting lower tax revenues and the continuation of state spending. The collapse of financialized growth was often also associated with banking crises, with public budgets bearing considerable costs for bailouts. The impact of the crisis on households and businesses is thereby transferred into a potential crisis for state finance. That is manageable, provided recovery is rapid, but cannot continue indefinitely. At some point, it could become difficult, and ultimately even impossible, to continue borrowing to cover those deficits. An internal fiscal crisis can then escalate into a crisis of international solvency for individual countries. This was the case for some countries during the first stage. It was manageable when only a few countries were affected and the IMF was willing and able to help. However, a prolonged period of economic depression could make this much more difficult, and the possibility of this stage serves as a warning against running high budget deficits over a number of years. This is, therefore, an ever-present constraint on policy options and a source of pressure for lower demand levels over quite a long time period.

STAGE 1: THE CREDIT CRUNCH

The credit crunch hit countries where the private-sector actors and/or the governments needed to raise capital to refinance their debt. The drying up of global liquidity led to major problems in the financialized regimes, where persistent current account deficits were financed by foreign credits. In such a context, the drop in financial inflows translated into a contraction of domestic consumer demand, based on borrowing abroad, and to a collapse of real estate prices and, thus, the construction sector. As shown later in Table 17.5, GDP in the financialized economies was already falling in the last quarter of 2008 (see also Table A.2). The biggest output contractions were initially experienced in Latvia, Ukraine, and Estonia. Refinancing problems also led a number of countries to seek emergency financing from the IMF and, in the CIS context, from Russia. This gave the IMF significant power through its conditionalities, discussed in Box 17.1, and it lent a geopolitical leverage to Russia.

The shock of the Lehman bank collapse triggered capital flight from the region, with the volume of loans reducing sharply worldwide and with lending shifting to "developed markets" (EBRD 2009, 48–50). In Kazakhstan and the Baltic republics, borrowing booms and capital inflows had already peaked in June 2007, even before the onset of the global crisis (8, 47), reflecting a degree of external concern over the viability of financialized growth in these countries. With banks dependent on funding from international markets, Kazakhstan was the first transition country to be directly affected by the crisis, as the cross-border credit flows and domestic credit plummeted from August 2007. As foreign inflows stalled or fell, domestic credit began to decline in Bulgaria, Romania, Russia, and Slovenia from the fourth quarter of 2007. In Russia, capital flows began to reverse in the summer of 2008, as armed conflict with Georgia and apparent violation of shareholders rights further weakened investors' confidence. Ukraine was shut out of international markets in September 2008, with domestic lending effectively frozen.

Countries that were in trouble were frequently those with long histories of building up international debt, meaning that they had failed to build an export potential to finance growth in domestic consumption, and of banking systems that consistently failed to match the growth in credits by a growth in deposits, a key issue outlined in Chapter 13. Table 17.1 shows the overall debt levels in 2008, with high figures in a number of countries that were to prove especially vulnerable (such as Hungary and the Baltic republics), but also in some that were in less danger—notably Slovenia. Countries with lower debt levels include some with higher incomes—the CEECs apart from Hungary—some that had not felt the need to borrow—such as Azerbaijan—and a number of lower-income countries that were less trusted internationally and, therefore, had less chance to borrow and to run into debt.

There were also differences in who had borrowed. Governments were, in all cases for which data are available, less important than the private sector. The

TABLE 17.1   **External debt and its structure as a percentage of GDP**

	2008 Total[a]	2008 (Q3)			
		Total	Government	Total private	Of which banks
Czech Republic	42.0[b]	36.2	8.7	27.5	12.8
Hungary	113.5	87.4	32.6	54.8	38.1
Poland	46.0	39.5	15.1	24.5	10.9
Slovakia	53.3	42.7	11.5	31.2	18.9
Slovenia	101.1	84.0	10.0	73.9	49.3
Bulgaria	103.5	71.4	8.3	63.1	27.1
Estonia	115.7	94.7	2.9	91.9	64.3
Latvia	124.2	118.3	6.2	112.1	84.9
Lithuania	68.7	65.0	9.9	55.2	37.2
Romania	35.4				
Bosnia and Herzegovina	43.6				
Croatia	82.7	77.4	17.0	60.5	19.6
Macedonia, FYR	49.1				
Montenegro	15.1				
Serbia	60.6				
Azerbaijan	13.8				
Kazakhstan	79.8				
Russia[c]	36.0	31.6	2.1	29.5	12.5
Turkmenistan[d]	7.7				
Belarus	24.6	24.0	3.9	20.1	5.6
Ukraine	57.3	59.9	8.4	51.5	25.1
Uzbekistan	13.6				
Albania	20.4				
Armenia[c]	23.3				
Georgia	35.6				
Kyrgyzstan	45.7				
Moldova	68.2				
Tajikistan	43.5				

Source: OTP Bank Hungary.

Note: Q3 = third quarter.

[a]Data are from EBRD economic statistics and forecasts, available at http://www.ebrd.com/country/sector/econo/stats/index.htm.

[b]Data are from Czech National Bank statistics, available at www.cnb.cz.

[c]Data are for 2007.

[d]Data are for 2006.

largest government share was for Hungary and the private sector was particularly dominant in the Baltic republics. Banks played an unusually important role in those countries. It was not crucial that they were foreign owned as the growth of credit was less marked in some other countries with foreign-owned banks, such as the Czech

Republic, and quite high in cases where there was substantial domestic ownership of banking, as in Slovenia.

However, total levels of debt are not a precise indicator of vulnerability. Liquidity problems depended on the pattern of debt maturities, which, in a few cases, led to dangers for countries with relatively low debt levels, as was the case in Belarus, following the escalation of capital inflows shown in the data on countries' financial accounts in Table 16.1. Table 17.2 provides an overview of the maturity imbalances and, thus, helps to identify countries with refinancing needs.

There are different ways of expressing the extent of difficulties that a country may face with repaying its debts. The first column in Table 17.2 shows the ratio of external debt to exports. This is a general indicator of how much has been borrowed relative to the means to earn foreign currency. However, that can be deceptive as it takes no account of exactly when debts need to be repaid. The column showing the ratio of short-term debt to foreign-exchange reserves gives an indication of whether substantial repayments are imminent that may strain a country's available resources. Debt refinancing needs, shown in the next column in Table 17.2, show the new loans needed to replace existing debt and are an alternative indicator of the most immediate problems that countries may face. This highlights difficulties for the Baltic republics, Hungary, and Belarus, the last of these suffering despite the low level of total debt because so much was due for repayment.

The data in Table 17.2 suggest that Russia was in a very sound position, given the size of its state reserves accumulated during the oil boom. The Russian state could act as a source of emergency financing for other CIS states. However, even these aggregate figures provide only a partial picture. The actual problems reflected the balance sheet situation of individual actors as much as they did economies as a whole. The credit crunch represented a major problem for Russian banks and businesses that had relied extensively on foreign financing. As indicated in Table 16.2, the level of indebtedness of the Russian private sector was remarkably low in relative terms, but it had been increasing very rapidly and was linked to financial inflows from outside the country, which, as implied by the data on countries' financial accounts in Table 16.1, had become very important by 2007. Refinancing of the short-term liabilities that were included here represented a major problem (Malle 2009, 258). The private-capital outflow in the fourth quarter of 2008 was largest in Russia ($130 billion), both in absolute terms and relative to GDP. Attempts to defend the currency led to major depletions of reserves, with losses exceeding $200 billion between September 2008 and January 2009 (EBRD 2009, 47). The state used its reserves to help the private sector cope with its liquidity problems, through debt-equity swaps, leading to scope for further subordination of the private sector to the state.

The ending of financial inflows across transition economies raised further difficulties from devaluations in countries with floating exchange rates. Among those hit the most, the national currency lost between October 2008 and March 2009 about 50 percent of its value in Ukraine, 30 percent in Poland, 25 percent in Russia, and more than 20 percent in Hungary. This exacerbated difficulties in debt refinancing. Cumulative losses to nonbank enterprises, households, and the government from devaluation between October 2008 and March 2009 amounted to 18 percent of GDP in Hungary and 8 percent in Poland (Auer and Wehrmuller 2009). Slovakia and Slovenia, countries that had adopted the euro, were protected from these devaluation

TABLE 17.2   Solvency risks and maturity structures

	Ratio of external debt to exports (%) 2008	Ratio of short-term debt to foreign-exchange reserves (%)[a] 2008	Debt refinancing needs (percentage of reserves)[b] 2009
Czech Republic		113	89
Hungary	138.7	177	101
Poland	133.9	124	141
Slovakia	67.0	137	
Slovenia	147.6		
Bulgaria	168.8	112	132
Estonia	151.7	358	346
Latvia	298.0	312	331
Lithuania	113.5	159	204
Romania	136.1	89	127
Bosnia and Herzegovina	113.5		
Croatia	214.5	87	136
Macedonia, FYR	102.4		
Montenegro	29.7		
Serbia	204.9		
Azerbaijan	20.2		
Kazakhstan	138.8		82
Russia	118.5		34
Turkmenistan	10.7[c]		
Belarus	39.7		150+
Ukraine	120.6		117
Uzbekistan	32.1		
Albania	73.9		
Armenia	123.8[d]		
Georgia	127.7		
Kyrgyzstan	73.7		
Moldova	165.3		
Tajikistan	274.6		

Source: IMF (2008b) and Moody's (2007); EBRD (2008), in Conolly (2009).

[a]Data are from Raiffeisen Research staff (personal communication, October 20, 2009) and central banks. Short-term debt is any debt that is due within one year. It is measured on the remaining maturity basis by adding the value of outstanding short-term external debt to the value of outstanding long-term external debt due to be paid in one year or less.

[b]Data are from IMF (2009b).

[c]Data are for 2006.

[d]Data are for 2007.

shocks but were at least potentially threatened by the decrease of cost competitiveness due to the significant appreciation relative to their competitors in Eastern Europe; evidence in the next section does not demonstrate any such effect in the short time period that could be followed.

Devaluation was particularly painful for some actors in countries with high shares of foreign currency loans, as shown in Table 17.3. The extent of private sector borrowing in foreign currency is indicated in the first columns which show exceptionally high levels in Baltic republics and also quite high levels in most other countries listed. Russia and the Czech Republic stood out as countries with low shares of loans in foreign currency.

The growth in foreign currency loans was a feature of the forms of integration into international financial systems in many transition economies. In most cases it was associated with high involvement of Western European banks that financed a large

TABLE 17.3   Loans in foreign currency as a percentage of total loans

	Loans in foreign currency (percentage of total bank loans)			
	2003	2006	2007	2008
Czech Republic	13.5	13.6	13.0	14.1
Hungary	25.0	43.6	52.4	63.8
Poland	30.3	27.1	24.4	34.3
Slovakia	20.3	22.0	23.6	21.8
Slovenia[a]	25.6	55.4	9.6	
Bulgaria	43.6	45.7	50.6	57.2
Estonia			80.0	85.3[e]
Latvia		70.0[c]	80+[d]	89.3[e]
Lithuania			50+	64.0[e]
Romania	45.0	47.3	54.3	57.8
Bosnia and Herzegovina		5.7	5.7	5.5
Croatia		69.5	59.9	63.8
Serbia	37.9	12.0	8.0	7.1
Kazakhstan	55.5	48.4	42.7	43.6[e]
Russia	33.8	28.7	25.2	32.0
Belarus	50.4	33.8	41.5	31.9
Ukraine	41.7	49.5	49.9	59.1
Albania			70.0	
Georgia			60+	

Source: Raiffeisen Research (2008, 2009); data shown in italics are estimates from EBRD (2008).

[a]Slovenia joined the Eurozone on 1 January 2007 so that loans previously denominated in foreign currency were then counted as domestic currency.

[b]Data are from Moody's (2008, 92–98).

[c]Data are from the *Vienna Institute Monthly Report*, no. 4/2007.

[d]Data are from Fitch Ratings.

[e]IMF data

part of foreign-currency lending (Bakker and Gulde 2010). Foreign-owned banks offered substantially higher interest rates on credits in domestic currencies, thereby encouraging businesses and households to take out loans in foreign currency. The banks thereby avoided any risk from currency devaluation. That was not an important consideration where credits were covered by a domestic deposit base, as in the Czech Republic and Slovakia, where there was little difference in interest rates. The data in Table 17.3 indicate that it was much more important in Hungary, the Baltic republics, and southeastern Europe. Credits in foreign currency in these countries were partly balanced by foreign currency deposits, but that did not resolve the extreme difficulties faced by debtors, should the currency devalue. The implications of this are developed further in a subsequent section.

Thus, the first stage had varying effects on transition economies depending on their forms of vulnerability to the external shock. For many of the worst affected, there was access to help from the IMF (Box 17.1), but that in turn was accompanied by conditions that led to further reductions in internal demand levels that had repercussions for the subsequent effects of the crisis in individual countries.

Box 17.1   IMF and the financial crisis

The IMF played a major role in providing emergency financing to countries hit by the financial crisis, with lending commitments in the emerging markets reaching a record level of more than $160 billion by August 2009. With 13 transition economies signing up for some form of IMF-administered program of assistance, the crisis brought the IMF back into the region. The IMF's standby arrangements, such as those implemented in transition economies in the 1990s, had been associated with one-size-fits-all conditionalities that emphasized macroeconomic restriction, often enforcing cuts in public spending.

The IMF claimed to have changed its approach in the context of the global financial crisis, overhauling its general lending framework to become more flexible and tailoring loan terms to suit country needs, putting the emphasis on social protection for the most vulnerable through social safety nets, and streamlining loan conditions, with more flexibility on fiscal policy and inflation (IMF 2009a, 2009d). The IMF became a strong supporter of government fiscal stimuli and expansionary monetary policies implemented in the European Union and the United States to counteract the world recession (2008a). It also introduced a new lending instrument, the conditionality-free and unphased flexible credit line for "well-run emerging market economies" (2009a, 1), which was approved for Colombia, Mexico, and Poland, with credits totaling $78 billion. In its review of crisis programs, the IMF concluded that fiscal policy was seen as "the main countercyclical instrument" (2009e, 14). However, critics have argued that the actual conditions enforced within the standby arrangements across the world were procyclical in their effects, aiming to reduce fiscal deficits and/or increase interest rates during a recession or significant slowdown (Weisbrot et al. 2009).

Table 17.4 provides an overview of IMF agreements of assistance in transition countries. In EU member states and accession countries, the European Commission

TABLE 17.4 IMF agreements in the aftermath of the 2008 crisis

Approval	Country	Facility	Duration	Amount of arrangement (millions $)				Balance drawn as of 8/6/2009	Estimated impact of fiscal measures		Impact of monetary policy measures	Conditionalities Notes
				IMF	EU	WB	Other		CEPR	IMF		
September 15, 2008	Georgia	SBA	32	1,172	184	328	606	452	E	E	E	Addresses capital flight after the August 2008 conflict in South Ossetia; social spending scheduled to increase from 7.2% of GDP to 8.2% in 2009 and 8.3% in 2010, but this will represent declines in real terms, as GDP is expected to fall by 4% in 2010.
November 5, 2008	Ukraine	SBA	24	17,253	1,000	1,750	1,250	10,979	C	C	C	Utilization of a flexible exchange rate regime; bank recapitalization; increase in bank deposit insurance.
November 6, 2008	Hungary	SBA	17	16,529	8,400	1,300	0	11,900	C	C	C	Focuses on public–deficit reduction.
December 10, 2008	Kyrgyzstan	ESF		100					E		C	Cut "nonpriority spending"; reduce public-sector wage bill; social fund expenditure to rise from 5.4% of GDP in 2008 to 5.9% in 2009.
December 23, 2008	Latvia	SBA	27	2,387	4,382	565	2,351	840	C	E	C	Maintain the peg to euro; nominal public-wage reductions; sizeable fiscal cuts, most notably through reducing pensions.
January 12, 2009	Belarus	SBA	15	3,560	0	200	1,000	470	C	C	C	Devaluation and a new peg; price liberalization; privatization; cutting of subsidies; social spending supported.

(continued overleaf)

TABLE 17.4 IMF agreements in the aftermath of the 2008 crisis (continued)

Approval	Country	Facility	Duration	Amount of arrangement (millions $)				Balance drawn as of 8/6/2009	Estimated impact of fiscal measures		Impact of monetary policy measures	Notes
				IMF	EU	WB	Other		CEPR	IMF		
January 16, 2009	Serbia	SBA	27	4,108	411	350	0	1,100	C	C	E	Fiscal restraint a cornerstone.
March 6, 2009	Armenia	SBA	28	838	0	525	637	416	E	E	C	Introduce a flexible exchange rate regime; liquidity to banking sector; increase social spending by 0.3% of GDP.
April 1, 2009	Mongolia	SBA	18	240	0	60	125	120	C	C	C	Improve targeted social safety net.
April 21, 2009	Tajikistan	ESF		116					C	C	C	Increasing social spending from 7.3% of GDP in 2008 to 8.7% in 2009 and to 10 % by 2012.
May 4, 2009	Romania	SBA	24	17,948	6,550	1,310	1,310	6,854	C	C	C	
May 6, 2009	Poland	FCL	12	21,472				0	C	C	C	No conditionalities.
July 8, 2009	Bosnia and Herzegovina	SBA	36	1,592	137	259	74	287	C	C	C	Strengthen the currency board; public-wage restraint; pensions and social benefits cuts.

Source: Reports on standby agreements, available at www.imf.org; IMF (2009e); CEPR, in Weisbrot et al. (2009).

Note: SBA = standby arrangement; ESF = exogenous shocks facility; FCL = flexible credit line. E = expansionary policy; C = contractionary policy.
Monetary policy: An increase in policy interest rates during a recession or significant growth slowdown was counted as contractionary (procyclical), and an interest rate cut was counted as expansionary (counter-cyclical; CEPR, in Weisbrot et al. [2009]). For money supply targets, some agreements did not target money supply growth and thus were not counted as procyclical or counter-cyclical on the basis of this measure. Some explicitly indicated a tightening of monetary policy.
Fiscal policy: A programmed reduction in the fiscal deficit (or an increase in the fiscal surplus) during a recession or significant growth slowdown was counted as contractionary (procyclical) fiscal policy. A programmed decrease in the fiscal surplus was counted as expansionary (counter-cyclical; CEPR, in Weisbrot et al. [2009]). The two columns show estimates by the Center for Economic and Policy Research and by the IMF.
Data on funding as of August 6, 2009.

had an important role in shaping these programs and in providing funding. Private-sector involvement was also sought in some of the programs, both informally and through the Bank Coordination Initiative established by the European Commission and the EBRD. This ensured that the European parent banks were committed to maintaining exposure in Eastern European host countries and to maintaining adequate capital and liquidity in subsidiaries.

Table 17.4 also shows a measure of the degree to which the anticrisis programs were expansionary or contractionary. The difference in policy interpretations between the IMF and its critics can partly be explained by the different methods of measurement (IMF 2009e, 25; Weisbrot et al. 2009, 7). However, the two competing evaluations of fiscal policies are surprisingly consistent for transition economies, with the Latvian program being the only exception. The IMF interpretation, thus, refers to its programs "on the whole," pointing to a "less restrictive" approach than in past crises (IMF 2009e, 24).

Nevertheless, the experience of the Eastern European countries does not indicate a major change in the IMF's approach. Conditionalities still put the emphasis on fiscal and monetary restriction. Ukraine, for instance, agreed that the budget deficit, excluding bank recapitalization costs, would not exceed 1 percent of GDP in 2008 and 0 percent in 2009. Hungary agreed to reduce the public sector deficit to 3.4 percent of GDP in 2008 and to 2.5 percent in 2009 and to introduce a rules-based fiscal framework. This was particularly harsh, as the government had undertaken budget cuts reducing a deficit from 10 to 3 percent of GDP in the previous two years. As in Ukraine, cuts in spending took place in the context of procyclical monetary tightening. In April 2009, signs of flexibility were observed, with the IMF and the European Union agreeing to lift the Hungarian deficit target to 3.9 percent of GDP.

However, it may be possible to speak about a new approach to emergency lending in low-income countries. In this context, agreements seemed to be less biased to procyclical—meaning, in this case, deflationary—policies, with agreements in Georgia, Kyrgyzstan, and Armenia including expansionary fiscal policies. Moreover, improving the social safety net and defending or increasing social spending played an important role in such agreements. These countries had previously failed to develop their welfare state systems. The IMF and WB intervention, may, thus play an important role in their future development.

The implications of IMF conditionalities may be most profound in Belarus, as there, the emphasis was on important structural reforms, including liberalizing prices, cutting price subsidies, and scaling down subsidies and lending directed to specific enterprises. Belarus had also continued supporting old means of welfare provision, such as utility and housing subsidies. The IMF wanted to see those policies scaled down and replaced by the targeted safety net.

On average, adjustments to the crisis in transition economies within IMF programs were more contractionary than in other countries (IMF 2009e, 24–26), but the role of the IMF should not be overestimated. First, its intervention was associated with other factors militating against anticyclical measures, such as higher initial debt levels and a lack of external financing. Therefore, IMF intervention did not necessarily lead to more restrictive policies. At the same time, however, its funding did not provide leeway for countercyclical anticrisis measures, as would be preferred by some of the IMF's critics. Second, policy makers in countries as varied as Belarus, Latvia, and Serbia seemed to prefer restrictive policies for reasons other than the IMF's conditionalities. Finally, there is a question of the degree of enforceability as far as the IMF's conditionalities are concerned. This is particularly relevant for the CIS countries, where Russia seemed to be willing to provide alternative sources of financing. Moreover, the IMF did not appear willing to enforce rigorously the conditionalities when its only hard sanction could cause economic catastrophe and political turmoil. In 2009, it seemed to be tolerating countries not fulfilling conditions, such as Ukraine, where fiscal policies—most importantly, increased social spending—were very remote from the agreed-on program. However, developments in Ukraine showed also the limits to the IMF's tolerance as the adoption of a law on social spending led to a freezing of the lending program in November 2009.

STAGE 2: THE DEMAND SLUMP

The second stage refers to the impact of the falling demand for physical goods following the first effects of the financial crisis. While U.S. growth was still positive in the second quarter of 2008, output declined in the European Union, the main trading partner for many transition economies. That impact was felt in domestic demand for exports, hitting particularly countries with high shares of exports relative to GDP (see Table 17.5). This included some countries already suffering from stage 1, such as Hungary, Ukraine, and the Baltic republics, and some that appeared to have escaped without much effect, including Slovakia and the Czech Republic.

A division can be made between countries with exports based on manufacturing—largely Eastern Europe—and countries exporting semimanufactures and raw materials, including Russia and Ukraine. Falls in exports and GDP are indicated in Table 17.5, with further general data in Table A.2. The data in Table 17.5 confirm the timing of the biggest drop in exports coming in early 2009. For some countries—those hit by the first stage of the crisis—GDP can already be seen falling in the last quarter of 2008. However, for the CEECs, apart from Hungary, and for Russia, there was much less impact until 2009. In these countries exports generally fell by substantially more than GDP which is consistent with falling demand for exports being the principal channel for spreading the effects of the crisis.

Eastern European countries recorded lower drops in exports than the natural resource exporters in the CIS. The export falls among the manufacturing exporters reflected the drop in the volume of goods exported, which immediately translated into a fall in industrial output and hence in GDP. In contrast, the decline in exports among the natural resource exporters, such as Russia, Kazakhstan and Azerbaijan, was associated with much greater falls in prices than in volumes. The impact on output (measured in constant prices in the GDP figures) was, thus, less severe and immediate. In fact, rising oil prices later in 2009 led to apparent improvements in export performances in those countries.

TABLE 17.5   Falls in exports and GDP contractions in 2008 to 2009

	Exports as a percentage of GDP in 2008[a]	Change in exports, year on year[a]		Changes in GDP, year on year[b]		
		2009 (Q1)	2009 (Q2)	2008 (Q4)	2009 (Q1)	2009 (Q2)
Czech Republic	67.1	−19.0	−19.4	0.0[a]	−4.4[a]	−5.8[a]
Hungary	68.8	−16.0	−13.5	−2.5	−6.7	−7.5
Poland	33.9	−2.4	−2.9	2.9	0.9	1.3
Slovakia	75.8	−29.6	−27.0	1.6	−5.7	−5.5
Slovenia	53.7	−22.4	−23.7	−0.8	−8.2	−9.2
Bulgaria		−26.9	−33.4	3.5	−3.5	−4.9
Estonia	53.5	−25.9	−27.8	−9.2	−15.0	−16.1
Latvia	28.4	−25.7	−27.4	−10.3	−17.8	−18.4
Lithuania	50.2	−24.9	−36.1	−2.2	−13.3	−19.5
Romania	24.5	−7.4	−9.3	−3.1	−6.2	−8.7
Bosnia-Herzegovina		−20.7	−26.3	12.0[a]	−10.9[a]	−9.9[a]
Croatia		−13.4	−23.9	0.2	−6.7	−6.3
Macedonia, FYR		−34.6	−33.2	1.0	−0.9	−1.4
Montenegro		−22.5	−58.2		−15.9[ac]	−28.0[ac]
Serbia	21.6	−13.5	−9.9	2.8	−4.2	−4.0
Azerbaijan	66.0	−50.4	−47.4	7.9	4.1	8.4
Kazakhstan	53.0	−49.2	−52.5	1.6	−4.5	−2.6
Russia	28.1	−47.9	−46.3	0.0	−9.4	−10.8
Turkmenistan						
Belarus	61.0	−48.9	−46.4	−2.5	−5.1	−10.1
Ukraine	37.5	−39.4	−51.5	−8.0	−20.2	−17.9
Uzbekistan		6.1	−6.3	7.8[a]	7.9[a]	8.5[a]
Albania		−13.5	−20.1	2.8	2.0	6.0
Armenia	9.2	−47.3	−44.8	−5.9	−6.1	−17.9
Georgia	18.8	−33.5	−36.6	−2.5	−5.1	−10.1
Kyrgyzstan	35.3	−9.8	−10.9			
Moldova	27.1	−17.8	−22.9	6.2	−6.9	−8.6
Tajikistan	8.5	−48.3	−47.6			

Note: Q1 = first quarter; Q2 = second quarter; Q4 = fourth quarter. Changes in exports are measured in local currencies in Eastern European countries and in the U.S. dollar in the CIS. This overestimates the decline in CIS, as the U.S. dollar appreciated by approximately 20 percent related to the Russian ruble. Changes in GDP are measured in real terms.

[a]*Source:* National authorities data reported in Economist Intelligence Unit Country reports.

[b]*Source:* EBRD (2010)

[c]Data are for industrial production.

The initial drop in manufacturing demand felt by Eastern European countries was ameliorated by the expansionary policies pursued in Western Europe. The German car-scrap scheme, in operation until September 2009, was particularly important for export demand in the Czech Republic and Romania, which produced the smaller and cheaper cars that the scheme favored. Poland's GDP was the least dependent on

TABLE 17.6   Exports as a share of GDP in CEECs, 2006

	Exports	Exports of machinery and complex products	Exports of motor vehicles and components
Czech Republic	66.8	36.5	11.2
Hungary	65.5	42.3	6.2
Poland	34.4	13.3	4.3
Slovakia	75.7	30.8	12.4

Note: The machinery and complex-products category includes SITC, revision 3, categories 7, 54, 87, and 88. Motor vehicles and components are taken as category 78.

exports, and had the smallest share in exports coming from the motor-vehicle industry. Slovakia appeared the most vulnerable due to an exceptionally high dependence on exports, in general, and on this sector, in particular, with the highest number of cars produced per capita in Europe (cf. Figure 4.8 and Table 17.6).

Table 17.7 brings together the effects of the second stage with the effects of the first, showing which countries were susceptible to the ending of financial inflows and which suffered from falling export demand. There is some overlap, with for example Hungary and SEECs appearing in two categories. Moreover, the effects of the second stage are not in all cases clearly differentiated from those of the first. As indicated, drops in output shown in Table 17.5 and Table A.2 were related also to the collapse in financialized growth.

STAGE 3: FURTHER DOWNWARD PRESSURES

The third stage includes the further pressures for depression, following on from the first two stages. It is necessarily heterogeneous, including further threats to financial systems, the possible withdrawal of MNCs, and the loss of earnings from remittances. In some cases, the third stage was associated with threats of international insolvency, but that was largely the case only in countries that had already suffered from the effects of earlier financialized growth. Moreover, the collapse of import demand based on external borrowing resolved the immediate current account problems of financialized economies at the expense of domestic consumption and living standards. In contrast, the current account became a concern among the natural resource exporters, which saw their export earnings reduced by the collapse of prices (compare Table A.13).

The third stage had the most immediate and severe consequences in countries that had been dependent on financial inflows and that had a significant share of credits in foreign currencies. The drop in domestic incomes and real estate prices, following from the previous stages, put a strain on the balance sheets of the private sector, with the increase in the stock of nonperforming loans undermining the banking system. The growth of nonperforming loans was particularly dramatic in Kazakhstan, Latvia, and Georgia (EBRD 2009, 14). Any currency devaluation then threatened the ability of debtors to repay, in turn undermining the stability of creditor institutions. This provided incentives for the governments to defend the exchange rate through restrictive policies rather than to compensate for the falls in the level of economic output through expansionary policies.

TABLE 17.7   Forms of integration and the nature of vulnerabilities to crisis

Form of integration	Nature of vulnerability	Countries where these forms are important or dominant
Manufacturing exports through producer-driven networks	Export demand: consumer products and capital goods dependent on credit (primary impact on domestic output)	CEECs, (Belarus)
Manufacturing exports through buyer-driven networks	Export demand (primary impact on domestic output)	Baltic republics, Southeast Europe
Commodity exporters	Export demand and large price fluctuations (primary impact via export earnings)	Russia, Ukraine, Kazakhstan, Azerbaijan, Turkmenistan (Belarus, Baltic republics, SE Europe)
Remittances and foreign aid	Dependence on low-tier labour markets abroad (impact via reduction in remittances)	Albania, Armenia, Georgia, Kyrgyzstan, Moldova, Tajikistan, Uzbekistan, Bosnia-Herzegovina
Financialised growth	Reduction of financial inflows and difficulties with refinancing debt, foreign currency loans make devaluation especially costly (impact via direct reductions in domestic demand levels and through public spending and wage cuts leading to further demand reductions)	Baltic republics, Southeast Europe, Ukraine, Hungary, Belarus, Kazakhstan (Russia)

Source: summary of authors' analysis

Note: countries and country groups shown in brackets indicate a lower level of importance for the form of integration.

The third stage took a different form in CEECs. Domestic demand levels fell as external finance was reduced and as output—and hence wages and employment—were reduced in export-oriented activities. However, that did not lead into further financial difficulties—for example, from a failure to repay loans to banks. That link between declining real output and further difficulties in the financial sector was limited, as foreign-owned MNCs had financed their operations without extensive credits from within CEECs.

Some banks saw their credit ratings downgraded, reflecting the difficulties of their customers in the face of collapsing demand, but the subsidiaries of foreign-owned banks in CEECs were seen as prudent, as they had not been allowed to buy into subprime markets or to buy the most risky assets. However, in countries with low deposit bases, concerns were raised about the lack of liquidity and capital. Moreover, the scarcity of capital provided mother banks with incentives to withdraw funds from the region (European Commission 2009, 22). Following intensive lobbying by banks with exposure to CEEC markets, the joint IFI Action Plan for Central and Eastern Europe (including the EBRD, the EIB Group, and the World Bank) was launched in March 2009 to address these concerns. It contained a pledge to provide up to €24.5 billion in support to the banking sectors in the region and to fund lending to businesses. Most transition countries, not only CEECs, also introduced guarantees for bank deposits, with Lithuania extending protection for individual deposits to €100,000 and Montenegro, Slovakia, and Slovenia even committing to unlimited coverage.

Credits were reduced gradually, reflecting greater caution from banks, but, by the end of 2009, the reversal in capital flows seemed to be modest (cf. EBRD 2009, 52–55). Difficulties with credits in foreign currency were generally handled by increasing payments and lengthening repayment periods from debtors. Therefore, the third stage meant lower living standards for the population, lower tax revenues for the state, and thus rising budget deficits, but no immediate further downturn. The effects on the trade balance remained unclear, as lower domestic demand cut imports, while lower export demand cut exports, with no certainty as to which reduction would be larger.

An open question remained over the fate and behavior of MNCs, which might rethink their strategies toward investment in CEECs. A reduction in inward investment—and more dramatically, decisions to pull out—would lead to lower employment and domestic incomes, to lower export levels, and to lower levels of financial inflow, which had helped to balance current account deficits. Multinational companies could become a net drain, as repatriated profits dominate over capital inflows and benefits from net export earnings. All of this is possible, and there were indications, based on aggregated company-level data, of substantial contraction in FDI inflows in 2009 in all Eastern European countries, except Slovakia.[1]

The largest declines were linked to investment in real estate and the automotive sectors, both shrinking to one third. Latvia and Slovenia experienced the largest drops in FDI inflows, 71 percent and 70 percent, respectively, linked to the collapse of investment in real estate. Lithuania, Estonia and the Czech Republic experienced more modest declines, at about 20 percent, and the shrinkage in the remaining countries amounted to about 50 percent. The exceptional 55 percent rise in Slovakia was driven by a single $2.3 billion real estate investment by a Hungarian developer. In the longer term, however, it is also possible that MNCs would continue to see CEECs as among their most desirable locations, as they continued to offer cheaper labor than in Western Europe.

The effects of the third stage in Russia were much more immediate and involved a closer interlocking of problems with financial flows and falling real output. As previously indicated, and in contrast to the CEECs, the key enterprises were under domestic rather than foreign ownership. This gave them a financial independence that was absent from the big firms—or rather, subsidiaries of MNCs—in CEECs, and they used this to raise finance in ways that carried risks for the domestic economy.

Growth in raw-material exports in the preceding years had been led by the large conglomerates controlled by oligarchs. Commodity prices rose in the years up to 2008, and this was in turn reflected in financial developments. Higher revenues for the conglomerates led to higher share prices—helping to create the impression of the

---

[1] The aggregated company-level data are provided by FDI Intelligence from the Financial Times Ltd, (as reported in PwC 2010).

rapidly developing stock market implied by Table 13.3—which in turn enabled the firms to borrow, using shares as collateral. They could thereby raise finance on international markets, bypassing the country's weakly developed banking system. Borrowing helped to finance purchases of further enterprises, increasing the concentration of Russian industrial ownership. It was also used by the big companies to diversify into construction and real estate, activities that expanded rapidly in the years up to 2008. The oligarchs were able to boost their economic power and personal wealth to such an extent that the accumulated wealth of the 87 Russian citizens listed by *Forbes* as billionaires in 2008 was equivalent to approximately one-third of Russian GDP.[2]

The downside was that these firms were very exposed to the effects of falling share prices—down by 70 percent from mid- to late 2008—and that was an inevitable and rapid consequence of falling commodity prices. Personal wealth levels plummeted, and the oligarchs also lost access to sources of external finance. FDI inflows fell by 48 percent in 2009, driven by a collapse in investment in the real estate and extractive industries (PwC 2010). The oligarchs were further hit by a falling exchange rate, which made repayments more difficult. The only option was to seek help from the state and to accept terms that meant surrendering shares. Thus, the state headed back to control over key exporting enterprises that had been privatized in the 1990s. This also spread into the other sectors in which oligarchs were well placed, including motor vehicles, which were also hit by the financial squeeze.

A heavy blow was also felt in countries dependent on remittances when production, and hence demand for labor, fell in the European Union, Kazakhstan, Russia, and other countries where those people had previously worked. The countries most dependent on remittances, set out in Table 4.2, included a number of smaller CIS countries and Albania. Kyrgyzstan, Moldova, and Tajikistan recorded remittance falls of 30 to 40 percent between the third quarter of 2008 and the beginning of 2009, using balance-of-payments statistics that frequently understate remittance levels (EBRD 2009, 50).

The remittance-dependent countries could be expected to suffer very severe falls in income levels. Based on the experience of the 1998 Russian crisis, O'Hara, Ivlevs, and Gentile (2009) suggested that by 2012, remittances to the region could fall to only one-third the 2008 level and that a return to precrisis levels of remittances could take almost a decade. Some transition economies will do better, able to lose the temporary migrant labor that had been important to economic growth in the previous years of expansion. For them—a group that included Slovenia and the Czech Republic—the rise in the domestic unemployed population was less than the fall in domestic employment. The same could apply for a number of CIS countries that were experiencing flows of labor in both inward and outward directions, including Russia, Kazakhstan, and, to a lesser extent, Ukraine.

STAGE 4: THE FISCAL AND SOLVENCY CRISIS

The fourth stage, the crisis in state budgets as a result of the effects of the world financial crisis, remained a permanent threat in limiting governments' scope for active intervention. The region started from a good position in terms of its public

---

[2]http://www.forbes.com/lists/2008/10/billionaires08_The-Worlds-Billionaires_Rank.html

indebtedness. However, in the aftermath of the crisis, the transition economies saw their revenues fall faster than the rate of GDP contraction, with the difference being attributed to the falls in imports, the declining asset bases, weak compliance, and—in some cases—tax reductions. This led to budget-deficit increases, albeit with differences between countries, depending on the impact of the crisis and the policies chosen by governments, in several cases under pressure from the IMF.

Data are consistent with generally rising budget deficits (see Table A.16).[3] Bulgaria was almost an exception, with a budget surplus in the first half of 2009, but it recorded a 3.9 percent deficit for the year as a whole. Information for CIS countries is rather fragmentary, and Russia's deficit—6.2 percent of GDP for 2009—was not a threat to the country's international position. In CEECs, the highest deficits were recorded in Poland (7.1 percent of GDP) and Slovakia (6.8 percent). Government deficit was lowest in Hungary (4.0 percent). Revenues fell, while spending increased or held steady. Apart from Hungary, these countries were not compelled by IMF conditions to impose cuts and made some gestures toward joining the efforts of richer EU members toward stimulating demand. An alternative of emphasizing the speedy restoration of budget balance was likely to face strong political and social opposition. However, spending was held back by fears that these small countries would face difficulties in raising finance to cover deficits. Therefore, governments generally regarded further increases in the levels of deficit as highly undesirable.

The Baltic republics faced larger deficits, reflecting the more severe depression in financialized economies, but these stabilized or fell in the later months of 2009. In Estonia, the deficit reached 7.5 percent of GDP in the first three months of the year but was back to 1.7 percent of GDP for the whole of 2009. There were also falls in Latvia and Lithuania, but deficits for 2009 remained equivalent to 9.0 percent and 8.9 percent of GDP, respectively. The key issue here was the ability of the government to transfer the costs of the crisis back onto the population by raising taxes and cutting spending.

Pressure to pursue this option was particularly strong in view of dangers of international insolvency. These were countries that had a large proportion of credits denominated in foreign currencies, and that effectively ruled out devaluation—normally an option in the face of balance-of-payments difficulties—as it would have left debtors with even less chance of repaying their loans. Governments in the Baltic republics, following international advice and particularly tough IMF conditions for Latvia, therefore, concluded that adjustment had to be done through cutting domestic demand for imports by cutting domestic spending.

The absence in these countries of strong interest representation made this easier, but even cuts negotiated and agreed with the IMF proved very difficult to implement. In June 2009, Latvia, the worst hit country, implemented spending cuts and tax increases of €712 million, designed to reduce the budget deficit by 10 percent of GDP in the next three to four years. It cut wages in the public sector by almost 40 percent and reduced pensions by 10 percent. It also reduced benefits and increased payments in health care. The Baltic republics seemed to have reached a dead end in their growth strategies, as the speculative boom was not likely to be repeated in the region in the foreseeable future. Options that remained included hoping wage reductions would lay a basis for low-wage export activities or hoping for more income

---

[3] Eurostat data (available at http://ec.europe.eu/eurostat) are used for EU member states EBRD (2010) data for others.

from remittances, should demand for labor revive in richer countries. There was little sign of either of these happening during 2009 and unemployment, using the ILO method of measurement, increased rapidly to 21.7 percent of the labor force in Latvia in February 2010, the highest of any European union country. Equivalent figures for Estonia and Lithuania were 15.5 percent and 15.8 percent (compare with Table A.4).

Summarizing from the analysis of these stages of crisis, the first effects reaffirmed the divergence between Eastern Europe and the CIS as well as within those very broad country groupings. Further development is difficult to predict, but, even with early recovery elsewhere in the world, many transition economies could be expected to face difficulties for years to come. The crisis of 2008 marked an end to one period of their development, and lasting recovery could be expected to be hampered by the weaknesses left behind by the transitions up to that date. Reliance on international finance proved to be a poor alternative to the development of competitive industry. Privatization, as pursued in the majority of cases, had not created firms that could compete with innovations and new technology on the international stage. The Eastern European states were better placed than CIS countries, thanks to inward FDI, but even in CEECs, the future was very uncertain.

CONCLUSION: A VERDICT ON TRANSITION?

The effects of the world financial and economic crisis upset comfortable verdicts on the results of transition. All countries were affected, bringing an end to the period of recovery from transformation depression and the quite rapid growth of the immediately preceding years. In some cases, recorded GDP was not much above, or even, below, the 1989 level before the impact of the crisis. Figures in Table A.2 show that it was brought close to, or below, that level in almost all transition economies, apart from most oil exporters—even Russia is not included here—CEECs, Estonia, and the two order states of Belarus and Uzbekistan.

The crisis exposed not only the limitations to the quantitative levels of growth since 1989 but also the potential instability of the forms it had taken. Transition had brought benefits to populations, with greater access to the outside world and all that went with that, but it had not led to robust and secure economies. Some were better placed than others, depending on the kinds of goods that they exported, but none had been able to join world leaders in key areas of modern technology. The best could be characterized as FDI-based economies, implying a high level of dependence on developments in more wealthy economies. Others are labeled on pp. 310–11 as peripheral market economies, emphasizing more clearly the instability of their positions and the extent to which their fate depends on developments elsewhere.

This was not the only possible outcome from the 20 years. Many other countries did rather well over that period. China stands out as one that built from a less-developed base to be able to export modern manufactured goods. Others, too, grew reasonably rapidly, both in Asia and other continents. The clear impression is that transition economies missed a chance, or at best, only some of them took some advantage of the possibilities that the world offered at the time. There is plenty of evidence in preceding chapters of where alternatives existed but were not chosen.

Contrasts among transition economies carry some surprising implications. It is remarkable that those that reformed the least—Belarus and Uzbekistan—were not the worst performers. Indeed, they did better than their most obvious comparators, countries that were their immediate neighbors. However, that is not because they did particularly well, much less because they chose the best policy mix. They clearly failed to exploit their full potential, as indicated by the slow development of new enterprises, followed in Chapter 12, and by the limited ability to take advantage of international contacts. However, they did avoid, or at least limited, the costs of extreme liberalization, of state breakdown, of giving wealth to owners without the interest or ability to develop enterprises, and—on this one, Belarus was also partially guilty—of covering up for their economies' weaknesses with financial inflows.

Taking account of contrasts between transition economies, and of development elsewhere in the world, the key mistake would appear to have been excessive faith in, and reliance on, free markets. That needed to be balanced with the development of stable state structures and the regulation of market processes. Where this was done, the transformation depression was shorter and recovery more persistent, that being the experience in CEECs. Where private enterprise was given the freest hand, controlled the least by a state, a legal framework, or an active civil society, the outcome was enrichment for some individuals, without much accompanying economic development.

The CEECs were relatively successful among transition economies, and overall growth was faster here than the average for EU countries. However, that could be expected in view of their potential for catching up, and growth was slow relative to the fastest-growing countries in the world. Indeed, much of the catching up that did occur was in the development of a service sector, often including quite basic services that had been neglected before, while industry performed remarkably badly relative even to EU countries (cf. Tiits et al. 2008). Here, too, opportunities were missed by the reluctance to accept the benefits of an active state in helping to create better environments for business, helping to develop a better qualified labor force, helping to improve the physical infrastructure, and helping to maintain and develop a research base. These are normal state roles in mature market economies and in rapidly developing economies. They were either avoided or undertaken only on a small scale, as governments complied with fashionable theories on the dangers of state involvement. This did not prevent rapid growth, especially in the last years up to 2008, but the result was a dependent status as outposts for foreign MNCs. Effectively no high-tech activities developed under domestic ownership, and MNCs brought little of their high-value activities into CEECs. The future of these economies was left uncertain, dependent on decisions made elsewhere.

Predicting the future would be hazardous, particularly after neither the form taken by the ending of state Socialism nor the nature and effects of the crisis of 2008 were widely predicted. Recovery from the resulting depression may be easier for countries exporting modern manufactured goods, although their dependent positions carry substantial risks and uncertainties. The fate of commodity exporters will depend on demand, and hence economic recovery, in the rest of the world; that, too, is uncertain. Recovery may be extremely difficult for countries that have been dependent on financialized growth. It is not possible to go back and correct for policy mistakes in the past, and the directions of future policy changes depend on political choices. It remains impossible to predict how populations will react to sharp falls in living standards and threats of still more austerity.

Table A.1 GNI per capita, PPP (current international $)

	1989	1990	1991	1992	1993	1994	1995	1996	1997	1998	1999	2000	2001	2002	2003	2004	2005	2006	2007	2008
Albania	3,040	2,820	2,080	1,950	2,280	2,620	3,010	3,380	3,100	3,540	3,940	4,370	4,820	5,000	5,390	5,820	6,250	6,890	7,350	7,950
Armenia		2,040	1,950	990	1,040	1,250	1,390	1,570	1,720	1,830	1,920	2,090	2,350	2,730	3,170	3,590	4,210	4,940	5,740	6,310
Azerbaijan					2,100	1,700	1,500	1,510	1,640	1,810	1,940	2,080	2,320	2,580	2,910	3,200	3,940	5,380	6,630	7,770
Belarus		4,650	4,750	4,380	4,130	3,720	3,410	3,590	4,070	4,480	4,720	5,120	5,510	5,930	6,530	7,520	8,560	9,700	10,790	12,150
Bosnia and Herzegovina						900	1,160	2,380	3,260	4,700	4,870	4,910	5,110	5,350	5,600	6,030	6,500	7,180	8,010	8,620
Bulgaria	5,490	5,000	4,670	4,900	4,980	5,180	5,390	4,980	4,850	5,210	5,470	6,000	6,730	7,580	8,070	8,760	9,260	10,080	10,790	11,950
Croatia		9,530	8,260	7,450	6,770	7,310	8,020	9,010	9,630	10,070	9,760	10,580	11,290	12,280	12,820	14,050	14,790	16,060	17,840	18,420
Czech Republic				10,540	10,490	11,170	12,810	13,480	13,620	13,710	13,970	14,640	15,630	16,070	17,150	18,220	19,380	20,730	22,160	22,790
Estonia							6,330	6,930	7,740	8,310	8,580	9,430	10,150	11,430	12,640	13,950	15,730	17,560	18,830	19,280
Georgia	4,400	3,900	3,210	1,830	1,330	1,240	1,290	1,520	1,830	1,960	2,070	2,150	2,270	2,450	2,810	3,130	3,550	4,090	4,680	4,850
Hungary	8,320	8,390	7,680	7,670	7,840	8,220	8,490	8,760	9,200	9,800	10,370	11,730	12,910	13,950	14,800	15,400	16,060	16,980	17,470	17,790
Kazakhstan		5,120	4,690	4,510	4,240	3,830	3,640	3,770	3,950	3,990	4,110	4,460	5,260	5,940	6,530	7,240	7,830	8,680	9,510	9,690
Kyrgyz Republic	1,680	1,810	1,700	1,480	1,280	1,030	980	1,050	1,140	1,140	1,170	1,250	1,370	1,380	1,500	1,620	1,670	1,790	1,980	2,140
Latvia	8,130	7,810	7,100	4,990	4,950	5,230	5,370	5,750	6,450	6,990	7,350	8,010	8,930	9,900	10,590	11,490	12,880	14,460	16,770	16,740
Lithuania		9,000	8,770	7,090	6,100	5,660	5,990	6,420	7,080	7,760	7,770	8,460	9,410	10,440	11,720	12,620	13,860	15,320	17,090	18,210
Macedonia, FYR		5,500	5,340	4,940	4,700	4,730	4,770	4,880	5,000	5,220	5,450	5,830	5,790	5,970	6,190	6,800	7,510	8,310	9,050	9,950
Moldova	2,780	2,800	2,430	1,760	1,780	1,250	1,250	1,280	1,330	1,260	1,260	1,320	1,530	1,710	1,990	2,260	2,530	2,770	2,900	3,210
Mongolia	1,560	1,500	1,450	1,310	1,060	1,130	1,490	1,550	1,620	1,700	1,760	1,790	1,880	1,970	2,120	2,380	2,550	2,810	3,170	3,450
Montenegro												6,320	6,550	6,930	7,390	8,000	8,350	10,160	12,560	13,920
Poland		5,160	5,050	5,380	5,720	6,040	7,330	8,010	8,730	9,310	9,850	10,410	10,880	11,450	11,790	12,590	13,480	14,430	15,600	17,310
Romania		5,180	4,700	4,440	4,600	4,900	5,360	5,690	5,460	5,290	5,280	5,610	6,370	6,940	7,590	8,550	9,280	10,620	12,350	13,500
Russian Federation		9,100	8,920	7,740	7,230	6,500	6,340	6,220	6,380	5,990	6,510	7,430	8,110	8,640	9,400	10,510	11,570	12,810	14,330	15,630
Serbia									6,420	6,720	5,610	6,000	6,400	6,760	7,080	7,870	8,590	9,310	9,830	11,150
Slovakia	7,570	7,730	6,810	6,470	7,190	7,730	8,320	9,020	9,690	10,250	10,250	10,800	11,880	12,730	13,550	14,540	15,510	17,340	19,220	21,300
Slovenia				10,740	11,500	12,430	13,100	13,850	14,800	15,620	16,630	17,460	18,390	19,600	20,310	21,960	23,260	24,580	26,230	26,910
Tajikistan	2,200	2,210	2,080	1,480	1,240	960	840	680	720	760	790	800	940	1,040	1,140	1,310	1,430	1,550	1,700	1,860
Turkmenistan	2,660	2,710	2,600	2,440	2,200	1,860	1,680	1,570	1,430	1,490	1,710	1,930	2,430	2,820	3,380	4,000	4,350	4,980	5,650	6,210
Ukraine	6,100	5,950	5,620	5,070	4,340	3,500	3,130	2,900	2,890	2,870	2,910	3,170	3,630	3,940	4,450	5,160	5,520	6,120	6,830	7,210
Uzbekistan				1,290	1,260	1,200	1,190	1,200	1,260	1,310	1,360	1,420	1,490	1,570	1,650	1,830	2,000	2,190	2,430	2,660

Source: World Bank International Comparison Program database.

Note: Gross national income (GNI) per capita is based on purchasing power parity (PPP); GNI PPP is gross national income converted to international dollars using purchasing power parity rates. An international dollar has the same purchasing power over GNI as a U.S. dollar has in the United States. The GNI is the sum of value added by all resident producers, plus any product taxes (less subsidies) not included in the valuation of output, plus net receipts of primary income (compensation of employees and property income) from abroad.

Table A.2 GDP (percentage change in real terms)

	1989	1990	1991	1992	1993	1994	1995	1996	1997	1998	1999	2000	2001	2002	2003	2004	2005	2006	2007	2008	2009	GDP level as percent of 1989[a]	
																						2008	2009
Albania	9.8	-10.0	-28.0	-7.2	9.6	8.3	13.3	9.1	-10.9	8.6	13.2	6.5	7.1	4.2	5.8	5.7	5.7	5.5	6.0	7.0	2.8	163	168
Armenia	14.2	-7.4	-11.7	-41.8	-8.8	5.4	6.9	5.9	3.3	7.3	3.3	5.9	9.6	13.2	13.9	10.1	14.0	13.2	13.8	6.8	-14.2	153	131
Azerbaijan	14.2	-7.4	-11.7	-41.8	-8.8	5.4	6.9	5.9	3.3	7.3	3.3	5.9	9.6	13.2	13.9	10.1	14.0	13.2	23.4	10.9	9.3	177	193
Belarus	8.0	-3.0	-1.2	-9.6	-7.6	-11.7	-10.4	2.8	11.4	8.4	3.3	5.8	4.7	5.0	7.0	11.4	9.4	9.9	8.2	10.0	0.2	161	161
Bosnia–Herzegovina		-23.2	-12.1	-50.0	-60.0	0.0	20.8	86.0	37.0	15.6	9.6	5.5	4.3	5.5	3.0	6.3	3.9	6.7	6.8	5.4	-3.4	84	81
Bulgaria	0.5	-9.1	-11.7	-7.3	-1.5	1.8	2.9	-9.4	-5.6	4.0	2.3	5.4	4.1	4.5	5.0	6.6	6.2	6.3	6.2	6.0	-5.0	114	108
Croatia	-1.6	-7.1	-21.1	-11.7	-8.0	5.9	6.8	5.9	6.8	2.5	-0.9	2.9	4.4	5.6	5.3	4.3	4.3	4.8	5.5	2.4	-5.8	111	105
Czech Republic	1.4	-1.2	-11.6	-0.5	0.1	2.2	5.9	4.2	-0.7	-0.8	1.3	3.6	2.5	1.9	3.6	4.5	6.3	6.8	6.1	2.5	-4.2	142	136
Estonia	8.1	-6.5	-13.6	-14.2	-8.8	-1.6	5.0	5.0	10.8	5.4	-0.1	9.6	7.7	7.8	7.1	7.5	9.2	10.4	7.2	-3.6	-14.1	147	126
Georgia	-4.8	-12.4	-20.6	-44.8	-25.4	-11.4	2.4	10.5	10.6	2.9	3.0	1.9	4.7	5.5	11.1	5.9	9.6	9.4	12.4	2.1	-3.9	61	59
Hungary	0.7	-3.5	-11.9	-3.1	-0.6	2.9	1.5	1.3	4.6	4.8	4.2	5.2	4.1	4.1	4.2	4.8	4.0	4.1	1.2	0.6	-6.3	136	127
Kazakhstan	-0.4	-0.4	-11.0	-5.3	-9.2	-12.6	-8.2	0.5	1.7	-1.9	2.7	9.8	13.5	9.8	9.3	9.6	9.7	10.7	8.9	3.2	1.2	141	143
Kyrgyzstan	2.8	5.7	-7.9	-13.9	-15.5	-20.1	-5.4	7.1	9.9	2.1	3.7	5.4	5.3	0.0	7.0	7.0	-0.2	3.1	8.2	7.6	2.3	102	104
Latvia	6.8	2.9	-10.4	-34.9	-14.9	2.2	-0.9	3.9	8.4	4.7	3.3	6.9	8.0	6.5	7.2	8.7	10.6	12.2	10.0	-4.6	-18.0	118	97
Lithuania	1.5	-5.0	-5.7	-21.3	-16.2	-9.8	1.2	5.1	8.5	7.5	-1.5	4.1	6.6	6.9	10.3	7.3	7.9	7.7	9.8	2.8	-15.2	120	102
Macedonia, FYR	0.9	-9.9	-6.2	-6.6	-7.5	-1.8	-1.1	1.2	1.4	3.4	4.3	4.5	-4.5	0.9	2.8	4.1	4.1	3.7	5.9	4.8	-0.7	102	101
Moldova	8.5	-2.4	-17.5	-29.1	-1.2	-30.9	-1.4	-5.9	1.6	-6.5	-3.4	2.1	6.1	7.8	6.6	7.4	7.5	4.8	3.0	7.2	-6.7	55	51
Mongolia	4.2	-2.5	-9.2	-9.5	-2.9	2.3	6.3	2.4	4.0	3.5	3.2	1.1	1.0	4.0	5.9	10.1	7.3	8.6	10.2	8.9	-1.6	167	164
Montenegro	1.3	-7.9	-10.8	-21.0	-24.9	0.7	6.2	13.9	4.2	4.0	-6.7	3.1	1.1	1.9	2.5	4.4	4.2	8.6	10.7	7.0	-5.3	92	87
Poland	0.2	-11.6	-7.0	2.6	3.8	5.2	7.0	6.2	7.1	5.0	4.5	4.3	1.2	1.4	3.9	5.3	3.6	6.2	6.8	5.0	1.7	178	181
Romania	-5.8	-5.7	-12.9	-8.8	1.5	3.9	7.1	3.9	-6.1	-4.8	-1.1	2.1	5.7	5.1	5.2	8.5	4.2	7.9	6.0	7.1	-7.1	128	119
Russia	1.6	-3.0	-5.0	-14.8	-8.7	-12.7	-4.0	-3.6	1.4	-5.3	6.4	10.0	5.1	4.7	7.3	7.1	6.4	7.4	8.1	5.6	-7.9	108	99
Serbia	1.3	-7.9	-11.6	-27.9	-30.8	2.5	6.1	7.8	10.1	1.9	-18.0	5.2	5.1	2.4	4.8	9.3	6.3	5.5	6.9	5.5	-3.0	72	70
Slovakia	1.4	-0.4	-15.9	-6.7	-3.7	6.2	5.8	6.1	4.6	4.2	1.5	2.0	3.4	4.8	5.2	5.2	6.6	8.5	10.4	6.2	-4.7	164	156
Slovenia	-1.8	-7.5	-8.9	-5.5	2.8	5.3	4.1	3.7	4.8	3.9	5.4	4.1	3.1	4.0	2.8	4.3	4.3	5.9	6.8	3.5	-7.8	156	144
Tajikistan	3.0	-32.6	-7.1	-28.9	-11.1	-21.4	-12.5	-4.4	1.7	5.3	3.7	8.3	10.2	9.1	10.2	10.6	6.7	7.0	7.8	7.9	3.4	61	63
Turkmenistan	-6.9	2.0	-4.7	-5.3	-10.0	-17.3	-7.2	-6.7	-11.3	6.7	16.5	18.6	20.4	15.8	17.1	14.7	13.0	11.4	11.6	10.5	6.0	226	240
Ukraine	4.0	-4.0	-10.6	-9.7	-14.2	-22.9	-12.2	-10.0	-3.0	-1.9	-0.2	5.9	9.2	5.2	9.6	12.1	2.7	7.3	7.9	2.2	-15.1	70	59
Uzbekistan	3.7	1.6	-0.5	-11.1	-2.3	-4.2	-0.9	1.6	2.5	4.3	4.3	3.8	4.1	4.0	4.2	7.7	7.0	7.3	9.5	9.0	7.0	163	174

Source: EBRD economic statistics and forecasts, available at http://www.ebrd.com/country/sector/econo/stats/index.htm, EBRD (2010), Eurostat figures for the Czech Republic from 2008, available at http://ec.europe.eu/eurostat
[a]Calculated from the annual percentage changes.

Table A.3 Inflation

	1989	1990	1991	1992	1993	1994	1995	1996	1997	1998	1999	2000	2001	2002	2003	2004	2005	2006	2007	2008	2009
Albania	0.0	0.0	35.5	226.0	85.0	22.6	7.8	12.7	33.2	20.6	0.4	0.1	3.1	5.2	2.4	2.9	2.4	2.4	2.9	3.4	2.2
Armenia	4.8	10.3	274.0	1,346.0	1,822.0	4,962.0	175.8	18.7	14.0	8.7	0.7	-0.8	3.1	1.1	4.7	7.0	0.6	2.9	4.4	9.0	3.4
Azerbaijan		7.8	107.0	912.0	1,129.0	1,664.0	412.0	19.7	3.5	-0.8	-8.5	1.8	1.5	2.8	2.2	6.7	9.6	8.3	16.7	20.8	2.5
Belarus	1.7	4.7	94.1	970.3	1,190.2	2,221.0	709.3	52.7	63.9	72.9	293.7	168.6	61.1	42.5	28.4	18.1	10.3	7.0	8.4	14.9	12.8
Bosnia-Herzegovina							-4.4	-24.5	14.0	5.1	-0.9	1.9	1.9	-0.2	0.1	-0.3	3.0	6.1	4.9	6.5	0.0
Bulgaria	6.4	26.3	333.5	82.0	73.0	96.3	62.0	123.0	1,082.0	22.2	0.7	9.9	7.4	5.9	2.3	6.1	5.0	7.3	8.4	12.3	2.7
Croatia		609.5	123.0	665.5	1,517.5	97.6	2.0	3.5	3.6	5.7	4.0	4.6	3.8	1.7	1.8	2.1	3.3	3.2	2.9	6.1	2.5
Czech Republic	1.4	9.7	52.0	11.1	20.8	9.9	9.6	8.9	8.4	10.6	2.1	3.8	4.7	1.8	0.1	2.8	1.9	2.6	3.0	6.3	0.6
Estonia	6.1	23.1	210.5	1,076.0	89.8	47.7	29.0	23.1	11.2	8.1	3.3	4.0	5.8	3.6	1.3	3.0	4.1	4.4	6.6	10.4	0.0
Georgia		3.3	79.0	887.4	3,125.4	15,606.5	162.7	39.4	7.1	3.6	19.2	4.1	4.6	5.7	4.9	5.7	8.4	9.2	9.3	10.0	1.7
Hungary	17.0	28.9	35.0	23.0	22.5	18.8	28.2	23.6	18.3	14.3	10.0	9.8	9.2	5.3	4.7	6.8	3.6	3.9	8.0	6.1	4.2
Kazakhstan			78.8	1,381.0	1,662.3	1,892.0	176.3	39.1	17.4	7.1	8.3	13.2	8.4	5.9	6.4	6.9	7.6	8.6	10.8	17.2	7.3
Kyrgyzstan		85.0	855.0	772.4	180.7	43.5	31.9	23.4	10.5	35.9	18.7	6.9	2.0	3.1	4.1	5.6	6.5	10.2	15.4	24.5	6.9
Latvia	4.7	10.5	172.2	951.2	109.2	35.9	25.0	17.6	8.4	4.7	2.4	2.5	1.9	2.9	3.1	6.2	6.8	6.5	10.1	15.4	3.5
Lithuania	2.1	8.4	224.7	1,020.5	410.4	72.1	39.6	24.6	8.9	5.1	0.8	1.0	1.5	0.3	-1.1	1.2	2.7	3.8	5.7	11.0	4.5
Macedonia, FYR	1,246.0	608.4	114.9	1,664.4	338.4	126.5	16.4	2.3	2.6	-0.1	-0.7	5.8	5.5	1.8	1.2	-0.4	0.5	3.2	2.3	8.3	-0.8
Moldova		4.2	98.0	1,276.4	1,184.0	487.0	30.2	23.5	11.8	7.7	39.3	31.1	9.6	5.2	11.6	12.5	12.0	12.8	12.4	12.8	0.1
Mongolia					268.4	87.6	56.8	46.9	36.6	9.4	7.6	11.6	8.0	0.3	5.1	8.3	12.7	5.1	9.0	26.8	6.3
Montenegro							97.0	80.2	23.4	32.4	67.6	97.1	22.6	16.0	6.7	2.4	2.3	3.0	4.2	7.4	3.4
Poland	251.1	585.8	70.3	43.0	35.3	32.2	27.8	19.9	14.9	11.8	7.3	10.1	5.5	1.9	0.8	3.5	2.2	1.2	2.5	4.3	3.5
Romania	1.1	5.1	170.2	210.4	256.1	136.7	32.3	38.8	154.8	59.1	45.8	45.7	34.5	22.5	15.4	12.0	9.5	6.9	4.8	7.9	5.6
Russia	2.0	5.6	92.7	1,526.0	875.0	311.4	197.7	47.8	14.7	27.6	86.1	20.8	21.6	15.7	13.7	10.9	12.7	9.8	9.1	14.1	11.7
Serbia						3.3	78.6	94.3	18.3	30.0	41.1	70.0	91.8	19.5	11.7	10.1	16.5	12.7	6.7	11.7	8.4
Slovakia	2.3	10.8	61.2	10.0	23.2	13.4	9.9	5.8	6.1	6.7	10.6	12.0	7.3	3.3	8.5	7.5	2.5	4.5	2.8	4.6	1.5
Slovenia	1,285.3	551.6	115.0	207.3	32.9	21.0	13.5	9.9	8.4	8.0	6.2	8.9	8.4	7.5	5.6	3.6	2.5	2.5	3.6	5.7	1.0
Tajikistan	2.0	5.6	111.6	1,156.7	2,600.7	350.4	612.5	418.5	88.0	43.2	27.5	32.9	38.6	12.2	16.4	7.2	7.3	10.0	13.2	20.4	6.4
Turkmenistan	2.1	4.6	103.0	493.0	3,102.0	1,748.0	1,005.3	992.4	83.7	16.8	24.2	8.3	11.6	8.8	5.6	5.9	10.7	10.5	8.6	12.0	5.5
Ukraine	2.2	4.2	91.0	1,210.0	4,734.0	891.0	377.0	80.0	15.9	10.6	22.7	28.2	12.0	0.8	5.2	9.0	13.5	9.1	12.8	25.2	15.9
Uzbekistan				645.2	534.2	1,568.3	304.6	54.0	70.9	29.0	29.1	25.0	27.3	27.3	11.6	6.6	10.0	14.2	12.3	12.7	12.5

Source: EBRD economic statistics and forecasts, available at http://www.ebrd.com/country/sector/econo/stats/index.htm, EBRD (2010), Eurostat figures for the Czech Republic from 2008, available at http://ec.europe.eu/eurostat

Table A.4 Unemployment (end year, % of labor force)

	1989	1990	1991	1992	1993	1994	1995	1996	1997	1998	1999	2000	2001	2002	2003	2004	2005	2006	2007	2008	2009[a]
Albania		9.5	8.3	24.4	18.6	16.0	10.2	12.4	14.9	17.8	18.4	16.8	16.4	15.8	15.0	14.4	14.1	13.8	13.2	12.7[a,b]	13.8[b]
Armenia				3.5	6.3	6.6	6.7	9.3	10.8	9.4	11.2	11.7	10.4	10.8	10.1	9.7	7.9	7.4	6.7	6.3	
Azerbaijan			15.4	0.5	0.5	0.6	0.7	0.8	1.0	1.1	1.1	1.1	1.3	1.4	1.4	1.4	1.4	6.8	6.5	4.3	
Belarus	0.0	0.0	0.1	0.5	1.4	2.1	2.7	3.9	2.8	2.3	2.1	2.1	2.3	2.9	3.0	1.9	1.5	1.2	1.0	0.8[a,c]	0.8[c]
Bosnia-Herzegovina										38.4	37.9	39.0	40.2	41.0	42.1	42.9	42.0	44.8	43.2	41.1	
Bulgaria		1.6	10.5	15.0	16.3	18.6	13.7	13.0	14.5	16.0	17.0	16.4	19.5	16.8	12.7	11.8	9.9	8.4	6.2	5.4[a]	8.3
Croatia		9.3	13.2	13.2	14.8	14.5	14.5	10.0	9.9	11.4	13.5	15.7	16.4	14.5	14.4	13.8	12.3	10.5	9.7	8.9[a]	9.5
Czech Republic		0.7	4.1	2.6	4.3	4.3	4.0	3.9	4.8	6.5	8.7	8.8	8.1	7.3	7.8	8.3	8.0	7.1	5.3	4.7[a]	7.4
Estonia	-0.6	0.6	1.5	3.7	6.6	7.6	9.7	10.0	9.6	9.8	12.2	13.6	12.6	10.3	10.0	9.6	7.9	5.9	4.7	7.6[a,b]	15.5
Georgia	0.0	0.0	0.1	5.4	9.1	3.6	3.1	2.8	7.5	12.5	14.8	10.4	10.3	11.9	10.7	12.5	13.8	13.6	13.3	12.9	10.7
Hungary	0.5	1.4	8.2	9.3	11.9	10.7	10.2	9.9	8.7	7.8	7.0	6.4	5.7	5.8	5.9	6.1	7.2	7.5	7.4	8.5[a]	10.7
Kazakhstan			0.1	0.4	0.5	8.0	10.1	7.6	6.5	13.1	13.5	12.8	10.4	9.3	8.8	8.4	8.1	7.8	7.3	6.6[a]	3.5
Kyrgyzstan					5.7					5.9	7.4	7.5	7.8	13.5	10.4	8.8	8.8	9.0	8.9		
Latvia		0.5	0.6	3.9	8.7	16.7	18.1	20.5	15.4	14.3	14.5	14.6	13.3	12.1	10.7	10.6	8.8	7.0	6.2	11.2[a]	20.4
Lithuania		0.3	0.3	1.3	4.4	3.8	17.5	16.4	14.1	13.2	14.6	16.4	17.4	13.8	12.4	11.4	8.3	5.6	4.3	7.9[a,b]	15.8
Macedonia, FYR	18.0	18.5	19.2	27.8	27.7	30.0	35.6	31.9	36.0	34.5	32.4	32.2	30.9	31.9	36.7	37.2	37.3	36.0	34.9	33.5[a]	32.4[b]
Moldova										10.1	11.1	8.5	7.3	6.8	7.9	8.1	7.3	7.4	5.1	3.9[a,b]	6.2[b]
Mongolia	3.8	5.5	6.5	6.3	8.5	8.7	5.4	6.5	7.7	5.9	4.7	4.6	4.6	3.4	3.5	3.6	3.3	3.2	2.8	3.3	
Montenegro			28.7	32.5	32.6	31.3	32.1	32.7	30.2	31.6	33.9	37.3	41.6	40.2	38.5	29.3	25.2	20.6	16.8	17.5	
Poland		6.5	12.2	14.3	16.4	16.0	14.9	13.2	10.1	11.0	15.1	16.6	18.5	19.7	19.3	18.0	16.7	12.2	8.5	7.1[a]	8.8
Romania		0.0	3.0	8.2	10.4	10.9	9.5	6.6	6.0	6.3	6.8	7.1	6.6	8.0	6.7	8.1	6.8	7.2	6.1	5.8[a,b]	7.6
Russia		0.0		5.3	6.0	7.7	9.2	9.3	10.8	11.9	12.9	10.2	8.9	8.5	7.8	7.9	7.1	6.7	5.6	7.7[a]	8.2
Serbia	17.9	19.7	22.2	23.8	23.1	22.7	24.2	25.4	24.1	24.6	25.5	25.6	26.8	29.0	31.7	31.6	32.4	33.2	29.9	31.0	
Slovakia		1.2	9.5	10.4	14.4	13.6	13.1	11.3	11.8	12.5	16.2	18.6	19.2	18.5	17.4	18.1	16.2	13.3	11.0	9.0[a]	14.2
Slovenia			7.3	8.3	9.1	9.1	7.2	6.9	7.1	7.4	7.4	6.4	7.0	6.6	6.8	6.6	7.4	5.7	4.8	4.4[a]	6.3
Tajikistan		0.0	0.0	0.4	1.2	1.7	2.0	2.6	2.8	3.2	3.0	2.7	2.3	2.5	2.4	2.0	1.9	2.2	2.2		
Turkmenistan	17.1		18.3	21.0	20.0	20.9	23.9	22.5	21.0	24.2	27.9	27.9	28.8	29.3	29.8	30.2					
Ukraine		0.0	0.0	0.2	0.3	0.3	0.3	1.3	2.3	3.7	4.3	11.6	10.9	9.6	9.1	8.6	7.2	6.8	6.4	6.4[a]	9.2
Uzbekistan	0.0	0.0	0.0	0.2	0.3	0.3	0.3	0.3	0.3	0.4	0.4	0.4	0.4	0.4	0.3	0.3	0.4	0.4	0.4	0.4	0.4

Source: EBRD economic statistics and forecasts, available at http://www.ebrd.com/country/sector/econo/stats/index.htm

Note: unemployment is measured by the ILO method as a percent of the active labor force.

[a] ILO data (http://www.ilo.org/pls/apex/f?p = 109:11:0) and Eurostat for EU member states (http://ec.europa.eu/eurostat)

[b] November data,

[c] registered unemployed

Table A.5 Average labor force participation rate (%), ages 15 to 64

	1989	1990	1991	1992	1993	1994	1995	1996	1997	1998	1999	2000	2001	2002	2003	2004	2005	2006	2007
Albania	80	82	65	65	66	66	66	67	66	66	66	66	66	66	66	66	66	66	67
Armenia	78	78	69	67	66	66	67	67	67	67	67	68	68	69	69	69	69	69	70
Azerbaijan	75	76	68	68	68	67	67	67	67	68	69	69	70	70	70	71	70	70	71
Belarus	78	77	76	76	75	74	73	73	72	71	70	70	70	70	71	71	71	71	70
Bosnia and Herzegovina	82	82	67	67	67	67	69	70	70	70	70	70	70	70	70	70	70	70	70
Bulgaria	72	72	69	69	68	67	66	65	63	62	60	59	63	63	61	62	62	65	63
Croatia	71	71	66	65	65	65	65	64	64	64	64	64	63	64	64	64	64	64	64
Czech Republic	82	82	72	72	72	73	72	72	72	72	72	72	71	71	71	70	70	70	71
Estonia	75	75	73	73	73	73	72	72	71	72	71	70	70	69	70	70	70	69	70
Georgia	79	80	72	70	68	67	67	68	69	69	69	66	69	67	69	67	67	68	68
Hungary	66	66	65	65	62	60	59	59	58	58	60	60	60	60	61	61	61	62	62
Kazakhstan	76	76	76	76	76	76	76	76	76	76	76	76	76	76	76	76	76	75	76
Kyrgyzstan	71	71	71	71	71	71	71	71	71	70	70	70	69	69	69	68	68	68	68
Latvia	80	79	78	76	75	74	72	70	70	69	69	67	68	69	69	70	69	71	72
Lithuania	76	76	75	75	74	74	73	73	72	73	74	71	70	70	70	69	68	68	67
Macedonia, FYR	69	69	63	62	62	61	61	61	61	60	60	60	60	61	61	59	61	62	62
Moldova	75	75	74	73	72	71	70	69	67	65	64	62	60	58	56	54	54	54	51
Poland	71	70	70	69	69	68	66	66	65	65	64	65	65	64	64	64	64	63	63
Romania	69	69	69	70	71	72	73	71	71	69	69	69	68	64	63	63	63	64	61
Russia	77	76	75	73	72	72	71	70	70	69	69	69	70	70	71	70	71	71	72
Serbia and Montenegro	79	79	65	64	64	64	65	66	67	67	67	68	68	68	69	69	69	70	70
Slovakia	83	83	76	74	72	70	69	70	69	69	69	70	70	70	70	70	69	69	70
Slovenia	76	76	68	65	61	67	68	68	68	69	68	68	68	69	67	70	70	71	70
Tajikistan	84	85	65	63	60	56	54	50	50	51	51	53	55	56	57	58	59	60	64
Turkmenistan	72	73	67	68	68	68	69	68	68	68	69	69	69	69	69	69	69	69	69
Ukraine	74	74	73	73	73	73	72	73	74	75	66	67	66	66	66	67	67	67	68
Uzbekistan	85	86	65	64	63	63	63	63	63	64	64	64	65	65	65	66	67	67	68

Source: ILO Economically Active Population Estimates and Projections (EAPEP) database, 5th edition (2008 revision), available at http://laborsta.ilo.org/applv8/data/ EAPEP/eapep_E.html. *Note*: Workforce is calculated as a percentage of population in the age category.

Table A.6 Industry, value added (% of GDP)

	1989	1990	1991	1992	1993	1994	1995	1996	1997	1998	1999	2000	2001	2002	2003	2004	2005	2006	2007	2008
Albania	44.8	48.2	42.7	23.3	22.9	21.7	22.5	20.2	18.7	16.0	16.8	19.0	19.8	18.5	21.1	21.2	21.5	20.4	20.0	19.7
Armenia		52.0	49.2	39.4	26.9	37.0	32.0	32.6	33.2	30.8	32.2	35.4	33.2	35.1	38.5	38.0	45.3	44.7	43.9	45.0
Azerbaijan		32.9	31.4	40.0	33.8	28.2	33.6	39.1	39.9	36.5	40.7	45.3	47.2	50.2	52.6	54.7	63.6	68.7	68.5	70.8
Belarus		47.1	49.9	47.8	38.4	36.0	37.0	38.6	41.2	40.6	39.2	39.2	37.2	37.0	38.7	40.9	41.8	42.4	41.7	38.6
Bosnia and Herzegovina[a]							23.9	21.4	22.6	22.5					16.1	16.4	16.3	16.0	16.3	16.0
Bulgaria	57.6	49.2	43.8	43.5	37.2	34.8	35.5	33.5	28.6	32.0	29.4	30.7	30.2	28.7	29.1	29.2	29.4	30.9	32.3	31.3
Croatia		35.8	34.6	32.9	36.1	33.3	31.4	30.5	31.3	29.7	28.4	28.4	28.2	27.4	27.9	28.9	28.3	28.4	28.2	28.4
Czech Republic		48.8	49.1	50.8	42.4	43.6	38.3	41.8	40.6	39.2	38.8	38.1	37.7	36.7	35.9	38.6	37.9	38.2	38.9	37.6
Estonia	40.6	49.7	40.1	34.7	31.0	30.2	33.0	31.2	31.0	29.2	27.0	27.8	28.4	28.4	28.6	28.1	29.0	29.7	30.4	
Georgia	38.7	33.5	37.2	23.9	22.0	10.3	15.8	23.7	23.6	22.9	22.5	22.4	22.0	24.4	25.6	26.4	26.8	24.9	24.1	23.7
Hungary	43.7	39.1	36.1	34.5	32.9	32.1	32.3	31.7	33.8	33.7	33.3	32.2	30.6	29.8	29.9	30.3	30.2	30.1	29.7	29.4
Kazakhstan				44.6	40.0	41.2	32.0	27.4	27.3	31.2	34.9	40.5	38.8	38.6	37.6	37.6	40.1	42.1	40.6	41.9
Kyrgyz Republic	43.9	35.8	35.5	37.8	32.0	25.5	19.5	18.3	22.8	27.6	25.0	31.4	28.9	23.3	22.3	24.1	21.6	20.1	18.9	
Latvia		46.2	43.9	34.9	35.0	31.3	30.4	28.6	29.5	27.6	24.8	23.6	23.1	22.7	22.3	22.3	21.6	21.9	22.0	
Lithuania		30.9	50.7	42.9	41.4	35.5	32.8	30.9	31.1	31.4	30.3	29.8	30.7	29.7	31.6	33.1	32.9	32.9	32.8	28.4
Macedonia, FYR		44.5	35.6	39.1	35.0	30.4	30.0	29.6	34.5	33.8	32.6	33.7	32.1	30.2	30.7	29.2	29.6	29.5	29.5	28.4
Moldova	39.2	36.7	33.3	31.5	44.0	38.4	32.2	30.7	29.0	24.5	19.0	21.7	24.1	23.2	24.5	17.3	16.3	15.6	14.8	15.0
Mongolia	38.8	40.6	34.2	33.9	27.7	28.5	29.4	22.1	27.2	21.5	21.7	20.3	20.7	22.0	25.0	29.8	34.4	42.3	41.5	
Montenegro												23.4	24.7	24.1	22.6	22.3	20.7	20.4	17.7	17.9
Poland		50.1	47.3	41.4	40.0	38.5	35.2	33.6	33.4	32.9	32.7	31.7	29.5	28.7	29.6	30.8	30.8	31.3	31.1	30.3
Romania		49.9	45.1	44.0	42.1	46.3	42.7	42.5	39.2	35.4	33.9	36.4	37.0	37.9	34.8	35.0	35.0	37.4	36.1	34.0
Russia	50.2	48.4	47.6	43.0	44.6	44.7	37.0	38.7	38.1	37.4	37.2	37.9	35.7	34.1	34.0	35.2	39.1	38.0	38.5	
Serbia												31.4	27.6	26.7	26.2	28.1	29.1	28.5	28.4	
Slovakia		59.1	60.1	37.9	33.0	33.6	37.8	39.0	35.2	34.6	35.3	36.2	34.8	34.0	35.0	36.5	36.5	39.0	40.5	41.2
Slovenia		42.4	45.0	40.9	38.8	40.2	35.1	35.4	35.8	36.4	36.1	35.8	35.5	34.8	35.1	34.5	34.1	34.4	34.4	
Tajikistan	36.2	37.6	36.9	46.1	46.5	41.0	39.3	31.6	28.7	27.0	29.6	38.9	40.1	39.4	37.4	31.8	31.3	27.4	27.5	22.9
Turkmenistan	33.8	29.6	31.0	11.9	64.0	46.7	62.6	68.8	48.0	42.2	46.0	44.4	44.3	42.4	41.3	40.1				
Ukraine	48.4	44.6	50.5	50.9	37.7	47.5	42.7	38.2	35.1	36.1	38.5	36.3	34.7	34.5	34.6	35.9	32.3	36.1	36.7	36.9
Uzbekistan	32.6	33.0	36.6	35.8	34.5	26.4	27.8	30.5	26.1	26.2	24.3	23.1	22.6	22.0	23.5	26.0	23.2	27.4	32.0	33.3

Source: World Bank national accounts data and OECD national accounts data files (available through World Bank world development indicators).

Note: Industry corresponds to the International Standard Industrial Classification (ISIC) divisions 10 through 45 and includes manufacturing (ISIC divisions 15 to 37). It comprises value added in mining, manufacturing (also reported as a separate subgroup), construction, electricity, water, and gas. Value added is the net output of a sector after adding up all outputs and subtracting intermediate inputs. It is calculated without making deductions for depreciation of fabricated assets or depletion and degradation of natural resources. The origin of value added is determined by the ISIC, revision 3.

[a] Data are from the EBRD (method of measurement differs).

Table A.7 Agriculture, value added (% of GDP)

	1989	1990	1991	1992	1993	1994	1995	1996	1997	1998	1999	2000	2001	2002	2003	2004	2005	2006	2007	2008
Albania	32.3	35.9	39.3	51.6	54.6	53.6	55.8	33.0	33.6	32.6	29.5	29.1	27.0	26.3	24.0	23.5	22.8	22.1	21.4	21.0
Armenia		17.4	25.0	31.0	51.4	44.9	42.3	36.8	32.0	34.0	29.5	25.5	28.3	26.0	23.7	24.7	20.9	20.5	20.3	17.8
Azerbaijan		29.0	32.3	28.5	28.5	33.0	27.3	27.5	21.7	18.9	19.2	17.1	16.1	15.2	13.5	11.8	9.9	7.5	5.9	5.9
Belarus		23.5	21.0	23.6	18.3	15.0	17.5	17.0	15.4	13.9	14.6	14.2	11.9	11.8	10.2	10.3	9.8	9.8	9.2	8.5
Bosnia and Herzegovina[a]							24.6	20.5	17.5	16.0					8.1	8.9	8.7	8.5	7.9	8.0
Bulgaria	10.6	17.0	16.9	12.9	11.3	13.3	14.5	16.4	26.8	19.1	16.6	14.2	13.7	12.2	11.7	11.0	9.4	8.5	6.2	7.3
Croatia		10.9	10.9	14.8	13.9	11.5	9.6	9.3	8.7	8.9	9.1	8.4	8.4	8.2	6.8	7.2	6.5	6.3	6.1	6.4
Czech Republic		6.2	6.0	5.1	5.6	5.3	5.0	4.7	4.2	4.2	3.9	3.9	3.9	3.3	3.1	3.3	3.0	2.6	2.4	2.3
Estonia	21.0	16.6	17.9	13.1	10.3	9.6						7.0	6.5	6.0	5.5	5.4	4.9	3.1	2.8	
Georgia	23.3	31.5	28.7	52.9	58.6	65.9	52.2	34.1	29.2	27.6	26.2	21.9	22.4	20.6	20.6	17.9	16.7	12.8	10.9	10.4
Hungary	15.6	14.5	8.9	7.5	6.8	7.0	7.1	6.9	6.1	5.7	5.0	5.4	5.3	4.6	4.3	4.8	4.2	4.1	4.0	4.3
Kazakhstan				26.7	17.5	15.5	12.9	12.8	12.0	9.1	10.5	8.7	9.4	8.6	8.4	7.6	6.8	5.9	6.1	6.2
Kyrgyz Republic	33.6	34.2	37.0	39.0	41.0	40.9	43.9	49.7	44.6	39.5	37.7	36.7	37.3	37.7	37.1	33.3	31.9	32.8	33.6	
Latvia	19.9	21.9	23.1	17.6	11.8	9.5	9.1	7.4	5.1	4.0	3.9	4.6	4.5	4.6	4.1	4.4	4.0	3.5	3.3	3.3
Lithuania	27.1		16.7	14.3	15.0	11.1	11.4	12.4	11.4	9.7	8.3	6.3	5.5	5.3	4.9	4.6	4.7	4.2	4.4	
Macedonia, FYR		8.5	13.6	17.1	11.8	13.3	13.2	13.2	12.8	13.2	12.9	12.0	11.8	12.4	13.4	13.2	12.8	12.7	12.0	11.3
Moldova	36.5	36.1	42.7	50.9	32.5	29.2	33.0	31.4	30.2	31.8	27.9	29.0	26.0	24.1	21.5	20.5	19.5	17.4	12.0	11.2
Mongolia	15.5	15.2	14.1	30.2	29.9	32.3	40.6	47.1	39.0	41.1	41.2	32.7	29.3	24.2	23.5	25.4	24.7	21.9	23.0	
Montenegro												12.5	11.9	12.2	11.6	10.9	10.5	10.2	9.3	8.9
Poland		8.3	6.6	6.6	6.6	6.9	8.0	7.5	6.6	6.0	5.2	5.0	5.1	4.5	4.4	5.1	4.6	4.5	4.3	4.2
Romania		23.7	20.1	19.4	22.6	21.5	21.4	20.6	19.6	16.2	15.2	12.5	15.0	12.8	13.0	14.3	10.1	10.5	9.0	8.0
Russia	16.8	16.6	14.3	7.4	8.3	6.6	7.2	7.2	6.4	5.6	7.3	6.4	6.6	5.7	5.4	5.0	5.5	5.1	4.8	
Serbia												20.6	19.7	15.9	14.4	14.2	16.0	14.8	13.0	
Slovakia	9.4	7.4	5.7	5.3	5.6	5.9	5.9	5.5	5.3	5.4	4.7	4.5	4.7	5.1	4.5	4.1	3.7	3.6	3.5	3.6
Slovenia		5.6	5.8	5.9	5.2	4.6	4.4	4.2	4.2	4.0	3.4	3.3	3.0	3.3	2.5	2.7	2.7	2.4	2.4	
Tajikistan	32.1	33.3	36.6	27.4	23.3	24.0	38.4	39.0	35.4	27.2	27.4	27.4	26.2	24.7	27.1	21.6	24.0	24.8	21.4	18.0
Turkmenistan	28.9	32.2	32.3	10.6	19.4	34.0	17.2	13.3	21.6	26.2	26.2	24.4	24.4	22.0	20.3	19.6	24.0			
Ukraine	22.9	25.6	22.8	20.4	21.7	16.2	15.4	13.8	14.4	14.2	14.3	17.1	16.4	14.6	12.1	11.9	10.4	8.7	7.5	8.3
Uzbekistan	31.1	32.8	37.0	34.8	30.4	37.4	32.3	26.1	32.2	31.3	33.5	34.4	34.0	34.3	33.1	30.8	28.0	26.1	24.0	23.4

Source: World Bank national accounts data and OECD national accounts data files (available through World Bank world development indicators).

Note: Agriculture corresponds to the International Standard Industrial Classification (ISIC) divisions 1 through 5 and includes forestry, hunting, and fishing, as well as cultivation of crops and livestock production. Value added is the net output of a sector after adding up all outputs and subtracting intermediate inputs. It is calculated without making deductions for depreciation of fabricated assets or depletion and degradation of natural resources. The origin of value added is determined by the ISIC, revision 3.

[a]Data are from the EBRD (method of measurement differs).

Table A.8 Services, value added (% of GDP)

	1989	1990	1991	1992	1993	1994	1995	1996	1997	1998	1999	2000	2001	2002	2003	2004	2005	2006	2007	2008
Albania	22.9	15.9	18.0	25.0	22.5	24.6	21.7	46.8	47.7	51.4	53.7	51.9	53.3	55.2	54.9	55.3	55.7	57.5	58.6	59.3
Armenia		30.7	25.8	29.6	21.7	18.2	25.8	30.6	34.8	35.2	38.3	39.0	38.5	39.0	37.8	37.4	33.8	34.9	35.8	37.2
Azerbaijan		38.1	36.3	31.5	37.7	38.8	39.1	33.4	38.3	44.6	40.1	37.5	36.7	34.6	34.0	33.4	26.5	23.8	25.6	23.3
Belarus		29.4	29.1	28.6	43.3	49.0	45.6	44.4	43.4	45.5	46.2	46.7	50.9	51.2	51.1	48.8	48.5	47.9	49.0	52.8
Bulgaria	31.8	33.8	39.3	43.6	51.5	51.9	50.0	50.1	44.6	48.9	54.0	55.1	56.1	59.1	59.1	59.8	61.2	60.6	61.5	61.5
Croatia		53.4	54.5	52.2	50.0	55.2	58.9	60.2	60.0	61.4	62.5	63.2	63.4	64.4	65.3	63.9	65.2	65.3	65.7	65.1
Czech Republic	38.4	45.0	44.9	44.1	52.0	51.1	56.7	53.5	55.2	56.6	57.4	58.0	58.3	60.0	61.0	58.1	59.1	59.2	58.7	60.1
Estonia		33.7	42.0	52.2	58.7	60.2						65.2	65.2	65.6	65.9	66.4	66.0	67.2	66.8	
Georgia	38.0	35.0	34.1	23.2	19.4	23.8	32.1	42.1	47.1	49.5	51.2	55.7	55.6	55.0	53.8	55.7	56.5	62.3	65.0	65.9
Hungary	40.7	46.4	55.0	58.0	60.3	60.8	60.6	61.4	60.2	60.6	61.8	62.4	64.2	65.5	65.8	64.9	65.6	65.9	66.3	66.2
Kazakhstan				28.7	42.5	43.4	55.1	59.8	60.7	59.7	54.6	50.8	51.8	52.8	53.9	54.8	53.1	52.0	53.3	51.9
Kyrgyz Republic		30.0	27.6	23.2	27.0	33.7	36.6	32.0	32.6	37.7	37.3	31.9	33.8	39.0	40.6	42.6	45.7	47.2	47.5	
Latvia	36.1	31.9	32.9	47.5	53.2	59.2	60.6	64.0	65.4	68.4	71.3	71.8	72.4	72.7	73.6	73.3	74.5	74.6	74.7	
Lithuania		42.1	32.5	42.8	43.7	53.4	55.8	56.6	57.6	58.9	61.4	63.9	63.9	65.0	63.5	62.4	62.4	62.9	62.8	
Macedonia, FYR		47.0	50.8	43.9	53.1	56.3	56.8	57.2	52.7	52.9	54.5	54.2	56.1	57.5	56.0	57.7	57.6	57.8	58.5	60.3
Moldova	24.3	27.2	23.9	17.6	23.5	32.4	34.8	37.9	40.8	43.8	53.1	49.2	49.9	52.7	54.0	62.2	64.1	67.0	73.2	73.8
Mongolia	45.7	44.2	51.7	35.9	42.3	39.3	30.0	30.8	33.8	37.4	37.1	47.0	50.0	53.8	51.4	44.8	40.9	35.9	35.6	
Montenegro												64.1	63.4	63.7	65.8	66.8	68.8	69.4	73.1	73.2
Poland		41.6	46.1	52.0	53.4	54.6	56.8	58.9	60.0	61.2	62.1	63.3	65.4	66.8	66.0	64.1	64.6	64.6	64.6	65.5
Romania		26.3	34.8	36.6	35.3	32.2	35.8	37.0	41.2	48.4	51.0	51.1	48.1	49.3	52.2	50.7	54.9	52.1	55.0	58.0
Russian Federation	33.0	35.0	38.1	49.6	47.1	48.6	55.9	54.1	55.5	57.0	55.5	55.6	57.7	60.2	60.7	59.8	55.3	57.0	56.8	
Serbia												48.1	52.7	57.4	59.3	57.7	54.8	56.7	58.6	
Slovakia	32.2	33.5	34.2	56.7	61.5	60.5	56.3	55.5	59.5	60.0	59.9	59.3	60.5	61.0	60.5	59.4	59.9	57.5	56.0	55.2
Slovenia		51.9	49.2	53.1	55.9	55.2	60.5	60.4	60.0	59.6	60.5	60.9	61.5	61.9	62.4	62.8	63.2	63.3	63.3	
Tajikistan	31.8	29.1	26.4	26.5	30.2	35.0	22.2	29.5	35.9	45.8	43.0	33.7	33.8	35.9	35.4	46.6	44.7	47.8	51.0	59.0
Turkmenistan	37.3	38.2	36.7	77.5	16.6	19.3	20.2	17.8	30.4	31.6	27.8	31.2	31.4	35.6	38.4	40.3				
Ukraine	28.7	29.9	26.7	28.7	40.6	36.2	41.9	48.0	50.5	49.6	47.2	46.6	48.9	50.8	53.3	52.2	57.3	55.2	55.8	54.8
Uzbekistan	36.3	34.3	26.5	29.4	35.1	36.1	39.9	43.4	41.7	42.5	42.2	42.5	43.4	43.7	43.4	43.3	48.9	46.5	44.0	43.4

Source: World Bank national accounts data and OECD national accounts data files (available through World Bank world development indicators.)

Note: Services correspond to International Standard Industrial Classification (ISIC) divisions 50 through 99 and include value added in wholesale and retail trade (including hotels and restaurants), transport, and government, financial, professional, and personal services such as education, health care, and real estate services. Also included are imputed bank service charges, import duties, and any statistical discrepancies noted by national compilers as well as discrepancies arising from rescaling. Value added is the net output of a sector after adding up all outputs and subtracting intermediate inputs. It is calculated without making deductions for depreciation of fabricated assets or depletion and degradation of natural resources. The industrial origin of value added is determined by the ISIC, revision 3.

Table A.9 Exports of goods and services (% of GDP)

	1989	1990	1991	1992	1993	1994	1995	1996	1997	1998	1999	2000	2001	2002	2003	2004	2005	2006	2007	2008
Albania	17.9	14.9	7.2	11.5	15.4	11.4	12.5	12.3	10.5	10.8	17.3	19.1	20.5	20.4	20.6	21.5	22.3	25.1	27.8	28.5
Armenia		35.0	40.7	39.8	47.2	39.3	23.9	23.2	20.3	19.0	20.8	23.4	25.5	29.4	32.2	27.4	28.8	23.4	19.2	14.8
Azerbaijan		43.9	45.7	86.2	57.4	24.7	27.9	29.5	29.0	22.7	28.0	39.0	40.9	42.8	42.0	48.8	62.9	66.5	68.1	67.6
Belarus		46.0	36.9	59.3	67.6	71.3	49.7	46.3	59.9	59.1	59.2	69.2	66.7	63.6	65.2	67.9	59.8	60.1	61.0	65.2
Bosnia and Herzegovina						15.4	20.4	23.6	27.8	27.3	27.6	28.7	28.4	24.3	26.1	29.4	33.0	36.6	39.1	34.6
Bulgaria	46.4	33.1	43.5	47.1	38.2	45.0	44.8	55.4	58.3	47.1	44.6	55.7	55.6	51.5	53.3	57.0	60.2	64.5	63.4	60.5
Croatia			77.7	59.6	52.4	45.8	33.0	35.8	35.5	35.1	36.5	42.0	43.8	41.0	42.9	43.3	42.6	43.4	42.8	41.9
Czech Republic		45.2	52.8	54.5	55.8	50.5	50.7	48.9	52.1	54.2	55.5	63.4	65.4	60.2	61.8	70.1	72.2	76.6	80.2	76.8
Estonia				60.3	66.6	71.8	68.3	62.1	72.0	74.9	70.8	85.4	80.5	71.1	69.4	73.0	80.0	80.9	74.4	
Georgia	42.4	39.9	27.8	35.7	46.9	57.8	25.5	13.3	15.6	16.5	19.1	23.0	24.5	29.2	31.8	31.6	33.7	32.9	31.5	30.8
Hungary	36.0	31.1	32.8	31.4	26.4	28.9	44.6	48.5	55.1	61.9	64.3	72.2	71.2	63.1	60.8	63.2	66.0	77.1	80.4	81.4
Kazakhstan				74.0	37.9	37.1	39.0	35.3	34.9	30.3	42.5	56.6	45.9	47.0	48.4	52.2	53.5	51.1	49.4	60.7
Kyrgyz Republic		29.2	35.3	35.6	33.5	33.8	29.5	30.7	38.3	36.5	42.2	41.8	36.7	39.6	38.7	42.6	38.7	41.7	44.7	
Latvia		47.7	35.2	79.9	73.2	46.5	42.7	46.8	46.8	47.2	40.4	41.6	41.6	40.9	42.1	44.0	47.8	44.9	41.9	
Lithuania	52.1		29.6	23.4	82.5	55.4	49.2	51.4	52.2	45.4	38.8	44.7	49.8	52.7	51.2	52.1	57.5	59.1	54.4	59.2
Macedonia, FYR		25.8	22.9	54.3	46.8	38.2	33.0	28.2	37.3	41.2	42.2	48.6	42.7	38.0	37.9	40.2	44.7	48.1	53.2	56.0
Moldova		48.2	32.4	38.9	21.1	38.2	49.3	55.3	54.8	48.5	52.1	49.8	49.9	52.7	53.5	50.7	51.1	45.2	45.6	43.7
Mongolia	22.5	22.4	64.6	34.3	69.3	52.6	48.0	40.5	59.0	55.3	58.6	56.4	54.6	55.7	57.7	66.7	64.3	65.3	64.3	
Montenegro												36.8	38.4	35.4	30.6	42.0	43.5	49.4	46.3	41.1
Poland		28.6	23.5	23.7	22.9	23.8	23.2	22.3	23.4	26.0	24.2	27.1	27.1	28.6	33.3	37.5	37.1	40.3	40.6	37.1
Romania		16.7	17.6	27.8	23.0	24.9	27.6	28.1	29.2	22.6	28.0	32.9	33.3	35.4	34.7	35.9	32.9	33.7	31.3	27.5
Russian Federation		18.2	13.3	62.3	38.2	27.8	29.3	26.1	24.7	31.2	43.2	44.1	36.9	35.2	35.2	34.4	35.2	33.8	30.5	33.4
Serbia	21.9								16.7	22.6	17.1	23.0	20.7	18.7	21.4	22.7	25.2	28.7	29.4	31.4
Slovak Republic	28.8	26.5	46.3	70.3	56.3	58.7	57.8	53.4	56.4	59.2	61.2	70.5	72.7	71.1	75.9	74.5	76.3	84.4	86.5	77.7
Slovenia		90.8	83.5	63.1	58.8	58.9	49.9	50.2	51.7	51.4	47.6	53.9	55.5	55.2	54.0	58.0	62.2	66.6	70.2	
Tajikistan	35.9	27.8	33.2	9.7	28.6	43.0	65.6	76.6	87.2	48.9	66.1	98.8	68.0	65.5	63.4	58.3	26.0	23.3	20.7	16.7
Turkmenistan					84.7	85.0	84.0	74.6	42.7	32.7	56.1	95.5	81.4	69.0	62.3	61.7	65.0	73.7	62.7	47.5
Ukraine	32.1	27.6	26.1	24.0	25.9	35.4	47.1	45.7	40.6	41.9	53.7	62.4	55.5	55.1	57.8	61.2	51.5	46.6	44.8	41.7
Uzbekistan		28.8	35.3	27.0	33.7	16.8	27.9	27.7	27.0	22.5	18.1	24.6	28.1	30.8	37.3	40.2	37.9	37.5	40.3	41.9

Source: World Bank national accounts data and OECD national accounts data files.

Note: Exports of goods and services represent the value of all goods and other market services provided to the rest of the world. They include the value of merchandise, freight, insurance, transport, travel, royalties, license fees, and other services, such as communication, construction, financial, information, business, personal, and government services. They exclude labor and property income (formerly called factor services) as well as transfer payments.

Table A.10 Imports of goods and services (% of GDP)

	1989	1990	1991	1992	1993	1994	1995	1996	1997	1998	1999	2000	2001	2002	2003	2004	2005	2006	2007	2008
Albania	20.7	23.2	27.6	88.5	62.3	39.0	34.5	35.2	36.7	34.4	32.0	37.5	38.7	46.7	45.9	43.3	46.3	49.2	54.3	55.0
Armenia		46.3	60.1	61.3	60.8	73.1	62.2	56.0	58.3	52.8	49.8	50.5	46.1	46.6	50.0	42.1	43.2	39.3	39.2	39.7
Azerbaijan		39.2	41.2	54.6	76.0	30.6	41.5	55.5	53.0	54.5	41.9	38.4	37.3	50.0	65.6	72.7	52.9	38.8	28.5	25.6
Belarus		43.6	33.4	57.8	83.4	84.1	54.1	50.4	65.7	63.9	61.6	72.4	70.3	67.4	69.0	74.3	59.1	64.2	67.1	71.2
Bosnia and Herzegovina						86.4	71.5	83.9	72.8	98.4	94.2	75.5	75.9	70.9	71.6	70.7	74.7	66.4	73.7	64.4
Bulgaria	48.2	36.7	39.2	52.9	45.8	45.7	46.3	50.0	53.7	46.8	50.3	61.1	63.1	59.9	64.0	68.5	76.4	83.3	85.5	83.4
Croatia			86.1	54.2	53.6	45.9	41.4	42.4	48.5	41.9	42.7	45.3	47.6	49.4	50.8	49.6	49.1	50.4	50.4	50.3
Czech Republic		42.6	45.7	53.6	54.3	53.2	55.1	54.8	57.3	55.3	56.6	66.4	67.9	62.3	64.1	70.1	69.0	73.1	75.1	71.8
Estonia				54.4	70.7	82.2	75.9	73.1	82.9	84.9	75.7	89.0	83.0	78.5	76.9	81.2	86.3	92.4	85.3	
Georgia	45.1	45.7	31.1	66.3	71.8	109.1	42.3	32.4	42.1	37.1	38.1	39.7	38.9	42.4	46.4	48.2	51.6	57.0	57.7	59.2
Hungary	32.7	28.5	33.7	31.7	34.6	35.4	44.7	48.0	54.1	63.4	67.0	75.8	72.5	65.1	64.7	66.5	67.8	77.8	78.8	80.2
Kazakhstan				75.3	46.7	47.1	43.5	36.0	37.4	34.9	40.1	49.1	47.0	47.0	43.0	43.5	44.7	40.4	42.6	40.7
Kyrgyz Republic		49.6	36.6	47.6	41.2	40.1	42.4	56.6	46.2	58.0	57.0	47.6	37.0	43.3	45.3	51.3	57.7	79.0	89.9	
Latvia		49.0	25.5	73.1	57.0	44.4	44.9	54.3	54.7	59.6	49.6	48.7	51.1	50.6	54.6	59.6	62.2	66.3	61.1	
Lithuania		60.7	21.0	19.9	90.4	61.4	60.1	60.9	62.4	56.8	48.9	51.0	55.3	58.4	57.0	59.1	64.6	69.3	67.8	70.6
Macedonia, FYR		35.9	25.9	53.4	54.7	48.4	42.8	38.5	50.8	56.1	52.2	63.5	56.6	58.2	54.8	60.5	62.0	66.8	72.2	77.3
Moldova		50.6	34.0	40.6	29.7	44.1	58.0	73.9	74.3	75.0	67.4	75.4	73.5	77.9	87.2	82.0	91.7	91.8	97.7	96.9
Mongolia	53.9	49.4	98.6	43.2	82.3	64.2	49.2	48.5	53.0	68.8	72.5	70.9	71.1	74.4	74.9	77.4	68.2	59.7	65.7	74.0
Montenegro												51.1	62.0	59.9	47.0	58.1	61.1	77.7	84.9	
Poland		21.5	25.4	22.2	22.0	21.6	21.0	23.7	27.3	30.8	30.1	33.5	30.7	32.1	35.9	39.5	37.4	41.0	43.3	40.4
Romania		26.2	21.5	36.2	28.0	27.0	33.2	36.6	36.2	30.6	32.9	38.5	41.1	41.1	42.2	45.0	43.3	44.1	43.7	37.1
Russia	21.0	17.9	13.0	48.3	30.5	23.2	25.9	21.8	22.5	24.6	26.2	24.0	24.2	24.4	23.8	22.1	21.5	21.0	21.8	22.5
Serbia									24.1	29.6	27.3	39.1	38.3	38.3	40.2	46.3	47.3	49.4	51.5	55.5
Slovakia	32.1	35.5	49.3	74.3	60.0	53.8	55.6	64.1	66.0	70.0	65.6	73.0	80.8	78.3	77.7	77.2	80.8	88.3	87.5	76.3
Slovenia		78.5	74.2	56.2	57.7	56.3	51.8	51.2	52.5	52.9	51.8	57.4	56.3	54.1	54.2	59.3	62.6	67.1	71.5	
Tajikistan	48.7	35.2	32.2	12.5	41.6	54.6	71.9	80.0	93.9	58.0	67.5	100.9	78.4	76.1	73.5	69.9	52.8	57.5	66.4	58.3
Turkmenistan					61.4	85.3	84.2	75.4	68.5	70.8	83.5	80.9	76.9	53.4	56.6	59.5	47.8	55.2	47.9	36.9
Ukraine	32.1	28.7	23.9	22.0	26.2	38.6	50.2	48.2	43.7	44.2	48.2	57.4	53.8	50.7	55.2	53.7	50.6	49.5	50.4	47.8
Uzbekistan		47.8	39.1	43.2	30.5	20.6	28.1	34.2	30.0	22.8	18.4	21.5	27.6	29.3	30.6	32.7	28.7	27.4	30.2	31.6

Source: World Bank national accounts data and OECD national accounts data files.

Note: Imports of goods and services represent the value of all goods and other market services received from the rest of the world. They include the value of merchandise, freight, insurance, transport, travel, royalties, license fees, and other services, such as communication, construction, financial, information, business, personal, and government services. They exclude labor and property income (formerly called factor services) as well as transfer payments.

Table A.11 Foreign direct investment (inward) as a percentage of GDP: Stock

	1989	1990	1991	1992	1993	1994	1995	1996	1997	1998	1999	2000	2001	2002	2003	2004	2005	2006	2007	2008
Albania	0.0	0.0	0.0	1.3	5.0	7.2	8.5	9.1	15.0	14.5	12.7	6.8	8.0	8.1	9.8	11.5	12.2	15.3	19.2	20.8
Armenia				2.6	2.9	3.4	5.1	5.2	8.3	18.8	25.9	30.5	30.8	32.1	31.5	30.8	27.8	27.8	26.7	29.6
Azerbaijan				0.0	0.0	0.0	10.7	30.1	52.7	69.6	78.7	70.8	69.4	85.9	118.7	140.5	90.1	54.1	21.1	14.4
Belarus				0.0	0.1	0.2	0.4	1.1	3.6	4.7	9.5	12.5	11.3	11.3	10.7	8.9	7.9	7.4	10.1	11.2
Bosnia and Herzegovina				0.0	0.0	0.0	0.0	0.0	17.8	17.5	19.6	23.5	24.6	25.8	25.8	27.9	27.5	33.1	45.8	43.5
Croatia				1.3	2.5	2.7	2.6	5.0	10.6	9.0	12.9	15.2	19.6	26.2	28.8	35.2	37.9	63.7	87.9	51.2
Czech Republic	2.5	3.1	5.8	7.6	9.2	10.4	13.3	13.8	16.2	23.2	29.2	38.2	43.8	51.4	49.6	52.3	48.6	55.8	65.4	53.2
Estonia				2.2	6.1	11.2	15.1	17.3	22.6	32.0	43.1	47.0	51.0	57.8	71.3	84.5	81.2	76.6	79.0	67.5
Georgia					0.6	1.0	1.2	2.2	7.0	14.2	21.2	24.9	27.3	30.9	35.0	37.3	37.1	46.0	53.0	54.0
Hungary	0.0	1.6	6.1	8.9	14.1	16.6	24.6	28.6	38.3	42.9	47.1	47.7	51.4	54.4	57.2	61.2	56.1	72.7	72.6	41.1
Kazakhstan				0.0	5.2	8.8	14.1	19.2	24.2	29.4	47.3	55.1	58.3	62.8	57.0	51.9	44.8	40.6	42.8	44.4
Kyrgyzstan				0.0	0.5	3.1	9.7	10.5	15.5	23.4	34.2	31.5	27.1	29.3	27.2	32.2	21.0	21.9	21.9	20.4
Latvia				3.2	4.6	8.9	12.4	16.5	20.3	23.1	24.6	26.6	28.0	29.5	29.3	32.9	30.7	37.5	39.2	35.9
Lithuania				1.4	2.1	5.2	5.4	8.6	10.4	14.5	18.9	20.4	21.9	28.2	26.7	28.4	31.9	37.0	39.3	27.5
Macedonia, FYR						2.3	1.9	2.2	4.2	8.9	9.8	15.0	26.6	31.9	34.9	40.8	35.9	43.4	49.5	47.8
Moldova				0.7	0.6	1.7	5.5	7.2	10.1	14.9	27.3	34.8	37.1	38.5	36.2	33.4	35.2	38.3	42.2	42.0
Poland		0.2	0.5	1.5	2.5	3.5	5.6	7.3	9.3	13.0	15.5	20.0	21.7	24.4	26.7	34.3	29.9	36.8	41.9	31.1
Romania		0.0	0.2	0.6	0.8	1.3	2.3	3.1	6.8	10.7	15.4	18.8	20.8	17.1	20.5	27.1	26.1	37.1	39.0	37.7
Russia				0.0	0.0	0.8	1.4	2.1	3.4	4.8	9.3	12.4	17.3	20.5	22.4	20.7	23.6	27.0	38.1	12.8
Serbia and Montenegro									3.3	4.1	7.1	8.9	7.9	9.0	12.8	14.3	19.8	31.2	34.0	38.1
Slovakia					4.7	5.7	6.6	9.6	9.8	13.0	15.5	23.2	26.4	34.8	44.2	52.1	49.9	61.0	61.3	49.2
Slovenia				14.1	14.8	13.9	12.7	13.2	11.0	8.0	10.4	14.8	12.9	18.2	22.3	22.9	20.6	23.5	30.6	29.8
Tajikistan				0.4	1.1	2.2	3.2	5.6	8.2	8.0	10.4	15.8	13.5	14.9	13.7	12.1	13.2	22.8	27.1	16.7
Turkmenistan					2.9	7.9	19.0	22.0	23.5	24.2	21.2	22.8	25.2	31.1	34.2	38.6	41.3	48.0	54.2	36.1
Ukraine				0.4	0.7	0.9	1.8	3.2	4.1	6.7	10.3	12.4	12.6	14.0	15.1	14.8	20.0	21.5	27.0	26.3
Uzbekistan				0.1	0.4	1.0	0.8	1.4	2.3	3.4	3.7	5.1	8.4	8.6	9.0	9.2	8.7	8.1	11.0	12.6

Source: UNCTAD major FDI indicators, available at http://stats.unctad.org/FDI/.
Note: FDI stock is the value of the share of their capital and reserves (including retained profits) attributable to the parent enterprise, plus the net indebtedness of affiliates to the parent enterprises.

Table A.12 Foreign direct investment (inward) as a percentage of GDP: Flows

	1989	1990	1991	1992	1993	1994	1995	1996	1997	1998	1999	2000	2001	2002	2003	2004	2005	2006	2007	2008
Albania	0.00	0.00	0.00	1.29	3.90	2.72	2.83	2.72	2.05	1.66	1.20	3.96	5.08	2.99	3.11	4.73	3.23	3.57	6.14	7.56
Armenia				0.20	0.07	0.78	1.97	1.10	3.17	11.67	6.61	5.45	3.30	4.66	4.31	6.93	4.88	7.10	7.20	9.52
Azerbaijan				0.00	0.00	0.64	5.03	18.61	26.52	21.32	7.75	0.57	3.85	22.34	44.35	40.72	12.68	-2.86	-15.42	0.02
Belarus				0.04	0.10	0.07	0.11	0.72	2.49	1.33	3.66	1.14	0.78	1.69	0.96	0.71	1.01	0.96	3.99	3.62
Bosnia and Herzegovina				0.00	0.00	0.00	0.00	0.00	0.00	1.58	3.78	3.23	2.48	4.73	5.37	7.02	5.70	5.85	14.32	5.64
Croatia				0.13	1.32	0.79	0.57	2.48	2.69	4.35	7.29	6.02	7.97	4.78	6.92	3.06	4.64	8.05	9.72	7.22
Czech Republic	0.00	0.31	1.56	2.49	1.76	1.99	4.64	2.30	2.28	6.01	10.51	8.79	9.12	11.28	2.21	4.55	9.30	3.82	6.07	4.99
Estonia				1.88	3.86	5.10	4.50	3.15	5.25	10.19	5.33	6.88	8.76	3.89	9.36	8.12	21.11	10.76	12.86	8.33
Georgia				0.00	0.00	0.31	0.22	1.78	6.91	7.34	2.94	4.29	3.41	4.72	8.38	9.60	7.06	15.11	17.20	12.21
Hungary	0.00	1.51	4.28	3.86	6.16	2.68	11.12	7.11	8.87	6.90	6.71	5.76	7.38	4.49	2.53	4.41	6.97	6.67	4.41	4.21
Kazakhstan				0.38	5.17	3.01	4.69	5.40	5.96	5.20	8.72	7.01	12.80	10.51	6.78	9.63	3.45	7.75	10.68	11.07
Kyrgyzstan				0.00	0.53	2.47	6.44	2.56	4.70	6.66	3.55	-0.17	0.33	0.29	2.37	7.93	1.73	6.42	5.55	4.67
Latvia				0.58	0.95	4.38	3.62	6.72	8.33	5.30	4.77	5.27	1.59	2.72	2.71	4.63	4.45	8.35	8.27	4.47
Lithuania				0.13	0.47	0.51	1.12	1.86	3.55	8.28	4.46	3.32	3.67	5.18	0.97	3.43	4.01	6.18	5.26	3.89
Macedonia, FYR	0.01			0.00	0.00	0.71	0.21	0.25	1.56	4.20	2.41	6.00	13.01	2.78	2.54	6.02	1.67	6.66	9.26	6.60
Poland	0.01	0.14	0.43	0.73	1.82	1.73	2.63	2.87	3.12	3.68	4.33	5.45	3.00	2.08	2.25	5.05	3.37	5.75	5.39	3.18
Republic of Moldova				0.69	0.56	0.69	3.79	1.40	4.08	4.45	3.23	9.90	3.68	5.06	3.72	3.38	6.38	7.37	11.23	11.64
Romania			0.00	0.39	0.35	1.13	1.17	0.74	3.42	4.82	2.89	2.85	2.88	2.49	3.69	8.52	6.55	9.27	6.15	6.98
Russia			0.14	0.24	0.26	0.17	0.52	0.66	1.20	1.02	1.69	1.05	0.90	1.00	1.84	2.61	1.69	3.02	4.27	4.21
Serbia and Montenegro[a]									3.28	0.54	0.83	0.45	1.18	2.90	5.63	3.46	6.52	13.72	9.29	
Slovakia				0.86	0.87	0.79	13.12	1.73	1.07	3.23	2.08	9.45	7.50	16.89	6.55	7.21	5.12	8.52	4.42	3.66
Slovenia				0.45	0.53	0.87	0.73	0.84	1.67	1.01	0.49	0.70	1.83	7.14	1.07	2.49	1.67	1.69	3.13	3.43
Tajikistan							0.81	1.72	1.95	2.27	0.62	2.74	0.88	2.95	2.03	13.10	2.36	11.96	9.63	7.27
Turkmenistan					2.89	4.46	10.65	4.54	4.02	2.18	3.24	3.15	3.83	6.14	4.77	6.91	7.22	11.22	11.08	6.24
Ukraine				0.25	0.29	0.29	0.55	1.17	1.24	1.77	1.57	1.90	2.08	1.63	2.84	2.64	9.06	5.20	7.01	5.99
Uzbekistan	0.01	0.07	0.14	0.07	0.35	0.55	-0.18	0.64	1.07	0.93	0.71	0.54	0.89	0.66	0.69	1.56	0.64	1.14	3.83	3.81

Source: UNCTAD major FDI indicators, available at http://stats.unctad.org/FDI/.

Note: FDI inflows are comprised of capital provided (either directly or through other related enterprises) by a foreign direct investor to a FDI enterprise or of capital received by a foreign direct investor from a FDI enterprise. Foreign direct investment includes the three following components: equity capital, reinvested earnings and intracompany loans.

Equity capital is the foreign direct investor's purchase of shares of an enterprise in a country other than that of its residence.

Reinvested earnings comprise the direct investor's share (in proportion to direct equity participation) of earnings not distributed as dividends by affiliates or earnings not remitted to the direct investor. Such retained profits by affiliates are reinvested.

Data on FDI flows are presented on net bases (capital transactions' credits less debits between direct investors and their foreign affiliates). Net decreases in assets or net increases in liabilities are recorded as credits (with a positive sign), while net increases in assets or net decreases in liabilities are recorded as debits (with a negative sign). Hence, FDI flows with a negative sign indicate that at least one of the three components of FDI is negative and not offset by positive amounts of the remaining components. This are called reverse investment or disinvestment.

[a] Data for 1988 to 1991 inclusively refer to Slovenia only, except for the FDI inflows that also cover other republics of the former Yugoslavia.

Table A.13 Current account (% of GDP)

	1989	1990	1991	1992	1993	1994	1995	1996	1997	1998	1999	2000	2001	2002	2003	2004	2005	2006	2007	2008	2009
Albania	-1.7	-5.6	-15.0	-8.1	1.2	-8.1	-0.5	-3.2	-11.3	-2.4	-4.5	-4.2	-5.3	-9.2	-7.1	-4.9	-6.9	-7.4	-7.6	-15.7	-15.3
Armenia					-14.3	-16.0	-17.0	-18.2	-18.7	-22.1	-16.6	-14.6	-9.4	-6.2	-6.7	-0.5	-1.1	-1.8	-6.2	-11.5	-15.2
Azerbaijan[a]			19.3		-10.2	-10.3	-13.2	-25.8	-23.1	-30.7	-13.1	-3.5	-0.9	-12.3	-27.8	-29.8	1.3	17.7	28.8	35.5	14.8
Belarus					-11.9	-9.1	-4.3	-3.6	-6.1	-6.7	-1.6	-3.2	-3.2	-2.3	-2.4	-5.2	1.4	-3.9	-6.8	-8.4	-13.1
Bosnia-Herzegovina								-24.0[a]	-26.6[a]	-7.5	-10.1	-7.5	-13.4	-19.3	-19.5	-16.4	-16.8	-7.9	-12.8	-15.0	-8.8
Bulgaria	-1.6	-8.2	-1.0	-4.2	-10.1	-0.3	-0.2	0.2	4.1	-0.5	-5.0	-5.6	-5.9	-2.0	-5.1	-6.8	-12.3	-18.5	-25.4	-24.0	-9.4
Croatia			-3.8[a]	3.4[a]	6.5	5.0	-6.3	-4.2	-11.9	-5.8	-6.7	-2.5	-3.2	-7.3	-6.4	-4.6	-5.7	-6.7	-7.6	-9.2	-5.2
Czech Republic					1.3	-2.0	-2.5	-6.7	-6.3	-2.1	-2.4	-4.7	-5.3	-5.7	-6.3	-5.2	-1.3	-2.7	-1.9	-3.1	-1.1
Estonia				3.4	1.3	-6.9	-4.2	-8.6	-11.4	-8.6	-5.3	-5.3	-5.2	-10.7	-11.4	-11.8	-9.8	-16.8	-18.0	-9.4	4.6
Georgia				-33.5[a]	-40.2[a]	-22.3[a]	-7.5[a]	-9.1[a]	-14.6	-6.6	-7.0	-8.8	-6.6	-7.1	-9.8	-8.3	-12.0	-16.1	-20.8	-22.7	-16.1
Hungary	-1.9	1.1	1.2	0.9	-11.1	-9.8	-3.7	-3.9	-4.5	-7.2	-7.9	-8.3	-6.0	-7.1	-8.0	-8.6	-7.5	-7.6	-6.4	-7.0	0.2
Kazakhstan	-7.6[a]	-8.7[a]	-0.9[a]	-25.0[a]	-7.8[a]	-7.6[a]	-1.3	-3.6	-3.6	-5.5	-1.0	2.0	-6.3	-4.2	-0.9	0.8	-1.8	-2.5	-7.8	5.1	-3.2
Kyrgyzstan				-6.9[a]	-10.0[a]	-7.6	-15.7	-23.3	-7.8	-25.1	-20.1	-9.0	-3.4	-3.8	-3.2	0.2	-2.4	-10.6	-6.9	-8.2	-7.9
Latvia					17.3	5.0	-0.3	-4.9	-5.5	-9.6	-9.0	-4.7	-7.5	-6.7	-8.2	-12.8	-12.4	-22.7	-22.5	-13.0	9.4
Lithuania					-3.4	-2.2	-9.5	-8.8	-9.8	-11.6	-10.9	-5.9	-4.7	-5.1	-6.9	-7.6	-6.9	-10.7	-14.6	-11.9	3.8
Macedonia, FYR		-9.2[a]	-5.5[a]	-0.8[a]	-3.3[a]	-7.8[a]	-6.7[a]	-6.5	-7.4	-7.8	-1.8	-2.7	-6.9	-10.0	-4.0	-8.4	-2.7	-0.9	-3.1	-12.8	-7.0
Moldova				-3.0[a]	-14.5[a]	-7.0	-6.1	-11.5	-14.2	-19.7	-6.7	-8.4	-2.5	-1.5	-6.6	-1.8	-8.3	-11.3	-17.0	-16.7	-10.7
Mongolia[a]	-35.2	-34.4	-5.2	-5.0	4.1	4.2	1.7	-2.8	4.7	-6.7	-5.8	-5.0	-6.6	-8.5	-6.8	1.5	1.3	7.0	6.7	-14.0	-5.6
Montenegro[a]												-4.5	-14.6	-12.3	-6.8	-7.2	-8.6	-24.7	-32.5	-33.6	-18.7
Poland	-1.7	4.9	-2.8	-3.7	-6.7	0.7	0.6	-2.1	-3.7	-4.0	-7.4	-6.0	-3.1	-2.8	-2.5	-4.0	-1.2	-2.8	-4.4	-5.1	-1.6
Romania	4.7	-8.5	-3.5	-7.7	-4.7	-1.5	-5.0	-7.3	-6.0	-6.9	-3.6	-3.7	-5.5	-3.3	-5.6	-8.5	-8.7	-10.4	-13.9	-11.6	-4.5
Russia						2.8	2.2	2.8	0.0	0.1	12.6	18.0	11.1	8.5	8.2	10.2	11.1	9.5	6.0	6.1	4.0
Serbia								-9.6[a]	-6.5[a]	-4.2[a]	-4.4[a]	-2.4[a]	2.4[a]	-4.1[a]	-7.5[a]	-13.5[a]	-8.4[a]	-9.8[a]	-15.5	-17.2	-5.5
Slovakia					-4.3	4.3	2.0	-9.9	-9.2	-9.5	-5.7	-2.4	-8.4	-5.6	-0.6	-5.9	-6.4	-5.7	-4.9	-6.6	-3.2
Slovenia	679.9[a]	49.6[a]	7.1[a]	17.8	2.7	6.3	-0.6	0.4	0.3	-0.7	-4.0	-3.2	0.2	1.1	-0.8	-2.7	-1.9	-2.8	-4.9	-6.2	-1.0
Tajikistan[a]				-17.0	-27.0	-17.8	-15.2	-7.8	-4.0	-7.3	-0.9	-1.6	-5.0	-3.6	-1.3	-3.9	-2.7	-2.8	-11.2	-7.9	-10.5
Turkmenistan[a]						4.0	0.7	0.1	-24.8	-34.3	-23.3	13.6	3.2	13.0	5.2	1.2	10.5	32.2	35.5	18.8	0.0
Ukraine				-12,075.1		-3.2	-3.1	-2.7	-2.7	-3.1	5.2	4.7	3.7	7.5	5.8	10.7	2.9	-1.5	-3.7	-7.1	-1.7
Uzbekistan[a]					-8.6	2.1	-0.2	-7.8	-5.4	-0.9	-2.0	2.7	-1.5	1.4	8.9	7.0	7.4	9.1	7.3	12.8	7.6

Source: Calculated from IMF International Financial Statistics database.

Note: The current account is the sum of the balance of trade (exports minus imports of goods and services), net factor income (such as interest and dividends), and net transfer payments (such as foreign aid, payments to the European Union, if applicable, and remittances). Also, there are inconsistencies in data reported by the IMF and EBRD. This indicates the low reliability of figures, particularly for the early 1980s.

[a] Data are from the EBRD (when IMF data are missing).

Table A.14 Financial account (% of GDP)

	1989	1990	1991	1992	1993	1994	1995	1996	1997	1998	1999	2000	2001	2002	2003	2004	2005	2006	2007	2008
Albania	15.4	−5.6	−16.1	−5.2	3.6	2.1	−16.6	1.8	6.3	0.6	1.0	5.1	2.7	4.8	3.5	5.4	4.7	5.8	6.8	
Armenia					12.4	13.9	17.7	13.6	20.4	20.6	15.5	13.1	8.3	6.2	6.2	0.5	3.3	6.8	10.7	
Belarus					8.0	3.0	1.9	2.6	5.2	2.3	3.3	1.4	2.7	5.2	2.4	5.0	−0.2	4.6	11.6	6.1
Bosnia-Herzegovina										−4.7	−1.0	1.6	17.9	8.9	12.6	13.9	16.7	10.1	14.4	
Bulgaria	−0.1	−13.6	−5.6	7.1	7.0	−10.5	2.5	−7.2	4.4	2.1	5.6	6.2	4.9	22.5	13.7	13.9	25.4	28.1	47.1	33.9
Croatia					−1.3	0.1	5.1	12.7	12.8	6.4	12.7	9.2	10.6	10.3	12.9	7.7	10.9	13.1	11.2	
Czech Republic					8.7	11.0	14.9	6.8	2.0	4.7	5.1	6.8	7.4	14.1	6.2	6.4	5.1	3.0	2.8	
Estonia				−0.1	11.0	6.9	6.2	11.6	16.3	9.2	7.5	7.0	4.4	10.3	13.0	13.5	11.2	18.1	16.7	12.3
Georgia								9.2	9.2	8.4	4.8	3.0	6.5	0.4	7.9	8.6	10.4	17.3	21.6	
Hungary	2.9	−2.2	4.4	1.1	15.8	8.1	12.8	−0.9	4.6	9.4	13.5	10.3	5.2	3.9	8.1	11.7	13.0	10.7	7.3	16.2
Kazakhstan							7.0	9.5	13.1	10.1	7.7	7.1	11.8	5.5	9.0	10.9	1.6	20.0	8.0	1.0
Kyrgyzstan					22.7	7.7	17.4	19.8	14.2	15.1	19.6	6.1	3.0	6.9	1.4	8.1	3.5	11.9	9.3	
Latvia					2.8	9.0	12.8	9.5	5.5	8.9	10.5	5.3	10.8	7.4	8.4	14.6	16.2	30.8	24.6	
Lithuania					11.8	5.6	8.2	7.9	10.1	12.9	9.7	6.1	6.4	7.4	8.8	5.1	8.6	15.5	16.1	11.8
Macedonia, FYR								3.9	5.0	9.5	1.4	8.9	9.3	6.6	6.1	8.7	9.9	6.8	6.0	
Moldova						18.1	−4.8	4.5	4.9	0.3	−3.0	9.8	1.3	1.2	4.3	4.3	6.7	10.5	22.2	
Poland	−2.2	−14.0	−5.4	−1.2	2.7	−9.8	6.7	4.3	4.7	7.7	6.2	6.0	1.7	3.6	4.0	3.2	5.0	3.8	9.4	20.9
Romania	−2.6	4.2	1.1	7.0	2.4	1.8	2.3	4.2	7.0	4.8	2.0	5.7	7.3	8.9	7.4	14.3	14.2	15.4	17.7	12.9
Russia						−10.8	−2.0	−5.2	0.8	−4.5	−8.9	−13.2	−1.2	0.6	0.7	−0.9	0.1	0.3	7.4	−8.1
Serbia																			18.8	
Slovakia					−1.1	0.5	6.2	10.7	8.3	8.6	8.8	5.1		15.1	3.6	8.6	10.0	1.7	8.4	
Slovenia				−0.2	−1.2	1.5	3.9	3.6	7.8	1.3	3.3	4.0	6.5	9.1	2.0	2.1	2.3	−0.3	5.7	
Tajikistan														6.0	4.0	4.5	4.4	9.8	21.9	
Ukraine						−1.5	−1.4	0.5	3.6	−3.0	−2.9	−2.7	−0.7	−2.5	0.3	−7.0	9.4	3.6	10.7	5.3

Source: Calculated from the IMF International Financial Statistics database.
Note: The financial account consists of asset inflows and outflows, such as international purchases of stocks, bonds, and real estate.

Table A.15 Financial account without FDI (% of GDP)

	1989	1990	1991	1992	1993	1994	1995	1996	1997	1998	1999	2000	2001	2002	2003	2004	2005	2006	2007	2008
Albania	15.4	−5.6	−16.1	−8.4	−1.1	−0.7		−0.9	4.3	−1.1	−0.2	1.2	−2.4	1.8	0.4	0.9	1.6	2.3	2.6	
Armenia										9.0			1.9	1.5	1.9	−6.4	−1.4	−0.2	3.3	
Belarus									2.8			0.2	1.9	2.1	1.5	4.3	−1.2	3.6	7.7	2.5
Bosnia-Herzegovina										−6.1		−1.2	15.8	4.6	8.1	6.8	11.1	4.3	0.6	
Bulgaria	−0.1			6.7	6.6	−11.6	1.7	−8.6	−0.4	−2.1	−0.6	−1.7	−1.0	16.9	3.3	2.2	10.7	4.2	18.2	16.9
Croatia		−13.6			−2.5	−0.6	4.6	10.7	11.3	3.1	6.7	4.0	4.5	8.2	7.2	5.9	7.4	6.6	3.2	
Czech Republic					7.1	9.1	10.3	4.7	−0.2	−1.1	−5.2	−2.0	−1.5	3.1	4.2	2.8	−4.2	0.1	−1.7	
Estonia			−7.6	−7.6	1.9	−1.9	0.9	9.3	13.6	−1.2	3.5	1.2	−1.2	8.2	5.2	7.7	−4.8	14.0	11.4	7.8
Georgia	2.9								2.3	2.0	1.9	−1.3	3.1	−4.2	−0.4	−0.7	1.9	3.5	5.3	
Hungary		−2.2	0.0	−2.9	9.7	5.5	2.2	−8.2	−3.5	2.9	7.1	5.8	−1.5	−0.2	7.5	8.3	8.1	9.7	3.9	13.8
Kazakhstan							1.2		7.1	4.9	−1.7	0.2	−1.1	−3.3	1.8	−1.7	−2.1	11.7	0.4	−7.2
Kyrgyzstan										9.8	16.5	6.6	3.1	6.6	−0.9	2.2	1.7	5.5	3.8	
Latvia					0.7	2.1	7.9	2.8	−2.7	4.4	6.0	0.2	9.4	4.7	6.1	10.8	12.6	23.3	17.9	8.2
Lithuania							7.1	6.0	6.8	4.7	5.3	2.9	2.8	2.5	8.1	2.8	6.0	10.3	12.5	
Macedonia, FYR										5.3	−1.0	2.9	−3.6	3.8	3.5	2.7	8.3	0.2	1.9	
Moldova							−6.5	3.2	0.9	−4.2	−6.2	−0.1	−2.4	−3.8	0.5	1.1	0.3	3.2	11.2	9.6
Poland	−2.2	−14.2	−5.7	−2.0	0.7	−11.8	4.1	1.4	1.6	4.2	1.9	0.5	−1.4	1.7	2.0	−1.5	2.7	0.7	5.1	
Romania	−2.6	4.3	1.0	6.7	2.1	0.6	1.1	3.5	3.5	0.0	−0.9	2.8	4.4	6.4	4.4	5.8	7.7	6.5	11.8	6.1
Russia						−10.9	−2.5	−5.6	0.4	−5.1	−9.5	−13.0	−1.3	0.8	1.1	−1.2	0.1	−0.4	6.7	−9.2
Serbia																			21.1	
Slovakia					−2.2	−1.2	5.0	9.3	8.0	6.7	5.2	−1.9		3.3	2.5	3.2	6.3	−3.8	4.8	
Slovenia			−2.3	−2.3	−2.7	0.1	2.7	2.5	5.8	0.0	3.0	3.6	4.5	2.2	2.6	1.2	2.6	0.3	5.9	
Tajikistan														3.0	2.0	−8.6	2.0	−2.2	12.2	
Ukraine						−1.9	−2.1	−0.7	2.4	−4.8	−4.4	−4.6	−2.7	−4.2	−2.5	−9.6	0.7	−1.7	4.2	−0.1

Source: Calculated from the IMF International Financial Statistics database.

Title A.16 General government balance (% of GDP)

	1989	1990	1991	1992	1993	1994	1995	1996	1997	1998	1999	2000	2001	2002	2003	2004	2005	2006	2007	2008	2009
Albania	−6.1		−20.7	−23.1	−15.5	−12.6	−10.1	−9.7	−12.4	−11.8	−12.1	−7.5	−6.9	−6.1	−4.9	−5.1	−3.5	−3.2	−3.8	−5.7	−6.9
Armenia			−1.9	−13.9	−54.7	−16.5	−9.0	−8.5	−5.8	−4.9	−7.2	−6.4	−3.8	−0.4	−1.1	−1.8	−2.6	−2.8	−2.2	−1.7	−7.5
Azerbaijan				2.7	−15.3	−11.2	−3.1	−2.4	−4.0	−3.9	−4.7	−0.6	−0.4	−0.5	−0.8	1.0	2.6	−0.2	2.4	25.5	9.4
Belarus				−2.0	−5.5	−3.5	−2.7	−1.5	−0.7	−1.0	−2.0	−0.1	−1.9	−2.1	−1.7	0.0	−0.7	1.4	0.4	1.4	0.4
Bosnia-Herzegovina							−3.3	−3.9	−0.4	−0.1	−4.0	−4.7	2.2	−4.2	1.6	1.5	2.1	2.6	1.3	−3.1	−4.0
Bulgaria	−1.0	−8.1	−4.5	−2.9	−10.9	−5.7	−5.6	−10.3	−0.3	1.7	0.4	−0.5	1.9	0.1	−0.9	2.2	1.9	3.3	3.5	1.8	−3.9
Croatia				−4.2	−0.9	0.6	−0.6	−0.4	−1.1	−3.0	−8.2	−7.5	−6.8	−4.9	−5.4	−4.2	−3.5	−2.6	−2.0	−1.4	−3.3
Czech Republic		−0.2	−1.9	−3.1	−27.4	−7.8	−13.4	−3.3	−3.8	−5.0	−3.7	−3.7	−5.7	−6.8	−6.6	−2.9	−3.6	−2.7	−0.7[a]	−2.7[a]	−5.9[a]
Estonia						1.2	−1.2	−0.4	1.9	−0.3	−3.7	−0.6	0.3	0.3	1.7	1.7	1.5	2.9	2.7	−2.8	−1.7
Georgia			−3.0	−25.4	−26.2	−7.4	−5.3	−7.3	−6.7	−5.4	−6.7	−4.0	−1.9	−2.0	−2.5	2.3	−1.5	−3.0	−4.2	−6.4	−9.4
Hungary		0.0	−2.9	−6.1	−6.0	−7.5	−6.7	−4.7	−6.2	−8.2	−5.5	−2.9	−4.0	−9.0	−7.2	−6.4	−7.8	−9.3	−4.9	−3.8	−4.0
Kazakhstan		1.4	−7.9	−7.3	−4.1	−7.4	−3.4	−5.3	−7.0	−8.0	−5.2	−1.0	2.7	1.4	3.0	2.5	5.8	7.2	4.7	1.1	−2.0
Kyrgyzstan	−3.1	−6.1	4.0	−17.5	−14.4	−11.6	−17.3	−9.5	−9.2	−9.5	−13.1	−10.4	−5.6	−5.3	−4.7	−4.4	−3.4	−2.5	−0.7	−0.1	−3.8
Latvia						−3.9	−2.0	−0.5	1.4	0.0	−3.9	−2.8	−2.1	−2.3	−1.6	−1.0	−0.4	−0.2	0.1	−4.1	−9.0
Lithuania					−5.5	−4.8	−1.6	−3.3	−11.9	−3.1	−2.8	−3.2	−3.6	−1.9	−1.3	−1.5	−0.5	−0.4	−1.0	−3.3	−8.9
Macedonia, FYR			−4.5	−9.8	−13.4	−2.7	−1.0	−1.4	−0.4	−1.7	0.0	2.5	−6.3	−5.7	−0.6	0.4	0.3	−0.5	0.6	−1.0	−2.9
Moldova			0.0	−26.6	−7.5	−10.6	−6.7	−8.0	−10.5	−7.4	−6.2	−1.8	−0.3	−2.2	1.0	0.4	1.5	−0.3	−0.3	−1.0	−6.8
Mongolia			−12.7	0.7	−5.9	−9.9	−4.5	−6.5	−7.9	−12.4	−10.6	−6.1	−4.7	−5.2	−3.7	−1.9	2.6	8.1	2.8	−4.9	−5.4
Montenegro												−4.0	−2.0	−1.9	−3.1	−1.9	2.1	4.2	6.3	1.5	−3.0
Poland	−7.4	3.1	−2.3	−5.3	−2.8	−2.8	−4.4	−4.9	−4.6	−4.3	−2.3	−3.0	−5.1	−5.0	−6.3	−5.7	−4.3	−3.9	−1.9	−3.7	−7.1
Romania				−4.6	−0.3	−2.2	−2.5	−3.9	−4.5	−3.2	−4.5	−4.6	−2.1	−2.0	−1.5	−1.2	−1.2	−2.2	−2.5	−5.4	−8.3
Russia				−18.9	−7.3	−10.4	−6.6	−9.4	−8.5	−8.1	−3.1	3.2	2.7	0.6	1.4	4.9	8.1	8.4	5.1	4.8	−6.2
Serbia												−1.0	−6.2	−43.0	−1.1	0.9	0.9	−2.6	−2.4	−2.4	−4.5
Slovakia				−11.9	−5.7	−1.4	0.4	−1.3	−5.2	−5.0	−7.1	−12.3	−6.5	−8.2	−2.7	−2.3	−2.8	−3.5	−1.9	−2.3	−6.8
Slovenia			2.6	1.2	0.9	0.0	0.0	0.3	−1.1	−0.7	−0.6	−3.7	−4.0	−2.5	−2.7	−2.2	−1.4	−1.2	0.5	−1.7	−5.5
Tajikistan	1.3	−3.0	−20.2	−31.2	−22.3	−10.1	−7.8	−5.8	−3.3	−3.8	−3.1	−5.6	−3.2	−2.4	−1.8	−2.4	−2.9	1.7	−6.2	−6.1	−8.5
Turkmenistan	0.0	1.7	3.0	−9.4	−3.5	1.7	0.4	0.3	−0.2	−2.6	0.0	−0.3	0.6	0.2	−1.3	1.4	0.8	5.3	4.0	11.3	5.3
Ukraine				−24.0	−16.2	−8.7	−4.7	−3.2	−5.4	−2.5	−2.3	−1.1	−0.9	0.1	−0.7	−4.4	−2.3	−1.4	−2.0	−3.2	−11.4
Uzbekistan	−0.9	−1.1	−3.6	1,757.2	−14.9	−5.6	−3.8	−7.9	−2.2	−3.8	−3.0	−2.5	−1.3	−1.9	0.1	1.2	2.8	6.8	5.7	10.5	2.0

Source: EBRD economic statistics and forecasts, available at http://www.ebrd.com/country/sector/econo/stats/index.htm,
[a]Data are from Eurostat.

Table A.17 Gini: Inequality

	1988 to 1989	1992 to 1994	1995 to 1997	1998 to 2000	2001 to 2003	2004 to 2006
Albania			29	29	28	31
Armenia			44	36	35	
Azerbaijan			35	35	37	
Belarus	23	22	27	29	30	28
Bosnia and Herzegovina						36
Bulgaria	23	28	31	26	32	
Croatia	23			29	31	29
Czech Republic	19	27	25			25
Estonia	23	40	30	37	35	36
Georgia			37	38	39	41
Hungary	25	28		27	27	30
Kazakhstan	26	33	35	35	33	
Kyrgyz Republic	26	54	41	34	30	
Latvia	22	27	31	34	37	36
Lithuania	22	35	32	31	34	36
Macedonia, FYR				31	39	
Moldova	24	34	37	39	35	
Mongolia			33	30	33	
Poland	27	30	33	33	33	35
Romania	23	27		30	31	32
Russian Federation	24	48	46	44	40	
Serbia					30	
Slovak Republic	20	19	26			28
Slovenia		29		28		31
Tajikistan				32	33	34
Turkmenistan	26	35		41		
Ukraine	23	26	37	29	28	28
Uzbekistan	25	33		45	36	

Source: World Bank world development indicators; data for Czech and Slovak republics are the 2006 Eurostat figures.

Note: The Gini index measures the extent to which the distribution of income (or, in some cases, consumption expenditure) among individuals or households within an economy deviates from a perfectly equal distribution.

This index also measures the area between the Lorenz curve and the hypothetical line of absolute equality, expressed as a percentage of the maximum area under the line. A Gini index of zero represents perfect equality, and a Gini index of 100 represents perfect inequality.

The figures in the table represent averages for estimates made in each period.

REFERENCES

Adserà, A., and C. Boix. 2002. Trade, democracy, and the size of the public sector: The political underpinnings of openness. *International Organization* 56 (2): 229–62.

Agell, J., T. Lindh, and H. Ohlsson. 1997. Growth and the public sector: A critical review essay. *European Journal of Political Economy* 13: 33–52.

————. 1999. Growth and the public sector: A reply. *European Journal of Political Economy* 15: 359–66.

Ahrend, R. 2006. Russia's post-crisis growth: Its sources and prospects for continuation. *Europe-Asia Studies* 58 (1): 1–24.

Aidis, R. 2006. From business ownership to informal market traders: The characteristics of female entrepreneurship in Lithuania. In *Enterprising women in transition economies*, ed. F. Welter, D. Smallbone, and N. Isakova (119–42). Aldershot, UK: Ashgate.

Aidis, R., and T. Mickiewicz. 2006. Entrepreneurs, expectations and business expansion: Lessons from Lithuania. *Europe-Asia Studies* 58 (6): 855–80.

Akimov, A., and B. Dollery. 2009. Financial development policies in Uzbekistan: An analysis of achievements and failures. *Economic Change and Restructuring* 42 (4): 293–318.

Alam, A., M. Murthi, R. Yemtsov, E. Murrugarra, N. Dudwick, E. Hamilton, and E. Tiongson. 2005. *Growth, poverty, and inequality: Eastern Europe and the former Soviet Union.* Washington, DC: World Bank.

Alcock, P., and G. Craig. 2009. *International social policy: Welfare regimes in the developed world.* 2nd ed. Basingstoke, UK: Palgrave.

Alexandrova, A., and R. Struyk. 2007. Reform of in-kind benefits in Russia: High cost for a small gain. *Journal of European Social Policy* 17 (2): 153–66.

Allan, D. 2002. Banks and the loans-for-shares auctions. In *Russian banking: Evolution, problems and prospects*, ed. D. Lane, 137–59. Cheltenham, UK: Edward Elgar.

Allen, F., and D. Gale. 2000. *Comparing financial systems.* Cambridge, MA: Massachusetts Institute of Technology (MIT) Press.

Alonso-Gamo, P., S. Fabrizio, V. Kramarenko, and Q. Wang. 2002. Lithuania: History and future of the currency board arrangement. International Monetary Fund (IMF) Working Paper no. 02/127. Washington, DC: IMF.

Amable, B. 2003. *The diversity of modern capitalism.* Oxford: Oxford University Press.

Amann, R., and J. Cooper. 1982. *Industrial innovation in the Soviet Union.* New Haven, CT: Yale University Press.

Amann, R., J. Cooper, and R. W. Davies. 1977. *The technological level of Soviet industry.* New Haven, CT: Yale University Press.

Amsden, A. H. (2000). *The rise of the rest: Challenges to the West from late-industrialization economies.* Oxford: Oxford University Press.

Amsden, A. H., J. Kochanowicz, and L. Taylor. 1994. *The market meets its match: Restructuring the economies of Eastern Europe.* Cambridge, MA: Harvard University Press.

Anderson, J. F. 2007. Representative democracy. In *Encyclopedia of governance*, vol. 2, ed. M. Bevir, 827–34. Thousand Oaks, CA: Sage.

Anderson, J. H., D. S. Bernstein, and C. W. Gray. 2005. *Judicial systems in transition economies: Assessing the past, looking to the future.* Washington, DC: World Bank.

Anderson, J. H., and C. W. Gray. 2006. *Anticorruption in transition 3: Who is succeeding . . . and why?* Washington, DC: World Bank.

Appel, H. 2004. *A new capitalist order: Privatization and ideology in Russia and Eastern Europe.* Pittsburgh: University of Pittsburgh Press.

————. 2006. International Imperatives and tax reform: Lessons from post-Communist Europe. *Comparative Politics* 39 (1): 43–62.

_____. 2008. Is it Putin or is it oil? Explaining Russia's fiscal recovery. *Post-Soviet Affairs* 24 (4): 301–23.

Åslund, A. 1991. Principles of privatisation. In *Systemic change and stabilization in Eastern Europe*, ed. L. Csaba, 17–31. Aldershot, UK: Dartmouth.

_____. 2002. *Building capitalism: The transformation of the former Soviet bloc*. Cambridge: Cambridge University Press.

_____. 2005. The economic policy of Ukraine after the Orange Revolution. *Eurasian Geography and Economics* 46 (5): 327–53.

_____. 2006. The Ancien Régime: Kuchma and the oligarchs. In *Revolution in orange*, ed. A. Åslund and M. McFaul, 9–28. Washington, DC: Carnegie Endowment for International Peace.

_____. 2007. *How capitalism was built: The transformation of Central and Eastern Europe, Russia, and central Asia*. Cambridge: Cambridge University Press.

_____. 2008. Reflections on Ukraine's current economic dilemma. *Eurasian Geography and Economics* 49 (2): 152–59.

Åslund, A., and N. Jenish. (2005). *The Eurasian growth paradox*. Washington, DC: Peterson Institute for International Economics.

Atkinson, A. B. 1995. *Incomes and the welfare state: Essays on Britain and Europe*. Cambridge: Cambridge University Press.

Atkinson, A. B., and J. Micklewright. 1992. *Economic transformation in Eastern Europe and the distribution of income*. Cambridge: Cambridge University Press.

Auer, R., and S. Wehrmuller. 2009. $60 billion and counting: Carry trade-related losses and their effect on CDS spreads in Central and Eastern Europe. Working Paper, Swiss National Bank.

Bair, J., and G. Gereffi. 2003. Upgrading, uneven development, and jobs in the North American apparel industry. *Global Networks* 3 (2): 143–69.

Baka, W. 2005. The economic agenda of the Polish round table 15 years later: Lessons for the Future. In *The Polish miracle: Lessons for the emerging markets*, ed. G. W. Kolodko, 49–62. Aldershot, UK: Ashgate.

Bakker, B. B. and A.-M. Gulde (2010). The Credit Boom in the EU New Member States: Bad Luck or Bad Policies? *IMF Working Paper* no. 10/130.

Balcerowicz, L. 1992. *800 dni: szok kontrolowany* [800 days: controlled shock]. Warsaw: Polska Oficyna Wydawnicza BGW.

_____. 1995. *Socialism, capitalism, transformation*. Budapest, Hungary: Central European University Press.

Bandelj, N. 2004. Negotiating global, regional, and national forces: Foreign investment in Slovenia. *East European Politics and Societies* 18 (3): 455–80.

_____. 2007. *From Communists to foreign capitalists: The social foundations of foreign investment in post-Socialist Europe*. Princeton, NJ: Princeton University Press.

Bank of Latvia. 1995. Origins of the banking crisis. Available at http://www.bank.lv/eng/main/all/pubrun/lbgadaparsk/1995gadpars/ku/originsbankcrisis/.

Bardhan, P. 1997. Corruption and development: A review of issues. *Journal of Economic Literature* 35 (3): 1320–46.

Barr, N., and P. Diamond. 2008. *Reforming pensions: Principles and policy choices*. Oxford: Oxford University Press.

_____. 2010. *Pension reform: A Short guide*. Oxford: Oxford University Press.

Barro, R. J. 1997. *Determinants of economic growth: A cross-country empirical study*. Cambridge, MA: MIT Press.

Baylis, T. C. (1994). Plus ca change? Transformation and continuity among East European elites. *Communist and Post-Communist Studies* 27 (3): 315–28.

Beck, T., and L. Laeven. 2005. Institution building and growth in transition economies. World Bank Policy Research Working Paper no. 3657.

Becker, J. 2007. Dollarisation in Latin America and euroisation in Eastern Europe: Parallels and differences. In *Dollarization, euroization and financial instability: Central and Eastern European countries between stagnation and financial crisis?* ed. J. Becker and R. Weissenbach, 223–78). Marburg, Germany: Metropolis-Verlag.

Begg, D., and R. Portes. 1992. *Enterprise debt and economic transformation: Financial restructuring of the state sector in Central and Eastern Europe.* London: Center for Economic Policy Research.

Berend, I. T. 1996. *Central and Eastern Europe, 1944–1993: Detour from the periphery to the periphery.* Cambridge: Cambridge University Press.

———. 2003. *History derailed: Central and Eastern Europe in the long nineteenth century.* Berkeley: University of California Press.

———. 2009. *From the Soviet bloc to the European Union: The economic and social transformation of Central and Eastern Europe since 1973.* Cambridge: Cambridge University Press.

Berglöf, E., A. Kunov, J. Shvets, and K. Yudaeva. 2003. *The new political economy of Russia.* Cambridge, MA: MIT Press.

Berle, A. A., and G. C. Means. 1968. *The modern corporation and private property.* Rev. ed.. New York: Harcourt, Brace and World.

Berlemann, M., and N. Nenovsky. 2004. Lending of first versus lending of last resort: The Bulgarian financial crisis of 1996/1997. *Comparative Economic Studies* 46 (2): 245–71.

Berliner, J. S. 1957. *Factory and manager in the USSR.* Cambridge, MA: Harvard University Press.

———. 1976. *The innovation decision in Soviet industry.* Cambridge, MA: MIT Press.

Bertelsmann Stiftung, ed. 2008. *Bertelsmann Transformation Index 2008: Political management in international comparison.* Gütersloh, Germany: Verlag Bertelsmann Stiftung.

Black, B., R. Kraakman, and A. Tarassova. 2000. Russian privatization and corporate governance: What went wrong? *Stanford Law Review* 52: 1731–1804.

Blanchard, O., M. Boycko, M. Dabrowski, R. Dornbusch, R. Layard, and A. Shleifer. 1993. *Post-Communist reform: Pain and progress.* Cambridge, MA: MIT Press.

Blanchard, O., and M. Kremer. 1997. Disorganization. *Quarterly Journal of Economics* 112 (4): 1091–1126.

Blasi, J. R., M. Kroumova, and D. Kruse. 1997. *Kremlin capitalism: The privatization of the Russian economy.* Ithaca, NY: Cornell University Press.

Bohle, D. 2008. Race to the bottom? Transnational companies and reinforced competition in the enlarged European Union. In *Contradictions and limits of neoliberal European governance: From Lisbon to Lisbon,* ed. B. Van Apeldoorn, J. Drahokoupil, and L. Horn, 163–86). Basingstoke, UK: Palgrave.

Bohle, D., and B. Greskovits. 2006. Capitalism without compromise: Strong business and weak labor in Eastern Europe's new transnational industries. *Studies in Comparative International Development* 41 (1): 3–25.

———. 2007. Neoliberalism, embedded neoliberalism, and neocorporatism: Paths towards transnational capitalism in Central-Eastern Europe. *West European Politics* 30 (3): 443–66.

Bollen, K. A. 1979. Political democracy and the timing of development. *American Sociological Review* 44 (4): 572–87.

Bonin, J. P., K. Mizsei, I. P. Szekely, and P. Wachtel. 1998. *Banking in transition economies: Developing market oriented banking sectors in Eastern Europe.* Cheltenham, UK: Edward Elgar.

Boycko, M., A. Shleifer, and R. Vishny. 1995. *Privatizing Russia.* Cambridge, MA: MIT Press.

Boyer, R. 2005. How and why capitalisms differ. *Economy and Society* 34 (4): 509–57.

Bräutigam, D. 2008. Taxation and state-building in developing countries. In *Taxation and state-building in developing countries: Capacity and consent*, ed. D. Bräutigam, O.-H. Fjeldstad, and M. Moore, 1–33. Cambridge: Cambridge University Press.

Briceño-Garmendia, C., A. Estache, and N. Shafik. 2004. Infrastructure services in developing countries: Access, quality, costs and policy reform. World Bank Policy Research Working Paper no. 3486.

Brīvers, I., T. Laizāns, K. Lešinskis, S, Šreibere, and T. Volkova. 2007. Thirteen hard years of transforming a heavily integrated economy: Latvia. In *Rebuilding the market economy in Central-East Europe and the Baltic countries*, ed. I. Kiglics, 319–70. Budapest, Hungary: Akadémiai Kiadó.

Brown, A. 1996. *The Gorbachev factor*. Oxford: Oxford University Press.

Brown, J. D., J. S. Earle, and S. Gehlbach. 2009. Helping hand or grabbing hand? State bureaucracy and privatization effectiveness. *American Political Science Review* 103 (2): 264–83.

Brus, W. 1972. *The market in a Socialist economy*. London: Routledge and K. Paul.

Brus, W., and K. Laski. 1989. *From Marx to the market: Socialism in search of an economic system*. Oxford: Clarendon.

Brym, R. J., and V. Gimpelson. 2004. The size, composition, and dynamics of the Russian state bureaucracy in the 1990s. *Slavic Review* 63 (1): 90–112.

Bučar, M., and M. Stare. 2006. From quantity to quality: Critical assessment of Slovenia's potential for knowledge-based growth. In *The knowledge-based economy in Central and East European countries*, ed. K. Piech and S. Radosevic, 239–58. Basingstoke, UK: Palgrave.

Buchen, C. 2007. Estonia and Slovenia as antipodes. In *Varieties of capitalism in post-Communist countries*, ed. D. Lane and M. Myant, 65–89). Basingstoke, UK: Palgrave.

Bunce, V. 1999. *Subversive institutions: The design and the destruction of Socialism and the state*. Cambridge: Cambridge University Press.

Bunce, V., and S. L. Wolchik. 2006. International diffusion and post-Communist electoral revolutions. *Communist and Post-Communist Studies* 39 (3): 283–304.

Burawoy, M. 1996. The state and economic involution: Russia through a China lens. *World Development* 24 (6): 1105–17.

Burawoy, M., and J. Lukács. 1992. *The radiant past: Ideology and reality in Hungary's road to capitalism*. Chicago: University of Chicago Press.

Busse, E. 2000. The embeddedness of tax evasion in Russia. In *Economic crime in Russia*, ed. A. V. Ledeneva and M. Kurkchiyan. London: Kluwer Law International.

Buyske, G. 2007. *Banking on small business: Microfinance in contemporary Russia*. Ithaca, NY: Cornell University Press.

Campos, N. F., and F. Coricelli. 2002. Growth in transition: What we know, what we don't, and what we should. *Journal of Economic Literature* 40 (3): 793–836.

Canning, D., and E. Bennathan. 2000. The social rate of return on infrastructure investment. World Bank Policy Research Working Paper no. 2390.

Carlin, W., J. V. Reenen, and T. Wolfe. 1994. Enterprise restructuring in the transition: An analytical survey of the case study evidence from Central and Eastern Europe. European Bank for Restructuring and Development (EBRD) Working Paper no. 14.

Cassette, A., and S. Paty. 2008. Tax competition among Eastern and Western European countries: With whom do countries compete? *Economic Systems* 32 (4): 307–25.

Chandler, A. D. 1977. *The visible hand: The managerial revolution in American business*. Cambridge, MA: Harvard University Press.

————. 1990. *Scale and scope: The dynamics of industrial capitalism*. Cambridge, MA: Belknap Press.

Chang, H.-J. 1995. Return to Europe? Is there anything for Eastern Europe to learn from east Asia? In *The transformation of the Communist economies: Against the mainstream*, ed. H.-J. Chang and P. Nolan, 382–99. New York: St. Martin's Press.

Christophe, B. 2007. Georgia: capitalism as organized chaos. In *Varieties of capitalism in post-Communist countries*, ed. D. Lane and M. Myant, 183–200). Basingstoke, UK: Palgrave.

Chu, K.-Y., and G. Schwartz. 1994. Output decline and government expenditures in European transition economies. IMF Working Paper no. 94/98.

Clarke, S. 1996. The enterprise in the era of transition. In *The Russian enterprise in transition*, ed. S. Clarke. Cheltenham, UK: Edward Elgar.

————. 1999. *New forms of employment and household survival strategies in Russia*. Coventry, UK and Moscow: Center for Comparative Labor Studies and Institute for Comparative Labor Relations Research.

————. 2007. *The development of capitalism in Russia*. London: Routledge.

Cliff, T. 1964. *Russia: A Marxist analysis*. London: International Socialism.

Collins, K. 2006. *Clan politics and regime transition in central Asia*. Cambridge: Cambridge University Press.

Colton, T. J. 1986. *The dilemma of reform in the Soviet Union*. Rev. and expanded ed. New York: Council on Foreign Relations.

————. 2008. *Yeltsin: A life*. New York: BasicBooks.

Comisso, E. 1979. *Workers' control under plan and market: Implications of Yugoslav self-management*. New Haven, CT: Yale University Press.

Commander, S., I. Dolinskaya, and C. Mumssen. 2002. Determinants of barter in Russia: An empirical analysis. *Journal of Development Economics* 67 (2): 275–307.

Connolly, R. 2009. Financial vulnerabilities in emerging Europe: An overview. *BOFIT Online*, 3/2009.

Cook, L. J. 2007. *Post-Communist welfare states: Reform politics in Russia and Eastern Europe*. Ithaca, NY: Cornell University Press.

Cornia, G., and F. Stewart. 1995. Two errors of targeting. In *Public spending and the poor: Theory and evidence*, ed. D. v. d. Walle and K. Nead, 350–86). Baltimore: John Hopkins University Press for the World Bank.

Coudouel, A., and S. Marnie. 1999. From universal to targeted social assistance: An assessment of the Uzbek experience. *MOCT-MOST: Economic Policy in Transitional Economies* 9 (4): 443–58.

Crouch, C. 2005. *Capitalist diversity and change: Recombinant governance and institutional entrepreneurs*. Oxford: Oxford University Press.

Crowley, S., and D. Ost, eds. 2001. *Workers after workers' states: Labor and politics in post-Communist Eastern Europe*. Lanham, MD: Rowman and Littlefield.

Cutright, P., and J. A. Wiley. 1969. Modernization and political representation: 1927–1966. *Studies in Comparative International Development* 5 (2): 23–44.

Czech National Bank (CNB). 2008. *Přímé zahraniční investice 2006* [Foreign Direct Investment 2006]. Prague: CNB.

Czech Statistical Office (CZSO). 1993. *Statistical yearbook of the Czech Republic*. Prague: Český spisovatel.

————. 1994. *Statistical yearbook of the Czech Republic*. Prague: Český spisovatel.

————. 2002. *Statistical yearbook of the Czech Republic*. Prague: Scientia.

————. 2008. *Statistical yearbook of the Czech Republic*. Prague: Scientia.

Dani, A. A., and A. d. Haan. 2008. Social policy in a development context: Structural inequalities and inclusive institutions. In *Inclusive states: Social policy and structural inequalities*, ed. A. A. Dani and A. d. Haan, 3–38. Washington, DC: World Bank.

Davidova, N., and N. Manning. 2009. Russia: State Socialism to marketized welfare. In *International social policy: Welfare regimes in the developed world*, 2nd ed., ed. P. Alcock and G. Craig, 190–209. Basingstoke, UK: Palgrave.

Demsetz, H. 1988. *Ownership, control and the firm*, vol. 2. Oxford: Basil Blackwell.

Derluguian, G. M. 2005. *Bourdieu's secret admirer in the Caucasus: A world-system biography*. Chicago: University of Chicago Press.

Deutscher, I. 1950. *Soviet trade unions: Their place in Soviet labour policy*. London: Royal Institute of International Affairs.

————. 1963. *The prophet outcast: Trotsky, 1929–1940*. London: Oxford University Press.

Diamond, P. 1998. The economics of social security reform. In *Framing the social security debate: Values, politics, and economics*, ed. R. D. Arnold, M. J. Graetz, and A. H. Munnell, 38–64. Washington, DC: Brookings Institution Press.

Djankov, S., and P. Murrell. 2000a. *The determinants of enterprise restructuring in transition: An assessment of the evidence*. Washington, DC: World Bank.

————. 2000b. Enterprise restructuring in transition: A quantitative survey. *Journal of Economic Literature* 40 (3): 739–92.

Djilas, M. 1957. *The new class: An analysis of the Communist system*. London: Thames and Hudson.

Dmitriev, M. 1997. *Biudzhetnaia Politika V Sovremennoi Rossii*. Moscow: Carnegie Center.

Dobbs, M. 1997. *Down with big brother: The fall of the Soviet empire*. New York: Alfred A. Knopf.

Drahokoupil, J. 2008a. *Globalization and the state in Central and Eastern Europe: The politics of foreign direct investment*. London: Routledge.

————. 2008b. Who won the contest for a new property class? Structural transformation of elites in the Visegrád Four region. *Journal of East European Management Studies* 13 (4): 361–77.

————. 2009. After transition: Varieties of political-economic development in Eastern Europe and the former Soviet Union. *Comparative European Politics* 7 (2): 279–98.

Durand, C. 2008. Between developmentalism and instrumentalization: The comeback of the producing state in Russia. *Journal of Innovation Economics* 2 (2): 171–91.

Eamets, R., and J. Masso. 2005. The paradox of the Baltic states: Labour market flexibility but protected workers? *European Journal of Industrial Relations* 11 (1): 71–90.

Earle, J. S., R. Frydman, A, Rapaczynski, and J. Turkewitz, eds. 1994. *Small privatization: The transformation of retail trade and consumer services in the Czech Republic, Hungary, and Poland*. Budapest, Hungary: Central European University Press.

Easter, G. 2002. Politics of revenue extraction in post-Communist states: Poland and Russia compared. *Politics and Society* 30 (4): 599–627.

————. 2006. Building fiscal capacity. In *The state after Communism: Governance in the new Russia*, ed. T. J. Colton and S. Holmes, 21–52. Lanham, MD: Rowman and Littlefield.

Ebrill, L., and O. Havrylyshyn. 1999. Tax reform in the Baltics, Russia, and other countries of the former Soviet Union. IMF Occasional Paper no. 182.

Economist Intelligence Unit (EIU). 2007. *Country report: Russia, June 2007*. London: EIU.

————. 2008a. *Country profile 2008: Moldova*. London: EIU.

————. 2008b. *Country profile 2008: Ukraine*. London: EIU.

Eder, M., A. Yakovlev, and A. Çarkoglu. 2003. Suitcase trade between Turkey and Russia: Microeconomics and institutional structure. Moscow State University, Higher School of Economics Working Paper no. WP4/2003/07.

EIROnline. 2003. 2002 annual review for Slovakia. Available at: http://www.eurofound.europa.eu/eiro/2003/01/feature/sk0301102f.htm.

Ellerman, D. 2001. Lessons from Eastern Europe's voucher privatization. *Challenge* 44 (4): 14–37

————. 2005. Can the World Bank be fixed? *Post-autistic economics review* 33: 2–16.

Elster, J. 1993. The necessity and impossibility of simultaneous economic and political reform. In *Constitutionalism and democracy*, ed. D. Greenberg. Oxford: Oxford University Press.

Epstein, R. A. 2008. Transnational actors and bank privatization. In *Transnational actors in Central and East European transitions*, ed. M. Orenstein, S. Bloom, and N. Lindstrom, 98–117. Pittsburgh: University of Pittsburgh Press.

Ernst, M., M. V. Alexeev, and P. Marer. 1995. *Transforming the core: State industrial enterprises in Russia, Central Europe and China*. Boulder, CO: Westview.

Esping-Andersen, G. 1990. *The three worlds of welfare capitalism*. Princeton, NJ: Princeton University Press.

Estrin, S. 1983. *Self-management: Economic theory and Yugoslav practice*. Cambridge: Cambridge University Press.

Estrin, S., J. C. Brada, A. Gelb, and I. Singh, eds. 1995. *Restructuring and privatization in Central Eastern Europe: Case studies of firms in transition*. Armonk, NY: M.E. Sharpe.

Estrin, S., K. E. Meyer, and M. Bytchkova. 2006. Entrepreneurship in transition economies. In *The Oxford handbook of entrepreneurship*, ed. M. Casson, B. Yeung, A. Basu, and N. Wadeson, 693–725). Oxford: Oxford University Press.

European Bank for Reconstruction and Development (EBRD). 1997. *Transition report 1997*. London: EBRD.

————. 2000. *Transition report 2000: Employment, skills and transition*. London: EBRD.

————. 2001. *Transition report 2001: Energy in transition*. London: EBRD.

————. 2004. *Transition report 2004: Infrastructure*. London: EBRD.

————. 2005. *Transition report 2005: Business in transition*. London: EBRD.

————. 2007. *Transition report 2007: People in transition*. London: EBRD.

————. 2008. *Transition report 2008: Growth in transition*. London: EBRD.

————. 2009. *Transition report 2009: Transition in crisis?* London: EBRD.

————. 2010. *Regional Economic Prospects in Ebrd Countries of Operation: May 2010 Update*. London: EBRD.

European Commission (EC). 2009. *EC spring forecasts 2009*. Brussels: EC.

Eurostat. 2007. *Taxation trends in the European Union: Data for the EU member states and Norway*. Luxembourg: Office for Official Publications of the European Communities.

————. 2008. Social protection in the European Union. *Statistics in focus*, no. 46.

————. 2009. Population and social conditions, labour force survey. Luxembourg: Eurostat.

Evans, P. 1995. *Embedded autonomy: States and industrial transformation*. Princeton, NJ: Princeton University Press.

Evans, P., and J. E. Rauch. 1999. Bureaucracy and growth: A cross-national analysis of the effects of "Weberian" state structures on economic growth. *American Sociological Review* 64 (5): 748–65.

Eyal, G., I. Szelenyi, and E. R. Townsley. 1998. *Making capitalism without capitalists: Class formation and elite struggles in post-Communist Central Europe*. London: Verso.

Faccio, M., and L. H. P. Lang. 2000. *The separation of ownership and control: An analysis of ultimate ownership in Western European corporations*. Paper presented at the European Finance Association Annual Meeting, 23-26 August 2000, London, United Kingdom. Available at http://ssrn.com/abstract = 222429.

Falkner, G., and O. Treib. 2008. Three worlds of compliance or four? The EU-15 compared to new member states. *Journal of Common Market Studies* 46 (2): 293–313.

Falkner, G., O. Treib, M. Hartlapp, and S. Leiber. 2005. *Complying with Europe: EU harmonisation and soft law in the member states*. Cambridge: Cambridge University Press.

Federální statistický úřad (FSÚ). 1992. *Statistická ročenka České a Slovenské Federativní Republiky* [Czechoslovak statistical yearbook]. Prague: SEVT (FSU).

Feige, E. L., and K. Ott, eds. 1999. *Underground economies in transition: Unrecorded activity, tax evasion, corruption, and organized crime*. Aldershot, UK: Ashgate.

Feldmann, M. 2006. Emerging varieties of capitalism in transition countries: Industrial relations and wage bargaining in Estonia and Slovenia. *Comparative Political Studies* 39 (7): 829–54.

Ferge, Z., and G. Juhasz. 2004. Accession and social policy: The case of Hungary. *Journal of European Social Policy* 14 (3): 233–51.

Filtzer, D. 1994. *Soviet workers and the collapse of perestroika: The Soviet labour process and Gorbachev's reforms, 1985–1991.* Cambridge: Cambridge University Press.

Fischer, S., and A. Gelb. 1991. The process of Socialist economic transformation. *Journal of Economic Perspectives* 5 (4): 91–105.

Fish, M. S. 2005. *Democracy derailed in Russia: The failure of open politics.* Cambridge: Cambridge University Press.

Fisher, S., J. Gould, and T. Haughton. 2007. Slovakia's neoliberal turn. *Europe-Asia Studies* 59 (6): 977–98.

Fitzsimons, V. G. 2009. A troubled relationship: Corruption and reform of the public sector in development. *Journal of Management Development* 28 (6): 513–21.

Fleming, A., and S. Talley. 1996a. The Latvian banking crisis: Lessons learned. World Bank Policy Research Working Paper no. 1590.

————. 1996b. Latvian banking crisis: Stakes and mistakes. *Beyond Transition: The Newsletter about Reforming Economies* 7 (3–4).

Franke, A., A. Gawrich, and G. Alakbarov. 2009. Kazakhstan and Azerbaijan as post-Soviet rentier states: Resource incomes and autocracy as a double "curse" in post-Soviet regimes. *Europe-Asia Studies* 61 (1): 109–40.

Friedman, J. 2009. A crisis of politics, not economics: Complexity, ignorance and policy failure. *Critical Review: A Journal of Politics and Society* 21 (2): 127–83.

Friedman, M. 1962. *Capitalism and freedom.* Chicago: University of Chicago Press.

Friedrich, C. J., and Z. K. Brzezinski. 1956. *Totalitarian dictatorship and autocracy.* Cambridge, MA: Harvard University Press.

Fries, S., T. Lysenko, and S. Polenac. 2003. The 2002 Business Environment and Enterprise Performance Survey: Results from a survey of 6,100 firms. EBRD Working Paper no. 47.

Friss, I. 1971. *Reform, of the economic mechanism in Hungary.* Budapest, Hungary: Akadémia Kiadó.

Frydman, R., C. W. Gray, M. P. Hessel, and A. Rapaczynski. 1997. Private ownership and corporate performance: Some lessons from transition economies. World Bank Policy Research Working Paper no. 1830.

Frydman, R., K. Murphy, and A. Rapaczynski. 1998. *Capitalism with a comrade's face.* Budapest, Hungary: Central European University Press.

Frydman, R., and A. Rapaczynski. 1994. *Privatization in Eastern Europe: Is the state withering away?* Budapest, Hungary: Central European University Press.

Frydman, R., A. Rapaczynski, and J. S. Earle. 1993a. *The privatization process in Central Europe.* Budapest, Hungary: Central European University Press.

————. 1993b. *The privatization process in Russia, Ukraine and the Baltic states.* Budapest, Hungary: Central European University Press.

Frye, T. 1997. Russian privatization and the limits of credible commitment. In *The political economy of property rights*, ed. D. Weimer, 84–108. Cambridge: Cambridge University Press.

Frye, T., and A. Shleifer. 1997. The invisible hand and the grabbing hand. *American Economic Review* 87 (2): 354–8.

Frye, T., and E. Zhuravskaya. 2000. Rackets, regulation and the rule of law. *Journal of Law, Economics, and Organization and Environment* 16 (2): 478–502.

Fultz, E. 2004. Pension reform in EU accession countries: Challenges, achievements, and pitfalls. *International Social Security Review* 57 (2): 3–24.

Gabrisch, H., and J. Hölscher. 2006. *The successes and failures of economic transition: The European experience.* Basingstoke, UK: Palgrave Macmillan.

Gaddy, C., and W. Gale. 2005. Demythologizing the Russian flat tax. *Tax Notes International*, March 14, 983–8.

Gaddy, C., and B. Ickes. 2002. *Russia's virtual economy*. Washington, DC: Brookings Institution Press.

Gadó, O., ed. 1972. *Reform of the economic mechanism in Hungary: Development, 1968–71*. Budapest, Hungary: Akadémia Kiadó.

————. 1976. *The economic mechanism in Hungary: How it works in 1976*. Budapest, Hungary: Akadémia Kiadó.

Gaidar, Y. (1999). *Days of defeat and victory*. Seattle: University of Washington Press.

Gebel, M. 2008. Labour markets in Central and Eastern Europe. In *Europe enlarged: A handbook of education, labour and welfare regimes in Central and Eastern Europe*, ed. I. Kogan, M. Gebel, and C. Noelke, 35–62. Bristol, UK: Policy Press.

Gehlbach, S. 2008a. *Representation through taxation: Revenue, politics, and development in post-Communist states*. Cambridge: Cambridge University Press.

————. 2008b. What is a big bureaucracy? Reflections on *Rebuilding Leviathan* and *Runaway State-Building*. *Czech Sociological Review* 44 (6): 1189–97.

Gelb, A. H., and C. W. Gray. 1991. *The transformation of economies in Central and Eastern Europe: Issues, progress and prospects*. Washington, DC: World Bank.

Gel'man, V. 2009. Leviathan's return: The policy of recentralization in contemporary Russia. In *Federalism and local politics in Russia*, ed. C. Ross and A. Campbell, 1–24. London: Routledge.

Gereffi, G. 1995. Global production systems and third world development. In *Global change, regional response*, ed. B. Stallings, 100–42. Cambridge: Cambridge University Press.

Gerschenkron, A. 1962. *Economic backwardness in historical perspective: A book of essays*. Cambridge, MA: Belknap Press of Harvard University Press.

Gimpelson, V. 2001. The politics of labor-market adjustment: The case of Russia. In *Reforming the state: Fiscal and welfare reform in post-Socialist countries*, ed. J. Kornai, S. Haggard, and R. R. Kaufman, 25–52. Cambridge: Cambridge University Press.

GKS. 2009. *Russia in figures: 2009*. Moscow: Russian State Statistics Service.

Główny Urząd Statystyczny (GUS). 1990. *Rocznik statystyczny Polski* [Concise statistical yearbook of Poland]. Warsaw: GUS (Central Statistical Office of Poland), Zakład Wydawnictw Statystycznych (Statistical Publishing Establishment).

————. 2008. *Mały rocznik statystyczny Polski* [Concise statistical yearbook of Poland]. Warsaw: GUS (Central Statistical Office of Poland), Zakład Wydawnictw Statystycznych (Statistical Publishing Establishment).

Goel, R., and J. Budak. 2006. Corruption in transition economies: Effects of government size, country size and economic reforms. *Journal of Economics and Finance* 30 (2): 240–50.

Goldman, M. I. 2003. *The piratization of Russia: Russian reform goes awry*. London: Routledge.

Golikova, V., K. Gonchar, B. Kuznetsov, and A. Yakovlev. 2008. *Russian manufacturing at the crossroads: What prevents firms from becoming competitive*. Moscow: State University, Higher School of Economics.

Górski, M. 2001. The new banking and financial sector: Its role, potential and weaknesses. In *Poland into the new millennium*, ed. G. Blazyca and R. Rapacki, 161–87). Cheltenham, UK: Edward Elgar.

Gorton, M., and J. White. 2009. Export strategies and performance in the CIS: Case study evidence from the dairy sector. *Post-Communist Economies* 21 (4): 475–94.

Gough, I. 2008. European welfare states: Explanations and lessons for developing countries. In *Inclusive states: Social policy and structural inequalities*, ed. A. A. Dani and A. d. Haan, 39–72). Washington, DC: World Bank.

Government Accountability Project (GAP). 2008. *Privatization and corruption: The World Bank and Azerbaijan*. Washington, DC: GAP.

Grabbe, H. 2006. *The EU's transformative power: Europeanization through conditionality in Central and Eastern Europe*. Basingstoke, UK: Palgrave Macmillan.

Grabher, G. 1992. Eastern conquista. In *Regional development and the contemporary industrial restructuring*, ed. H. Ernste and V. Meier. London: Belhaven Press.

Grafe, C., and K. Richter. 2001. Taxation and public expenditure. In *Russia's post-Communist economy*, ed. B. Granville and P. Oppenheimer, 131–72). Oxford: Oxford University Press.

Gramsci, A. 1971. *Selections from the prison notebooks*. New York: International Publishers.

Granick, D. 1975. *Enterprise guidance in Eastern Europe: A comparison of four Socialist economies*. Princeton, NJ: Princeton University Press.

Greskovits, B. 1998. *The political economy of protest and patience: East European and Latin American transformations compared*. Budapest, Hungary: Central European University Press.

———. 2005. Leading sectors and the variety of capitalism in Eastern Europe. *Actes du GERPISA* 39: 113–28.

Grzymala-Busse, A. 2007. *Rebuilding Leviathan: Party competition and state exploitation in post-Communist democracies*. Cambridge: Cambridge University Press.

Guriev, S., and A. Rachinsky. 2005. The role of oligarchs in Russian capitalism. *Journal of Economic Perspectives* 19 (1): 131–50.

Gylfason, T. 2001. Natural resources, education, and economic development. *European Economic Review* 45 (4–6): 847–59.

Haggard, S., and R. R. Kaufman. 2008. *Development, democracy, and welfare states: Latin America, east Asia, and Eastern Europe*. Princeton, NJ: Princeton University Press.

Haggard, S., R. R. Kaufman, and M. Shugart. 2001. Politics, institutions, and macroeconomic adjustment: Hungarian fiscal policy making in comparative perspective. In *Reforming the state: Fiscal and welfare reform in post-Socialist countries*, ed. J. Kornai, S. Haggard, and R. R. Kaufman, 75–110. Cambridge: Cambridge University Press.

Hall, P. A., and D. W. Soskice, eds. 2001. *Varieties of capitalism: The institutional foundations of comparative advantage*. Oxford: Oxford University Press.

Hall, R. E., and A. Rabushka. 2007. *The flat tax*. Rev. ed. Stanford, CA: Hoover Institution Press.

Hamm, P., and L. P. King. 2007. *Post-Manichean Economics: Foreign Investment, State Capacity and Economic Development in Postcommunist Society*. Unpublished manuscript.

Hankiss, E. 1990. *East European alternatives*. Oxford: Oxford University Press.

Hanley, E., N. Yershova, and R. Anderson. 1995. Russia: Old wine in a new bottle? The circulation and reproduction of Russian elites, 1983–1993. *Theory and Society* 24 (5): 639–68.

Hannah, L. 1983. *The rise of the corporate economy*. 2nd ed. London: Methuen.

Hanson, P., and K. Pavitt. 1987. *The comparative economics of research development and innovation in East and West: A survey*. New York: Harwood Academic.

Hanson, P., and E. Teague. 2005. Big business and the state in Russia. *Europe-Asia Studies* 57 (5): 657–80.

———. 2007. Russian political capitalism and its environment. In *Varieties of capitalism in post-Communist countries*, ed. D. Lane and M. Myant, 149–64). Basingstoke, UK: Palgrave.

Haraszti, M. 1977. *A worker in a worker's state: Piece-rates in Hungary*. Harmondsworth, UK: Penguin Books.

Hardy, J. 1998. Cathedrals in the desert? Transnationals, corporate strategy and locality in Wroclaw. *Regional Studies* 32 (7): 639–52.

Hare, P. G., H. K. Radice, and N. Swain, eds. 1981. *Hungary: A decade of economic reform*. London: Allen and Unwin.

Harrison, M., and B.-Y. Kim. 2006. Plans, prices, and corruption: The Soviet firm under partial centralization, 1930 to 1990. *Journal of Economic History* 66 (1): 1–41.

Hausner, J., B. Jessop, and K. Nielsen, eds. 1995. *Strategic choice and path-dependency in post-Socialism: Institutional dynamics in the transformation process.* Aldershot: Edward Elgar.

Havrylyshyn, O. 2006. *Divergent paths in post-Communist transformation: Capitalism for all or capitalism for the few?* Basingstoke, UK: Palgrave.

Hayek, F. v. 1935. *Prices and production.* 2nd ed. London: Routledge and Sons.

Heclo, H. 1998. A political science perspective on social security reform. In *Framing the social security debate: Values, politics, and economics,* ed. R. D. Arnold, M. J. Graetz, and A. H. Munnell. Washington, DC: Brookings Institution Press.

Heitlinger, A. 1979. *Women and state Socialism: Sex Inequality in the Soviet Union and Czechoslovakia.* London: Macmillan.

Hellman, J., G. Jones, and D. Kaufmann. 2000. Seize the state, seize the day: State capture, corruption, and influence in transition economies. World Bank Policy Research Working Paper no. 2444.

Hellman, J., and M. A. Schankerman. 2000. Intervention, corruption, and capture. *Economics of transition* 8: 545–76.

Helmenstein, C., ed. 1999. *Capital markets in Central and Eastern Europe.* Cheltenham, UK: Edward Elgar.

Hendley, K. 2009. Rule of law, Russian-style. *Current History* 108 (720): 339–40.

Higley, J., J. Kullberg, and J. Pakulski. 1996. The persistence of post-Communist Elites. *Journal of Democracy* 7 (2): 133–47.

Hlavacka, S., R. Wágner, and A. Riesberg. 2004. *Health care systems in transition: Slovakia.* Copenhagen: World Health Organization Regional Office for Europe on behalf of the European Observatory on Health Systems and Policies.

HNB. 2009a. Balance of payments, international investment position. *Statistical Time Series,* available at http://english.mnb.hu/Engine.aspx?page = mnben_statisztikai_idosorokand-ContentID = 12282.

———. 2009b. Foreign direct investment. *Statistical Time Series,* available at http://english.mnb.hu/Engine.aspx?page = mnben_statisztikai_idosorokandContentID = 11138.

Hoffman, D. E. 2002. *The oligarchs: Wealth and power in the new Russia.* Oxford: Public Affairs.

Holzmann, R., and J. Stiglitz, eds. 2001. *New ideas about old age security: Toward sustainable pension systems in the 21st century.* Washington, DC: World Bank.

Hope, K., and N. Petrov. (2009). Anti-fraud fight is stuck in the courts. *Financial Times,* June 19, pp. S1–2.

Hosking, G. A. 2006. *Rulers and victims: The Russians in the Soviet Union.* London: Belknap.

Hrubos, I. 2000. Transformation of the Hungarian higher education. *International Higher Education* 2 (20): 8–10.

Huber, E., and J. D. Stephens. 2001. *Development and crisis of the welfare state: Parties and policies in global markets.* Chicago: University of Chicago Press.

Hyde, M. 2001. Putin's federal reforms and their implications for presidential power in Russia. *Europe-Asia Studies* 53 (5): 719–43.

Iglesias, A., and R. Palacios. 2001. Managing public pension reserves: Evidence from the international experience. In *New ideas about old age security,* ed. R. Holzmann and J. Stiglitz, 213–53. Washington, DC: World Bank.

Inglot, T. (2008). *Welfare states in East Central Europe, 1919–2004.* Cambridge: Cambridge University Press.

International Fund for Agricultural Development (IFAD). 2007. *Sending money home: Worldwide remittance flows to developing countries.* Rome: IFAD.

International Iron and Steel Institute (IISI). 2007. *Steel statistical yearbook*. Brussels, UK: IISI, Committee on Economic Studies.

International Monetary Fund (IMF). 2004. Republic of Kazakhstan: Statistical appendix. IMF Country Report no. 04/363.

————. 2000a. *Russian Federation: Selected issues*. Washington DC: IMF.

————. 2000b. *World economic outlook: Focus on transition economies*. Washington, DC: IMF.

————. 2007. *Government finance statistics yearbook 2006*. Washington, DC: IMF.

————. 2008a. IMF spells out need for global fiscal stimulus. IMF survey online, December 29.

————. 2008b. *World economic outlook*. New York: IMF.

————. 2009a. A changing IMF: Responding to the crisis. IMF Factsheet, September.

————. 2009b. *Global financial stability report: Responding to the financial crisis and measuring systemic risks*. Washington, DC: IMF.

————. 2009c. *Government finance statistics yearbook 2008*. Washington, DC: IMF.

————. 2009d. The IMF's role in helping protect the most vulnerable in the global crisis. IMF Factsheet, October.

————. 2009e. *Review of recent crisis programs*. Washington, DC: IMF.

————. 2009f. *World economic outlook: A Survey by the staff of the international monetary fund*. Washington, DC: IMF.

International Monetary Fund, World Bank (WB), Organization for Economic Cooperation and Development (OECD), and European Bank for Reconstruction and Development (EBRD). 1991a. *A study of the Soviet economy*, vol. 2. Paris: OECD.

————. 1991b. *A study of the Soviet economy*, vol. 1. Paris: OECD.

Intriligator, M. 1997. Round table on Russia: A new economic policy for Russia. *Economics of Transition* 5 (1): 225–31.

Ioffe, G. 2004. Understanding Belarus: Economy and political landscape. *Europe-Asia Studies* 56 (1): 85–118.

Ivanova, A., M. Keen, and A. Klemm. 2005. The Russian flat tax reform. IMF Working Paper no. 05/16.

Iwasaki, I. 2004. Evolution of the government-business relationship and economic performance in the former Soviet states: Order state, rescue state, and punish state. *Economics of Planning* 36 (3): 223–57.

————. 2007. Enterprise reform and corporate governance in Russia: A quantitative survey. *Journal of Economic Surveys* 21 (5): 849–902.

Iwasaki, I., and T. Suzuki. 2007. Transition strategy, corporate exploitation, and state capture: An empirical analysis of the former Soviet states. *Communist and Post-Communist Studies* 40 (4): 393–422.

Jackson, J. E., J. Klich, and K. Poznańska. 2005. *The political economy of Poland's transition*. Cambridge: Cambridge University Press.

Jessop, B. 1990. *State theory: Putting the capitalist state in its place*. University Park: Pennsylvania State University Press.

Johnson, C. 1982. *Miti and the Japanese miracle*. Stanford, CA: Stanford University Press.

Johnson, J. 2000. *A fistful of rubles: The rise and fall of the Russian banking system*. Ithaca, NY: Cornell University Press.

Johnson, S., J. McMillan, and C. Woodruff. 2002. Property rights and finance. *American Economic Review* 92 (5): 1335–56.

Journal of Communist Studies and Transition Politics. 2009. Rethinking the "Coloured Revolutions." Vol. 25, issues 2–3.

Journal of Communist Studies and Transition Politics. 2010. Federalism and Intergovernmental Relations in Russia. Vol. 26, issue 2.

Journal of Democracy. (2007). Is East-Central Europe backsliding? Vol. 18, issue 4.

Kaczmarczyk, P., and M. Okólski. 2008. Economic impacts of migration on Poland and the Baltic states. Fafo-paper no. 2008:01.

Kahanec, M., A. Zaiceva, and K. F. Zimmermann. 2009. Labor mobility in the enlarged EU: Who wins, who loses? In *EU labor markets after post-enlargement migration*, ed. M. Kahanec and K. F. Zimmermann, 3–46). Berlin: Springer.

Kahanec, M., and K. F. Zimmermann, eds. 2009. *EU labor markets after post-enlargement migration*. Berlin: Springer.

Kalyuzhnova, Y., A. M. Kutan, and T. Yigit. 2009. Corruption and economic development in energy-rich economies. *Comparative Economic Studies* 51 (2): 165–80.

Karl, T. L. 1997. *The paradox of plenty: Oil booms and petro-states*. Berkeley: University of California Press.

Kaser, M. C. 1986. *The economic history of Eastern Europe, 1919–1975*, vol. 3, *Institutional change within a planned economy*. Oxford: Clarendon.

Kaufman, R. R. 2004. Corruption, governance and security: Challenges for the rich countries and the world. In *Global competitiveness report 2004/2005*, ed. World Economic Forum (WEF), 83–102. Geneva: WEF.

Kaufmann, D., A. Kraay, and M. Mastruzzi. 2009. *Governance matters*, vol. 8, *Governance indicators for 1996–2008*. Washington, DC: World Bank.

Keen, M., Y. Kim, and R. Varsano. 2006. The "flat tax(es)": Principles and evidence. IMF Working Paper no. WP/06/218.

Kenedi, J. 1981. *Do it yourself: Hungary's hidden economy*. London: Pluto.

Keune, M. 2009. EU enlargement and social standards: Exporting the European social model? In *The European Union and the social dimension of globalization*, ed. J. Orbie and L. Tortell, 45–61. London: Routledge.

Kim, Y. 2003. *The resource curse in a post-Communist regime: Russia in comparative perspective*. Aldershot, UK: Ashgate.

King, L. P. 2007. Central European capitalism in comparative perspective. In *Beyond varieties of capitalism: Conflict, contradictions, and complementarities in the European economy*, ed. B. Hancké, M. Rhodes, and M. Thatcher, 307–27. Oxford: Oxford University Press.

King, L. P., and I. Szelenyi. 2005. Post-Communist economic systems. In *Handbook of economic sociology*, ed. N. J. Smelser and R. Swedberg, 206–32). Princeton, NJ: Princeton University Press.

King, L. P., and A. Sznajder. 2006. The state-led transition to liberal capitalism: Neoliberal, organizational, world-systems, and social structural explanations of Poland's economic success. *American Journal of Sociology* 112 (3): 751–801.

King, L. P., and J. Treskow. 2006. Understanding the Russian oil sector. *Canadian Foreign Policy* 13 (2): 77–92.

Klenow, P. J., and A. Rodríguez-Clare. 1997. Economic growth: A review essay. *Journal of Monetary Economics* 40 (3): 597–617.

Knell, M. 2000. FIEs and productivity convergence in Central Europe. In *Integration through foreign direct investment: Making Central European industries competitive*, ed. G. Hunya, 178–96). Cheltenham, UK: Edward Elgar.

Knell, M., and M. Srholec. 2007. Diverging pathways in Central and Eastern Europe. In *Varieties of capitalism in post-Communist countries*, ed. D. Lane and M. Myant, 40–62. Basingstoke, UK: Palgrave.

Knöbl, A., and R. Haas. 2003. IMF and the Baltics: A decade of cooperation. IMF Working Paper no. 03/241.

Knöbl, A., A. Sutt, and B. B. Zavoiceo. 2002. The Estonian currency board: Its introduction and role in the early success of Estonia's transition to a market economy. IMF Working Paper no. 02/96.

Kohli, A. 2004. *State-directed development: Political power and industrialization in the global periphery*. Cambridge: Cambridge University Press.

Kokoszczynski, R. 1999. Poland. In *Capital markets in Central and Eastern Europe*, ed. C. Helmenstein. Cheltenham, UK: Edward Elgar.

Kolodko, G. W. 2000. *From shock to therapy: The political economy of post-Socialist transformation*. Oxford: Oxford University Press.

Kornai, J. 1959. *Overcentralization in economic administration: A critical analysis based on experience in Hungarian light industry*. Oxford: Oxford University Press.

———. 1980. *Economics of shortage*. Amsterdam: North Holland.

———. 1982. *Growth, shortage, and efficiency: A Macrodynamic model of the Socialist economy*. Berkeley: University of California Press.

———. 1990a. *The road to a free economy: Shifting from a Socialist system; The example of Hungary*. New York: W.W. Norton.

———1990b. *Vision and reality, market and state: Contradictions and dilemmas revisited*. New York: Harvester Wheatsheaf.

———. 1992. *The Socialist system: The political economy of Communism*. Oxford: Clarendon.

———. 1995a. *Highway and byways: Studies on reform and post-Communist transition*. Cambridge, MA: MIT Press.

———. 1995b. Transformational recession: The example of Hungary. In *Eastern Europe in crisis and the way out*, ed. C. T. Saunders, 29–77. Basingstoke, UK: Macmillan in association with the Vienna Institute for Comparative Economic Studies.

Korosteleva, J. 2007. Belarus: Heading towards state capitalism? In *Varieties of capitalism in post-Communist countries*, ed. D. Lane and M. Myant, 221–38). Basingstoke, UK: Palgrave.

Kotz, D. M., and F. Weir. 2007. *Russia's path from Gorbachev to Putin: The demise of the Soviet system and the new Russia*. London: Routledge.

Kowalik, T. 2008. George Blazyca on shock therapy and the Third Way. In *Reinventing Poland: Economic and political transformation and evolving national identity*, ed. M. Myant and T. Cox, 10–17. London: Routledge.

Krejčí, J. 1972. *Social change and stratification in postwar Czechoslovakia*. New York: Columbia University Press.

Kronenberg, T. 2004. The curse of natural resources in the transition economies. *Economics of Transition* 12 (3): 399–426.

Krugman, P. 1991. Increasing returns and economic geography. *Journal of Political Economy* 99 (3): 483–99.

Kryshtanovskaya, O., and S. White. 1996. From Soviet nomenklatura to Russian elite. *Europe-Asia Studies* 48 (5): 711–33

———. 2003. Putin's militocracy. *Post-Soviet Affairs* 19 (4): 289–306.

———. 2005. The rise of the Russian business elite. *Communist and Post-Communist Studies* 38 (3): 293–307.

Kubicek, P. 2004. *Organized labor in post-communist states: From solidarity to infirmity*. Pittsburgh: University of Pittsburgh Press.

Kurth, J. R. 1979. The political consequences of the product cycle: Industrial history and political outcomes. *International Organization* 33 (1): 1–34.

Kuzio, T. 2007. Oligarchs, tapes and Oranges: "Kuchmagate" to the Orange Revolution. *Journal of Communist Studies and Transition Politics* 23 (1): 30–56.

Kvapilová, E. 2007. Práca: Boj s nezamestnanosťou ako hlavná stratégia boja proti chudobe a sociálnemu vylúčeniu. In *Kniha o chudobe: Spoločenské súvislosti a verejné politiky*, ed. D. Gerbery, I. Lesay, and D. Škobla. Bratislava, Slovakia: Priatelia Zeme CEPA.

Lajtai, G. 1997. Successful waves of employee ownership in Hungary. In *Privatization surprises in transition economies: Employee-ownership in Central and Eastern Europe*, ed. M. Uvalic and D. Vaughan-Whitehead, 136–64. Cheltenham, UK: Edward Elgar.

Landesmann, M. A., and J. Burgstaller. 1997. Vertical product differentiation in EU markets: The relative position of East European producers. Vienna Institute for International Economic Studies Research Report no. 234a.

Lane, D. 1971. *The end of inequality? Stratification under state Socialism*. Harmondsworth, UK: Penguin.

————. 1978. *Politics and society in the USSR*. 2nd ed. Oxford: Martin Robertson.

————. 1985. *Soviet economy and society*. Oxford: Basil Blackwell.

————. 2002. The evolution of post-Communist banking. In *Russian banking: Evolution, problems and prospects*, ed. D. Lane, 9–35. Cheltenham, UK: Edward Elgar.

————. 2005. Social class as a factor in the transformation of state Socialism. *Journal of Communist Studies and Transition Politics* 21 (4): 417–35.

————. 2008. From chaotic to state-led capitalism. *New Political Economy* 13 (2): 177–84.

————. 2009. "Coloured Revolution" as a political phenomenon. *Journal of Communist Studies and Transition Politics* 25 (2): 113–35.

Lane, D., and I. Lavrentieva. 2002. The view from the ground: Case studies of three major banks (Sberbank, Uneximbank/Rosbank, Bank of Moscow). In *Russian banking: Evolution, problems and prospects*, ed. D. Lane, 79–115. Cheltenham, UK: Edward Elgar.

Lane, D., and C. Ross, eds. 1999. *The transition from Communism to capitalism: Ruling elites from Gorbachev to Yeltsin*. Basingstoke, UK: Macmillan.

Lange, O., and F. M. Taylor. 1938. *On the economic theory of Socialism*. Minneapolis: University of Minnesota Press.

Lavoie, D. 1985. *Rivalry and central planning: The Socialist calculation debate reconsidered*. Cambridge: Cambridge University Press.

Ledeneva, A. V. 1998. *Russias economy of favours: Blat, networking and informal exchange*. Cambridge: Cambridge University Press.

————. 2000. Continuity and change of practices in Soviet and post-Soviet Russia. In *Bribery and Blat in Russia: Negotiating reciprocity from the early modern period to the 1990s*, ed. S. Lovell, A. Rogachevski, and A. V. Ledeneva, 183–205. Basingstoke, UK: Macmillan.

————. 2006. *How Russia really works: The informal practices that shaped post-Soviet politics and business*. Ithaca, NY: Cornell University Press.

Ledyard, J. O. 2008. Market failure. In *The new Palgrave dictionary of economics online*, ed. S. N. Durlauf and L. E. Blume. Basingstoke, UK: Palgrave.

Leinsalu, M., D. Vågerö, and A. E. Kunst. 2003. Estonia, 1989–2000: Enormous increase in mortality differences by education. *International Journal of Epidemiology* 32: 1081–87.

Lerner, A. P. 1944. *The economics of control: Principles of welfare economics*. New York: Macmillan.

Levcik, F. 1995. Economic transformation in the East: A critical appraisal of its development and suggestions for a possible way out. In *Eastern Europe in crisis and the way out*, ed. C. T. Saunders, 13–28. Basingstoke, UK: Macmillan in association with the Vienna Institute for Comparative Economic Studies.

Levitsky, S., and L. A. Way. 2002. The rise of competitive authoritarianism. *Journal of Democracy* 13 (2): 51–65.

Lewis, M. 2000. *Who is paying for health care in Eastern Europe and central Asia?* Washington, DC: World Bank.

Lindholm, C. 1986. Kinship structure and political authority: The Middle East and central Asia. *Comparative Studies in Society and History* 28 (2): 334–55.

Linz, J. J. 2000. *Totalitarian and authoritarian regimes*. Boulder, CO: Lynne Rienner.

Linz, J. J., and A. C. Stepan. 1996. *Problems of democratic transition and consolidation: Southern Europe, South America, and post-Communist Europe*. Baltimore: Johns Hopkins University Press.

Lipset, S. M. 1959. Some social requisites of democracy: Economic development and political legitimacy. *American Political Science Review* 53 (1): 69–105.

Lipton, D., and J. Sachs. 1990a. Creating a market economy in Eastern Europe: The case of Poland. *Brookings Papers on Economic Activity* 20 (1): 75–133.

————. 1990b. Privatization in Eastern Europe: The case of Poland. *Brookings Papers on Economic Activity* 20 (2): 293–341.

Lissovolik, B. 1997. Rapid spread of employee ownership in the privatized Russia. In *Privatization surprises in transition economies: Employee-ownership in Central and Eastern Europe*, ed. M. Uvalic and D. Vaughan-Whitehead, 204–29). Cheltenham, UK: Edward Elgar.

Lithuanian Development Agency (LDA). 2006. *Foreign direct investment*. Vilnius: LDA.

Lopez-Claros, A., M. E. Porter, K. Schwab, and X. Sala-i-Martin. 2006. *The global competitiveness report, 2006–2007*. Basingstoke, UK: Palgrave.

Lyakh, A. 2007. The evolution of the industrial structure in Donetsk region: Maroeconomic, microeconomic and institutional factors. In *Re-constructing the post-Soviet industrial region: The Donbas in transition*, ed. A. Swain, 78–96. London: Routledge.

Maddison, A. 2006. *The world economy*. Paris: OECD.

Madrid, R. L. 2003. *Retiring the state: The politics of pension privatization in Latin America and beyond*. Stanford, CA: Stanford University Press.

Malle, S. 2009. Soviet legacies in post-Soviet Russia: Insights from crisis management. *Post-Communist Economies* 21 (3): 249–82.

Mann, M. 1993. *The sources of social power*, vol. 2. Cambridge: Cambridge University Press.

March, A. F. 2003. From Leninism to Karimovism: Hegemony, ideology, and authoritarian legitimation. *Post-Soviet Affairs* 19 (4): 307–36.

Marples, D. R. 1996. *Belarus: From Soviet rule to nuclear catastrophe*. London: Macmillan.

Marrese, M., and J. Vanous. 1983. *Soviet subsidization of trade with Eastern Europe: A Soviet perspective*. Berkeley: Institute of International Studies, University of California.

Martinez-Vazquez, J. 1994. Expenditures and expenditure assignment. In *Russia and the challenge of fiscal federalism*, ed. C. I. Wallich, 96–128. Washington, DC: World Bank.

Martinez-Vazquez, J., and R. M. McNab. 2000. The tax reform experiment in transitional countries. *National Tax Journal* 53 (2): 273–98.

Marx, K. 1990. *Capital: Volume I*. London: Penguin Books.

Matejko, A. J. 1974. *Social change and stratification in Eastern Europe: An interpretive analysis of Poland and her neighbors*. New York: Praeger.

Mathews, J. A. 2006. Catch-up strategies and the latecome effect in industrial development. *New Political Economy* 11 (3): 313–35.

Matthews, M. 1978. *Privilege in the Soviet Union: A study of elite life-styles under Communism*. London: Allen and Unwin.

Mau, V. 1996. *The political history of economic reform in Russia, 1985–1994*: London: Center for Research into Communist Economies.

————. 2005. *From crisis to growth*. London: Center for Research into Post-Communist Economies.

McDermott, G. A. 2002. *Embedded politics: Industrial networks and institutional change in post-Communism*. Ann Arbor: University of Michigan Press.

McKinnon, R. I. 1993. *The order of economic liberalization: Financial control in the transition to a market economy*. 2nd ed. Baltimore: Johns Hopkins University Press.

Meardi, G. 2007. More voice after more exit? Unstable industrial relations in Central Eastern Europe. *Industrial Relations Journal* 38 (6): 503–23.

Mencinger, J. 1995. Slovenia: A new state and its prospects. In C. *Eastern Europe in crisis and the way out*, ed. T. Saunders. Basingstoke, UK: Macmillan in association with the Vienna Institute for Comparative Economic Studies.

_____. 2007. Addiction to FDI and current account balance. In *Dollariziation, euroization and financial instability: Central and Eastern European countries between stagnation and financial crisis?* ed. J. Becker and R. Weissenbacher, 109–28). Marburg, Germany: Metropolis Verlag.

Merlevede, B., K. Schoors, and B. V. Aarle. 2009. Russia from bust to boom and back: Oil price, Dutch disease and stabilisation fund. *Comparative Economic Studies* 51 (2): 213–41.

Mickiewicz, T. 2005. *Economic transition in Central Europe and the Commonwealth of Independent States*. Basingstoke, UK: Palgrave Macmillan.

Mikhailovskaya, I. B. 1994. Crime and statistics: Do the figures reflect the real situation? *Demokratizatsiya* 2 (3): 412–25.

Milanovic, B. 1998. *Income, inequality, and poverty during the transition from planned to market economy*. Washington, DC: World Bank.

_____. 1999. The role of social assistance in addressing poverty. In *Poverty and social assistance in transition countries*, ed. J. Braithwaite, C. Grootaert, and B. Milanovic, 99–156. New York: St. Martin's Press.

Miller, J. B., and S. Tenev. 2007. On the role of government in transition: The experiences of China and Russia compared. *Comparative Economic Studies* 49 (4): 543–71.

Minsky, H. P. 1982. *Inflation recession and economic policy*. Brighton, UK: Wheatsheaf.

Mises, L. von 1935. Economic calculation in the Socialist Commonwealth. In *Collectivist economic planning*, ed. F. v. Hayek, 87–130. London: George Routledge and Sons.

_____. 1949. *Human action: A treatise on economics*. London: W. Hodge.

Mitra, P., and N. Stern. 2003. Tax systems in transition. World Bank Policy Research Working Paper no. 2947.

Mizobata, S. 2002. Bank sector restructuring. In *Russian banking: Evolution, problems and prospects*, ed. D. Lane, 36–55. Cheltenham, UK: Edward Elgar.

Mlynář, Z. 1980. *Night frost in Prague: The end of humane Socialism*. London: C. Hurst.

Moene, K. O., and M. Wallerstein. 2001. Targeting and political support for welfare spending. *Economics of Governance* 2 (1): 3–24.

Moody's. 2007. *Moody's statistical handbook: Country credit*. New York: Moody's Investor Service.

_____. 2008. *Moody's statistical handbook*. New York: Moody's Investor Service.

Morrison, C. 2008. *A Russian factory enters the market economy*. London: Routledge.

Munnell, A. H., and A. Sundén. 2001. Investment practices of state and local pension funds: Implications for social security reform. In *Pensions in the public sector*, ed. O. S. Mitchell and E. C. Hustead, 153–94). Philadelphia: University of Pennsylvania Press.

Munteanu, I., T. Lariushin, V. Ionita, and A. Munteanu. 2008. *Moldova: Decentralisation of the education reform and spending for education*. Chisinau, Russia: Research Center of the Institute for Development and Social Initiatives (IDIS) "Viitorul."

Murphy, K. M., A. Shleifer, and R. W. Vishny. 1992. The transition to a market economy: Pitfalls of partial reform. *Quarterly Journal of Economics* 107 (3): 889–906.

Murphy, M., M. Bobak, A. Nicholson, R. Rose, and M. Marmot. 2006. The widening gap in mortality by educational level in the Russian Federation, 1980–2001. *American Journal of Public Health* 96 (7): 1293–99.

Murthi, M., J. M. Orszag, and P. Orszag. 2001. Administrative costs under a decentralized approach to individual accounts: Lessons from the United Kingdom. In *New ideas about old age security*, ed. R. Holzmann and J. Stiglitz, 308–37. Washington, DC: World Bank.

Murthi, M., and E. R. Tiongson. 2009. Attitudes to income equality: The "Socialist Legacy" revisited. *Comparative Economic Studies* 51(3).

Myant, M. 1981. *Socialism and democracy in Czechoslovakia: 1945–1948* Cambridge: Cambridge University Press.

————. 1982. *Poland: A crisis for Socialism*. London: Lawrence and Wishart.

————. 1985. Yugoslavia: Self-management and economic crisis. Paisley College Economics and Management Working Papers no. 4.

————. 1989a. *The Czechoslovak economy, 1948–1988: The battle for economic reform*. Cambridge: Cambridge University Press.

————. 1989b. Poland: The permanent crisis? In *Poland: The economy in the 1980s*, ed. R. Clarke. London: Longman.

————. 1993. *Transforming Socialist economies: The case of Poland and Czechoslovakia*. Aldershot, UK: Edward Elgar.

————. 1997. Enterprise restructuring and policies for competitiveness in the Czech Republic. *Ekonomický časopis* 45 (6–7): 546–67.

————. 1999a. Czech enterprises: The Barriers to Restructuring. *Prague Economic Papers* 8 (2): 163–77.

————. 1999b. Inward investment and structural transformation. In *Institutional change and industrial development in Central and Eastern Europe*, ed. A. Lorentzen, B. Widmaier, and M. Laki, 61–84. Aldershot, UK: Ashgate.

————. 2003. *The rise and fall of Czech capitalism: Economic development in the Czech Republic since 1989*. Cheltenham, UK: Edward Elgar.

————. 2007. The Czech Republic. In *Trade union revitalisation: Trends and prospects in 34 countries*, ed. C. Phelan, 335–46. Oxford: Peter Lang.

Myant, M., and J. Drahokoupil. 2008. International integration and the structure of exports in central Asian republics. *Eurasian Geography and Economics* 49 (5): 604–22.

Myant, M., F. Fleischer, K. Hornschild, Z. Souček, R. Vintrová, and K. Zeman. 1996. *Successful transformations? The creation of market economies in Eastern Germany and the Czech Republic*. Aldershot, UK: Edward Elgar.

Mykhnenko, V. 2007. Poland and Ukraine: Institutional structures and economic performance. In *Varieties of capitalism in post-Communist countries*, ed. D. Lane and M. Myant, 124–48). Basingstoke, UK: Palgrave.

————. 2009. Class voting and the Orange Revolution: A cultural political economy perspective on Ukraine's electoral geography. *Journal of Communist Studies and Transition Politics* 25 (2–3): 278–96.

Mykhnenko, V., and A. Swain. 2009. Ukraine's diverging space-economy: Post-Soviet development models and regional trajectories, 1990–2009. *European Urban and Regional Studies* 17: 141–65.

National Bank of Poland (NBP). 2006. *Foreign direct investment*. Warsaw: NBP.

Neef, R., and M. Stanculescu, eds. 2002. *The social impact of informal economies in Eastern Europe*. Aldershot, UK: Ashgate.

Nellis, J. 2002. *The World Bank, privatization and enterprise reform in transition economies: A retrospective analysis*. Washington, DC: World Bank.

Nijkamp, P., and J. Poot. 2004. Meta-analysis of the effect of fiscal policies on long-run growth. *European Journal of Political Economy* 20: 91–124.

Nölke, A., and A. Vliegenthart. 2009. Enlarging the varieties of capitalism: The emergence of dependent market economies in East Central Europe. *World Politics* 61 (4): 670–702.

North, D. C. 1981. *Structure and change in economic history*. New York: Norton.

————. 2005. *Understanding the process of economic change*. Princeton, NJ: Princeton University Press.

Nove, A. 1977. *The Soviet economic system*. London: Allen and Unwin.

_____. 1992. *An economic history of the USSR, 1917–1991*. 3rd ed. London: Penguin Books.

Nuti, D. M. 1981. The Polish crisis: Economic factors and constraints. In *The Socialist register 1981*, ed. R. Miliband and J. Saville, 104–43. London: Merlin.

_____. 1997. Employee ownership in Polish privatizations. In *Privatization surprises in transition economies: Employee-ownership in Central and Eastern Europe*, ed. M. Uvalic and D. Vaughan-Whitehead. Cheltenham, UK: Edward Elgar.

_____. 2007. Belarus: Prototype for market Socialism? In *The transformation of state Socialism: System change, capitalism or something else?* ed. D. Lane, 221–32). Basingstoke, UK: Palgrave Macmillan.

Obradović, J., and W. N. Dunn, eds. 1978. *Worker's self-management and organizational power in Yugoslavia*. Pittsburgh: University of Pittsburgh Press.

O'Dwyer, C. 2006. Reforming regional governance in East Central Europe: Europeanization or domestic politics as usual? *East European Politics and Societies* 20 (2): 219–53.

O'Dwyer, C., and B. Kovalčík. 2007. And the last shall be first: Party system institutionalization and second-generation economic reform in post-Communist Europe. *Studies in Comparative International Development* 41 (4): 3–26.

Offe, C. 1991. Capitalism by democratic design? Democratic theory facing the triple transition in East Central Europe. *Social Research* 58 (4): 865–92.

O'Hara, S., A. Ivlevs, and M. Gentile. 2009. The impact of global economic crisis on remittances in the Commonwealth of Independent States. *Eurasian Geography and Economics* 50 (4): 447–63.

Okun, A. M. 1981. *Prices and quantities: A macroeconomic analysis*. Oxford: Blackwell.

Olsson, M.-O. 2008. The Russian virtual economy turning real: Institutional change in the Arkhangelsk forest sector. *Europe-Asia Studies* 60 (5): 707–38.

Orenstein, M. 2008. *Privatizing pensions: The transnational campaign for social security reform*. Princeton, NJ: Princeton University Press.

Orenstein, M., S. Bloom, and N. Lindstrom. 2008. A fourth dimension of transition. In *Transnational actors in Central and East European transitions*, ed. M. Orenstein, S. Bloom, and N. Lindstrom, 1–18. Pittsburgh: University of Pittsburgh Press.

Organization for Economic Cooperation and Development (OECD). 1982. *OECD economic surveys: Yugoslavia*. Paris: OECD.

_____. 1995. *Mass privatisation: An initial assessment*. Paris: OECD.

_____. 2001. *The social crisis in the Russian Federation*. Paris: OECD.

_____. 2008. *Labour Force Statistics 1987-2007*. Paris: OECD.

Orszag, P., and J. Stiglitz. 2001. Rethinking pension reform: Ten myths about social security systems. In *New ideas about old age security*, ed. R. Holzmann and J. Stiglitz, 17–56. Washington, DC: World Bank.

Osborn, E. A., and K. M. Słomczyński. 2005. *Open for business: The persistent entrepreneurial class in Poland*. Warsaw: IFiS Publishers.

Ost, D. 1992. Labour and societal transition. *Problems of Communism* 33 (5–6): 48–51.

_____. 2005. *The defeat of solidarity: Anger and politics in post-Communist Europe*. Ithaca, NY: Cornell University Press.

_____. 2009. The Consequences of post-Communism: Trade unions in Eastern Europe's future. *East European Politics and Societies* 23 (1): 13–33.

Özcan, G. B. 2006. Djamila's journey from Kolkhoz to Bazaar: Female entrepreneurs in Kyrgyzstan. In *Enterprising women in transition economies*, ed. F. Welter, D. Smallbone and N. Isakova, 93–118. Aldershot, UK: Ashgate.

Pädam, S. 2007. Transformation from a centrally planned to a market economy: Developments in Estonia, 1989–2003. In *Rebuilding the market economy in Central-East Europe and the Baltic countries*, ed. I. Kiglics, 255–317. Budapest, Hungary: Akadémiai Kiadó.

Panitch, L., and S. Gindin. 2005. Euro-capitalism and American empire. In *Varieties of capitalism, varieties of approaches*, ed. D. Coates, 139–60. Basingstoke, UK: Palgrave Macmillan.

Papava, V. G. 2005. *Necroeconomics: The political economy of post-Communist capitalism (lessons from Georgia)*. New York: iUniverse.

Pappe, Y. 2000. *Oligarchi: Ekonomischeskaya Chronika 1992–2000*. Moscow: VSE.

Parker, E., and J. Thornton. 2007. Fiscal centralisation and decentralisation in Russia and China. *Comparative Economic Studies* 49 (4): 514–42.

Pavlínek, P. 2004a. Regional development implications of foreign direct investment in Central Europe. *European Urban and Regional Studies* 11 (1): 47–70.

————. 2004b. Transformation of the Central and East European passenger car industry: Selective peripheral integration through foreign direct investment. In *Foreign direct investment and regional development in East Central Europe and the former Soviet Union: A Collection of essays in memory of professor Francis "Frank" Carter*, ed. D. Turnock, 71–102. Aldershot, UK: Ashgate.

————. 2008. *A successful transformation? Restructuring of the Czech automobile industry*. Heidelberg, Germany: Springer Verlag.

Pavlínek, P., B. Domański, and R. Guzik. 2009. Industrial upgrading through foreign direct investment in Central European automotive manufacturing. *European Urban and Regional Studies* 16 (1): 43–63.

Pavlínek, P. and J. Ženka. 2010. Industrial upgrading in the Czech automotive industry. *Journal of Economic Geography* Advance Access published June 21, 2010, doi:10.1093/jeg/lbq023.

Pereira, L. C. B., A. Przeworski, and J. M. Maravall. 1993. *Economic reforms in new democracies: A social-democratic approach*. Cambridge: Cambridge University Press.

Petrov, N., and K. Hope. 2009. Frustration at slow progress in EU. *Financial Times*, June 19, p. S1.

Peyrouse, S. 2007. Nationhood and the minority question in central Asia: The Russians in Kazakhstan. *Europe-Asia Studies* 59 (3): 481–501.

Phelan, C., ed. 2007. *Trade union revitalisation: Trends and prospects in 34 countries*. Oxford: Peter Lang.

Pickles, J., A. Smith, P. Roukova, R. Begg, and M. Bucek. 2006. Upgrading and diversification in the East European industry: Competitive pressure and production networks in the clothing industry. *Environment and Planning* 38 (12): 2305–24.

Piech, K., and S. Radosevic, eds. 2006. *The knowledge-based economy in Central and Eastern Europe: Countries and industries in a process of change*. Basingstoke, UK: Palgrave.

Pilkington, H. 1998. *Migration, displacement and identity in post-Soviet Russia*. London: Routledge.

Pinto, B., M. Belka, and S. Krajewski. 1993. Transforming state enterprises in Poland: Evidence on adjustment by manufacturing firms. *Brookings Papers on Economic Activity*, issue no. 1: 213–70.

Pinto, B., V. Drebentsov, and A. Morozov. 2000. Dismantling Russia's nonpayments system: Creating conditions for growth. World Bank Technical Paper no. 471.

Pistor, K. 1999. Supply and demand for law in Russia: A comment on Hendley. *East European Constitutional Review* 8 (4): 105–8.

Pohl, G., S. Claessens, and S. Djankov. 1997. Privatization and restructuring in Central and Eastern Europe. World Bank Technical Paper no. 368.

Polanyi, K. 1957. *The great transformation*. Beacon Hill, MA: Beacon Press.

————. 1977. *The livelihood of man*. New York: Academic Press.

Pomfret, R. 2006. *The central Asian economies since independence*. Princeton, NJ: Princeton University Press.

_____. 2009. Using energy resources to diversify the economy: Agricultural price distortions in Kazakhstan. *Comparative Economic Studies* 51 (2): 181–212.

Pomfret, R., and K. Anderson. 1997. Uzbekistan: Welfare impact of slow transition. United Nations University, World Institute for Development Economics Research (UNU-WIDER) Working Paper no. 135.

Pontusson, J. 2005. Varieties and commonalities of capitalism. In *Varieties of capitalism, varieties of approaches*, ed. D. Coates, 163–88. Basingstoke, UK: Palgrave Macmillan.

Popov, V. 2000. Shock therapy versus gradualism: The end of the debate (explaining the magnitude of transformational recession). *Comparative Economic Studies* 42 (1): 1–57.

_____. 2007. Shock therapy versus gradualism reconsidered: Lessons from transition economies after 15 years of reforms. *Comparative Economic Studies* 49: 1–31.

Porket, J. L. 1982. Retired workers under Soviet-type Socialism. *Social Policy and Administration* 16 (3): 253–69.

Porter, M. E. 1990. *The competitive advantage of nations*. London: Macmillan.

Potůček, M. 2008. Metamorphoses of welfare states in Central and Eastern Europe. In *Welfare state transformations: Comparative perspectives*, ed. M. Seeleib-Kaiser, 79–95. Basingstoke, UK: Palgrave Macmillan.

Poznanski, K. Z. 1996. *Poland's protracted transition: Institutional change and economic growth, 1970–1994*. Cambridge: Cambridge University Press.

PricewaterhouseCoopers (PwC). 2010. *Foreign Direct Investment in Central and Eastern Europe: A Case of Boom and Bust?* London: PwC.

PRO INNO Europe. 2009. *European innovation scoreboard 2008: Comparative analysis of innovation performance*. Luxembourg: Office for Official Publications of the European Communities.

Przeworski, A. 1991. *Democracy and the market*. Cambridge: Cambridge University Press.

Radaev, V. 2000. Corruption and violence in Russian business in the late 1990s. In *Economic crime in Russia*, ed. A. V. Ledeneva and M. Kurkchiyan. London: Kluwer Law International.

_____. 2002. Entrepreneurial strategies and the structure of transaction costs in Russian business. In *The new entrepreneurs of Europe and Asia: Patterns of business development in Russia, Eastern Europe and China*, ed. V. E. Bonnell and T. B. Gold, 191–213. Armonk, NY: M.E. Sharpe.

Radnitz, S. 2006. Weighing the political and economic motivations for migration in post-Soviet space: The case of Uzbekistan. *Europe-Asia Studies* 58 (5): 653–77.

Raiffeisen Research. 2008. *CEE banking sector report: Size matters ... as deposits move into the spotlight*. Vienna: Raiffeisen Zentralbank Österreich AG.

_____. 2009. *CEE banking sector report: Rough playing field ... committed players*. Vienna: Raiffeisen Zentralbank Österreich AG.

Ramanauskas, G. 2007. Experience of dramatic systemic and structural changeover until the EU accession: Lithuania. In *Rebuilding the market economy in Central-East Europe and the Baltic countries*, ed. I. Kiglics, 371–413. Budapest, Hungary: Akadémiai Kiadó.

Rapacki, R. 1996. Enterprise culture in Poland in transition: A cautionary diagnosis. In *Enterprise culture in a transition economy: Poland 1989–1994*, ed. R. Rapacki, 24–40. Warsaw: Warsaw School of Economics.

Rauch, J. E., and P. B. Evans. 2000. Bureaucratic structure and bureaucratic performance in less developed countries. *Journal of Public Economics* 75 (1): 49–71.

Reinhart, C. M., and K. S. Rogoff. 2008. Is the 2007 U.S. sub-prime financial crisis so different? An international historical comparison. Nation Bureau of Economic Rsearch (NBER) Working Paper no. 13761.

Remmer, K. L. 1991. The political impact of economic crisis in Latin America in the 1980s. *American Political Science Review* 85 (3): 777–800.

Research Center for Competitiveness of Czech Economy (RCCCE) and National Observatory of Employment and Training (NOET). 2008. *The competitiveness yearbook: The Czech Republic 2006–2007*. Prague: RCCCE and NOET.

Rhodes, M., and M. Keune. 2006. EMU and welfare adjustment in Central and Eastern Europe. In *Enlarging the Euro area: External empowerment and domestic transformation in East Central Europe*, ed. K. Dyson, 279–300. Oxford: Oxford University Press.

Rodrik, D. 2006. Growth strategies. In *Handbook of economic growth*, vol. 1A, ed. P. Aghion and S. N. Durlauf, 967–1014). Amsterdam: North Holland.

Roland, G. 2000. *Transition and economics: Politics, markets, and firms*. Cambridge, MA: MIT Press.

Roma Education Fund (REF). 2007. *Advancing Education of Roma in Hungary: Country Assessment and the Roma Education Fund's Strategic Directions*. Budapest: REF.

Romer, P. 1986. Increasing returns and long-run growth. *Journal of Political Economy* 94 (5): 1002–37.

Rose-Ackerman, S. 1999. *Corruption and government: Causes, consequences, and reform*. Cambridge: Cambridge University Press.

Rossiaud, S., and C. Locatelli. 2009. The obstacles in the way of stabilising the Russian oil model. *Post-Communist Economies* 21 (4): 425–38.

Ruble, B. A. 1981. *Soviet trade unions: Their development in the 1970s*. Cambridge: Cambridge University Press.

Rudra, N., and S. Haggard. 2005. Globalization, democracy, and effective welfare spending in the developing world. *Comparative Political Studies* 38 (9): 1015–49.

Rueschemeyer, D., and P. Evans. 1985. The state and economic transformation: Toward an analysis of the conditions underlying effective state intervention. In *Bringing the state back in*, ed. P. Evans, D. Rueschemeyer, and T. Skocpol, 189–210. Cambridge: Cambridge University Press.

Rueschemeyer, D., E. H. Stephens, and J. D. Stephens. 1992. *Capitalist development and democracy*. Chicago: University of Chicago Press.

Rutland, P. 2010. The oligarchs and economic development. In *After Putin's Russia: Past imperfect, future uncertain*, ed. S. K. Wegren and D. R. Herspring, 159–82. Lanham, MD: Rowman and Littlefield.

Rutland, P., Z. Y. Gitelman, and R. Sakwa. 2005. Putin's economic record. In *Developments in Russian politics*, vol. 6, ed. S. K. Wegren and D. R. Herspring, 186–203. Basingstoke, UK: Palgrave Macmillan.

Sachs, J. 1990. Eastern Europe's economies: What is to be done? *Economist*, January 12, pp. 19–24.

———. 1992. Privatization in Russia: Some lessons from Eastern Europe. *American Economic Review* 82 (2): 43–48.

———. 1993. *Poland's jump to a free market economy*. Cambridge, MA: MIT Press.

Sachs, J., and D. Lipton. 1990. Poland's economic reform. *Foreign Affairs* 69 (3): 47–65.

Sakwa, R. 2008. Putin and the oligarchs. *New Political Economy* 13 (2): 185–91.

Sanford, J. E. 2003. Russia and the international financial institutions: From special case to a normal country. In *Russia's uncertain economic future*, ed. J. P. Hardt, 425–64. Armonk, NY: M.E. Sharpe.

Satter, D. 2003. *Darkness at dawn: The rise of the Russian criminal state*. New Haven, CT: Yale University Press.

Saxonberg, S., and T. Sirovátka. 2009. Neo-liberalism by decay? The evolution of the Czech welfare state. *Social Policy and Administration* 43 (2): 186–203.

Schaffer, M. E., and G. Turley. 2000. Effective versus statutory taxation: Measuring effective tax administration in transition economies. William Davidson Institute Working Paper no. 347.

Schiavo-Campo, S., G. d. Tommaso, and A. Mukherjee. 1997. An international statistical survey of government employment and wages. World Bank Policy Research Working Paper no. 1806.

Schmidt, V. A. 2002. *The futures of European capitalism*. Oxford: Oxford University Press.

Schumpeter, J. A. 1952. *Capitalism, Socialism and democracy*. 5th ed. London: Allen and Unwin.

————. 1954. *Capitalism, Socialism and democracy*. 4th ed. London: Allen and Unwin.

Schütte, C. 2000. *Privatization and corporate control in the Czech Republic*. Cheltenham, UK: Edward Elgar.

Schwartz, A. 2006. *The politics of greed: How privatization structured politics in Central and Eastern Europe*. Lanham, MD: Rowman and Littlefield.

Schwartz, H. 2000. *States versus markets: The emergence of a global economy*. 2nd ed. Basingstoke, UK: Palgrave.

Shafer, D. M. 1994. *Winners and losers: How sectors shape the developmental prospects of states*. Ithaca, NY: Cornell University Press.

Shishkin, S. V., T. V. Bogatova, E. G. Potapchik, V. A. Chernets, A. Y. Chirikova, and L. S. Shilova. 2003. *Informal out-of-pocket payments for health care in Russia*. Moscow: Moscow Public Scientific Foundation and Independent Institute for Social Policy.

Shkaratan, O. 2007. The Russian transformation: A new form of etacratism? In *The transformation of state Socialism: System change, capitalism or something else?* ed. D. Lane, 143–58. Basingstoke, UK: Palgrave Macmillan.

Shlapentokh, V. 2004. Wealth versus political power: The Russian case. *Communist and Post-Communist Studies* 35 (2): 135–60.

Shleifer, A. 1997. Agenda for Russian reforms. *Economics of Transition* 5 (1): 227–31.

Shleifer, A., and R. Vishny. 1997. A survey of corporate governance. *Journal of Finance* 52 (2): 737–83.

————. 1993. Corruption. *Quarterly Journal of Economics* 108 (3): 599–617.

————. 1998. *The grabbing hand: Government pathologies and their cures*. Cambridge, MA: Harvard University Press.

Sim, L.-C. 2008. *The rise and fall of privatization in the Russian oil industry*. Basingstoke, UK: Palgrave Macmillan.

Smallbone, D., and F. Welter. 2008. *Entrepreneurship and small business development in the post-Socialist economies*. London: Routledge.

Smith, G. 2008. Tractor giant pulls weight. *Financial Times*, November 18.

Smith, H. 1976. *The Russians*. London: Times Books.

Smith-Sivertsen, H. 2004. Latvia. In *The handbook of political change in Eastern Europe*, 2nd ed., ed. S. Berglund, J. Ekman, and F. H. Aarebrot, 95–131. Cheltenham, UK: Edward Elgar.

Solnick, S. L. 1998. *Stealing the state: Control and collapse in Soviet institutions*. Cambridge, MA: Harvard University Press.

Sommers, J. 2009. The Anglo-American model of economic organization and governance: Entropy and the fragmentation of social solidarity in twenty-first century Latvia. *Debatte: Journal of Contemporary Central and Eastern Europe* 17 (2): 127–42.

Spechler, D. R., and M. C. Spechler. 2009. A reassessment of the burden of Eastern Europe on the USSR. *Europe-Asia Studies* 61 (9): 1645–57.

Spechler, M. 2008. *The political economy of reform in central Asia: Uzbekistan under authoritarianism*. London: Routledge.

Stalker, P. 2000. *Workers without frontiers: The impact of globalization on international migration*. Boulder, CO: Lynne Rienner.

Staniszkis, J. 1991. *The dynamics of breakthrough in Eastern Europe: The Polish experience*. Berkeley: University of California Press.

Stanojevic, M. 2003. Worker's power in transition economies: The cases of Serbia and Slovenia. *European Journal of Industrial Relations* 9 (3): 283–301.

Stark, D., and L. Bruszt. 1998. *Post-Socialist pathways: Transforming politics and property in East Central Europe*. Cambridge: Cambridge University Press.

Steen, A. 1997. *Between past and future: Elites, democracy and the state in post-Communist countries; A comparison of Estonia, Latvia and Lithuania*. Aldershot, UK: Ashgate.

Stiglitz, J. 1988. On the relevance or irrelevance of public financial policy. In *The Economics of public debt*, ed. K. J. Arrow and M. J. Boskin, 4–76. New York: St. Martin's Press.

————. 1994. *Whither Socialism?* Cambridge, MA: MIT Press.

————. 2002. *Globalization and its discontents*. London: Allen Lane.

————. 2009. The anatomy of the murder: Who killed America's economy? *Critical Review: A Journal of Politics and Society* 21 (2): 329–39.

Stoner-Weiss, K. 2006. *Resisting the state: Reform and retrenchment in post-Soviet Russia*. New York: Cambridge University Press.

Stuckler, D., L. King, and M. McKee. 2009. Mass privatisation and the post-Communist mortality crisis: A cross-national analysis. *Lancet* 373 (9661): 399–407.

Sutela, P. 1991. *Economic thought and economic reform in the Soviet Union*. Cambridge: Cambridge University Press.

————. 2003. *The Russian market economy*. Helsinki, Finland: Kikimora Publications.

Sutherland, H., F. Figari, and A. Paulus. 2007. The effect of taxes and benefits on income distribution in the EU. In *Social inclusion and income: Distribution in the European Union, 2007*. Brussels, Vienna, Budapest, and Colchester: European Observatory on the Social Situation.

Swain, A., and V. Mykhnenko. 2007. The Ukrainian Donbas in "transition." In *Re-constructing the post-Soviet industrial region: The Donbas in transition*, ed. A. Swain, 7–46. London: Routledge.

Swain, N. 1985. *Collective farms which work?* Cambridge: Cambridge University Press.

————. 1992. *Hungary: Rise and fall of feasible Socialism*. London: Verso.

Szelenyi, I., and S. Szelenyi. 1995. Circulation or reproduction of elites during the post-Communist transformation of Eastern Europe: Introduction. *Theory and Society* 24 (5): 615–38.

Tanzi, V., and L. Schuknecht. 2000. *Public spending in the 20th century*. Cambridge: Cambridge University Press.

Tiits, M., R. Kattel, T. Kalvet, and D. Tamm. 2008. Catching up, forging ahead or falling behind? Central and Eastern European development in 1990–2005. *Innovation: The European Journal of Social Science Research* 21 (1): 65–85.

Tilly, C. 1990. *Coercion, capital and European States, AD 990–1990*. Cambridge, MA: Basil Blackwell.

Tompson, W. 2005. Putin and the "oligarchs": A two-sided commitment problem? In *Leading Russia: Putin in perspective*, ed. A. Pravda, 179–203. Oxford: Oxford University Press.

Tóth, I. G. 2009. The demand for redistribution: A test on Hungarian data. *Czech Sociological Review* 44 (6): 1063–87.

Treisman, D. 1999. *After the deluge: Regional crises and political consolidation in Russia*. Ann Arbor: University of Michigan Press.

Trotsky, L. 1972. *The revolution betrayed: What is the Soviet Union and where is it going?* 5th ed. New York: Pathfinder Press.

Tsygankov, A. P. 2007. Modern at last? Variety of weak states in the post-Soviet world. *Communist and Post-Communist Studies* 40: 423–39.

Tucker, J. A. 2007. Enough! Electoral fraud, collective action problems, and post-Communist Colored Revolutions. *Perspectives on Politics* 5 (3): 535–51.

Tyson, L. D. A. 1980. *The Yugoslav economic system and its performance in the 1970s.* Berkeley, CA: Institute of International Studies.

————. 1983. Investment allocation: A comparison of reform experience of Hungary and Yugoslavia. *Journal of Comparative Economics* 7: 288–303.

United Nations (UN). 1992. *Statistical yearbook.* 39th ed. New York: UN.

————. 1993a. *International trade statistics yearbook, 1992.* New York: UN.

————. 1993b. *Statistical yearbook.* 40th ed. New York: UN.

————. 1995. *Statistical yearbook.* 42th ed. New York: UN.

————. 1997. *Statistical yearbook.* 44th ed. New York: UN.

————. 1998. *Statistical yearbook.* 45th ed. New York: UN.

————. 2006. *Statistical yearbook.* 50th ed. New York: UN.

————. 2008. *Statistical yearbook.* 52th ed. New York: UN.

United Nations Conference on Trade and Development (UNCTAD). 2007. *World investment report: Transnational corporations, extractive industries and development.* New York: UNCTAD.

————. 2009. *World investment report: Transnational corporations, agricultural production and development.* New York: UNCTAD.

United Nations Development Program (UNDP). 1998. *Poverty in transition.* New York: UNDP.

————. (2006). *At Risk: Roma and the Displaced in Southeast Europe.* New York: UNDP.

————. (2007). *Report on the Living Conditions of Roma Households in Slovakia.* New York: UNDP.

————. (2010). *Vulnerable Groups in Central and Southeast Europe: Statistical Profiles.* Available at http://vulnerability.undp.sk/

United Nations Educational, Scientific, and Cultural Organization (UNESCO). 2006. *UNESCO statistical yearbook 2006.* Paris: UNESCO.

————. 2009. *Global education digest 2009: Comparing education statistics across the world.* Montreal: UNESCO.

Uvalic, M., and D. Vaughan-Whitehead, eds. 1997. *Privatization surprises in transition economies: Employee-ownership in Central and Eastern Europe.* Cheltenham, UK: Edward Elgar.

Uzagalieva, A., and A. Menezes. 2009. The poverty effect of remittance flows: Evidence from Georgia. *Post-Communist Economies* 21 (4): 453–74.

Vanhuysse, P. 2006. *Divide and pacify: Strategic social policies and political protests in post-Communist democracies.* Budapest, Hungary: Central European University Press.

Vaughan-Whitehead, D. C. 2003. *EU enlargement versus social Europe? The uncertain future of the European social model.* Cheltenham, UK: Edward Elgar.

Vishnevsky, A. G. 1999. *Serp i rubl'.* Moscow: OGI.

Vliegenthart, A., and H. Overbeek. 2008. Corporate tax reform in neoliberal Europe: Central and Eastern Europe as a template for deepening the neoliberal European integration project? In *Contradictions and limits of neoliberal European governance: From Lisbon to Lisbon,* ed. B. v. Apeldoorn, J. Drahokoupil, and L. Horn, 143–62. Basingstoke, UK: Palgrave.

Volkov, V. 2002. *Violent entrepreneurs: The use of force in the making of Russian capitalism.* Ithaca, NY: Cornell University Press.

Vorobyov, A. Y., and S. V. Zhukov. 2006. The Russian way of adjustment: Mechanisms of economic growth in 1999–2001 and patterns of poverty and income distribution. In *External liberalization in Asia, post-Socialist Europe, and Brazil,* ed. L. Taylor, 346–68. Oxford: Oxford University Press.

Wade, R. 1990. *Governing the market: Economic theory and the role of government in east Asian industrialization.* Princeton, NJ: Princeton University Press.

————. 2008. The first-world debt crisis of 2007–2010 in global perspective. *Challenge* 51 (4): 23–54.

————. 2009. From global imbalances to global reorganisations. *Cambridge Journal of Economics* 33 (4): 539–62.

Wallace, C., and R. Latcheva. 2006. Economic transformation outside the law: Corruption, trust in public institutions and the informal economy in transition countries of Central and Eastern Europe. *Europe-Asia Studies* 58 (1): 81–102.

Wallich, C. I. 1994a. Russia's dilemma. In *Russia and the challenge of fiscal federalism*, ed. C. I. Wallich, 1–18. Washington, DC: World Bank.

————, ed. 1994b. *Russia and the challenge of fiscal federalism*. Washington, DC: World Bank.

Walton, J., and D. Seddon. 1994. *Free markets and food riots: The politics of global adjustment*. Oxford: Blackwell.

Way, L. A. 2005. Authoritarian state building and the sources of regime competitiveness in the fourth wave: The cases of Belarus, Moldova, Russia, and Ukraine. *World Politics* 57: 231–61.

Weber, M. 1968. *Economy and society: An outline of interpretive sociology*. New York: Bedminster Press.

Večerník, J. 2009. *Czech Society in the 2000s: A Report on Socio-Economic Policies and Structures*. Prague: Academia.

Weisbrot, M., R. Ray, J. Johnston, J. A. Cordero, and J. A. Montecino. 2009. *IMF-supported macroeconomic policies and the world recession: A Look at forty-one borrowing countries*. Washington, DC: Center for Economic and Policy Research.

Welfens, P. 1992. The Socialist shadow economy: Causes, characteristics, and role for systemic reforms. *Economic Systems* 16 (1): 113–47.

Weresa, M. A. 2008. Foreign direct investment and the competitiveness of Polish manufacturing. In *Reinventing Poland: Economic and political transformation and evolving national identity*, ed. M. Myant and T. Cox, 30–41. London: Routledge.

Wesołowski, W. 1979. *Classes, strata and power*. London: Routledge.

White, S. 2000. *Russia's new politics: The management of a post-Communist society*. Cambridge: Cambridge University Press.

————. 2009. Is there a pattern? *Journal of Communist Studies and Transition Politics* 25 (2–3): 396–412.

Whitten, D. O. 2002. Russian robber barons: Moscow business, American style. *European Journal of Law and Economics* 13 (3): 193–201.

Wiles, P. J. d. l. F. 1962. *The political economy of Communism*. Oxford: Basil Blackwell.

————. 1968. *Communist international economics*. Oxford: Blackwell.

Williamson, J. 1990. What Washington means by policy reform. In *Latin American adjustment: How much has happened?* ed. J. Williamson. Washington, DC: Institute for International Economics.

Williamson, J. B., and M. Williams. 2003. The notional defined contribution model: An assessment of the strengths and limitations of a new approach to the provision of old age security. Boston College, Center for Retirement Research Working Paper no. 18.

Winiecki, J. 1988. *The distorted world of Soviet-type economies*. London: Routledge.

Wolosky, L. 2000. Putin's plutocrat problem. *Foreign Affairs* 70 (2): 18–31.

Woo-Cumings, M., ed. 1999. *The developmental state*. Ithaca, NY: Cornell University Press.

Woodruff, D. M. 1999. *Money unmade: Barter and the fate of Russian capitalism*. Ithaca, NY: Cornell University Press.

————. 2000. Rules for followers: Institutional theory and the new politics of economic backwardness in Russia. *Politics and Society* 28 (4): 437–82.

_____. 2004. Property rights in context: Privatization's legacy for corporate legality in Poland and Russia. *Studies in Comparative International Development* 38 (4): 82–108.

_____. 2005. Boom, gloom, doom: Balance sheets, monetary fragmentation, and the politics of financial crisis in Argentina and Russia. *Politics and Society* 33 (1): 3–45.

_____. 2007. The expansion of state ownership in Russia: Cause for concern? *Development and transition* 7: 11–13.

Woolfson, C., D. Calite, and E. Kallaste. 2008. Employee voice and working environment in post-Communist new member states: An empirical analysis of Estonia, Latvia and Lithuania. *Industrial Relations Journal* 39: 314–34.

World Bank (WB). 1990. *World development report 1990: Poverty*. Washington, DC: WB.

_____. 1994. *Averting the old age crisis: Policies to protect the old and promote growth*. Washington, DC: WB.

_____. 1997. *World development report 1997: The state in a changing world*. Oxford and Washington, DC: Oxford University Press and WB.

_____. 1998. *Kazakhstan: Living standards during transition*. Washington, DC: WB.

_____. 2000. *Making transition work for everyone: Poverty and inequality in Europe and Central Asia*. Washington, DC: WB.

_____. 2001. *World development report 2002: Building institutions for markets*. Vol. 1. Washington, DC: WB.

_____. 2003. *World Development Indicators*. CD-ROM. Washington, DC: WB.

_____. 2005. *Russian Federation: Reducing poverty through growth and social policy reform*. Washington, DC: WB.

_____. 2006. Dimensions of urban poverty in the Europe and central Asia region. World Bank Policy Research Working Paper no. 3998.

_____. 2007. *Fiscal policy and economic growth: Lessons for Eastern Europe and central Asia*. Washington, DC: International Bank for Reconstruction and Development and WB.

_____. 2008a. *World Development Indicators*. CD-ROM. Washington, DC: WB.

_____. 2008b. *The financial crisis and mandatory pension systems in developing countries*. Washington, DC: WB.

World Bank and PricewaterhouseCoopers (PwC). 2008. *Paying taxes 2008: The global picture*. Washington, DC and London: WB and PwC.

Yakovlev, A. 2006. The evolution of business: State Interaction in Russia; From state capture to business capture? *Europe-Asia Studies* 58 (7): 1033–56.

_____. 2008a. Interest groups and economic reform in contemporary Russia: Before and after Yukos. In *Politics and the ruling group in Putin's Russia*, ed. S. White, 87–119. Basingstoke, UK: Palgrave Macmillan.

_____. 2008b. *Shuttle trade and entrepreneurship development in CEE and Russia at Local and regional level*. Unpublished presentation at Workshop 2, Joint European Master in Comparative Local Development, Trento University, October 2008,

_____. 2009. State-business relations and improvement of corporate governance in Russia. In *Organization and development of Russian business: A firm-level analysis*, ed. T. Dolgopyatova, I. Iwasaki, and A. Yakovlev, 284–306. Basingstoke, UK: Palgrave.

Yudaeva, K., and M. Gorban. 1999. Health and health care. *Russian Economic Trends* 8 (2): 27–35.

Yurchak, A. 2002. Entrepreneurial governmentality in post-Socialist Russia: A cultural investigation of business practices. In *The new entrepreneurs of Europe and Asia: Patterns of business development in Russia, Eastern Europe and China*, ed. V. E. Bonnell and T. B. Gold, 278–324. Armonk, NY: M.E. Sharpe.

Zudin, A. 2002. *Rezhim Vladimira Putina: Kontury novoi politicheskoi sistemy*. Moscow: Carnegie Center.

Zweynert, J. 2007. Conflicting patterns of thought in the Russian debate on transition: 1992–2002. *Europe-Asia Studies* 59 (1): 47–69.

Subject Index

Acquis communautaire, 91–92
Agriculture, under state socialism, 26
Aid, 67–68, 306
Alpha Group, 146, 155
ArcelorMittal, 293. *See also* Mittal Steel Company
Asset stripping, in Georgia, 249
Association Agreements, 90–91
August Coup in Russia (1991), 149
Austrian school of economics, 18, 85
Authoritarianism(s), *see* Competitive authoritarianism(s)

Balance of payments, 63, 67, 282–83, 326
Balcerowicz Program, 95
Baltic republics, transition strategies, 100–101
Bank Baltija, 273
Bank of Latvia , 273
Bank Stolichny, 146
Bank(s), xxii-xxiii, 259–75
  in Belarus, 265, 274
  credits, *see* Credits
  crises, 259, 260, 267–70, 272–73, 313–14
  in Czech Republic, 267–70
  deposits, *see* Deposits
  in economic theory, 259–60
  and financial crisis, 316–320
  foreign ownership, 262, 266–67, 269–70, 272
  in Hungary, 267
  in Kazakhstan, 265
  in Latvia, 273
  in market economies, 259
  numbers in transition economies, 261–62, 268, 271
  in Poland, 266
  privatization, 260, 266–71
  regulation, 266, 268–71, 273–74
  in Russia, 224, 265, 270–72
  in Ukraine, 265, 274
  in Uzbekistan, 274
Bankruptcy laws in Hungary, 220
Barter, between Russian enterprises, xxi, 140, 150, 223–24
Bertelsmann Stiftung, 136, 138, 144
Blat, 22
Bureaucracy, 123–27, 134. *See also* State apparatus
  in Russia, 150, 152
Business capture, 151–52, 154
Business Environment and Enterprise Performance Survey (BEEPS) 132, 133–35, 235

Capitalists, creation of, 230–31, 256–57
Cayman Islands, 270

Central banks, 266, 268–71, 273–74
Central planning, 16. *See also* Market reform
  enterprises under, 16
  failings of, 17
  money and banking under, 16
  prices under, 17
  and state capacity 126
  taxation under, 17
Central Statistical Office of Poland (GUS), 170
CEPR (Centre for Economic Policy Research), 322
Česká spořitelna (ČS), 269
Československá obchodní banka (ČSOB), 268, 270
China, 124–25
  economic reform strategy, 96, 112
Circular flow of income, 58
Citibank, 196
Civil society, 5–6, 94, 108, 114
Clans, in Central Asia, 127
Clientelism, 145–49, 151–52. *See also* Corruption
Colored revolutions, 148. *See also* Orange revolution
Comecon, *see* Council for Mutual Economic Assistance (CMEA)
Command economy, 7
Communist Party(ies), 125, 127
  end of power, 9–10, 37–41
  in power, 3
  in Russia 149
  after state socialism, 8
Communist Union of Youth, *see* Komsomol
Comparative advantage, 300, 302–3
Competition state 173
Competitive authoritarianism(s), 148–49. *See also* Political regime(s)
Competitiveness 300. *See also* Comparative advantage
Cooperatives, in Russia, 229–30, 247
Corporate exploitation, 133–35. *See also* Corruption
Corporate governance, 239–41, 243
  in Russia, 157–58, 174
Corruption, 22, 125, 128, 132–35, 141–42, 145, 149
  in Bulgaria, 141–42
  causes, 132, 135
  in Russia, 97
Council for Mutual Economic Assistance (CMEA), 24
  breakdown, 59, 70, 73
Credits, bank, 263–65, 268–72
  in foreign currencies, 319–20
  nonperforming, 267, 268–70

Name Index